Curriculum and Instruction

The Secondary School Physical Education Experience

DEBORAH A. WUEST, Ed.D.

Associate Professor,
School of Health Sciences and Human Performance,
Ithaca College, Ithaca, New York

BENNETT J. LOMBARDO, Ed.D.

Professor, Department of Health,
Physical Education, and Recreation,
Rhode Island College, Providence, Rhode Island

with 165 illustrations

 **Mosby**

St. Louis Baltimore Boston Chicago London Madrid Philadelphia Sydney Toronto

Mosby

Dedicated to Publishing Excellence

Editor-in-Chief: James M. Smith
Editor: Vicki Malinee
Developmental Editor: Michelle Turenne
Project Manager: Patricia Tannian
Production Editor: Suzanne Fannin
Manufacturing Supervisor: Theresa Fuchs
Cover Illustration: Tony Stone Worldwide/Lori Adamski Peek
Cover Design: Rokusek Design
Senior Book Designer: Gail Morey Hudson

Printed in the United States of America

Composition by Graphic World, Inc.
Printing/binding by Maple-Vail Book Manufacturing Group

Mosby–Year Book, Inc.
11830 Westline Industrial Drive
St. Louis, Missouri 63146

Library of Congress Cataloging in Publication Data

Wuest, Deborah A.
    Curriculum and instruction : the secondary school physical
  education experience / Deborah A. Wuest, Bennett J. Lombardo.
        p.   cm.
    Includes bibliographical references (p.) and index.
    ISBN 0-8016-5729-6
    1. Physical education—Study and teaching (Secondary)
  I. Lombardo, Bennett J.   II. Title.
  GV361.W84 1993
  796'.071'2—dc20   93-36733
                                                      CIP

94 95 96 97 98 / 9 8 7 6 5 4 3 2 1

Preface

Physical education is an important part of the secondary school curriculum. As an integral component of the total education of students, it contributes to the overall goals of education. Additionally, physical education makes a unique contribution to the education of the student; it is the only subject area in the school devoted to the study of human movement, the acquisition of motor skills, and the promotion of fitness. It is concerned with the total development of the individual, encompassing development in the psychomotor, cognitive, and affective domains. The development of motor skills, fitness, knowledge, and attitudes conducive to a lifetime of participation is a commonly acknowledged goal of the secondary school physical education program.

The importance of leading a physically active lifestyle is increasingly recognized. The incorporation of regular and appropriate physical activity, such as that associated with participation in sports, aquatics, dance, outdoor, and fitness activities, can have a beneficial effect on one's health. National public health goals presented in *Healthy People 2000* recognize the important contribution that health-related fitness can make to enhancing the quality and length of life. School physical education programs represent the best avenue for reaching millions of adolescents and educating them about health-related fitness and the effects of exercise on the human body. Involving students with vigorous activity during classes, teaching them motor skills for use outside of school, and providing experiences conducive to forming positive attitudes toward physical activity are some of the important contributions that physical education can make to the health of the nation.

The secondary school years are an important time for physical education. During this time adolescents should have the opportunity to be exposed to a variety of sports, dance, and outdoor activities and to develop competence in a few selected ones. Gaining knowledge about human movement is an important part of the physical education experience. Since one of the major goals of education is to prepare students to be lifelong learners, knowledge of factors affecting movement is essential to future learning. Since physical activity habits are formed early in life, attention must be given within the physical education program to helping students incorporate physical activity into their lifestyles at this age. Experiences that promote mastery, enjoyment, and satisfaction contribute to formation of positive activity habits.

This text emphasizes the teaching of motor skills, fitness, knowledge, and attitudes as part of the comprehensive secondary school physical education experience. The focus of attention is on the unique needs of adolescent boys and girls. The adolescent student is used as a focal point in discussing the many factors required to effectively teach physical education to secondary school youths.

SPECIAL CONTENT FEATURES

Users of *Curriculum and Instruction: The Secondary School Physical Education Experience* will find several content areas that may be particularly helpful in teaching secondary school students.

Student-Centered Approach

Meeting the needs of the individual student is emphasized throughout the text. Adolescent students and their unique needs are the focal point for secondary school physical education. For example, Chapter 2 identifies the characteristics of secondary school students with respect to development in the psychomotor, cognitive, and affective domains. Chapter 11 is devoted to understanding the needs of students with disabilities and describing how these needs can be fulfilled within the physical education program.

Developed for Beginning Teachers

Chapter 3 is written for the beginning teacher. It is designed to help teachers become familiar with the school and community and the responsibilities incumbent upon them as educators. Some of the challenges that beginning teachers face are discussed, and various strategies that can be used to meet these challenges are presented. The satisfactions to be realized from teaching are many, and they make teaching a rewarding career.

Teaching Styles and Strategies

A variety of teaching styles are introduced in Chapter 9. These styles offer teachers a multitude of approaches for accomplishing program goals and accommodating individual student's needs. Examples help clarify how each style may be used to teach various activities and enhance individual learning. Various strategies are presented to help teachers effectively accomplish their goals. A variety of approaches that teachers can use to improve their teaching and enhance their effectiveness are presented in Chapter 14.

Curriculum Approaches

Several different approaches to the design of the secondary school physical education curriculum are introduced in Chapter 4. From the various models presented, physical education teachers can choose the model that best fits the needs of their program and students. Guidelines for developing a curriculum are delineated, and information on how to translate planning into practice is given. An overview of the various program components comprising the comprehensive physical education program helps teachers understand the total physical education program.

Wellness and Fitness

Part IV, which consists of Chapters 16, 17, and 18, is devoted to wellness and the health-related components of fitness. An overview of wellness is provided, the various dimensions of wellness are discussed with reference to the secondary school student, and the new food pyramid is included. Each of the health-related components of fitness is defined and discussed, along with their overall importance to health. Activities to assess and improve each fitness component are presented.

Variety of Activities

A variety of activities are included for selection in achieving program goals for secondary school students and to provide a helpful resource. Numerous activities are included to assist teachers in preparing lessons in the areas of sports, fitness, dance, and outdoor pursuits. Additional references are included to facilitate locating further information.

ORGANIZATION

Curriculum and Instruction: The Secondary School Physical Education Experience is comprised of five parts. Part I is divided into three chapters. The first chapter provides an overview of contemporary physical education. Chapter 2 presents the psychomotor, cognitive, and affective characteristics of secondary school students and the implications for the physical education program. The third chapter is written for beginning teachers and focuses on orientation to the school and community, challenges facing them, and satisfactions to be realized from teaching.

Part II discusses the secondary school curriculum. Various curriculum models are presented in Chapter 4. Program planning is discussed in Chapter 5, and translating plans into action is addressed in Chapter 6. Chapter 7 focuses on the total physical education program, including intramurals, sports clubs, and interscholastic sports.

Chapters pertaining to instruction and the program in action are contained in Part III. Chapter 8 presents selected concepts from motor learning and the implications for the design and conduct of the program. Various teaching styles and strategies are contained in Chapter 9. Communication, motivation, and discipline are the focus of Chapter 10. So that teachers may meet the special needs of students with disabilities, Chapter 11 presents a brief overview of significant legislation and its implications for the physical education program. Specific disabling conditions are also presented with suggestions for effective instruction. The topics of safety and administration are covered in Chapter 12. Chapter 13 introduces evaluation techniques for assessing students' needs, the effectiveness of teaching, and the success of the physical education program. In Chapter 14 various approaches are presented to help teachers improve their teaching effectiveness. The importance of promoting the physical education programs and several approaches that can be used are contained in Chapter 15.

Part IV focuses on wellness and fitness. Three chapters present information on these timely areas. An overview of wellness is given in Chapter 16. This is followed by information about fitness and its development in Chapter 17. Chapter 18 discusses guidelines for incorporating wellness and fitness activities in the secondary school physical education program and examples of curricular programs in action. Teachers who are concerned with helping their students acquire the skills, knowledge, and attitudes conducive to learning a healthy lifestyle will find the material in these chapters helpful in accomplishing this goal.

Chapters 19, 20, 21, and 22 make up Part V. They present information on various physical education activities—team sports, individual sports, dual sports, and outdoor adventure activities. Skills are presented with suggestions for teaching and activities to be used for their development.

PEDAGOGICAL FEATURES

Pedagogical aids have been included to assist the teacher and student in using each chapter of the text.

Part Openers

Each of the five parts of the text begins with an overview of the material covered in that part. Information is presented about the relationship between the topics included in each part and the importance of them to secondary school physical education.

Chapter Objectives

At the beginning of each chapter, objectives are listed to assist the student in identifying the chapter's key points. Accomplishing the objectives indicates fulfillment of the chapter's intent.

Chapter Summaries

Summaries at the close of each chapter highlight the main points and reinforce salient concepts for the student.

For Review

Questions and topics for discussion are provided to help students review and analyze material for overall understanding.

References

Accurate and current documentation is provided at the end of each chapter.

Annotated Readings

Selected resources are provided with annotations to help students locate additional information to supplement the material presented within the chapter.

SUPPLEMENTARY MATERIALS

An Instructor's Manual and Test Bank accompanies the text. This manual has been carefully planned and developed to assist instructors in using and getting the most benefit from the text.

Prepared by Paul Cardoza, Ed.D., of Cranston Public Schools in Cranston, Rhode Island, the Instructor's Manual includes the following features for each chapter:

Chapter Overview. The chapter overview presents the salient points covered within the chapter.

Chapter Objectives. Additional objectives for each chapter are identified.

Chapter Outline. Each chapter is succinctly outlined to provide the instructor with the fundamental concepts and ideas contained within each section.

Suggested Learning Activities. Suggested in-class activities and outside assignments are presented.

Test Bank. Constructed by a specialist in measurement and evaluation, June Nutter, Ph.D., of Rhode Island College, the Test Bank contains a variety of questions (with answers provided). The questions include multiple choice, true/false, matching, and essay test items.

Transparency Masters. Fifty transparency masters conclude the manual and include many of the most important diagrams and charts from the text to help explain the concepts presented.

We believe that the teachers who use this manual will recognize the excellent job performed by Dr. Cardoza and Dr. Nutter.

ACKNOWLEDGMENTS

A project such as this could not have been completed without the many contributions of others. Our thanks are gratefully extended to the publisher's reviewers for their insightful comments, constructive criticism, and numerous helpful suggestions. They include:

Tim Chandler
Syracuse University

John Cheffers
Boston University

Suzi D'Annolfo
Farmington Public Schools

Linda Griffin
Kent State University

Ron McBride
Texas A&M University

Tom Steen
University of North Dakota

Hans van der Mars
Arizona State University

Kay M. Williamson
University of Illinois at Chicago

We would also like to acknowledge our contributing authors. Appreciation is extended to Dr. Victor Mancini for his work on Chapter 4, to Dr. Kathy Pinkham for her preparation of Chapters 19 and 22, and to Ms. Joy Buffan for authoring Chapters 20 and 21. Appreciation is also extended to Dr. Sarah Rich for her critical review of the manuscript.

A special recognition is extended to the outstanding professionals at Mosby. Their professional expertise and advice were invaluable in completing this first edition. We are especially indebted to Michelle Turenne for seeing this project through to completion.

Deborah A. Wuest
Bennett J. Lombardo

Contents

Detailed Contents

PART I

Value and Overview

Physical education is an important part of the secondary school curriculum, and it contributes in many ways to the overall goals of education. It also makes a unique contribution to the education of students as it is the only subject in the curriculum devoted to the study of human movement, development of motor skills, and promotion of fitness. The contribution of physical education to students' development in the affective, cognitive, and psychomotor domains assists in attainment of educational goals.

The unique characteristics of adolescents must be considered in planning and conducting a quality physical education program. Designing meaningful physical education experiences requires consideration of the psychomotor, cognitive, and affective developmental characteristics of each student.

Beginning teachers should orient themselves to the nature of the school and the community and acquaint themselves with their many professional responsibilities. Many challenges await teachers. Those teachers who are aware of these challenges can more effectively use a variety of strategies to meet them.

OUTLINE

1 Physical Education in the Secondary Schools
2 Secondary School Students
3 Beginning Teachers

CHAPTER 1

Physical Education in the Secondary Schools

CHAPTER OBJECTIVES

◆ To describe the goals of secondary school physical education

◆ To relate the goals of secondary school physical education to those of education

◆ To discuss selected factors influencing the nature and conduct of secondary school physical education

◆ To present an overview of salient features of quality physical education programs

Contemporary secondary school physical education is best characterized by the word *diverse*. Physical education programs at the secondary level range from high-quality, exemplary programs to "throw out the ball," play-type programs. Some curriculums include a wide variety of activities, building on a foundation of fundamental skills and leading progressively toward proficiency in several physical activities, focusing on the goal of promoting lifetime participation. Other curriculums are more limited in scope, are haphazardly constructed, and lack clearly defined goals.

Dedicated, committed teachers conduct excellent programs in a variety of settings, many in conditions that fall short of ideal. Other teachers struggle to accomplish their goals, because they are confronted with overwhelming demands, and they experience isolation and burnout. Still other teachers are teaching by "going through the motions," simply striving to make it through the day. Differences in teaching styles are noted as well. Some teachers employ a diversity of teaching styles, which are designed to accommodate the wide range of individual differences found in a typical secondary school physical education class. Other teachers tend to use exclusively a direct style of teaching, focusing their efforts on reaching the majority of students. Some teachers are a role model for what they profess; they exemplify a healthy, active lifestyle. Other teachers fail to "practice what they preach," exhibiting a lifestyle and level of fitness at odds with what they advocate for their students.

Students are in the throes of adolescence; some are struggling to master various developmental tasks, while others are finding the transition from childhood to adulthood relatively smooth. Students enter secondary school physical education classes with varied backgrounds and skills. Some students have mastered the fundamental motor skills, acquired prerequisite knowledge, and developed positive attitudes toward physical activity; other students lag behind in these areas. Some are excited and challenged by the secondary school physical education program. They are motivated to improve their skills and fitness levels, find personal satisfaction in moving, and incorporate physical activity into their lives. The attitudes of other students could be described as dissatisfied and apathetic. Some of these students are only too glad to finish their physical education requirement and may make a silent vow never to participate in sports again.

Support for secondary school physical education programs varies as well. In some schools, it is securely enmeshed as an integral part of the secondary school curriculum and appreciated for its contribution to the total development of the students. In other schools, physical education hovers on the fringes of acceptability, tolerated and included only because it is required by state mandate.

Physical education, at times, suffers from an image

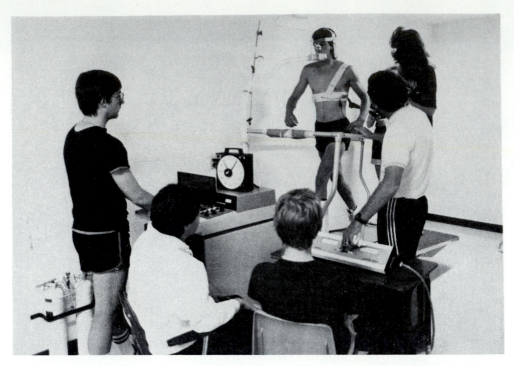

Students conduct an exercise test under supervision of the teacher at Rock Springs High School, Rock Springs, WY.

Courtesy of Paul Grube, Rock Springs High School, Rock Springs, WY.

problem. It is often misunderstood. While some people are familiar with the instructional nature of physical education and the outcomes being sought, other people mistakenly equate physical education with athletics or conceive of physical education as play or recess.

The diverse nature of secondary school physical education throughout the country presents a challenge to professionals. In many cases, this challenge involves addressing improvements in the curriculum, employing a variety of teaching styles to meet the needs of all students, and convincing the public, school personnel, parents, and students that physical education is an important part of the total educational experience.

Physical Education Defined

Physical education is a learning process designed to foster the development of motor skills, health-related fitness, knowledge, and attitudes relative to physical activity through a series of carefully planned and conducted experiences. The learning environment is thoughtfully structured to enhance the overall development of each student within the three learning domains—psychomotor, cognitive, and affective. These learning experiences help students understand how humans move and how to execute movements safely, efficiently, and effectively. These experiences are conducted in such a way as to promote positive feelings toward oneself as a mover and

an appreciation for the contribution that physical activity can make to one's quality of life (Fig. 1-1).

Physical education is an integral part of the total educational curriculum. It is the only area of the school curriculum that teaches motor skills and an understanding of human movement and provides opportunities to facilitate their development. Furthermore, physical education, when thoughtfully planned and taught, can support learning across the curriculum. For example, physical education can integrate information about anatomy and physiology as well as nutrition that is taught in science and health classes. Some teachers have further built on this knowledge by offering their students a course in applied exercise physiology. It can also provide an opportunity for students to apply their mathematical skills, for example, in calculating caloric cost of various physical activities and the amount of energy expended. A well-designed and sequenced K-12 physical education program helps students develop the skills and attitudes conducive to lifelong learning, an important educational goal. Physical education is an essential component of any curriculum designed to educate the whole person.

Broadly defined, the physical education program encompasses the instructional program and other related programs: intramurals, sports clubs, recreational programs, and interscholastic programs. Intramurals, sports clubs, and recreational programs provide extended opportunities for all students who voluntarily choose to

A physically educated person:

HAS learned skills necessary to perform a variety of physical activities
- Moves using concepts of body awareness, space awareness, effort, and relationships
- Demonstrates competence in a variety of manipulative, locomotor, and nonlocomotor skills
- Demonstrates competence in combinations of manipulative, locomotor, and nonlocomotor skills performed individually and with others
- Demonstrates competence in many different forms of physical activity
- Demonstrates proficiency in a few forms of physical activity
- Has learned how to learn new skills

IS physically fit
- Assesses, achieves, and maintains physical fitness
- Designs safe personal fitness programs in accordance with principles of training and conditioning

DOES participate regularly in physical activity
- Participates in health-enhancing physical activity at least three times a week
- Selects and regularly participates in lifetime physical activities

KNOWS the implications of and the benefits from involvement in physical activities
- Identifies the benefits, costs, and obligations associated with regular participation in physical activity
- Recognizes the risk and safety factors associated with regular participation in physical activity
- Applies concepts and principles to the development of motor skills
- Understands that wellness involves more than being physically fit
- Knows the rules, strategies, and appropriate behaviors for selected physical activities
- Recognizes that participation in physical activity can lead to multicultural and international understanding
- Understands that physical activity provides the opportunity for enjoyment, self-expression, and communication

VALUES physical activity and its contributions to a healthful lifestyle
- Appreciates the relationships with others that result from participation in physical activity
- Respects the role that regular physical activity plays in the pursuit of lifelong health and well being
- Cherishes the feelings that result from regular participation in physical activity

FIG. 1-1   Characteristics of a physically educated person.

Reprinted by permission of National Association for Sport and Physical Education, Physical Education Outcomes Committee: *Definition of the physically educated person: outcomes of quality physical education programs,* Reston, Va, 1990, AAHPERD.

participate in physical activities conducted before, during, and after school hours. These activities may include both those activities taught in physical education class and activities of special interest to students.

Interscholastic sports or athletics encompass those programs for highly skilled students. Extensive training, practice, and commitment are required for these programs, which emphasize performing and competing at a high level of skill.

Goals of Physical Education

Throughout the years professionals have set forth many purposes for secondary school physical education. These purposes or general aims provide direction for the program and offer a basis for designing the curriculum and teaching for achievement. Goals are statements of intended outcomes that, when attained, will lead to the fulfillment of our purposes.

As a young professional, it may be helpful to consider the following questions:

◆ What is the primary purpose of secondary school physical education?
◆ What are our goals?
◆ What are our priorities?
◆ At the end of 13 years of physical education, encompassing grades K-12, what should students have achieved?

From our perspective, the primary purpose of secondary school physical education is to assist each individual to develop the skills, attain the knowledge, and acquire the attitudes that will result in a lifetime of participation in physical activity. It is our mission to help all students incorporate meaningful physical activity into their lives. Physical activity encompasses a diversity of sports, dance, outdoor pursuits, aquatics, and fitness activities. Regular participation in appropriate physical activity is important to attain an optimal level of health and well-being and achieve a high quality of life.

How can this purpose be achieved? What goals or outcomes will lead to its attainment? The National Association of Sport and Physical Education (NASPE) has identified a series of instructional outcomes for physical education that are helpful to teachers in developing and implementing their programs (Fig. 1-1).[1]

How can these outcomes best be achieved? There are many approaches that will lead to their attainment. Effective teachers achieve these outcomes in ways that are appropriate to the schools in which they teach, their students' characteristics, and their personal teaching styles.

These outcomes embrace the acquisition of physical skills, promotion of participation, achievement of fitness, attainment of knowledge, and development of attitudes. When viewed from the more traditional perspective, the goals of physical education relate to the student development in three interrelated domains: psychomotor, cognitive, and affective.

Psychomotor development. The acquisition and refinement of motor skills essential for everyday activities (for example, posture or lifting objects) and for movement in a variety of physical activities, such as dance, sports, aquatics, or outdoor pursuits, are important outcomes associated with this domain.

Teachers will find that their students exhibit a wide range of differences with respect to motor skill development. Some students have mastered the fundamental manipulative, locomotor, and nonlocomotor skills that serve as a foundation for the more specialized sport skills that are typically emphasized at this level. Other students lack competency in the fundamental skills. Teachers must assess students' abilities at the start of instruction, accept students at their entry level, and provide a sequential progression of activities to allow each individual to attain the stated motor skill objectives. Effort and participation should be encouraged, extra help should be provided if

necessary, and personal accomplishments should be recognized. Learning experiences that provide for success while developing skill proficiency increase the probability that students will incorporate physical activity into their lifestyle.

Health-related fitness, with its objectives of cardiorespiratory efficiency, flexibility, appropriate body composition, and muscular strength and endurance, should receive strong emphasis in the secondary school physical education curriculum because of its significant impact on the health of individuals and their quality of life.[2] A progressive, systematic approach to fitness should be used, with the program adapted to the needs of the individual student. It may be helpful to expose students to a wide range of physical activities and explain their potential to contribute to the development of fitness. Following this exposure, students can select activities in which to develop proficiency. By allowing students to have a choice of activities, students can select those that are best suited to their abilities and needs as well as being personally meaningful and enjoyable. No matter what the positive outcomes of participation in terms of fitness, if students do not like to do an activity, they will be unlikely to continue participation on a regular basis and incorporate it into their lives.

Cognitive development. Acquisition of knowledge is an important outcome of physical education. Development of knowledge encompasses the learning of rules, strategies, and safety considerations for various physical activities. Problem-solving, critical thinking, and analytical skills are also important outcomes to be achieved. Physical education teachers must provide students with guidance and experiences that will help them understand the relationship between movement concepts (time, space, relationships, and effort) and principles and the performance of motor skills. Teaching for transfer of knowledge and skills from one situation to another is also important, that is, teachers must help students make the connection between skills and knowledge previously learned and new learnings. When performing skills, students should be able to identify key elements of the skill, analyze their performances, and prescribe necessary changes to enhance the performances; this is essential to promoting lifelong learning in physical education.

Understanding of the health-related benefits of physical activity is necessary if students are to incorporate physical activity into their lifestyles. By understanding the benefits and being aware of the contribution of physical activity to one's quality of life, students can strengthen purposes and motivation for being active, and the likelihood that they will continue participation increases. Knowledge is essential if students are to become self-educative. For example, students should know how to develop a personal exercise prescription in terms of the frequency, duration, and intensity of exercise as well as be able to evaluate the potential of various physical activities in terms of their contribution to fitness. How-

A par cours provides students with opportunity to participate in many different exercises and promotes physical fitness.
Courtesy of Kathy Pinkham.

ever, if students do not know the benefits of physical activity to their health and its contribution to one's quality of life, or if they are unable to make the appropriate adjustments in their exercise prescription as their needs change, the probability that they will be lifelong participants is diminished.

Affective development. Psychosocial and emotional development, development of moral reasoning, and formulation of values, interests, and attitudes are encompassed within the affective domain. Development in this domain should not be left to chance but actively sought through carefully planned approaches designed to promote growth in this area. In selecting learning experiences and teaching processes to develop skill and knowledge, physical education teachers must also consider how they will have an impact on affective development.

Physical education has the potential to develop such desirable characteristics as cooperation, fair play, courtesy, responsibility, acceptance, and appreciation of one's efforts and abilities as well as those of other students. The enhancement of self-concept, self-respect, self-confidence, and self-responsibility are important and should not be overlooked. Students who perceive themselves as competent and have confidence in their abilities as movers are more likely to seek involvement in physical activities.

Developing an appreciation for the contribution that regular physical activity makes to lifelong health and well-being is also an important outcome for which to strive.

Teachers must model the behaviors and values they aspire to develop in their students.[3] Consideration for the needs and feelings of others, respect for each individual, and enjoyment of physical activity are some of the behaviors teachers should exhibit in working with their students if they desire to promote affective development. Acknowledgment and reinforcement of appropriate student affective behavior, such as a student assisting another student on a learning task or praising the performance of a classmate, is important as well, because it strengthens and encourages the desired behavior.

Psychomotor, cognitive, and affective development are the focus of secondary school physical education. Physical education teachers need to be cognizant of the close relationship that exists between the three learning domains. The types of activities taught and the manner in which they are taught can positively or negatively affect students' feelings about the activity and physical education. These feelings will, in turn, influence students' feelings about themselves as movers and their participation in physical activities. In teaching, physical education teachers must assess their efforts in light of their impact on achievement in the three domains. It is also important to remember that physical education is not taught in isolation. The outcomes achieved through physical education must also be viewed as an integral part of the broader goals of education.

Physical Education and Goals of Education

As part of the total education of the students, the curriculum in physical education should be congruent with the educational philosophy of the school and meaningfully contribute to the school's educational goals. Education is viewed by many as the backbone of our nation.

In our society, contemporary education has many aims.[4] One of its primary purposes is to provide experiences that will help all individuals develop to their fullest potential, regardless of their ability, race, sex, religion, or economic status. This purpose typically encompasses development in the three educational domains. Helping each individual attain a high quality of life is another important outcome. Skills, knowledge, and attitudes that enable students to attain a high level of health and well-being are necessary. Another goal is to prepare individuals for life. Schools are charged with preparing each individual to function as an effective, contributing member of society, both socially and vocationally, both now and in the future. In our rapidly changing society, one of the most important educational aims is to prepare individuals to be lifelong learners, to be self-educative. Schools must help individuals acquire the foundation and self-responsibility for lifelong learning.

National commissions and noted authorities have set forth many specific goals for education over the years.[3,4] In general, schools should develop the basic skills of reading, writing, computation, social studies, science, and computer competency, because these skills form the foundation for future learning. Development of critical and creative thinking, decision-making skills, ethical principles, and values have also been cited as important goals of education. Schools are also charged with helping students develop skills in human relations, fostering global human concern, and appreciating other cultures. Students must also be provided with experiences that will enable them to develop a sense of self-worth, to value human life, and to respect the worth, dignity, and unique potential of each individual. Respect for the environment, worthy use of leisure time, and an appreciation for beauty

---

Participation in appropriate kinds and amounts of physical activity:
- Promotes changes in brain structure and functions in infants and young children. Sensory stimulation through physical activity is essential for the optimal growth and development of the young nervous system.
- Promotes early cognitive function through imitation, symbolic play, the development of language, and the use of symbols.
- Assists in the development and refinement of perceptual abilities involving vision, balance, and tactile sensations.
- Enhances the function of the central nervous system through the promotion of a healthier neuronal network.
- Aids the development of cognition through opportunities to develop learning strategies, decision making, acquiring, retrieving, integrating information, and solving problems.
- Fortifies the mineralization of the skeleton and promotes the maintenance of lean body tissue, while simultaneously reducing the deposition of fat.
- Leads to proficiency in the neuromuscular skills that are the basis for successful participation in games, dances, sports, and leisure activities.
- Is an important regulator of obesity because it increases energy expenditure, suppresses appetite, increases metabolic rate, and increases lean body mass.
- Improves aerobic fitness, muscle endurance, muscle power, and muscle strength.
- Is an effective deterrent to coronary heart disease because of the effects on blood lipids, blood pressure, obesity, and capacity for physical work.
- Improves cardiac function as indicated by an increased stroke volume, cardiac output blood volume, and total hemoglobin.
- Is associated with a reduction in atherosclerotic diseases.
- Promotes a more positive attitude toward physical activity and leads to a more active lifestyle during unscheduled leisure time.
- Enhances self-concept and self-esteem as indicated by increased confidence, assertiveness, emotional stability, independence, and self-control.
- Is a major force in the socializing of individuals during late childhood and adolescence.
- Is instrumental in the development and growth of moral reasoning, problem solving, creativity, and social competence.
- Is an effective deterrent to mental illness and alleviates mental stress.
- Improves the psychosocial and physiological functions of mentally and physically handicapped individuals.
- Deters depletion of bone mineral and lean body tissue in elderly individuals.
- Prevents the onset of some diseases and opposes the debilitating effects of old age.

FIG. 1-2   Contributions of physical activity to well-being.
From Seefeldt V, Vogel PG: *The value of physical activity*, Reston, Va, 1986, AAHPERD. Reprinted by permission of the National Association for Sport and Physical Education.

and nature are also mentioned as desired educational outcomes.

Preparing individuals for vocations and helping them achieve occupational competence are important outcomes of education. Preparation for a career is viewed as critical by students and parents. The most recent educational goals set forth by former President Bush for the year 2000 emphasize excellence in education and preparation of students to enable our country to remain economically competitive in the global economy. These goals include (1) all children beginning school ready to learn, (2) increasing the high-school graduation rate to 90%, (3) demonstrating competence in critical subjects as assessed through periodic testing, (4) students being the first in the world in the areas of mathematics and science, (5) every adult will be literate and possess the skills to compete in our economy, and (6) the schools will be drug and violence free.

Physical education contributes to the aims and goals of education in many significant ways. However, whether the potential of physical education to contribute to educational goals is fulfilled rests heavily on the shoulders of teachers, their commitment to conducting a quality program, and support received from within the school system.

If education is concerned with the development of the total person, the unique contribution of physical education to this endeavor cannot be overlooked. Physical education is the only area of the school curriculum that promotes the development of motor skills and fitness. The contribution of physical education to psychomotor development is unparalleled by any other curricular area.

A quality physical education experience supports learning by enhancing individual attributes important to learning. Seefeldt and Vogel,[5] in the text *The Value of Physical Education,* identify outcomes that can be attained through participation in the appropriate type and amount of physical activity (Fig. 1-2). These outcomes are based on evidence in the biological and behavioral sciences supporting the relationship of physical activity to well-being. After one reviews these outcomes, it becomes increasingly apparent how a thoughtfully designed and competently implemented physical education program can promote the development of qualities that will assist children and youth to learn across the curriculum. These outcomes offer strong support for the significant role of physical education in the school curriculum.

Physical education can also contribute to the promotion of lifelong learning. All areas of school curriculum should strive to enhance positive feelings toward lifelong learning as well as provide foundational skills and knowledge. This can be accomplished by helping students set realistic goals for achievement, by providing for the needs of students at various levels of development and ability, by encouraging acceptance of responsibility, by fostering creative and critical thinking, by nurturing students' self-esteem, and by enabling them to gain confidence in themselves as learners. A quality physical education program certainly can support this endeavor.

There is increased recognition by all segments of society of the significant contribution of physical activity to well-being and one's quality of life. Regular and appropriate physical activity is an important component of health. Inactivity has been identified as a significant risk factor in disease. If we are to socialize people into lifespan involvement in sport and fitness activities, if we are to

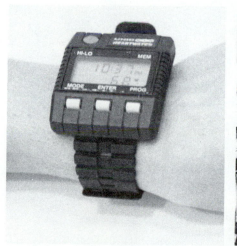

Just as in other areas of the educational curriculum, technology is being increasingly incorporated into physical education. Students at Tilford Middle School, Vinton, IA use heart rate monitors to monitor their exercise efforts.

Courtesy of Beth Kirkpatrick, Tilford Middle School, Vinton, IA.

help people understand the relationship between physical activity and health, then the critical role of school physical education cannot be overlooked. This effort must begin in preschool programs and be supported and strengthened at each level of education. The schools are our best hope of educating all people, regardless of race, sex, or economic status, about the importance and positive outcomes of incorporating physical activity into their lifestyles—it may be our best avenue for improving the health of all Americans and enhancing their quality of life.

While it is important to understand how physical education contributes to the education of the individual, it is equally important to appreciate that physical education is a worthy subject to study in its own right. Appreciation for the elegance of movement, satisfaction from physical exertion and efforts directed toward achieving movement competence, and the sheer joy of participation in sport should not be overlooked. These and other outcomes are worthy in and of themselves. Moreover, as the body of knowledge comprising physical education continues to grow in depth and breadth, it is likely that classes involving the study of the discipline of physical education will begin to appear in the secondary school curriculum. In some schools students can elect to enroll in a class in exercise physiology; perhaps classes in sports sociology or psychology will be offered as well in the future.

PHYSICAL EDUCATION IN THE SCHOOLS

It is clear that physical education can contribute in many significant ways to the goals of education and the total development of the individual. Yet, support for inclusion of physical education in the secondary school curriculum is not overwhelming. As Siedentop[6] states,

. . . in too many places, physical education exists precariously as a marginal aspect in secondary education. What is most disturbing is that at a time in American culture when sport, fitness, and physical active leisure experiences are increasingly valued, school physical physical education is so often devalued, generally lacking in credibility within the secondary school culture, and too often ridiculed by those outside of the school.

There are several factors that have the potential to influence the status of secondary school physical education. These factors include the educational reform movement, the fitness movement, legislation, and public health goals.

Status of Physical Education in the Schools

In the 1980s cries for educational reform abounded. Secondary schools were called upon to establish more rigorous academic standards and to devote more time to helping students achieve competency in the educational basics, specifically reading, writing, science, social studies, math, and computer sciences. Despite the significant contributions that physical education can make to the total development of the individual, it is not seen by many educational experts as a basic.

Physical education's status as an integral part of the secondary school curriculum is being challenged. Although the National Association of Secondary School Principals emphasized the worth of physical education and its important role in a curriculum designed to educate the whole person, support for physical education is diminishing.[7] As curriculums are being restructured to include more time for academics, time allotted to physical education and other subjects such as music and art is being decreased.

In 1986 to 1987 AAHPERD, in a study entitled *The Shape of the Nation*,[8] assessed each state's physical education requirement. Illinois was the only state that met the AAHPERD recommended requirement of 30 minutes of physical education a day for students in grades K-6 and 50 minutes of physical education a day for students in grades 7-12. Only 12% of the states require high-school students to participate in physical education all 4 years; 44% of the states require that physical education be taken only 1 year. Other data revealed that the number of students enrolled in physical education declined as

Teachers use community resources near the school to increase variety of program offerings.
Courtesy of Kathy Pinkham.

grade level increased; in fifth grade 97% of students were enrolled, while in twelfth grade only about 52% of the students were enrolled.

Within the past decade, national studies of youth fitness have raised a great deal of concern among the public and professionals. The National Children and Youth Fitness Study I, released in 1985, was designed to elicit information about the health and fitness of fifth through twelfth grade.[9] The data revealed that the fitness levels of youths need improvement. For example, when the data for the body composition measure were examined, the average score for both males and females approached or was in the moderately high range. On the cardiopulmonary measure, the average score revealed that many completed the 1-mile run-walk at a slow jog. The study also revealed that secondary school programs tended to focus more on competitive and team sport activities rather

than on lifetime and individual activities that can be used by adults for participation throughout life. Because of the link between youth health fitness and adult degenerative disease, it is imperative that we focus our efforts on health-related fitness and providing our students with the skills, knowledge, and attitudes that will promote lifespan participation in physical activity.

Yet while enthusiasm for exercise and fitness appears to be at an unprecedented level in the United States today, when the data about adult participation patterns are examined, the extent of participation is not as pervasive as it seems. Available data indicate that only 10% to 20% of adults exercise with sufficient frequency, intensity, and duration (e.g., exercise involving large muscles in dynamic movement for a minimum of 20 minutes, 3 or more days per week at an intensity of 60% or greater of cardiovascular capacity) to develop and maintain ade-

---

Senate Resolution 43
House Resolution 97

To encourage state and local governments and local educational agencies to provide quality daily physical education programs for all children from kindergarten through grade 12.

Whereas physical education is essential to the physical development of the growing child;

Whereas physical education helps improve the overall health of children by increasing cardiovascular endurance, muscular strength and power, flexibility, weight regulation, improved bone development, improved posture, skillful moving, increased mental alertness, active lifestyle habits, and constructive use of leisure time;

Whereas physical education helps improve the mental alertness, academic performance, readiness to learn, and enthusiasm for learning of children;

Whereas physical education helps improve self-esteem, interpersonal relationships, responsible behavior, and independence of children;

Whereas children who participate in quality daily physical education programs tend to be more healthy and physically fit;

Whereas physically fit adults have significantly reduced risk factors for heart attacks and strokes;

Whereas the Surgeon General, in Objectives for the Nation, recommends increasing the number of school-mandated physical education programs that focus on health-related physical fitness;

Whereas the Secretary of Education, in First Lessons—A Report on Elementary Education in America, recognized that elementary schools have a special mandate to provide elementary school children with knowledge, habits, and attitudes that will equip the children for a fit and healthy life; and

Whereas a quality daily physical education program for all children from kindergarten through grade 12 is an essential part of a comprehensive education: now, therefore, be it

Resolved by the Senate (the House of Representatives concurring), that Congress encourages state and local governments and local educational agencies to provide quality daily physical education programs for all children from kindergarten through grade 12.

FIG. 1-3   Resolution supporting daily, quality physical education.

quate levels of health-related fitness.[10-12] Furthermore, the extent of participation is influenced by such factors as age, sex, race, education, economic level, occupation, community setting, and geographic location.[10-13] The prevalence of physical activity decreases with age, is higher among men than women, and is greater among whites than nonwhites. High-school and college graduates, middle- and upper-middle-income people, and professional persons tend to participate more. Higher participation rates are also noted for those individuals who live in suburban settings and those who live in the western part of the United States. School physical education programs offer us perhaps the greatest opportunity to address disparities in participation, especially those linked to sex, race, and socioeconomic status.

Support for physical education is not lacking however. In 1987 the U.S. House of Representatives and the U.S. Senate passed resolutions encouraging states to provide quality, daily physical education for all children in grades K-12 (Fig. 1-3). This resolution arose out of concern for the health and fitness of our children and youth. While the resolution does not require daily physical education, it does offer strong support for our programs. In addition to AAHPERD, this resolution was also endorsed by such prestigious organizations as the American Medical Association, American Academy of Pediatrics, American Heart Association, and the National Education Association.

Within the last decade public health goals have reflected an increased emphasis on promoting health and preventing disease. Three national health reports, *Healthy People,*[14] *Objectives for the Nation,*[15] and *Healthy People 2000,*[10] clearly articulate national health goals and specific objectives to be achieved. The goals set forth in the latest document *Healthy People 2000* reflect an increased emphasis on reduction of preventable morbidity and chronic disability. Reducing health disparities between population groups is emphasized. Furthermore, the goals reflect a concern about improving the quality of life, not only increasing longevity. Long life, without health, is not acceptable. Achieving a full range of functional capacity throughout the lifespan is the goal.

Like its predecessors, the goals and objectives for improving the health of Americans by the year 2000 set forth in this latest report acknowledge that physical fitness and exercise are fundamental to a healthy people and a healthy society. Lifestyle is increasingly being recognized as a critical factor in disease. When the 10 leading causes of potential life lost before age 65 are examined, lifestyle is estimated to account for more than 50% of this problem.[16] Given the strong relationship between lifestyle and disease, it is evident that appropriate modifications in one's lifestyle can have a significant influence on one's health, as well as one's length and one's quality of life. Physical activity and fitness has been identified as one of 22 priority areas where lifestyle modifications can help in the attainment of these public health goals.

Increasing the amount of time physical education teachers spend teaching lifetime sports is one of the Year 2000 objectives.
Courtesy of Suzi D'Annalfo, Conard High School, West Hartford, CT.

For each priority area, such as physical activity and fitness, specific objectives were established that would provide direction to professionals in these efforts to attain the stated health goals. The objectives for physical activity and fitness, as shown in Table 1-1, are based on health-related fitness.

Physical education teachers are in a unique position to provide leadership to the rest of the community in achieving our national health goals. School programs provide the best means to reach millions of people and reduce the disparities in health among different segments of the population. Physical education programs can be instrumental in helping children establish physical activity patterns that are beneficial to their health and incorporating them into their lifestyle at an early age. Moreover, as schools increasingly take on the role of a community center, the potential of school-based physical education programs to reach people of all ages, races, and economic status will increase.

The conduct of physical education programs in the schools has also been significantly affected by legislation. In 1972 Title IX of the Educational Amendments Act was passed. This act stated, in part, that no person shall, on the basis of sex, be excluded from participation or discriminated against under any educational program or activity receiving federal assistance. This legislation was the impetus for coeducational classes in physical education at the high-school level, which historically had been separated by gender. According to the law, in physical education classes objective standards of performance can be used to group students by ability as long as the standards are applied without regard to gender. During contact sports, such as wrestling, boxing, rugby, ice hockey, football or basketball, students may be separated by sex. Title IX has also led to greater equality of opportunity

T A B L E   1-1

Year 2000 Objectives for the Nation: Physical Activity and Exercise

Specific Objectives	Goal	Baseline (Year)
Health Status Objectives		
Reduce deaths due to coronary heart disease.	100/100,000 people	135/100,000 people
Reduce prevalence of overweight.	20% for people 20 years and older; 15% for youths 12-19 years	26% for people 20 years or older; 15% for youths 12-19 years (1976-1980)
Risk Reduction Objectives		
Increase number of people who engage regularly, preferably on a daily basis, in light to moderate physical activity for at least 30 minutes/day.	30% for people 6 years and older	22% for people 18 years or older who were active 5 or more times/week; 12% active 7 or more times/week (1985)
Increase number of people who engage in vigorous physical activity that promotes the development and maintenance of cardiorespiratory fitness 3 or more days/week for at least 20 minutes/session.	30% for people 18 years or older; 75% for children and youths 6-17 years	12% for people 18 years or older (1985); 66% for children and youths 10-17 years (1984)
Reduce number of people 6 years and older who engage in no leisure-time physical activity.	15%	24% for people 18 years or older (1985)
Increase number of people 6 years and older who regularly engage in physical activities that promote and maintain muscular strength, muscular endurance, and flexibility.	40%	
Increase number of people 12 years and older who are overweight and have adopted sound dietary practices combined with regular physical activity to attain an appropriate body weight.	50%	30% of women and 25% of men 18 years or older (1985)
Services and Protection Objectives		
Increase number of children and youths in grades 1-12 who participate in daily school physical education.	50%	36% (1984-1986)
Increase proportion of school physical education class time that students spend actively engaged in physical activities, preferably in lifetime physical activities.	50%	27% (1983)
Increase number of worksites offering employer-sponsored physical activity and fitness programs.	20%-80% depending on size of worksite	14%-54% depending on size of worksite (1985)
Increase availability and accessibility of community physical activity and fitness facilities.		
Hiking, biking and fitness trails (miles)	1/10,000 people	1/71,000 people
Swimming pools	1/25,000 people	1/53,000 people
Parks and recreation open space (acres)	4/1,000 people	1.8/1,000 people

From Public Health Service, US Department of Health and Human Services: *Promoting health/preventing disease: year 2000 objectives for the nation,* Washington DC, 1989, US Government Printing Office.

for girls in interscholastic sports, and the number of participants has grown dramatically since the law's inception.

It has been over 20 years since the passage of Title IX. Have we achieved gender equity in physical education? Many suggest that while significant progress has been made, Title IX has fallen short of its goal.[17-19] The content and conduct of coeducational classes, in many instances,

reflect sexist practices that, overtly and covertly, perpetuate stereotypes. Teachers persist in grouping students by gender, although a wider range of abilities exists within each gender than between genders.[3] Even when classes conform to the requirements of the law, they fail, in many instances, to realize the spirit of Title IX.

Another law that promotes equity for all students and has had significant impact on the conduct of physical education classes is the Education of All Children Act of 1975, often referred to as PL (Public Law) 94-142 (see Chapter 11 for a fuller discussion). This landmark legislation and the laws that have followed it mandated a free, appropriate, quality education be provided for all children, regardless of disability. This legislation has increased opportunities for meaningful participation in physical education and athletics for students with disabilities. It requires that each child be educated in the least restrictive environment and promotes the integration of children with disabilities with their peers.

Federal legislation requires equal educational opportunities for all students, regardless of gender, ability, socioeconomic status, race, and ethnic background. Today we are seeing an increased emphasis on multicultural education in the schools. Designed to promote an understanding of cultural diversity and cultural pluralism, multicultural education emphasizes respect for individual differences and accommodation of them in a thoughtful, sensitive manner so that each student's needs can be met. As our society grows in diversity, commitment to equity for all individuals becomes increasingly important.

Equity is a multifaceted issue. Establishing programs that meet the requirements of the law may satisfy the legal issue, yet these programs may not be truly equitable (e.g., even though the class is coeducational, the class is separated into boys and girls for instruction; even though the child is mainstreamed, the teacher assigns the child to keep score rather than modifying participation for inclusion). Attaining equity requires commitment to the spirit of the law—an abiding conviction that each child has the right to a quality education and a commitment to work toward attainment of this goal.

Harrison and Blakemore[3] offer several suggestions about what teachers can do to foster an equitable approach to physical education. Teachers can:

1. Use teaching styles that provide for accommodation of a diversity of students' needs.
2. Be sensitive to individual differences and avoid embarrassing or belittling students in front of their peers.
3. Focus on students' abilities and work to strengthen areas of need.
4. Use activities to help overcome stereotypes and to enable students to learn to appreciate themselves and their peers.
5. Modify activities and rules to provide for meaningful participation by all students.
6. Become aware of students' interactions with other students.
7. Choose students for class leaders, role models, skill demonstrators equitably—do not always choose males or athletes, for example.
8. Promote self-responsibility while encouraging students to be supportive of other's efforts.
9. Help students appreciate the uniqueness of each person.
10. Model positive, equitable interactions with all students.

Equity requires teachers to strive to value rather than remediate differences, to see students as individuals with a diversity of needs to be met, and to make a commitment to meeting these needs. Equity means treating students so that their abilities are used to the fullest and their needs are met in such a way as to help each achieve their fullest potential.

CONTEMPORARY SECONDARY SCHOOL PHYSICAL EDUCATION

Secondary school physical education programs have been criticized by the public and professionals alike. Criticism has focused on the worth of the subject matter, the outcomes realized, the manner in which the program is conducted, and its contribution to the education of students.[3,6,19-22] Unfortunately, this criticism obscures the fact that there are many outstanding programs of secondary school physical education being conducted throughout the nation.[23-29] Dedicated teachers work hard toward achieving the desired outcomes for their programs, using a variety of approaches that adhere to the basic tenets of curriculum and instruction and are sensitive to the context in which they teach.

Curriculum

Outstanding programs have well-defined goals, and efforts are directed toward their attainment.[23] Whether the curriculum emphasizes sport education, health-related fitness education, motor skill acquisition and noncompetitive activities, outdoor pursuits, or an integrated academic approach, these programs have a clear focus that is communicated to school administrators, parents, and students. Moreover, there is a clear expectation that students will acheive these goals and an accountability system that furthers their attainment. Additionally, these programs tend to marshal their efforts toward pursuit of well-defined objectives; rather than trying to accomplish a multitude of goals, their efforts are focused on attaining those goals identified as most important to students' needs.

The content of these programs is varied. Some schools embrace a traditional multiactivity team sport approach at the junior high-school level, moving toward an in-depth approach to lifetime activities at the high school. Other programs emphasize health-related fitness and wellness in their endeavors. Activities such as aerobic dance, weight training, yoga, and progressive relaxation training are offered, drop-in and recreational fitness opportunities are available, and information about wellness is integrated within the curriculum. Yet other schools offer activities that focus on outdoor pursuits, such as Project Adventure, climbing, rappelling, and orienteering.

Some teachers make arrangements to use off-campus facilities to broaden program offerings. Students from Camp Hill High School, PA use community health club facilities during physical education classes.

Courtesy of Emily Leonardo, Camp Hill High School, Camp Hill, PA.

Increasingly, schools are broadening their curriculum offerings by using community facilities. Schools without pools offer swimming in cooperation with the local YMCA, community tennis courts and commercial bowling alleys are used for instruction, and the natural resources associated with the community provide opportunities for instruction in sailing, canoeing, skiing, hiking, and other outdoor pursuits. Community members with expertise in specific activities, such as karate, are being used to conduct classes for secondary school students in another effort to broaden activity offerings.

Careful sequencing of activities is evident in the curriculum. From the foundation in basic skills, students are progressively introduced to more advanced skills. The tenth-grade curriculum builds on the ninth-grade, and is different from the eleventh-grade curriculum, and so on.

In many successful programs, choice is a salient feature. At the upper secondary level, students can choose from an array of activities. Allowing student choice enables a better match between students' abilities, needs, and interests and the activity. Motivation is also enhanced when students are genuinely interested in learning.

Arrangement of activities. Various arrangements of instructional time are used in these programs. Typically, short instructional units of 3 to 4 weeks in length are used at the junior high-school level to allow students to become familiar with a variety of activities. This short exposure introduces students to many activities and allows them to identify activities in which they have an interest. At the high-school level, longer instructional units are offered, ranging from 4 weeks to semester-long units. The increased length of time devoted to an activity helps students attain competency in an activity suited to their ability and interest and furthers chances for continued participation. Mastery appears to be closely associated with the development of desired affective outcomes such as personal satisfaction, self-esteem, and self-confidence.

Providing opportunities for students to achieve mastery appears to be critical if we are to promote integration of activity into one's lifestyle. In addition to using units of increasing length to accomplish this objective, some schools have chosen to offer activities for different ability levels, such as beginning, intermediate, and advanced. This approach allows students to start at an appropriate level as well as receive more focused instruction according to their needs. This helps promote long-term mastery.

Schools have also used instructional time differently. Some schools have decreased the weekly frequency in which physical education is offered while doubling the class period, allowing for extended instruction. Where community facilities are used, this arrangement of extending the instructional period from the typical 50 minutes to 1½ hours to even an afternoon allows time for transportation to the facility as well as extended instruction and practice.

Additional opportunities for student practice are also provided. Drop-in programs and intramural opportunities further students' skills as well as encourage students to make a decision to incorporate physical activity consciously into their lifestyle.

Instructional Approaches

Teachers employ a variety of instructional approaches to better teach program content and to meet the unique needs of every student, whether they are highly or poorly skilled, able or disabled, or even the often forgotten average-skilled learner. Sensitivity to the special developmental tasks of adolescents guides their decisions. Individualized instructional strategies and sequential learning tasks allow students to start at their level of ability and progress at their own pace, achieving well-defined instructional objectives that contribute to overall learning goals. As students practice, teachers provide individual attention, skill feedback, encouragement for their efforts, and recognition for their accomplishments. Assessment of students' progress is a regular and important feature of these programs. Student activity is purposeful and productive. Students experience satisfaction from working hard and joy derived from competency.

Teachers have high, positive expectations for all students, and hold students accountable for learning. Self-responsibility for learning is fostered as opportunities are provided for self-direction. A warm, supportive instructional climate facilitates learning and stimulates the development of desired affective behaviors.

Some teachers have incorporated a strong conceptual component of physical education into their programs. Students are taught the concepts and principles underlying human movement and knowledge pertaining to the discipline of physical education. Movement activities are used to illustrate some principles, such as those pertaining to the laws of motion. Minilectures and opportunities for application are used to present other material, such as that pertaining to the development of a personal exercise prescription or a comprehensive wellness plan. In other schools, classes in exercise physiology are offered.

Other teachers have incorporated "Basic Stuff" into their curriculum. The "Basic Stuff" series presents the disciplinary knowledge of physical education covering such areas as motor development, motor learning, kinesiology, psychosocial aspects of movement, exercise physiology, and humanities. Specially designed learning experiences integrate this disciplinary knowledge with activity.

Still other teachers have sought to emphasize the cognitive aspect of physical education through bulletin boards or through the incorporation of 2- or 3-minute talks into the physical education lesson, or both. Cardiovascular concepts pertaining to circulation can be presented. Using "the muscle system of the month" furthers students' knowledge. During the month, information about the muscles' function, activities that use the muscles, exercise to strengthen the muscles, and activities to stretch the muscle can be incorporated into the program and reinforced. Teachers who dress in appropriate clothing or paint their muscles so that students can see the muscle's action during movement provide another creative approach to enhance students' learning.

Some programs provide additional opportunities for students with a strong interest in physical education, perhaps who are even considering careers in this area. Students are given an opportunity to develop their teaching and leadership skills through fieldwork or internship experiences, which involve working with their peers or children in the elementary grades as assistants in physical education classes.

Technology

Technology is having an increasing impact on activities in the gymnasium. Microcomputers are used by teachers to increase their effectiveness and efficiency. Teachers use them to manage student records, keep track of student fitness data, monitor student achievement, and to create tests. Students can use microcomputers to input their fitness data and receive immediate feedback on their performance as well as suggestions for improvement.

Videotape recorders are used to record students' performances and provide them with feedback for improvement. Instructional videotapes are becoming increasingly available for a variety of activities and grade levels.

Teachers' Characteristics

Strong programs have strong leadership. Teachers' efforts are coordinated and focused on fulfilling their program's mission. These teachers reflect a strong commitment to their students and a sense of pride. They are effective spokespersons for physical education because of their quality programs. There is congruence between what teachers say physical education can accomplish and contribute to the total development of the individual and what actually happens in physical education classes. Students achieve in physical education and are excited about their accomplishments. Furthermore, these students communicate a positive image of physical education to their parents, school, and community.

Physical education teachers involved in these programs serve as positive role models for students to emulate. They are active, fit, and enthusiastic, and they "practice what they preach" and share their experiences with their students. They are excited about teaching, are genuinely concerned about their students as well as their achievements, and put forth that extra effort that so often makes a difference. They are committed to excellence.

These programs and teachers indicate that there are many exciting directions in secondary school physical education today. Outstanding programs and exemplary teachers provide direction for young professionals seeking to provide their students with quality physical education.

SUMMARY

Physical education is a learning process designed to assist each individual to develop the skills, attain the knowledge, and acquire the attitudes that will result in a lifetime of participation in physical activity. An integral part of the secondary school curriculum physical education can contribute in many significant ways to the goals of education, including the development of each individual to his or her fullest potential and enhancement of each person's quality of life.

Physical education programs in the secondary schools are best characterized by their diversity. The conduct of these programs has been influenced to various extents by the educational reform movement, fitness movement, health promotion efforts, and legislation promoting equity.

Despite the potential contributions of physical education to the education of secondary school students, support for the inclusion of physical education in the curriculum is equivocal. In many schools, physical education's status as part of the education curriculum is questioned. Critics have characterized many secondary school physical education programs as ineffective. However, there are many secondary school programs throughout the country that are of high quality and conducted under the guidance of outstanding teachers. These programs and teachers reflect exciting, positive directions for secondary school physical education and serve as models for excellence.

FOR REVIEW

1. At the end of 13 years of physical education instruction, encompassing grades K-12, what should students have achieved? Specifically, what skills, knowledge, and attitudes should a physically educated person possess?
2. Many members of the public mistakenly equate physical education with athletics. What are the similarities and differences between these two programs?
3. Physical education programs have been criticized for serving only 10% of the students—the highly skilled. What can physical education teachers do to make sure that the needs of all students are met in the secondary school program?
4. List 10 characteristics associated with quality physical education programs. To what extent were these characteristics evident in your own secondary school physical education program?

REFERENCES

1. NASPE: *Definition of a physically educated person: outcomes of a quality physical education program,* Reston, Va, 1990, AAHPERD.
2. Seefeldt V, Vogel P, editors: *Physical activity and well being,* Reston, Va, 1986, AAHPERD.
3. Harrison JM, Blakemore CL: *Instructional strategies for secondary school physical education,* Dubuque, 1992, William C Brown.
4. Spring J: *American education: an introduction to social and political aspects,* New York, 1991, Longman.
5. Seefeldt V, Vogel P, editors: *The value of physical activity,* Reston, Va, 1986, AAHPERD.
6. Siedentop D: Thinking differently about secondary physical education, *JOPERD* 63(7):69-71, 77, 1992.
7. Mesenbrink R: *Curriculum report, National Association of Secondary School Principals,* 4:2, 1974.
8. AAHPERD: *The shape of the nation: a survey of state physical education requirements,* Reston, Va, 1987, AAHPERD.
9. Ross JG, Gilbert GG: The national children and youth fitness study: a summary of the findings, *JOPERD* 56(1), 45-50, 1985.
10. U.S. Department of Health and Human Services, Public Health Services: *Promoting health/preventing disease: year 2000 objectives for the nation,* Washington, DC, 1989, US Government Printing Office.
11. Blair S, Kohl H, Powell K: Physical activity, physical fitness, exercise, and public's health, *The Academy Papers* 20:53-69, 1987.
12. Montoye H: How active are modern populations? *The Academy Papers* 21:34-45, 1988.
13. Lupton CH III, Ostrove NM, Brozzo RM: Participation in leisure-time activities: a comparison of the existing data, *JOPERD* 55(9):19-23, 1984.
14. US Department of Health, Eduation, and Welfare. *Healthy people: the surgeon general's report on health promotion and disease prevention,* Washington, DC, 1979, US Government Printing Office.
15. US Department of Health and Human Services: *Promoting health/preventing disease: objectives for the nation,* Washington, DC, 1980, US Government Printing Office.
16. Powell KI, Christenson GM, Kreuter MW: Objectives for the nation: assessing the role physical education must play, *JOPERD* 55(6):18-20, 1984.
17. Geadelmann PL: Physical education: stronghold of sex stereotyping, *Quest* 32(2):192-200, 1980.
18. Durrant SM: Title IX—its power and its limitations, *JOPERD* 63(3):60-64, 1992.
19. Siedentop D: High school physical education: still an endangered species, *JOPERD* 58(2):24-25, 1987.
20. Griffey DC: Trouble for sure: a crisis—perhaps, *JOPERD* 58(2):20-21, 1987.
21. Lambert L: Secondary school physical education problems: what can we do about them? *JOPERD* 58(2):30-32, 1987.
22. Johnson MW: Physical education—fitness or fraud, *JOPERD* 56(1):33-35, 1985.
23. Rink JE: The plan and the reality, *JOPERD* 63(7):67-68, 73, 1992.
24. Greene L: One tree, many branches: the varieties of quality programs, *JOPERD* 54(7):46-48, 56, 1983.
25. Mancuso J: Model of excellence, *JOPERD* 54(7):24, 26, 1983.
26. Smith TK, Cestaro N: Saving future generations—the role of physical education, *JOPERD* 63(8):75-79, 1992.
27. Placek JH: A conceptually-based physical education program, *JOPERD* 54(7):27-28, 1983.
28. Kirkpatrick B: *Ultra physical education—the practical approach,* presented at the American Alliance for Health, Physical Education, Recreation and Dance National Convention, Kansas City, Mo, 1988.
29. Owens-Nauslar J: *Ultra physical education—technology and accountability,* presented at the American Alliance for Health, Physical Education, Recreation and Dance National Convention, Kansas City, Mo, 1988.

ANNOTATED READINGS

Haywood KM: The role of physical education in developing active lifestyles, *Research Quarterly for Exercise and Sport* 62(2):151-156, 1991.

Discusses a developmental approach to developing a grades K-12 curriculum to promote active lifestyles.

Morris HH: The role of school physical education in public health, *Research Quarterly for Exercise and Sport* 62(2):143-47, 1991.

Identifies the contribution that physical education can make to attainment of the public health goals presented in Healthy People 2000.

Sallis JF, et al: Determinants of physical activity and interventions in youth, *Medicine and Science in Sports and Exercise* 24(suppl 6):248-257, 1992.

Explores factors that influence physical activity levels of children and presents directions for physical education programs.

Smith TK, Cestaro N: Saving future generations—the role of physical education, *JOPERD* 63(8):75-79, 1992.

Presents a comprehensive lifetime fitness curriculum for secondary school students.

CHAPTER 2

Secondary School Students

CHAPTER OBJECTIVES

◆ To describe psychomotor, cognitive, and affective characteristics of secondary school students and their implications for program content and conduct

◆ To discuss some special concerns relative to teaching secondary school students

Understanding the developmental characteristics of students is essential if teachers are to be effective in helping students to learn. During the secondary school years, all aspects of human development—motor, cognitive, and affective—undergo profound changes. It is during these years that students experience adolescence, a period of development that serves as a transition from childhood to adulthood. Adolescence and the myriad changes that accompany it presents a unique challenge to teachers.

In addition to understanding the developmental characteristics of the students, teachers at this level may find it helpful to be familiar with some of the special concerns of students that may hold implications for the teaching of physical education. These include coping with stress, alienation, and child abuse. Teachers also need to be sensitive to the needs of students from other cultures and to those of youths who have disabilities.

DEVELOPMENTAL CHARACTERISTICS OF STUDENTS

Development is a continuous, multifaceted process that occurs throughout one's lifespan. In normal development, individuals follow a relatively uniform sequence of progression. Individuals experience the same changes in relatively the same order. However, although development proceeds sequentially, there is considerable variation in its rate. Chronological age is often used as a reference point to indicate when certain developmental changes are likely to occur, but individuals may experience these changes earlier or later than this age.

The broad variations in individual development are particularly noticeable during the early secondary school years. When observing seventh-grade students from a developmental perspective, the teacher would notice a great deal of variation in the students' maturity, despite their similar chronological age (approximately 12 to 13 years). Great variations in height and weight are evident as are differences in motor skill ability. Furthermore, a student may be more mature in some areas than others. For instance, students exhibiting similar levels of physical maturity may be functioning at different levels of cognitive or social development. Thus, the total development of the student must be considered in planning and implementing instruction.

Because of the great variation in individual development, a wide range of differences exist among students both within and across developmental domains, age, gender, and grade levels.[1,2] Combined with differences in students' backgrounds and experiences, the diverse nature of the students you will teach becomes readily apparent.

Successful teaching, from our perspective, requires that activities are selected after thoughtful examination of the characteristics of the students whom you are teaching and that various pedagogical strategies that accommodate individual differences and provide for student success are used. All too often teachers have used the chronological age of the students in selecting activities to teach and have utilized instructional styles that fail to take into account individual differences in the students. As Hellison and Templin[3] suggest, successful teaching requires discounting traditional notions of homogeneity and understanding the heterogeneity of the students you will teach.

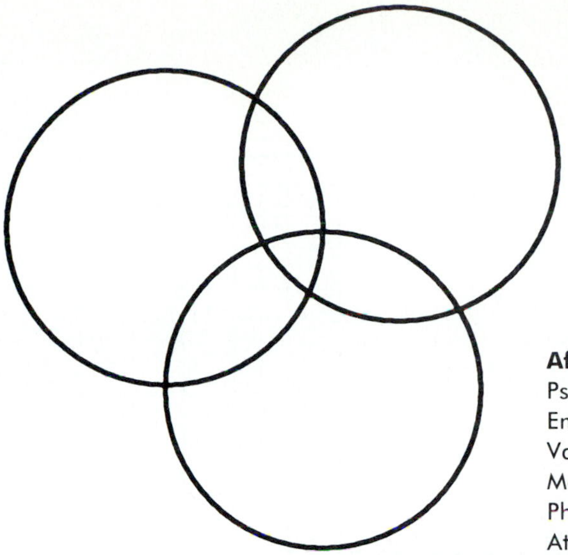

Cognitive Development
Intellectual function
Memory
Language skills
Cognitive operations

Psychomotor Development
Physical and physiological development
Motor skill development
Perceptual motor development
Fitness

Affective Development
Psychosocial development
Emotional development
Values
Moral reasoning
Philosophy
Attitudes

FIG. 2-1   Interaction of psychomotor, cognitive, and affective development.

It rests on the recognition of individual differences in development, skills, and backgrounds. It asks that you not only accept but appreciate, value, and respect differences. All students can and should have the opportunity to learn.

For ease of reading, the developmental characteristics of students are discussed in terms of psychomotor, cognitive, and affective development. However, it is important to remember that these areas are interrelated, as shown in Fig. 2-1. These developmental characteristics are discussed on a continuum, ranging from the early secondary school years (grades 7 and 8) to the late secondary school years (grades 11 and 12).

Psychomotor Development

Students experience numerous physical and physiological changes during their secondary school years. These changes are summarized in Box 2-1.

Height and weight. One of the most noticeable changes is in height and weight. Youths experience rapid changes in height and weight during pubescence, a period of 2 years that precedes puberty. There is rapid acceleration of the growth process, commonly referred to as a growth spurt. There is considerable variation in the timing of this growth spurt, with girls experiencing this growth spurt approximately 2 years earlier than boys.[1,4] Fig. 2-2 illustrates the growth patterns for height and weight, showing changes over time as well as variability in rate.

For girls, this rapid increase in height may begin as early as 9 years of age or as late as 15 years of age.[1,4] Typically, it occurs at 10.5 years, with the rate of growth accelerating until about 12 years of age.[1,4] At this time,

---

BOX 2-1

SUMMARY OF PSYCHOMOTOR DEVELOPMENT

Physical Development
- Height and weight increase
- Skeletal maturation occurs
- Attainment of mature adult figure
- Muscles increase in length and breadth; strength gains occur
- Adipose tissue distribution changes
- Primary and secondary sex characteristics develop
- Various systemic changes to adult functioning

Motor Skill Development
- Refinement of fundamental motor skills
- Achievement of proficiency in specialized sports skills

Fitness Development
- Focus on achieving and maintaining an optimal level of fitness

---

the increase in height becomes more gradual, with growth ceasing around age 17.[1]

Boys may experience the growth spurt as early as 10.5 years of age or as late as 16 years of age.[1,4] Typically, boys experience the growth spurt at 12.5 years of age, and this period of rapid growth continues until about 14 years of age (Fig. 2-3).[1,4] A slower rate of growth follows, with growth ceasing around 21 years of age.[1,4]

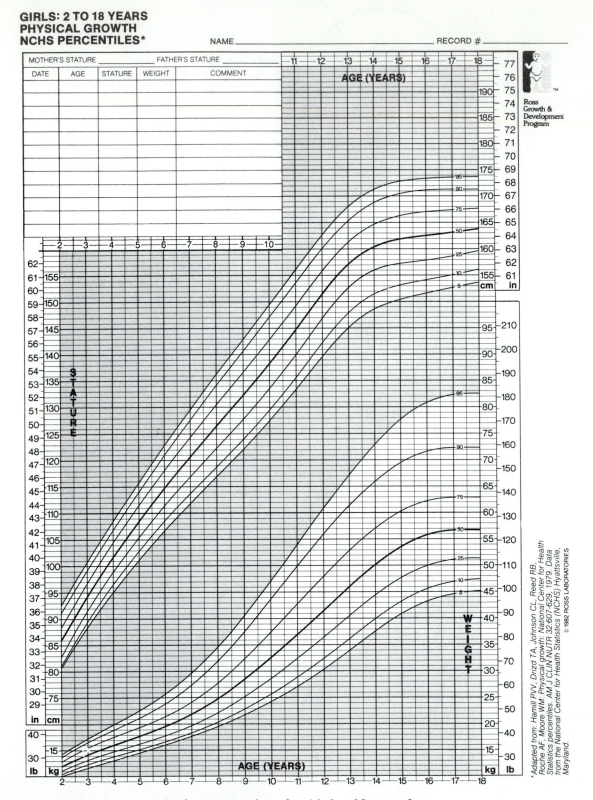

FIG. 2-2 Percentiles for stature and age for girls 2 to 18 years of age.
Reprinted with permission from Ross Laboratories, Columbus, Ohio.

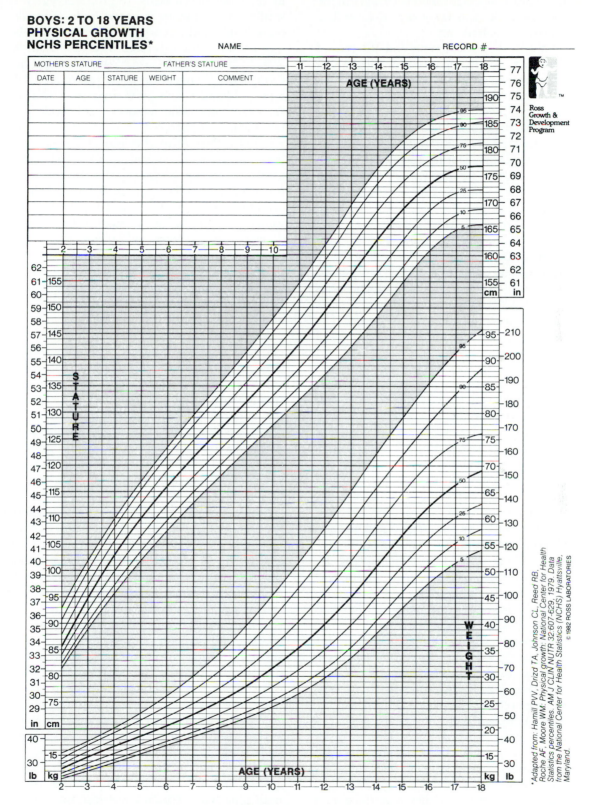

FIG. 2-3 Percentiles for weight and age for boys 2 to 18 years of age.
Reprinted with permission from Ross Laboratories, Columbus, Ohio.

Changes in height are accompanied by rapid changes in weight. This increase in weight reflects changes in the size of the bones, muscle, and body organs as well as increases in subcutaneous body fat.

Individual differences in the timing and the rate of growth lead to tremendous variations in height and weight among early adolescents, both within and between genders. In the early secondary school years, teachers will readily notice these differences when observing students in their classes. Some students have experienced their growth spurt, others are just starting, and yet others may not have begun theirs. During this time, girls are typically taller, heavier, and more physically mature than boys.[5] During the later secondary school years, boys will be taller and heavier than girls.[5]

During this period of rapid growth, students are very concerned about their appearance. "How tall will I be?" and "Why haven't I started to grow?" as well as "Why do I weigh so much?" are concerns that may be expressed by students. Students may be intensely self-conscious about their height; students who are taller than their peers may adopt poor posture to minimize the difference. The short, late-maturing boy and the tall, early-maturing girl may feel particularly out of place.

Teachers who are sensitive to individual differences and take the time to reassure these early secondary school students that wide variation in physical maturity is normal can do much to alleviate students' anxieties and foster self-acceptance. Because many students are self-conscious about their appearance, activities must be planned carefully to minimize any potential for embarrassment or failure. Individual sport activities, such as badminton, where an individual's size is not a factor in achieving successful participation, should be introduced at this time. Teaching strategies that take into account individual differences and are structured to enhance students' opportunity for success will help contribute to a comfortable learning environment. As the secondary years progress and students attain physical maturity, opportunities for students to attain proficiency in selected lifetime sports suited to their individual abilities should be emphasized.

Skeletal development. Many skeletal changes are experienced during the secondary school years. Bones begin as soft cartilaginous tissue. As the body matures, they ossify or harden. During the early secondary school years, students' bones are still not completely ossified, but the process is usually complete at the end of the secondary school years.

Vigorous activity is needed to stimulate normal bone growth. Care should be taken, however, to avoid injury to the bones during the developing years. Injuries to the epiphysis or growth centers of bones may result in a disturbance of growth in youths whose bones have not fully matured.

Body proportions. Changes in body proportions are evident during this time. Body segments grow and mature at different rates. This asynchronous growth results in body segments being disproportionately larger or smaller in relation to the total body. The adolescent's head, hands, and feet attain their mature size before the legs and arms; the legs reach their full length before the arms.[4] Changes in the size of shoulders and hips occur. Comparatively, males' shoulders grow larger than their hips, and females' hips grow larger than their shoulders.[4] As adolescents attain maturity, their body proportions become more congruent.

Because of the many changes in the skeletal system and body proportions, adolescents may feel and look ungainly, physically awkward, and uncoordinated. They may experience difficulty in performing skills they could previously perform quite well. This is because motor performance is affected by changes in height and weight, development of bone and muscle mass, and uneven growth of body segments.[1,5,6] Adolescents may need help in adjusting to the changes in their bodies and in learning how to use their bodies efficiently to perform physical skills. As they approach adulthood, their coordination improves.

Muscle tissue. Muscle strength increases as the individual grows. Before puberty, there is generally little difference between the strength of boys and girls.[8] As they approach puberty, both girls and boys increase in strength. At puberty the increase in the production of the hormone testosterone influences muscle development. It is found in higher levels in males than females. After the onset of puberty, boys exhibit greater strength than girls. It should be noted that, to some extent, strength differences in males and females are influenced by society.[1,4,5,7,8]

Society encourages adolescent males to participate in sports and engage in vigorous activity to a greater degree than girls.[4,7,8] Before puberty, if boys and girls were subjected to equal expectations and experiences, their physical performances would be similar, and the difference in their abilities would likely be less pronounced during adolescence.[4,7]

During the growth spurt, it is not uncommon for adolescents to experience low muscle endurance and strength.[9] Coupled with the awkwardness and uncoordination that often is experienced during this time, students' motor skill performance may be adversely affected. They may also find it difficult to learn new skills. As youths mature, muscular strength and endurance improve as does coordination, facilitating the acquisition of new skills.

Adipose tissue. During adolescence, variations in the amount and distribution of adipose (fat) tissue become noticeable. Girls typically develop more adipose tissue than boys. In girls, this tissue is primarily distributed around the hips, thighs, upper arms, abdomen, and breasts. In boys, adipose tissue accumulates mostly around the abdomen.

Many adolescents place high value on appearance.
Courtesy of Joy Buffan, SUC Oswego, Oswego, NY.

This increase in adipose tissue may lead adolescents to complain that their body is too "fat." It is important that teachers explain to their students that a certain amount of adipose tissue is essential for good health. Too little or too much adipose tissue can have detrimental effects on one's health. Adolescents need assistance in developing a healthy regard for their weight and body composition.[1] An obsessive preoccupation with weight can contribute to eating disorders such as anorexia nervosa and bulimia.

Sexual maturity. Another significant change that students experience during the secondary school years is puberty and the attainment of sexual maturity. In females, menarche, the first menstrual period, occurs at approximately 12 to 13 years of age. As females mature, the reproductive organs mature, breasts develop, hips broaden, and the growth of pubic and axillary hair occurs. For males, the onset of puberty usually occurs about 2 years later than females. It occurs at approximately 14.5 years of age and is marked by the ability to produce sperm and ejaculate. Complete sexual maturation occurs at about 18 years of age. Males experience genital development; broadening of the shoulders; deepening of the voice; and the growth of pubic, axillary, and facial hair.

The diverse and rapid physical transformations that occur during this period can cause considerable anxiety for some students. Students who mature earlier or later than their peers may experience difficulty. Until students become comfortable with their bodies, they may be very self-conscious. Students may seek to avoid physical education classes because of the anxiety and embarrassment that may accompany the changing of clothes and show-

ering in the locker room. Given the increased interest in personal appearance and grooming by adolescents, it may be helpful to shorten the time at the beginning of the class for dressing out and provide more time at the end of the class for grooming. Teachers must also be prepared to handle requests to be excused from participation that may be presented by girls who have their menstrual periods.

Systemic changes. Besides the muscloskeletal and reproductive systems, other physiological systems undergo developmental changes during this time. For example, within the circulatory system, the heart grows dramatically, increasing in size and weight. Respiratory system changes also occur; the size of the lungs and their respiratory capacity increase. The nervous system, while more fully developed before adolescence than any other system, continues to mature until late adolescence. The digestive organs also continue to grow during this time.

These systemic changes should be considered part of the total adolescent developmental picture. Appropriate aerobic activity to fully develop the cardiorespiratory system is important. To sustain the growth of the body, proper nutrition is needed. Adolescents' appetites are usually large, but they may seek to satisfy their nutritional needs with an assortment of low nutritional value, high-caloric junk foods. Teachers can provide adolescents with guidance in these areas.

Motor skill development. During the secondary school years, physical education teachers should emphasize the acquisition and refinement of specialized sport skills. To accomplish this objective, physical education teachers need to build on the skill foundation laid during the elementary school years. Typically students in elementary school learn fundamental motor skills (running, kicking, throwing, striking, and jumping) and begin to apply these skills in sports situations, usually team sports (soccer, basketball, and softball).

As students enter the early secondary school grades, physical education teachers should assess their motor skill competencies. Can the student execute the fundamental motor skills correctly? If not, what can be done to help these students? Teachers who emphasize an individualized approach to physical education accept each student's level of ability and provide the appropriate, developmental experiences to help these students learn and achieve. Extra help and attention or even a special class for those students who need it are strategies used by other physical education teachers to help meet students' needs. If these problems are not addressed now, these students may fall further behind in motor performance, experience less success, and become disinterested in incorporating physical activity into their lives.[5] Dealing with a diversity of motor skill competencies coupled with the pronounced variability in development typical of students at this time presents a real challenge to the teacher.

During the early secondary school years, traditional

team sports activities, such as soccer and volleyball, usually dominate the curriculum. Individual and dual sports activities, such as tennis, golf, and badminton, are introduced and the time devoted to these lifetime pursuits increases as the secondary school years progress.

The early secondary school program is typically structured to introduce students to a variety of activities. This allows students to begin to develop many sport skills while allowing them to identify activities suited to their abilities and interests. The teacher must carefully balance the curriculum to ensure that students have the opportunity to be exposed to a diversity of activities and yet also have the opportunity to develop proficiency in some activities. Units of instruction that are too short may accomplish the objective of exposing students to a variety of activities but could prove frustrating because they provide little time for skill development. Units that are too long provide opportunity for skill development but limit the exposure to a number of activities. Students who are having difficulty in performing the skills involved may find long units to be frustrating.

At the upper secondary levels, students are usually given the opportunity to refine specific sport skills even further and develop a high level of proficiency in selected skills through in-depth instruction. Advanced skills and strategies are taught, and units of instruction are often longer to provide an opportunity to master skills. Consideration of students' abilities and interests is important at this level. Many schools allow students to select the activities they wish to learn from a list of offerings.

Fitness. It is critical that health-related fitness be a priority at the secondary level. The secondary school years are the last opportunity to teach millions of students about the benefits of fitness and provide them with the skills and knowledge to maintain fitness throughout their lifespan.

Secondary school students vary greatly in their fitness levels. Differences in muscle strength and endurance, body composition, cardiorespiratory endurance, and flex-ibility are common. These differences coupled with the wide range of individual differences caused by physical maturation suggest that the best approach to fitness development and maintenance is an individualized one. The secondary school years are an opportune time to help students learn how to develop an individualized fitness program and to gradually assume responsibility for their own fitness.

Cognitive Development

During their adolescent years, individuals' cognitive abilities continue to develop. Cognitive changes include an increase in intellectual functioning, memory language capabilities, and conceptual thinking. These changes are summarized in Box 2-2.

Intellectual development. Adolescents' development brings them to the upper limits of their intellectual potential, and this occurs usually between 16 and 25 years of age.[4] The growth toward intellectual maturity is extremely varied, and this variability must be considered by the teacher in planning for instruction.

Secondary school students have a greater knowledge base than elementary school students. This increased knowledge and diversity of experiences contribute to their enhanced intellectual abilities. Physical education teachers will find it helpful to build upon the students' past experiences to facilitate learning, pointing out similarities in the new material to be learned and previously learned material. For example, physical education teachers teaching students the overhead tennis serve should illustrate how elements of the serve are similar to the elements of the previously learned overhand volleyball serve. This approach is called transfer of learning and can help students learn new skills and knowledge more readily.

Memory. The adolescent's memory is equivalent to that of an adult in terms of the ability to absorb, process, and retrieve information. Compared to elementary school students, students at this level are capable of comprehending more and increasingly complex information, concentrating for longer periods of time, and retaining more of what is seen and heard. Teachers can plan for slightly longer explanations and demonstrations (although not long-winded) as the students can remember more cues and skill sequences. They are better able to follow directions and understand more complex concepts.

Language. During adolescence, students improve their capacity for self-expression. Their language becomes increasingly sophisticated and refined. Their vocabulary increases. Presentations should be appropriate to adolescents' increased language capabilities. Students resent being talked down to and appreciate being treated like young adults.

Conceptual thinking. As youths mature, they gain in the ability to reason abstractly, to generalize information,

B O X   2 - 3

SUMMARY OF AFFECTIVE DEVELOPMENT

- ◆ Socialization in preparation for adulthood
- ◆ Decrease in egocentrism
- ◆ Adjustment of self-concept and self-esteem in light of developmental changes and experiences
- ◆ Experience of a greater range and intensity of emotions
- ◆ Learns to express emotions appropriately
- ◆ Personal system of values becomes more integrated
- ◆ Moral reasoning becomes increasingly sophisticated
- ◆ Formulation of attitudes in light of experiences

to apply knowledge, and to analyze situations critically. These expanded cognitive abilities enhance adolescents' problem-solving and decision-making skills. These students are capable of assuming increased responsibility for their learning.

Secondary students are interested in the "whys" underlying requests to perform an action. "Why are we warming up?" or "Why are we doing this drill?" are examples of questions that may be posed. These "why" questions present an opportune time for teachers to introduce students to the conceptual basis of physical activity. Concepts pertaining to exercise physiology and motor learning can be related to students. Once learned, students can learn to apply the concept to the new situations they encounter. Conceptually based programs such as Basic Stuff[11] may be helpful to practitioners in designing appropriate learning experiences that help students "learn how to learn."

Affective Development

Numerous changes within the affective domain are experienced by secondary school students. These are highlighted in Box 2-3.

Socialization. The process of learning behaviors that are appropriate to a cultural setting, including how to interact with people in society, is termed *socialization*.[10] Although this process continues throughout life, the period from birth to adolescence is particularly critical.[7]

Much of socialization occurs through the modeling or imitating of the behavior of others. Three major socializing forces impinging on adolescents are the family, the school, and the peer group. Although peers influence individuals' behaviors throughout their lives, their impact during adolescence is particularly notable.

During the early secondary school years, as youths be-

come increasingly autonomous from their families, peers exert more influence on their behavior. Peer group activities become more dominant in the lives of adolescents. Dating activities increase. Within the peer group, adolescents learn interpersonal and social skills and how to manage mature relationships with peers of both sexes.

Friendships are very important during this time. Success to many adolescents is defined in terms of their popularity. Physical attractiveness, possession of social and leadership skills, and participation in athletics for boys and increasingly so for girls all favorably influence one's popularity.[7]

As adolescents mature, peer groups become less influential in their lives. As their personal identities coalesce and their values systems become more developed, adolescents become increasingly autonomous and self-reliant as they move toward adulthood and independence.

Secondary school physical education teachers can contribute to students' social development in several ways. Opportunities to work cooperatively with others, to assume responsibility with appropriate guidance, to make decisions, and to lead and to follow contribute to the development of social skills. There is a need to be sensitive to individuals who are loners and who have not yet developed appropriate social relationships with their peers. These individuals may suffer from shyness and perhaps low self-esteem. Participation in physical activities provides a common interest and means for helping adolescents learn how to interact with their peers.

Dating and forming serious relationships are important during adolescence.

Courtesy of Cathy Haight, Lansing High School, Lansing, NY.

Peer group influence can be used to establish and maintain appropriate behaviors in class. Opportunities for leadership and provision for students to experience success frequently can help channel the need to impress and to be respected by members of the peer group in a healthful direction.

Students' interest in their appearances and bodies provides an opportune time to discuss the many physiological changes that are occurring and to help students gain an appreciation for individual differences. Information on nutrition, weight control, and exercise may be well received by students.

Egocentrism. Egocentrism is quite prominent in early adolescence. Students become centered on their own point of view and are unable to accept or see the viewpoints of others. Adolescents spend hours analyzing their thinking, appearance, actions as well as thoughts, intentions, appearance and actions of others.[12] They assume they are the center of attention. This is often reflected in the early adolescent's extreme self-consciousness. Adolescents are easily embarrassed and acutely sensitive to criticism. Teachers should try to avoid situations in which there is a possibility of confirming adolescents' worst fears that everyone is looking at them and laughing.

As individuals mature, egocentrism decreases. Through social interactions adolescents learn they are not the sole focus of attention. They become aware of the feelings and beliefs of others, gradually learning that others may hold views different from or similar to their own. Although adolescents may continue to reflect on their thoughts and feelings, they are able to adopt a broader perspective.

Self-perceptions. The enhanced cognitive abilities of adolescents influence their self-perceptions. These perceptions or interpretations of reality, rather than reality itself, significantly influence adolescents' behavior, feelings, and self-image.[13] Teachers need to be cognizant of how their students may interpret the many events that occur during the course of the class and how students' perceptions can positively or negatively influence their learning.

An individual's perception of his or her abilities and the strength of the belief that he or she can perform the required task are reflected in one's self-confidence. One's self-confidence interacts with an individual's level of competence to influence participation and involvement in activities. The choice of activities, the amount of effort expended, and persistence at a task are influenced by one's perception. Increased competence positively affects self-confidence, which, in turn, positively influences one's willingness to participate, work hard, and persist.[14] These efforts result in gains in achievement or increased competence and, subsequently, increased self-confidence.[14] Teachers who help their students learn skills as well as enhance their self-confidence help their students acquire positive perceptions of themselves as skillfull movers. This belief is important in realizing our goal of encouraging lifespan participation in physical activity.

Secondary school physical education teachers may be faced with the difficult task of helping students change their negative perceptions of themselves as movers. Students may be disinterested in physical education because at an early age they were placed in situations in physical education class where they experienced little success and were perhaps humiliated. Their unsuccessful performances and the accompanying feelings of inadequacy led to the attitude, "Why bother—I can't do it anyway!" These negative perceptions and attitudes may be overcome by providing learning experiences that use sound progressions to enhance skill development and provide frequent opportunities for success. Recognition and acceptance of individual differences and a supportive atmosphere where encouragement is offered and one's accomplishments and efforts recognized can help students improve their skills, develop more positive perceptions of their movement abilities, and enhance positive attitudes toward participation.

Self-esteem. Enhancement of students' self-esteem or their sense of value and worth is an important contribution that teachers can make to the students' development in this domain. Providing opportunities for students to achieve success is important. This can be accomplished through the use of activities that are appropriate to the developmental levels of students, through proper use of skill progressions, and structuring skills into smaller, meaningful tasks that allow students to experience success more frequently. A curriculum that offers a diversity of activities helps students find activities appropriate to their abilities and in which they can succeed.

Teachers can also enhance students' self-esteem by assisting them to appraise their abilities realistically and set challenging goals for themselves. Teaching approaches that provide for the use of checklists that specify tasks to be achieved and offer opportunities for frequent self-evaluation can help students see their abilities clearly while providing them with tangible evidence of their accomplishments.[13] Praising students for their effort as well as the outcomes achieved can help students gain pride in their ability to work diligently toward a goal. Teaching strategies that provide for student problem solving and help students acquire self-control promote social development.[13]

Teachers who communicate positive expectations for their students help them achieve to their fullest potential. Teachers must be aware of what they are communicating as well as sensitive to how they are communicating. What teachers say and how they say it makes a difference in how their message is perceived by students. Constructive feedback, delivered in a positive manner with respect for the dignity of the individual, promotes skill development while respecting the students' feelings. Feedback that is negative and belittling can be devastating to the student who has low self-esteem. Because of the acute self-consciousness of students, it may be better to deliver feedback privately whenever possible.

Emotional development. The emotional development of secondary school students is just as complex as development in other areas. Adolescents are faced with adjusting to and integrating the numerous physical, cognitive, and affective changes they are experiencing into a sense of self. Their emotional responses to these changes are varied and, at times, intense. The more sophisticated cognitive abilities of adolescents enable them to think more fully about their feelings and critically examine them.[10] Their awareness of their feelings about themselves and others becomes heightened. Furthermore, they come to learn that their feelings are legitimate and a valuable, integral part of their lives.

Adolescents are also faced with the task of learning how to regulate their emotions. This involves both acquiring skill in expressing one's feelings and knowing the appropriate time and place to express them. Controlling one's emotions when involved in a game, experiencing the exhiliaration associated with success, and learning how to accept and respect individual differences in skill ability are some opportunities for emotional growth within physical education. The opportunity to express one's emotions through the medium of physical activity and the use of physical activity as a cathartic, leading to

the release of tension, are also outcomes that can be beneficial to emotional growth.

The emotional responses of adolescents are also influenced by the various needs, held in common with all human beings, that must be satisfied. These include a need for affiliation, achievement, adventure, security, and well-being.[10] These needs can be met in the physical education program in several ways. In terms of affiliation needs, physical activity provides a shared area of interest as well as numerous opportunities for social interactions, thus promoting the development of friendships and interpersonal competence. Participation as a member of a group, cooperative efforts toward common goals, and chances to gain approval of one's peers contribute to the meeting of affiliation needs.

Adolescents have a strong need for achievement. They find satisfaction in meeting challenges and in the accomplishments that occur as a result of hard work. Sufficient time should be provided for students to master the skills presented so that students may develop competence. A varied program that provides all students with an opportunity to find an activity in which to achieve is important.

Adolescents' need for excitement and adventure may be met through the challenges and thrills associated with various sports as well as through competition. After-school activities should be offered on a broad scale for

Promoting positive attitudes toward participation in lifetime activities is an important objective of secondary school physical education.
Courtesy of Emily Leonardo, Camp Hill High School, Camp Hill, PA.

all students who are interested, not only the highly skilled. Activities that afford opportunities for risk taking under controlled safe conditions, such as structured outdoor pursuits, should be offered within the curriculum.

Adolescents seek security. This is a time of many changes and demands for adjustment. Many adolescents experience worries about their normalcy, doubts about their abilities, anxiety because of the uncertainities of life, and turmoil as they search for their identity—their insecurities are many. Physical education teachers can be helpful during this time by fostering feelings of security in their students. This can be accomplished by letting students clearly know what is expected of them, creating a warm and supportive class climate, and exhibiting consistency in dealing with discipline problems and everyday occurrences. Encouragement of self-discipline, self-responsibility, and self-reliance helps students feel secure and confident.

Attitude development. One important goal of secondary school physical education is the promotion of participation in meaningful physical activity throughout one's lifespan. In attempting to accomplish this objective, teachers must assist their students in acquiring the necessary motor skills and knowledge pertaining to physical activity. However, the likelihood that students will continue to participate in physical activities once they have left school is strongly influenced by their attitudes toward physical activity. Students with more favorable attitudes are more likely to participate in these activities than students with less favorable attitudes. Thus fostering favorable attitudes toward physical activity is a desirable outcome of secondary school physical education programs. Teachers must not only be concerned with the development of positive attitudes, but also with changing negative attitudes held by some students.

Attitudes encompass one's feelings toward a particular situation, one's likes and dislikes, and one's beliefs. Attitudes are reflected in one's behaviors, specifically one's tendency to act in a certain manner. Positive attitudes are expressed when an individual chooses to become involved in a specific activity and seeks out opportunities to participate; this may be termed *an approach tendency.*[4] Negative attitudes are evidenced when an individual chooses to ignore or avoid an opportunity to participate in an activity; this may be referred to as *an avoidance tendency.*[4] A secondary school student reflects a positive attitude toward tennis, for example, when the student expresses a liking for tennis, participates enthusiastically during class, and seeks out additional involvement in tennis through intramural activities. Teachers would label a student as possessing a negative attitude when the student voices a dislike for tennis, tries to avoid participation by getting excused from class, and participates only in a half-hearted manner. Attitudes are also reflected when the student is given a choice of activities and expresses a preference for one activity over another.

Acquisition of attitudes may be conceptualized as proceeding through a hierarchical sequence of three processes: compliance, identification, and internalization.[4] Compliance refers to an individual becoming involved or doing something with the objective of receiving a favorable reaction from another person. Assuming an attitude or behavior because it is valued by others is termed *identification*. Internalization relates to valuing a behavior and incorporating this value into one's value system.

Acquisition of a positive attitude toward physical activity may be illustrated by this example. Sara, a student in a fitness class, may follow the prescribed workout to achieve a good grade, even though working out is not enjoyable to her *(compliance)*. However, several of Sara's friends enjoy working out and decide to participate in weight training intramurals in the afternoon. Sara decides to participate in intramurals to join her friends (identification). As she continues to work out, Sara finds out she really enjoys this activity and continues to participate because she chooses to do so *(internalization)*. Helping students to appreciate and value participation in activities for their own satisfaction and the pleasure to be derived is an important task of teachers at this level.

Student's attitudes can either enhance their ability to learn or adversely affect it. Teachers who are aware of the important influence that students' attitudes hold in their learning can take steps to design learning experiences that encourage the development of favorable attitudes. Learning experiences should be constructed with special concern paid to enhancing students' self-esteem and self-confidence. Challenging instruction, specification of the goals to be achieved, instruction appropriate to one's abilities, appreciation for effort, frequent monitoring of progress, opportunities for mastery and success, positive expectations for achievement, and consideration of students' interests in selecting activities and instructional approaches contribute to a positive learning experience.

Learning experiences that cause students to lose self-respect and decrease their self-esteem are not conducive toward developing favorable attitudes toward physical activity. The lack of challenge and variety in content, the absence of feedback, placing students in embarrassing situations, utilization of poor grading practices, holding negative expectations for achievement, using physical activity as a punishment, and providing too little time to learn the material presented are some situations that contribute to the development of negative attitudes and adversely affect students' participation.

Values and moral development. During adolescence several significant changes take place in an individual's moral development. During early adolescence, youths often face a conflict between peer group and adult values.[15] As they develop, a more integrated system of values and more mature moral behavior are achieved.

Values serve as a guide for behavior, help determine priorities and goals, and form the basis for making moral decisions. Teachers have typically expressed the belief that the development of values is an important goal of physical education. Fair play, honesty, respect for others, cooperation, hard work, and sportsmanship have long been held as values that can be achieved through physical education. In order for these values to be achieved, these outcomes must be actively sought within the programs.

Attainment of these outcomes requires that opportunities are provided to discuss and deal with values questions. Teachers can design experiences that provide an opportunity for students to examine their own values. Using this approach, students may officiate their own games or play games with an uneven number of players on the team. The management of these situations during game play encourages participants to make moral judgments as well as incorporate these judgments into their actions during play. Meaningful follow-up discussion of events and actions taken, feelings of participants, and behavioral alternatives can help students gain insight into their values. Discussions of events that occur during class can also help students examine their values. Situations such as conflict over taking turns, cheating, belittling the efforts of others, competitiveness versus cooperation, and assuming responsibility for calling one's own fouls during games can be discussed. Physical education teachers who provide their students with opportunities to discuss values questions and make judgments about right and wrong

As officials, students have the opportunity to apply their knowledge of rules and to promote fair play and sportsmanship among peers.
Courtesy of Beth Kirkpatrick, Tilford Middle School, Vinton, IA.

assist their students in developing their individual value systems.

During the secondary school years, individuals experience changes in their level of moral reasoning. Throughout life, individuals are confronted with making moral choices requiring judgments about the "rightness" or "justness" of an act, calling into play such concepts as good and bad, right and wrong, and just and unjust. During the early secondary school years, students' actions are influenced by the expectations from their family and peer groups. The desire to please others and win their approval exerts considerable influence on the individual's actions. The desire for peer approval may result in some adolescents acting not in accordance with their moral beliefs but according to the social conventions of the group. As adolescents mature, their moral judgments become more guided by their consciences. At this level an individual's conscience determines right and wrong, based on respect for humanity and the dignity of each individual.[15]

Secondary school students need to recognize the consequences of their behavior and its impact on others. To help students view their behavior from another's perspective role playing can be used. This tactic is often used by teachers to allow other students to experience the challenges confronting individuals with disabilities. It may be useful in helping adolescents identify and understand the restrictions male and female stereotypes place on individuals' behaviors. Teachers can also help adolescents internalize their values and make choices by shifting some of the authority in the gymnasium from themselves to the students, thus promoting a more autonomous environment. Emphasizing high ethical standards and serving as a positive role model are other ways in which teachers can contribute to their students' moral development.

SPECIAL CONCERNS OF ADOLESCENTS

While some adolescents achieve the developmental tasks of this period without too much trouble, other adolescents find this time period fraught with challenges. Adolescents may experience difficulty in dealing with developmental changes and societal, familial, and educational demands. They may need assistance in coping with the many stresses in their lives. Other problems include drug abuse, alienation, and child abuse. Teachers who are sensitive to the special needs of students from minority groups and those who have a disability will enhance their students' opportunities to learn.

Stress and Coping

Meeting new expectations, competently handling the increased responsibilities and demands associated with this time, and adjusting to the many significant physical, cognitive, and affective changes can be stressful to adolescents. During this time they are expected to accomplish many developmental tasks and make great strides toward maturity; it often seems that success and failure looms on every front. Because adolescents are caught up in their own experiences and lack the broader perspective of adults, the effects of these stresses are often magnified. Stress that is prolonged and intense can have detrimental effects on adolescents' health.[16]

Physical education teachers can assist students in dealing with their stresses in several ways. One important resource in dealing with stress is the use of physical exercise as a means to increase the body's resistance to stress as well as a means to release stress. Units on physical and mental relaxation techniques can provide students with a lifelong resource to help them manage stress effectively in the future. Physical activity can also be used to help students resolve some of the problems that are causing them stress. Dissatisfaction with one's appearance, low self-esteem, and loneliness are significant causes of stress. Physical activity can aid adolescents in improving their appearance, enhance their self-concept, and provide them with opportunities to develop social skills and friendships. Secondary school physical education programs have the potential to help students develop skills to manage stress effectively throughout their lives.

Alienation

For some secondary school students, alienation is a problem—it reflects adolescents' disillusionment with society and its values and dissatisfaction with themselves. Some adolescents from the upper and middle classes rebel against society's preoccupation with materialistic goods and social status.[12] Among minorities and the poor of this country, alienation occurs in response to discrimination, rejection, and feelings that the American dream has passed them by.[17] Adolescents who have failed to achieve a sense of identity may be viewed as being alienated from themselves.[7] These adolescents may experience confusion about who they are, frustration, emptiness, and lack of direction and hope for the future.[12] The belief that no one cares about them and that their problems are overwhelming may leave adolescents feeling very alone or adrift in an uncaring world.

Adolescents who feel alienated may engage in antisocial behaviors, such as delinquency and acts of violence. In class they may appear to be sullen, disrespectful of authority, cynical, or unwilling to try. These students are hard to reach because they perceive themselves as not having a future, and thus it is not worthwhile for them to try to learn. On the other hand, some alienated youths may seek to change society and conditions by working actively to promote change. They may become involved in political groups and social agencies in an effort to make a difference.

Some schools have established programs to prevent alienation.[18] These programs focus on helping adolescents gain an understanding of the changes they are experiencing and to see their concerns and anxieties from a different perspective. These programs emphasize gaining control of one's behavior, social responsibility, communication skills, relationship skills, and the development of self-confidence. Alienated youths present a challenge to all teachers. Helping these youths to realize that they are unique and worthy individuals is a difficult task. Physical education teachers can assist these students by incorporating some of the skills used in alienation prevention programs into the physical education experience.

Drug Use

Adolescent drug use and abuse is a serious problem today. Alcohol, tobacco, marijuana, and cocaine are the most frequently used drugs. However, some adolescents may use inhalants, amphetamines, hallucinogens, sedatives, and heroin. Besides its harmful effects on health, drug use can adversely affect development in many areas of the individual's life.

Numerous reasons exist for drug use by youths. One of the most significant influences on youths beginning to use drugs is peer pressure.[19,20] Belonging and feeling accepted by others is especially important to adolescents. Socially insecure adolescents may begin to use drugs out of curiosity and the need to experiment. Unfortunately, experimentation often leads to chronic use and abuse. Adolescents may use drugs as a form of rebellion against parents and in defiance of societal norms. Often, adolescents may turn to drugs to escape from tensions, frustrations, and fears. Some adolescents use drugs because of the pleasurable sensations associated with their use or as a means to promote self-awareness. Low self-esteem and a lack of self-discipline have often been cited as risk factors in substance abuse.[20,21]

One alarming national trend is the increasing use of anabolic steroids by junior and senior high-school students, particularly males.[22] Obtained illegally and typically taken in megadoses, anabolic steroids along with a training diet and a comprehensive body building program can increase weight and muscle size dramatically. While often taken in hopes of improving athletic performance, they are increasingly being used by nonathletes to improve their appearances. For teens beset with the insecurities that often accompany adolescence, steroids provide a quick way to improve one's appearance and, subsequently, in the adolescent's mind, one's popularity and self-confidence. Teachers need to discuss the use of steroids with their students, emphasizing the serious health consequences of such use.

Teachers need to be knowledgeable about the various signs that indicate drug use by students. Some of these signs include dramatic changes in appearance, redness around the eyes and dilated pupils, lack of motivation, short attention span, declining grades, and excessive absences.[19,20] Furthermore, they need to be familiar with school policies for handling suspected drug use by students and for assisting students with this problem. Finally, teachers should be aware of the profound influence that their behavior has on their students. Drug use should not be condoned through silence or inaction.

Physical education teachers can incorporate drug prevention strategies into the physical education curriculum to reinforce the schoolwide prevention program. Physical activity can be used to help reduce the risk factors associated with substance abuse.[21] Programs that focus on increasing competence in all domains and that emphasize affective outcomes such as enhancement of self-esteem, self-discipline, and self-responsibility have the potential to contribute to drug prevention efforts.

Students from Minority Cultures

The U.S. public school population is marked by increasing ethnic and racial diversity. There are approximately 40 million students in the public schools. About 75% of the students are white, 16% are Afro-Americans, 8% are Hispanic, 2% are Asian Americans, and 0.8% are Native Americans.[23] In some schools, minority students outnumber white students. Because all students do not share the white, middle-class background and values, teachers need to familiarize themselves with various minority cultures. This is particularly important because the majority of teachers are white and from a middle-class background.[3] The students that they are teaching may hold values that are different from theirs.

One factor exerting a profound influence on the lives of minority students is socioeconomic status. In comparison to white youths, a disproportionate number of minority youths live below the poverty level.[23] Low socioeconomic status has been found to be associated with low levels of academic achievement. Futhermore, educational disparities exist between white and minority youths. Minority youths are less likely to complete high school and more likely to be suspended from school for various offenses.[10] They may be victims of prejudice, both subtle and overt. However, many minority students are academically successful. Parental encouragement and positive educational expectations have been shown to contribute to their success.

In working with minority students, teachers need to be aware of racial and ethnic stereotypes that may adversely affect minority students' achievement. Teachers also need to be aware of genuine differences in values that exist between different cultures and how these values serve to influence adolescents' behaviors.

A multicultural educational approach encourages respect for all cultures. It emphasizes similarities between cultures as well as appreciation of cultural differences. It requires that teachers make a commitment to understanding different cultural perspectives and provide opportunities for students to do so as well. The goals of multicultural education can be incorporated into the physical education program in several ways. Physical activities from other cultures can be included as part of the curriculum, for example, cricket, yoga, and European handball. Teachers can also explain how the same activities are viewed differently by other cultures. For example, field hockey is played predominately by females in the United States and by males in other cultures, such as in India and Pakistan. Soccer is termed *football* in other cultures, where it is much more popular than in the United States. Providing information about the background of activities taught in the physical education program can also enhance cultural appreciation.

Teachers can also support multicultural education by taking the time to learn a little about the backgrounds of their students. Learning to pronounce students' names correctly communicates respect for the individual. Awareness of differences in cultures with respect to learning styles, interaction patterns, and values helps teachers to more effectively work with all students. Teachers need to be cognizant that not all students are proficient in English. Teachers who are patient while students endeavor to comprehend what is being said and who help students to develop proficiency in the English language can help their students to learn more effectively.

As the diversity of the population increases, the ability to incorporate a variety of multicultural approaches into the educational process is necessary. Teachers who are committed to multicultural education send a powerful message to their students—that their differences are not only accepted but valued.

Adolescents with Disabilities

Adolescence may be a particularly challenging time for individuals who have a disability. Adolescents with disabilities are often sterotyped or stigmatized, leading to discrimination. They may be unfairly labeled and their disability generalized to other aspects of their development.[6] For example, an individual who is visually impaired may be perceived as mentally handicapped and treated as such, even though the individual is of normal intelligence.

Adolescence is a time when individuals attach a great deal of importance to physical appearance and attractiveness. Adolescents are concerned about their physical characteristics because they are perceived to play an important role in social acceptance and, subsequently, can affect one's self-esteem. Adolescents with physical disabilities, such as cerebral palsy, scoliosis, or spina bifida, may perceive themselves as less attractive than others. At a time when belonging to a group is highly valued, adolescents who are perceived as unattractive or different may find themselves excluded and suffer painfully from this rejection. Adolescents whose disabilities adversely affect their communication, such as those who have speech deficits or hearing impairments, may also find themselves isolated from their peers. Furthermore, the egocentricism typical of early adolescence may heighten these students' self-consciousness about their disability. Feeling unattractive, being "different" at a time when identification with a group is important, and heightened self-consciousness may lead to a negative self-concept and feelings of low self-regard.

Fortunately, society's acceptance of individuals with disabilities has improved during the last 20 years. Federal legislation, such as PL 94-142, has guaranteed equal access to education. Students with disabilities may be mainstreamed into the physical education class. Physical education teachers, therefore, need to be cognizant of the characteristics of each disability and their implications for physical education. Students with disabilities should be included in class activities in a meaningful way, not just assigned to keep score on the sidelines. Meaningful inclusion requires a sound understanding of the individual's disability and creative teaching. Knowledge of developmental progressions, task analysis, and activity modification, such as changing the equipment, rules, and roles of the players, help teachers provide successful experiences for students with disabilities.

Child Abuse

One of the most serious problems confronted by students is that of abuse. Approximately 10% of all children and youths are abused by a member of their family each year, and this figure may be even higher because much of the abuse goes unreported.[24] Physical, sexual, and emotional abuse may profoundly affect the lives of students. Physical education teachers should be familiar with the signs of abuse, cognizant of the reporting processes, and aware of how they may personally help abused adolescents deal with this severe problem.

The signs of physical, sexual, and emotional abuse are shown in Box 2-4. Physical education teachers may be in a unique position to detect child abuse. Because students are often required to wear shorts and a T-shirt for physical education class, physical signs of abuse such as severe bruises and pattern burns may be readily displayed. Teachers who are required to supervise dressing in the locker rooms may also notice signs of abuse. On the other hand, a student who refuses to dress out for class or repeatedly asks to be excused from participation may be trying to cover up signs of abuse.

Sometimes a case of child abuse may also be uncovered when a student chooses to confide in a teacher. Listen carefully, show feelings of genuine concern, and reassure the student about his or her decision to confide in you. It is important to assure the student that he or she is not responsible for the abuse. Try to obtain as much infor-

---

BOX 2-4

SIGNS OF CHILD ABUSE

Physical Indicators

Unexplained bruises, burns, wounds, and fractures
Hunger, poor hygiene, inappropriate dress
Medical needs that are not met, lack of care
Difficulty in walking, sitting, or moving—soreness
Bruises or bleeding in the genital area
Pseudomature sexual behavior
Venereal disease
Delayed development

Behavioral Indicators

Apprehensive toward adults
Afraid to go home, perhaps arriving at school early or staying late
Wears clothing that covers the body when inappropriate
Chronic runaway or leaving home to live on their own at an early age
Frequent absences, decrease in school performance
Suicide attempts
Substance abuse
Behavioral extremes and disruptive conduct

Modified from Broadhurst DD, Edmunds M, MacDicken RA: *Early childhood programs and the prevention and treatment of child abuse and neglect,* The User Manual Series, 1979, Washington, DC, US Department of Health, Education and Welfare.

---

mation about the abuse as possible while allowing the student to talk about his or her feelings and fears. After a student confides in you, he or she may ask you to maintain the secret. It is important to explain in a sensitive way why you must report the abuse to the appropriate authorities.

All teachers are mandated by law to report suspected child abuse.[24] Because the procedures for reporting child abuse vary from state to state and from school to school, teachers should be familiar with the reporting process in their own school. Be prepared to cooperate with professionals in helping to resolve this problem. The time to find out about these procedures and the process to be followed is before you, as a teacher, have to deal with this issue.

SUMMARY

To design effective programs, teachers must first and foremost consider students' characteristics and needs. During the secondary school years, students experience the many developmental changes associated with adolescence. Because of the intricate and complex relationship between the psychomotor, cognitive, and affective domains, teachers must be familiar with the important changes that are taking place in each of these areas and understand their implications for the conduct of the physical education program.

In terms of physical development, adolescence is marked by rapid changes in height and weight, alterations in body proportions, skeletal maturation, changes in muscle tissue and the distribution of adipose tissue, attainment of mature function in many of the body's systems, and development of primary and secondary sex characteristics. Motor skill performance becomes increasingly refined, and the development of specialized sport skills should be emphasized in physical education. Helping students attain and maintain an optimal level of fitness is an important priority.

Cognitively, adolescents' levels of intellectual function increase. Their memories are similar to those of adults in terms of the ability to absorb, process, and retrieve information, and they possess a greater attention span. Language and communication skills become increasingly sophisticated. Cognitive functions are enhanced; students are better able to conceptualize, reason, and analyze.

During this period many changes take place in affective development. Adolescents learn the roles associated with being an adult in our society as well as experience changes in their self-esteem and perceptions. Emotionally, adolescents experience increases in the range and intensity of their emotions as well as learn how to express them in an appropriate manner. Students at this time are involved in formulating personal systems of values and have attained higher levels of moral reason.

Several problems may be experienced by students as they move through this period of development. Some of the problems include coping with stress, alienation, and drug abuse. Adolescents from minority groups and those with disabilities may have special needs and concerns.

Consideration of the many developmental changes that occur at this time is important if sound physical education programs are to be planned to meet secondary school students' needs and contribute to their total development. To help all students reach their fullest potential, physical education teachers must consider students' characteristics and needs when selecting and implementing physical education content and instructional strategies.

FOR REVIEW

1. Describe the changes in physical development that occur during the secondary school years. Select one activity and specifically describe the implications of these changes for the conduct of the activity. How would the manner in which the content is taught need to be changed to accommodate individual differences in development?
2. Identify the cognitive changes associated with this period of development. Discuss the impact of these changes on development in the psychomotor and affective domains.

3. Affective development is often overlooked in physical education programs. Discuss the changes in affective development that occur during the secondary school years. Specifically describe how physical education teachers can contribute to development in this domain.
4. Reflect back on your adolescent years. What were some problems that you and your friends experienced? How did you resolve these problems? Now that you are preparing to be a teacher, how could you effectively assist students with similiar problems?

REFERENCES

1. Gallahue DL: *Understanding motor development: infants, children, adolescents,* ed 2, Indianapolis, 1989, Benchmark.
2. Harrison JM, Blackmore CL: *Instructional strategies for secondary school physical education,* Dubuque, Iowa, 1992, William C Brown.
3. Hellison DR, Templin TJ: *A reflective approach to teaching physical education,* Champaign, Ill, 1991, Human Kinetics.
4. Zaichkowsky LD, Zaichkowsky LB, Martinek TJ: *Growth and development: the child and physical activity,* St Louis, 1980, Mosby.
5. Malina RM: Physical growth and maturation. In Seefeldt V, editor: *Physical activity and well-being,* Reston, Va, 1986, AAHPERD.
6. Sherill C: *Adapted physical education and recreation: a multidisciplinary approach,* ed 3, Dubuque, Iowa, 1986, William C Brown.
7. Lloyd MA: *Adolescence,* New York, 1985, Harper & Row.
8. Nichols B: *Moving & learning: the elementary school physical education experience,* ed 2, St Louis, 1990, Mosby.
9. Pangrazi RP, Darst PW: *Dynamic physical education for secondary school students: curriculum and instruction,* New York, 1991, Macmillan Publishing.
10. Nielsen L: *Adolescent psychology: a contemporary view,* New York, 1987, Holt, Rinehart, & Winston.
11. American Alliance for Health, Physical Education, Recreation and Dance: *"Basic Stuff" Series,* Reston, Va, 1989, AAHPERD.
12. Offer D, Ostrov E, Howard K: *The adolescent: a psychological self-portrait,* New York, 1981, Basic Books.
13. Pope AW, McHale SM, Craighead WE: *Self-esteem enhancement with children and adolescents,* New York, 1988, Pergamon Press.
14. Bressan ES, Weiss MR: A theory of instruction for developing competence, self-confidence, and persistence, *Journal of Teaching in Physical Education* 2(1):38-47, 1982.
15. Kohlburg L: From is to ought. In Mishel T, editor: *Cognitive development and epistemology,* New York, 1971, Academic Press.
16. Levy MR, Digman M, Shirreffs JH: *Life and health: targeting wellness,* New York, 1992, McGraw-Hill Book.
17. Conger JJ, Peterson AC: *Adolescence and youth,* ed 3, New York, 1984, Harper & Row.
18. Gerler ER, Jr: Teaching young teenagers skills for adolescence, *Phi Delta Kappan* 67:426-39, 1986.
19. Weiner IB: Psychopathology in adolescence. In Adelson J, editor: *Handbook of adolescent psychology,* New York, 1980, John Wiley & Sons.
20. Towers RL: *How schools can help combat student drug and alcohol abuse,* Washington DC, 1987, National Education Association.
21. Collingwood TR et al: Enlisting physical education for the war on drugs, *JOPERD* 63(2):25-28, 1992.
22. Great Plains Sports Medicine and Rehabilitation Clinic: Illinois High School students: anabolic steroid study. In Kuznik F, editor: The steroid epidemic, *USA Weekend* 3(7):15-17, 1992.
23. US Bureau of the Census: *Statistical abstract of the United States,* ed 111, Washington DC, 1991, US Government Printing Office.
24. Tower CC: *Child abuse and neglect,* Washington DC, 1984, National Education Association.

ANNOTATED READINGS

Collingwood T et al: Enlisting physical education for the war on drugs, *JOPERD* 63(2):25-28, 1992.

Describes the use of a physical fitness program in conjunction with the DARE drug education program in reducing substance abuse risk factors and decreasing use patterns.

Gallahue DL: *Understanding motor development: infants, children, and adolescents,* Indianapolis, 1989, Benchmark.

A comprehensive approach to motor development with some reference to social development across these age spans. Implications for the content and conduct of physical education programs are presented.

Luke MD, Sinclair GD: Gender differences in adolescents' attitudes toward school physical education, *Journal of Teaching in Physical Education* 11(1):31-46, 1991.

Discusses curriculum content, teacher behavior, class atmosphere, student self-perceptions, and facilities as determinents of attitudes toward physical education and factors in the selection of physical education as an elective offering.

Pope AW, McHale SM, Craighead WE: *Self-esteem enhancement with children and adolescents,* New York, 1988, Pergamon Press.

Describes the theoretical foundations of self-esteem and presents a variety of approaches that contribute to a positive self-esteem.

Tower CC: *Child abuse and neglect: a teacher's handbook for detection, reporting, and classroom management,* Washington, DC, 1984, National Education Association.

Describes signs of child abuse and neglect and presents guidelines for effectively dealing with this problem.

CHAPTER 3

Beginning Teachers

CHAPTER OBJECTIVES

◆ To orient physical education teachers to the importance of understanding the school and community environment

◆ To describe the myriad responsibilities associated with teaching

◆ To identify challenges facing beginning teachers

◆ To reflect on the satisfactions and rewards associated with teaching

One of the most important determinants of the success of a physical education program is the teacher. For physical education teachers to function effectively in the schools, they must be familiar with the various facets of the school organization. Teachers will also find it helpful to understand the dynamic relationship that exists between the school and the community.

Beginning physical education teachers need to be cognizant of the many responsibilities they are expected to fulfill as faculty members in the school. In addition to teaching, physical education teachers may coach, supervise a study hall, serve on schoolwide committees, and actively participate in professional organizations.

Many challenges are faced by today's secondary school educators. First-year physical education teachers are challenged with making the transition from a student to a teacher and establishing positive relationships with their students, colleagues, and administrators. Beginning and experienced teachers alike must address the challenges of teacher stress and burnout and successfully working for change. Despite these challenges, the many satisfactions associated with teaching secondary school physical education make it a rewarding career.

ORIENTATION
Orientation to the School

An understanding of school governance and the manner in which schools operate is essential if physical education teachers are to function effectively in the school setting. Decisions made by administrators can affect one's effectiveness as a teacher in many ways. Secondary school physical education teachers also need to be aware of the manner in which schools are financed, because finances have a direct and often profound impact on the nature and quality of the entire educational program, including physical education.

As faculty members, physical education teachers should strive to establish congenial professional relationships with all school personnel and become cognizant of each person's contribution to the total educational effort. Knowledge of school policies, procedures, and rules is important information for teachers to possess.

Beginning teachers are faced with assimilating a tremendous amount of information about their school. Some schools provide an orientation period, in which much of the necessary information is covered. Experienced faculty may be assigned or take it upon themselves to acquaint new teachers with various aspects of school life and ease their transition into the school setting. Teachers' handbooks provide further insight into the organizational structure and regulations governing school. Box 3-1 presents some guidelines to serve as a starting point to familiarize yourself with a new school.[1]

School governance. In the United States, education is a state function, with each of the 50 states responsible for operation of the schools within its boundaries. Within each state, the state board of education and its chief executive officer, the commissioner or superintendent of education, and the state department of education are responsible for establishing guidelines and overseeing the education of its children.

BOX 3-1

ORIENTATION TO THE SCHOOL

Size and population
   Number of students in the school system
   Number of schools in the system
   Number of students in the secondary school
Personnel
   Names and responsibilities of school personnel
     including:
     Superintendent
     School board members
     Director of physical education
     Principals and assistant/vice principals
     Physical education department chairperson
     Physical education faculty
     Instructional faculty
     Support personnel
Administrative structure
   School district organizational chart
   School organization chart
School policies and procedures pertaining to teachers
   Time teachers report to school and depart
   Sign in and sign out procedures
   Procedures to be followed in case of illness or use of
     personal days
   School calendar
   School time schedule and special schedule (e.g., for as-
     semblies, conference days)
   Teaching schedule and related responsibilities (e.g.,
     homeroom)
   Requirements pertaining to lesson plans
   Requirements pertaining to attendance at faculty meet-
     ings and in-service programs
   Frequency and types of teacher evaluation
   Tenure guidelines
School policies and procedures pertaining to students
   Student code of conduct
   Student legal rights
   Discipline policies and procedures
   Suspected child abuse
   Suspected student alcohol or drug abuse
   Student absences from classes
   Student tardiness
   Accidents
Policies and procedures pertaining to institutional respon-
   sibilities

Homeroom procedures
Supervision of hallways, study halls, cafeterias
Fire and disaster drills
Arranging and conducting parent conferences
Availability and use of student support services
Marking periods and grading procedures
Policies and procedures pertaining to professional respon-
   sibilities
   Requirements and financial support available for contin-
     uing education
   Leaves of absence and sabbaticals for study
   Approval for conference attendance and financial sup-
     port
Physical education department information
   Documents
     Department handbook for teachers
     Physical education handbook or policies for students
     Curriculum guide
   Department personnel
     Areas of expertise
     Teaching assignments
     Coaching responsibilities
     Related responsibilities—directing intramurals, sports
       clubs, drop-in recreation, and physical education
       clubs
     Membership and involvement in professional organi-
       zation
   Department committees and assignments
   Departmental in-service programs
   Procedures for input into scheduling, budget, etc.
   Department policies and procedures
     Student dress
     Time for dressing at beginning and end of class
     Attendance procedures
     Make-up classes
     Grading procedures
     Maintenance of student records
     Locker room supervision
     Equipment use, storage, and repair
     Preparation of instructional materials (e.g., handouts,
       tests)
     Preparation of teaching stations (e.g., marking of
       fields, setting up of equipment)

The influence of state educational officials is widely felt at the local level. The state establishes local school districts, and these school districts are charged by the state with carrying out the educational program in compliance with the state's educational policies and regulations. As a result of this delegation of control to local communities, the nature and quality of education vary widely within individual states a well as across the nation.

The school districts within each state are controlled by local boards of education. School board members represent the citizens of the community and are either elected or appointed to this position. Heading the school board is the superintendent of schools. As the educational leader and administrator of the school district, the superintendent is the most powerful officer in the local school organization. School boards are typically charged with such responsibilities as hiring school personnel, establishing school policies, approving the curriculum, overseeing the budget, and planning for building programs.

The school board operates the schools according to state mandates and ensures that minimum state requirements are met. However, within these guidelines the school board can make policies to meet the local needs and desires of the community's citizens. For example, the state may require physical education for secondary school students for only 90 minutes (2 periods) a week. The local school board, however, may require daily physical education for secondary school students, thus exceeding the state requirement.

Understanding the responsibilities and authority vested in the local school board is critical to physical education teachers. The actions and decisions of the school board directly affect the school's programs. Favorable support by the school board can enhance the status of physical education in the secondary school curriculum and exert a positive influence on the program in many ways, such as through proper scheduling of students, time allocation, and resource distribution.

Funding. Public education is funded through a combination of federal and state government monies and local revenues. State aid and local revenues are the primary sources of funds for each school district. Local funds are obtained largely from property taxes.

The reliance of school funding on local property taxes has contributed to unequal educational opportunities. School districts where property values are high generate more money to finance their schools than districts whose property values are low. Inequities in financing lead to educational disparities as reflected in teacher-student ratios, training and experience of teachers, availability of facilities of equipment, curricular offerings, and support services.

Currently, a majority of states require that citizens in a school district vote either on the property tax rate or the school budget itself. In recent years, passing school budgets and tax referendums has become increasingly difficult. When taxpayers reject proposals to increase funds for education, school districts are forced to adopt austerity budgets.

Adoption of austerity measures typically leads to cutbacks in curricular offerings, extracurricular activities, school personnel, and resources. Unfortunately, in some school districts, perceived "frills" or "nonessential" programs such as physical education or music are disproportionately affected by such measures. Physical education offerings may be reduced, transportation to community recreation facilities for instruction eliminated, and necessary equipment not purchased as a result. In school districts where physical education is perceived as an integral part of the curriculum and support for it is strong, physical education programs will not be as severely affected, and reductions will be similar to those experienced by other curricular areas.

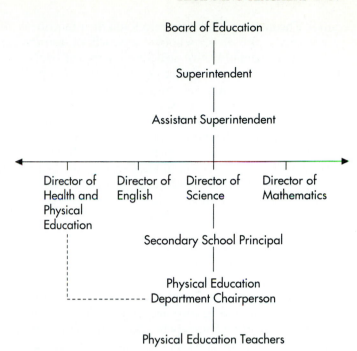

FIG. 3-1   Administrative structure of school district with a director of health and physical education.

Organizational structure and personnel. Understanding the organizational structure of the school system can be helpful to beginning teachers. The formal organization of the school is hierarchical (Fig. 3-1). The superintendent reports to the school board, and the principals are accountable to the superintendent and the teachers to the principal. Typically, the larger the school system is, the more administrators employed and the more levels of control. The lines of authority are clearly defined, and school personnel are expected to follow the "chain of command" and utilize appropriate channels of communication.

A knowledge of the channels through which problems, questions, requests, and innovative ideas can be presented is helpful to teachers. Animosity and ill will may be generated toward individuals who bypass the appropriate channels of communication in quest of an answer. Often, too, the school may appear to be excessively bureaucratic. Certain procedures must be followed, time-consuming paper work must be completed, and "red tape" may accompany the smallest of requests. Beginning teachers may find that experienced teachers can offer helpful advice about how to work effectively within the structure of the school organization.

Many school personnel are involved in working toward the accomplishment of the school's educational objectives. Administrators, direct instructional personnel, and support personnel have various responsibilities that contribute to the attainment of desired educational outcomes.

Administrators are charged with the operation of the

school. The number of administrators and their functions vary with the size of the school. Large school districts may have an administrative structure composed of the superintendent, several assistant superintendents charged with administration of specific areas (for example, finance or curriculum), directors of specific instructional areas (for example, English, mathematics, or physical education), principals for the specific schools within the district, and perhaps assistant principals within each school charged with specific responsibilities such as discipline. In such a structure, the director of physical education coordinates the program and supervises all physical education teachers in the district. In smaller school districts, there may be fewer administrators who are responsible for performing a diversity of tasks.

In addition to their teaching, some teachers may have various administrative responsibilities, such as being a department chairperson. A physical education department chairperson may be responsible for supervising the work of the department members, scheduling of program offerings, curriculum development, and budget administration in addition to teaching.

Individuals who work as direct instructional personnel have primary responsibility for the education of students. Teachers, teacher aides, librarians, and other personnel are responsible for working directly with students.

Support personnel contribute to the education of students in many diverse ways. Guidance counselors, social workers, psychologists, and nurses provide valuable services to students. Some professionals contribute to instructional efforts, such as media specialists, or to administrative efforts, such as executive assistants.

Individuals involved with the maintenance of the building are also considered to be support personnel. A safe and clean environment is important for learning. Custodians' performance can have a direct impact on the physical education program. Clean gymnasiums and locker rooms, well-maintained and marked fields, proper temperatures in instructional areas, and prompt repair of equipment can enhance instruction.

Many individuals work in the schools and contribute to the attainment of its educational objectives. Education can be viewed as a collaborative effort of school personnel working in conjunction with the students, parents, and members of the community. Although school personnel may differ in responsibilities, they share a common mission—to help all students attain their fullest potential.

Policies, procedures, and rules. As a faculty member, the physical education teacher has the responsibility to uphold school policies (Box 3-1). These policies may pertain to the school as a whole, or to the department, faculty, or students. Policies govern many aspects of school life such as student conduct.

School policies also influence the lives of teachers. Policies pertaining to gaining tenure, supervisory visits, attendance at in-service workshops, supervision of extracurricular activities, maintenance of lesson plans, and grading affect the conditions under which teachers work.

School procedures and rules often detail how school policies should be implemented. Procedures for handling disruptive students are often specified as are those for dealing with suspected cases of child abuse and drug and alcohol misuse. It is important to be knowledgeable about these procedures before being confronted with the situation. Physical education teachers also need to be aware of the procedures to be followed for handling fire drills, checking out audiovisual equipment, getting instructional handouts and tests copied, and securing parental permission for transportation to community recreational facilities for instruction. The faculty handbook and experienced teachers are good sources of information about school procedures.

Rules and regulations established by physical education teachers for the conduct of students in physical education classes must be consistent with those for the school. As faculty members, teachers are expected to abide by school regulations and enforce them. Teachers who do not agree with certain regulations should try to ascertain the reasons underlying them and, if necessary, seek change through the appropriate mechanism. Additionally, lack of consistency in implementing school policies, adhering to school procedures, and enforcing rules leads to difficulties and problems such as poor relationships with colleagues or students perceiving the teacher as unfair.

Policies, procedures, and rules are an integral part of school life. Knowledge of these many regulations will help instructors function effectively as members of the school faculty. Beginning teachers will also find it helpful to be aware of the numerous factors that influence the schools.

Influences on the schools. Education at the local level is influenced by federal, state, and local governments. Individuals and groups, some formal and some informal in nature, can also exert a significant influence on education.

Education can be directly influenced by the federal government through the passage of federal legislation and by judicial rulings. Title IX of the Education Amendments Act in 1972 and of Public Law 94-142, the Education for All Children Act, in 1974 are two examples of the impact of the federal government on local education and physical education. Title IX legislation had a direct influence on physical education and athletic programs. It mandated equal educational opportunities for children of both sexes, resulting in increased coeducational offerings for physical education and more athletic teams for girls. PL 94-142 resulted in expanded educational opportunities for children with disabilities, with students, when appropriate, being integrated or mainstreamed into the regular school setting, including physical education classes.

Beginning teachers must be aware of the contributions of other members of the school staff to the education of students.
Courtesy of Joy Buffan, SUC Oswego, Oswego, NY.

State mandates have a direct impact on education at the local level. Of particular concern to physical education teachers are the state requirements for physical education. As many states respond to pressures to increase the time allocated to educational "basics" such as English and mathematics in the curriculum, time allotted to "nonessentials" such as physical education and music is being curtailed. In some states the minimum weekly time requirement for physical education is being decreased and amount of physical education required for graduation reduced. To counteract this move, physical education teachers need to adopt proactive strategies. The state and the public must be convinced that physical education is a "basic" essential for all students and required for all grade levels.

At the local level, citizens and various groups exert a profound influence on the education of their children. Groups such as the parents-teachers association and teachers' unions may lobby school board members in support of certain decisions.

Teachers' unions have considerable influence in some school districts. The two largest unions that represent teachers are the National Education Association (NEA) and the American Federation of Teachers (AFT). On behalf of teachers, the union negotiates with the school board for the teachers' contracts, discussing such issues as salaries, fringe benefits, and working conditions. Unions seek to resolve teacher concerns relative to such work issues as maximum class size, clerical assistance, and in-service training. Through their unions, teachers have sought to gain additional involvement in the various de-

cision-making processes of their schools, such as appointment of department chairpersons, policy decisions, and curricular decisions. Unions also work to protect the legal rights of the teachers they represent.

Because of the profound influence the local community exerts on the schools, beginning teachers would benefit from understanding its characteristics. Once oriented to the school setting, young professionals should seek to acquaint themselves with the community.

Orientation to the Community

Community size, economic conditions, and political forces are just a few of the many community characteristics that influence the education of its children. The sociological and cultural background of community citizens, educational institutions within the community, and the attitude of the community toward education can exert considerable influence on the school's programs. The recreational and sports facilities and programs available can have a direct impact on a school's physical education program. An awareness of the influence of various community factors on the schools can enhance the effectiveness of secondary school physical education teachers. By learning about the community in which they work, physical education teachers will be better able to meet the needs of their students. Further, any suggestions offered for the improvement of the program or facilities will be more meaningful if they reflect an understanding of local community conditions (Box 3-2).

Community demographics. The size of the community

BOX 3-2

ORIENTATION TO THE COMMUNITY

Community size _____   Type—urban, suburban, or rural
School-aged population _____
Governance structure
Political groups
State mandates
Local media
Economic status
  Major businesses and industries
  Employment level
  Income level
Sociocultural background
Attitude toward schools
Educational institutions
  Private elementary and secondary schools
  Colleges and universities
Recreational and sport facilities and programs
  Facility size (number of tennis/racquetball courts, size
    of swimming pool)
  Director
  Programs offered
  Participants—number and ages
  Facility schedule and times of peak usage
  Distance from school
  Natural resources—mountains, rivers, and parks

is one factor that influences the nature of its educational programs and schools. Compared to a larger community, often schools in small communities hold a much more central role in the life of the community. The school is often used as a primary meeting place for community activities for all ages. Community members identify more closely with the school and the accomplishments of its students; they have a greater sense of ownership.

Another aspect of the community to be considered is its school-age population. If this population is growing, it is necessary to determine what changes need to be made in the school programs and facilities to meet the future needs of the students. Failure to take projected growth into account can result in overcrowding in the schools, inadequate monies for instruction, and other situations that can adversely affect learning conditions. Declining enrollments can result in the closing of some schools and the consolidation of students in the remaining schools. Faculty positions may be cut back, budgets reduced, and other constraints imposed that may lead to a less effective learning environment.

The characteristics of the community's population are important to take into account. For example, consider the impact of the age of the community members on the schools. When there are a large number of older residents in a community who no longer have school-aged children,

these residents may have little sympathy for public school problems. This may translate into a reluctance to support increased school budgets designed to remedy these problems, because increased budgets raise taxes, a burden for many residents on fixed incomes.

Economic status. The influence of the economic level of the community on its schools is considerable. The state of the nation's economy, the economic soundness of local businesses and industries, and the level of employment within the community are some of the economic factors that can positively or negatively affect various school programs and the quality of the education students receive.

In a community that is economically sound, it is more likely that educational expenditures will be met. In relation to physical education, this means well-planned physical plants, adequate equipment, and enough qualified personnel with salries high enough to attract and retain them. It also means an appropriate class size for learning, a varied instructional program, an inclusive intramural program, and a full interscholastic program. Where communities are experiencing hard economic times, the school budget may not be supported. Over a period of time, this lack of financial support can have a severe impact on the quality of education. With reference to physical education, the consequences can include inadequate facilities, shortages of equipment and supplies, overcrowded classes, and fewer personnel working at lower salaries. The instructional program may offer fewer activities and the physical education requirement for graduation may be reduced. Intramural and interscholastic programs may be limited.

Sensitivity to different economic conditions within the community is important to teachers trying to meet the needs of their students. While some students may come from very wealthy backgrounds, other students may be living at or below poverty level. These students may face the problems of hunger, fear, and insecurity that may interfere with their ability to learn.

Politics. Political groups and local politics may exert varying degrees of influence on the local schools. Candidates for local government positions may use educational issues as part of their platform for election. Politics also play a role in the determination of school board members. Because the school board wields considerable power and control over the schools, where the board is ineffective because it is politically motivated, the education of the children suffers.

Politics may also influence hiring decisions. Sometimes political connections lead to the hiring of less qualified personnel at the expense of more highly qualified personnel. Ultimately, it is the children who experience the consequences of these decisions.

Sociological and cultural backgrounds. Our society is a multicultural one. Throughout the United States communities are becoming increasingly culturally diverse. By the year 2020 it is estimated that nearly half of school-aged children will be members of ethnic minorities.[2]

As cultural diversity grows, it is important that teachers become informed about the values and mores of the various cultures within the community. It may be helpful to examine dominant societal views and one's own views pertaining to different cultures and how these views may serve to enhance or detract from the educational opportunities provided to the students one teaches.[3] Try to see the educational experience through the eyes of individuals from other cultures rather than just your own.[4]

Support for multicultural education is growing throughout the United States. The essence of multicultural education is respect for people of all cultures. Multicultural education values cultural diversity, stresses individual uniqueness, and seeks to foster an appreciation for other cultures. Teachers are sensitive to individual differences and provide for these differences in learning. Understanding and appreciation of cultural diversity are important if equitable learning opportunities are to be provided for all children.

Attitude toward education. The attitude of a community's citizens toward education shapes in many ways the educational experience it provides its children. Is the community conservative or liberal? Is it supportive of educational trends? Is the employment of outdated methods by teachers tolerated, or is the use of innovative techniques by teachers encouraged? The citizens' attitude to-

ward education can also be discerned by reviewing the items included in the school budget and the community's voting record on recent referendums.

What is the community's attitude toward physical education? Often based on their own negative experiences, some adults may perceive physical education as a waste of time and not worthy of inclusion in the educational curriculum. Or they may mistakenly equate the instructional program with athletics and thus believe that physical education does not meet the needs of 90% of the students. These perceptions can have disastrous consequences for the physical education program.

The burden rests on physical education teachers to interpret accurately their program to the community. Interpreting a quality program to the public, promoting effective school-parent communication, and sending home happy and knowledgeable students are probably among the best ways to create a positive attitude toward physical education in the community.

Educational institutions. The presence of institutions of higher education in the local area can positively influence educational programs. These institutions can serve as valuable resources for the community's teachers. Through cooperative programs, teachers can gain access to the latest instructional resources and benefit from the expertise of college and university faculty members. Public school teachers may have the opportunity to serve as adjunct faculty members at these institutions and share their experience with preservice teachers. Teachers may also serve as cooperating teachers for physical education majors completing their early field and student teaching experiences. Having an institution of higher education nearby also makes it easier for teachers to continue their education and attain advanced degrees.

Community recreational and sport facilities and programs. Secondary school physical education teachers should be knowledgeable about the public and commercial recreational and sport facilities within the community. The use of community facilities can broaden physical education offerings, allowing teachers to satisfy a greater variety of physical activity interests and provide increased opportunities for students to develop their skills.

An inventory of community facilities should include public and private facilities. In addition to information about the facility itself, information should be gathered about their distance from school, their personnel, schedule of use, and current programs and their participants. This information should be integrated with that pertaining to the school district. Physical education teachers can then form a comprehensive picture of facility usage and program offerings within the community as well as become aware of how the school physical education program fits into the total picture.

The use of school facilities by members of the community should be also encouraged and actively promoted. If education is indeed a lifelong activity, school programs should be expanded to meet the needs of adults and preschoolers. School physical education programs can help adults develop physical activity skills to pursue their leisure interests and fitness to enhance their quality of life. Preschool motor development programs can introduce young children to the joys of physical activity. School-community programs can be scheduled during the many hours when the school facilities are not being used, such as on the evenings, weekends, and vacations. Not only will program participants benefit from participation, but such programs can generate increased community support for physical education.

The utilization of community facilities can have a positive effect on the secondary school physical education program. The broadening of school physical education programs to meet the diverse needs of community members of all ages is a positive trend whose growth should be encouraged. Collaborative efforts between the school and the community can pay tremendous dividends not only for the students but also for all members of the community.

RESPONSIBILITIES OF SECONDARY SCHOOL PHYSICAL EDUCATION TEACHERS

Teaching physical education is more than instructing students and helping them attain the desired educational outcomes of skill proficiency, physical fitness, knowledge, and appreciation for the value of physical activity. Physical education teachers must also fulfill a number of responsibilities incumbent upon them as faculty members in the school. These obligations may be categorized into pedagogical, institutional, and professional responsibilities (Table 3-1).

Pedagogical Responsibilities

In a broad sense, pedagogical responsibilities are those activities that are related, either directly or indirectly, to teaching physical education classes and the physical education program. These responsibilities include teaching, planning, administration, coaching, directing, curriculum development, and program promotion.

Teaching. Secondary school physical education teachers typically teach four to six classes a day. The length of each class, class size, and frequency of class meeting varies from school to school. Teachers engage in many different activities and perform a diversity of functions when teaching their students. Rink[5] categorizes these teachers' functions into content and management behaviors.

Content behaviors are those tasks performed by the teacher that directly contribute to the development of physical education content and the intended outcomes of the lessons.[5] These instructional activities include such tasks as explaining and demonstrating a skill, using questions to check students' comprehension, and engaging students productively in activity. Teachers must also ac-

TABLE 3-1		
Responsibilities of Secondary School Physical Education Teachers		
Pedagogical Responsibilities	Institutional Responsibilities	Professional Responsibilities
Teaching	Supervision	Growth and devel-
Planning	Advisement	opment
Administration	Counseling	Involvement
Coaching	Parent conferencing	
Directing	Committee work	
Curriculum development	Community involvement	
Program promotion		

tively monitor students' efforts and provide them with feedback to facilitate improvement. They must be alert to modify learning tasks to meet individuals' needs and to accommodate a wide variety of individual differences. Provision must be made to assess students' progress and evaluate learning. Teachers must seek to maximize the amount of class time they spend engaged in instructional activities.

Management behaviors facilitate learning of physical education content indirectly by exerting an influence on the learning environment.[5] These behaviors focus on two areas: student conduct and organizational arrangements. Teachers who reinforce appropriate student behavior or who act to intervene to prevent a discipline problem are managing the learning environment to make it conducive for learning. Teachers who direct the students on how to get equipment for practice or how to move from one activity to the next are also engaging in managerial behaviors. Efficient performance of these tasks ensures that the time available for instruction is maximized.

Planning. Teaching is a goal-oriented activity in which specific outcomes are actively sought.[5] Planning can contribute to the attainment of desired instructional outcomes by helping teachers focus on objectives and identify strategies to achieve them. Planning gives direction to one's efforts and contributes to the wise use of instructional time.

When viewed from the perspective of safety and legal liability, planning is critical. Creation of a safe learning environment is of paramount concern. The potential problems and risks inherent in various physical activities should be carefully assessed. Utilizing appropriate progressions for activities and considering individual differences in abilities are important planning concepts from the safety and legal liability standpoint.

Schools generally provide their teachers with one daily planning period. Often, this period is not used for plan-

Planning is an important teacher responsibility.
Courtesy of Mary Beth Steffen, Shaker High School, Colonie, NY.

ning but to accomplish other tasks such as repairing equipment or talking to students. Teachers who coach may use this time to prepare for the afternoon's practice, schedule contests, or contact officials.

Beginning teachers should be aware that some school systems require that teachers have a certain number of preplanned lessons ready for use by substitute teachers. In other schools, weekly lesson plans are subjected to being checked by the department chairperson or the principal.

Administration. The administrative functions that physical education teachers perform are numerous. Maintaining student records is one administrative responsibility that may involve considerable time. Information on students' achievement on fitness and skills tests and ancetodal records of behavior, attendance, and test grades need to be recorded. Teachers must also prepare and submit grades for students at the end of each marking period. To facilitate record keeping, some physical education teachers use microcomputers.

In schools where students are allowed to select from an array of courses for physical education, teachers are often involved in conducting student interest surveys to determine course offerings and enrolling students in courses. Other administrative functions may include ordering equipment, conducting equipment inventories, and overseeing the department budget.

Coaching. Many teachers also coach interscholastic sport teams in addition to teaching their physical education classes. Coaching is a demanding responsibility, especially when it is viewed in conjunction with the many other responsibilities associated with teaching.

Teachers often coach two or three sports a year, serving as either the head or assistant coach. Thus for many teachers, the coaching season lasts year round. Coaching extends the school day by several hours. After teaching for 6 to 7 hours, practice activities occupy the teacher's time for an additional 3 or more hours. The conclusion of practice may be followed by conversations with athletes, supervision of the locker room, and meetings with assistants to evaluate the day's practice and decide on plans for tomorrow's. On days when there are contests, coaching consumes more time. Planning practices, scheduling contests and officials, scouting opponents, attending league meetings, working with booster clubs, and participating in clinics are other responsibilities typically associated with coaching.

Teaching and coaching impose numerous responsibilities on physical education teachers; for many individuals, it is like having two full-time jobs. Some teachers skillfully balance the various demands, dividing their time and efforts fairly between teaching and coaching. They bring to both positions dedication and enthusiasm and find tremendous satisfaction in meeting the needs of both their students and their athletes.

Other individuals may choose to address their efforts predominately toward one job, often at the expense of the other. Career aspirations and an effort to cope with often overwhelming demands may influence this decision. When teachers choose to direct their time and energy to coaching, often the quality of the physical education instructional program suffers.

Directing. Directing intramurals, sports clubs, and drop-in recreational programs are responsibilities also un-

Coaches spend many hours preparing for games and practices.
Courtesy of Suzi D'Annalfo, Conard High School, West Hartford, CT.

dertaken by physical education teachers. An important part of the total physical education curriculum, these activities provide additional opportunities for students to receive instruction and to practice. Further, they may be helpful in developing approach tendencies in students, that is, the desire to want to participate. This is important to the achievement of the goal of having students incorporate physical activity into their lifestyle.

In directing intramurals, teachers may perform such tasks as determining students' interests, scheduling activities, conducting intramural events, record keeping, and recognition of achievement through presentation of awards. Traditionally, intramurals are offered after school. Space and equipment limitations as well as students' obligations (for example, work) have led some schools to conduct intramural programs during evening hours, lunch periods, and even before school.

Sports clubs (for example, skiing, karate, or weight training) provide faculty and students with opportunities to engage in activities of interest to them. Although these clubs may be governed by students, physical education teachers may serve as club advisors, assisting with such matters as facility usage, insurance, travel arrangements, and scheduling. They may also provide instruction to club members.

Drop-in recreation programs are becoming more common in the schools. During their free time, students can independently pursue a variety of physical activities or work out. Scheduling times, publicizing, and supervising

are some ways in which physical education teachers are involved in these programs.

Directing student clubs related to physical education is another responsibility that may be undertaken. These include officiating clubs, athletic associations, and leaders' clubs. Students in these clubs contribute in many ways to the conduct of the physical education program. Physical education teachers may work directly with these club members, instructing them in officiating techniques, skills, and teaching methods so that they may provide assistance within the physical education program.

Curriculum development. A part of physical education teachers' pedagogical responsibilities is the development of a well thought out curriculum and a continuous revision of the curriculum to meet students' needs. This critical function may be carried out by the individual teacher or may occur through a committee process.

Curriculum development requires the physical education teacher to gather input from a variety of sources. Model curriculums, programs offered by other schools, information about students' needs and interests, and input from colleagues and administrators aid in the development process. Consideration of facilities, equipment, budget, time allotments, and scheduling constraints is important. Curriculum development that involves teachers from all education levels, elementary through secondary, in the process helps ensure that continuity and progression are provided for within the curriculum, K-12. The development of new units of instruction and timely revisions of the existing curriculum contributes to a viable physical education program that is exciting and meaningful to teachers and students alike.

Program promotion. Physical education teachers must assume the responsibility for actively promoting their programs. Program promotion starts with a quality program.

Sending a newsletter to parents, making a videotape for a local television station about the instructional program, conducting physical education demonstrations, and offering fitness assessments to community residents are some examples of program promotion efforts. A variety of different approaches will be effective in informing students, parents, and community members about the merits of a quality physical education program.

As part of their promotion efforts, physical education teachers should discuss with administrators and other teachers the significance of physical education and its contribution to the education and health of students. Another way to demonstrate the positive contribution of physical education to individuals' lives is to help set up an on-site wellness program for school personnel. More schools are offering health promotion programs for their employees. Teachers who take an active part in this endeavor will find it an excellent means to communicate to school personnel the value of physical education.

Institutional Responsibilities

As faculty members in an educational institution, physical education teachers must assume other responsibilities in addition to their pedagogical responsibilities. Some of these responsibilities are explicitly stated in teacher contracts, while others are unwritten expectations for teachers. These institutional responsibilities are wide ranging, encompassing such tasks as supervision, advisement, counseling, parent conferencing, and participating on schoolwide committees.

Supervision. For many teachers, part of the school day is taken up performing supervisory functions. Some teachers are assigned to homerooms, where they take attendance and inform students about school events. Teachers are often assigned to monitor hallways, supervise study halls, and oversee cafeterias. In these situations, the emphasis is on maintaining student order and discipline. Before the need arises, beginning teachers need to familiarize themselves with accepted procedures for dealing with such incidents as fighting in the hallways, smoking in the restrooms, food fights and other disruptive behaviors in the cafeteria, and excessive noise and misbehavior in study halls.

Advisement. Many teachers act as advisors to extracurricular student activities, such as student dramas, yearbook, student government, or special interest clubs such as the photography club, science club, or Students Against Drunk Driving (SADD). In some schools teach-

Physical education teachers may be required to assume various institutional responsibilities, such as supervision of hallways, study halls, and cafeterias.
Courtesy of Joy Buffan, SUC Oswego, Oswego, NY.

ers are required to serve as advisors for a certain number of extracurricular activities. In other schools, serving as an advisor is voluntary. Depending on the school and the activity, teachers may receive a small remuneration for their services. For many physical education teachers, the directing of intramurals or the coaching of a sport fulfills their extracurricular obligations.

Counseling. As part of the physical education program, teachers often counsel individual students as to their activity choices or improvement of their fitness levels. Often this counseling process extends to a variety of other issues. Adolescence is a difficult developmental stage for some students. Students may find themselves facing numerous problems pertaining to their physical development, emotional state, relationships with others, educational plans, and future careers. Often students will seek out teachers they respect to talk about some of their concerns. Teachers need to be prepared to deal with a myriad of problems such as eating disorders, depression, suicidal thoughts, substance abuse, child abuse, future career plans, relationships, and problems at home. During the counseling process, teachers should respect the student's right to privacy and uphold ethical standards. Teachers must understand their own limits for dealing with problems and know where, when, and how to refer students for additional, trained help.

Parent conferencing. Meeting with students' parents or guardians is another responsibility that must be carried out in a professional manner. At parents' evenings, teachers have the opportunity to meet students' parents and present information about their programs. Information about activities that will be covered during the year, objectives for student learning, and evaluation procedures can be shared with parents. This is also a good time to elicit parents' help in developing students' skills or fitness levels. Parent evenings are excellent opportunities for teachers to present a positive image of physical education and elicit parental support for their program.

Physical education teachers may also have to schedule individual parent conferences to deal with student problems such as misbehavior, inadequate skill development, or poor fitness levels. In preparing for a conference, gather pertinent materials (anecdotal records of behavior, attendance reports, fitness and skill assessments) and carefully review them. During the conference, each individual should have the opportunity to address the issue, and an acceptable solution to the problem should be sought.

Committee work. School faculty are expected to serve on school committees. These committees may be subject specific, for example, physical education, or schoolwide. Various physical education committees may deal with such issues as curriculum revision, student dress, or whether athletes should be excused from physical education classes during their season.

Schoolwide committees encompass the development of policies pertaining to such issues as student behavior and discipline, multicultural education, or extracurricular activity policies. It is important that physical education teachers not reinforce the impression of some faculty members regarding their nonacademic status by refusing to serve on a schoolwide committee. To be fully accepted as a faculty member, physical education teachers need to take an active part in school.

Community involvement. Because of their expertise, physical education teachers are frequently approached by community members to provide leadership for community sport or wellness activities. This may include serving as a member of the community recreation commission, conducting preseason clinics for volunteer youth sport coaches, instructing in continuing education evening classes for adults desiring to improve their skills or fitness, or serving as a member of a community health organization (for example, American Heart Association). Although physical education teachers already have an imposing list of demands placed upon them, involvement in some way in community activities can do much to create a positive impression of physical education.

Professional Responsibilities

In addition to fulfilling their pedagogical and institutional responsibilities, physical education teachers must also be mindful of their professional obligations. These obligations encompass activities pertaining to one's professional growth and development as well as involvement in professional organizations.

Professional growth and development. Continued study for professional growth and development is a major responsibility of every teacher. Continuing education is one means to fulfill this obligation. Many physical education teachers pursue advanced education degrees related to their area of interest—pedagogy, coaching, or sports medicine. In many states, a master's degree is required to gain a permanent teaching certificate or maintain a valid teaching license. Some school systems reimburse teachers for their educational expenses, and some schools recognize credits earned past the bachelor's degree with a pay increase.

Taking advantage of conferences and clinics offered by professional organizations such as AAHPERD and various coaching associations is another way to keep abreast of the latest advances in the profession. Reading professional periodicals offers another opportunity to gain new ideas to improve one's teaching.

Professional involvement. Physical education teachers should strongly consider being an active member of a professional organization. Many professional organizations, such as AAHPERD, have associations at the regional and state level in addition to the national level. Membership provides professionals with opportunities to communicate with each other as well as opportunities to share and learn new ideas. Professional organizations can also be helpful in gaining support for physical education, for example, lobbying against proposed changes to reduce physical education requirements within a state.

However, membership alone is not enough. To reap the greatest benefit and to aid in advancing the profession, involvement of each person in the activities of the association is necessary. Participating on committees, serving as an officer, and sharing ideas and research at workshops and conventions are just some of the ways in which physical education teachers can contribute to the advancement of the profession.

To be a teacher in today's secondary schools requires the undertaking of numerous pedagogical, institutional, and professional responsibilities. While these responsibilities are common to most secondary schools, the expectations held by a school for teachers' behaviors and the procedures to be followed in fulfilling these obligations vary from school to school. Information about each school's expectations and procedures can be found in the faculty handbook and through school orientation and inservice programs. Experienced teachers are also a valuable source of information and can be of great assistance to beginning teachers. Beginning teachers may have many concerns and face a variety of challenges as they start their careers. However, teaching secondary school physical education can be a highly satisfying and rewarding experience.

CHALLENGES AND SATISFACTIONS

The first year of teaching is an exciting one. Finally, after all those years of preparation, you're a teacher! Just think . . . starting your first job, taking charge of your own classes, and being responsible for your students' learning from the first day of school to the last. It's an opportunity to put theory into practice, to take what you have learned and apply it to your own teaching. The first year of teaching also marks the start of a tremendous opportunity to learn and grow as a professional. It is a time of many exciting challenges as well as one of many satisfactions.

Challenges

Beginning teachers face many challenges. Many first-year teachers have concerns about their competence. Beginning teachers also find learning the teacher's role, establishing positive relationships with colleagues and administrators, and developing productive relationships with students are important tasks in their adjustment to teaching. All teachers, beginning and experienced alike, should be aware of the serious problems of teacher stress and burnout as well as be familiar with ways to prevent its occurrence. Finally, understanding how to work effectively to bring about change in the schools is essential if teachers are to improve professional practice.

These concerns and challenges are presented to acquaint beginning teachers with the realities of teaching, not to discourage them. Not all beginning teachers face these challenges; it depends on the individual teacher and the school in which he or she is working. But these concerns and challenges, as well as many others, exist, and beginning teachers should be cognizant of them. Unaware of them, beginning teachers may be disillusioned, overwhelmed, or even shocked about the realities of teaching. Awareness is the first step in developing effective strategies to deal with these situations. Mastering these challenges can give one a sense of satisfaction and accomplishment.

Developing as a teacher. Becoming an excellent teacher requires dedication, practice, and the ability to reflect upon and learn from one's experiences. The first year of teaching provides numerous opportunities for young professionals to improve their teaching skills and further develop as a teacher. Effective physical education teachers establish productive relationships with their students, provide learning experiences and a supportive learning environment in which students can successfully engage in relevant motor behavior, and communicate positive expectations for student achievement.

A growing physical education teacher may experience various concerns. These concerns—anxieties, doubts, fears, apprehensions, feelings, ideas, and questions—initially focus on personal survival and later tend to center around teaching and student learning.[6]

During their first months of teaching, beginning teachers are preoccupied with concerns about their survival, their ability to cope, and their adequacy.[6] Some teachers experience a crisis of confidence as they question their own ability to teach: "Can I do it?" "Am I ready?" Concerns about being accepted as a professional by their colleagues and their students surface as well. "Will I be respected?" is a question that is asked often. Uppermost in many beginning teachers' minds is the question of whether they can maintain an appropriate degree of class control and uphold class discipline. Other concerns pertain to teaching evaluations, such as teaching well when a supervisor is present.

As beginning teachers resolve their initial concerns, they shift their focus to concerns about their teaching. Teachers' thoughts focus on mastering the tasks of teaching and the day-to-day routines within the gymnasium and the school. Within the context of the school and specifically the physical education setting, teachers may ask themselves "How can I teach effectively?" Limitations such as inadequate facilities, insufficient equipment, and overcrowded classes are concerns at this level. Teachers may feel under pressure, dissatisfied with the number of noninstructional duties they are required to perform (paperwork and supervising study halls), and overworked. Ways to make the job easier are sought.

Teachers are also concerned about the impact of their teaching, that is, their effectiveness in promoting student learning.[6] They may wonder how their teaching is affecting their students and may question if they are meeting the needs of their students. Challenging students, especially those who are disinterested or unmotivated, are a concern as well. These various expressions of concern about student achievement are a hallmark of development as a teacher.

Learning the role. As part of the socialization process, young professionals learn the behaviors and expectations associated with their roles as teachers in the complex, dynamic school environment. Essentially, they learn what teachers do or don't do in school—what is acceptable and what is not.

Often these expectations are learned informally by beginning teachers through astute observation and thoughtful examination of the behaviors exhibited by experienced teachers. At times, however, experienced teachers will take the "rookies" aside and offer them some advice. "Be sure to stay on the good side of the principal's secretary," "Don't arrive at school too early," and "Don't cross the custodian" are typical of helpful "hints" that are offered.

Naturally, all teachers are not in agreement about which behaviors are desirable. This may be particularly noticeable in the area of student control and teacher-student relationships. Some teachers may advocate an authoritarian approach, with students strictly controlled and a distance maintained in teacher-student relationships. Other teachers may believe in a laissez faire approach to student control and the development of close faculty-student relationships.

Beginning teachers who fail to live up to the expectations imposed upon them may face sanctions, either formal or informal, from other teachers and administrators. For example, a hard-working beginning teacher may face mild disapproval from some faculty; or a teacher who adopts a relaxed, informal style of class management with students may be perceived as incompetent or unable to maintain order by experienced teachers who advocate more firm class control.

Once the norms for behavior as an educational professional are learned, beginning teachers can modify or personalize the role to meet their own unique characteristics and reflect their beliefs. Personal adjustments to the working situation are made.

Initial adjustments to a new role can follow several avenues: internalization, compliance, and noncompliance.[7] Teachers who find the expectations for behavior or school policies compatible with their own beliefs and congruent with their values internalize the expectations of others and comply with them.

Teachers who find certain aspects of the job at odds with their beliefs may adopt a strategy of compliance. They "go along" with things and "don't make waves" at least on the surface. They comply and carry out their responsibilities in the accepted manner, even though they may not really believe in what they are doing. Compliance may be a short- or a long-term strategy.

Some beginning teachers, when faced with values or behaviors that are at odds with their beliefs about how teachers should act, may choose not to conform or comply. They may resist the pressure to "fit in" and continue to "march to the beat of their own drummer." Before embarking on this path, beginning teachers should step back and take time to evaluate their decision for noncompliance.[7] Look at the situation from a variety of perspectives and try to determine the reasons for such policies and behaviors. Consider whether the issue is important enough to challenge. If it is not important, perhaps it is better to comply with the policy or accepted norms that have other professionals form negative judgments. If it is important, beginning teachers should abide by their principles while conducting themselves in a professional manner.

Voicing dissatisfaction with the job or behaviors of other teachers may create problems for beginning teachers. Disapproval of the way in which things are done or failure to conform to expected behavioral norms may alienate other teachers. Another consequence may be receiving less than adequate teaching evaluations from the principal and peers no matter how good their teaching may be; this could lead to teachers not being rehired. Unless teachers have strong convictions against a certain policy or behavior, compliance may be an effective short-term strategy for beginning teachers to adopt.[7] Compliance allows teachers some time to familiarize themselves with the school environment and to establish credibility with their colleagues. Once beginning teachers have established themselves and demonstrated their ability to teach in the "real world," they will be able to work more effectively for change.

Professional relationships. Establishing congenial professional relationships with other members of the school staff is an important task for beginning teachers. New teachers are entering a situation where affiliation networks have already been established. A look at the informal organization of the school reveals that teachers are organized into groups, with some teachers belonging to several groups.

Teachers commonly form close affiliations with teachers from the same subject area. Other groups are formed when teachers share common attitudes, similar years of seniority, or compatible interests. Different degrees of power and prestige are associated with each group, as are different expectations for behavior. Beginning teachers need to discover the various groups within the school, their status, and behavioral expectations as well as to determine to which groups they belong. Being a part of a group should not lead to ignoring other colleagues. Pleasant professional relationships with all members of the school are important.

A serious problem facing teachers is professional isolation. Within the school day, little time is set aside for formal interaction (for example, staff meetings) with one's peers on a regular basis. Many interactions occur informally, often through conversations in teachers' lounges or over lunch. Physical education teachers may even be more isolated because of the location of the gymnasium on the periphery of the school and the perceived nonacademic status accorded by some teachers. Thus in addition to developing positive, professional relationships with other members of the physical education department, beginning teachers must take the initiative to establish professional relationships with other faculty in the school. Such interactions provide opportunities for physical education teachers to gain a comprehensive understanding of the function of the school and the curriculum as well as to promote physical education as an integral part of the educational experience.

Professional isolation hinders professional development because it deprives teachers of the opportunity to exchange ideas pertaining to curricular and instructional matters. Experienced teachers can gain from the infusion of new ideas and fresh perspectives that beginning teachers bring to the school. Beginning teachers can benefit from the wealth of knowledge possessed by veteran teachers. Importantly, teachers also provide each other with emotional support to get through the day "where nothing is going right"; they are also someone with whom to share the joy of your successes. Good relationships with one's peers enhance teachers' enjoyment of the school environment and contribute to the satisfaction that they derive from their work.

Determining administrators' expectations and establishing a professional relationship with them is also an important task of beginning teachers. The principal is one of the most powerful figures in the school. Knowing the principal's philosophy, educational priorities, and beliefs regarding characteristics of effective teaching is important because these can substantially influence evaluations of one's performance.

The principal's philosophy and perceptions of physical education should be ascertained. If the principal, because of past experiences, conceives of physical education as students neatly lined up in squads performing exercises, followed by teacher skill instruction, student drilling, and game play, then any deviation from this approach may be perceived as unsatisfactory teaching. Sharing with the principal your approach to physical education is helpful in clarifying expectations regarding the purpose and the teaching of physical education.

Teacher–student relationships. The establishment of a positive working relationship with their students is one aspect of teaching that may cause beginning teachers some concern. Good rapport with students and a collaborative productive relationship contributes to a successful physical education experience.

Mutual respect is important in establishing rapport with students. Gaining the respect of students requires that beginning teachers exhibit expertise, emotional maturity, confidence, leadership, and genuine concern for each student.

Establishing relationships with students and determining the appropriate social distance is often difficult for new teachers. Some teachers choose to be formal, strict, aloof, and extremely businesslike, while others decide to be informal, easy going, and a friend, with little distinction made between teacher and student. Both of these extremes have consequences. Being too strict and too aloof makes it difficult for students to readily perceive a teacher's concern for their well-being. Being too much like a student's pal may lead to charges of favoritism by some students and a lack of respect. Faculty colleagues may perceive such a relationship as nonprofessional, and this perception may threaten one's credibility as a teacher. Each teacher has to find the right social distance for himself or herself. Remember that students hold certain expectations for teacher's behaviors; they want teachers to be teachers. Secondary school students who are in the midst of coping with the uncertainties of adolescence especially need mature, caring adults whom they can respect.

Beginning teachers need to be prepared to treat all students fairly. This may be difficult because all teachers encounter students who they do not particularly like. This dislike may manifest itself in teachers being overly critical of the efforts and minimizing the accomplishments of these students. Students are very astute observers of behavior. Evidence of dislike or favoritism by a teacher adversely affects the establishment of rapport and respect.

Look for the good in each student you encounter. See students as individuals and appreciate individual differences. Make an effort to learn about each student as a person—their background, interests, and abilities. Learn each student's name as soon as possible. Knowing students' names helps teachers better maintain class control. The use of students' names by teachers personalizes the learning experience and helps make students feel important as an individual and not just another student in a class.

One problem faced by some beginning teachers is how to deal with the sexual attraction between themselves and their students. Because of the small age difference between beginning teachers and their adolescent students, teachers may find themselves attracted to a student or the object of a student's infatuation or romantic intentions. Be aware of the possibility of these occurrences and deal with these situations in a sensitive, professional manner.

Be cognizant that students will test beginning teachers. Students are interested in determining how a new teacher will react to misbehavior. Students can sense hesitancy and uncertainty and will capitalize on it as a means of finding out the new teacher's limits. New teachers will find it helpful to have a clear picture in their minds of acceptable and unacceptable student actions and a plan to deal with student misbehavior before it occurs.

On the first day it is critical that beginning teachers exhibit leadership and confidence in their abilities (even if you do not feel confident). Communicate to students class rules, define acceptable behavior, and express positive expectations for student learning. Plan an activity for the first day that is exciting and that allows students to experience enjoyment and success. "Getting off on the right foot" can pay positive dividends during the year.

Excessive demands can lead to burnout among teacher-coaches. Courtesy of Ben Lomardo, Rhode Island College, Providence, RI.

Good teacher-student relationships can be carried over to areas outside of the gymnasium. Teachers who attend school functions, such as concerts and athletic competitions, and help chaperone dances and other social affairs have the opportunity to further develop positive relationships with their students. Students will respond in kind to respect, understanding, and interest.

Stress and burnout. Teacher stress and burnout are two problems confronting educators today. Essentially, stress is caused by individuals having to adapt to various demands and events in their life. How one views these incidences—the outlook or perspective one adopts— often determines whether they are perceived as positive or negative occurrences. The same event may be interpreted in different ways. For example, a teacher may view student discipline as a challenge (a positive perspective) or as a burden (a negative perspective). The effectiveness of one's coping behaviors also influences the amount of stress experienced.

Stress can have positive effects, adding excitement to our lives, motivating us to excel, and serving as a stimulus for personal growth. However, prolonged and intense stress can have debilitating consequences, resulting in physical and psychological disorders. There are numerous demands and events in teachers' personal and professional lives that can cause stress.

Beginning teachers may experience stress caused by the many changes that occur in their life during the first year of teaching. Moving to a new location, living on one's own, and making new friends are just some of the many personal adjustments that are made by beginning teachers.

Professionally, beginning teachers encounter many demands that must be met. They must learn the norms for behavior within the school, become familiar with school policies and procedures, and establish themselves as a professional with their colleagues and administrators. Earning the respect of one's students, handling discipline problems, and dealing with many other professional concerns such as supervisory evaluations may contribute to feeling stressed. The first year of teaching typically has a high workload because teachers must prepare instructional units for many activities that they have not previously taught.

The many tasks and demands experienced may leave the first-year teacher feeling, at times, exhausted and stressed. Yet, for many beginning teachers the first year may be an energizing and exhilarating experience. Being on one's own, meeting new people, being able to teach as one likes and place personal beliefs into practice, and helping students learn and achieve success is for many satisfying and rewarding.

Stress is not unique to the beginning teacher. Beginning and experienced teachers alike may encounter events in the school environment that can lead to the development of stress. The many pedagogical, institutional, and professional responsibilities faced by teachers and the lack of time in which to perform them can contribute to the feeling of being overwhelmed. Managing disruptive students, dealing with many bureaucratic demands and the accompanying red tape, lack of support from parents, incompetent administrators, lack of supervisory feedback, little appreciation for a job well done, and fears for personal safety are some other causes of stress.[8,9] The lack of time to accomplish the many tasks associated with teaching can also create value conflicts. Having to compromise between what one would like to do for students and what one can realistically do given one's personal limitations and available time can be stressful.

For physical education teachers who also have coaching responsibilities, the demands impinging upon them and the time required to fulfill the responsibilities of both roles are even greater. Stress may also arise because of role conflict. Role conflict occurs when the expectations associated with various roles are incompatible. Teachers who are also coaches may be unable to satisfy the many and often conflicting demands. Thus, they have to make decisions about how to apportion their efforts, whether to give most of their time and energy to teaching or to coaching, or to try to strike a successful balance between both sets of demands.

When stresses are unresolved, are intense, and occur over a prolonged period of time, teachers' abilities to cope effectively with them are impaired, and their resources to do so are depleted. One consequence of prolonged stress is burnout, which is characterized by physical, emotional, and attitudinal exhaustion. Professionals who are suffering from burnout often experience never-ending fatigue and may exhibit symptoms of various physical and psychological disorders. Emotionally drained and lacking enthusiasm for their work, burned out professionals may perceive themselves as no longer making a meaningful contribution and accomplishing little with their efforts.

Burnout is becoming increasingly prevalent among teachers and coaches. The most critical impact of burnout may be on instruction. Burned-out secondary school physical education teachers may cope with the demands of teaching by "going through the motions," sitting on the sidelines, and "throwing out the ball."[8] They may plan carelessly, if at all. Burned-out teachers may cease to care what happens in their classes; complacency becomes the norm, and "making it through the day" becomes the goal. Concern for students is replaced by impersonal or even negative attitudes toward them. Students are given little encouragement for their efforts, and lower expectations for student achievement are held. Dissatisfaction with one's teaching and the conviction that they are wasting the best years of their life are common feelings of burned-out teachers.

Stress and burnout can result in serious deterioration of teachers' health. Hypertension, ulcers, anxiety, depression, and other stress-related disorders may manifest themselves. Inappropriate methods of coping with stress and burnout, such as the excessive use of alcohol and abuse of drugs, may be harmful as well.

Many school systems recognize the serious nature of teacher stress and burnout. Stress management programs are offered to help teachers cope with the personal and professional stress they are experiencing. These programs emphasize stress reduction approaches such as relaxation training, physical fitness, nutritional counseling, and development of psychological coping skills. In-service workshops may help teachers learn more effective discipline approaches, new instructional strategies, problem-solving techniques, and how to manage their time more effectively.

Many suggestions have been advanced to assist teachers to combat burnout. The varied causes and consequences of burnout require a diversity of solutions for professional renewal. Certainly, learning appropriate techniques to manage stress is helpful. Supervisors can help alleviate burnout by providing teachers with feedback about their teaching, recognizing and appreciating their efforts, and giving them the opportunity to assume a different teaching load or to undertake different responsibilities. For coaches, perhaps taking a season off, rather than coaching year-round, or relinquishing head coaching responsibilities in one sport and assuming an assistant's role may be helpful in reenergizing oneself.

Attending professional meetings offers burned-out teachers an opportunity for growth. Exchanging ideas with colleagues and learning new instructional approaches can help rekindle some excitement and enthusiasm for teaching. Arranging a leave of absence or a sabbatical to attend graduate school may be helpful. Taking time off in the summer to revitalize oneself or developing new hobbies and leisure time interests are other successful strategies for alleviating burnout.

Beginning teachers need to be aware of the causes of stress and burnout. Awareness can help teachers become cognizant of some of the stress in their lives and lead them to take steps to reduce the potential for burning out. The pervasiveness of teacher stress and burnout and their serious consequences makes combating them an important professional priority.

Working effectively for change. Beginning teachers enter the school setting with a fresh perspective, new ideas, and enthusiasm. Because of their recent exposure to the teacher education program, they have clear ideas of "the way things are supposed to be." Eager to try out their new ideas, they may question some of the routines and practices experienced teachers accept or take for granted. In short, they may seek to change the ways things are done.

Beginning teachers are an important source of new ideas that can lead to improvements in the program. But, before trying to institute change, they should take the time to familiarize themselves with the school setting and the various constraints inherent within the school.

Whether the potential that each beginning teacher has to be a change agent is realized depends to a great extent on the manner in which the teacher seeks to create change.[7] Beginning teachers who are quick to criticize and eager to change the way things are done may alienate experienced teachers and administrators. By their actions they may generate hostility toward themselves and reduce any chance for change. Physical education teachers who have struggled to build a program in the face of numerous obstacles (such as a small budget, lack of administrative support, or outdated facilities) will resent beginning teachers criticizing what it took them so long to achieve.

Establishing credibility as a teacher before trying to change the status quo can positively affect the likelihood for success.[7] Beginning teachers need to demonstrate that they can teach effectively in the "real world." Unless they are accepted as professionals by their colleagues, efforts to promote change may be met with skepticism and resistance.

Once the beginning teacher has gained credibility and acceptance as a professional, the time is favorable to try to effect change. Change involves clearly defining the problem and the generation of possible solutions. Potential solutions are evaluated in terms of their practicality given the constraints of the school, their ability to solve the problem, and their acceptability to individuals affected by the change—students, teachers, administrators, and parents. Once a solution is agreed upon and implemented, its effectiveness should be evaluated and modifications made where appropriate.

As a change agent, the beginning teacher may choose to involve others in the process. Participation by others in resolving the problem could generate a greater number and diversity of solutions. Greater participation engenders a sense of ownership and leads to greater support and commitment to the eventual solution.[7] The respect and support of colleagues, particularly if they have considerable power and respect within the school, can facilitate the change process. In working for change, be careful to follow the appropriate channels and chain of command.

Beginning teachers can also create change by starting with their own classes. Adopting new procedures or introducing students to a new unit (given permission) may serve as the impetus for other teachers to try different approaches. Realize too that change is a slow process. Patience, commitment, and perseverance are often needed to bring about change.

There are many challenges facing beginning teachers. Often, beginning teachers may become disillusioned with teaching when the teaching situation is less than ideal or different than expected. Teaching requires a great deal of reflection, adaptation, and flexibility. While upholding the basic tenets of various theories guiding teachers' efforts and keeping in mind "the way things are supposed to be," teachers have to make adroit adaptations in light of the local school context to achieve their educational goals. The first year of teaching is truly a challenging learning experience. Beginning teachers will find it helpful to adopt a positive perspective and welcome this opportunity for growth and development.

Satisfactions

Teaching can be a very rewarding career. Although many challenges face teachers today, many teachers derive tremendous satisfaction from their work. What teachers do is important and significant, and can have an impact in measurable ways on the quality of students' lives, not only when they are in school but also in the future.

There are many satisfactions associated with teaching secondary school physical education. Unlike the business world, where satisfactions may be measured in monetary rewards, the rewards of teaching cannot be measured in terms of dollars and cents. Teaching has its triumphs and rewards, but they often come from events that occur each day. It is these events that contribute in numerous ways to making teaching a fulfilling career. Satisfactions may be derived from the job itself, from the accomplishments of students, from personal achievements, and from the recognition of a teacher's efforts.

Many physical education teachers derive satisfaction from the job itself. They enjoy the opportunity to be active and to maintain their own fitness level. Being able to teach the skills and appreciation of physical activities that they enjoy to others is rewarding. Knowing that physical education can have a significant impact on the quality of life adds significance and meaning to our efforts. Additionally, the opportunity to work with adolescents during the important transition to adulthood can be very satisfying. Physical education teachers can be instrumental in helping adolescents resolve some of their developmental concerns and ease their "growing pains," thus assisting them to grow and reach their fullest potential.

For many physical education teachers, the impact on their students' behavior, as reflected in their students' accomplishments, is a measure of their success. Satisfaction is obtained not only from the students' mastery of physical skills, but from their pride and joy in their achievements. Satisfaction can be derived from seeing unfit adolescents, barely able to walk a mile in September, improve their fitness during the year, and raise their arms in triumph as they run across the finish line of the mile in June. There is the satisfaction of helping individuals become skillful movers. There is pleasure in seeing students learn to master the skills in an activity that you've taught them. Joy can also occur from seeing a change in the attitudes of students in your classes, where cooper-

Attending conferences can help professionals keep abreast of changes in the field. Professionals discuss a poster presentation at an AAHPERD national convention.
Courtesy of Deborah A. Wuest, Ithaca College, Ithaca, NY.

ative behavior has become the norm, and sounds and expressions of students encouraging each other's efforts fill the air. Another source of satisfaction is the pleasure experienced when students report that they have been successful in using the information you taught them in class about fitness to persuade their parents to embark on an exercise program.

Yet another measure of our successes is not immediately apparent but may come after students have graduated. Seeing former students in the community still participating in a sport that they learned in your physical education class indicates that you have succeeded in your goal of incorporating physical activity into the lifestyle of the students.

Satisfaction may also be obtained from one's own growth as a teacher. Looking back on the first year and seeing how you've improved and what you have accomplished can be inspiring. Mastering the many teaching skills is satisfying. Attaining goals you have set for yourself, such as speaking to each student in the class by name each day, reducing waiting time, or increasing the time students are active in class, is rewarding. Feeling you've taught well and having that feeling reinforced by praise from your supervisor can really make your day.

Recognition of one's efforts and effectiveness as a teacher can also help one feel that teaching is a meaningful and worthwhile profession. This recognition can come from many different avenues. It may come as a "thank you" from a student you have counseled about a problem or from the evident joy on students' faces as they master a challenging task. A phone call from a parent indicating how pleased they are with their son's or daughter's improvement in fitness can be gratifying. Recognition of the impact you have made may come from the student who asks you to fill out a college recommendation and aspires to be a physical education teacher. A peer's acknowledgment of your efforts as a real professional may bring a sense that you are appreciated and accepted. And, finally, a principal who, after observing your class, comments, "I wish I had a physical education program like this one when I was in school" can make your hard work and efforts worthwhile.

There are many satisfactions that can be gained from teaching secondary school physical education. Students' successes are gratifying. The satisfaction derived from seeing students master skills, develop a high level of fitness, become knowledgeable about various physical activities, and exhibit enjoyment while participating is sustaining. Recognition of your efforts and acknowledgment of the importance of your contributions to the lives of your students is uplifting. Although teaching is a demanding profession, it is also a very rewarding one. Teachers can make a difference.

SUMMARY

The success of the secondary school physical education program depends to a tremendous extent of the effectiveness of its teachers. To enhance their effectiveness, beginning teachers should take responsibility to familiarize themselves with the schools and communities in which they work. This knowledge will help them more readily understand the constraints of the local situation and to design a program to meet the specific needs of the students they teach.

As a faculty member in the school, physical education teachers perform many pedagogical, institutional, and professional responsibilities. Pedagogical responsibilities include instructing students, planning, administration, coaching, directing, curriculum development, and program promotion. Institutional responsibilities encompass such activities as supervision, advisement, student counseling, parent conferencing, committee work, and community involvement. Additionally, teachers want to grow and develop professionally and should consider being actively involved in professional organizations.

Many challenges face beginning teachers. Growing as a teacher, making the transition from student to teacher, establishing professional relationships with school personnel and students, dealing with stress, and working successfully for change are just a few of the many challenges that often need to be addressed.

There are many satisfactions to be gained from teaching secondary school physical education. The opportunity to work with adolescents to help them attain the desired goals of physical education and to share in their achievement is rewarding. Knowing that what you do can affect students' quality of life adds significance to your work. Although teaching is demanding, it is a rewarding and fulfilling career.

FOR REVIEW

1. Why is it important that beginning physical education teachers orient themselves to the school environment and the community? Examine how three aspects of the school organization can positively or negatively influence the school physical education experience. It may be interesting to ask practitioners in the schools for their perceptions. Discuss how three community characteristics can positively or negatively influence the school physical education program. How did various aspects of your community influence your secondary school experience, including physical education?

2. How can secondary school physical education teachers ensure their acceptance as faculty members within the school? What strategies can physical education teachers employ to gain recognition by other faculty of physical education's contribution to the school curriculum?

3. Select two challenges that face secondary school physical education teachers. (Try to think of other challenges than those presented in the text.) How can teachers successfully meet these challenges?

4. The satisfactions derived from teaching are often related to the reasons individuals decide to pursue a teaching career. What are your reasons for choosing teaching as a career? What aspects of teaching do you think will give you the greatest satisfaction?

REFERENCES

1. Adapted from Department of Health and Physical Education: *Ithaca College Student Teaching Handbook*, Ithaca College, Ithaca, NY, 1992.
2. US Bureau of the Census: *Statistical abstract of the United States* ed 111, Washington, DC, 1991, US Government Printing Office.
3. Matiella AC: *Positively different*, Santa Cruz, Calif, 1991, Network.
4. Hellison DR, Templin TJ: *A reflective approach to teaching physical education*, Champaign, Ill, 1991, Human Kinetics.
5. Rink J: *Teaching physical education for learning*, St Louis, 1985, Mosby.
6. Fuller FF: Concerns of teachers: a developmental conceptualization, *American Educational Research Journal* 4:154-159, 1969.
7. Bain LL, Wendt JC: *Transition to teaching: a guide for the beginning teacher*, Reston, Va, 1983, AAHPERD.
8. Mancini VH et al: A comparison of the interaction patterns and academic learning time of low- and high-burnout secondary school physical educators. In Templin TJ, Olson JK editors: *Teaching in physical education*, Champaign, Ill, 1983, Human Kinetics.
9. Wendt JC, Bain LL: Physical educators' perceptions of stressful teaching events, *Journal of Teaching and Physical Education* 8:342-346, 1989.

ANNOTATED READINGS

Bain LL, Wendt JC: *Transition to teaching: a guide for the beginning teacher,* Reston, Va, 1983, AAHPERD.

Strategies to help teachers to adjust to the realities of teaching, including how to function effectively within the school, learning the daily routine, coping strategies, and professional growth.

Fahs ME, Lapkin B, Rothstein A: Can teachers help? *Strategies* 2(2):6-9, 29, 1988.

Presents practical ideas for teachers who want to help their students cope with stress.

Griggs R: *Professional balance: the careerstyle approach to balanced achievement,* Mountain View, Calif, 1989, MANFIT.

Suggestions for reaching one's goals while combining personal and professional successes.

Raxter LM: Keeping your edge: maintaining excellence, *Strategies* 5(8): 24-26, 1992.

Offers suggestions for balancing the many professional demands associated with teaching with personal demands so that burnout does not occur.

Templin TJ, Schempp PG, editors: *Socialization into physical education: learning to teach,* 1989, Indianapolis, Benchmark.

Provides a multidimensional perspective of the teacher socialization process with implications for teachers and professional practice.

Van Oteghan S, Forrest M: Adolescent stress, *Strategies* 2(2):5-9, 1988.

Describes causes of stress among junior high school students.

Wendt JC, Bain LL: Physical educators' perceptions of stressful teaching events, *Journal of Teaching in Physical Education* 8(4): 342-346.

Examines concerns of preservice and inservice teachers of physical education.

PART II

Curriculum

A variety of curricular models are available for teachers' use in designing the physical education program to meet the needs of their students and achieve desired goals. Carefully setting goals, delineating objectives, and selecting content to achieve them are important to good teaching. Translating curriculum into practice requires careful planning so that desired outcomes are achieved. The total physical education program is comprised of the instructional program, the adapted program, and the extracurricular program. Teachers should be cognizant of each facet of the total program and the contribution of each to educational goals.

O U T L I N E

CHAPTER 4

Curriculum Models

CHAPTER OBJECTIVES

◆ To describe and discuss various curriculum concepts
◆ To compare and contrast selected curriculum models

Schools exist to help students acquire the interests, skills, attitudes, and knowledge that will enable them to live happy and productive lives. The school curriculum is the vehicle that is utilized to help students acquire these competencies. Educators involved with any aspect of the educational process must ultimately consider the curriculum, which is the keystone of educational theory and practice.[1]

This chapter will define the term *curriculum* and present selected models that will serve as guidelines to aid in the development of a secondary school curriculum. Three theoretical curriculum models—the activity-based curriculum, the competency-based curriculum, and the concept-based curriculum—will be reviewed and analyzed.

CURRICULUM

Curriculum is often thought of by physical education teachers as the whole body of courses offered or identified as the course of study. The most common definition of curriculum is stated by Willgoose[2] as a work schedule or a body of experiences that lies between objectives and teaching styles. Jewett and Bain[3] describe school curriculum in a broader sense, which includes the total experiences conducted under schools' auspices, from classroom instruction to interscholastic athletics. They further discuss curriculum as the planned sequence of formal instructional experiences presented by the teacher to whom responsibility is assigned. Lawson and Placek[4] and Hellison[5] refer to curriculum as the selection of subject matter to be taught. (Additional interpretations can be found in Chapter 5.)

Some other curriculum perspectives that have been used to describe the nature and conduct of programs are (1) the traditional, (2) the functional, and (3) the hidden curriculums. The traditional curriculum usually makes little attempt to relate one school subject to another. Students study each subject that is offered in the school for a certain amount of time each day, that is, periods of English, health, math, science, and physical education. This approach tends to have students learn isolated facts and skills in one area without seeing them as a part of total education for lifetime learning.

The functional curriculum focuses on the amount of instructional time the student is appropriately engaged in learning tasks. Within the physical education setting, this approach studies the relationship between content, the teaching styles used by the physical education teacher in a class, and the amount of time a student is engaged in an appropriate physical education task in a manner maximizing potential success.[6]

The third curriculum term is identified as the hidden curriculum. The curriculum of the secondary school physical education program reflects the expressed values and precise decisions of educators regarding what is to be taught and what is to be learned. The term *hidden curriculum* refers to unplanned and unrecognized values that

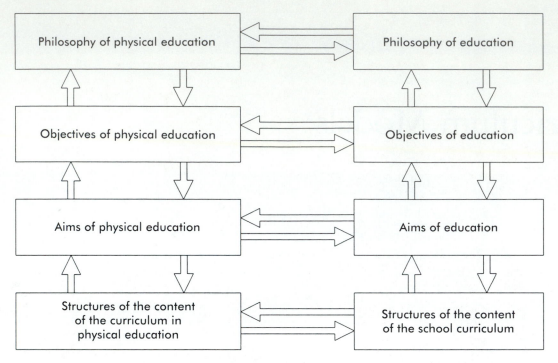

FIG. 4-1 Interrelationship of philosophy, objectives, aims, and content structure between education and physical education curriculums.

are taught and learned through the process of education. Physical education teachers should become aware of the values that are being taught through selected activities and make sure that there is congruence between the expressed values of an activity and the actual values that the student learns. Some factors influencing the hidden curriculum are procedures and regulations, administrative decisions, curricular content, and teacher behavior.[7]

For our purposes, the concept of curriculum will denote those experiences and activities that are devised by the school for the purpose of modifying learners' behavior in a desirable manner. The physical education curriculum is part of the total school curriculum and does contribute to the philosophy, the objectives, and the aims of education that comprise the total education program of the secondary school. The structure of the physical education curriculum must coincide with the philosophy, aims, and objectives of the educational institution in which the curriculum is located. Fig. 4-1 illustrates this concept.

The curriculum is a guide or a blueprint of learning experiences (content) that enables students to achieve the objectives of the secondary physical education program, whereas teaching refers to the procedures employed by teachers to help students achieve the program's objectives. The teacher structures the content (curriculum) according to the students' needs and then selects the most appropriate teaching style (instruction) that will produce optimum learning for the student (Fig. 4-2).

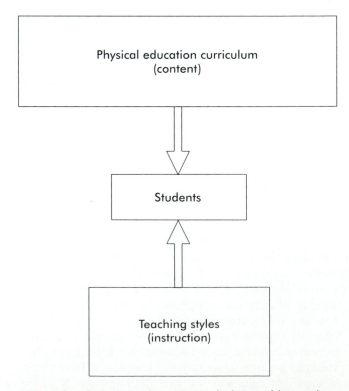

FIG. 4-2 Articulation between curriculum and instruction.

CURRICULUM ORGANIZATION

The physical education curriculum should be organized according to the logical development of its subject matter—human movement. Each learning experience should be built upon the previous learning experience of the student and should develop a basis for performance required in subsequent learning experiences. In other words, the teacher should know where he or she and the class have been and where the total educational experience in which they are engaged is going. The total educational experience of each student is the primary consideration in planning the school curriculum.

The focal points for curriculum are called *organizing centers*. An organizing center provides a frame of reference, emphasis, or themes around which the subject matter is designed.[8] Some of the traditional organizing centers for secondary physical education have been (1) facilities and equipment, (2) student-teacher ratio, (3) seasons, and (4) activities (for example, sports, games, and dance).

It is argued by Wuest and Bucher[1] and Willgoose[2] that physical education is an integral part of every school's curriculum because it makes a unique and vital contribution to the students' total education. Physical education can offer a variety of learning experiences that certainly contribute toward the development of physical, social, emotional, and intellectual growth. Griffey[9] and Taylor and Chogioji[10] cite three educational reforms that may help us to realize the goals in secondary physical education. Physical education teachers must emphasize student learning of the principles and concepts that underlie physical activities, integrate the physical education program into the general high-school curriculum, and encourage learning for mastery.

As far back as 1969, Mackenzie[11] called for major revisions in physical education programs. He discussed the need to examine the substance and purpose of the curriculum. The knowledge explosion had caused schools to overhaul the entire curriculum and to place values and priorities on what should be taught. Further, physical education must rid itself of meaningless repetition and trivia and develop a lean and purposeful curriculum. The physical education program should focus on the development of basic movement skills, an understanding of basic movement concepts, and, in general, the study of human movement.

Physical education should provide for instruction in basic skills, movement concepts, and fundamental skills in 20 to 30 different activities. Mackenzie also emphasized the achievement of specific, selected outcomes rather than adhering to traditional blocks of time (the three-week unit) for the organization of instruction. Proficiency examinations, the provision of advanced, indepth instruction in two or three activities, the use of master teachers, and student selection of activities were also suggested. Mackenzie's ideas are still relevant today. Teachers must revise their programs by constructing their curriculums to be congruent with the body of knowledge in physical education, to be relevant to present and future societies, and to meet student needs. Without such changes, the secondary physical education program may lack quality and direction.

Horizontal and Vertical Plans

Organizing centers can be structured in the secondary physical education curriculum in either a vertical or horizontal plan. The manner in which the school curriculum is designed for one year is referred to as the *horizontal organizational plan*. Some of the most widely utilized horizontal patterns for organizing the yearly plan have been the simple block plan, the concurrent unit plan, the cycle plan, and the elective/selective plan.

The simple block plan is the most common pattern used in secondary school physical education. The block plan is followed by all students for a predetermined block of time. Students are often classified by grade within this plan. The cycle plan is typically used in smaller schools where enrollment may be too small to schedule separate physical education classes for each grade level. To avoid repetition in the learning activities offered from year to year, the yearly program varies in alternate years. When physical education teachers want to present more variety during the same period of instruction or when facility constraints are present, they may utilize the concurrent unit plan. In this approach two units are scheduled concurrently (for example, swimming and volleyball or soccer and tennis).

Finally, if physical education teachers wanted to maximize student input, they would use an elective/selective plan to organize the yearly plan. In this planning approach, students participate in the activity identification and selection process.

The relationship between what is learned from one grade level to another determines the *vertical organization plan* of curriculum and learning. The teacher utilizes organizing centers to provide a basis for vertical articulation and sequence. The vertical plan is concerned with the scope and sequence of the curricular offerings from kindergarten through grade 12. The scope and sequence of activities should be organized according to the philosophy, aims, and objectives of the program and the students' needs. A strong articulation must exist between the secondary school, the middle or junior high school, and the elementary school programs (for more information about planning see Chapter 6).

Student Needs

A constructive emphasis in curriculum development should be placed upon attempts to satisfy the needs of

Teachers from all elementary, middle, and secondary schools are involved in revising the curriculum.

Courtesy of Victor Mancini, Ithaca College, Ithaca, NY.

each student. To provide sound learning experiences, it is necessary to know each student's interests and needs as well as to understand the way that each student grows and develops. Chapter 2 provides a comprehensive analysis of secondary school students and their characteristics.

A basic task for the secondary physical education department is to decide what is essential for everyone to know (cognitive), to perform (psychomotor), and to be (affective). The school curriculum should provide for each student the opportunities needed for growth and development of the full extent of the individual's potential abilities in the educational domains—cognitive, psychomotor, and affective. In the secondary school physical education program, students should be given the chance to apply the skills learned at the elementary level.[1]

CURRICULUM FOCUS

The curriculum should focus on program content in terms of its objectives and activities. Curriculum designers make decisions about (1) the scope—what content will be included; (2) the structure—how the content will be clustered into units; and (3) the sequence—how the content will be put in order. Curriculum theories and models provide systematic assistance for these decisions.

If physical education is to continue to share a place in the total school curriculum of all students, physical education teachers must define and structure the physical education experiences in a formal curriculum blueprint. The plans and framework should be developed and implemented cooperatively by physical education personnel at all levels—teachers, administrators, students, and par-

ents—preferably under the leadership of a qualified physical education teacher.

CURRICULUM GUIDELINES

In 1985 the Society of State Directors of Health, Physical Education, and Recreation produced a document entitled *The School Programs of Health, Physical Education, and Recreation: A Statement of Basic Beliefs*.[12] Their beliefs are offered as a set of guidelines for state and local school systems, agencies, institutions, organizations, and other interested individuals in health, physical education, and recreation. Their beliefs emphasize the school's responsibility regarding the physical education program. Box 4-1 outlines their statement about the role of physical education.[12]

Further, in 1986 the National Association for Sport and Physical Education (NASPE), an association of the American Alliance for Health, Physical Education, Recreation and Dance (AAHPERD), also presented a position paper entitled *Guidelines for Secondary School Physical Education*.[13] This position paper focuses on the need for and the role of the teacher in developing and implementing physical education programs at the secondary level. Within this document are standards for the curriculum in secondary physical education. These standards should serve as a guide for physical education teachers in the study of curriculum in the schools and are presented in Box 4-2.

These two documents provide much direction for physical education teachers, who would do well to utilize them in the evaluation of current physical education programs. Schools should give careful thought to the rec-

BOX 4-1
STATEMENT OF BASIC BELIEFS

Physical education is an essential part of the total education program and makes significant contributions toward the achievement of desirable educational outcomes through the medium of physical activity and related experiences. It is education through, as well as of, the physical. An effective and comprehensive physical education program:

- Promotes the physical growth and development of children and youth while contributing to their general health and well-being.
- Makes a major contribution to the personal and physical fitness of each student, including cardiorespiratory efficiency, endurance, flexibility, agility, balance, muscular strength, speed, power, coordination, and rhythmic responses.
- Teaches efficient, graceful, and useful movement skills at all developmental levels.
- Is a planned sequence of experiences in a variety of activities beginning with basic movement skills and progressing toward complex skills in sports, dance, aquatics, and other forms of human movement.
- Offers many opportunities to help individuals develop a wholesome self-concept and appreciation of others.
- Is education for the constructive use of time, including leisure hours, keeping fit, and enjoying forms of recreation during the school years and continuing throughout adult life.
- Helps students to understand and appreciate expressive, creative aesthetic movement from the standpoint of both the participant and the observer.
- Makes important contributions to the emotional, social, mental, moral, and ethical development and adjustment of students.

BOX 4-2
STANDARDS FOR SECONDARY SCHOOL PHYSICAL EDUCATION

- Instructional activities should be selected to maximize the potential of achieving established program goals.
- Program activities should be sequenced to provide continuity and progression within each unit of instruction, as well as from unit to unit and year to year.
- Students should be introduced to a variety of physical activities to ensure that all students meet appropriate individualized performance standards in skills common to survival, work, and leisure pursuits.
- The curriculum should be structured to include a variety of fitness activities and to ensure that all students meet appropriate individualized, health-related fitness standards.
- Students should have opportunities to develop intermediate and advanced skills in activities personally selected.
- Students should have opportunities to develop participation skills on a personal selective basis in high-adventure and high-challenge activities.
- Students should receive guidance in developing self-direction and seeking personal meaning in conducting their individual lifelong physical activity program.
- Secondary school physical education should be granted unit credit toward graduation on a basis comparable to other subject matter areas.
- Quality standards for credit in physical education should reflect the same quality as those established by local boards or state departments of education for other areas of instruction.
- Schools should make certain that their offerings and procedures are consistent with accrediting by which they are governed.[13]

ommendations and standards presented in these documents in order to enrich and shape the secondary physical education offerings to better address the needs of every student.

The physical education program must be a planned and organized series of learning experiences implemented with (1) a physical education specialist assigned primary responsibility, (2) a budget, (3) an integrated set of objectives sufficiently detailed to allow evaluation, and (4) administrative support. It is important that the students and all physical education teachers recognize that the school physical education program is a vital part of the whole school program. Through the coordination of various school personnel, the provision of a positive school environment, and the development of a sound, comprehensive, physical education instruction, students can best profit from the total school experience.

CURRICULUM MODELS

Models are prescriptive strategies designed to accomplish particular instructional goals. A model can be prescriptive in the sense that the teacher's responsibilities during the planning, implementing, and evaluating stages are clearly defined.[14] Joyce and Weil[15] defined a model as a pattern or plan that can be used to shape a curriculum or course, to select instructional materials, and to guide a teacher's selection. As Eggen, Kauchak, and Harder[14] explain:

When a teacher identifies a goal and selects a particular strategy designed to reach a goal, we can say that the teacher is using a model's approach. The use of a model requires an ability to identify different types of instructional goals so that a specific model can be selected to match a particular goal.

A model consists of guidelines for designing educational activities and environments. It describes ways of teaching and learning that are intended to achieve certain kinds of goals. Joyce and Weil[15] state that a model should include a rationale, a theory that justifies it, and a description of what it is good for and why. A curriculum model is further discussed by Joyce and Weil[15] as a method for integrating or making inseparable the process of instruction and the outcomes of instruction, using a specific value system or learning theory as the unifying agent. They further define a model as providing definite ideas for creating an environment in which students are likely to learn certain kinds of things. While there is no single model for all programs, for all classrooms, or for all teachers, the use of a model can enhance clarity and stability via internal logic and consistent practice.[16] A model-based approach to program development requires the teacher to select a model and to use it to develop a cohesive, logically consistent pattern of classroom activities.

The model that one selects will provide the general structure for the physical education program. Developing a specific model into specific objectives will require that physical education teachers have complete information about the current characteristics of their students. A curriculum model can be compared with an engineer's blueprint. When considering a project, an engineer must identify the structure to be built (a road, a bridge, or a building). The engineer puts in all the needed ingredients and develops a blueprint to complete his tasks. A curriculum model can be considered a type of blueprint for teaching. As the builder, the teacher is responsible for accomplishing the goals of the program, a unit of instruction, or a single lesson. Data about the preprogram knowledge, attitudes, and skills of the students will help the physical education teacher define program objectives. The data blueprint will help in selecting the most appropriate model to incorporate in the physical education program.

Bank, Henerson, and Eu[17] suggest that the educator answer the following questions in considering a model for a program:

◆ Does the model express a point of view about learning consistent with what I agree?
◆ Is this model suitable for the kind of program I have in mind?
◆ Does the model call for the teacher behavior I have in mind?
◆ Does the model call for activities appropriate for my students?
◆ Can I achieve the classroom organization and develop the materials called for in this model?
◆ Can I handle the problems that might arise by using this model?

After these questions have been satisfactorily answered, the educator should be ready to select the model that appears most suitable for the program.

TABLE 4-1

Common Curriculum Models and Associated References/Sources

Model	Reference(s)/Source(s)
Activity-based curriculum	Cheffers[18]
Adventure program	Siedentop, Mand, Taggart[19]
Competency-based curriculum	Cheffers[18]; Melograno[8]; Willgoose[2]; Miller, Cheffers, Whitcomb[20]
Concept-based curriculum	Cheffers[18]; Melograno[8]; Lawson, Placek[4]; Miller, Cheffers, Whitcomb[20]; Siedentop, Mand, Taggart[19]; Willgoose[2]
Developmental curriculum	Jewett, Bain[3]
Exploration curriculum	Cheffers[18]
Humanistic curriculum	Hellison[21]; Willgoose[2]; Jewett, Bain[3]; Miller, Cheffers, Whitcomb[20]
Independence curriculum	Cheffers[18]
Kinesiological studies	Jewett, Bain[3]; Lawson, Placek[4]
Mini-course approach	Willgoose[2]
Movement education	Jewett, Bain[3]
Multi-activity	Siedentop, Mand, Taggart[19]
Personal meaning and purpose process curriculum	Jewett, Bain[3]; Jewett, Mullan[22]
Physical fitness	Jewett, Bain[3]; Lawson, Placek[4], Siedentop, Mand, Taggart[19]
Play and lifetime	Jewett, Bain[3]; Lawson, Placek[4]; Siedentop, Mand, Taggart[19]
Retroaction curriculum	Cheffers[18]
Separate subject curriculum	Willgoose[2]
Traditional physical education curriculum	Hellison[20]; Lawson, Placek[4]; Siedentop, Mand, Taggart[19]

Most physical education teachers use models developed throughout the history of physical education as their starting point. Just as there are many definitions of a curriculum within physical education literature, there are also numerous curriculum models, as well as varied terminology used to describe these "models," "frameworks," or "patterns." Table 4-1 summarizes some of the most commonly identified physical education curriculum models and physical education teachers who have analyzed them. The reader should refer to the sources indicated for additional information about the models.

Three theoretical curriculum models (and their stages of development) that we believe incorporate many of the models identified above will be further discussed. These three models are (1) the activity-based curriculum, (2) the competency-based curriculum, and (3) the concept-based curriculum.[18,20]

Many schools utilize the activity-based curriculum model.
Courtesy of Suzi D'Annalfo, Conard High School, West Hartford, CT.

The Activity-Based Curriculum

In the study of curriculum design, substance is generally referred to as *the content*. All content should reflect or embrace the three learning domains—cognitive, affective, and psychomotor. However, curricular content is often confused with curriculum activity. Curricular content is comprised of the major activity areas that the secondary school program will be centered around, that is, aquatics, sport skills, outdoor living, dance, fitness, and gymnastics. Contrast this with curriculum activity, which is the specific unit of instruction within a major activity area, for example, badminton is a specific unit of instruction within the major activity area of lifetime sports. Understanding this distinction requires that educators view activity (that is, curricular offerings) as a process through which students are guided to reach desired outcomes (that is, content).

Activities provide learning experiences that enable students to achieve program objectives. In learning to hit a baseball, a student may watch a demonstration; listen to a lecture; practice hitting; utilize feedback from a peer, a video recorder, or an instructor; and perform a variety of other batting activities. The activity-based curriculum prepares students for a variety of physical activities, for performance of fitness activities, and for learning of selected physical, social, and intellectual skills. The major core of the activity-based program is patterned movement centered around sports, dance, fitness, gymnastics, and aquatics. The activity-based curriculum stresses the development of the fine and gross motor skills, locomotor activities, and especially sports skill fundamentals. The

eventual goal of this curriculum model is the motor proficiency of the learners, with all other goals receiving minimal attention. Problems associated with the activity-based curriculums are related to its inherent disregard for the quality of movement, time restriction, and scope and its relative avoidance of cognitive and affective learning as an equally important outcome of the program. As a

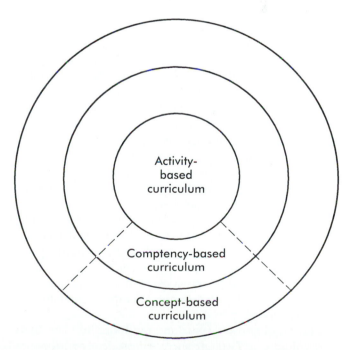

FIG. 4-3 Cheffers' centripetal curriculum model.

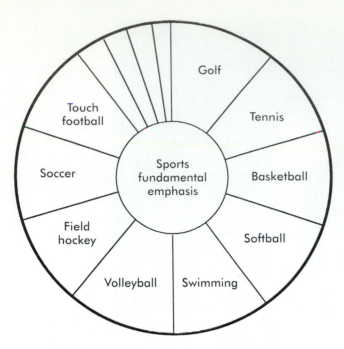

FIG. 4-4 Sports fundamental emphasis.

result, activity-based curriculums occasionally lose momentum because of a lack of direction and purpose. Cheffers'[18] centripetal curriculum model does, however, provide secondary physical education teachers with a reminder that activities are central to the goals and objectives of physical education (Fig. 4-3).

Harrison and Blakemore[23] identify the activity-based curriculum as among the most popular for the organization of activity units encompassing fitness, dance, and sports. Harrison and Blakemore[23] and Evaul[24] believe that meaningful participation in activity is the primary goal of physical education. Consistent with the precepts of sound instructional planning, they view activity as a pathway leading to the achievement of goals reflective of physical, cognitive, emotional, and social development. However, the ever-growing variety of activities available to physical education teachers requires its advocates to accept that even the most comprehensive of activity-based curriculums must be partially limited in their offerings. It would be truly impossible to offer the entire range of activities within the model's format.

Retaining "their most popular status" among the content areas identified previously are sports fundamentals. Forming the core of most secondary curriculums, sports fundamentals include team sports, such as basketball or soccer, and individual activities, such as swimming, tennis, or golf. Fig. 4-4 demonstrates the sports fundamental curricular focus.

The major thrust of teaching the sports fundamentals curriculum is to facilitate successful student performance in each sport. In this approach, emphasis on performance of skill (not the value or knowledge of the sport) is of

primary importance, while growth in the other domains often becomes incidental and secondary.

For purposes of effective programing, physical education teachers have found it beneficial to categorize activity into related groupings, sometimes referred to as major activity areas. Table 4-2 lists examples of major activity areas and a suggested list of activities that may be included in a secondary curriculum.

When presented with a list as comprehensive as the one in Table 4-2, physical education teachers will invariably be challenged by still more questions regarding the nature and scope of effective activity selection. For example, how much time shall be devoted to a particular activity area? Which activities within these areas should be included? What percentage of the available time should

TABLE 4-2

Suggested Activities for Secondary Physical Education*

Activity Area	Activity
Team sports	Angleball, baseball, basketball, bobsledding, cageball, cricket, team handball, field hockey, fistball, flickerball, football, hockey, korfball, lacrosse, pickleball, soccer, softball, speed-a-way, speedball, rugby, ultimate frisbee, volleyball
Lifetime sports	Archery, badminton, body building, bowling, boccie, croquet, equestrian, fencing, golf, horseshoes, paddle tennis, racketball, self-defense, shuffleboard, skeet shooting, squash, handball, tennis
Aquatics	Aquatic fitness, ball tag, boating, canoeing, crew, diving, lifesaving, scuba, surfing, sailing, sail boarding, wind surfing, water polo, water skiing, synchronized swimming
Outdoor living	Angling, backpacking, ballooning, camping, casting, rock climbing, cycling, project adventure, hiking, snowshoeing, orienteering, skiing, cross-country skiing
Rhythm/dance	Basic rhythms, ballet, contemporary, country, creative/expressive, disco, folk, jazz, modern, round, ballroom/social, ethnic, square, tap
Games	Billards, horseshoes, shuffleboard, tabletennis, tetherball
Fitness	Aerobics, running, calisthenics, isometrics, weight training, weight lifting, power lifting, body building, wrestling, martial arts, walking, cycling, fitness trail, dancercize
Gymnastics	Acrobatics, balance beam, floor exercise, horizontal bar, parallel bars, ropes, pummel horse, vaulting, trampoline, rings

*Some activities applicable in multiple categories.

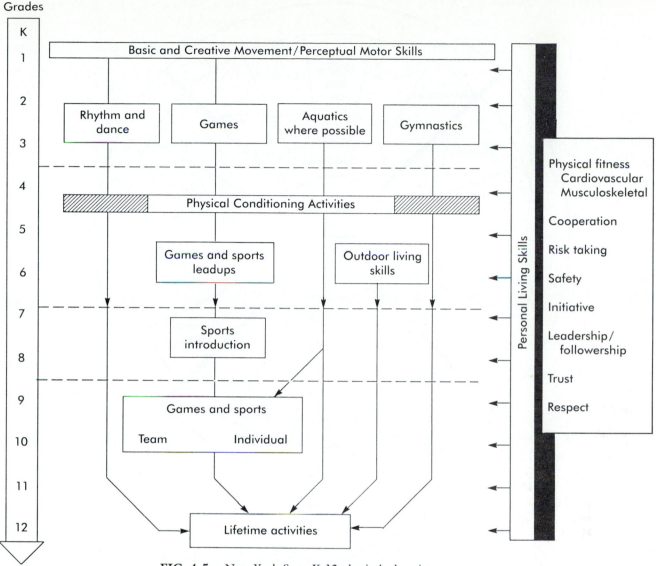

FIG. 4-5   New York State K-12 physical education program.
From the State University of New York, the State Education Department.

be allotted to fitness? To dance? To outdoor pursuits? To lifetime sports? One approach to answering these questions is to refer to the State Education Department's program recommendations for secondary school physical education. The New York State K-12 physical education program is presented as an example of such a plan (Fig. 4-5).[26]

Balance within each of the activity areas is essential and can be identified in the Suggested Activity Schedule of the New York State Department of Education Syllabus for grades K-12 (Fig. 4-6).

Physical education teachers should review each major activity area, selecting activities from each area for utilization in their own individual physical education program. Chapter 5 reviews the processes used to determine which activities should be included and guidelines for attaining content balance in curriculum offerings. Upon completion of such study, physical education teachers should develop a yearly plan for their school. Table 4-3 is an example of such a yearly plan.

The Competency-Based Curriculum

The competency-based curriculum approach to physical education is viewed as a way of defining various curricular areas in terms of minimum skills and knowledge necessary for a student to function in today's world. The competency-based approach to education received wide acclaim in the 1970s. Prompted by a massive public outcry for greater accountability in the functioning of educational systems, competency-based curriculums require students to meet standards identified in specific behavioral and instructional objectives. For purposes of this discussion, a competency-based design is goal di-

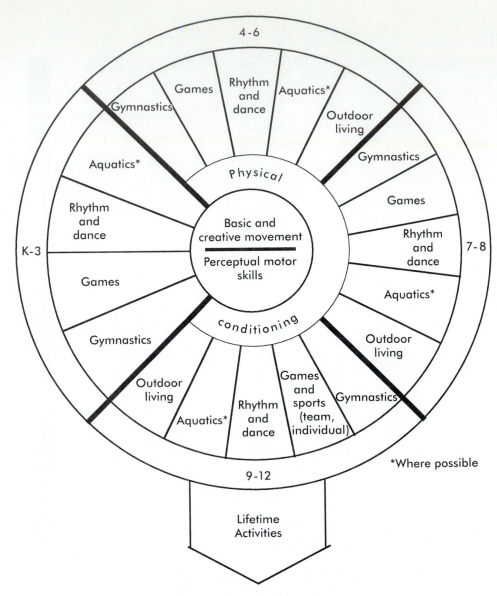

FIG. 4-6   New York State suggested activity schedule.
From the State University of New York, the State Education Department.

rected with the competencies being the goals. They are the criteria by which successful performance is to be measured. One of the major characteristics of a competency-based program is its use of behavioral objectives. Concise statements of what students are expected to do and the conditions under which they are expected to do it, behavioral objectives provide both teachers and students with a well-defined process for achievement and evaluation.

Behavioral objectives should be designed to be consistent with instructional objectives. A behavioral objective is a statement of what the student should be able to do after instruction. Specifically, behavioral objectives focus on the learners' performance. The three main functions of an instructional objective are (1) to provide a focus of attention for both the student and the teacher, (2) to

serve as a guide for selection of content, and (3) to provide the criteria for evaluating the learner's performance. The writing of behavioral objectives is covered in more detail in Chapter 6.

Behavioral objectives written with a competency as the desired outcome are far more likely to focus on meaningful subject matter (activity). Additionally, the focus is more apt to be on doing and performing rather than only knowing. If competence is to be the outcome of a set of objectives, then the form and quality of those statements must be very precise and written in language for student comprehension. Chapter 6 contains a full description of the three components of a behavioral objective as well as several examples of behavioral objectives written for each of the three domains (cognitive, affective, and psychomotor).

TABLE 4-3

Yearly Block Selector Plan for Liverpool High School, 1988-1989

Block #1	Block #2	Block #3	Block #4	Block #5	Block #6	Block #7	Block #8
Football (B)*	Flickerball (B)	Basketball (B)	Volleyball (B)	Basketball (B)	Paddleball (B)	Weight training (B)	Softball (B)
Soccer (B)	Weight training (B)	Eur. handball (B)	Weight training (B)	Floor hockey (B)	Weight training (B)	Badminton (B)	Team competition (B)
Field hockey (G)†	Slimnastics (G)	Badminton (G)	Basketball (G)	Weight training (G)	Floor hockey (G)	Aerobic dance (G)	Softball (G)
Soccer (G)	Eur. handball (G)	Weight training (G)	Dance (G)	Paddleball (G)	Slimnastics (G)	Paddleball (G)	Golf (G)
Co-ed tennis	Co-ed volleyball	Co-ed volleyball	Co-ed cross-country skiing	Co-ed cross-country skiing	Co-ed badminton	Co-ed volleyball	Co-ed tennis
Co-ed swim (non-swimmers)	Co-ed swim (diving & interval swim)	Co-ed swim (water games)	Co-ed swim (team competition)	Co-ed swim (recreation)	Swim (canoeing)	Co-ed swim (kayaking & sail boating)	Co-ed swim (scuba-fins)

A two-week block for physical fitness testing will be administered between Block I and Block II.
Activities will be offered according to the number of teachers available per period.

From John Johnstone, with permission.
*(B), Boys.
†(G), Girls.

In the competency-based approach, students must demonstrate that they have mastered certain competencies before receiving a grade. The purposes of competency-based learning are multidimensional. They are (1) to identify the competencies required of learners, (2) to provide educational experiences conducive to the attainment of the competency, and (3) to develop procedures and techniques by which students can be evaluated and rewarded when mastering the skills comprising the competency.

In addition to identifying the competencies to be taught, physical education teachers must also select or develop an accurate and appropriate method of assessment to determine the degree of mastery. What is important is that the student reach a given standard of performance and that such performance be measurable. According to Cheffers,[18] a competency-based curriculum requires students to attain a specified standard of minimal competency as they strive for the attainment of instructional goals. Cheffers[18] continues and suggests that this curriculum approach is concerned with the specific activities performed and also requires achievement of minimal criteria levels before success can be proclaimed.

The competency-based curriculum has the added advantage of permitting all students opportunities to reach the same minimal grade for their effort. Most often, in the activity-based curriculum, time becomes the important criterion separating graded levels of achievement. Additionally, the competency approach places emphasis for achievement on measurable student ability, not on subjective criteria. In carefully planned competency-based programs, students are informed well in advance about expectations for their learning, they know exactly what is required to receive a specific reward or assessment, and typically their efforts are evaluated in a more objective manner with fairer assessments resulting. This can be stated with confidence, because the competency model is dependent upon clearly stated learning objectives, thereby providing teachers and students with carefully designed plans, which will assist and enhance student learning. Fig. 4-7 presents a graphic portrayal of the interrelationships of the aims, developmental objectives, performance objectives, and outcomes experienced by students in physical education.[27]

In a competency-based curriculum, performance or behavioral objectives are used to chart the instructional objectives. Within the activity-based curriculum, the important aspect is the time devoted to each activity or the length of an activity unit required for the student to achieve skill mastery. In the activity-based curriculum, the student would have to progress with the rest of the class at a pace defined by others (for example, the teacher or the group). In contrast, the competency-based curriculum focuses on the mastery of the competency as the most important factor, rather than time as the criterion for success. Specifically stated, the competency-based curriculum is a self-paced approach to skill acquisition with many opportunities for individualization as well.

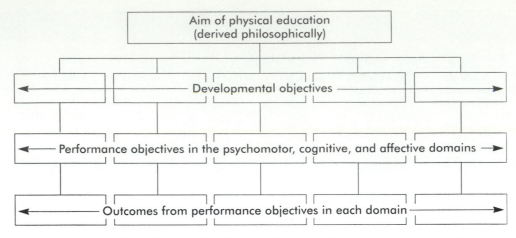

FIG. 4-7 Interrelationships of the aims, development objectives, performance objectives, and outcomes.

Wessel and Kelly[28] developed an Achievement-Based Curriculum (ABC) model combining a competency-based approach with a systems approach (Fig. 4-8). The ABC model allows physical education teachers to plan, implement, and evaluate instructional programs for individual students based on selected goals and objectives. The implementation of this model requires a series of five steps. Within a given content area, the five steps are to:

1. Assess the entry skill level of students.
2. Prescribe competencies for student attainment.
3. Discuss the manner in which the content is to be taught.
4. Provide ample opportunities for learning.
5. Maintain an ongoing process of evaluation to ensure that student needs are being addressed.

By specifying the competencies to be achieved in each educational domain, the students have goals to guide their efforts and clear criteria for achievement. This process will produce specified outcomes reflecting consideration of individual differences.

The Concept-Based Curriculum

What is a conceptual approach to curriculum in physical education? Simply stated it is one that employs concepts, generalizations, themes, ideas, or conceptual statements as the organizing elements in physical education rather than activities or competencies. Concepts are generalizations derived from facts expressed in understandable form. Wuest and Bucher[1] believe that the more basic the concept, the broader the situation to which it can be applied. Concepts allow individuals to generalize findings from one situation to another and provide the learner with a sound base from which to make many applications of the material learned.[27]

In recent years there has been an attempt to teach the "why" of physical activity as well as the "how" to participants. The teaching of the why is the focus of the concept-based curriculum model. The conceptual approach to physical education also helps students to understand why certain activities are selected for the program. A conceptual curriculum means that basic concepts need to be learned for growth to take place, rather than well-ordered, multivaried competency skills.[18,19,29] The activities selected by the physical education teacher offer a medium through which to teach concepts. Stated yet another way, the activities are the vehicle through which the learning of concepts is conveyed and developed. For example, students would participate in aerobic exercise because it can serve as a vehicle to improved cardiovascular fitness and for its potential to develop the concepts of balance or coordination as well as facilitate the students' understanding of these concepts.

The conceptual approach gives the teacher and student meaning to a physical activity area and illustrates a theoretical rationale for inclusion of physical activities into the school curriculum. Why do we teach basketball, weight training, dance, and other activities? One value of this approach is to enable the student to learn general ideas. The selection of activities may vary from one school district to another and, indeed, from one sport to another, but the underlying concepts remain the same. The concepts of stability remain the same whether the student is learning tennis or golf. In this model, the physical education teacher's prime concern is to select skills from various activities to help students attain the conceptual understanding. In effect, the instructor "uses" the specific activity to explicate the underlying concept(s) manifest and inherent in the motor activity.

The concept-based curriculum will be utilized by the physical education teacher who seeks to develop students'

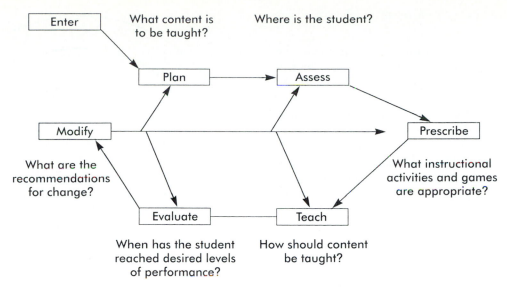

FIG. 4-8   Five-step procedural guide to implement the ABC model components.[28]
From Wessel JA, Kelly LE: *Achievement-based curriculum development in physical education*, Philadelphia, 1986, Lea & Febiger.

ability to understand, synthesize, analyze, and evaluate their psychomotor experience.[18,19,29] Dougherty and Bonanno[29] believe that once a concept is learned, "the concept must be transferrable to new skills and situations yet to be encountered, and they must be meaningful enough to justify the time and effort expended on their development." Because the concept-based curriculum focuses on more than mere participation in an activity, it

provides a firmer, more rational basis for the physical education curriculum than the more narrowly focused activity-based curriculum.[17,18,29]

The concept-based curriculum refocuses physical activities and the quality of performance around important ideas. Educators should emphasize the "why" and not just the "how" in the education of students. Illustrative of the concept-based teaching approach is the following example. A teacher desiring that students acquire knowledge and understanding of the concept of teamwork may select a series of team sports for the primary purpose of providing experience in group and cooperative activities and then have the class analyze and discuss how teamwork influences individual performance, etc. Specific examples of conceptual lessons, units, and other related instructional materials are provided in Chapter 6.

Kate Barrett,[30] a past chairperson of the NASPE Curriculum and Instruction Academy, expressed the point that all models appear to focus on the various "substantive aspects of a curriculum, the 'what' the teacher will teach or the 'what' the students will learn or experience."[30] The activity-based curriculum focuses on the activities that students will experience or the process of activity itself. Barrett[30] agreed with Cheffers[18] in that "both ideas are considered central to the curriculum development process and starting points from which all curricula emanate." She continues:

The competency curriculum model indicates activities but suggests some structure within which specific substance may be identified; for example, minimum standards, predetermined behaviors, and accountability. The concept curriculum model focuses on both substance and structure of substance. Physical activity is the substance, but the way it is structured may now be different in nature: it focuses on "concepts" and uses them

Some schools emphasize a conceptual approach to physical education within programs. Students enter the physical/motor fitness laboratory at Rock Springs High School, Rock Springs, WY.

Courtesy of Paul Grube, Rock Springs High School, Rock Springs, WY.

as an organizing device with the intent to integrate all substance.[30]

However, Barrett[30] made some suggestions toward improving the core, or center, of Cheffers'[18] three models. Identifying the focal point as physical activity, Barrett suggested that it marked the starting point and that the first concentric circle should be the activity-based curriculum model, followed by the competency- and concept-based curriculum models. Therefore an acceptance of the model's center as physical activity, and not as a model for curriculum development, permits the other three models to exert an influence on one another, eventually causing an attraction to the center core (physical activity). The resulting effects evolve into a major model for curriculum development (Fig. 4-9).[30]

Physical education teachers who desire to teach the why as well as the how of physical education are directed to several sources.[3,5,33,39] Initially published in 1981 and revised in 1987, the very successful *Basic Stuff Series I and II* is a convenient source for physical education teachers to use in the development of a concept-based model.[34-38] Another text, *Fitness for Life* by Corbin and Lindsey,[32] developed physical fitness concepts for secondary students.

To enhance the reader's insight into the conceptual approach, three examples of this method in physical education will be presented. These are the Purpose Process Curriculum Framework,[3,22,32] the Basic Stuff Series,[35,36] and Hellison's Social Development Curriculum.[5]

The personal meaning curriculum model by Jewett and Bain[33] purports that for an experience to be educational, it must have meaning and significance for the individual. Jewett and Mullan recommended that the focus and organization of curriculums are what must change.[21] Jewett and Bain[3,34] present a theoretically conceptual framework, the Purpose Process Curriculum Framework (PPCF), to serve as a guide to the physical education teacher in the development of a concept-based program. Jewett and her colleagues provide us with a thorough description of the personal meaning curriculum in the PPCF.

The PPCF was designed as a conceptual framework for curriculum decision making based upon a theoretical model. The conceptual framework for physical education curricular decision making, the PPCF, was presented as a resource to guide curriculum planners through a systematic process of curriculum development and instruction planning.[33] The PPCF is divided into two major dimensions: the purpose and the process. The purpose dimension focuses on achieving the goals of humankind: personal development, environmental coping, and social interaction. These three key concepts are divided into seven major purposes and 22 purpose elements. The seven major purposes are described as physiological efficiency, psychic equilibrium, spatial orientation, object manipulation, communication, group interaction, and cultural involvement.[33]

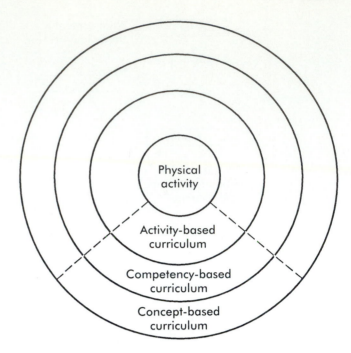

FIG. 4-9 As the total curriculum grows outward from the core, the best features of previously identified curriculums are incorporated.

Developed from Cheffers J: The beginnings of a centripetal curriculum. In Harrington WM (editor): *Proceedings of the Second Conference on Curriculum Theory in Physical Education*, Athens, Ga, 1981, University of Georgia, and Barrett KR: *Reaction: proceedings of the Second Conference on Curriculum Theory in Physical Education*, Athens, Ga, 1981, University of Georgia.

The process dimension of the PPCF provides for sequence in physical education content in terms of desired movement process outcomes.[33] The process dimension focuses on learning processes, and the attempt has been to differentiate important learning operations in order to facilitate improvement in instruction.[31] The process dimension of the PPCF is divided into three key concepts: generic movement (perceiving and patterning), ordinative movement (adapting and refining), and creative movement (varying, improvising, and composing).

Fig. 4-10 and Table 4-4 are examples of a middle-school and a high-school plan identifying physical education activities and the concept in which activity develops in the PPCF.

In Table 4-5, Heitman[40] illustrates one of the key purpose concepts from Jewett and Mullan,[22] object manipulation: man moves to give impetus to and to absorb the force of the object, in a unit that includes throwing, striking, catching, receiving, and kicking.

The concept-based curriculum stresses the knowing of the "how" and "why" of an action and is therefore distinctly different from the other two models that emphasize "doing." Teachers advocating the guided-discovery and problem-solving approaches to teaching, as discussed

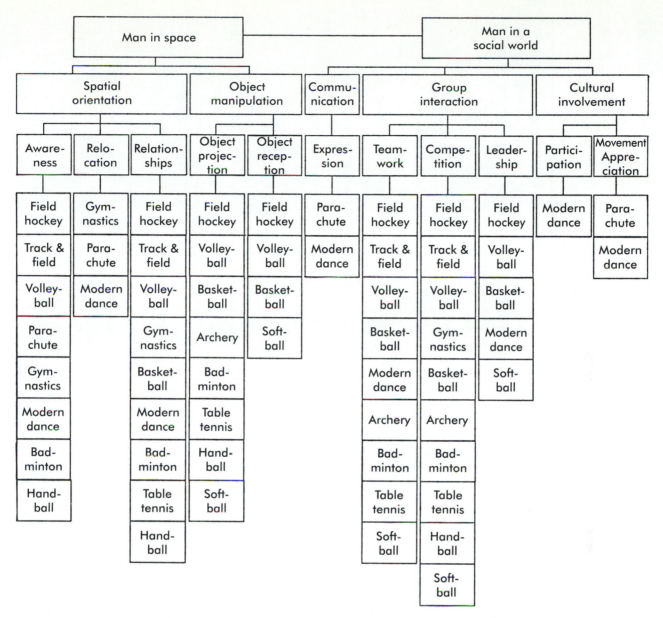

FIG. 4-10 Middle school physical education curriculum plan.
Reprinted with permission of the American Alliance for Health, Physical Education, Recreation, and Dance.

in Chapter 9, will use these concepts in their teaching of physical activity.

The second most significant contribution to the development of a concept-based curriculum model for physical education is the *Basic Stuff Series I and II*. *The Basic Stuff Series* was developed by teachers working under the guidance of NASPE of AAHPERD. *The Basic Stuff Series* presents a conceptual approach that offers valuable information focusing on the "why" of physical education for students. Basic Stuff attempts to summarize the appropriate concepts and provides teachers with methods to assist their instructional efforts. Concepts were selected by public school teachers and scholars for "relevance to students" in physical education programs. The authors

of the series identified several common motives as purposes for participation. They are (1) health (feeling good), (2) appearance (looking good), (3) achievement (doing better), (4) social (getting along), (5) aesthetics (turning on), and (6) coping with the environment (surviving).[36] Concepts were selected to provide information useful to students in accomplishing these purposes.

The Basic Stuff Series is comprised of two separate parts. Series I is composed of the following six volumes: Exercise Physiology, Kinesiology, Motor Learning, Psycho-Social Aspects, Humanities (art, history, philosophy), and Motor Development. Series I offers a summary of basic information around concepts salient to student purposes.[37] Series II is comprised of three volumes: Basic

T A B L E 4 - 4

High School Education Curriculum Plan

Activities	Physiological Efficiency	Teamwork	Participation	Others*	Process (Motor Domain) to be Developed
Soccer	X	X			Skills strategy-creative movement (varying, improvising, composing)
Field hockey	X	X			Skills strategy-creative movement (varying, improvising, composing)
Speedball	X	X			Skills strategy-creative movement (varying, improvising, composing)
Flag football		X	X		Fundamentals-application (perceiving, adaptation)
Basketball tournaments	X	X		Competition	Skills strategy (improvising, composing)
Volleyball tournaments		X	X	Object projection/competition	Skills strategy (improvising, composing)
Softball		X	X		Skills strategy-application (refining, improvising)
Archery			X		Fundamentals-application (perceiving, refining)
Tennis			X	Object projection/object reception	Fundamentals-application-skills strategy (perceiving, composing)
Golf			X	Object projection	Fundamentals-application (perceiving, refining)
Weight training	X				Fundamentals (perceiving, pattern)
Gymnastics I	Mechanical efficiency			Relocation maneuvering/interest	Fundamentals-application (perceiving, varying)
Gymnastics II				Challenge expression/interest	Application-skills strategy (refining, composing)
Swimming	X Mechanical efficiency		X		Fundamentals-application (perceiving, refining)
Floor hockey		X		Interest professional/team in area	Fundamental-application (perceiving, adaption)
Outdoor education			X		Cognitive domain fundamentals (perceiving, pattern)
Jogging	X				Application-refining (cognitive awareness of self)
Badminton			X		Fundamentals-application-skills (perceiving, composing)
Yoga	X		X		Fundamentals-application (perceiving, refining)
Judo self-defense			X		Fundamentals-application-skills (perceiving, refining)
Senior life saving			X		Fundamentals-application (perceiving, refining)
Recreational games			X		Fundamentals-application (perceiving, refining)
Bowling			X		Fundamentals-application (perceiving, refining)
Slimnastics	X				Cognitive learning-fundamentals (perceiving, patterning)
Orienteering	X				Cognitive learning-about fitness
Bicycling	X		X		Fundamentals-application
Backpacking	X		X		Fundamentals-application
Outdoor recreational games			X		

Purposes

Reprinted with permission from the American Alliance for Health, Physical Education, Recreation, and Dance.
*Purposes served other than the three emphasized in the curriculum plan.

TABLE 4-5

Conceptual Organizing Center Built on Throwing, Striking, Catching, Receiving, Kicking

Unit of Study	Projected Objects	Variables	Unit of Study	Received Objects	Variables
Object projection with			Object reception with		
Hands	Bowling ball	For distance	Hands	Softball	From others
	Basketball	For accuracy		Basketball	Wall
	Handball	With others		Volleyball	Floor
Balls	Volleyball	Environment		Football	Grass
	Baseball	Air		Water polo ball	Ice
	Shot put	Ground		Handball	Water
	Football	Floor	Feet	Soccer ball	Varying force, spin
	Water polo ball	Ice	Implements		
		Snow	Gloves	Baseball	
Missiles	Discus	Water	Cesta	Lacrosse ball	With locomotion
	Javelin	Grass	Hockey	Puck	Without locomotion
	Darts		stick		
Feet	Soccer ball	With locomotion			
	Football	Nonlocomotion			
		With spin			
		Without spin			
Implements	Bat				
	Racket				
	Stick				
	Club				
	Bow				

Object manipulation: man moves to give impetus to and to absorb the force of the object.

From AAHPERD: *JOPERD* 2:46, 1981.

Unit: Folk Dance

Volume	Concepts
Kinesiology	Smaller strides increase stability on slippery surfaces. (V2,P68)
Psychosocial aspects	Aesthetic movement experiences help an individual feel good. (V4,P10)
Motor learning	Mental practice can improve performance. (V3,P35)

Unit: Volleyball

Volume	Concepts
Psychosocial aspects	Fear of failure affects performance in physical activity. (V4,P20) (V2,P68)
Motor development	Development of body awareness, balance, spatial awareness, and tactile location aids performance. (V6,P29)
Kinesiology	Force is needed to produce or change motion. (V2,P1)
Humanities	Specific activities emphasize different characteristics of beauty. (V5,P9)

Unit: Tennis

Volume	Concepts
Psychosocial aspects	Self-talk can aid in doing better. (V4,P34)
Kinesiology	Force will be reduced if firm contact is not maintained at the moment of contact of release. (V2,P49)
Kinesiology	A follow through facilitates projection at maximum velocity. (V2,P49)

FIG. 4-11 Outline of sample *Basic Stuff* concepts.

Reprinted with permission of the American Alliance for Health, Physical Education, Recreation, and Dance.

Stuff in Action for: Grades K-3, Grades 4-8, and Grades 9-12. Each provides examples of instructional activities to aide teaching physical education concepts appropriate to a particular age group (Fig. 4-11).[38]

The Basic Stuff Series was written for teachers. Kneer[39] stated that the "teachers decide what it is that students ought to learn." This could provide learning experiences about fitness, knowledge, or lifetime skills. On the students' part, "they should decide what they want to learn, and then internalize learning relative to their needs and interests."[39]

Basic Stuff was designed for a variety of curricular uses. Some school systems may employ the content of the series to establish the value and direction of their physical education program and to thwart efforts to eliminate these programs by demonstrating the conceptual basis of the program of instruction. The series can also stimulate other professionals to foster conceptual learning through which to implement this body of knowledge. With regard to the application of a conceptual curriculum, Heitmann[40]

demonstrated how Basic Stuff concepts may be organized within a unit. Concepts are integrated into (1) a basketball unit (Table 4-6); (2) a throwing, catching, striking, receiving, and kicking unit (Table 4-5); and (3) a personal fitness unit (Table 4-7). Fig. 4-12 illustrates some basic skills showing how their implied concepts link activity centers.

Table 4-5 shows how to integrate various concepts from the *The Basic Stuff Series* in a unit using basketball as the organizing center. When utilized as the organizing center, the concept becomes the unit theme, whereas sports, exercise, or rhythmic forms illustrate the concepts and link various concept units.[40]

Table 4-6 illustrates how to integrate Basic Stuff concepts into a personal fitness unit.

Physical education teachers are well aware that they must also adapt physical education to the demands of this era. They have found that today's students require and react well to a conceptualized approach to teaching. Such a realization reinforces the professionals' movement to-

TABLE 4-6

Basic Stuff Integrated Into a Basketball Unit

Skill	Foundational Movements	Subdiscipline	Basic Stuff Concepts
Dribbling	Eye-hand coordination	Motor development	Readiness
	Locomotion	Kinesiology	Production of force
	Agility	Motor learning	Dynamic balance
			Information processing
			External-internal environment
		Psycho-social	Modeling
		Exercise physiology	Endurance/strength
Shooting	Eye-hand coordination	Motor development	Kinesthetic awareness
	Throwing	Kinesiology	Production of force
			Trajectory
			Angle of incidence
			Timing
		Motor learning	Challenges
		Humanities	Achievement motives
		Psycho-social	
Passing	Throwing	Motor development	Spatial awareness
	Bouncing		Integration
	Catching	Kinesiology	Absorption of force
		Motor learning	External environment
		Humanities	Artistry
		Psycho-social	Self-control
Game play	Teamwork	Humanities	Sportsmanship
			Cooperation/competition
	Strategy	Motor learning	External environment
		Psycho-social	Attentional focus
			Controlling aggression
		Motor development	Visual perception

From AAHPERD: *JOPERD* 2:43, 1981.

T A B L E   4 - 7

Basic Stuff Integrated Into a Personal Fitness Unit

Subthemes	Activities	Basic Stuff Concepts
Cardiorespiratory	Calisthenics Track Jogging-aerobics Cycling Dancing Endurance swimming Cross-country skiing–running Circuit training Rope jumping	Physiology of exercise Training rules
Mechanical efficiency	Gymnastics	Mechanical analysis of movement
Flexibility, joint mobility	Weight lifting Track and field	Force production
Static and dynamic strength	Self-defense Aikido Wrestling	
Tension control	Relaxation Yoga	Principles of stress control
Aquatic competency	Survival swimming Beginning, intermediate, and advanced swimming	Principles of buoyancy and propulsion
Rhythmic response	Free exercise Fundamental dance patterns	Aesthetic qualities Body as subject/object Artistry
Self-knowledge	Physical fitness testing Neuromuscular testing Depth perception Peripheral vision Height-weight Reaction time Competition Psychological set	Understanding of status Maturity Weight control Nutrition Achievement motives Self-concept
Balance-agility	Stilts Tumbling–stunts Skating Unicycle Balance beam/apparatus Obstacle course	Effect of center of gravity and base of support on static and dynamic balance
Eye-hand, eye-foot	Object projection and reception Hands–feet Implements–racket, cesta, club, glove	Information processing Whole–part–whole Force production Force absorption Trajectory Open/closed skill
Locomotor	Walking, running, leaping, skipping, sliding, hopping	Spatial awareness Friction

From AAHPERD: *JOPERD* 2:44, 1981.

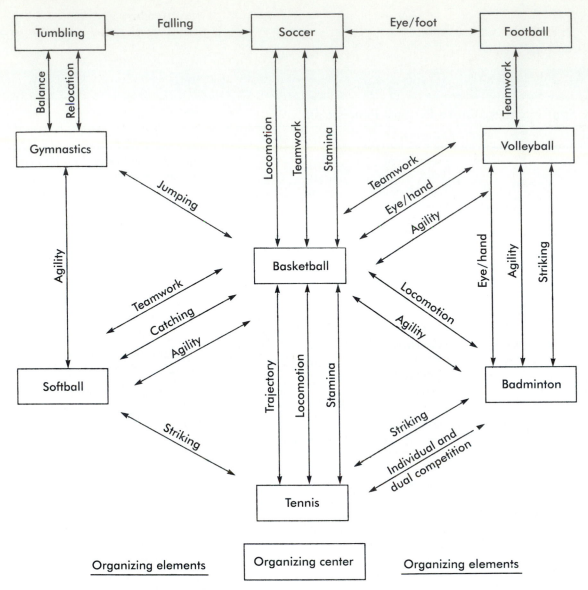

FIG. 4-12 Concept link to activity center. Activity organizing centers with fundamental skill as organizing elements.
From AAHPERD: *JOPERD* 2:42, 1981.

ward curriculum reform of secondary school physical education.

Current physical education teachers realize that their primary task is to educate students about their bodies, the principles that are foundational to the use of the body, effective and efficient methods of maintaining health and fitness, in short to teach the discipline of human movement studies. The conceptualized approach integrates the previously described cognitive and intellectual aspects with the physical.

When using the conceptual approach, the teacher serves as a guide rather than a storehouse of information. Students learn, for example, the principles of body leverage, hip rotation, generation of momentum, and foot and leg placement in throwing a softball via exploration

and experimentation. The physical principles involved are best understood when students conceptualize the principles for themselves. This approach depends upon the background and preparation of instructors and their willingness to place much of the responsibility for learning on the students themselves. It also demands that the physical education teacher use instructional materials, such as *The Basic Stuff Series I and II,* geared to secondary school students and that each student be assigned readings and outside work based on the text and related experiences in the physical education classroom.

Hellison[5] describes yet another conceptual curriculum model, one that has had an impact on the curriculum field. His Social Development model has as its goal students progressing through a series of five interrelated

BOX 4-3

HELLISON'S SOCIAL DEVELOPMENT CURRICULUM MODEL: DEVELOPMENTAL LEVELS

Level 0: Irresponsibility

This level describes students who are unmotivated and undisciplined. Students who operate at Level 0 are not motivated to participate in the program. Typical behaviors manifested are: interrupting, intimidating, manipulating, and verbally or physically abusing others.

Level I: Self-control

Students at this level may not participate in the day's activity but they are able to control their behavior at least to the point of not interfering with other students' right to learn and/or the teacher's right to teach.

Level II: Involvement

Students at this level not only show self-control, but are involved in the program and the lesson activities. They willingly, even enthusiastically, play, accept challenges, practice skills, and train for fitness under the teacher's supervision.

Level III: Self-responsibility

Level III emphasizes the need for students to learn to take more responsibility for their own learning and linking the choices made to their own identities. Students at this level not only show self-control and involvement, but they are also able to work without direct supervision, eventually taking responsibility for their intentions and actions.

Level IV: Caring

This level deals with the need for social stability in students' lives by encouraging students to reach beyond themselves to others and to commit themselves to caring about others. Students at this level are motivated to extend their sense of responsibility by cooperating, giving support, showing concern, and helping. Level IV is built upon the assumption that students must meet some of their own needs before they can reach out to others.

Modified from Hellison DR: *Goals and strategies for teaching physical education*, Champaign, Ill, 1985, Human Kinetics.

teachers who employed his suggested levels. In this way, his text can assist physical education teachers interested in applying the conceptual approach to secondary school physical education.

The conceptual approach to physical education helps students to understand why certain activities are selected for inclusion in the program and why such activities as physical fitness and lifetime sports receive such emphasis. In this atmosphere students are drawn closer to the program, which helps to make physical education activities a respected and pleasurable aspect of the school day.

The process of education is undergoing a series of reforms in many areas of the curriculum. The sciences, mathematics, and the languages especially are utilizing new teaching methodology and new technological devices, drastically revising existing curricula. Today's secondary school students are familiar with concepts and areas of knowledge that formerly were reserved for college level courses. Cheffers[18] explains that as the total curriculum grows outward from its core, it incorporates the best features of previously identified curricula—activity based, competency based, and concept based. Consideration of individual student needs, philosophical foundations, staffing, and facility and equipment use as well as community preferences are all of essential importance when one is designing revising, and changing a physical education curriculum.

SUMMARY

The national curriculum reform movement currently taking place combined with increased emphasis on educational priorities dictates that physical education teachers rethink their positions in regard to their place in the educational system.[1] Instructors should reexamine how they can contribute their best efforts and make their greatest contributions in today's changing world. They must decide what are the most important objectives they wish to accomplish in their curriculum. What curriculum framework will guide them in their efforts to reach these objectives? What is the content needed to meet the needs of students?

The material reviewed here should help professionals make such decisions based on a sound, rational basis. From such a basis, clearly designed, positive, and effective programs will emerge that will support physical education and its contributions to the development of secondary students.

levels of responsibility. These levels are carefully delineated and are, in truth, broadly defined concepts of social behavior (Box 4-3).

Hellison's work adds yet another series of practical examples of the implementation of the conceptual curriculum in physical education. In his book, Hellison analyzes, describes, and outlines examples from several school

FOR REVIEW

1. Describe the values of lesson plans.
2. What are the major differences between the activity-based, the concept-based, and the competency-based curriculums?
3. Describe the various expectations for the teacher's instructional behavior and role differentiation when conducting

lessons within an activity-based curriculum and a concept-based curriculum.

4. Why is the activity-based curriculum the dominant model currently employed in physical education? Be sure to address the social, political, administrative, and economic factors as well as the curricular variables that might account for this situation.

5. Which curriculum model do you favor? Why?

REFERENCES

1. Wuest DA, Bucher CA: *Foundations of physical education and sport,* ed 10, St Louis, 1987, Mosby.
2. Willgoose CE: *The curriculum in physical education,* ed 4, Englewood Cliffs NJ, 1984, Prentice Hall.
3. Jewett AE, Bain LL: *The curriculum process in physical education,* Dubuque, Iowa, 1985, William C Brown.
4. Lawson HA, Placek JH: *Physical education in the secondary schools: curricular alternatives,* Boston, 1981, Allyn and Bacon.
5. Hellison DR: *Goals and strategies for teaching physical education,* Champaign, Ill, 1985, Human Kinetics.
6. Siedentop D: *Developing teaching skills in physical education,* ed 2, Palo Alto, Calif, 1983, Mayfield.
7. Bain LL: Description of the hidden curriculum in secondary physical education, *Research Quarterly* 47(2):154-160, 1976.
8. Melograno V: *Designing the physical education curriculum: a self-directed approach,* ed 2, Dubuque, Iowa, 1985, Kendall/Hunt Publishing.
9. Griffey DC: Trouble for sure—a crisis perhaps: secondary school physical education today, *JOPERD* 58(2):20-21, 1987.
10. Taylor JL, Chiogioji EN: Implications of educational PE programs, *JOPERD* 58(2):22-23, 1987.
11. Mackenzie MM: *Toward a new curriculum in physical education,* New York, 1969, McGraw-Hill Book.
12. The Society of State Directors of Health, Physical Education and Recreation: *A statement of basic beliefs,* Kensington, Md, 1985, SSDHPER.
13. National Association for Sport and Physical Education: *Guidelines for secondary school physical education,* Reston, Va, 1986, AAHPERD.
14. Eggen PD, Kauchak DD, Harden RJ: *Strategies for teachers: information processing models in the classroom,* Englewood Cliffs, NJ, 1979, Prentice Hall.
15. Joyce B, Weil M: *Models of teaching,* Englewood Cliffs, NJ, 1972, Prentice Hall.
16. Weil M, Joyce B: *Information processing models of teaching: expanding your teaching repertoire,* Englewood Cliffs, NJ, 1978, Prentice Hall.
17. Bank A, Henerson M, Eu L: *A practical guide to program planning: a teaching models approach,* New York, 1981, Teachers College, Columbia University.
18. Cheffers J: The beginnings of a centripetal curriculum. In Harrington WM, editor: *Proceedings of the Second Conference on Curriculum Theory in Physical Education,* Athens, Ga, 1981, University of Georgia, AAHPERD.
19. Siedentop D, Mand C, Taggert A: *Physical education: teaching and curriculum strategies for grades 5-12,* Palo Alto, Calif, 1986, Mayfield.
20. Miller AG, Cheffers, J, Whitcomb V: *Physical education in the elementary school,* Englewood Cliffs, NJ, 1974, Prentice Hall.
21. Hellison D: *Humanistic physical education,* Englewood Cliffs, NJ, 1973, Prentice Hall.
22. Jewitt AE, Mullan MR: *Curriculum design: purposes and processes in physical education,* Washington, DC, 1977, AAHPERD.
23. Harrison JM, Blackmore C: *Instructional strategies for secondary school physical education,* Dubuque, Iowa, 1989, William C Brown.
24. Evaul, T: How do we help others by structuring programs in human movement? In Cheffers J, Evaul T, editors: *Introduction to physical education: concepts of human movement,* Englewood Cliffs, NJ, 1978, Prentice Hall.
25. Nixon JE, Jewett AE: *Physical education curriculum,* New York, 1964, The Ronald Press.
26. The University of the State of New York: *Physical education syllabus: grades K-12,* Albany, NY, 1988, The State Education Department—Bureau of Curriculum Development.
27. Kizer DL, Piper DL, Sauter WE: *A practical approach to teaching physical education,* Ithaca, NY, 1984, Movement Publications.
28. Wessel JA, Kelly L: *Achievement-based curriculum development in physical education,* Philadelphia, 1986, Lea & Febiger.
29. Dougherty NJ, Bonanno D: *Contemporary approaches to the teaching of physical education,* ed 2, Scottsdale, Ariz, 1987, Gorsuch Scarisbrick.
30. Barrett KB: Reaction to the beginnings of the centripetal curriculum model. In Harrington WM, editor: *Proceedings of the Second Conference on Curriculum Theory in Physical Education,* Athens, Ga, 1981, University of Georgia, AAHPERD.
31. AAHPERD: *Knowledge and understanding in physical education,* Washington, DC, 1969, AAHPERD.
32. Corbin C, Lindsey R: *Fitness for life,* ed 2, Glenview, Ill, 1983, Scott, Foresman.
33. Jewett AE, Bain LL, editors: The purpose process curriculum framework: a personal meaning model for physical education, *JOTPE* Special Monograph 6(3):1-366, 1987.
34. AAHPERD: *Basic Stuff Series I and II,* Reston, Va, 1981, AAHPERD.
35. AAHPERD: *Basic Stuff Series I and II* ed 2, Reston, Va, 1987, AAHPERD.
36. Bain LL: Basic Stuff Series, *JOPER* 52(2):33-34, 1981.
37. Rothstein A: Basic Stuff Series I, *JOPER* 52(2):35-37, 46, 1981.
38. Trimble TR, Mullan M: Basic Stuff Series II, *JOPER* 52(2):38-39, 46, 1981.
39. Kneer ME: Basic Stuff: a collaborative project for a "new game," *JOPERD* 53(7):27-29, 1982.
40. Heitmann HH: Integrating concepts into curricular models, *JOPER* 52(2):42-45, 1981.

ANNOTATED READINGS

AAHPERD: *Basic Stuff Series I and II,* ed 2, Reston, Va, 1987, AAHPERD.

Basic Stuff Series I and II presents a conceptual approach, offering valuable information that focuses on the "why" of physical education for elementary and secondary school students. The Basic Stuff Series I covers such areas as exercise physiology, kinesiology, movement in the humanities, psychosocial aspects of movement, motor development, and motor learning. Series II identifies concepts from the various disciplines in Series I and relates them to the three basic age groups: early childhood (grades K-3), childhood (grades 4-8), and adolescence (grades 9-12).

Burns RW: *New approaches to behavioral objectives,* Dubuque, Iowa, 1972, William C Brown.

This text deals extensively with the objectives for instructional settings, their selection, creation, writing, evaluation, and use. This is a how-to-do-it type of book; it is designed for use in college and university curriculum and methods courses and also for in-service training of educators at all levels. Special attention has been given to writing objectives, an area of concern to many teachers.

Carlson RP, editor: *Ideas II for secondary school physical education,* Reston, Va, 1984, AAHPERD.

Forty-six ideas for secondary school physical education are presented in this text. The purpose of the text is to share, with physical education teachers, these new ideas, new teaching practices, or new wrinkles that could be used within their own school setting. The authors of each idea share their school's program experience by describing why they made a change, how they accomplished the change, and the evaluation of the change to the reader. The ideas are presented in five major sections: Curriculum Ideas: Concepts and Designs; Instructional Ideas: Teaching

Notions and Concepts; Games and Activities Ideas; Adaptations and Contemporary, Alternative Content Ideas: Curricular Nontraditional Activities; and Fitness-Related Ideas: Curricular and Teaching Concepts.

Dougherty NJ, editor: *Physical education and sport for the secondary school students,* Reston, Va, 1983, AAHPERD.

This text was written to provide the secondary student with a comprehensive and authoritative book on contemporary physical education and sports concepts. This book was designed to provide the student with an overview of various sports, information on skill and technique acquisition, safety, scoring values and etiquette, strategies, equipment, and related terminology.

Jewett AE, Bain LL: *The curriculum process in physical education,* Dubuque, Iowa, 1985, William C Brown.

The authors of this text have attempted to present a classification of value perspectives, to review the major curriculum models that have been proposed, and to provide examples and illustrations of applications of these models in a wide range of educational settings. The authors do not endorse a single curriculum model, but attempt to encourage the reader to examine critically the models that are available. The intent of the text is to help the reader clarify his or her own beliefs, to guide the reader in learning to design his or her own physical education program, and to enhance the reader's ability to make sound professional judgments about his or her physical education curriculum. The text has three major sections: Part 1 provides a theoretical base, Part 2 leads the reader through the process of curriculum design, and Part 3 deals with practical and theoretical issues related to curriculum development in physical education.

Jewett AE, Bain LL: The purpose process curriculum framework: a personal meaning model for physical education, *JOTPE* 6 (3): Special Monograph, 1987.

This monograph represents the combined efforts of 19 authors illustrating the development of a personal meaning model for physical education curriculum development: the Purpose Process Curriculum Framework (PPCF). The monograph is organized in four sections: (1) the Development of the Framework, (2) Purpose Studies, (3) Process Studies, and (4) Future Directions. The monograph serves as a useful resource to all who are intrigued by the challenge and stimulated by the need for increasingly meaningful physical education curriculum theory and research.

Jewett AE, Mullan MR: *Curriculum design: purposes and processes in physical education,* Washington, DC, 1977, AAHPER.

This monograph presents the Purpose Process Curriculum Framework (PPCF) for physical education. The PPCF is the only curriculum framework available to physical education teachers that is based on the building of curriculum theory by a large number of scholars over a long period of time. The PPCF and its development through a logical, philosophical analysis of the common human purposes for moving is presented. The PPCF is based upon three major purpose concepts, which are made up of 22 purpose elements, and 3 key process concepts that consist of 7 movement process categories. AAHPER recommends this publication as a basic construct in the area of curriculum planning.

Kryspin WJ, Feldhusen JF: *Writing behavioral objectives: a guide to planning instruction,* Minneapolis, 1974, Burgess.

This is a programmed text for students learning to become teachers. The book focuses on behavioral objectives in a manner that the learner is guided through a sequential series of learning stages, from distinguishing among objectives to using a specification chart as a guide to writing objectives.

Lawson HA, Placek JH: *Physical education in the secondary schools: curriculum alternatives,* Boston, 1981, Allyn and Bacon.

The authors provide the reader with a critique of current operations and beliefs in secondary school physical education. The book illustrates the process and products of designing alternatives for physical education and presents a way in which theory and practice can be interwoven with discipline and profession along with pedagogy and kinesiology and sport studies. The authors provide a conceptual framework for alternatives and give teachers some plans that can be modified for local use.

Mager RF: *Preparing instructional objectives,* Palo Alto, Calif, 1962, Fearon.

This text provides a step-by-step approach to writing behavioral objectives. It provides a valuable approach to the task of goal specification and to solutions to development of one's own instructional objectives.

Curriculum Development: A Systematic Approach

CHAPTER OBJECTIVES
- To describe a systematic approach to curriculum construction
- To discuss procedures to determine and prioritize curriculum objectives
- To identify methods of selecting and sequencing educational activities

Few would argue that at the heart of the educative process lie the many face-to-face interactions students experience daily with teachers. The varied exchanges between physical education teachers and their secondary students receive near-consensual support from professionals as the most significant aspect of the high school experience.

It is the specific content of such interactions that is the concern of this chapter. The curriculum, or course of study as it is often defined, includes the content, subject matter, and learning experiences that generate the numerous student-teacher interactions characteristic of the learning climate in physical education. The school curriculum, however operationalized, is the essential vehicle of the educative process. It is the medium by which abstract, theoretical, and philosophical concepts are translated into effective procedures and plans that will affect the instructional process.[1]

The program of study in physical education in secondary schools is, in effect, a collection of learning activities, information, and subject matter, which reflects the collective wisdom of the community, the school system, the administration, the faculty, and the physical education teachers about not only what is important for students to learn, but also the process by which learning should take place. Teaching professionals are responsible to students and the community for offering coordinated and sequential experiences designed to facilitate student achievement of educational goals. Without a formal pro-

gram, as specified in the written curriculum, secondary school physical education can quickly succumb to a mode of operation dominated by disparate, discrete lessons, and independent, idiosyncratic teacher behavior and pedagogical practice.

For the physical education curriculum to be transformed into, and perceived as, coherent, relevant, and meaningful learning episodes and, in short, to be worth studying, interpreted, and experienced by students as more than a series of vaguely focused activities, explicit procedural steps must be employed. These procedures, known collectively as systematic curriculum development, are the focus of this chapter.

The school curriculum is a great concern of parents, taxpayers, and the general community. Such concern is reflected in recent polls, which reported that curricular problems were ranked fourth by those responding.[2,3] Also implicit in these data is the concern that an ever-broadening, more intensely packed curriculum makes schooling in the United States more difficult than ever.

The development and implementation of well-founded curricula is critical if physical education in secondary schools is to continue to evolve in consistent, logical, and positive directions. Failure to address this task appropriately will continue to reinforce the view held by many that physical education in high school is superfluous and irrelevant when contrasted with other educational imperatives.

In this chapter, techniques will be suggested for developing the high-school physical education curriculum. The results of such systematic curriculum development endeavors should promote student growth, maximize individual growth across the various domains of learning, and nurture the acceptance and inclusion of physical activity within a balanced, thoughtfully designed lifestyle. The procedures described will facilitate the generation of a set of guidelines that reflects sound judgment, manifests strong internal consistency, and enhances evaluative efforts. Finally, a sound curriculum development system should possess and provide for the necessary flexibility and responsiveness to change at local and regional levels while paralleling the current accelerated pace of change within society.

APPROACHES TO CURRICULUM DEVELOPMENT

The absence of a national physical education curriculum in conjunction with the rare imposition of state or regional curricular mandates has provided professionals with an opportunity that calls to mind the proverbial double-edged sword. On one hand, some physical education teachers have used the curricular void to develop unique programs that truly address specific student needs. Indeed, in some isolated cases, the lack of explicit expectations or outcomes has stimulated unique, often inspired physical education programs. On the other hand, the isolation, lack of supervision, and inadequate monitoring related to curriculum development have influenced programs negatively. Some programs possess few identifiable or defensible goals, which others have not been guided by, or are even incongruent with, stated educational objectives.

The autonomy that accrues because of neglect, inattention, and isolation, however, is often achieved at the expense of colleagueship and support.[4] Circumstances such as these often create other significant problems that curriculum planners and teachers alike must, at some point, address.

In light of these circumstances, if physical education teachers were to create or revise a curriculum, where should they begin? What steps should be taken to prepare an adequate and appropriate curriculum document? The first step is actually simultaneous with the recognition of a need to change, revise a current curriculum, or create a new program of study where none existed before. Once a need for change has been recognized and agreed on, systematic curriculum development can help ensure congruence between stated goals and instructional practice, as well as provide guidance to physical education teachers, who often perform in isolation with minimal professional collaboration and in parts of the institution usually hidden from the public. Significant improvement of the curriculum, not mere tinkering, requires that attention be directed not only to the needs and interests of teachers,

the requirements related to specific activities, or to students' abilities and interest, but to all of these variables that must be analyzed, studied, and reviewed concurrently.

Curriculum development refers to a process that will eventually determine how the formulation or construction of the curriculum will proceed. The curriculum development process centers on the following questions[5]:

◆ Who will be involved in the curriculum building process? Teachers? Administrators? Students? Parents?
◆ What procedures will be employed in curriculum construction?
◆ How are the committees to be utilized?

The intent of the curriculum writing process is to produce a document that is in touch with reality, internally consistent with the day-to-day contingencies of the local situation, easily comprehended by teachers, and useful to secondary school physical education teachers in the daily interactive situations that consume much of their time.

CURRICULUM COMMITTEE

At the earliest point possible, the chief administrator responsible for curriculum development within the system should appoint a committee to follow through with the task of curriculum building or revision. This committee should be considered a working group and consist of approximately 6-12 members. Members should be selected on the basis of technical skills and competencies

Communication among physical education faculty is important in developing and implementing the physical education curriculum.

Courtesy of Ben Lombardo, Rhode Island College, Providence, RI.

required for the job, with major consideration given to ensuring that the group is representative of the types of professional roles within the school system.

Therefore it is suggested that the curriculum committee should include a curriculum specialist, a principal or other systemwide administrator, possibly a building administrator, and several knowledgeable physical education teachers. Also, to ensure appropriate articulation with elementary and middle/junior high–school programs, a professional from the system who possesses such knowledge and familiarity and can facilitate and address the issues related to articulation should be invited to join the group. Finally, it is highly recommended that the curriculum committee group engage the services of a qualified consultant. The consultant should be an individual who can (1) provide an objective, scholarly perspective to the work of the committee and (2) provide an independent, external view of the proceedings without being encumbered by systemwide or districtwide loyalties and political allegiances.

To ensure effective and efficient operation, the committee must be provided with a clearly defined curricular task, a timeline or calendar of specific checkpoints for resolution and implementation, and resources appropriate and commensurate to the accomplishment of the task. The provision of time, the key resource other than the work of the professional personnel, is critical to the achievement of a meaningful document. These elements should be considered foundational to the success of the curriculum committee's functioning.

COMMON MODELS OF CURRICULUM DEVELOPMENT

Three commonly observed curriculum development approaches will be introduced next. The first two approaches are somewhat similar, and are definitely more educationally sound, more complex, and at least at the outset, depend greatly on reflective thought and a clearly composed rationale. However, the rewards and outcomes are more commensurate with productive, relevant, and scholarly endeavors, and they certainly impact students in a more profound manner. A third alternative, more firmly grounded in day-to-day practice, occurs with much regularity within the profession, and although serving pragmatic ends often mitigates against professional, scholarly efforts to improve curricular endeavors in physical education.

The first general approach to curriculum development is identified as the Tyler model. Some claim that the Tyler rationale has become the overwhelmingly dominant mode of responding to curriculum development in recent years.[6] The Tyler model is a way of viewing, analyzing, and interpreting the program, and although not originally intended for use as such, this approach has been transformed into and accepted as the most favored form of curriculum development.[7]

The Tylerian approach suggests a clear set of organizing maneuvers that enhance the curriculum development process. Tyler recommended the following systematic process:
1. Identify aims and objectives.
2. Select learning activities that will support and enable students to achieve the objectives.
3. Organize educational experiences in a coherent and logical manner.
4. Determine the effectiveness of the curriculum.

This approach, driven as it is by objectives, reflects Tyler's commitment to a highly rationalized, comprehensive *method* for arriving at logical and justifiable curriculum.[8] This technique is linear and comprehensive in resolving the curriculum development task. Objectives are identified early in the process, thereby guiding each of the successive steps in development. In addition, this model includes several factors that further recommend its use. It is goal based, ensuring that curricular development is undertaken with general outcomes clearly in mind. The model also emphasizes feasibility, and it is systematic. The planning decisions are cast in a rational framework that emphasizes orderly progression.[9]

Examples of the Tylerian curriculum development model are plentiful in the physical education literature. Berg's[9] suggested plan for a national physical education curriculum implies a preeminent position of Tyler's model for curriculum building. Formulation of national objectives as a necessary prerequisite is recommended followed by their sequential presentation and regular evaluation.

The ABC Curriculum Development Procedures put forth by Wessel and Kelly[10] provide a plan for curriculum development commonly found in the professional literature, and also reflect the Tylerian concept. Early in this collaborative approach, the school district must determine program goals and accompanying supportive rationale. These goals then guide the entire process from that point.[10] (Chapter 4 provides additional information about the ABC Curriculum Development Model.)

Vogel and Seefeldt's[11] work in curriculum design provides another example of how imbued the Tylerian model has become in the thinking and cognition of curriculum specialists. In their description of a twelve-step procedural model for curriculum development, they suggest that program goals should be established by the curriculum team. This should be accomplished, they continue, before the selection and organization of program objectives and learning experiences.[11]

A second general approach to the task of developing the curriculum is one in which planners identify their shared beliefs and images. In other words, physical education teachers would start the curriculum development process by responding to, elaborating on, and specifying their individual orientation to curricular concepts. Miller[12] calls this the development of a curriculum orientation. Included would be clarifying analyses about

BOX 5-1

CURRICULUM ORIENTATION

Educational aims
Conception of the learner
Conception of the learning process
Conception of the instructional process
Conception of the learning environment
The teacher's role
Conception of how learning should be evaluated

Adapted from Miller J: *The educational spectrum: orientations to curriculum,* New York, 1983, Longman.

their beliefs related to the subject matter; about students and learners, their needs, and how students learn; beliefs about schools, gymnasiums, and teachers; about society and its needs; and images of good teachers. Box 5-1 outlines several aspects of a curriculum orientation.[12]

As a result of this reflective and clarifying process, a proposal of an action plan consisting of specific directions and curricular imperatives should evolve. While the products of the two approaches would possibly bring curriculum planners to the same approximate point, the methods are quite different. The latter approach is less linear, more free form, includes much give and take and comparative analyses before the delineation of more specific objectives takes place. The initiatives resulting from the collective wisdom of the group would drive the remaining aspects of the curriculum building process.

A recent National Association for Sport and Physical Education (NASPE) curriculum project provides an example of this second technique. The NASPE Physical Education Outcomes Committee has attempted to define a physically educated person to facilitate the development of curricular initiatives.[13] By developing this composite image of a physically educated person before the delineation of specific competencies, objectives, and educational outcomes, NASPE utilized this second approach to curriculum building. The definition of a physically educated person (see Chapter 1 and Box 5-2), should lead to and facilitate the specific description of a physically educated high-school student, which will then drive future courses of action.

The third method of curriculum development usually results in a compilation of games, drills, and activities organized according to grade level and completed by the physical education staff within a school. In many cases such documents do not clearly delineate what material should be taught, the specific objectives to be addressed, or explicit outcomes that are expected. Such curricula usually provide little overall direction to programs and, in effect, become a resource list of activities for teachers. While the secondary teacher might select the games and activities from the same guide, the goals, objectives, and

emphases of each program depend on the particular interests, needs, abilities, and perceptions of the physical education teacher in each respective school. Research conducted on how teachers plan shows little support for the classical ends-means, four-stage model of planning proposed by Tyler.[14]

Without clearly stated goals or expectations to provide a conceptual framework for activity selection, such curricula provide program options without providing rationale for activity selection. Such plans provide teachers with the means (activities) but not the ends (goals), which leave this latter, important component to the discretion of the teacher.

Such practice often leads to programs that are idiosyncratic in form, devoid of an internal logic, lacking in continuity, and atheoretical in essence. Curricula formed in this manner are difficult, if not impossible, to defend, assess, and coordinate.

Another common result of such practice is that content coverage varies greatly from school to school. Articulation problems quickly surface that undermine continuity and have the potential to destroy or confuse students' understanding of the purposes of the program.

This latter approach to curriculum building, while a common method of development, is curriculum building by default. Faculty charged with producing a written curriculum and who put forth these activity-based compendia usually do so because of a failure to receive one or more of the following necessary prerequisites to curriculum building: adequate support in terms of released time, financial resources, administrative, psychological, and clerical support or encouragement consultant services (so important to implementation and follow-through). As a result, teachers often put forth documents such as these by settling quickly on the path of least resistance, creating minimally expensive, least threatening, extremely practical, and feasible programs. A quick review of curriculum guides produced by various school systems in-

BOX 5-2

MAJOR CHARACTERISTICS OF A PHYSICALLY EDUCATED PERSON

A physically educated person:
- ◆ **has** sufficient skills to perform a variety of physical activities
- ◆ **participates** regularly in physical activity
- ◆ **is** physically fit
- ◆ **knows** the benefits, costs, risks, and obligations of physical activity involvement
- ◆ **values** the effects of regular physical activity in maintaining a healthy lifestyle

Courtesy of Franck DM: Physical education outcomes, project making progress, *UPDATE* Reston, Va, 1989, AAHPERD.

dicates this collection of activities as curriculum approach is produced often without any pretense to a conceptual framework (curriculum orientation).

For curriculum planners to do otherwise in circumstances characterized by minimal administrative encouragement and commitment would be self-defeating and frustrating. To design truly new curricular directions without access to consultant services and appropriate inservice resources, and without various support and services for professionals, possibly threatened by change, would certainly not only doom their efforts to sure failure, but would incur needless frustration as well. One only needs to analyze the success of the implementation of recent legislated mandated curricular changes. The implementation of PL 94-142, The Education for All Children Act, received massive federal and state support in many forms over many years. Mandated changes were nurtured in an era of generous support and numerous opportunities for supervised, monitored, guided change were provided. On the other hand, the failure of Title IX legislation in some school systems can be attributed to the failure or refusal of federal and state government agencies to provide similar resources and support to local educational agencies. School districts and state agencies should not expect meaningful, relevant curricular changes and revisions without appropriate support and an environment that will nurture successful curriculum development.

In the next section, specific aspects of curriculum construction will be reviewed. Explicit steps in the formulation of curriculum will be discussed for the purpose of providing readers with a plan to enhance curriculum development.

STEPS IN CURRICULUM CONSTRUCTION

Curriculum development activities, regardless of approach employed, generate an educational plan that translates educational philosophy and epistemological knowledge into instructional and pedagogical practice that can serve to guide teachers in all aspects of the program. According to Anderson,[16] such a process "holds the prospect of yielding a carefully crafted plan that can be used to shape future programs."

The question arises, then, of how to formulate the curriculum. At this point procedures pertinent to the accomplishment of the curriculum construction task will be presented.

Once the decision to change has been made and a curriculum committee has been organized, the next critical step in the curriculum construction process is the identification and specification of a conceptual framework, a belief system, and a curriculum orientation or philosophy (or whatever the organizing group cares to title it), regardless of the specific nature of these organizing beliefs. This is especially important for physical

education teachers, if the profession is to maintain its legitimate place within the educational hierarchy. Kelly[17] indicates that early in the curriculum building process, planners must address six objectives:

1. Develop a working draft of a program philosophy.
2. Identify program goals.
3. Determine program goal emphasis across grade levels.
4. Determine how many objectives (content) could be realistically addressed in the program.
5. Identify the essential objectives for each goal.
6. Recruit a cadre of teachers to continue curriculum development process.[17]

Anderson[18] refers to this process as the logical-sequential approach, which starts with the conceptualization of an educational philosophy and a derived statement of program goals.

The process of formulating an educational philosophy or reaching consensus about beliefs, which should be reflected in the program, requires much reflection and competent leadership. First of all, program planners must understand that when they prepare, revise, or select a curriculum, they are adopting a philosophy of physical education, and this philosophy consists of the beliefs inherent, hidden, and overtly expressed in the curriculum. The beliefs of the principal authors of the curriculum document will be reflected in the end product, that is, the curriculum and the resultant learning experiences.

With this in mind, those in charge of curriculum development should select or develop a program consistent with that of the school system, the department, and the teachers leading the program. In other words, the resultant curriculum must "fit" within the mission of the school system and reflect an amenable consensus among the professionals who will be charged with the task of implementation.

The development or selection of a curriculum will influence decisions about such elements of the program as methodology, organization, equipment, administration, and staff development. All of these components should be in keeping with the basic beliefs that the group holds. Only then will the physical education program be coherent and effective.

Determination of Objectives

How does a physical education department (or teacher) develop an outstanding curriculum? How does a department or school make the right decisions—the decisions that are right for the teachers, the school, and the district; in selecting or designing a curriculum; establishing instructional methods; and setting organizational policies and procedures?

A successful secondary school program will result only if the individual parts of the program are congruent and articulate well. These components must be consistent with each other and support each other well. It should be obvious that a successful physical education curriculum will not evolve from a policy that addresses each decision individually, on an ad hoc basis. Solid guidelines must be established to set the stage for consistent, congruent, and logical decision making and to prepare the foundation for continual review and analysis of such precepts. Such a situation calls for the development of a philosophy, a system of beliefs about the secondary school physical education program.

The development of a curriculum will influence decisions about other elements of the physical education program including methodology, organization, equipment, administration, and staff development. All of these components should be in keeping with the basic beliefs that the group holds. Only then will the program be coherent and effective.

The process of developing a system of beliefs about physical education of necessity should expose opposing points of view among the curriculum committee members. This is natural and, if committee membership is truly representative, inevitable. The various professionals, having all been prepared in different institutions and trained in various materials, have their own views and causes to champion.

Having different belief systems is useful, particularly in the early stages of the committee's deliberations, for one of the first tasks of the committee is to define and list the questions and issues that need to be answered in a complete statement of beliefs. Some of the issues and concerns will take form more definitely and become more readily apparent when committee members hold different positions. Box 5-3 provides the reader with a list of typical issues, concerns, and problems that a curriculum committee needs to address.

From this analytical group experience and other similar values clarifying activities, a consensus must emerge. The committee cannot progress if some minimal level of agreement is not attained. How long this process takes depends greatly on the committee members' seriousness of purpose and their willingness to compromise when necessary. The quality of the leadership will have a significant impact on this aspect of curriculum development as well. This latter point reaffirms the need to provide qualified and experienced consultants to curriculum planning groups.

The final statement of beliefs will become a basis for decision making by the school or district. The document can serve as the criterion for assessing the existing program. It can be an impetus for change, a guide for choosing a new program, and a standard for measuring progress. It can even be a tool in hiring new staff, because if a candidate cannot subscribe to the beliefs of a school, neither the candidate nor the school is likely to be satisfied.

Another benefit of the philosophical document is that it makes public the direction the program is taking. Staff

BOX 5-3

ASPECTS OF A PHILOSOPHY OF PHYSICAL EDUCATION

1. What is the place of physical education in the educational hierarchy?
2. How important is physical education in relation to other areas of study?
3. What are the purposes of movement, play, and physical education?
4. What is the role of the physical education teacher?
5. What is the role of student decision making in physical education? In athletics? In sport?
6. What is the role of the coach?
7. Curriculum concepts in physical education.
8. The place of enjoyment/fun in physical education.
9. Beliefs related to the teacher-coach role conflict.
10. What is the relationship between health and physical education?
11. Views on athletics and sport for females.
12. Grading in physical education.
13. Behavior management and discipline in physical education.
14. Administrative practice in physical education (style? methods?).
15. Views on intramurals?
16. Views on competition?
17. What is the relationship/role of competition in the instructional program?
18. Views on dance?
19. Views on interscholastic athletics.
20. What is the relationship between interscholastics and the instructional program? Between intramurals and the instructional program? Between athletics and intramurals?

and clients have the opportunity to know before, rather than after the fact, why certain actions are taking place.

Most important, however, the statement of beliefs or philosophy will serve as a guide to action. It will help the school or district to plan, develop, and implement its program in an intelligent, reflective, and consistent manner. The program can be expected to improve, and so can the achievement of the students.

Authorities who have worked extensively with school curriculum groups have discovered that teachers were not inclined to follow the logical-sequential approach. Typically, administrators and teachers, from the outset, addressed the specific content and activities, and they employed nonlinear thinking. Such practitioners dealt with several curricular factors concurrently.[19] Therefore curriculum consultants suggest as an alternative starting point, an analysis of the real-ideal match of the current curriculum as documented in the available written materials and the actual or "live" curriculum, as reflected in current instructional practice.

A comparative analysis of the written versus the taught curriculum could be a fruitful avenue for curriculum planners to explore. The results of such analyses should identify several general and specific courses of action:

1. A need to revise program goals and objectives (the "ideal" program versus the "written" curriculum)
2. A need to modify program activities in light of written curriculum goals (revise "taught" curriculum)
3. A revision, more encompassing, which entails revising selected goals and objectives, as well as selected activities

Once a curriculum planning group has determined its curriculum orientation or education philosophy, several steps become more obvious and emerge to create the next developmental stage in the construction process. These include validating and prioritizing objectives, conducting a needs assessment, and collecting relevant data to select activities.

Validation and prioritization of objectives

The process of determining whether goals and objectives are acceptable as appropriate or "right" for the school system or the physical education program proposing them is known as validation.[20] After goals and objectives have been identified and selected (as a result of the development of an educational philosophy or a curriculum orientation), the curriculum development process should continue to validate these goals and objectives and place them in order of priority.[21]

The determination of priority is actually the placement of the goals and objectives in order of relative importance in the school system. Realistically, the development of a curriculum framework and the clarification of beliefs about secondary physical education should result in a long list of potential curriculum directions. It is impossible for programs of secondary school physical education to address and implement all the objectives determined by the analysis of the wealth of data collected. The proposed objectives must be evaluated in terms of the values (stated or implied) in the philosophies of the district, school, and the department. Objectives that do not match the philosophy should be deleted. Those that match well should be retained. Schools exist in an era of the knowledge explosion, and physical education's knowledge has paralleled such growth. Such an explosion has had an impact on all curriculum ventures and has influenced instructional practice as well. Physical education professionals should utilize flexible curriculum models[17,22] as well as attend to movements such as Sizer's Essential Schools[23] as a way to keep curricular objectives at a manageable level and to assist in the task of prioritization.

Numerous efforts have been made in this vein.[24-30] Results of surveys and interviews with various populations (preservice and in-service teachers, administrators, and parents) revealed that priorities varied within narrow limits, with most individuals more concerned that students learn lifetime fitness concepts, the motor skills related to, and supportive of, participation in lifetime sports, and healthful living knowledge.

Efforts like those just described, whether national, regional, or local in scope, are required to facilitate endeavors to rank, order, or prioritize program objectives. Curriculum designers must plan on gathering similar information or data in an effort to clarify and resolve issues related to program emphasis and preparing comprehensive lists of ranked objectives.

The task of prioritization can be facilitated if the curriculum committee can establish clear criteria for this purpose. Pratt[21] suggests that curriculum objectives should meet the following criteria: objectives should (1) identify learning outcomes, (2) be consistent with the curriculum aim, (3) be precise, (4) be feasible, (5) be functional, (6) be significant, and (7) be appropriate.

Various groups concerned about the educational system should be enlisted to help identify suitable goals and objectives and to set priorities.[20] That the goals and objectives should be submitted by the curriculum developers to a broad sampling of groups is good practice. It is vitally important that the goals of a school curriculum be validated, prioritized, and ranked. This can be accomplished by submitting the curriculum to a sizable number of educators and noneducators for review. Such a sampling should include (1) lay persons, (2) parents, (3) students, (4) teachers, (5) administrators, and (6) curriculum specialists. The curriculum committee must endeavor to discover whether consensus and agreement exist about the goals formulated and what the priorities of the respective groups are. Data thereby generated should be analyzed by a committee representative of the various groups surveyed.

The curriculum committee has the critical responsibility of attempting to reach consensus among its own members about the goals and objectives under consideration. The curriculum planners must decide—based on data collected, opinions reviewed, and the polling of curriculum specialists—which goals are valid and which are to be assigned priority. To set priorities is to claim that some goals or objectives are more important than others and deserve more time, attention, and emphasis in the program.[20]

Needs assessment

Whether the logical-sequential strategy is used or an alternative, reality-based, pragmatic approach is employed, the next step mandates the collection, analysis, and assessment of relevant data. This stage of curriculum development is known as a *needs assessment*. According to Oliva,[19] ". . . a needs assessment is a process for identifying programmatic needs that must be addressed by program planners." Kaufman[31] defines needs assessment as the "process of identifying gaps between what is and what should be." The needs assessment process, as clarified by English and Kaufman,[22] results in the delineation and specification of the desired ends or outcomes of a curriculum.[20] They continue and offer several other insights into the needs assessment process.

A needs assessment:

◆ Identifies what schooling should be and how it can be assessed.

◆ Can result in a set of criteria by which curricula may be developed and compared.

◆ Can facilitate the validation of objectives.

◆ Can identify the gaps between current outcomes and desired results, and can prioritize these gaps.

Why should a curriculum planning group invest time and energy in the completion of a needs assessment? Based on the previous suggestions, a needs assessment is required to answer the following questions:

◆ What is going on at the present time?

◆ What does the current curriculum accomplish?

◆ What is not addressed in the current plan?

◆ How satisfied are the students? Parents? Taxpayers? Administrators? The community?

◆ What are the perceptions of the curriculum held by the various groups?

◆ What does the evaluative data (formative, summative) suggest, if available?

◆ What does the professional literature recommend?

Additional information that will assist curriculum planners to assess needs can be derived by a careful analysis of the items indicated in Box 5-4.

A thorough needs assessment should address information related to the environment, the school, the learners, and the subject matter and how it is learned. Specific aspects of each area are discussed more thoroughly in the next section.

Environment

The curriculum committee should review the social forces that have an impact on students and the school curriculum. Such national trends as increased frequency of one-parent families, substance use and abuse, and increased leisure time must be assessed in light of their influence at the local and community level.

Local resources and interests also have an impact on curriculum developers. A determination must be made of the local commitment and level of support for program modifications related to athletics, fitness, and lifestyle change. Committee members must discern whether local resources will support recreation and athletic opportunities for the disabled, quality instructional and intramural programs, and a balanced interscholastic program. A comprehensive survey of local interests and needs should be taken. The survey results assessment should reveal information about the various items indicated in Box 5-4.

BOX 5-4

ASPECTS OF A NEEDS ASSESSMENT

The Community

1. Community history
2. Philosophy of local population
3. Community willingness to support education and the physical education program
4. Fiscal status (major industries, businesses; average household income; unemployment rate)
5. Ethnic identity, racial composition
6. Religious orientation
7. Educational background, average level of education
8. Demographic trends, population trends
9. Geography (weather patterns)
10. Setting (urban, rural, suburban)
11. Resources (institutions of higher education, public libraries, parks, playgrounds, swimming pools, resorts, commercial recreation clubs, etc.)
12. Community activities, pastimes, leisure pursuits

The Students

1. Ethnic identity
2. Eligibility for federal or state assistance
3. Parents' occupations
4. Academic abilities
5. Talents, skills, special interests
6. School achievement (standardized test scores, curriculum referenced test scores)
7. Fitness scores, motor ability test results
8. English proficiency, native language
9. Limitations (physical, emotional, learning abilities)
10. Career and educational aspirations
11. Extracurricular activities, participation/involvement rates

The Faculty

1. Subjects and grades certified/licensed to teach
2. Age, gender ratios, experience
3. Present assignments (instructional, intramural, interscholastic)
4. Special interests and skills
5. Recent professional development (coursework, workshops, conferences attended)
6. Philosophy of education and of physical education
7. Morale

School

Several factors influence the resources in schools, which in turn, have an impact on the physical education curriculum. Specifically, items such as finances (the operating budget and salaries), faculty and staff (number, philosophy, and morale), equipment and facilities (type, location, number, size, and portability), district, school, and department policies (student behavior and administrative policies), and the total school curriculum (schedule and time distribution) all directly or indirectly affect the physical education curriculum.

Learners

The characteristics and needs of students should be the primary source of goals and curricular objectives in a physical education program. Information outlined and discussed in Chapter 2, which relates to the interests, needs, and abilities of the secondary school student, should guide the program planners in their efforts to understand the learner and to design appropriate curricula.

Embarking on this stage of development is quite an undertaking. Curriculum authorities strongly suggest that homework be assigned, projects be cooperatively addressed, and work groups be assembled (probably in addition to the original curriculum committee) to ensure an adequate completion of these difficult, often arduous, yet invaluable undertakings. It is important to reiterate the need for the administration's support, in various forms (time, clerical assistance, fiscal resources, and consultant services). Such support will often be the determining factor as to the effectiveness and results of the committee's work.

In addition, the issue of ownership, so important in any curriculum revision, is critical to the future implementation of the written document. Those professionals who will be responsible for implementation must invest in and be committed to the curriculum. By cooperating in the design and construction of the curriculum, professionals are more likely to view the curriculum as something they helped to create, will be more likely to believe in it, and are more likely to attempt to implement it as it was formed, rather than attempt to subvert or circumvent its intentions.

Selection of activities to be included within the curriculum should reflect the goals and objectives of the program and the students' needs.

Courtesy of Ben Lombardo, Rhode Island College, Providence, RI.

Activity selection

The next step in the curriculum development process is the selection of learning experiences and activities that will facilitate the achievement of the desired outcomes by the students. For example, if a curriculum objective states, "Students will demonstrate an intermediate level of proficiency in a lifetime activity," teachers and curriculum planners need to provide the conditions, instructional environment, and specific activities to nurture the students' accomplishment of the objective.

The essence of this stage of curriculum construction is the determination of the selection and organization of the physical education content. In the sections to come, design features that contribute to the creation and implementation of quality physical education programs (for example, the congruence between the end of a previous learning sequence and those scheduled next; the relationship among lesson objectives, methods employed by the teacher, and supportive learning resources, equipment, and supplies such as media, practice jerseys, field markers, and work sheets) will be addressed. Specifically, the concepts of scope and sequence, as applied to the physical education curriculum, will be examined.

Scope

The scope of the physical education curriculum refers to the spectrum of exposures to the content deemed important to the accomplishment of educational goals. In physical education, the scope of the program would include every activity that is thought to contribute to the students' attainment of curricular objectives. The determination of the extent and depth of content coverage (scope) is a major function of the curriculum committee and, given the rapid pace of social and cultural change, is a challenging task. The modification of school curricula must attempt to keep pace with the accelerated pace of educational changes and the growth of knowledge in physical education and related fields (for example, sports psychology, biomechanics, and pedagogy). Professionals would do well to employ flexible curricular models for use of instructional time and to identify a feasible set of essential objectives, which can be realistically addressed, given current constraints on school time.

Scope decisions relate to the entire secondary school curriculum (grades 9 to 12) and relate to the content elements in physical education that should be included at each grade level and how much time should be allocated to each. Table 5-1 provides the reader with a scope and sequence chart typically found in physical education curricular documents. Additional examples of scope and sequence charts can be found in Chapters 4 and 6.

State legislation or board of education policy decisions often inform or mandate scope decisions. Such dictates may require that certain instructional time or an exact number of minutes per week be devoted to specific content or particular types of learning activities. For example,

TABLE 5-1

Typical Scope and Sequence Chart in Physical Education

Activity	Team	Individual	Lifetime	Grade Level 9	10	11	12
Aquatics		X	X	X	X	X	X
Archery		X	X			X	X
Badminton		X	X			X	X
Basketball	X			X	X		
Bowling		X	X			X	X
Creative movement		X	X			X	X
Cycling		X	X			X	X
Dance aerobics		X	X	X	X	X	X
Dance/rhythms		X	X	X	X		
Fencing		X	X			X	X
Field hockey	X			X	X		
Golf		X	X			X	X
Gymnastics		X		X	X	X	X
Team handball	X			X	X		
Orienteering		X	X			X	X
Self-defense		X	X			X	X
Soccer/speedball	X			X	X		
Softball	X			X	X		
Tennis		X	X			X	X
Track and field		X		X	X	X	X
Volleyball	X		X	X	X		
Weight training		X	X	X	X	X	X
Wrestling		X		X	X		

the Rhode Island Department of Education mandates that students participate an average of 20 minutes each day in health and physical education.[15]

However, physical education teachers almost always have some control over the scope of the subject matter they address, regardless of how district or state level scope decisions are made. Teachers make many decisions on a day-to-day basis about how much material to cover related to a specific activity or topic, and how much to expect of learners as a result of instruction on this topic. For example, at the level of an individual class, physical education teachers may implement their scope priorities by preparing a larger number of or more specific learning objectives for the volleyball unit, when contrasted with the expectations and planned outcomes of the dance aerobics unit. A larger number of objectives will guide planning that can assure more breadth and depth of coverage of these priority areas.[32]

Scope-related decisions are particularly potent because they have a direct impact on instructional time. When teachers or curriculum designers decide to expand opportunities in one area, time must be taken away from the instructional time in another. In this way, scope decisions involve important value choices, significantly influencing views relative to the merits of learning experiences.

Sequence

The sequencing of learning experiences relates to the underlying logic on which specific units or courses of study are arranged. When the subject matter has been appropriately structured in a hierarchical order, it can be stated by program planners that a relevant sequence exists. Sequence decisions attempt to provide continuity and progression within and between learning units and from year to year.

In public educational systems, curriculum committees, including curriculum specialists and administrators, will often be responsible for determining which courses and learning experiences must precede others. However, even within individual lessons and classes, physical education teachers regularly make decisions about the order of the lesson.

Sequencing decisions are important in the physical education curriculum. Nixon and Jewett[33] believe that sequencing issues are often at the root of criticisms often leveled at physical education programs, specifically citing the repetition of a restricted few activities from year to year, and mindless seasonal rotation of traditional sport units.

Typically within the physical education curriculum, some sequencing decisions are almost self-identifying because tradition, difficulty, or the logic of the content suggests an ordering that few will challenge. For example, few would dispute the need for a beginning level of skill and knowledge of swimming before embarking on an intermediate or advanced course of study.

In other cases the sequence decisions are not so clear. Some instructional experiences are more or less freestanding and depend more on general motor development and understanding rather than on the mastery of specific and critical prerequisite content (cycling, hiking, weight training, cross-country running, the standing long jump).

Traditionally, the sequencing of content in physical education emerges from progressions derived from analyses of various forms of activities (dance, team/individual sports, and gymnastics) specifically related to specific motor skills required, difficulty, and complexity. Teachers commonly employ such information in conjunction with current data pertaining to age-appropriate standards and typical developmental levels for comparable populations, readily available in the professional literature. These techniques for ordering the learning experiences within a curriculum appear to be the usual approaches employed by physical education teachers, as evidenced by a review of curricular documents within the discipline of physical education. Material presented in Chapter 8, related to the enhancement of skill acquisition, can assist physical education teachers in their endeavor to sequence learning experiences appropriately for students.

Continuity and articulation

Continuity and articulation are critical dimensions of sequencing in that they are potent factors that have a significant impact on curriculum development. While sequencing is the logical arrangement of subject matter within units, courses, and grades, continuity refers to efforts to associate prior learning to present subject matter as well as present lesson content to anticipated future topics. Articulation, on the other hand, is the planned sequencing of units from one grade level to the next to assure that the next grade level takes up where the previous grade level left off.[19] For example, experiences in the tenth grade fitness unit should be related to and contiguous to those of the eleventh grade fitness unit, and be based on the learnings accomplished in the ninth grade unit. It certainly would be an ineffectual curriculum that provided the same learning experiences or the same content at each grade level.

In the secondary program, continuity and articulation concerns arise specifically from the need to coordinate prior learning that takes place in the elementary and middle-school programs with those at the secondary level. Furthermore, careful attention must be directed to correlate learning experiences in the physical education curriculum between the high-school grades.

The concepts of continuity and articulation suggest a need for instruction to be organized so that the ending points of a set of learning experiences mesh well with the beginning points of the next one. For example, a class that has just finished a unit on the physiological bases of physical fitness could logically move to units such as aerobic fitness or weight training, which relate well to, and could serve as an arena for, direct and immediate application of knowledge and skills studied previously. However, in contrast, curricula that move students from one activity to another, for example, soccer to volleyball, often do not manifest continuity, appropriate sequencing, or an apparent logic to students, thereby creating the potential for confusion.

Curriculum planners must attend to these aspects of sequencing if new or revised programs are to better serve students. In addition, a well-planned, clearly articulated curriculum will do much to convey a clear sense of purpose to the community and thereby do much to gain the confidence of the public.

In this latter endeavor, Berg's[9] call for a concerted effort to design a national curriculum makes much sense. If for no other purpose than to serve as a model of a properly conceived, logically focused, sequential, and well-articulated secondary school physical education curriculum for planners across the nation, the results of such efforts could contribute much to legitimize and gain support for secondary physical education programs. In this way major criticisms regularly directed at physical education can be addressed and responded to in a meaningful manner. Physical education professionals will be in a stronger position to respond to criticism and will be better prepared to enhance learning in physical education.

Curriculum implementation

The next step, once a curriculum document has been prepared, is a crucial one. The production of a curriculum guide or the written curriculum is not the final stage in the process, as many feel it is. Rather, implementation of the curriculum or, as some state, "bringing the curriculum to life" comes next. Moreover, unless careful steps are taken to support such implementation via regular and appropriate staff development activities, change will not occur. Rather, the new program will be consigned to the proverbial circular file!

As stated previously, neither the production of the curriculum document nor the implementation of it should signify the end of the curriculum development process. It is critical at the point of implementation to select judiciously a school or grade that could serve as an appropriate field test site. After selecting a field testing site, plans must be devised to formatively monitor and assess the implementation of the program.

The curriculum committee would do well to select a school or program that presents the best opportunity to successfully implement and demonstrate the effectiveness of the new program, as intended by its designers. This process of selection should include consideration of the personnel who will be in charge of the program. The

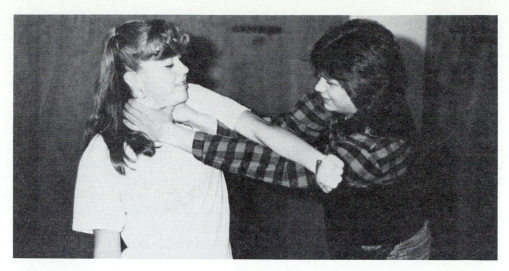

Self-defense is a popular offering within the secondary school physical education curriculum.
Courtesy of Suzi D'Annalfo, Conard High School, West Hartford, CT.

chances of success, obviously, will be dramatically maximized if competent teachers can be utilized to implement the new program. Later on, these competent physical education teachers could well be employed to assist others (to facilitate staff development).

A common error in judgment made by ambitious, overzealous curriculum developers is to implement widely a new or revised program. For several reasons, this usually constrains continued development or refinement with the new curriculum initiatives.

One problem resulting from a decision to implement widely a program still in its infancy relates to staff development. A new or revised curriculum implies the need for change. Virgilio[34] suggests that this is often a major weakness in curriculum development endeavors in physical education. Most professionals, novice or experienced, require guidance and assistance as they progress through change. Those initiating or mandating the curriculum development process (curriculum directors and principals) must include the funding, time, and access to consultant services required to support professionals through this often anxiety-provoking, if not threatening, process of professional change. Adding to an often frustrating process, such as curriculum development, is the infrequent or insufficient systematic help provided either in understanding the rationale for the changes or in the development of specific instructional strategies which might facilitate and enhance the acceptance, the understanding, and the implementation of the program changes. Staff development activities must be provided for (for example, in-service training, access to knowledgeable consultants, and consultation with program designers).

A second potential problem can emerge if the curriculum committee recommends implementation too widely. The assessment process could be greatly inhibited, because the implemented changes must be accomplished carefully and meticulously, results noted, and data collected and analyzed to facilitate further modifications, revisions, and fine-tuning. Vogel and Seefeldt[11] recommend this pilot testing approach before a more all-encompassing systemwide attempt at implementation is made.

An additional benefit can emerge if systems employ a cautious approach to program implementation. By employing a conservative approach, the number of individuals familiar with the new program will be increased gradually (that is, with program developers and professionals implementing the changes). The teachers actually involved in the first wave of implementation can become additional, in-house resources for professionals whose involvement will take place in the later rounds of implementation. They, in effect, can become "turnkey" trainers, who can become useful in the process of staff development. Also, the initial group of professionals involved in the implementation stage can serve others by providing a live demonstration of the new curriculum. As such, these teachers and the pilot program can serve as a visual model for those professionals who will be asked to implement the program at a later time and a source of valuable experience related to the curricular revamping.

As suggested previously, the evaluative stage should commence almost simultaneously with the implementation stage of curriculum development. Program planners need to assess the program based on a comparative analysis of educational outcomes with the program objectives. The basic question at this point is, "Does the implementation of the intervention (revisions or new curriculum) result in student achievement of the stated objectives?"[11]

The curriculum committee should follow up this assessment of the initial field testing site with program revisions as indicated, and implement the program in another setting with similar opportunities and prerequisites (such as competent personnel and positive educational circumstances) to achieve success. Staff development and support services must be continued concurrently with these activities. Replication continues in this manner, with continued assessment, revision, support services, and in-service educational opportunities, until the entire system has implemented the program.[11]

The evaluative process continues with a systemwide assessment that is scheduled to determine the effectiveness of the program at a broader, all-inclusive scale. While this may suggest a finality to the process of curriculum building, this is not the case. Curriculum evaluation should be a continual process, and professionals should assume that the curriculum is perpetually changing. It is a serious professional error to even assume that the ultimate in curriculum has been achieved. Students change continually; the professional staff regularly fluctuates, resulting in a varied combination of skills and abilities at any one point in time; society is always moving ahead and evolving; and all of these factors must be reflected in the curriculum. Such variables, impermanent as they may be and which of necessity have an impact on instructional practice and curricular endeavors, mandate that curricula be continually reviewed for development and revision.

Evaluation of the curriculum

In the previous section, reference was made several times to the evaluation process as it pertains to the implementation stage of curriculum development. Indeed, the process of bringing a new curriculum or program revision to life must be accomplished concurrently with the imposition of a well-conceived monitoring system of evaluation. Curriculum monitoring is the attempt to ensure that the new program is actually employed in the recommended manner. Those implementing the new program should be working toward the goals and objectives delineated in the new curriculum. Specifically, the task is to appraise the extent to which, through curricular activities, the program and faculty make good on their promise in the way of pupil growth and development.[1] In this section the process of determining the effectiveness of a new program or curricular initiative will be reviewed.

Evaluation must be viewed by all concerned parties as a formative, continual, and ever-evolving process. When curriculum evaluation is perceived as a one-time, summative process, it reveals a program philosophy that will fail to maintain its support, will fall short of its goals, and will quickly become irrelevant.

For the purposes of this section, curriculum evaluation will be directed to evaluation of the set of educational experiences offered at a particular level of schooling (for example, high school), or at a systemwide level, in a particular discipline (such as physical education).[35] This process should include an extensive review of all the critical elements of the curriculum: the students, the program, the teachers, instructional practices, and facilities. Concepts and factors introduced and discussed previously in this chapter (the development of a curriculum orientation and the completion of a thorough needs assessment) should be relied on to provide the program data, qualitative and quantitative insights, and other information required to complete a meaningful and complete evaluation of the curriculum changes designed.

Those responsible for evaluation should generate a comprehensive list of evaluation questions. These questions should be used to survey administrators, supervisors, and teachers. The curriculum leadership team should review the results of such data collection and identify the evaluation issues to be addressed. This approach should produce a comprehensive yet manageable set of evaluative concerns.

The results of the evaluation process (the data collection) should inform the curriculum committee of the need for change and the extent of change required in the curriculum. Decisions regarding a major overhaul, minor revisions, or refinement would thus be made. It must be emphasized that evaluations should be made regularly and should be considered a task to be addressed continually. Second, the evaluation must be viewed as an ever-evolving process through the K-12 curriculum. Regular efforts should be made to ensure congruence, articulation, and proper sequencing throughout the total program. Such a practice will maintain the rigor, effectiveness, and relevance of the curriculum.

Several approaches, both qualitative and quantitative, can be employed to facilitate the data collection and information-generating process that are critical in completing the evaluation. Surveys, rating scales, questionnaires, and checklists can be devised and employed to provide relevant information to those charged with monitoring and supervising the new program.

Data derived from the application of a variety of these techniques should indicate the extent to which the students' needs are met; the strengths and weaknesses of the program objectives; the quality of instruction; the qualitative and quantitative degree of students' achievement; and whether there is effective utilization of staff, facilities, and equipment.[1]

After such data is collected, a thorough analysis must occur using appropriate statistical methods. Then the curriculum assessment team must interpret the results in light of the aforementioned curricular standards. That is, the curriculum committee must determine if the data collected and analyzed indicate achievement of the desired objectives.

Finally, decisions concerning the program relative to effectiveness, strengths, weaknesses, and revisions must be made. The degree to which standards have been met or objectives achieved will influence the recommendations put forth by the assessment team. When, as it usually happens, some of the objectives have been achieved, decisions will need to be made concerning whether the objectives are valid, whether the program can be further revised or modified in some way to achieve the objectives, or whether to adopt yet another approach.

Recommendations emanating from this process provide a basis for administrative action as to further implementation, modification, or revision. The outcome of the appraisal process, with specific recommendations, must be communicated to all interested and concerned parties.

SUMMARY

The curriculum has been, is, and will remain a focus of attention for educational reformers, concerned citizens, business leaders, parents, students, and teachers. At the present time, the public is demanding more rigorous standards for all students and more comprehensive and complex programs. Performance expectations are being raised, while simultaneously the student population is becoming more diverse and problematic than ever before, thereby requiring broader, more intensive, and improved services. Added to these circumstances is the rapid pace of social and cultural change, which requires that schools and programs change at comparable rates. When students change, societal forces change. Constituents supporting education change and therefore school programs must reflect and respond to such changes as well. A curriculum that is not continually changing, maturing, and growing in response to such forces soon becomes outdated and indefensible. Systematic curriculum development in physical education can and should be an instrument, not only to respond to such initiatives for change, but also to facilitate specific program revisions.

FOR REVIEW

1. With the help of the information provided in Box 5-1, describe your curriculum orientation.
2. In your opinion, what factors have the greatest impact on curriculum development? On curriculum implementation?
3. To what extent is it essential for teachers to agree with the philosophy of the school (or school system) in which they teach?
4. What makes an effective secondary school physical education curriculum? Be prepared to defend your position.
5. Examine various curriculum guides from different school systems. Describe the differences and similarities among the guides reviewed. Describe the curriculum orientation and program emphasis of each guide.
6. Suppose you were charged with the responsibility of evaluating a secondary school physical education program. What kinds of evaluation data would you seek? How would you gather data? When would you be satisfied that you had enough information? Prepare an evaluation plan in the form of a written report and present it to your instructor for review.

REFERENCES

1. Annarino A, Cowell C, Hazleton HW: *Curriculum theory and design in physical education,* ed 2, Prospect Heights, Ill, 1980, Waveland Press.
2. Gallup A, Elam S: The 20th annual Gallup poll, *Phi Delta Kappan* 70(1):33-46, 1988.
3. Gallup A, Elam S: The 21st annual Gallup poll, *Phi Delta Kappan* 71(1):41-54, 1989.
4. Locke L: Analysis and discussion: what can we do? *JOPERD* 57(4):60-63, 1986.
5. Zais R: Conceptions of curriculum and the curriculum field. In Giroux H, Penna A, Pinar W, editors: *Curriculum and instruction: alternatives in education,* Berkeley, Calif, 1981, McCutcheon Publishing.
6. Walker D, Soltis J: *Curriculum and aims,* New York, 1986, Teachers College Press.
7. Tyler R: *Basic principles of curriculum and instruction,* Chicago, 1950, University of Chicago Press.
8. Walker D: The process of curriculum development: a naturalistic model, *School Review* 80:51-65, 1971.
9. Berg K: A national curriculum in physical education, *JOPERD* 59(8):70-75, 1988.
10. Wessel J, Kelly L: *Achievement-based curriculum development in physical education,* Philadelphia, 1986, Lea & Febiger.
11. Vogel P, Seefeldt V: Redesign of physical education programs: a procedural model that leads to defensible programs, *JOPERD* 58(7):65-69, 1987.
12. Miller J: *The educational spectrum: orientations to curriculum,* New York, 1983, Longman.
13. Franck M: Physical education outcomes project making progress, *UPDATE* 9:9, 1989.
14. Placek J: A multicase study of teacher planning in physical education, *JOTPE* 4:39-49, 1984.
15. Rhode Island Department of Education: *Basic education program for RI public schools,* Providence, RI, 1983, Rhode Island Department of Education.
16. Anderson W: Curriculum and program research in physical education: selected approaches, *JOTPE* 8(2):113-122, 1989.
17. Kelly L: Curriculum design model: a university-public school cooperative model for designing a district-wide elementary physical education curriculum, *JOPERD* 59(6):26-32, 1988.
18. Anderson W: Preparing and using the written curriculum, *JOPERD* 59(2):67-72, 1988.
19. Oliva P: *Developing the curriculum,* ed 2, Glenview, Ill, 1988, Scott, Foresman.
20. English F, Kaufman R: *Needs assessment: a focus for curriculum development,* Washington, DC, 1975, Association for Supervision and Curriculum Development.
21. Pratt D: *Curriculum: design and development,* New York, 1980, Harcourt Brace Jovanovich.
22. Harrison J, Blakemore C: *Instructional strategies for secondary school physical education,* ed 3, 1992, Dubuque, Iowa, William C Brown.
23. Sizer T: Putting ideas into practice: an interview with Ted Sizer, *Harvard Educational Letter* IV(4):5-7, 1988.
24. Arrighi M: Learning in the gymnasium: teacher perspectives, *The Physical Educator* 43(3):137-140, 1986.
25. Loper D et al: Healthful living the goal: physical education the means? *JOPERD* 60(2):58-61, 1989.
26. Hedlund R: Kansas secondary physical education teachers ranking of the goals of physical education. In Carre F, Mordy A, editors: *Teacher and teaching in physical education: proceedings of the 1986 international conference on research in teacher education and teaching in physical education,* Vancouver, 1988, University of British Columbia, *JOPERD* 60(5):8, 1989.
27. Petrakis E, Newman I, LeGrande J: Nebraskans' perceptions of physical education, *Nebraska Journal* 16(1):7-9, 1985.

28. Austin D, Novak N: Lincoln public school needs assessment survey. Healthful living the goal: physical education the means? *JOPERD* 60(2):58-61, 1987.

29. Hetherington C: The school program in physical education, Yonkers-on-the-Hudson, NY, 1922, World Book Company. In Colfer G, et al (editors): *Contemporary physical education,* Dubuque, Iowa, 1986, William C Brown.

30. Colfer G et al: *Contemporary physical education,* Dubuque, Iowa, 1986, William C Brown.

31. Kaufman R: Needs assessment. In English F, editor: *Fundamental curriculum decisions,* Alexandria, Va, 1982, Association for Supervision and Curriculum Development.

32. Armstrong D: *Developing and documenting the curriculum,* Boston, 1989, Allyn and Bacon.

33. Nixon J, Jewett A: *An introduction to physical education,* Philadelphia, 1980, WB Saunders.

34. Virgilio S: A paradigm for curriculum implementation, *JOTPE* 4:57-63, 1984.

35. Glatthorn A: *Curriculum leadership,* Glenview, Ill, 1987, Scott, Foresman.

ANNOTATED READINGS

Anderson W: Preparing and using the written curriculum, *JOPERD* 59(2):67-72, 1988.

This article reports on the work of The Physical Education Program Development Center, at Teachers' College, Columbia University, with several school districts focused on updating and rewriting curriculum plans. Anderson shares the successes and the setbacks and presents many relevant ideas for curriculum development. Suggestions are pertinent to physical education teachers and supervisors, as well as school administrators.

Harrington W: Making it happen: connecting theory and practice, *JOPERD* 55(6):32-33, 1984.

The purpose of this article is to provide guiding questions and activities to facilitate making necessary connections between curriculum theory and practice. Harrington makes a strong pitch for asserting the unique and important contribution teachers who face the students every day can make to the curriculum development process.

Vogel P, Seefeldt V: Redesign of physical education programs: a procedural model that leads to defensible programs, *JOPERD* 58(7):65-69, 1987.

This article describes a twelve-step procedural model for curriculum development. The model employs programmatic needs as the foundation upon which to design the program, with a concurrent emphasis on inservice education. This very explicit and well-documented work puts forth a well-conceived plan for curriculum change and makes a strong case for long-term cooperative efforts between public schools and college/university faculty.

CHAPTER 6

Instructional Planning: Translating Curriculum into Practice

CHAPTER OBJECTIVES

◆ To describe the process by which goals for secondary school physical education are identified and specified

◆ To describe procedures that facilitate the translation of the secondary school physical education curriculum into appropriate annual, unit, and lesson plans

◆ To describe a process for analyzing motor tasks and activities

Planning is an important pedagogical function that enhances instructional practice and teachers' satisfaction and, quite possibly, motivation. Teaching can be extremely satisfying for many, and regular observance of students' growth in many areas attributable to the teachers' endeavors can be a continuing source of joy. The administration of well-designed lessons, which nurture students' potential, can be tremendously rewarding. The formulation of meaningful and effective plans, including the identification of relevant objectives, will maximize students' engagement time and will ensure student achievement. In effect then, diligent planning not only can contribute significantly to student development, but can also have an impact on teachers' satisfaction from their professional endeavors.

In view of the often cited criticisms directed at secondary school physical education, planning becomes even more significant. A commonly voiced criticism relates to the outcomes attributed to secondary school physical education. Recently critics have suggested that the educational value of secondary school programs is overrated and that students could easily do without such programs. The public in general is confused about the purpose and contributions of high-school movement programs, often equating them with athletics. Students also have difficulty discerning the differences between instructional and interscholastic programs. Professionals also disagree about the purposes of secondary programs, often rationalizing their existence based on the instructional programs' contributions to athletic programs.

With such issues and problems placing the secondary physical education teacher regularly on the defensive and often influencing the conduct of secondary programs, the role of instructional planning takes on even greater importance. The ability to translate the curriculum into meaningful learning experiences and to address concurrently the many dimensions of the student should be central concerns of teachers in secondary schools.

This chapter will address the conversion of the instructional process into meaningful learning experience for students by focusing on the many and varied aspects of the planning process. Specifically, the establishment of goals for the secondary program will be reviewed, the types of plans usually found in schools will be described, and a systematic approach to analyzing motor tasks and activities will be presented.

PLANNING PROCESS

In response to the many calls for change in the secondary physical education curriculum, legislators, taxpayers, professionals in physical education, and curriculum specialists have identified demands for accountability, that is, evidence that teachers and programs are accomplishing what they claim to be achieving. The call for accountability, although not a new phenomenon, has led to curricular efforts typified by programs that lean heavily on behavioral objectives, the precise specification and measurement of outcomes, and performance-based instructional programs.

The curriculum—the course of study in physical education—is the vehicle by which teachers facilitate student achievement. Central to the instructional endeavor, which includes implementation of the physical education curriculum, is the planning process.

Pedagogical responsibilities of the high-school physical education teacher include planning for appropriate instruction[1]:

Planning can help maximize instructional time and have a positive effect on student learning by helping physical educators reduce the time spent on managerial tasks, while increasing the time spent on productive behaviors. Physical educators must spend time planning so that they use their instructional time wisely.

Planning can be time consuming (especially for novice teachers) and usually requires some time outside the confines of the school day. Teachers who are reflective, who possess a significant level of professionalism, and certainly those who care for their students invest much time in anticipating, reflecting on, and planning for their instructional assignments. This does not necessarily mean long, written lesson plans. Depending on the professional maturity of the instructor (preservice, novice, or experienced), written plans will vary. Typically, preservice teachers, novice teachers, teachers unsure about their abilities, or teachers who possess little confidence about their teaching assignment require much more active reflection about their lessons, and this typically translates into more precisely written plans. As physical education teachers gain in confidence with the subject matter and their pedagogical skills, the length, intensity, and depth of the planning usually decrease.

While planning is an essential competency for all teachers to possess, planning alone will not guarantee effective teaching or positive instructional endeavors. While it is safe to say that all effective teachers execute a variety of planning functions before confronting the teaching assignment, planning skills alone cannot convert an ineffective teacher to one who is effective.

What exactly should be included in the planning process? What procedures are encompassed in sound planning? To be thorough and to design instruction congruent with curricular beliefs, planning should include goal setting (selection and identification of goals): identification and preparation of objectives (both instructional and student performance objectives); and development of annual, unit, and lesson plans. The flow or sequence of the planning process is depicted in Fig. 6-1.

Each stage in the flow of activities is predicated on and directly influenced by the completion of the specific planning tasks that precede it. In other words, the identification and preparation of instructional objectives must await the identification of program goals, and student behavioral objectives should be prepared only after the teacher has selected instructional objectives. To do otherwise would incur the risk of destroying the congruence between adjacent planning components and the inherent logic of the process. The planning process has as its purpose the articulation of the student's involvement with the subject matter and the efforts of the teacher. Such a three-pronged interaction requires much reflection and insight by the professional directly involved to ensure student achievement. It is in this way that the planning process can enhance the pedagogical endeavor and affect student achievement.

The purpose of planning is to promote purposeful and consistent action so that the instruction is efficiently conducted with minimal interruption of the education process. Plans should be vehicles that guide the presentation of movement experiences to ensure sequence and organization. In the sections that follow, each specific component of the planning process will be examined and procedures for development discussed.

Goal Setting

The essence of the planning process centers about the ability to select and establish goals and priorities for secondary school physical education. While much rhetoric clouds this process, the act of specification is truly at the heart of the planning process. While goal setting can be arduous and a struggle at times, there is nothing that will inhibit an instructional program more than a lack of clarity about the direction or goal desired.

Factors influencing goal setting. The process of goal setting is influenced by several factors, including (1) the perceived general values of secondary school physical education; (2) the role of physical education within the general school curriculum; (3) the needs, interests, and characteristics of the learners; and (4) the conception of physical education held by the faculty.

Goals selected must be congruent with the general education aims and purposes of the school system and the community. In effect, then, the goal-setting process should result in a confluence of ideas related to beliefs, needs, and characteristics of students, the community, the value orientation of the local educational institution,

1. Goal —— 2. Objectives —— 3. Annual —— 4. Unit —— 5. Lesson —— 6. Lesson
   Setting   Identification   Plan   Plan   Plan   Execution
                and
                Preparation

FIG. 6-1 The flow of planning tasks.

and the faculty's conception of the role of physical education within the broader, more general school curriculum.

The responsibility for bringing the curriculum to life rests with the secondary school practitioner. Therefore it is imperative for curriculum builders and teachers charged with the task of administering programs to develop a clear notion of the outcomes of such processes. Questions that should be addressed (and periodically revisited) by teachers concerned with curriculum planning are the following: What skills, abilities, knowledges, and attitudes should the secondary school student possess at the various stages of secondary school? At graduation? Can the faculty describe a physically educated high-school graduate? A physically educated adult? What must a physically educated high-school graduate be able to do in the future to ensure an active, healthy lifestyle?

The responses to these and similar questions and the accompanying analysis will facilitate the goal-setting process by establishing broadly painted guidelines for future delineation and action. Goal statements should be broad, generally stated educational outcomes, so as to provide general direction and guidance to the program. Examples of well-prepared goals can be seen in a position paper produced by NASPE in 1986 entitled: *Guidelines for Secondary School Physical Education.* One such goal states, "The instructional program should provide students with opportunities to develop and refine movement skills in a wide range of activities beyond the exposure level."[2]

The previous goal is effective because it provides general guidelines that can assist teachers to develop effective, comprehensive programs of secondary school physical education.

Once the selection, identification, and establishment of such goals have been completed, more specific instructional and behavioral objectives can be identified. Of course these objectives would be directly related to the exact nature of the goals selected and provide guidance and direction at a more specific level. Before examining commonly suggested goals for secondary school physical education, it would be helpful to keep in mind four basic guidelines that should be of assistance in the establishment of goals.

Goal-setting guidelines. *Goals must be clearly identified and should be understood by the students, the community, and the administrators.* All those concerned with or participating in physical education should have a clear understanding of the purpose of the program and the benefits and values resulting from such curricula. Carefully prepared goals should elicit immediate recognition of their present and future importance from students and others.

Because students are at the center of the curriculum and the primary concern of the instructor, they should be reminded regularly of the goals of the program. An ongoing dialogue between students and teachers about the relationship between the various learning experiences and the program goals will (1) enhance motivation and interest by clarifying goals and thereby enhance student goal setting and (2) respond effectively to the students' search for relevance and meaningfulness. This search, characteristic of adolescent behavior, is manifested in efforts to relate personally to all their activities, including those in the physical education program. Such a dialogue may, at times, range from simple (and quite repetitive) explanations to more complex, sometimes impassioned, justifications of the program.

Goals should be relevant to society, education, and the student. As discussed in Chapters 1 to 3, the aims or statements of goals should be grounded in and mirror society at large, as reflected in the local community, the local educational agency, and the characteristics of the student population. Physical education teachers will be remiss if they fail to consider these factors in their curricular endeavors. Each community, for example, has unique characteristics and patterns that need to be recognized by curriculum planners. This becomes readily apparent when educators examine, for example, school districts as to their tax base, indoor and outdoor facilities, the student population's employment needs, local geography, and differing community interest and participation in recreational activities. Physical education teachers need to attend to such information and plan accordingly.

Goals should have support from the professional literature. Goals selected should have merit and be supported by available research literature. The history of physical education is replete with unsupported claims for movement programs, from within and outside the profession, which may not be substantiated. The profession must move beyond mere rhetoric as a basis for goal selection. Careful analysis of acutal programs and pertinent literature should be employed as sources of goals.

Acquisition of knowledge and development in the cognitive domain is an important outcome of physical education.
Courtesy of Cathy Haight, Lansing High School, Lansing, NY.

Goals should relate to the cognitive, affective, and psychomotor domains. Goal statements, when considered as a group, should reflect the interdependence of the cognitive, affective, and psychomotor domains in relation to student learning. Individuals think and behave across the three dimensions simultaneously, not in a univariate manner, as is often assumed by teachers and other professionals dealing with students. Goal statements composed by physical educators should reflect an understanding that students respond as integrated, total beings in their reactions to the secondary school curriculum. Goals that emphasize one dimension and ignore the multifaceted nature of the human psyche should be avoided. Once determined, the set of goals, when considered as an entity, must address the whole student. Specifically, this guideline means that reference needs to be made to the students' physical, emotional, social, and intellectual development.

Goals. To what ends should secondary school physical education be directed? A goal commonly found in high-school physical education programs is (as stated in Chapter 1): "To assist each individual to develop the skills, attain the knowledge, and acquire the attitudes that will result in a lifetime of participation in physical activity."

While this goal is broadly defined, it does provide an explicit notion of expected outcomes of the secondary program. It is explicit to the point of providing a central theme and focus for the program. Melograno[2] refers to such goals as "organizing centers" for they represent broad educational goals and purposes. The specific content of the physical education curriculum should be structured in accordance with the goals identified as a result of the goal-setting process.

Other goals that are often included in secondary programs include the development of physical fitness, motor skill proficiency, knowledges, and affective behavior. In 1986 NASPE produced a position paper entitled *Guidelines for Secondary School Physical Education*,[3] which specifically outlined goals for the instructional program in physical education. Among these goals are:

1. Opportunities to develop and refine movement skills in a wide range of activities beyond the exposure level
2. Experiences that assist in developing personal programs for gaining and maintaining a high level of physical health and enjoyment of movement activities
3. Knowledge of the scientific principles related to physical activity, exercise, and health
4. Experiences that help in understanding the role of physical activity and sport in society

The point to be made here is the importance of preparing a clearly defined set of goals. Programs that fail to establish such goal statements will mirror the actions of a ship sailing the high seas without the benefit of navigation instruments, foundering, its crew unaware of

their destination, and making many false starts and stops. The goal-setting process is the first step in prevention of such situations.

Goals and their derivatives and behavioral objectives can be classified into three related domains: the psychomotor domain (doing), the cognitive domain (knowing), and the affective domain (feeling). It is imperative that secondary school physical education programs promote and encourage learning, growth, and development in each of these domains. If physical education teachers are concerned with the total development of the student and wish to nurture growth of the *whole* person, then professionals must address each of these domains of learning. To do less would be failure to follow through on our promise and to commit a disservice to the students.

Writing Objectives for Learning

Learning is generally defined as an observable change in behavior as an outcome of the teaching process. In this next section, the results of the teaching process, or the outcomes of learning, will be analyzed. The trend toward greater and more specific levels of accountability for actions in the learning setting makes it imperative that actual learning be identified. How does a teacher know that learning has occurred in the gymnasium? How does a physical education teacher know for certain that a student has achieved specified educational goals?

It is the purpose here to assist the teachers in their efforts to evaluate the teaching process by identifying learning outcomes. These learning outcomes are in the form of observable, measurable behaviors that the teacher has brought about through the establishment of two types of objectives: instructional and behavioral. *Instructional objectives are those goals or aims that the teacher defines* for the program of activities or the unit under study. The presentation of instructional objectives will be addressed first. Later in this chapter the process of writing specific *behavioral objectives—those outcomes of the learning process that the student should achieve during a particular unit or class* will be discussed.

Development of Instructional Objectives

Although objectives have long been a part of the educational process, the classification of educational objectives into a taxonomy, or hierarchical form, using developmental theories as a basis for structuring objectives, was a totally new approach when put forth by Bloom.[4] However, it was not until quite a few years later that educators capitalized on Bloom's work to facilitate efforts to respond to the calls for increased accountability. As a result of these earlier efforts, methodological changes in educational technology have been instituted, specifically behavioral objectives derived from various taxonomies, which have had such an impact on educational practice and policy that they are now considered the sine qua non of educational planning.

Learning in the cognitive (or thinking) domain was the focus of the first taxonomy. From the research of developmental psychologists, theories about stages of development emerged, indicating at what point in the developmental process a learner would begin to assimilate facts and then process to higher levels of cognitive functioning. Development of specific cognitive skills could then be fostered at appropriate stages of intellectual development.

Educators like Krathwohl, Bloom, and Masia[9] further recognized that an individual does not learn facts or develop cognitive abilities without the influence of other factors. Realizing that how a person feels—both about self and surrounding—has a definite relationship to learning, they next developed a taxonomy of educational objectives in the affective or feeling domain. Here again, the developmental nature of the individual was taken into account in classifying objectives in hierarchical form.

The third learning domain, the psychomotor domain, has been classified by several authorities in several disciplines. Because of the complex nature of development in this domain, the process of identification of a single taxonomy of educational objectives has been slow. However, the taxonomy put forth by Harrow[5] has received apparent acceptance among physical education teachers at the present time.

Physical education teachers historically have been dedicated to the teaching of the *whole* person. Therefore it might seem that a discussion of objectives within three learning domains would not be innovative to teachers in the field. However, by thoroughly analyzing student outcomes and employing concepts in the three domains discussed, the physical education teacher can establish a firm foundation on which to plan, conduct, and assess a progressive and meaningful curriculum. Moreover, the implications of motor learning research (see Chapter 8) support the importance of precise specification of what is to be learned, to what extent (quality? quantity? characteristics of the student performance anticipated?), and the exact conditions the student must perform under to facilitate learning in the psychomotor domain. Clearly formulated objectives can enhance physical education teachers' efforts in these activities. Furthermore, to meet the pervasive demands for accountability, physical education teachers, like all professionals in education, have to provide relevant, meaningful evidence that learning indeed has taken place. Therefore the development of a taxonomy of instructional objectives leading toward measurable behaviors can assist in responding to the calls for accountability. With the utilization of the following series of instructional objectives in the three domains of learning, the teacher of physical education is able to initiate measures toward promoting changes in behavior. The second step, measurement of the specific outcomes of the

Provision for warm-up activity should be made within the lesson plan.
Courtesy of Patricia Quinn, Notre Dame High School, Elmira, NY.

TABLE 6-1

The Cognitive Domain

Category	Description
1. Knowledge	Memory; ability to recall; bringing to mind appropriate information; represents lowest level of learning outcomes in cognitive domain
2. Comprehension	To grasp the meaning of material; understanding without perceiving implications; interpret; translate; estimate; predict; one step beyond memory; represents lowest level of understanding
3. Application	Ability to use learned information in new situations; can apply rules, methods, and concepts; higher level of understanding
4. Analysis	To break down material into its component parts; organization and relationships between parts made clear; identifying; selecting; inferring; higher intellectual level
5. Synthesis	To put parts together to form a new whole; produce new patterns, routines, or structures; creative behaviors stessed
6. Evaluation	Judge value of ideas, concepts, based on definitive criteria or standards; highest learning outcome because it contains elements of all other categories and judgments based on specific criteria

TABLE 6-2

The Affective Domain

Category	Description
1. Receiving	Sensitivity to the existence of certain events, stimuli; awareness; willingness to receive or attend to phenomena
2. Responding	Actively attending to stimuli; reacts to situation beyond mere perception; overt response
3. Valuing	Stimuli or phenomena assigned worth; learner places a value on events; characteristics of a belief or an attitude; appreciation
4. Organizing	Internalization of values and organizes them into a system; determines interrelationship among values; arranges values in hierarchical form; compares, relates, synthesizes values
5. Characterizing by a value or complex	Acts in accordance with internalized values; behavior consistent with accepted values and becomes a part personality; highest level of affective domain

learning process through behavioral objectives, will then be addressed.

Cognitive domain. Developers of the taxonomy of educational objectives within this learning domain recognized that cognition increases in complexity at each developmental stage of the individual.[4] Initial stages of development allow learning of basic facts, while the mature individual is later able to understand and apply total concepts. Six basic levels of cognitive learning are identified so that teachers can incorporate educational objectives on a hierarchical basis (Table 6-1).

Affective domain. The affective learning domain encompasses the development of attitudes and appreciation for a particular subject or activity. With the acceptance of affect into the educational scene came recognition of the role of a student's feelings and interests in relation to achievement and a heightened awareness among educators of the importance of this learning domain.

Formulation of the taxonomy of instructional objectives in the affective domain combined the work of developmental psychologists with the work of sociologists

studying the changing patterns of society. It should be noted that within this taxonomy individuals are first aware of their being and their own response to surroundings, gradually developing a value structure in an ever-increasing social sphere. The taxonomy of objectives in the affective domain is organized under the headings described in Table 6-2.

Psychomotor domain. The taxonomy of objectives in the psychomotor domain of learning provides the foundation of programs in physical activities. Again, the taxonomy presented here is developmental in nature, relying on theories of physical development for its hierarchical structure.

Although teachers have traditionally used objectives in their instructional programs, the application of this hierarchy of objectives can provide for an appropriate individualization of learning activities. By allowing students opportunities to develop motor tasks organized from simple to complex, a distinct progression in psychomotor abilities can be achieved.

The taxonomy in Table 6-3, suggested by Harrow,[5] is relevant to physical activity and to the development of physical skills. Its application to physical education should be obvious to the reader.

These taxonomies of educational objectives provide concrete guidelines to develop levels of behavior or improvement in the learner. Moreover, the organization and systematic ordering of behaviors found within each taxonomy also provide a framework for other important teaching functions such as serving as a basis of compar-

TABLE 6-3

The Psychomotor Domain

Category	Description
1. Reflex movements	Actions elicited without conscious volition in response to some stimuli; flexing, extending, stretching, postural adjustments; provides base for movement behavior
2. Basic fundamental movements	Inherent movement patterns based on combinations of reflex movements; patterns provide starting point for improvement of perceptual and physical abilities; basis for complex skilled movement
3. Perceptual abilities	Interpretation of stimuli from various modalities so adjustments can be made; includes auditory, visual, tactile kinesthetic, coordinated perceptual abilities
4. Physical abilities	Characteristics that, when developed to a high degree, provide learner with a sound, efficiently functioning body; organic vigor essential to development of highly skilled movement; endurance, strength, agility, flexibility
5. Skilled movements	Degree of efficiency in performing a complex movement task; consists of a vertical and horizontal continuum, based on inherent movement patterns
6. Nondiscursive communication	Movement expressions that are part of a movement repertoire; movement interpretations that include any efficiently performed skilled movement; movement patterns designed to communicate a message to the viewer; ranges from facial expressions through sophisticated choreographies

ison of programs and allowing for judgment and evaluation of curricular offering. Taxonomic instructional materials also provide necessary information for test development, which may be similarly organized to measure levels of development in the three learning domains and at the same time pinpoint needs of individual students.

Classifications of instructional objectives have been used successfully for the development of physical education programs and for the organization of instructional units within those programs.

Development of instructional objectives in taxonomic form for the many activities incorporated in a program of physical education is a demanding task. Yet the out-

comes, as evidenced by concrete measurement of learning by students, are of extreme importance to students, administrators, and the community. Evidence that learning has taken place because instructional objectives have been met thus provides more than an adequate response to the demands for accountability.

But how does a teacher determine that instructional objectives have been achieved? This is accomplished by evaluating student performance. For example, a lesson within a tennis unit might include the following instructional objective: "The student will learn the forehand stroke."

To determine whether students have accomplished the instructional objective, the teacher would assess achievement of the following behavioral objective:

Behavioral objective: After a review of mechanical principles, the student will return seven of ten balls into the backcourt area of the singles court using the forehand stroke and exhibiting proper technique.

In effect, then, teachers can determine that instructional objectives have been achieved by employing behavioral objectives that describe the desired student performance/behaviors and, when attained, provide evidence that learning has occurred.

The second step, that of writing specific behavioral objectives for students based on outlined instructional objectives, is essential for completion of the teaching process. The students in the learning setting must show evidence of learning by doing something specific and measurable. Therefore after formulating instructional objectives for a unit of study, the teacher must next establish specific behavioral objectives for students to master in each daily lesson.

Writing Behavioral Objectives

Instructional objectives, specific behavioral objectives, and daily lesson plans as well as the resultant student behaviors should emerge from and contribute to the attainment of overall unit objectives that curriculum planners seek. Well-prepared unit objectives should be the basis for the development of congruence among the components of planning (for example, objectives, lesson activities, and desired and actual student learning). Teachers need to be certain that students comprehend these relationships and understand the additive nature of lesson objectives in light of the unit under consideration. Fig. 6-2 clarifies the relationship between the levels of curricular objectives.

A behavioral objective, sometimes referred to as a performance objective, may be defined as an intended learning outcome achieved through the performance (for example, an observable, measurable behavior) of a specified task. When a student accomplishes the established task, this behavior represents an outcome of the educational

The sum of all lesson objectives = UNIT objectives
The sum of all UNIT objectives = CURRICULAR objectives
The sum of all CURRICULAR objectives = total SCHOOL objectives
The sum of all SCHOOL objectives = SYSTEM-WIDE objectives

FIG. 6-2 The relationship of educational objectives.

process; in other words, the student shows that learning has taken place.

For example, in a tennis unit, an instructional objective in the cognitive domain such as "the student will know the rules of the game" is written from the point of view of the teacher, who intended that the students would learn the rules of tennis. However, for the teacher to determine that this learning has occurred, the students have to demonstrate this knowledge by doing something, such as taking a written exam, answering questions orally in class, or performing some similar measurable behavior. These test results or performances in the cognitive domain would then indicate not only what each student had learned but also would show to the teacher how well instructional objectives had been met. Evidence of higher levels of cognitive skills should also be evaluated while students actually play their tennis matches and while they are analyzing each other's play. Student activities or performances should be based on written behavioral objectives, established to ensure that learning has taken place.

Translation of instructional objectives (the teacher's goals) into behavioral objectives (the student's goals) requires careful and thoughtful planning, because these behavioral objectives become the formula for planning individual lessons. The fact that behavioral objectives then play a major role in the conduct and organization of the instructional process must not be overlooked. If a behavioral objective in the psychomotor domain involves learning to stroke a tennis ball, then within the lesson plan some activities must be organized that will develop that stroking ability. If an affective objective for that day is to develop sharing of equipment with a partner, then the activities during class must include sharing opportunities. Student achievement of established behavioral objectives, therefore, is synonymous with the learning process. They *are* the outcomes of learning.

Components of Behavioral Objectives

The preparation of a behavioral objective based on instructional objectives requires careful delineation of four specific components or elements. It must first be stated *who* will be performing the behavior—the student, the tenth-grade boy or girl, or whoever it might be. Next, *what* the student will be doing is identified, and third,

the *conditions* under which the activity will be performed must be described. The fourth element is perhaps the most significant from an instructional standpoint. Here the quality of performance is measured by including a description of *how well* the performance must be demonstrated.

The following are three behavioral objectives taken from a beginning tennis unit and include an objective in each domain. All four elements are incorporated in each objective.

◆ *Cognitive:* After studying instructional materials, the student will correctly explain (according to a partner's judgment) the concept "sweet part of the racket."
◆ *Affective:* The ninth-grade student will choose to practice the forehand stroke against the tennis backboard throughout the class period.
◆ *Psychomotor:* The beginning tennis student will execute a controlled stroke against the tennis backboard by not losing the ball for 5 minutes.

Each of the above objectives contains the four necessary components. To clarify the factors further, the objectives have been rewritten with each element defined (Table 6-4).

When writing a behavioral objective, the teacher must be careful to include:

1. A behavior that can be performed. The student must do something. Knowing how to do it is important, but it is not enough because it is difficult to ascertain what a student knows.
2. A behavior that can be clearly measured. Students must demonstrate learning by performing in ways that can be clearly observed by others. Students learn many things in school. Some learned behaviors are easy to perceive. Others, such as changes in attitude, are difficult to detect. The teacher must prepare behavioral objectives that provide clear criteria by which changes in student behavior can be determined.
3. A behavior that is described, with limiting specifications. How did the student explain? Verbally? In writing? Where did the student run? On the track? Out of the stadium?
4. Behavior that can meet certain established criteria or standards for evaluation purposes. Judgment of the quality of performance is required here, as in successfully hitting a target 3 out of 5 attempts or running a distance of 1 mile within 12 minutes.

The evaluation element is a critical component of a behavior objective. If the major underlying purpose for establishing these behavioral objectives is to identify results of the teaching process (the learning outcomes), then measurement of performance must be obtained.

Selection of action verbs is another important aspect in the formulation of behavioral objectives. General verbs, such as *know, learn, appreciate,* and *comprehend* are appropriate for instructional objectives. However, more

TABLE 6-4

Components of Behavioral Objectives

| | Objective | | |
Component	Cognitive	Affective	Psychomotor
Who will do it?	Student	Ninth-grade boy or girl	Beginning tennis student
What will be done?	Will explain verbally the concept of "sweet part of racket"	Will choose to practice the forehand	Will execute a controlled forehand stroke
Under what conditions?	After studying instructional materials	Against the tennis backboard	Against the tennis backboard
How well will it be done? Criteria? To what extent?	Correctly, according to judgment of a partner	Throughout the class period	By not losing the ball for 5 minutes

specific verbs must be included in behavioral objectives. In the cognitive domain, such verbs as *explains, describes, lists, identifies, diagrams, analyzes,* and *evaluates* are acceptable. In the affective domain a student might *follow, respond, obey, practice, select, volunteer, share,* or *prefer* an activity. Psychomotor verbs are more easily included since they already involve actions as in *run, walk, swing, hit, catch, pass,* and *jump.* Table 6-5 provides the reader with a list of verbs for possible use in each of the three domains.

Factors Affecting Planning

Several factors must be considered when one is planning learning activities and experiences. The learner, community influences, geography, facilities, scheduling patterns, and the faculty are all significant factors that have an impact on the planning process and the curriculum. Each has either a direct or indirect influence on the planning process.

The learner. The needs, interests, and experiences of the students should be of utmost concern to teachers when planning curricular activities. Instruments such as needs assessment, preassessment inventories, and teacher observation scales can maximize the accuracy of teachers' efforts to develop plans that are congruent with the student population and reflect its educational needs. Jewett and Bain[6] provide an example of a preassessment inventory that can be utilized for the purpose of gaining a clearer understanding of the student population. This inventory is presented in Box 6-1.

Community influence. Teachers and curriculum specialists must design experiences and lessons that take into account the specific local (for example, city, town, or regional educational initiatives), context (for example, school or administrative support), and sociocultural milieu of the school and students (ethnic composition and socioeconomic level of the community). Communities vary as to the value and expectations of the high-school physical education program, interest in specific activities, and support for programs that reinforce proper attitudes toward an active lifestyle.

Geography. The local climate, natural surroundings and resources, and the length of the seasons and their potential for influencing the conduct of the instructional program are important.

Facilities and equipment. Do the available facilities, equipment, and teaching stations enhance or inhibit program variety? Program flexibility? Do they offer students opportunities to select from a wide array of activities and topics? Do the facilities and equipment foster or discourage coordination with elementary and middle-school programs? Are off-campus sites, which can expand pro-

TABLE 6-5

A Selection of Action Verbs in Each of the Learning Domains

Affective Domain	Cognitive Domain	Psychomotor Domain
Accept	Assess	Demonstrate
Agree	Compare	Execute
Choose	Contrast	Swing
Compliment	Classify	Volley
Contribute	Change	Dribble
Cooperate	Define	Pitch
Follow	Differentiate	Hit
Help	Discriminate	Throw
Join	Distinguish	Toss
Listen	Evaluate	Catch
Permit	Interpret	Kick
Reinforce	Judge	Run
Share	List	Jump
Sympathize	Name	Pass
Take turns	Design	Serve
Volunteer	Select	Swim

UNDERSTANDING THE LEARNER LOCAL DATA SOURCES

School Records

What is the rate of absenteeism?

Which students are absent most often?

What health problems occur most frequently?

How does academic achievement compare with national norms? With other area schools?

Who gets in trouble for what?

How are discipline problems dealt with?

Who are the students who participate in various activities?

Departmental Records

What is the rate of attendance and participation?

Which students are out most often?

Which teachers or activities have highest rates of nonparticipation?

How does fitness performance compare to norms?

What evidence exists regarding cognitive and motor achievement?

What patterns are evident in the awarding of grades?

How do students evaluate the physical education program?

When allowed to choose activities, what preferences do students indicate?

Other Agencies

What content is taught in elementary and middle schools in the district?

What organized recreational programs exist for secondary students?

Which students participate in community or private recreation programs?

What items are big sellers at area sporting goods stores?

What health problems are prevalent in the community?

gram offerings, available for use by school personnel? Can individualized instructional strategies be supported given current facilities and equipment? Can initiatives in lifetime activities requiring special resources (for example, golf or archery) be supported adequately? Responses to these questions can elucidate the potential influence of these factors on the planning of the curriculum.

Scheduling patterns. Of concern with scheduling patterns is the time allocated for instruction. How many meetings per week are students scheduled for physical education? Every day? Twice per week? How long is each class session? 40 minutes? 52 minutes? Does the schedule rotate? If so, how does it rotate? Across the week? Within each day? Both? Is modular scheduling in place?

Faculty. What skills do the faculty possess as a whole? Individually? Do the competencies complement each other? Does the faculty as a whole present a balanced, yet varied set of abilities and expertise to facilitate a broad set of offerings, variety in methodology, and opportunities for individualization? Can the faculty work together and produce a coherent curriculum plan? Are faculty members flexible in their approach to instruction and curriculum planning? In their responses to change?

Types of Plans

The most common plans found at the secondary level are the annual plan, the unit plan, and the lesson plan. At this point a brief discussion of each will follow, and samples of each type of plan will be presented. It should be made clear, however, that although formats for each type of plan will be presented, no one type of format has received widespread acceptance. Although most lesson plan and unit plan formats are similar and contain the essential elements, future teachers should be advised to consult with the formats employed or in use within their system as a starting point, and then use common sense and experience from there. Employed wisely, each of the suggested plans has the potential to contribute to the success of the instructional program.

Annual plan. If one assumes that the goals of the secondary program have been determined, most programs attempt to identify a plan for the year. The annual plan facilitates the teacher's endeavors to chart the year's experiences for the secondary student.

The employment of the annual planning process can facilitate the planning process. Specifically, it:

1. Ensures the emphasis for each aspect of the curriculum.
2. Helps determine the amount of time to be devoted to each area or component of the program.
3. Assists in blocking out the units of instruction.
4. Facilitates and coordinates equipment and facility usage by faculty and staff.
5. Helps insure a well-rounded, varied program.
6. Assists in the coordination between various schools (elementary, middle, and secondary) and programs within the secondary school itself (grades 9-12).

The lack of articulation among the various educational programs continues to be a major problem in physical education. School programs, from elementary through secondary, should be coordinated, sequential, and flow logically from year to year and from school to school if educators are to maximize the growth and development of students. Communication is required among professionals situated in schools to ensure appropriate, sequential development of skills, knowledge, and attitudes based on experiences in physical education.

Often administrative and contextual constraints inhibit

Teachers must have enthusiasm, a strong belief in the value of their endeavors, and the ability to convey these values to others. Teachers run with their class at Tilford Middle School, Vinton, IA.

Courtesy of Beth Kirkpatrick, Tilford, Middle School, Vinton, IA.

the attainment of such articulation. The former is often readily evidenced by a lack of administrative interest and support, sometimes combined with a failure or inability to understand the contributions of physical education to student development, while the latter set of constraints sometimes emerges from the immediate environment of physical education, such as unprofessional attitudes of colleagues, and the physical education faculty's lack of support or concern for quality programs. Articulation between programs must be accomplished if the legitimacy of secondary programs is to be maintained and support is to be generated from the various publics served.[8]

Curricular materials must be obtained, reviewed, and analyzed to avoid unnecessary duplication and overlap and to ensure presentation, development, and learning across the three domains that will be meaningful, beneficial, and productive. Tables 6-6 and 6-7 provide the reader with examples of annual plans; Chapter 4 also contains annual plans.

Unit plan. The development of unit plans, the next logical step in the planning process, evolves from the annual plan and eventually facilitates the development of daily plans and lesson plans.

A unit plan or unit of instruction is a series of related learning experiences based on a common theme or in-

structional focus. In secondary school physical education, the most common themes focus on specific activities (for example, units of soccer, basketball, or swimming) and are known as activity-based units. Examples of such units commonly observed in secondary physical education are shown in Box 6-2. Less common are themes with a conceptual focus, such as the concept of spatial awareness, the concept of force production, or the concept of courage. These latter themes lead to conceptual units. Examples of conceptual themes are found in Box 6-3.

The purpose of the unit plan is to enable the teacher to organize a series of related learning experiences into lessons that follow a logical progression.[2] The process of planning and constructing a unit involves addressing the items included below, within a format similar to that outlined in Box 6-4. One unit plan is included in this chapter for the reader's perusal (Box 6-5).

Lesson plan. Earlier in this chapter, the values of planning were delineated. The identification of broad areas of content (goals) to be addressed, followed by the formulation of instructional goals to be achieved at regular intervals during the year, gave the curriculum plan its definitive structure. Finally, the development of learning units through which the identified goals could be attained were discussed.

Annual Plan of Instruction: Activity-Based Units for Grades 9-12

Number of Weeks in Unit	Grades 9 and 10	Grades 11 and 12
3	Wellness; lifestyle assessment and management	
6	Choice: soccer, speedball, flag football, adventure activities I	Tennis I, golf I, softball, field hockey, adventure activities I
6	Choice: swimming, aerobics, weight training I, volleyball I, floor hockey	Swimming, aerobics, team handball, badminton, volleyball I
6	Choice: swimming, aerobics, gymnastics I, badminton, folk/square dance	Swimming, aerobics, creative dance, bowling, weight training I, gymnastics I, volleyball II
6	Choice: swimming, aerobics, weight training I, creative dance, wrestling, basketball	Swimming, aerobics, bowling, gymnastics II, folk/square dance, weight training II
6	Choice: softball, team handball, adventure activities I, track and field	Adventure activities II, golf II, tennis II, track and field, archery
3	Wellness; lifestyle assessment and management	

Annual Plan of Instruction: Conceptual Units for Grades 9-12

Number of Weeks in Unit	Concepts	Activities
Grades 9 and 10		
2	Wellness concepts	Aerobics, weight training, biking
3	Physiological aspects, principles of physical fitness (overload, specificity, progression)	Speedball, soccer
7	Movement education concepts: time, flow, force, space	Flag football, softball, creative dance, tumbling/gymnastics
7	Process of motor skill acquisition, concepts of motor skill development (practice, feedback, transfer, retention)	Volleyball, basketball, team handball, bowling, swimming
7	Analysis of motor performance, kinesiological concepts, applied anatomy, posture and body mechanics	Swimming, tennis, track and field, badminton, wrestling, gymnastics/tumbling
7	Psychosocial aspects of motor performance	Cooperative games, adventure activities, archery, golf, folk/square dance
3	Wellness concepts	Aerobics, hiking, biking
Grades 11 and 12		
2	Wellness and lifestyle management	Aerobics, weight training II, biking, hiking, cross-country running
3	Physiological aspects of motor performance—II, principles of fitness	Soccer, track, swimming, tennis II, basketball, field hockey
7	Movement education concepts: time, space, flow, force	Creative dance, tumbling II, gymnastics II, pickleball, wrestling
7	Psychological aspects of motor performance: anxiety, aggression, relaxation, courage	Cooperative games, volleyball I, adventure activities II, folk/square dance
7	Biomechanical concepts of motor performance: stability, force, leverage, friction	Swimming, badminton, volleyball II, bowling, field events
7	Sociological aspects of motor performance: cooperation, cohesion, affiliation, competition	Archery, cooperative games, adventure activities, track and field
2	Wellness and lifestyle management concepts	Aerobics, swimming, jogging, hiking, biking

BOX 6-2

ACTIVITY UNITS IN PHYSICAL EDUCATION

Aerobic dance	Gymnastics
Archery	Speedball
Badminton	Swimming
Basketball	Team handball
Bowling	Tennis
Football	Track and field
Golf	Volleyball

BOX 6-3

CONCEPTUAL UNITS IN PHYSICAL EDUCATION

Accuracy	Momentum
Balance	Responsibility
Cooperation	Spatial awareness
Courage	Trust
Flow	Weight transfer
Force absorption	

Goals, however significant, remain no more than important generalities. It should be understood that, to achieve curricular goals, secondary school physical education teachers must design daily plans that address the goals of the program, but which are transformed into more specific terms. Each daily lesson plan should be designed to achieve a particular part of the unit, as defined by the unit objectives. Unit plans, moreover, are comprised of a series of daily lesson plans.

Derived as it is from the content-oriented unit plan, a lesson plan specifies the experiences students must undergo to learn the lesson of the day. In other words the lesson plan is a set of strategies, presented in a logically sequenced manner, employed to facilitate students' accomplishment of the goals of the unit. Henson's[7] view is very pertinent here:

For a teacher to attempt to teach a class without the aid of a lesson plan is analogous to a pilot's taking off to a new direction without a map. Like the map, the lesson plan provides direction toward the objectives. If the lesson begins to stray, the lesson plan enables you to steer it back to the main course.

Lesson plans should assist teachers' efforts to conduct relevant, meaningful, and thought-provoking learning experiences for students. While serving as a guide, it should nonetheless be flexible enough to respond to the needs of the students and the inherent unpredictability and volatility of interactive teaching.

The lesson planning process involves addressing items similar to those included in the suggested lesson plan format in Fig. 6-3.

In this chapter there is a sample lesson plan (Fig. 6-4). In addition, there are other lessons outlined within the sample unit plan provided for the reader. Careful review of these plans should elucidate the fact that the lesson plan is a fully developed version of the unit plan and provides much more precise translation of the activities listed in the unit plan. Each lesson plan is like a brick in the unit plan structure, and while it is derived from and owes its essence to the unit plan structure, it nevertheless focuses more on the immediacy and interactive nature of the teaching-learning environment.

Task Analysis

Once instructional goals and objectives have been formulated, the teacher needs to focus on the next component in the planning process, namely, the sequential arrangement of various learning tasks. How does the teacher proceed to develop a unit plan? What procedures should be employed to facilitate the decisions about what is to be taught and when? At this point the teacher would do well to complete a task analysis for the instructional goals identified in the unit plan. The planner must analyze the motor tasks and activities in an effort to sequence activities appropriately and select and organize learning experiences, which not only facilitate learning, but in terms of complexity, difficulty, and motor prerequisites, are logical. In effect, the teacher must be able to match students to movement experiences that are congruent with the students' motor abilities and knowledge. Inherent in this process is the determination of hierarchical arrangements to enhance the effectiveness of the presentation of skills, tasks, or concepts.

By employing the three taxonomies outlined previously, teachers can place learning tasks into a logical sequential order in which those tasks easily learned must be achieved first. By incorporating the results of the task analysis within the plans for individual lessons, teachers can ensure appropriate progression for their students.

Moreover, upon completion of the sequential arrangement of the tasks and activities included in the unit plan, the preparation of behavioral objectives for each lesson will be facilitated. Because a task analysis starts with an instructional objective and breaks down and identifies the essentials of the skill, each element identified contributes and is prerequisite to the achievement of the instructional

Text continued on p. 113.

BOX 6-4

SUGGESTED FORMAT FOR UNIT PLANNING

Title of Unit Plan (Name of unit plan that reflects its emphasis of theme)

Grade Level_____ Number of Classes_____

Class Size_____ Time per Class____

I. Primary goals or purposes
   The most important general educational goals to be achieved in all domains should be identified.

II. General behavioral objectives
   List the affective, cognitive, and psychomotor behaviors and skills that will direct and shape the material and methods of the unit. General behavioral objectives are those objectives the teacher wishes to accomplish. The objectives differ from specific, lesson behavioral objectives in that they are not as precisely stated and refer more to the teacher's goals than to specific student performance.

III. Block plan
   A brief outline of the activities to be covered in the lessons should be provided here. The block plan should reflect an appropriate progression for the grade and skill level of the students.

IV. Lesson development
   Anticipated progressive sequence of learning experiences.
   A. Lesson #1
      1. Specific behavioral objectives for this lesson
         Using the general unit objectives, the teacher identifies the specific knowledges, patterns, sequences, skills, and behaviors that the students should achieve in this lesson.
      2. Activities (presented in progressive order)
         a. Introductory activities
            (warm-up, review of past lessons)
         b. Body of lesson (learning experiences presented in progression, including breakdown of specific tasks, patterns, sequences, concepts, skills, games, questions, and problems to be presented)
         c. Questions/discussion (provide list of questions to be employed; how discussion is to be conducted, activities to reinforce cognitive and other objectives)
         d. Organization for dismissal
   B. Repeat lesson development for each lesson to be planned for in the unit.
      1. Specific behavioral objectives
      2. Learning experiences
         a. Introductory activities
         b. Body of lesson (new material)
         c. Questions/discussion
         d. Organization for dismissal

V. Special activities and alternative plans
   Plans for special activities or alternative lessons (in addition to the regularly planned lessons for the unit) in the event of inclement weather, temporary displacement or loss of teaching station should be described here.

VI. Equipment, supplies, space requirements
   A. List of all floor and wall markings needed
   B. List of all equipment and quantity of each needed
   C. Space requirements

VII. Motivational techniques (How will interest in unit activities themes, or concepts be generated? Maintained?)
   A. List of all audiovisual aids to be employed
   B. Tournaments, meets, and performances
   C. Special events (field days, playdays, demonstration by specialists, assembly programs, awards)
   D. Other

VIII. Health and safety precautions
   A. List of safety rules for students
   B. Health and safety precautions to be taken by instructor

IX. Teacher behavior
   A description of the teacher behavior/style(s) to be employed during each lesson in the unit. The teacher should describe how he/she plans to behave in as specific a manner as possible, employing behavioral terminology (teacher lecture, types of questions, and feedback).

X. Evaluation of student learning
   This section should describe how the teacher will assess the achievement of students in light of the behavioral objectives of the unit.
   A. Psychomotor domain
      1. Standardized tests (motor ability, fitness, sport skills)
      2. Subjective ratings/checklists
      3. Use of behavioral objectives and criteria
   B. Cognitive domain
      1. Movement response
      2. Verbal and written knowledge tests
      3. Discussion questions in class
   C. Affective domain
      1. Subjective assessment of desired behavior
      2. Value assessments
      3. Sociograms
      4. Self-evaluation instruments

XI. Evaluation of teacher's performance
   A. Self-evaluation
   B. Peer evaluation
   C. Student evaluations
   D. Supervisor evaluation

XII. References (all materials used to formulate the unit and assist the student)
   A. Sources of information for the teacher, used to prepare the unit (books, periodical literature)
   B. Sources of information for the student within the unit (within the learning experiences in each lesson), for example, handouts, rules, strategies, worksheets, task cards
   C. Other

BOX 6-5

A CONCEPTUAL UNIT PLAN

Teacher_____   Unit: <u>Concepts of Force</u>   Activity <u>Volleyball</u>
Grade <u>10th</u>   Class Size <u>36</u>   Number of Classes <u>8</u>
Time per class <u>50 minutes</u>

I. Primary goals or purposes
  A. To enhance the motor proficiency of students
  B. To enhance the cognitive growth of students
  C. To develop students' physical fitness
  D. To contribute to the development of a positive self-concept through physical education activities
  E. To enhance students' awareness of the contributions of physical activity to a healthy lifestyle
  F. To strengthen students' affection for, and appreciation of, physical activity

II. General behavioral objectives
  A. Psychomotor
    1. The student will demonstrate the following volleyball skills:
      a. Underhand serve
      b. Overhand serve
      c. Overhead pass/set
      d. Bump pass
      e. Spike
      f. Dig
    2. The student will participate in a volleyball match.
  B. Cognitive
    1. The student will demonstrate an understanding of the mechanical principles of force as it relates to volleyball skills.
    2. The student will apply the concepts of force production, application of force, force absorption, and rebound forces, to the following skills: serve, bump, set, spike, dig.
    3. The student will demonstrate an understanding of the rules and strategies of volleyball.
    4. The student will assess volleyball, other sport skills, and everyday activities as to their specific manner of applying, producing, absorbing, and rebounding forces.
  C. Affective
    1. The student will cooperate with other students.
    2. The student will follow directions.
    3. The student will demonstrate responsible behavior at all times.
    4. The student will assist others during the class experiences.
    5. The student will demonstrate empathy regarding the performance of others.

III. Block plan—progression chart
  A. Lesson #1
    Introduce the game of volleyball (history, values, development)
    Introduce the concepts of force (magnitude, production, absorption, rebound forces, and application)
    Introduce serve—underhand and overhand
    Introduce rules pertaining to service
    Preassessment—serve

Problems and questions:
    How can force be varied when serving? Specify body actions? What is the relationship between force modulation and accuracy? Effectiveness? What is the relationship between force production and point of application of force?
Game/drill—"calling serves"
  B. Lesson #2
    Review concepts of force as they relate to the serve
    Review serves
    Drill—wall serve drill
    Drill—serve placement drill
    Introduce concepts related to force absorption and rebound forces
    Explain and demonstrate the bump pass
    Preassessment—bump pass
    Problems and questions:
      Discuss role of force absorption, rebound forces and effective bump passing skills. How is force absorbed, in general, by the body? What actions indicate absorption? How is force absorbed in the bump pass? How is the direction of force reversed in the bump pass? Describe the specific body actions.
  Bump pass drill (from a toss)
    Introduce basic volleyball rules and strategies
    Game—modified—serve and bump only
  C. Lesson #3
    Review concepts of force as they relate to serve and bump
    Drill—serve and bump pass
    Introduce overhead set/pass
    Relate force concepts to overhead set/pass
    Preassessment—overhead set/pass
    Problems and questions:
      How is force produced in the overhead pass? How does this resemble or differ from previous skills?
      Describe body actions in overhead that:
        a. Generate force
        b. Absorb force
        c. Change the direction of force
        d. Cause a rebound effect
    Overhead wall drill
    Drill—overhead (off a toss)
    Drill—keep it up
    Introduce rules of volleyball
    Game—serve, overhead, bump
  D. Lesson #4
    Review concepts of force as related to the overhead pass/set
    Drill—keep it up
    Explain and demonstrate spike
    Relate concepts of force to spike
    Discuss relationship of overhead to spike
    Preassessment—spike

Continued.

BOX 6-5

A CONCEPTUAL UNIT PLAN—cont'd

Problems and questions:

Discuss horizontal and vertical components of force in the spike. How is force generated in spike? Describe body actions in spike that:

   a. Create force

   b. Redirect force

   c. Absorb force

Drill—spike (from a toss; one-step approach)

Drill—serve—bump—set—spike

Explain and demonstrate volleyball rules and strategy

Game—spiking

E. Lesson #5

Review previous concepts of force as related to spike

Drill—overhead set and spike

Explain and demonstrate dig

Relate concepts of force to dig

Discuss dig in relationship to spike

Problems and questions:

Describe relationship of dig actions to force (magnitude, production); how is force redirected in dig? Describe body actions in dig that create or absorb force

Drill—dig (off-toss)

Drill—set—spike—dig

Explain rules, strategy and rotation

Game play

F. Lesson #6

Assign homework—written self-evaluation of volleyball skills

Review force concepts as related to all volleyball and general volleyball strategy

Review all volleyball skills

Review rules, strategy, scoring

Problems/questions:

Relate force concepts to:

   a. Other sport activities

   b. Other physical activities

   c. General daily activities

Select tournament teams, practice with teams, game play (half of class)

Postassessments—psychomotor (half of class)

G. Lesson #7

Review rules, strategy, scoring

Relate study of force to game play

Psychomotor postassessment (half of class)

Tournament play (half of class)

H. Lesson #8

Written examination (concepts of force, skills, rules, scoring, strategy)

Collect student self-evaluations

Psychomotor postassessment (continued from Lesson #7)

Tournament play (continued from Lesson #7)

IV. Lesson development

A. Lesson #1

1. Specific behavioral objectives

   a. Cognitive

     (1) After a discussion of the history of volleyball and viewing an instructional video of a typical match, the student will demonstrate an understanding of the general concept of volleyball by responding correctly to teacher initiated questions.

     (2) After a discussion of the concepts of force, the student will:

- Define the term *force*.
- Differentiate among force production, absorption, application, and rebound.
- Assess the contribution of force to the underhand and overhand serves.

Criteria: Student responses to teacher questions.

     (3) After a class discussion, the student will describe specific body actions involved in varying force production during the serve by responding correctly to teacher-initiated questions.

     (4) After participating in a discussion of the concepts of force as they relate to the volleyball serve, the student will identify two other activities with similar mechanical aspects.

   b. Psychomotor

     (1) Given an explanation and demonstration, the student will execute the following skills employing the techniques introduced in class:

- Underhand serve
- Overhand serve

     (2) After an explanation and demonstration, the student will serve seven of ten balls into the backcourt area with either the underhand or overhand style, utilizing appropriate techniques as reviewed in class.

     (3) After an explanation and demonstration, the student will serve the ball to an area identified prior to execution with 80% accuracy.

   c. Affective

Given specific expectations for behavior in class by the instructor, the student will:

     (1) Cooperate with others at all times.

     (2) Follow directions 100% of the time.

     (3) Demonstrate responsible behavior when required.

     (4) Assist others in their efforts to master both skills and concepts when appropriate.

     (5) Demonstrate empathy when observing the performance of others.

2. Activities

   a. Introductory activities (5 minutes)

Take attendance as students enter the courts. Students jog four laps around perimeter of courts. Individualized stretching routines with teacher supervision.

   b. Body of lesson (37 minutes)

     (1) Discuss goals of the conceptual unit. Video of history, values, and typical match. Class seated in front of teacher and monitor (5 minutes).

     (2) Introductory lecture and discussion of the concepts of force (application, magnitude, production, rebound, and absorption) (5 minutes).

     (3) Presentation of underhand and overhand serves, and rules pertinent to serving (5 minutes).

BOX 6-5

A CONCEPTUAL UNIT PLAN—cont'd

(4) Preassessment—serve (10 minutes).
Students, 12 to a court, attempt 10 serves, using either style and try to place ball in the backcourt area. Record best set of trials and report to teacher. Students not serving assist by retrieving balls, feeding server, etc. Teacher circulates and provides feedback, encouragement, and clarification.

(5) During the next activity students are expected to observe other student performance. Problems and questions to be analyzed and considered by students as they perform the game/drill "Calling Serves" (12 minutes):

- How can force be varied on the serve? Identify specific body actions that serve to modulate force.
- What is the relationship between force modulation and accuracy? Explain the relationship between force variation and effectiveness.
- What is the relationship between force production and the point at which force is applied? Explain.
- What is the result when the ball is contacted at the top? bottom? right? left? center? Explain.

Calling serves: server identified player on opposite team to whom the ball will be served. One point is scored if server is successful. If the server is successful, play continues to resolution. If the server is unsuccessful, the serve is lost, and the ball goes to the other team. Teacher supervises and encourages student analysis, observation, and assessment. The teacher strives to keep students focused on analytical/conceptual questions and problems as they practice serving.

c. Questions/discussion (8 minutes)
First 4 minutes the class is organized in groups of four, discussing the following questions:

(1) What is the general concept of volleyball?
(2) How do force and associated concepts relate to volleyball?
(3) What are the aspects of serving that relate specifically to force production? force absorption? rebound forces? application of force?
(4) Compare the effects of striking the ball at different points during the serve. Explain.

The last 4 minutes, the class comes together to discuss the same questions and summarize ideas and concepts. The teacher leads the discussion and summarizes the results of the conceptual efforts for the day.

d. Dismissal
Next class; the bump pass will be presented, along with additional conceptual work on force absorption and rebound forces. Lead class to changing area.

B. Lessons #2-8 developed in a similar way.

V. Special activities and alternative plans
In the event of a temporary loss of the use of the volleyball courts or other such emergency, the following options will be put into effect:

A. Use of a classroom to:
1. View video and loop films on volleyball skills
2. Discuss concepts of force
3. Discuss rules, strategy, scoring, rotation
4. Prepare class to write self-evaluation.
B. Use of wrestling/weight room
1. A session on the relationship of physical fitness and volleyball
2. Presentation on the dig with dive and roll technique

VI. Equipment, supplies, and space requirement
A. Full gymnasium (three volleyball courts)
B. 3 nets
C. 18 volleyballs
D. Videotape recorder and monitor
E. Instructional video
F. Blackboard
G. 6 mats

VII. Motivational techniques
A. Instructional video on volleyball
B. Tournament play
C. Use of self-assessment for evaluation
D. Use of written self-evaluation
E. Conceptual approach, which requires a highly interactive approach and an instructor who will listen to students

VIII. Health and safety precautions
A. Students
1. Proper dress and footwear
2. Retainers or protective goggles for those wearing glasses
3. Warmup properly before vigorous activities
4. Limit movement to perimeter of courts when not participating
B. Teacher
1. Daily inspection of equipment, facilities, and playing surfaces for potential hazards
2. Proper supervision of all activities
3. Stress spatial awareness during unit
4. Appropriate warm-up activities each day, including individualized stretching routines
5. In special cases, match groups and individuals by size and motor competence (spiking–dig drill)

IX. Teacher behavior
Direct teacher behavior will be employed to initiate most lessons, but indirect behavior will characterize this unit. In general, the teacher will pose questions for analysis, encourage discussion, interpretation and application of concepts addressed, through the vehicle of volleyball. This behavior is directed at eliciting student cognitions of a higher level (evaluation, synthesis). During drills and discussion, the teacher will encourage, provide feedback to individuals and groups, and support student to student exchanges and analytical thinking. Group discussions will serve as a forum for student thinking as well as assist the teacher's efforts to check student comprehension of the concepts as well as game-related knowledges.

Continued.

BOX 6-5

A CONCEPTUAL UNIT PLAN—cont'd

X. Evaluation of student learning
  A. Psychomotor domain
  The following items will comprise the psychomotor skills test battery:
    1. Serving: from the legal service area, the student will make 10 attempts to serve into the backcourt area, using either the underhand or overhand serve. Each successful underhand serve equals 1 point; each successful overhand serve equals 3 points. Score equals total points earned on 10 attempts.
    2. Bump pass: from the center backcourt position, the student will make 10 attempts to bump pass to the front court area, from a tossed ball. Each successful return equals 3 points. Score equals total number of points in 10 attempts.
    3. Overhead set: from a front court position, the setter will make 10 attempts to set a ball, tossed to the student, to a player preparing to spike the set. Each successful set equals 3 points. Score equals the total number of points earned in 10 attempts.
  B. Cognitive domain
    1. Cognitive development will be subjectively evaluated by the teacher, based on the student's participation and performance in class discussions and analyses.
    2. Each student will submit a written self-evaluation of strengths and weaknesses.
    3. A written examination on concepts of force as applied to volleyball, and the rules, strategy, skills of volleyball, will be administered.
  C. Affective domain
    1. The teacher will observe students and make subjective assessments of desired behaviors employing stated behavioral objectives.
    2. The written examination will include a few items that will ask students to evaluate their achievement of the affective objectives.
  D. Grading
    1. Psychomotor skills (30%)
      Skill Test Battery 1–4 (Score = total number of points on battery)
      Score of 81–90 = A
              71–80 = B
              61–70 = C
              51–60 = D
    2. Cognitive (40%)
      Written examination = 15%
      Self-evaluation = 15%
      Class discussions = 10%
    3. Affective (30%)
XI. Evaluation of teacher's performance
  A. Self-evaluation
    1. After each lesson, notes will be recorded in the lesson plan book as to class progress, problems, etc.
    2. At the end of the unit, daily notes will be summarized and recorded.
    3. Checklist of unit behavioral objectives will be employed.
  B. Students will evaluate the unit by responding to course evaluation items at the time of the cognitive examination.
XII. References
  Cox RH: *Teaching volleyball,* Minneapolis, 1980, Burgess.
  Slaymaker T, Brown VH: *Power volleyball,* Philadelphia, 1983, Saunders.

When planning, attention should be given to how to distribute and collect equipment so that it will be done in an efficient manner.
Courtesy of Suzi D'Annalfo, Conard High School, West Harford, CT.

Teacher _____ Unit _____ Lesson _____ Date _____

Grade _____ Time of Lesson _____ Number of Students _____

Space Requirements _____ Equipment Needs _____

Lesson Objective _____

Behavioral objectives: List behavioral objectives in psychomotor, affective, and cognitive domains.

Evaluation of objectives: Indicate methods of assessing achievement of behavioral objectives

Time: Indicate the anticipated time for each section of the lesson

Teaching and learning experiences: List all activities, experiences, and topics to be included in the lesson.

Teacher and student class organization: Describe how the students will be grouped, formations to be employed, and diagrams if necessary.

Skill analysis and description of skills and activities: The specific aspects of the skills, knowledges, and rules to be addressed in the lesson should be described here.

Teaching cues: Describe the teaching cues to be emphasized in the learning experiences.

Safety, motivation, and provisions for individual differences: In this section, safety concerns to be emphasized, provisions for generating, increasing, and maintaining interest in the lesson topics, and items related to dealing with individual students and variations in student response to the topics should be addressed.

Culminating activities and lesson conclusion: The teacher should indicate here those activities specifically directed to bringing the lesson to a close—activities such as discussion and review, summary and review of the class, checking for student comprehension before departure, gathering equipment, reporting scores, and dismissal to lockers.

Alternate plans: The teacher should describe here an alternate set of activities in preparation for a temporary loss of a teaching station, inclement weather, or other such emergencies.

FIG. 6-3   Suggested format for lesson planning.

objective. Teachers, then, can readily transform these elements into relevant behavioral objectives.

What is a task analysis? A task analysis responds to questions that should be of foremost concern in the planning efforts of teachers: What skills and knowledge must the student possess to perform efficiently? What abilities must the learner bring to the novel situation to have an opportunity to deal effectively with the criteria specified in the behavioral objectives of the lesson?

There are two kinds of task analysis, each with a different purpose. The first is the procedural task analysis, which facilitates the development and presentation of an individual motor task, because it involves breaking down a motor task into its basic elements and then ordering such elements from simple to complex (Box 6-6).

A second type of task analysis known as a hierarchical task analysis would seem to enhance efforts at planning a series of lessons (a unit plan). In this task analysis the teacher attempts to arrange a number of motor tasks or skills in a logical sequence in such a way that indicates to the learner the skills, subskills, and prerequisite motor abilities that must be mastered to achieve the instructional goal. From this point, the teacher can then prepare individual lessons that can maximize student learning of

each of the hierarchically arranged tasks (Figs. 6-5 and 6-6).

It is suggested here that the hierarchical analysis would contribute much to the planning process, in general, and specifically to unit planning. Competencies in this area would appear to be vital to the functioning and effectiveness of physical education teachers.

The major contribution of task analysis relates to its use as a preassessment guide. Teachers completing the process will be in a position to pretest students and thereby be better informed about the needs and abilities of the learners. In this way, lessons will be enhanced, student learning should be facilitated, and the learning experiences should be successful.

Task Analysis Competencies

To analyze tasks completely, teachers must develop the following competencies, abilities, and knowledge:
1. Knowledge of content (sports skills, concepts, and basic movements)
2. Familiarity with biomechanical and kinesiological concepts to arrange skills, subskills, and components into progressive order

Text continued on p. 117.

Teacher _____

Date _____ Grade: 10th Time: 50 minutes Unit: Tennis Lesson: Force production Number of Students: 24

Equipment: 24 tennis rackets; 72 tennis balls

Space requirements: six tennis courts

Lesson objective: Students will understand the concept of force production.

Behavioral objectives:

1. After a discussion on the topic, the student will apply the concept of force production to the execution of the tennis forehand stroke on each attempt.
2. Given an explanation, several demonstrations, and some practice, the student will return 7 of 10 balls into the backcourt area of the singles court, using the forehand stroke.
3. After participating in class discussions, the student will determine how force is produced in tennis and other activities.
4. Students will demonstrate a sense of caring by assisting students who need help during the lesson.

Evaluation of objectives:

1. Class discussion of the concept of force production.
2. Results of student self-testing.
3. Teacher observation.

Time (Min)	Teaching/Learning Experiences	Teacher/Class Organization	Skill Analysis Description of Skills and Activities	Teaching Cues	Safety, Motivation Individual Differences
5	Warm-up activities and review	Scattered in view of the teacher	Grip: Eastern shake hands with racket; hold racket perpendicular to the ground; grasp handle as if shaking hands; "V" formed by base of thumb and index finger should point slightly to the right side of the middle of bevel of racket grip	Shake hands with racket; racket perpendicular to ground; forehand grip; relax; weight on balls of feet; small steps; maintain balance; light on feet	Spatial awareness; keep distance from others
	Forehand grip and regrip; grip without looking down at racket	In place	Index finger is spread from others and thumb rests between index and other fingers; heel is on right bevel with base knuckle of index finger on right vertical bevel		
	Stance: ready position	In place in pairs; observe each other for proper stance	Ready position: racket off hand supports at throat of racket; arms and elbows close to the body; weight forward; feet spread shoulder width apart; relaxed, yet maintain springiness		
	Footwork: move with teacher's movement; shuffle to right, then left	Scattered on own spot	Movement/footwork from ready position for ball close to player; skip/shuffle after first step to that side; strive to get sideways; turn before stroke; step to ball with foot closest to ball; take small steps; try to keep feet shoulder width apart		Spatial awareness; safety; maintain distance

8	Self-assessment self-hit from self-toss; attempt to hit into backcourt area; best of ten attempts	Four students per court; one executing stroke; others assisting	Underhand drop of ball in front of body; full stroke; step into ball; eye on ball at point of contact with racket	Toss ball away from body; eye on ball; firm grip	Insure spacing; record and report scores to teacher; assist others when not stroking
3	Explanation and demonstration of task; students are to analyze what body movements are made to increase/decrease force placed on the tennis ball	Seated and scattered in front of instructor	Forehand: pivot on ball of foot: turn shoulders sideways so nonracket shoulder points to net; front foot in line with back foot; pivot is made. Backswing: take racket back until head of racket points to back fence; step forward; transfer weight to forward foot; racket travels forward through slightly low to high motion; tighten fingers at time of contact; contact ball 6-12 inches in front of forward foot; continue forward through contact and toward direction of intended flight of ball	Prepare racket; firm grip; shift weight; keep racket head on edge during stroke; point with nonracket hand to point of contact; follow through	Check for student understanding of task. Encourage student analysis; support student to interaction and discussion; reinforce students helping students
10	Forehand practice off self-toss; analyze body actions for force production; observe and help other students when not practicing	Students work with partner; share court with others; observe and analyze; teacher works with groups and individuals posing additional questions and providing feedback to facilitate analytical efforts of students	Same skill descriptions as those in the previous section	Same as above	Same as above; check for student understanding; reinforcement; encourage analysis; pose questions to check student comprehension
10	Discussion: What did you discover? What do we do to increase/decrease force? Why? What are effects of such actions? How do these actions relate to tennis forehand stroke force production? Be specific. Can you demonstrate such actions?	Group discussion: listen to students; continue to pose questions; probe to elicit higher level of thinking; avoid providing answers too soon; employ guided discovery method	Points of analysis: complete, full backswing; weight transfer; hip rotation; point of contact; follow through	Same as above	Same as above; check for student understanding
10	Practice newly discovered concepts of force production; count consecutive backcourt placements with forehand stroke; report individual scores to teacher	Four per court; forehand stroke with partner from a self-toss	Same skill information and descriptions as in previous section	Full backswing; transfer weight; contact in front of forward foot; rotate hips; follow through	Reinforcement; encourage analysis; pose questions to check student comprehension

Culminating activities/lesson conclusion: 4 minutes
Discussion: review force production: How defined? How varied? How applied to tennis? Can you provide examples of how force production is varied in other tennis skills? The backhand? In other sports? In everyday activities of life?
Review and summarize teaching cues
Gather equipment
Dismiss class to changing area
Alternate plans (inclement weather): (1) move to wrestling room indoors; (2) video series on tennis forehand stroke; (3) introduce rules, strategy, and etiquette of tennis.

FIG. 6-4 A conceptual lesson plan.

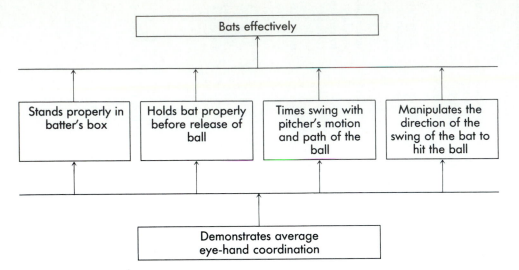

FIG. 6-5   A hierarchical task analysis. The goal is for students to bat effectively in a softball game.

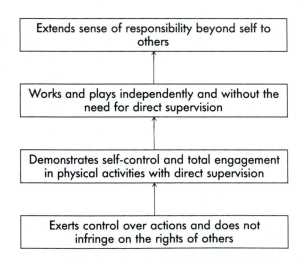

FIG. 6-6   Task analysis–affective domain. The goal is for students to extend their sense of responsibility by cooperating, giving support, showing concern, and assisting others.

BOX 6-6

A PROCEDURAL TASK ANALYSIS: THE BOWLING THROWING MOTION

Goal: The student will throw a bowling ball using the technique studied and practiced in class (as indicated below).

1. Rotate the ball on the ball return unit until finger holes are visible.
2. Place proper fingers into the holes in the ball.
3. Place support hand (nondominant) underneath the ball as positioned on the ball return unit.
4. Grip and lift the ball to the resting position in front of the body at waist height.
5. Walk to the approach line while holding the ball.
6. Place the feet in the proper stance.
7. Take one step while lowering the ball to the throwing side.
8. Take a second step while swinging the ball behind the body (backswing preparation).
9. Take a third step while swinging the ball in a forward motion even with the hips.
10. Take a fourth step while swinging the ball in front of the body.
11. Release the ball in the direction of the pins.
12. Follow through with the throwing motion unit; the throwing hand is in front of the body at shoulder height after pointing fingers at pins.

3. Analytical abilities to be able to break down movements and skills into their component elements
4. Familiarity with the characteristics of the student population

SUMMARY

Planning relevant and appropriate learning experiences is a challenging endeavor. Effective planning and related procedures can contribute much to student learning and achievement, provide necessary coherency to the program, and serve as a vehicle for the generation of data supportive of the effectiveness of the instructional faculty and the curriculum. These aspects make it necessary that secondary school physical education teachers attend to the particulars related to planning as addressed in this chapter.

Professionals who attend to and carefully select program goals, prepare worthy instructional objectives, and translate the objectives into relevant behavioral objectives that can direct and motivate student efforts will reap many benefits in return. Foremost among these benefits will be enhanced student learning, maximized student interest, and a concomitant heightened public awareness of the efforts of the physical education profession. Carefully formulated task analyses leading to appropriately selected and designed lessons will convey, in an effective manner, the worthiness of the goals of physical education in secondary schools and will support physical education's legitimate place in the educational experience of the high-school student.

REVIEW ACTIVITIES

1. Obtain a copy of a physical education curriculum from a local high school. Examine the units of instruction outlined or suggested therein. Analyze the units. What activities are emphasized? Are units focused on concepts and conceptual development? Are students supported in their growth across the three learning domains? Can you identify the concepts emphasized? How might you modify the units in the curriculum?
2. Discuss the contribution of each of the following to the secondary school physical education program:
   a. Curriculum goals
   b. Instructional objectives
   c. Behavioral objectives
   d. Task analysis
3. Prepare or obtain copies of a conceptual unit plan and an activity-based unit plan. Discuss the differences in the two forms of unit plans.
4. Discuss the advantages and disadvantages of behavioral objectives as they relate to physical education in high school.
5. Select an open and a closed skill and write a task analysis for each. Prepare several behavioral objectives that could be addressed in a physical education class related to each skill.

REFERENCES

1. Insley GS: *Practical guidelines for the teaching of physical education,* Reading, Mass, 1986, Addison-Wesley Publishing.
2. Melograno V: *Designing curriculum and learning: a physical coeducation approach,* Dubuque, Iowa, 1979, Kendall/Hunt Publishing.
3. National Association for Sport and Physical Education: *Guidelines for secondary school physical education,* Reston, Va, 1986, AAHPERD.
4. Bloom BS, editor: *Taxonomy of educational objectives: the classification of education goals, handbook I: cognitive domain,* New York, 1956, David McKay.
5. Harrow A: *A Taxonomy of the psychomotor domain,* New York, 1964, David McKay.
6. Jewett AE, Bain LL: *The curriculum process in physical education,* Dubuque, Iowa, 1985, William C Brown.
7. Henson KT: *Secondary teaching methods,* Lexington, Mass, 1981, DC Health.
8. Doughtery NJ, Bonanno D: *Contemporary approaches to the teaching of physical education,* Minneapolis, 1979, Burgess Publishing.
9. Krathwohl DR, Bloom BS, Masia BB: *Taxonomy of educational objectives handbook II: the affective domain,* New York, 1964, David McKay.

ANNOTATED READINGS

Kneer ME, Heitmann HM: *The basic stuff in action for grades 9–12,* vol 9, Reston, Va, 1987, AAHPERD.

This practical handbook presents concepts, principles, and developmental ideas extracted from the body of knowledge for physical education and sport. It is intended for use by undergraduate major students and instructors in physical education. The guidebook supports the idea that disciplinary knowledge about how and why the body moves is worthwhile in the curriculum. The materials include many sample lessons, each one describing topics and conceptual information, suggested learning experiences, materials needed, evaluation techniques, and related concepts.

NASPE: *Guidelines for secondary school physical education,* A position paper, Reston, Va, 1986, AAHPERD.

A well-prepared document that outlines recommended program goals, curriculum standards, teacher competencies, student health and safety guidelines, scheduling recommendations, standards for facilities and equipment, measurement and evaluation guidelines, and suggestions for accreditation. This position paper is an excellent starting point for program planners. It has the support of the National Association of Secondary School Principals.

Hautala RM: The tape recorder teacher: high tech that we don't need, *JOPERD* 60(2):25-28, 1987.

A succinct review of the planning process that examines the values of careful reflection by teachers. The author, however, cautions against inflexibility and rigidity once plans have been developed and emphasizes lesson planning procedures which can be responsive to the immediacy of interactive teaching.

CHAPTER 7

The Integrated Program

CHAPTER OBJECTIVES

◆ To describe the relationship of the instructional program to the total secondary school physical education curriculum

◆ To identify various approaches to conducting intramural and club sports programs

◆ To describe characteristics of interscholastic sports programs based on sound educational principles

The comprehensive secondary school physical education program is composed of many components: the instructional program, the adapted physical education program, the intramural and club sports program, and the interscholastic program. The instructional program is perceived by most physical education teachers as the foundation for the other programs that comprise the total secondary school physical education program. The instructional program focuses on the teaching of motor skills, fitness, knowledge, and attitudes to all students.

The adapted physical education program is designed for individuals whose developmental needs cannot safely or successfully be met through the regular instructional program. This program offers students with unique needs, that is, those students who are differently abled because of a permanent disability, such as cerebral palsy, or a temporary disability, such as a broken leg, opportunities to participate safely and to experience success while attaining desired physical education outcomes. Adapted physical education emphasizes individualized instruction to meet the unique needs of each student in the program.

The intramural and club sports program and the interscholastic program provide opportunities for students to utilize skills, concepts, and strategies presented in the instructional program in organized recreational and competitive situations. These aspects of the physical education program are often thought of as providing a laboratory for students to apply and develop further what has been learned in the instructional program. These programs have the potential to enrich greatly the physical education experience provided to students through the instructional program.

The adapted, intramural and club, and interscholastic sports programs are integral phases of the total physical education program in a school. Each of the component parts has an important contribution to make to the achievement of the educational objectives. However, it is necessary to maintain a proper balance so that each phase enhances and does not detract from other aspects of the total program.

ADAPTED PHYSICAL EDUCATION

Provision of quality physical education programs for all students is a professional priority. To help all students—males and females; the high-, average-, and low-skilled; the physically fit and unfit; the abled and the disabled; and the socioeconomically advantaged and disadvantaged—develop to the fullest of their abilities requires relevant instruction and utilization of teaching techniques that accommodate individual differences.

The essence of good teaching is the essence of adapted physical education: modifying the curriculum and instructional process to accommodate a diversity of individual needs while ensuring each student the opportunity to participate fully, successfully, and safely in physical education.[1] Adapted physical education may take place in a variety of placements ranging from the regular phys-

Opportunities to participate in physical activity, including competitive athletics, have grown tremendously for individuals with disabilities.

Courtesy of Sarah Rich, Ithaca College, Ithaca, NY.

ical education class or the mainstream setting to a separate class or to a combination of educational settings.[2,4,5]

When students' needs are such that they cannot be safely and successfully met within the regular physical education program, an adapted physical education program is needed. The adapted program should be diversified in its scope and suited to the needs of students with various disabilities, limitations, and capacities.[1] Developmental in nature, it includes exercises, games, rhythms, aquatics, and sports designed to meet the unique physical education needs of students.[1] It is designed to provide a learning environment that is safe and the opportunity for each individual to experience success and achievement. The adapted physical education program will be addressed fully in Chapter 11.

INTRAMURALS

The intramural program is the phase of the total program that provides students of all abilities with the opportunity to participate in organized activities outside of the instructional program. Participation in the intramural program is voluntary. A diversity of activities is usually offered, and they may be conducted on a recreational or competitive basis, or both.

The intramural program as an extension of the instructional program offers all students the opportunity to apply the skills and knowledge acquired in the instructional

program, further enhancing their psychomotor development. Students can further develop their skills and acquire competency in activities that they can enjoy and use throughout their lifetime. Competency encourages participation in activities after the school years have ended; individuals who have not developed skills and confidence in their ability to use them are less likely to participate in recreational activities after they graduate.[1] Moreover, the additional opportunity to be active can further contribute to the development of fitness.

The intramural program can also contribute a great deal to the attainment of the social and affective development objectives of physical education. The intramural setting provides a social setting for students to participate with their peers in physical activities. Friendships are encouraged as students find a common meeting ground in their enjoyment of the activity. Students learn to cooperate and compete with each other in a wholesome manner, without the undue pressure of winning and losing. Opportunities for leadership and followership encourage personal growth in these areas. Students given the opportunity for involvement in the management and direction of the intramural program learn to accept and carry out responsibilities in an appropriate manner.[6]

Cognitive development is further enhanced as students have increased opportunities to apply information and knowledge gained in the instructional program to situations encountered in the intramural setting. Furthermore, many intramural programs provide students with the opportunity to officiate. As an official, students further their knowledge of the rules and are given opportunities to interpret and apply them to regulate the conduct of the activity. Students also have the opportunity to serve as a coach of a team, which offers them a chance to apply strategies learned in the instructional program and the opportunity to create new strategies.

The organization and the conduct of the intramural program involves determining the nature and scope of the program, selecting activities, scheduling, determining eligibility, establishing awards, maintaining records, providing for officials, planning health examinations, financing, directing publicity and promotion, and conducting evaluations.

Nature and Scope of the Program

One issue that must be addressed is the orientation of the program. Should competition be featured or should the emphasis be recreational in nature? The needs and desires of the students must be considered in answering this question.

If the program is oriented toward competition, winning is featured. League standings are monitored closely, tournaments are conducted with a view toward naming a champion, and trophies and other awards are typically given. The best participants dominate the playing time, teams may devote considerable time to practice, and avoiding mistakes as much as possible is emphasized.

When the program is oriented toward recreation, emphasis is on maximizing the participation of all students. League standings are not posted, and each game is played as an entity in itself. All students play an equal amount of time, and awards and trophies are not offered. However, in some cases certificates of participation are given.

The emphasis on competition and recreation within a given program depends on the needs and desires of the students and the nature of the activity. Some students join the intramural program for the enjoyment of competition, and this often includes students who have been eliminated from the athletic program. Other students join for the experience of taking part in enjoyable activities with their friends. Perhaps the best answer is a balanced program that provides appropriate competitive experiences and recreational opportunities so that students can select the experience that best meets their own personal needs.

Activities. The type and variety of activities offered to participants are the keystones of the intramural program. Activities are a strong factor in determining the amount of resulting participation. Therefore it is important to select the right activities for inclusion within the program. Furthermore, the scope of intramural activities should be determined by students. Because students chose to participate in intramurals during their free time, intramural

---

BOX 7-1

POSSIBLE ACTIVITIES FOR AN INTRAMURAL PROGRAM

Adventure activities	Fencing	Riflery
	Flag football	Roller hockey
Aerobic dance	Floor hockey	Roller skating
	Frisbee	Rowing
Archery	Golf	Sailing
Badminton	Gymnastics	Shuffleboard
Billiards	Handball	Skiing
Bowling	Horseback riding	Soccer
Cooperative games		Softball
	Horseshoes	Swimming
Cross-country running	Ice hockey	Table tennis
	Ice skating	Tennis
Cross-country skiing	Judo	Track and field
	Karate	Volleyball
Curling	Lacrosse	Water games
Cycling	Orienteering	Weight lifting
Dancing	Paddle tennis	Wrestling
Deck tennis	Racquetball	

---

activity offerings should reflect students' desires and needs.

One means to determine students' interests is through the use of a survey. Copies of the survey could be distributed through the homeroom teacher or administered in the physical education classes. After compiling the results, this information should be posted so that students can clearly see that the activities being offered are a result of their expressed interests.

Although student interest is of considerable importance in selecting activities, consideration must also be given to the ability and safety of the participants.

A variety of activities should be offered. Activities can be modified to offer novel events, increased participation, and additional competitive opportunities. Basketball may be offered as a team sport, one on one, or free throw contest, for example. A list of activities that could be offered is shown in Box 7-1.

The intramural program should also provide opportunities for self-directed activities. Students should have the opportunity to come to a facility and work out or conduct an activity without having to enter a competitive tournament. Students should be able to check out equipment and use it during their free time under properly supervised conditions.

Scheduling. The time when activities are scheduled will depend on the facilities, the season of the year, instructional offerings, the community, faculty availability, student needs, and budget requirements. Consideration must also be given to the instructional offerings when planning the schedule. Ideally intramural activities should be closely coordinated with activities in the instructional program to provide students with opportunities to further develop and refine skills and knowledges presented in class.

Facilities and equipment. Proper facilities and adequate equipment are critical to the success of the intramural program. This becomes an important consideration in the scheduling of program activities. Priority is often given to interscholastic athletics in terms of the scheduling of facilities. As the number of boys and girls athletic teams continues to grow, obtaining facilities for the use of the intramural program becomes more difficult. This may be particularly true in the afternoon, one of the most desirable times for intramurals. There are several ways to deal with this problem.

One approach is to schedule intramural activities out of season relative to the interscholastic program, for example, to schedule intramural volleyball in the spring, rather than in the season when interscholastic teams typically play. Another approach to resolving this problem is to schedule intramurals during the low-demand times. This may involve before school, during lunch, or in the early evening when facilities are available. Another approach is to extend the program from the secondary school to the community setting. Nearby elementary schools, churches, youth-serving agencies, parks, and recreation areas can be used to conduct the intramural program. Sometimes commercial facilities are used, such as bowling alleys, swimming pools, golf courses, ski slopes, and skating rinks. Schools are typically accorded special rental rates for the use of these facilities.

Eligibility. A few simple eligibility rules are needed to ensure a wholesome experience for participants. However, these rules should be kept to a minimum, be easy to administer, and provide for participation for the vast majority of students under fair conditions.

Eligibility rules should require medical clearance to participate in activities. There are activities that by their nature should not be engaged in by individuals with certain health problems. Additionally, students should be cleared by the school health department when returning to school from a serious illness before being allowed to participate. Such rules are essential to ensure the safety and well-being of program participants.

Awards and point systems. Arguments have been advanced by professionals in support of and against the granting of awards for intramural competition. Awards can stimulate interest, provide an incentive for participation, and serve to recognize achievement. On the other hand, awards make programs more expensive, typically recognize the achievements of a few participants rather than many, and may be unnecessary because individuals would participate even if no awards were given. Professionals who oppose awards also stress that there should be no expectation of awards for participation in volun-

tary, leisure-time activities; joy and satisfaction received from participation should be reward enough.

Record keeping. Record keeping is important to the efficient management of the program. Information needed to determine the worth of the program and to evaluate its effectiveness should be maintained. Records allow physical education teachers to determine the degree to which the program is providing for the needs of the students and the extent of participation. They show activities that are popular and those that are not favored. They focus attention on the best units of competition, needs of the program, effective management procedures, and leadership strengths and weaknesses. Record keeping is an important phase of the program that should not be overlooked.

Use of computers. An increasing number of schools are using computers to assist in the management of the intramural program. There are a diversity of computer programs available to help in various aspects of this task.

Computers can be used to assist in scheduling. Programs are available that will expedite the scheduling process, the assigning of teams to various tournament structures, and the printing of final copies for distribution. Information on participants, team statistics, eligibility, and officials can be easily stored and recalled quickly when needed. The use of the computer, particularly in large programs, can result in the elimination of much of the paperwork while contributing to the more efficient administration of the program.

Health examinations. To safeguard their health, all participants should be required to have a health examination. The annual physical examination, commonly completed before the start of the school year, is often used as a basis to clear students for participation. In other schools a special examination may be required before the start of the activity.

Finances. Because intramurals contribute to the attainment of educational objectives, they should be financed out of the board of education and central administration funds, just as other phases of the program are financed. They should be included in the regular physical education budget, and they should be supported through the regularly budgeted school income.

In some schools the cost of the program is incorporated into the regular activity fee that includes such student activities as dramatics, interscholastic athletics, band, and the school newspaper. Other schools finance intramurals from athletic gate receipts, equipment rental, required participant entry fees, and special fund-raising projects.

Program promotion. One aspect of the intramural program that should not be neglected is publicity. A well-planned promotional effort can encourage student involvement, engender administrative support, and inform the public about the contributions of the program to students' lives. Information must be disseminated about the activities offered and the benefits of participating.

BOX 7-2

CHECKLIST FOR EVALUATION OF INTRAMURAL PROGRAMS

1. Do students have major responsibility for the leadership of the intramural program?
2. Are the students provided with leadership opportunities within the program?
3. Is the program guided by an intramural council?
4. Do students serve as assistant directors or supervisors?
5. Do students serve as game officials?
6. Are procedures in place to prepare students to serve as game officials?
7. Do the policies and procedures employed serve the needs and interests of students?
8. While the intramural program should be available to students, faculty, and staff, is the major emphasis on the students?
9. Does the program foster fair play and sportsmanship?
10. Does the program emphasize educational outcomes in addition to other related objectives?
11. Are adequate measures in place to ensure the health and safety of all participants?
12. Are competitive events equalized as much as possible?
13. Do the majority of the participants view the intramural program/experience as rewarding?
14. Is there sufficient variety built into the program offerings?
15. Are qualified officials provided?

Newspapers should be encouraged to give appropriate coverage to these activities. Students can write articles about the program for the school and local newspapers. Attractive bulletin boards located throughout the school can be used to display schedules, post standings, and inform students about upcoming events. Brochures, notices, or handbooks explaining the various aspects of the program can be distributed to interested students and parents. Holding clinics on various sports is another way to generate interest in the program. Orientation sessions can be held at school assemblies and at the beginning of the year in homerooms or physical education classes. Special days incorporating activities, such as a predicted time running or walking event, team challenges, or faculty-student competitions or activities, can be held with considerable publicity. A good job of program promotion will result in greater student participation and better public understanding.

Program evaluation. To ensure that the program meets its stated objectives, periodic evaluations should be conducted. The philosophy, organization and administration, competition, program activities, time periods, rules and regulations, finances, and publicity are all aspects of the program that should be carefully scrutinized. A checklist to help in the evaluation of the intramural program is shown in Box 7-2.

For a program to be successful, it is important that it meets the needs and interests of the students for whom it was designed. Activity offerings should be evaluated periodically to determine if student interest is growing or waning, if the manner in which the activity is conducted needs to be changed, or if activities should be added or removed from the program.

Numerous evaluation techniques can be employed. Generally speaking, the process should include definition of program objectives; data collection and evaluation of the number of participants, teams, and games played; appraisal forms; estimates of cost-effectiveness; and participant opinion about specific activities. It is important to evaluate regularly the program to determine how it can be improved to serve the students better.

Officials. Capable officials are critical to the success of the intramural program. Intramurals should be officiated by students. The director of intramurals, the intramural council, or an officiating committee can be used to recruit and train student officials. Some students who love the sport but who do not wish to play competitively may enjoy being involved in the intramural program as an official.

Administration. In many schools the intramural program is under the jurisdiction of the director of intramurals. This individual typically reports to the director of physical education.

The director is responsible for planning programs; securing adequate funding; organizing tournaments and other forms of competition; actively supervising the program; and monitoring the maintenance of facilities, equipment, and supplies. Additionally, the director often plans intramural council meetings; interprets the program to the students, school administration, and the public; prepares budgets; and evaluates the worth and effectiveness of the program.

Students have increasingly become involved in the leadership of the program. One way to involve students in the conduct of the intramural program is to develop an intramural council. The council may consist of elected students, representative of the various grade levels, who will work closely with the director of intramurals. The intramural council is often accorded responsibility for developing policies, rules, and procedures to guide the program. Additional students may be involved in the conduct of the program through the formulation of student committees that report directly to the intramural council. Committees can be developed to deal with many aspects of the program such as activity selection and scheduling, rules and regulations, and preparation of officials, publicity, and record keeping. The intramural council can be of tremendous assistance to the director, and it provides an excellent means for students to be involved in the conduct of the program.

Units of competition. There are many ways for organizing and equating competition for the intramural program. In grouping students for competition, it is important that the teacher not lose sight of the purposes of the intramural program—promoting student involvement, enhancing individual development, and providing an enjoyable experience for all participants.

At the secondary level, several units of organization are possible. Organization may be made by grades, homerooms, residential districts, or physical education classes. Homerooms provide an easy and heterogeneous means of grouping. Students of various skill levels participate on the same teams. In some cases where it is warranted, homerooms could be divided into two or more teams by ability, size, or age. Teams would be assigned to different leagues based on salient characteristics.

Regardless of the method used to form teams, members should never be selected in such a fashion that students are publicly embarrassed about their poor ability or humiliated by being chosen last. Care must be taken to provide for healthy competition and enjoyable participation for all students.

Tournaments and Leagues

There are several different ways to organize competition that are appropriate for the intramural and instructional program. Leagues and tournaments are popular in many sports. The type of competition used will depend on the number of entries, the number of days available for play, the facilities and equipment available, and the number of officials. Teachers should keep in mind the guiding tenets of the intramural program when deciding on the type of structure to be used. Additionally, teachers should not be afraid to modify activities (shorten games or increase variations for scoring) to provide for increased opportunities for students to participate.

Round robin tournament

The round robin tournament is probably one of the most widely used tournaments. This tournament allows every team or individual to play every other team or individual, and thus it is one of the best structures because it provides for maximum play. It is a good choice when adequate time is available for play. It is frequently used in recreational leagues, in which it works best with no more than eight teams or individuals. Because each team or individual plays every other team or individual at least once during the tournament, everyone involved continues to play until completion of the schedule. The winner is the team or individual with the highest won-lost percentage at the end of play.

To calculate the number of games to be played, the following formula can be used where N equals the number of entrants (teams or individuals): $E = (N - 1) \div 2 =$ number of games. For an eight-team tourney, the formula indicates that $8(8 - 1) \div 2$ or 28 games would need to be scheduled.

To schedule a tournament for eight teams, for example, each team should be assigned a number. Teams should

---

Rotation for eight teams

Round 1	Round 2	Round 3	Round 4
1-8	1-7	1-6	1-5
2-7	8-6	7-5	6-4
3-6	2-5	8-4	7-3
4-5	3-4	2-3	8-2

Round 5	Round 6	Round 7
1-4	1-3	1-2
5-3	4-2	3-8
6-2	5-8	4-7
7-8	6-7	5-6

Rotation for seven teams illustrating the use of a bye

Round 1	Round 2	Round 3	Round 4
1-bye	1-7	1-6	1-5
2-7	bye-6	7-5	6-4
3-6	2-5	bye-4	7-3
4-5	3-4	2-3	bye-2

Round 5	Round 6	Round 7
1-4	1-3	1-2
5-3	4-2	3-bye
6-2	5-bye	4-7
7-bye	6-7	5-6

FIG. 7-1 Round robin tournament.

be numbered down the right-hand column and up the left. Team 1 is kept stationary, while the other teams are moved one place counterclockwise on the schedule until all games are complete (Fig. 7-1).

When the number of teams or individuals is uneven, a bye (an exemption from playing a round) is given to one of the entrants. As the schedule rotates, the team that is last each time is assigned a bye (Fig. 7-1).

Elimination tournaments

Elimination tournaments do not allow for maximum participation. The winners continue to play while the losers drop out. A team or individual is eliminated after one or two losses depending on the type of tournament selected. Usually the poorly skilled teams and less proficient individuals are eliminated first and relegated to sitting on the sidelines. The better teams or individuals have increased time to participate and further improve their

skills. It is important to balance the need to promote student involvement with time constraints.

There are several types of elimination tournaments. They include the single elimination, consolation, and double elimination tournaments. When there are an uneven number of entrants or not enough to fill all the brackets, byes are used.

Single elimination tournament

As illustrated in Fig. 7-2, in the single or straight elimination tournament, one defeat leads to the elimination of the entrant. This type of tournament is quick to conduct because half of the entrants are eliminated after the first round. However, there is no provision for selecting second- and third-place finishers, and it does little to promote participation because it eliminates so many participants early in the competition.

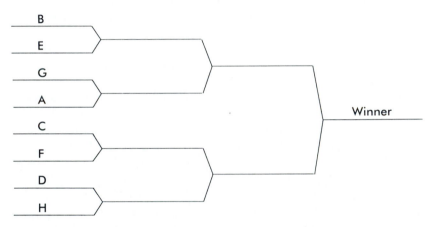

FIG. 7-2   Single elimination tournament.

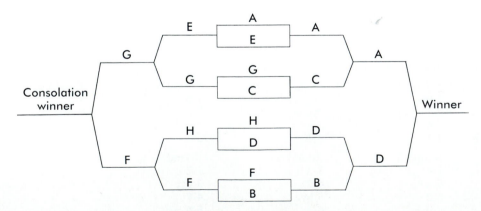

FIG. 7-3   Consolation tournament.

Consolation tournament

There are many types of consolation tournaments. Generally, when an entrant loses in the first round, the entrant continues to play to determine a consolation winner. It should be noted that the consolation winner is not the third-place winner, but the winner of the consolation tournament. An example of a consolation tournament is shown in Fig. 7-3.

Double elimination tournament

The double elimination tournament requires two losses before the entrant is eliminated (Fig. 7-4). It provides additional opportunities for participants to play because it does not eliminate them so quickly.

Challenge tournaments

Ongoing tournaments in which competition occurs by entrants challenging as many other entrants as possible during the alloted time are known as challenge tournaments. Entrants are ranked and usually are restricted to challenging other participants who are one or two ranks above their present ranking. Winners exchange places with the losers. Challenge tournaments allow the best players to move to the top. Placement in the initial rankings may be done by a draw, seeding, or the order in which entrants sign up. Types of challenge tournaments include ladder, pyramid, and funnel tournaments.[6]

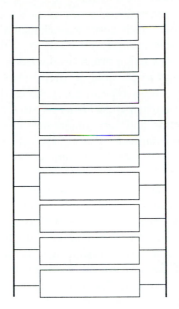

FIG. 7-5   Ladder tournament.

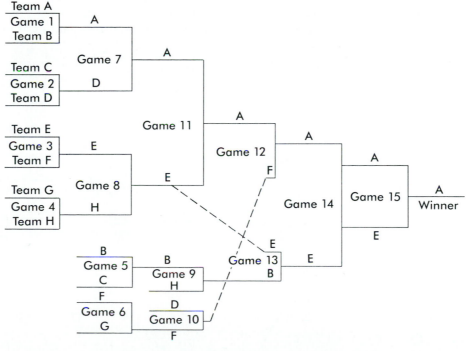

FIG. 7-4   Double elimination tournament.

Ladder tournament

The ladder tournament is well suited for individual and team competition. As illustrated in Fig. 7-5, the contestants are arranged in a ladder or a vertical formation, one above the other. Each entry may challenge the one directly above, or in some cases, two above. If the challenger wins, the names change places on the ladder. The goal is to move as high as possible up the rungs of the ladder. This is a continuous type of tournament that does not eliminate any participants. However, this type of tournament may drag and participants may lose interest.

Pyramid tournament. Although similar to the ladder tournament, the pyramid tournament can accommodate a large number of participants (Fig. 7-6). It is similar to the ladder tournament except instead of having one name on a rung or a step, several names are on the lower step, with the number of participants decreasing at each level. A participant may challenge anyone in the same horizontal row on the tournament chart or anyone to the immediate left or right on the level above.

Funnel tournament. The features of the ladder and pyramid tournaments are combined in a funnel tournament (Fig. 7-7). This type of structure can accommodate large numbers of participants as well as ranked players. The bottom portion of the funnel is governed by rules for the pyramid structure, and the top portion of the funnel is governed by rules of the ladder structure.

Special events. In addition to tournaments and challenges, special events may add excitement to the intramural program. This could include a schoolwide activity such as a fitness challenge for all students and faculty in the school or a sports day with another nearby school. Additionally, participants involved in self-directed activities, such as jogging, can form a club to provide companionship in the activity and recognition for accomplishments such as jogging 200 miles.

The type of tournament structure adopted should be best for the group, activity, and student interest. The goal should be to have as much participation as possible for all skill abilities within the local constraints imposed by the facilities and time available. Tournaments encourage participant interest and enthusiasm and are an important part of the intramural and instructional program.

Sports Clubs

The concept of a sports club, in which students meet to pursue their common interest in a particular sport or an activity, originated in Europe. Clubs have increased in popularity in the United States and provide another means to extend the physical education program to meet the interests and needs of many more students. A club is typically devoted to one activity such as mountain climbing, skiing, or tennis, and it encourages students and other individuals to participate at all levels of skill. Clubs are typically established, funded, and run by students under the guidance of a club advisor. School clubs are typically required to follow guidelines set for the conduct of extracurricular activities set forth by the administration.

Sports clubs offer many advantages. They present opportunities for students and others, such as school faculty, to engage in activities that interest them and that are not provided for in the physical education program. Sports clubs offer students the chance to plan and to govern their own programs. Clubs are often funded by club membership—the students—and provide students with the chance to practice sound fiscal management. Clubs

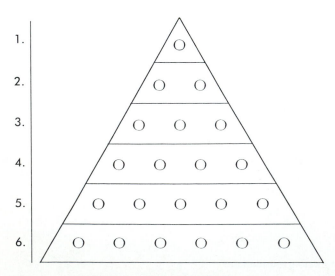

FIG. 7-6 Pyramid tournament.

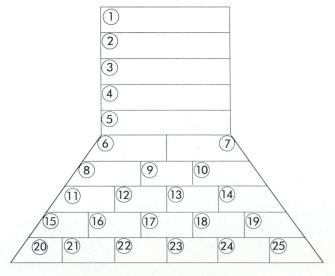

FIG. 7-7 Funnel tournament.

Some high schools have leaders clubs whose members provide invaluable assistance in various aspects of the physical education program. Here the teacher at Evanston Township High School, IL, is holding a seminar with the senior leaders.
Courtesy of Ann Stevens, Evanston Township High School, Evanston, IL.

also provide an opportunity for students to socialize with their friends while enjoying a particular activity or sport.

Interscholastic Sports

Interscholastic sports, or athletics, provide the opportunity for highly skilled students to compete against their peers in other schools. Similar to the other facets of the physical education curriculum, the interscholastic program should be educational in nature. It is an integral part of the total physical education curriculum and should grow out of the instructional and intramural programs.

In recent years there has been a great deal of attention focused on the interscholastic sports program. Concerns have been raised regarding the actual outcomes of interscholastic athletics and their educational nature. Can interscholastic athletics contribute to the growth and development of its participants? Or are athletics detrimental in nature, adversely affecting the health and well-being of youths who participate? It appears that athletics are neither inherently good nor bad. The quality of the leadership provided is critical in determining the program outcomes—whether the experience will be positive or negative for the partipants.

Values of Interscholastic Athletics

There have been many values ascribed to participation in interscholastic athletics. The positive outcomes that many suggest derive from the interscholastic athletic experience are briefly summarized in the next section.

Cooperation. Competitive sports can provide a social laboratory for the student to learn how to work with others in a cooperative manner and to contribute toward the common purposes of the team. Attainment of team goals requires cooperation and commitment on the part of all participants. Athletics can also promote social consciousness and can develop an understanding of the feelings and rights of others.

Acceptance. Athletics may teach the appreciation of all persons in terms of their ability and performance regardless of race, creed, or origin. Individuals may be applauded for their achievement and recognized for their accomplishment without regard for their skin color, religion, nationality, or socioeconomic status. Athletics can alleviate discrimination and prejudice provided that their structure and leadership emphasize the attainment of these important outcomes.

Good citizenship. Competitive athletics can help to develop traits of good citizenship essential to democratic living. These include qualities such as initiative, trustworthiness, dependability, social consciousness, loyalty, and respect for the individual.

Leadership and followership. Competitive athletics can promote leadership qualities in students. Athletics may provide opportunities for accepting responsibilities, making decisions, influencing others, and developing other personal qualities important to leadership. Athletics may

Athletic opportunities for women have increased in recent years.
Courtesy of Barbara Armstrong.

also help students develop traits of successful follower-ship, including such qualities as respecting authority, abiding by rules, and cooperating with those in leadership positions. Athletics may promote a recognition for the rights of others and a sense of fairness.

Self-discipline. Athletics help develop qualities of self-discipline and determination. The rigorous training involved forces individuals to push themselves to achieve maximum effort. Athletes must be disciplined to make sacrifices and work hard, and they must have the determination necessary to achieve personal and team goals.

Skill development. Athletics contribute to the development of physical skills. The acquisition of skill through sports leads to a higher level of proficiency. The development of skill, furthermore, results in recognition, a feeling of achievement, and an enhancement of self-esteem. Students who develop their athletic skills to a high level may also be accorded the opportunity to continue their athletic participation at the collegiate level.

Physical development. Participation in athletics contributes to the development of physical attributes. Through the intensive training provided for competition, various components of physical fitness such as strength, speed, endurance, and coordination are developed.

Cognitive development. Opportunities to learn advanced knowledge relative to skills and strategies are provided through athletics. Numerous occasions are available to apply knowledge and concepts learned to one's performance.

Social development. Athletics contribute to social poise, self-composure, and confidence. Participation also promotes the value of healthy competition and the need to cooperate with others to attain one's goals. Under effective leadership such qualities as fairness, adherence to the rules, understanding and respect for others, acceptance of decisions, and graciousness in victory and defeat may be developed. Participants in athletics are accorded recognition by their peers and parents. Athletics convey status on individuals.

Athletics can contribute to the formulation of friendships. A deep bond of friendship may develop between teammates as they practice and compete together day after day, working toward commonly held goals. Sports provide a shared experience to be enjoyed by friends.

Values. Participation in athletics may contribute to the development of values. The athlete develops a concern for teammates and opponents. The athlete learns the importance of respecting others. Athletics may promote a way of life that fosters morality, ethical behavior, and concern for individual dignity and worth. Values concerning what is right and what is wrong become familiar as athletics provide opportunities to put one's beliefs into practice.

Individual development. Self-discipline, self-realization, and a desire to achieve are individual values that can be developed through sports. Self-control may be increased through athletics. Athletics provide a highly charged atmosphere in which individuals may test and develop their ability to exercise self-restraint. The ability to withstand or cope with emotional stress and to function effectively under pressure are skills that can be learned by virtue of participation in athletics. Athletics can also provide opportunities for participants to learn how to make decisions and live with the consequences.

The benefits of athletics have been extolled by many professionals within the field. Sports can be a positive experience for its participants. Athletics are a source of fun and enjoyment and an acceptable outlet for excess energy. They can provide a common bond for unifying a school and a community. They can also be instrumental in encouraging students to remain in school. They provide youths with the opportunity to be involved with the school community.

Athletics can contribute to the total development of the individual and enhance educational outcomes in all three learning domains. Athletics provide students with the opportunity to learn worthwhile skills, develop physical abilities and fitness, grow intellectually, and enhance personal development.

Suggested Harm Caused by Athletics

Although there are many positive benefits typically ascribed to participation in athletics, there are also many potential detrimental outcomes. The following is a brief description of the most salient of these concerns.

Ego-centered athletes. The star athletes tend to be glorified by the school and the community. They are frequently singled out from the team to receive special attention and recognition. Subsequently these athletes may develop inflated ideas about themselves. They begin to develop an attitude that they are special and better than other students in the school. They may assume that they should receive personal favors and special attention because of their reputations as outstanding athletes.

Winning at all costs. In the desire to have winning teams, some coaches adopt unethical and undesirable practices. Academic irregularities may be overlooked, undue pressure may be exerted on athletes to play when injured, athletes may be physically or psychologically abused, and long practice sessions may be held. A professional rather than an educational perspective may pervade the athletic arena. Winning may dominate the program as opposed to efforts to foster personal growth.

Deemphasis of educational values. Educational values may become deemphasized because of the focus placed on athletics. Athletics may become more important to the individual than any educational activity. Highly skilled athletes, believing they are destined to become a collegiate star or eventually a professional athlete, may devote all of their energies to this endeavor. For some of these individuals, education becomes a low priority. Moreover, athletic trips often may require leaving school

early, athletes may receive release time to practice, and time required for athletics decreases the time available for educational pursuits.

Harmful pressures. When parents and members of the community develop the kind of interest in the sports program that has winning as its main objective, unhealthy pressures on athletes are likely to result. Athletes may feel constant pressure to achieve to meet adult expectations and goals.

Loss of identity. Although it appears that coaches are becoming less authoritarian, some coaches still employ authoritarian procedures that prevent athletes from making their own decisions and leading their own lives. Athletes may begin to wonder if they have the capability to make decisions and the right to lead their own lives. Loss of individual identity and freedom often occurs in programs that overemphasize winning—in programs where winning is the primary objective and where athletes are used as instruments to achieve this end.

Inequitable allocation of resources. Athletics are only one phase of the total physical education program. Yet the resources (funds and personnel) devoted to sports are often distributed in an unequitable amount to the athletic program. A disproportionate amount of resources are allocated to serve only a small number of students out of the entire student body.

Role conflict. Athletes may experience conflicts between the expectations associated with their role as a student and their role as an athlete. They may have difficulty resolving the disparate demands of both roles. For example, an athlete with an important examination the next day may experience role conflict when the coach calls for a mandatory team meeting after a particularly poor practice. The athlete then faces the dilemma of deciding which demands to meet: the academic or the athletic. Often academics suffer as athletes feel overtly or subtly pressured to meet athletic demands.

Overspecialization. Increasingly, athletes are specializing in one sport on a year-round basis. Athletes used to participate in more than one sport during the school year; some athletes played on a different sports team during each season. Specialization often did not occur until college. Now more athletes train year round for a particular sport. Off seasons are devoted to training. Furthermore, athletes may seek out additional opportunities for competitions in community and summer leagues and camps. This increased specialization may lead to overuse injuries and athletic burnout. Moreover, this concentration on athletics leaves youths little time to develop other interests or other facets of their lives.

Aggression and violence. Athletics may encourage the expression of aggression and promote violence. Intense rivalries between schools can precipitate destructive and violent acts by athletes, students, and adult fans. Coaches who promote winning at all costs and "killing an opponent" encourage aggression and violence. Athletes should be coached to do their best within a healthy and competitive environment.

The manner in which the athletic program is conducted and the leadership provided greatly influence whether participation will be a positive or negative experience for the students. When conducted in accordance with desirable standards and directed toward the attainment of educational outcomes, athletics increase an individual's potential for accomplishing beneficial effects. However, when undesirable standards govern the program, athletics can be detrimental and harmful to students.

GUIDELINES FOR CONDUCTING A QUALITY INTERSCHOLASTIC SPORTS PROGRAM

To ensure that the developmental needs of the students are met and educational outcomes are realized, the interscholastic sports program should be carefully designed and conducted by qualified and dedicated professionals. The following guidelines may be helpful in structuring and implementing the athletic program to ensure a positive and meaningful experience for all participants.

1. The athletic program should represent a natural outgrowth of the instructional and intramural programs. These programs should function effectively for all students before interscholastic athletics are considered.

2. Qualified and dedicated leadership is essential if the educational outcomes of the athletic program are to be realized. It is essential that the coach be knowledgeable about the growth and developmental characteristics of the athletes. The physical, mental, emotional, and social developmental characteristics of the athletes must be taken into account when one is designing and implementing the athletic program. The coach should also be knowledgeable about the activity, instructional techniques, and conditioning of the sport. Competency in the medical aspects of athletics is also important. Finally, the coach should be a positive role model for the athletes to emulate.

3. All students who choose to participate in athletics should have the opportunity to compete. Students who are willing to make the necessary commitment to the program and to practice should have the opportunity to compete in interscholastic athletics. Students who do not have the necessary skills to participate on the varsity teams should be provided with other opportunities to develop their skills and compete. These opportunities may include junior varsity teams, "B" or "C" squads, or class teams such as a freshman team. All interested students should be able to compete at their levels of ability. If athletics are indeed educational in nature, all students have the right to participate in that experience and realize desired educational outcomes.

4. Opportunities must be provided for students with disabilities to participate in the athletic program. Care must be taken not to make the assumption that if students are disabled in some way, they do not have the ability to participate in athletics. Students' abilities, not disabilities, should be emphasized. Students with disabilities have the right to attain the same educational benefits and personal values as other students who participate in sports.

5. The athletic program must be based on the developmental characteristics of the student. The program should meet the needs of the students and be appropriate for their age, maturity, and physical, mental, social, intellectual, and emotional characteristics.

6. The athletic program should be conducted during after-school hours. A regular class period should not be used for practice, nor should practice be conducted during the physical education class period. Also, athletes should not be excused from physical education classes.

7. A broad spectrum of activities based on the needs of interests of students should be offered. The number of students that can be accommodated in a wide variety of sports should be the basis on which the interschool athletic program is founded and developed. The greater the number of sports that are offered, the greater the number of participants. Team and individual sports activities should be a part of the program.

8. The athletic program should be organized and administered with the needs of the participant in mind. Concerns for entertainment value and spectators should not influence the program.

9. The health and well-being of the participants should be of primary consideration. All students should have medical clearance from a physician before being allowed to participate. Proper safety practices and procedures should be followed at all times. A written emergency care plan to deal with accidents is essential. The participants and their parents should be informed of the procedures that will be followed should an accident occur. Typically, parents must sign a waiver of responsibility before their child can participate. Provision for medical supervision during practices and competition is necessary. When possible, a certified athletic trainer should be available to provide necessary care at practices and games. Some form of insurance for the athletes should be available at all schools.

10. The program should emphasize healthful participation and fun. Development of the individual and enjoyment of the experience should be stressed, not "winning at all costs." An educational focus should be maintained in all aspects of the program.

11. Adequate preconditioning and practice sessions before the start of each sports season is essential for the health and safety of the athletes. Proper principles of exercise should be followed in designing and conducting the conditioning program. Coaches should also be familiar with special precautions required by exercising in

certain environmental conditions, such as in high heat and humidity.

12. Adequate facilities and equipment should be provided. Moreover, facilities and equipment should be shared with all facets of the physical education program. The needs of all individuals in the physical education program should be considered, and facilities and equipment should be allocated in a fair and acceptable manner.

13. All athletic programs should be financed as other educational activities are—with funds provided by the local educational agency. However, in difficult economic times, schools may operate with a limited budget. In these circumstances other sources of revenue may need to be considered. Often this is raised through various fundraising activities such as car washes, candy sales, or increasingly by charging participants a fee to play.

14. Awards should be used judiciously. They should be simple and inexpensive such as medals, ribbons, and trophies. Athletes should be encouraged to participate for the intrinsic values and personal satisfaction associated with the athletic experience, rather than to attain an award.

15. The philosophy, the policies, and the procedures governing the athletic program should be clearly written. Lines of authority for the administration of the program need to be delineated. The responsibilities of the school administration, director of athletics, coaches, parents, and participants should be clearly identified and understood.

16. The rules and regulations of national, state, and local athletic associations under whose aegis the program is conducted should be followed.

17. The program should constantly be evaluated and improved. Periodic evaluations can be instrumental in preventing potential problems. Moreover, evaluation can provide information that can help improve the program and make it a more positive experience for all those involved. A checklist for evaluating interscholastic programs is shown in Box 7-3.

These guidelines can help school districts plan and implement worthwhile programs that contribute to the educational mission of the school.

Sound and qualified leadership is essential to the properly functioning athletic program. Leadership plays an important role in preventing undesirable practices and keeping the interscholastic sports program in a proper perspective. Leaders must see that the program is always conducted with regard to the best interest of the students. Whether the students experience positive benefits of participation in athletics, as opposed to negative, ultimately depends on the leadership provided.

Administration of the Program

The director of athletics is the key administrator in the interscholastic sports program. Other personnel involved

---

> **BOX 7-3**
>
> ## CHECKLIST FOR EVALUATION OF INTERSCHOLASTIC SPORT PROGRAMS
>
> 1. Is the sports program financially supported by the physical education budget?
> 2. Are all sports in the program provided by equitable funding?
> 3. Are interscholastic sports available to all students on an equitable basis?
> 4. Are adequate health and safety standards being met with respect to the number and length of practices, number of games, fitness of the participants, and type of competition?
> 5. Are adequate and appropriate medical services and supervision provided for the interscholastic program?
> 6. Is an athletic trainer available to the interscholastic program pre-, during, and postseason?
> 7. Is competition provided by schools of similar size?
> 8. Is the program justifiable as an important educational tool?
> 9. Does the program emphasize educational outcomes in addition to competitive outcomes?
> 10. Are academic standards for participants maintained?
> 11. Are good public relations with the community furthered through this program?
> 12. Are the needs and interests of the participants central to the program?
> 13. Are various forms of intrinsic and extrinsic rewards provided for the participants?
> 14. Are student athletes provided with leadership opportunities within the program?

---

in program administration include the coach, the athletic trainer, and the athletic council.

Director of athletics. The athletics director implements the athletic policies established by the school board and athletic council. Responsibilities of the athletics director include preparing the budget for the sports program, purchasing equipment and supplies, supervising eligibility requirements, arranging for transportation, seeing that athletes receive medical approval and that insurance is adequate, instituting and monitoring procedures for crowd control, supervising the staff, evaluating the program and its personnel, and monitoring the program in general.

In schools with a large athletics program, the director may work closely with an assistant director and delegate some responsibilities to this administrator. The assistant

A greater number of qualified women coaches and athletic administrators is needed.
Courtesy of Coakley J: *Sport and society: issues and controversies,* ed 4, 1990, Mosby.

director may help with such responsibilities as scheduling, staff supervision, transportation, and purchasing.

The coach. One of the most popular careers within the realm of physical education is coaching. Many students who show exceptional skill in an interscholastic sport would like to become a physical education teacher to coach. They feel that because they have been outstanding high-school athletes, they will be successful in coaching. This is not necessarily true. There is insufficient evidence to indicate that exceptional skill in any activity necessarily guarantees success in teaching that activity. Many other factors are essential to coaching success (for example, interest in youth; personality; knowledge of human growth, development, and psychology; intelligence; integrity; leadership; and an empathetic attitude).

Coaching should be recognized as teaching, and coaches of sports teams should be hired for their abilities as teachers as well as their expertise as coaches. Because of the nature of the job, a coach may be in a better position to teach concepts that affect daily living than any other member of the school faculty. Youth, with their inherent drive for activity and their quest for excitement and competition found in sports, look up to their coaches and, in many cases, feel that they are the type of individual to be emulated. Therefore coaches should recognize their influence and see the value of such attributes as integrity, personality, and character. Although coaches must know thoroughly the sport they are coaching, these other characteristics are equally important.

Coaching is characterized in some schools by insecurity of position. Whether a coach feels secure depends to a great extent on the administration. In schools that emphasize producing winning teams and evaluate a coach's effectiveness on the basis of won-lost record, a coach's position may be insecure. A losing season could place the coach's job in jeopardy. On the other hand, in schools where the administration accentuates the educational outcomes of sport, a coach who places the attainment of educational objectives as a priority may find security.

Four qualifications characterize the outstanding coach. First, this person has an ability to teach the fundamentals and strategies of the sport; he or she must be a good teacher. Second, there is a need to understand the athlete: how a person functions at a particular level of development—with full appreciation of skeletal growth, muscular development, and physical and emotional limitations. Third, the coach understands the sport that is being coached. Thorough knowledge of techniques and rules is basic. Fourth, the coach should be a model for the athletes, a person of strong moral character. Patience, understanding, kindness, honesty, a clear sense of right and wrong, courage, cheerfulness, affection, humor, energy, and enthusiasm are imperative characteristics.

Many physical education programs do outstanding jobs of preparing professionals to work with these young athletes. However, there are an increasing number of individuals coaching in high school today who do not have a background in physical education or in teaching. These individuals may have little preparation and training for the positions they hold. Unfortunately, the only qual-

Self-evaluation: to be completed before the start of coaching assignment.

I. Statement of personal and program goals as they relate to the coaching assignment.

II. Statement of self-evaluation on applicable criteria relative to completion of goals statement: to be completed at the conclusion of your coaching assignment.

III. Athletic coordinator's evaluation: to be completed subsequent to the coaching assignment, then reviewed with the coach.

	High				Low
A. Administration					
1. Care of equipment	5	4	3	2	1
2. Organization of staff	5	4	3	2	1
3. Conduct of practices	5	4	3	2	1
4. Communication skills	5	4	3	2	1
5. Adherence to district and school philosophy and policies	5	4	3	2	1
6. Public relations	5	4	3	2	1
7. Supervision	5	4	3	2	1
B. Skills					
1. Knowledge of fundamentals	5	4	3	2	1
2. Presentation skills	5	4	3	2	1
3. Conditioning	5	4	3	2	1
4. Game preparation	5	4	3	2	1
5. Care and prevention of injuries	5	4	3	2	1
C. Relationships					
1. Enthusiasm					
a. Working with students	5	4	3	2	1
b. Working with staff	5	4	3	2	1
c. Working with academic staff	5	4	3	2	1
d. For the sport itself	5	4	3	2	1
2. Discipline					
a. Fairness	5	4	3	2	1
b. Consistency	5	4	3	2	1
3. Communication with players					
a. Individuals	5	4	3	2	1
b. As a team	5	4	3	2	1
D. Performance					
1. Appearance of team	5	4	3	2	1
2. Execution of team	5	4	3	2	1
3. Attitude of team	5	4	3	2	1
4. Conduct of coach during game	5	4	3	2	1
E. Self-improvement					
1. Attends local professional meetings	5	4	3	2	1
2. Attends out-of-district professional meetings	5	4	3	2	1
3. Familiarity with current professional literature	5	4	3	2	1

IV. Review by building athletic coordinator with coach (district athletic coordinator will review all evaluations before forwarding to the principal).

FIG. 7-8 Form for evaluation of coaches.

ification some coaches possess is the fact that they played the game in high school, college, or the professional ranks. It is generally recognized that the best preparation is training. In light of this, several states require that coaches have at least some instruction in the field of physical education.

AAHPERD's Task Force on Certification of High School Coaches, established to set standards for coaching certification, identified five essential areas: (1) medical aspects of athletic coaching, (2) social and psychological aspects of coaching, (3) theory and techniques of coaching, (4) kinesiological foundations of coaching, and (5) physiological foundations of coaching. The trend toward certification of coaches is growing. All individuals aspiring to coach should make sure they are carefully prepared to handle all aspects of the position.

Many athletes now participate in their sport on a year-round basis. Here athletes are attending a summer sports school to further develop their skills.
Courtesy of Joy Buffan, SUC Oswego, Oswego, NY.

Evaluation of coaches should be conducted periodically. Coaches should be encouraged to spend some time assessing their effectiveness. Athletic directors may evaluate coaches periodically to ascertain strengths and to determine areas where improvements need to be made. A form for the evaluation of coaches is shown in Fig. 7-8.

The athletic trainer. The profession of athletic training has taken on greater significance in recent years with the increase in sports programs and the recognition that the health of the athlete is an important consideration. Today's athletic trainers need special preparation to handle duties that include the prevention of injuries, administration of first aid, and postinjury treatment and rehabilitation. Certification by the National Athletic Trainers Association (NATA) is increasingly required to be hired as a professional. Furthermore, trainers should have such personal qualifications as emotional stability under stress, ability to act in a rational and productive manner in an emergency, and a standard of ethics that places the welfare of the participant first.

The financial situation of many schools prohibits the hiring of a full-time athletic trainer. Some schools, however, find it feasible to provide this service by hiring a qualified individual who plays a dual role. Such an individual might have another part-time school assignment (for example, a coach or a teacher). Some schools contract for the services of an athletic trainer through sports medicine clinics or local hospitals. Cooperative arrangements between colleges that offer an athletic training curriculum and the schools may be another means to secure the services of an athletic trainer.

The athletic council. Many schools have some type of athletic council or committee that establishes athletic policies for the institution. In some cases the principal may serve as chairperson; in other areas this position may be held by the director of athletics, the director of physical education, or another faculty member. The group may include coaches, students, parents, faculty members, members of the board of education, or members of the community.

Some of the functions of athletic councils include (1) making policy, (2) advising the athletic department on a wide variety of problems and issues, (3) approving awards, (4) endorsing and approving schedules and budgets, (5) evaluating the sports program, (6) interviewing and recommending coaches to athletic directors, (7) developing eligibility guidelines, and (8) developing a code of ethics.

SUMMARY

The comprehensive secondary school physical education curriculum is composed of the instructional, adapted, intramural and club, and interscholastic program components. The instructional program is typically perceived by leaders within the field as providing the foundation for these program components.

The adapted physical education program is designed to provide physical education instruction in a safe environment to those students who have disabilities. The adapted physical education program provides instruction in a diversity of sports and recreational activities. The program is structured to provide a safe learning environment and successful learning experiences in the least restrictive environment. An individualized educational plan (IEP) guides the physical education teacher in providing services to students with unique needs.

The intramural and club sports programs provide opportunities for all students regardless of skill ability to participate in sports and recreational activities. The emphasis of these programs is maximizing participation while providing opportunities to enhance one's skills further. Several types of organizational formats may be utilized to accomplish this objective.

The interscholastic program offers highly skilled students the opportunity to compete against their peers from other schools in a structured, competitive setting. Leadership is critical in this program so that the potential benefits of participation may be realized and possible harmful effects avoided. The program should keep winning in perspective and emphasize the contribution of athletics to the realization of educational goals.

FOR REVIEW

1. Prepare a short essay that describes the relationship of the instructional and the adapted components of the secondary school physical education program to the intramural and club and interscholastic sports program.
2. Identify ten guidelines that should be followed in designing and conducting an intramural program.
3. Describe the psychological, social, and emotional characteristics of secondary school students and the implications of these characteristics for the conduct of the interscholastic sports program.
4. List and briefly describe the potential positive outcomes and the possible detrimental effects that might be realized through participation in an interscholastic sports program. Identify ten suggestions for leaders of these programs to follow to ensure that the potential positive benefits are realized by the program's participants.

REFERENCES

1. Sherrill C: *Adapted physical education, recreation, and sport: a multidisciplinary approach,* ed 4, Dubuque, Iowa, 1993, William C Brown and Benchmark.
2. Long E, Irmer L: *Peopel,* Phoenix, Ariz, 1984.
3. Vodola T: *Teacher training manual: Project ACTIVE,* Oakhurst, NJ, 1976, Township of Ocean School District.
4. Winnick JP, Short FX: *Physical fitness testing of the disabled: Project UNIQUE,* Champaign, Ill, 1985, Human Kinetics.
5. Wessel J: *Planning individualized educational programs in special education with examples from I CAN,* Northbrook, Il, 1977, Hubbard.
6. Jensen CR: *Administrative management of physical education and athletic programs,* ed 3, Philadelphia, 1992, Lea & Febiger.

ANNOTATED READINGS

Auxter D, Pfyer J, Huettig C: *Principles and methods of adapted physical education and recreation,* ed 9, St Louis, 1993, Mosby.

This textbook integrates assessment, programing, and implementation procedures while offering practitioners task-specific information to facilitate the teaching of physical education to individuals with disabilities.

Byl J: *Organizing successful tournaments,* Champaign, Ill, 1990, Human Kinetics.

A comprehensive resource to tournament managers, this book includes information on single, double, multilevel, round robin, and extended tournaments. It also includes draw sheets, seeding charts, and playing schedules.

Houseworth SD, Davis ML, Dobbs RD: A survey of coaching education program features, *JOPERD* 61(5):26-30, 1990.

This report reviews the results of a study conducted to determine coaches' preferences in coaching education. Results indicated that coaching education would be welcomed and valuable to high-school coaches. Professionals are concerned about the apparent lack of adequate preparation of some high-school coaches.

Martens R: *Successful coaching,* Champaign, Ill, 1990, Human Kinetics.

This book offers a practical guide for the coaching of secondary school athletes.

Seefeldt V: Coaching certification: an essential step in reviving a faltering profession, *JOPERD* 63(5):29-30, 1992.

Seefeldt discusses steps that can be implemented to reestablish coaching as a legitimate educational endeavor. He identifies several issues pertinent to this problem including the current demand for trained professionals, the identification of requisite coaching competencies, and the professional remuneration of coaches. Seefeldt continues and discusses five ingredients required for coaching to acquire professional status.

Shepard RJ: *Fitness in special populations,* Champaign, Ill, 1990, Human Kinetics.

This is resource for the physical education teacher on fitness assessment, programing, and performance for people with various disabilities.

Sherrill C: *Adapted physical education, recreation, and sport: crossdisciplinary and lifespan,* ed 4, Dubuque, Iowa, 1986, William C Brown and Benchmark.

This is a comprehensive approach to conducting adapted physical education experiences for individuals with a diversity of special needs.

Wessel JA, Kelly L: *Achievement-based curriculum development in physical education,* Philadelphia, 1986, Lea & Febiger.

This text offers a step-by-step approach to designing individualized programs in physical education for students with disabilities.

Winnick JP, Short FX: *Physical fitness testing of the disabled: Project UNIQUE,* Champaign, Ill, 1985, Human Kinetics.

This text offers a complete program of activities and fitness tests for physical education teachers to use with students with cerebral palsy, spinal neuromuscular conditions, visual impairments, and auditory disorders.

Teaching

Implementation of the physical education program requires consideration of many different facets of teaching. Understanding the process by which individuals learn skills offers teachers guidance in the selection of teaching styles and strategies. The teacher's interactions with students influence learning, the class climate, motivation, and discipline. Teachers must thoughtfully consider how they will meet the needs of all students within the program, including those with special needs.

Safety is a foremost consideration in conducting the physical education program. Effective administrative procedures can help teachers be more efficient and accomplish required tasks in a more timely manner. Evaluation should be an integral part of the program so teachers can determine the extent of achievement of learning goals. Teachers who are determined to improve their teaching will benefit from employing a diversity of techniques to evaluate their own performance. Promotion of the physical education program through the use of various public relations strategies is an important responsibility of each physical education teacher.

OUTLINE

Motor Learning

CHAPTER OBJECTIVES

◆ To describe selected principles of motor learning
◆ To illustrate how motor learning principles can be applied to the teaching of secondary school physical education

One of the primary goals of secondary school physical education teachers is to help students acquire motor skills. Attaining an adequate level of skill competence is important if students are to become active participants in their adult lives.

As a field of study, motor learning offers physical education teachers insights into how learning occurs in the psychomotor domain, specifically how skills are acquired. Physical education teachers who successfully apply tenets from motor learning to their teaching facilitate their students' learning. It is equally important, however, that teachers give attention to providing students with experiences that offer them opportunities to realize satisfaction and success.

Within this chapter, selected information about the nature and process of learning motor skills is presented to guide the design and conduct of learning experiences. In teaching for achievement, instructors need to be familiar with the nature, process, and stages of skill learning. Teachers must also be concerned with motivation, practice organization, transfer of learning, provision of feedback, reinforcement, and retention.

NATURE OF LEARNING

Learning can be defined as a change in the internal state of the individual as a result of experience or practice.[1] Because these changes at the fundamental level are neurological in nature, they cannot be discerned directly by the teacher. Therefore learning must be inferred from changes in an individual's behavior or performance. From this perspective, learning can be viewed as a relatively permanent change in behavior or performance achieved as a result of experience or practice.

Performance curves are commonly used to make inferences about learning. The performance of an individual over a period of time of practices is plotted (Fig. 8-1). Examination of the slope of the curve provides insight as to the individual's progress in learning the skill. A relatively horizontal line or a curve that gradually changes represents a slow rate of learning. A steep or near vertical change in the curve depicts a rapid rate of learning. Typically, performance curves reflect rapid improvements at first and a more gradual rate of improvement over time.[1]

A performance curve will either increase or decrease with practice, depending on the performance measure used. Selection of the performance measure is influenced by the skill being learned and the goal of instruction. Performance measures may be quantitative or qualitative in nature.

Quantitative measures yield objective performance scores expressed in units of time, errors, or magnitude.[2] Time performance measures yield information about the amount of time needed to complete a task or the duration of the response (for example, the time it takes to swim the front crawl 500 yards or to dribble a soccer ball through an obstacle course). Error performance measures provide information about the accuracy or the variability of the performance (for example, the number of successful tennis serves out of a specified number of trials). Last, magnitude performance measures reflect the extent of the performance—how far, how much, or how many (for

FIG. 8-1   Performance curve.
Courtesy of Nichols B: *Moving & learning: the elementary school physical education experience*, ed 3, St Louis, 1994, Mosby.

example, the distance a golf ball is driven). Quantitative performance measures make it relatively easy for teachers and their students to gather information about their learning.

At times, qualitative performance measures may be more appropriate. Qualitative measures compare an individual's performance against established criteria or detailed descriptions of the skill. For example, a student's dance performance may be evaluated on the basis of artistic impression, an individual's form when executing a gymnastics skill may be evaluated according to specific criteria on a checklist, or a learner's performance of a badminton serve may be evaluated for the presence of certain critical elements.

The employment of various performance measures can be helpful to teachers in assessing students' progress toward stated goals. Selection of the performance measure to be used during a unit of instruction should be an integral part of the planning process.

It is important that teachers are aware of one other feature that may be apparent when inspecting a student's performance curve: a performance plateau, which is represented by a near horizontal line. A plateau represents a period of little or no improvement. It may reflect the loss of interest by the student, a shift from learning the fundamental aspect of the skill to the more advanced phases that require greater effort, inappropriate pacing of instruction, or failure to attend to an important aspect of the skill.[3]

Plateaus can be frustrating to teachers and students alike. Plateaus can be minimized by teachers who provide for individual differences in learners, utilize an array of motivational strategies, provide encouragement and feedback, and employ a variety of challenging learning activities. Teachers may find it helpful to review with students their progress to date and assure students that plateaus are typically followed by another period of improvement.

The use of performance observations is one of the most popular methods for making inferences about learning.

Performance scores are recorded and reviewed for salient characteristics indicative of learning. First, teachers should look for an improvement in performance following a period of practice.[2] Next, this improvement should be characterized by persistence, that is, the improvement should be relatively stable or long-lasting.[2] Additionally, the scores should vary less than those scores after little or no practice.[2] Fluctuations in performance should decrease, and performance should become more consistent. Physical education teachers who observe their students exhibiting increased levels of performance that are characterized by persistence and consistency may infer that learning has occurred.

This process can be facilitated by the selection of performance measures that can easily be used by students to make assessments of their own performance or that of their classmates. Quantitative performance measures easily allow students to record their efforts, for example, the number of volleyball serves placed in a specified area of a court. With qualitative performance measures, well-designed checklists can assist students in assessing their own performance or that of their classmates.

Repeated performance assessments should be made throughout the unit, and performance scores should be recorded on cards or sheets designed for this purpose. This enables students to discern the progress they have made throughout the unit and teachers to readily monitor students' skill development.

Understanding the nature of learning and how it is assessed is important for teachers. This knowledge should be incorporated into the planning process and has numerous implications for the design and conduct of instructional experiences.

INFORMATION-PROCESSING MODEL OF LEARNING

Throughout the years, numerous models have been developed to explain how individuals acquire and perform motor skills. Familiarity with the specific components of a system, understanding of the interrelationship between them, and knowledge of how the system operates can be helpful to teachers desiring to assist their students in learning more efficiently and effectively. One popular approach to describe how individuals learn skills is the information-processing model. This model is based on the premise that in order for individuals to learn and perform motor skills, they must first be able to process information.[4] The model, its four components, and the relationship among them, are shown in Fig. 8-2.

The first step in the model involves sensory input. Through their senses, individuals receive information from the environment, which is then transmitted to the central nervous system. Visual stimuli such as information about the flight of the ball; auditory stimuli such as the sound of the ball striking the tennis racquet; tactile stimuli

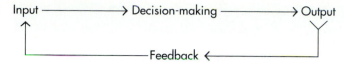

FIG. 8-2   Information-processing model.

from the pressure of the water on the palms of the hands and the soles of the feet in swimming; and proprioceptive information, such as information about the "feel" associated with the performance of a gymnastic movement are examples of sensory information available to individuals to guide their motor performance.

The second step, decision making, involves perception. Sensory information is analyzed and interpreted. In the brain, sensory information about the present conditions is associated with information on past relevant experiences. Information about responses that have been used previously in similar situations and the consequences of these responses, successes or failures, assist the individual in deciding on an appropriate action.

During the output step, the planned response is executed. A motor response results. As the movement is performed, the individual receives feedback or sensory information about the response. Feedback, the last step in the model, provides the individual with critical information about the movement itself and its outcome—did the individual move correctly and was the intended goal accomplished? This information serves to help the individual adjust the next movement attempt to attain the desired goal.

To illustrate the model, imagine you are receiving a serve from your tennis opponent. You receive sensory information about the sound of the ball striking your opponent's racquet, the flight of the ball, and the location of your opponent. Your past experiences help you judge where the ball is going and how fast it is moving. The sensory information plus your past experiences are used to help you decide where to move to receive the ball and what type of stroke to use to return it. As you execute the desired stroke, you receive information about the movement itself and its outcome—a winner!

There are several implications of this model for teaching. First, teachers should help their students become aware of the multitude of sensory information available to guide one's performance. Students' attention should be drawn to the relevant cues to the environment that are critical to performance. Direct students to concentrate on critical cues and ignore less critical and irrelevant ones. Second, help students become wise decision makers so the likelihood of selecting the best response from the many available is enhanced. This can be accomplished by helping students see similarities between the present sit-

uation and previous situations, by assisting students to analyze their successful and unsuccessful performances in terms of the decisions they made, and by teaching students the "whys" underlying various strategies. Third, provide sufficient opportunities for students to practice and learn a wide array of movement responses. Last, offer students frequent feedback to improve the quality and effectiveness of their movements. Equally important, help students learn how to identify and interpret the feedback available to them as performers. Students need to learn how to use this valuable information to evaluate their performance and to make the necessary adjustments in their response to achieve the desired goal.

STAGES OF LEARNING

As individuals learn motor skills, they generally progress through three stages: cognitive, associative, and autonomic.[4] The rate of progress varies for each individual. These stages, delineated by changes in learners' focus of attention and performance, hold significant implications for physical education teachers regarding the design of practice (Table 8-1).

Cognitive Stage

In this initial stage, students are concerned with understanding the nature and goal of the skill. These concerns are reflected in questions typically posed by students, such as "How do I hold the racquet? How do I score in this game? What is the sequence of actions in the front crawl?"

Providing students with a model of the desired skill performance is critical at this stage. Simple explanations and demonstrations that provide an overview of the skill followed by identification of the critical elements involved are helpful. Provide just enough information to get the student started; progressively add more information to develop the skill further. Helping students draw on past experiences, transferring their knowledge and movement skills to this new situation, can facilitate progress.

The goal of practice is to have the students develop an approximation of the skill. Performances are quite variable, inconsistent, and error prone. For example, a student hitting a tennis forehand may successfully place one drive into the opponent's court and see the next effort go into the net, or way out of bounds, or even miss the ball entirely. While students may remember the sequence of movements, their timing is not refined, giving the appearance of awkwardness. Much of the students' attention is absorbed in trying to remember what to do.

Frequent feedback to correct gross errors in movement patterns is critical at this stage. The feedback should be congruent with the critical elements of the skill emphasized in the instructions and provide the learner with clear information about what to do the next time to improve

TABLE 8-1

Characteristics Associated with Stages of Learning

Cognitive	Associative	Autonomic
Students' Focus		
Cognitive understanding of the goal of the skill	Concentration on temporal aspects or timing of movements	Concentration on use of the skill in performance situations, use of strategies
Concentrate on spatial aspects or sequence of skill components		
Performance Characteristics		
Lacks smoothness, inefficient, variable, large number of gross errors	Smoother, less variability, more efficient, reduction of extraneous movements, fewer and reduced range of errors	Smooth, efficient, highly refined and well organized spatially and temporally, adaptable to environmental demands
Teacher's Focus		
Provide overview of nature of skill and goal; feedback on intent of skill; information and demonstration of skill, cognitive understanding	Direct students' attention to critical cues and feedback available, provide numerous practice opportunities, accommodate individual differences	Focus on refinement of response, consistency for closed skills and flexibility open skills, use of skill in performance situations, feedback for refinement of movements

performance. Focus on one or two elements at a time; do not overwhelm the student with too much advice. Supportive and encouraging comments are helpful in motivating students in their practice endeavors.

Progress through the cognitive stage is usually fairly rapid. Once students have an understanding of the nature and goal of the skill and are able to perform the basic movement pattern, they advance to the associative stage.

Associative Stage

Efforts at this stage are focused on skill development. The emphasis shifts from learning the sequence of movements to learning the temporal patterning or timing of the movements. With practice, skill performance improves in coordination and consistency. For example, students can now execute the tennis forehand so that it lands in the opponent's court, although they are not able to place the ball consistently in a particular spot. The number of errors committed is reduced, and students begin to be able to detect some of their errors and make appropriate adjustments.

Practice should initially emphasize the production of the desirable movement pattern. As performance becomes more refined, opportunities to practice the skill under the conditions in which it will ultimately be performed should be stressed. The students' attention should be drawn to relevant, critical cues in the environment. Students are also capable of using a greater array of cues to guide their performance.

Feedback about the movement itself and its outcome is helpful to the students. Now is a good time to help students learn how to evaluate their own performances and use the wide array of feedback available to them to improve. Viewing videotapes of their performance may be helpful.

During this stage of learning, considerable variation in performance can be expected in a typical class of secondary school students. Some students may progress rapidly, others may exhibit steady but slow improvement, and others may experience difficulty and require more time to demonstrate appreciable performance gains. The rate of progress is influenced by such factors as previous experience with similar skills, skill complexity, teaching methods, practice structure and opportunities, and motivation. Because of the increasingly heterogeneous proficiency of the students, it is suggested that teaching strategies that accommodate individual differences be employed during this stage.

During this stage, students make great strides toward becoming skilled performers. After considerable practice, they reach the autonomic stage.

Autonomic Stage

This advanced stage is characterized by almost automatic performance of the skill. The high level of integration of the sequencing and timing of the movement components makes skill performance appear effortless.

Unlike the previous stages of learning, students do not

have to concentrate consciously on the production of the skill and can execute most of the skill without thinking about it. Consequently, students can direct their attention to how to use the skill and other features of performance. Thus in performing the tennis forehand drive, students at this level are freed from thinking about such fundamentals as the grip and body position. Instead they can focus their attention on game tactics, such as faking a shot down the line while sending the ball cross court.

Depending on the goal of the performance, practice should emphasize production of a high level of response consistency or adaptation of the response to the wide variety of conditions encountered during performance. Teachers can focus their efforts on helping their students fine-tune their performances. Feedback for further refinement is necessary. Students also increase in their ability to use feedback from the movement itself or its outcome to make adjustments in their performances.

Extended practice is necessary for the attainment of the high degree of proficiency commonly associated with this stage. Units of instruction that are too short and lack opportunities for sufficient and appropriate practice may result in the majority of the class remaining at the associative stage of learning rather than advancing to the autonomic stage.

Highly skilled performers exemplify the autonomous stage of learning.

Courtesy of Deborah A. Wuest, Ithaca College, Ithaca, NY.

READINESS

Students' ability to acquire new skills successfully is influenced by their readiness to learn. Readiness is defined as the level at which each individual learns most efficiently and experiences the least difficulty in accomplishing the learning goals. Readiness reflects the individual's capability, preparedness, and willingness to learn. Individual in nature, readiness is influenced by such factors as developmental level, possession of prerequisite skills and abilities, interest and attitude, and level of arousal.

Developmental Level

Considerable variation in development exists among students at each grade level. Students' physical development as well as their intellectual, social, and emotional characteristics must be carefully weighed when one is choosing what to teach as well as how to teach it.

Thoughtful consideration of developmental levels leads to learning experiences that allow students to experience success rather than frustration from trying to learn something that is developmentally inappropriate. Progressions should reflect students' developmental levels while leading in sequential steps to the achievement of the desired skill. Teaching approaches that provide for individual differences in development and rate of learning effectively meet students' needs and contribute to a positive learning experience.

Prerequisite Skills and Abilities

Students enter secondary school from elementary school physical education programs with differences in philosophy, program content and emphases, and quality of instruction. This can lead to a wide range of differences in skill competence. Therefore secondary school physical education teachers should determine the students' mastery of the fundamental motor skills (for example, throwing and running) and knowledge and use this information as a foundation for constructing learning experiences. Secondary students who are proficient in the fundamental motor skills will find it easier to perform the more advanced skills and experience more success applying them in sport situations. Those students who have not attained an adequate level of proficiency in the fundamental skills, like throwing, will find learning more advanced sport skills, such as throwing the softball from first to third base, a difficult and frustrating experience.[5]

Consideration of the students' level of physical fitness is important. Students who possess a high level of physical fitness may be able to perform motor skills better and practice for a longer period of time without undue fatigue. Students' status relative to a specific fitness component also has an impact on their learning. Different skills place a premium on different fitness components.

Students who possess a high level of the fitness component critical for performance will likely be more successful than students who do not possess as high a level. For example, in activities where flexibility is important, such as in gymnastics, or where cardiovascular endurance is important, such as in soccer, students who possess a high level of these components are likely to be more successful.

Interest and Attitude

Students are more receptive to learning activities that they perceive to be relevant to their lives. In selecting activities for instruction, the potential of the activity to contribute to the goals of physical education should be considered as well as its ability to meet the needs and interests of students. As students become involved in the physical education program, teachers should seek to expand their interests by offering new activities and broadening curricular opportunities.

Students' attitudes toward learning also need to be taken into account. Some students have a favorable disposition toward learning new skills, while others are reluctant to try new things. Past experiences in physical education can positively or negatively influence the attitudes students bring to the class. Students who have enjoyed their past experiences may be more favorably disposed toward learning than those students whose experiences have been negative.

Favorable attitudes toward learning can be created by teachers who take the time to establish a positive set toward learning. Orient the students toward what they will be doing and why at the start of a new unit and in every class. Students who understand the lesson's goals will be better prepared to learn. Include activities of interest to students. Build on previously learned material and help students to be successful. Learning and enjoyment are not mutually exclusive.

Teachers must also be prepared to deal with students' fears. For example, a student may be fearful of the water, an obvious disadvantage when learning how to swim. Other students may be extremely fearful of performing poorly in front of their peers. These fears must be addressed in a sensitive manner and resolved; do not belittle or make fun of students' fears.

Level of Arousal

Arousal can be conceptualized as the individual's level of activation, alertness, or energy.[1,3] For each task there is an optimal level of arousal. Students whose level of arousal matches that which is required for the task are able to perform at their highest level. Generally, low levels of arousal aid in performing tasks that are complex and intricate in nature, such as a gymnastics routine on the balance beam. High levels of arousal are beneficial to performing tasks of a simple and repetitive nature or that require explosive power, for example, shot putting.

The level of arousal needed is also influenced by the stage of learning. Students who are learning a new skill may find the process easier if they are at a low level of arousal. Once students gain some proficiency in the skill and begin to apply it in various performance situations, higher levels of arousal may be needed.

Level of arousal can also be influenced by one's emotional state. Teachers who create a supportive, collaborative class climate and provide their students with progressively more difficult challenges that can be resolved by working hard help create an emotional state in their students that is conducive to learning. A class situation that evokes high levels of anxiety in students, such as one that is threatening, potentially embarrassing, highly competitive, or offers few opportunities for student achievement, hinders learning.

MOTIVATION

A critical factor in learning, motivation can be defined as the inner drive or intention to behave or to perform in a particular way.[6] The underlying reasons for such actions are called motives. Although internal in nature, motives may be influenced by external and internal factors. Teachers do not give students motivation, but rather create circumstances and alter factors that contribute to an individual's level of this desirable characteristic.

Extrinsic influences on motivation are those that are external to the individual. Rewards, such as teacher approval, peer recognition, and grades, exert a powerful influence on students' level of motivation and behavior. However, these motives can result in short-lived achievement.[5] For instance, a student may work hard to receive an A in a unit, yet have no intention of participating in the activity once the unit is ended.[5] If lifelong participation in physical activity is our goal, teachers need to help students become internally motivated to be active.

Intrinsic influences arise from within the individual. A genuine desire to learn and take pride in doing one's best can exert a significant and positive influence on one's level of motivation.

Intrinsic motives appear to be more conducive to learning and sustained participation than extrinsic motives. When students seek to improve their performance for their own sake, when they truly believe in the importance of a personal exercise program, they are more likely to be motivated to learn the necessary skills and attitudes and to continue to use them throughout their life.

Motivation plays a significant role in the initiation, maintenance, and intensity of behavior.[5] Teachers face many situations where it is helpful to understand why a student initiates a particular form of behavior. For example, why does a student start a personal fitness program—to improve appearance or to maintain health? Or, why does a student begin to misbehave in class—it is because of boredom, a need for attention, or a problem at home?

Persistence is critical to achievement. Students who work hard during practice, concentrate on what they are doing, and practice longer learn more. Students who are unmotivated devote little effort to practice and go through the motions with little attention to what they are doing and thus learn less. Understanding why individuals continue to behave in certain ways may be helpful in addressing such questions as, "Why do some students work hard on a task until they are successful?" "Why do others give up so easily?" and "What can be done to encourage students to persist until they have attained their goals?"

The intensity of behavior reflects the effort of the individual and is closely related to the level of arousal. As previously discussed, teachers need to determine what the best level of arousal is for an individual while learning a specific task. Knowledge of how anxiety and tension affect arousal and, subsequently, performance is also important if students are to achieve at their optimal level.

A reciprocal relationship exists between learning and motivation.[6] To elaborate, motivation may influence an individual to learn, and learning may cause an individual to become motivated to learn more. To take this further, some students may not be excited about learning a particular activity, such as badminton. But a teacher who makes the activity interesting and structures the learning experience to be challenging while providing for frequent successes helps students learn; this learning leads to the development of the desire to learn more.

Because motivation is critical in learning, teachers must help students develop the desire to learn. Creating interest and consideration of students' needs, establishing a favorable class climate, teaching for success, and setting goals are several approaches conducive to enhancing student motivation. The use of reinforcement and the provision of feedback are other strategies that can be successfully employed; they will be discussed later in this chapter.

Create Interest and Consider Students' Needs

If students are interested in a particular activity, they will be more motivated to learn. Students' interests vary widely. Athletic ability is highly valued by our society.[7] Some students may be interested in learning an activity in order to be a member of a sports team. Physical ability may also be important for being included in a desired peer group.[7] A desire to learn skills for leisure time pursuits, to maintain one's health, or to improve one's appearance are other reasons students may be interested in an activity. In many secondary schools, elective programs are offered in the upper grades so students may select activities according to their interests.

Teachers may also find that it helps student motivation when they explain the purpose and future application for an activity. Because of the strong orientation many high school students have to team sports such as basketball or volleyball, teachers may find it difficult to interest them in learning lifetime activities such as golf or tennis. Pointing out how these lifetime activities will be more important to them in the future helps create student interest in learning. The teacher can describe the contribution of certain activities to one's life, for example, the contribution of cardiovascular fitness to one's health and vitality. Students are motivated to learn when what they are doing is personally meaningful or for which they can see a purpose.

Teachers can create interest in several other ways. Introducing a tennis unit with a videotape of the U.S. Open or a self-defense unit with a demonstration by a local expert can create enthusiasm for learning. Culminating a unit with a special activity can have a positive effect on student interest. Ending a golf unit with a tournament on a local course, a swimming and water safety unit with a trip to a local lake to apply skills, or a fitness unit with a visit to a local health club to discuss factors to be considered in joining a club are just a few of the many ways teachers can stimulate their students' interest.

Create a Supportive Learning Climate

Students' feelings toward learning influence their level of motivation.[3] The nature of the learning environment— the class climate—affects students' feelings.

Teachers who are sincere and genuinely interested in their students' well-being help create positive feelings in their students toward learning. When students' efforts are recognized and supported by both their teachers and their peers, motivation is enhanced. Where there is mutual respect between the teacher and the students and where individual differences are accepted and respected, positive feelings toward learning occur.

A supportive learning environment helps all students learn without undue pressure or fear of failure or embarrassment. This is particularly critical during the early secondary school years. At the time when they are experiencing the many changes associated with adolescence, students especially don't want to look foolish in front of their peers. A supportive climate also helps students maintain an optimal level of arousal for learning. Class environments that elicit feelings of apprehension or anxiety in students create negative feelings, reduce motivation, and hinder learning.

Teach for Success

Success is powerful. Careful thought should be given to ensuring students' success when planning a unit. Select activities that are appropriate to the age, maturity, and interests of the students. Be sure students possess the necessary prerequisite skills and competencies for the activities. Plan units and daily lessons to ensure a logical progression of skills from simple to complex. Break large tasks down into challenging, relevant subtasks so that success is achieved more often. Use a variety of teaching styles and thoughtfully provide for individual differences.

To achieve success, students must have plenty of opportunities to practice. Structure class to utilize maximally the time allocated for learning and to provide for maximum participation. Reduce time spent on noninstructional activities (for example, transitions, attendance, and equipment distribution) through effective class management. Use instructional time to its fullest. Select teaching strategies that provide for high levels of purposeful student practice. Use all equipment, reduce the number of students interacting with each piece of equipment, employ minigames to involve participants, monitor students' efforts closely, and provide appropriate feedback.

Success that arises from working hard at a challenging task and succeeding positively affects students' self-esteem. Success helps students feel confident about their abilities as a mover.

Goal Setting

Motivation is enhanced when students know what is to be learned and why it is important. Establish and communicate to the students goals and specific objectives for each unit and lesson. By relating these learning goals to students' interests, to other subjects in the school curriculum, and to outside of the school activities, teachers positively influence their students' motivation. When students see meaning and value in what they are learning, motivation is enhanced.

Involve students in the goal-setting process by helping them establish realistic goals for their performance. Goals that are challenging, yet attainable through hard work, contribute to motivation. Goals that are unrealistic or too easy lead to a loss of motivation. Furthermore, goals should reflect individual differences in abilities and past experiences.

When goals are being established, objective performance measures should be used whenever possible. This allows students to monitor their progress more easily. Establish specific goals rather than encouraging students just "to do their best"; this approach appears to elicit higher levels of achievement.[5] Break major goals down into smaller subgoals. This lets students experience success more frequently and encourages continued efforts.

Record keeping is an important aspect of goal setting. Either the student or the teacher should keep a record of the student's performance. Records provide tangible evidence of progress and allow students to see readily what they have accomplished during each class.

DESIGN OF PRACTICE

Effective learning requires practice sessions that are designed to accomplish the lesson's goals and objectives. There are many decisions that must be made by teachers as they plan and conduct practices. Consideration must be given to the nature of the skills being learned, the manner in which they are presented, the emphasis given to different aspects of each skill, the use of practice time, and the provision for transfer.

Skills Analysis

The nature of the skill to be learned influences many decisions teachers must make in planning practice. Skill classification systems categorize skills based on specific criteria or common elements, with skills usually placed along a continuum according to the degree of affiliation with a category.[2] One common approach is to classify motor skills according to the environmental conditions under which performance occurs.

Closed skills are performed in a relatively stable, unchanging environment. Examples of closed skills are basketball free throw shooting, bowling, target archery, diving, swimming, yoga, and gymnastic movements. Open skills are performed in an environment that is constantly changing and unpredictable. Many of the skills involved in team and dual sport activities are open skills, because it is difficult to predict in advance what will happen moment to moment. Dribbling the basketball down the court during game play, executing a tennis forehand in a match, shooting on a goal in soccer, batting a ball, and defending oneself against an opponent in karate are examples of open skills. A sport may involve open and closed skills. For example, in badminton the serve can be regarded as a closed skill, but once the shuttlecock is in play, the various strokes used can be regarded as open skills.

The predictable environment associated with closed skills means that the critical elements or regulatory cues that control movement do not change between the time the skill is planned and executed. For example, in bowling, the alley and the location of the pins do not change as the skill is performed; you can plan your response and execute it as planned because the environment remains constant. Movements must conform to spatial demands; the archer must match the flight of the arrow to the distance from the target.

In teaching closed skills, the focus is on developing consistency of movement under stable environment conditions. Emphasis should be placed on the development of the movement itself, and the student should practice the skill until it becomes habitual, nearly automatic. Practice sessions should be as similar as possible to the situation under which the skill will actually be performed. Further, provision must be made to rehearse movements for a variety of different conditions under which the skill will be performed. For instance, in bowling have students practice various spare combinations, and in golf practice have students putt from different lines and distances from the hole.

The unpredictable environment characteristic of open skills means that the skills are executed under conditions that are changing. The critical elements or cues change in position and in timing. The individual must adjust the movement to changing spatial and temporal demands. To illustrate, when executing a tennis forehand, the player must match the position of the racquet and the timing of the stroke to the position, spin, and speed of the ball hit by the opponent. Additionally, the player has to make a decision about the return shot, selecting the type of the shot to be hit and desired court placement. Because it is virtually impossible to practice the response to all possible situations that may occur in an open environment, the ability to interpret environmental demands accurately and to modify one's response according to these demands should be stressed in teaching.

In teaching open skills, emphasis should be given both to the development of the skill itself and to the development of response flexibility. Students must be taught how to identify and interpret the spatial and temporal demands controlling the skill and how to adjust their movements to match environmental conditions in order to achieve the desired goal. Providing students with varied practice conditions is important to achieving the goal of response flexibility.

Sometimes during the early stages of learning an open skill, it may be practiced under closed conditions to help students learn the movements involved. As learning progresses, conditions become more open in nature. For example, in teaching the tennis backhand, the instructor may begin by having students hit a ball tossed by a partner, with the ball being tossed with relatively the same height and speed to the same location. From here, more variability is systematically introduced (for example, moving from hitting a tossed ball to an opponent hitting to a specific court area) until the environment resembles actual performance conditions. Students learn to hit tennis balls coming with different speeds and spin, at dif-

ferent heights and landing in different locations, and to make a return to a specific location on their opponent's court. Once the basic movement is learned, it is important to move to open conditions. Failure to do this will hinder learning. Students will experience difficulty because they will not learn how to identify accurately the spatial and temporal environmental cues and to adjust their movements accordingly.

Whole Versus Part Practice

When teaching a new skill, teachers must decide whether to present the skill as a whole or to divide it into meaningful segments and teach it by parts. Which approach will help students learn in the most efficient manner? Both the nature of the task and the characteristics of the students are considered in answering this question.

Motor skills are composed of varying number of component parts combined in a prescribed sequence.[2] For example, the tennis serve is made up of seven parts: grip, stance, backswing, ball toss, forward swing, ball contact, and follow-through. Motor skills may be described in terms of their complexity and organization. Complexity refers to the number of components comprising the skill and the associated information-processing demands.[2] Skills low in complexity are comprised of relatively few components and require a limited amount of information processing, such as shooting an arrow or executing a bench press in weight lifting. Highly complex skills are composed of many components and demand a high level of information processing. Examples of highly complex skills include the tennis serve or executing a particular offensive pattern in soccer.

Organization refers to the manner in which the component parts of the skill are interrelated.[2] In low-organization skills, the components are independent of each

Viedotape feedback is a valuable learning tool. Omaha public schools use videotape equipment in physical education classes.
Courtesy of Omaha public schools.

other, such as steps comprising a dance routine. In highly organized skills, the components are highly related or associated, such as in a basketball jump shot.

Thus in deciding whether a skill should be practiced as a whole or part, both complexity and organization are considered. Skills low in complexity and high in organization should be practiced as a whole (for example, shooting an arrow). Skills high in complexity and low in organization may be more efficiently learned utilizing part practice (for example, serving a tennis ball).

If the decision is made to have students practice by the part method, another decision must be made—which parts should be combined for practice. If the parts are relatively independent, they may be practiced individually. If they are highly dependent and have a natural flow or rhythm, combine them for practice. For example, with the golf swing, the grip and the stance can be practiced as parts; the swing itself, ball contact, and follow-through are highly related, and whole practice may be more beneficial.

Student characteristics need to be considered when one is making the decision to teach by the whole or the part method. If the students are highly skilled and have had previous experience with an activity, the whole method may be used successfully. The whole method may also be used successfully with students who are capable of concentrating for long periods of time and can remember relatively long sequences of movements or information. The part method may be advantageously employed with students who have a short attention span and limited capability to remember sequences. When teaching by the whole method, teachers should be alert to students having difficulty in learning. These students may benefit from part instruction.

When using part practice, one should provide students with a demonstration of the whole skill before learning the various component parts. This helps students understand the goal of the skill and makes practice more meaningful. When working on skills to be used later in a game, students may benefit from seeing a demonstration of the game or actually playing the game in some form. This aids students in understanding the context in which specific skills will actually be performed. However, take care to not spend too much time on developing the parts of a skill without integrating them into the whole, nor too much time on developing game skills without providing some opportunities for students to use them in game situations such as minigames.

Speed Versus Accuracy

Each skill has different requirements, in terms of speed and accuracy, that must be met to achieve optimal performance. In some skills, accuracy is more critical than speed of movement, such as executing a drop shot in badminton. Other skills emphasize speed of movement, such as many of the throwing events in track and field.

And yet other skills require a high degree of accuracy and speed; pitching a ball into a strike zone requires both of these qualities. Which of these qualities should be emphasized in practice?

In general, skills are to be practiced as they are to be performed. Thus the practice tasks must reflect the speed and accuracy requirements of the skill. This is relatively straightforward when the skill places a premium on one quality or the other—the practices emphasize the development of the critical quality.

When one is practicing skills where both speed and accuracy are of paramount concern, equal and simultaneous emphasis should be placed on both speed and accuracy. Students should practice these skills using a moderate degree of speed and attempting to maintain a moderate degree of accuracy. Ballistic skills, such as striking an object with an implement, as in batting, throwing, or kicking should be practiced at the required speed when possible.[5] Sometimes, if students are having difficulty in learning a skill or if the skill is extremely complex or dangerous, teachers may slow down the movements and work on form for a short period of time and then move back to regular speed.

Organization of Practice Time

Organize practices carefully to take full advantage of the time available for learning. Practices for optimal learning are goal oriented. Teachers and students have a clear idea of what is to be accomplished during practice and why. Effective practices engage students in purposeful activity and keep students focused on what is to be learned. Students are provided with assistance in correcting their errors and encouragement to motivate their efforts.

Students need many opportunities to rehearse the skill for learning to occur. During the initial or cognitive stages of learning, practice should emphasize acquiring the basic movement pattern. Practice trials should be structured to allow numerous repetitions of a given skill. As students progress, the practice structure may be altered depending on the nature of the skill. Where skills are open in nature, more variable practice should be introduced. Students are given experience in adjusting the skill to a variety of environmental demands. For skills that are closed in nature, achieving consistency of the movement pattern should be emphasized in practice. Remember that practice must prepare students for how the skill will ultimately be used.

Keep practices interesting and maintain motivation by varying activities. Use different challenges to stimulate students' interest. Different formations, maximum use of equipment, variety in teaching approaches, and minigames that reproduce various performance situations help maintain students' involvement during practice.

Careful thought should be given to the length of the practice period and provision of rest periods. Massed practice occurs when practice is relatively continuous, and there are relatively short or no rest periods between trials.[8] Distributed practice refers to the spacing out of practice over a period of time, with a relatively large amount of rest allowed between practice trials.[8] Within a given class period, under a massed practice schedule, one activity may be practiced for the entire time. Under a distributed schedule, an activity is practiced a relatively short period of time. This is followed by practice of alternative activities or rest periods.

When time is limited, employing a massed practice schedule would allow as much practice as possible to be completed during that time. However, when massed practice would lead to student fatigue and increased risk of injury, use a distributed practice schedule. The shorter and more frequent practice sessions associated with distributed practice may be more appropriate to use when the task is simple, repetitive, or demands intense concentration. Longer, massed schedules may be effective when the task is complex or requires a long warm-up period. Student characteristics also influence this practice decision. If students are highly skilled, able to concentrate and work purposefully for relatively long periods, and do not tire easily, then massed practice would be the appropriate choice.[8] When students have a short concentration span or may fatigue easily when performing the task, then a distributed practice schedule may be best.[8] Distributed practice sessions are often preferred for beginners. This practice schedule may result in less frustration for students when learning new skills and more positive feelings toward learning.

Transfer

One factor that influences students' rate of progress is the ability to apply previous learning to the new situation. The influence of previous learning on subsequent learning is called transfer. Previous learning can facilitate, hinder, or have no effect on new learning.

Transfer is positive when it enhances new learning. For example, the concept of passing ahead of the receiver in basketball may transfer to soccer or lacrosse; practice drills are structured to enhance the transfer of skills to actual game situations. When previous learning interferes with new learning, negative transfer occurs. Students who learn badminton first, which requires a flexible wrist action, may experience difficulty initially in learning tennis, which requires a fairly firm wrist. However, negative transfer effects are typically temporary in nature and can be overcome readily with practice.[2] Zero transfer occurs when previous learning has impact on new learning; no transfer from swimming skills to golf skills occurs.

Teachers must analyze the skills they teach to identify factors that will elicit transfer. Practice can then be structured so that positive transfer is maximized and the effects of negative transfer minimized.

Movement patterns that are similar transfer from one skill to another. For example, the overarm throwing pattern underlies many sports skills where objects are forcefully thrown or struck—serving a tennis ball, spiking a volleyball, smashing the shuttle in badminton and throwing a softball, to name a few.[1]

Teachers are also concerned with transferring the skills learned in practice to the actual performance situation. To realize the greatest positive transfer, practice conditions should reflect the conditions under which the skill will eventually be performed.

Concepts, rules, strategies, and principles can also positively transfer. Understanding concepts underlying the performance facilitates learning both now and in the future. For example, teachers who help their students understand the relationship between balance, the center of gravity, and the base of support or the mechanical principles governing the production of force or the rebound of objects help their students become more skillful movers. Teachers who help their students identify common strategic elements in games, such as principles of guarding an opponent, creating passing lanes in a team sport, or receiving service in a racquet sport, assist their students to learn more readily.

Teaching to maximize positive transfer is critical to student achievement. Maximum transfer occurs when teachers teach for transfer. Do not assume that transfer will automatically occur; plan instruction carefully to ensure that it will transfer. There are several guidelines that will be helpful to teachers to accomplish this goal.

First, make sure students have sufficient opportunities to develop their skills and knowledge. The greater the degree of the original learning, the more likely it will transfer to new situations.[2] Mastery of the fundamental skills of an activity should be emphasized, because these will form the basis for the more advanced skills. Students who understand concepts and principles and have had numerous opportunities to practice their application will more likely be able to use this information in new movement situations. The potential for transfer to new situations is increased when the original skills and information are well learned.

Second, teachers must make a conscious effort to teach for transfer. Help students perceive the connection between the previous situation and the new situation. Identify similarities and common elements; ask students questions that will help them analyze the new situation and relate it to previous and future learning.

Third, realize that the greater the similarity between the previous and new situation, the higher the potential for transfer. Analyze skills to discover similarities. Similarities involved in the use of the body, an implement, application of mechanical principles such as production of force, or movement principles such as balance can facilitate transfer. Motor skills are complex and are composed of many different component parts. The more components a new skill has in common with a previously learned skill, the greater the amount of transfer.

Teachers who structure the practice situation to be as similar to the ultimate performance situation help their students gain the experience necessary to execute the skill in the actual situation. Skill drills that are realistic help transfer from practice to performance.

Last, concepts and principles are more likely to transfer when students have had the opportunity to apply them in a variety of situations. Learning situations in which examples of concept application are provided and problem-solving situations where students must correctly apply the concept to be successful can help enhance transfer.

Transfer of learning is also an important consideration in curriculum development. When one is developing a curriculum, skills and material to be learned should be sequenced in such a manner that positive transfer is optimized. Consideration should be given to how positive transfer can be facilitated from unit to unit during the school year and from lesson to lesson within the unit.[9] Equally important, consideration should be given to creating positive transfer from what is learned one year to the next year.[9] At the secondary level, teachers should build upon the fundamental skills and knowledge learned at the elementary level. In addition, when teaching a unit for 2 years in a row, such as a soccer unit to seventh and eighth graders, strive to optimize transfer from the previous year's instruction to the current year. This will allow students to progress more rapidly and learn new material, rather than repeating the same material for 2 years.

Finally, if educators are to prepare students to be lifelong learners, teaching for transfer is an important pedagogical goal. Because it is not possible to prepare students for every movement situation they will encounter in their lifetime, students must have a sound understanding of movement concepts and principles, have competency in the fundamental motor skills, and possess analytical skills so they can see the relationship between their previous learning and the new situation.

FEEDBACK

Broadly defined, feedback is sensory information about the movement response that is available to the student. The feedback that is available as a result of a movement can be classified as intrinsic or extrinsic in nature, according to its source.

Intrinsic feedback is inherent within the skill itself, that is, the performance of the skill provides information about its outcome.[1] Proprioceptive feedback associated with the movement of the body during the execution of the skill or seeing its results is a type of intrinsic feedback. "Feeling right" when executing a gymnastics movement, placing the ball in the service court in tennis, or seeing the basketball miss the basket are examples of intrinsic feedback available to the student.

Extrinsic feedback, often referred to as augmented feedback, is information about an individual's perfor-

mance that is provided by an external source that supplements the intrinsic feedback available. Corrections by a teacher, a skill checklist completed by another student, or videotape replays of a performance are examples of extrinsic feedback. This information is critical in helping students correct errors, allowing them to make adjustments in their response in the next practice attempt to move closer to the achievement of the desired goal. Extrinsic feedback can take two forms: knowledge of results and knowledge of performance.

Knowledge of results, often referred to as KR, provides information about the performance relative to goal attainment, that is, whether or not the goal of the movement was achieved. Knowledge of performance, or KP, is information about the movement itself, such as the movement pattern or the spatial, temporal, or force aspects of the movement. A teacher who tells a student that performed a dance movement or a yoga posture that the intended goal was not accomplished is providing KR. Telling a batter that the swing was too late, a swimmer that the arm stroke needs to be longer, or a thrower to follow through to improve accuracy are examples of KP.

Extrinsic feedback functions to facilitate learning in three ways. First, it provides students with information about their performance. It should clearly prescribe what needs to be done to correct movement errors. Second, it can affect students' motivation, encouraging them to try harder and to persist in their efforts. It can inspire students to practice longer and with sufficient intensity to achieve desired outcomes. Last, feedback serves to reinforce a response, increasing the probability that the response will be repeated. A teacher who informs the student that the response was performed correctly encourages the student to respond in the same way during the next skill attempt. Teachers who use both KR and KP to inform, motivate, and reinforce behavior help their students attain their optimal levels of achievement.

The stage of learning, characteristics of the students, and nature of the skill should be considered when one is providing feedback. During the early stages of learning, direct feedback to the execution of the movement pattern. Attention should be focused on aspects of the movement that are most critical for success. As students learn, shift the focus of the feedback to the outcome of the movement and less critical features of the task. At the higher levels of learning, students should be helped to learn how to advantageously use the intrinsic feedback available to adjust and "fine-tune" their own performances.

If feedback is to be effective, the characteristics of the students must be taken into account. Sufficient information must be provided to help students correct their errors, but too much information is overwhelming and confusing. Address only one or two errors at a time; start with the most critical problems and work from this point. Provide feedback that is congruent to the focus of the task. Relate information to the critical cues that students

Teachers should provide students with appropriate feedback about their performance.
Courtesy of Ben Lombardo, Rhode Island College, Providence, RI.

were asked to concentrate on during their practice attempts. Communicate clearly, in terms that are understandable to the students. Key words and phrases that readily bring to mind the correct movement are preferable to long explanations. Be specific in giving feedback; "good try" is encouraging but offers little information about how to adjust one's performance. Students must also be allowed time to process the information given and to decide how to adjust their responses for the next attempt to produce the desired result.

The nature of the skill offers teachers guidance in selecting the appropriate feedback for their students. Generally, for closed skills, knowledge of performance is preferred.[10] Because closed skills require consistent execution of a prescribed sequence of movements, information about the spatial and temporal aspects of the movement pattern itself is the most helpful in improving performance. Successful performance in open skills requires the ability to select the correct response and to execute the selected response effectively. In the early stages of learning, knowledge of performance may be beneficial to help students learn the movement pattern. However, once the general movement pattern is learned, knowledge of results should be emphasized. Because success depends on appropriately interpreting and responding to environmental events, information about the consequence of their movements (KR) can help students refine their performance.[10]

Students should be provided with frequent feedback about their performances. If possible, this should be given at the conclusion of each performance. When delayed, it is difficult for the student to associate the feedback com-

ments with the performance itself. With a large class, the teacher must work hard to provide each student with feedback. When many students experience a similar problem, it may be helpful to stop practice and reemphasize critical cues. However, individual feedback is preferable. Individual feedback, offered privately and in an encouraging way, can be helpful in remediating errors. More teachers are using videotape replays to provide their students with feedback. Students can view their performances individually or in small groups. Teachers can provide their students with cues to direct their attention to relevant aspects of their performance.

Teaching styles that maximize opportunities for feedback should be employed. Styles that free up the teacher to work individually with students, that utilize students to provide feedback to their peers, and that provide for the structuring of tasks to maximize intrinsic feedback should be incorporated into the secondary school program.

REINFORCEMENT

Teachers who give careful consideration to the use of reinforcement in their teaching can enhance their effectiveness. Reinforcement is any action or behavior, such as reward or praise, that increases the probability of the occurrence of a behavior or maintains the strength of a behavior, such as the correct execution of a skill or appropriate conduct.[2]

To be effective, reinforcers must be meaningful to the individual. Students respond differently to reinforcers. What is a reinforcer for one student may have little impact on another student. Teachers who know their students as individuals can determine which reinforcers work best with each one. If a student is indifferent to a reinforcer, its effectiveness in strengthening the desired response is diminished.

Positive reinforcers that promote feelings of self-worth are desired.[3] Recognition of sportsmanship, praise following successful execution of a skill, and expressing appreciation for hard work are examples of positive reinforcers. These reinforcers increase the probability that the desired behavior will be strengthened as well as serve to motivate students to continue their efforts. Special opportunities can be used effectively as reinforcers. Many teachers give students free time to work on physical education activities of their own choosing as a reinforcer.

Although negative reinforcement, such as a teacher ceasing critical remarks when a student finally successfully performs a skill, may strengthen the correct response, the use of negative reinforcers may have adverse consequences. Negative reinforcers may make the class climate uncomfortable, lower students' self-esteem, and have an unfortunate impact on students' attitude toward learning.

The effectiveness of a reinforcer is influenced by its timing. Reinforcement that is given immediately after the desirable response is more effective than when it is delayed.[2] When reinforcement is delayed, students may be unsure which response is being rewarded. Immediate reinforcement helps students link the response and the reinforcer.

If many students are in the class, the teacher is unable to reinforce all correct responses made by each student. Often partial reinforcement is used and a schedule for reinforcement established. A ratio, interval, variable, or fixed schedule can be used. Teachers utilizing a ratio schedule provide the student with reinforcement after attainment of a specific number of appropriate responses. When one is employing an interval schedule, responses are reinforced after a specific period of time. When reinforcement is provided on an irregular basis, a variable schedule is being employed. The presentation of reinforcement on a regular basis is characteristic of a fixed schedule.

Reinforcement assists in the learning of skills and appropriate behavior. However, students often require a period of time before they can execute a skill correctly or exhibit the desired behavior consistently. Teachers can use reinforcement to strengthen student responses leading to the desired end result or goal; this is called shaping behavior. When shaping behavior, reinforcement is given when the response is somewhat similar or approximates the desired end goal.[2] Teachers who provide students with reinforcement as they progress toward learning a skill shape their students' behavior.

Appropriate and inappropriate behaviors may be strengthened by reinforcers. A teacher may inadvertently reinforce students' inappropriate behavior by their response to it. If a student misbehaves, and the negative response of the teacher provides the attention desired, the inappropriate behavior is reinforced, and the student may continue to behave in that manner. Teachers must be aware of the potent effects of their behaviors on their students. Specific strategies should be planned to strengthen appropriate behavior and reduce inappropriate behaviors of students. Reinforcement should not be haphazard. Careful thought should be given to the incorporation of reinforcement into each lesson. Additionally, teachers must decide what behaviors they will reinforce.

When a behavior is not followed by a reinforcer, it is weakened or extinguished. Inappropriate student behavior can often be eliminated by ignoring the behavior. Often students try to capture the teacher's attention by behaving in an inappropriate behavior. If the teacher responds to that behavior, it may be strengthened. However, if the inappropriate behavior is ignored and appropriate behavior carefully reinforced, students may be encouraged to behave in a more acceptable manner.

RETENTION

In planning instructional experiences, factors that influence students' ability to retain skills and the information presented must be considered. Retention refers to the extent that learning is remembered over time.[1]

Teachers are concerned about how much their students retain from one year to the next as well as from lesson to lesson. If we are to attain our goal of preparing students for a lifetime of physical activity, how can we ensure that students will remember what they have learned once they graduate? The proficiency attained, meaningfulness, and nature of the task influence the amount of retention.[1]

The level of proficiency attained during the original learning significantly influences retention of skills. The greater the proficiency attained, the greater the retention of the skill. A similar relationship has been found for knowledge. Sufficient time to learn is important to retention. Achievement of proficiency is enhanced when teachers take the time to reemphasize salient points, employ logical progressions, transfer old learning to new learning, stress thinking and concentrating while practicing, and provide for frequent review and practice. Overlearning, that is, continuation of practice after the attainment of a specified level of performance, facilitates retention. Remember, what is not learned cannot be retained.

Meaningfulness influences retention. Skills and information that are meaningful to the student are retained better than those that are not. Meaningfulness can be enhanced when students are helped to transfer previous learning to new learning. Presenting material in a logical progression, rather than in haphazard fashion, enhances retention. Structuring practice sessions to be similar to the situation in which the skill will ultimately be performed favorably influences retention. Taking a brief time to explain the *whys* of an activity helps students see its purpose and makes practice more meaningful. Finally, skills and knowledge that have personal importance to the student are retained longer. Students will remember learning that which is personally important to them and that for which they can see a use. Teachers who take the time to identify the personal interests of their students and help students to see the relevance of what they are learning to their lives foster retention.

Retention is also affected by the order in which the material to be learned is presented. Motor skills are composed of a series of movement components combined in a specified order. Skills may also be combined in a certain sequence, as in the case of a dance routine. When there are a large number of components or a long series of skills combined, students may have trouble remembering what to do and the proper order in which to do it. Often the beginning and final components of the skill or sequence are remembered best, while difficulty is experienced in recalling the middle portion. If this occurs, teachers can help students by reemphasizing the middle portion and reteaching as necessary. Breaking the skill or sequence into smaller and more manageable parts can help students learn the task.

Careful thought should be given to maximizing retention when one is planning for instruction. Opportunities to attain proficiency are essential and efforts to enhance the meaningfulness of learning contribute to retention.

SUMMARY

Secondary school physical education teachers who apply principles of motor learning to their teaching help their students acquire motor skills more easily. When planning instruction, teachers need to be familiar with how students learn, stages of learning, and methods of assessing learning. Teachers must also be concerned with individual factors that may affect learning such as readiness and motivation.

When one is designing practice sessions, consideration should be given to the nature of the skill, the manner in which the material to be learned is presented, the emphasis given to various aspects of the skill, and the optimal arrangement of practice time. Teaching for transfer can help students more readily learn the new material being presented.

Feedback and reinforcement play a critical role in learning. They strengthen behavior and help students adjust their responses to attain desired goals. Strategies to enhance the retention of the material learned should be incorporated into the learning experience.

FOR REVIEW

1. Select an open and closed skill. Describe how the information-processing model can be applied to the learning of each of these skills. For each skill, what performance measures would you employ to determine the extent of learning?
2. What strategies can secondary school physical education teachers employ to accommodate differences in readiness among their students?
3. Describe several strategies that teachers can employ to help motivate the reluctant participant in secondary school physical education class.
4. Select an open and closed skill. Design a practice session for each of these skills taking into consideration the characteristics of these skills, use of the whole and part method, degree of emphasis placed on speed and accuracy, schedule of practice, provision of feedback, and incorporation of the principles of transfer and reinforcement.

REFERENCES

1. Schmidt RA: *Motor learning and performance: from principles to practice,* Champaign, Ill, 1991, Human Kinetics.
2. Magill RA: *Motor learning concepts and applications,* ed 2, Dubuque, Iowa, 1989, William C Brown.
3. Nichols B: *Moving and learning: the elementary school physical education experience,* ed 2, St Louis, 1990, Mosby.
4. AAHPERD: *Motor learning: Basic Stuff Series I,* Reston, Va, 1987, AAHPERD.
5. Rink J: *Teaching physical education for learning,* St Louis, 1985, Mosby.
6. Sage GH: *Motor learning and control: a neuropsychological approach,* Dubuque, Iowa, 1984, William C Brown.
7. Sage GH: Social development. In Seefeldt V, editor: *Physical activity and well-being,* Reston, Va, 1986, AAHPERD.
8. Harrison JW, Blakemore CL: *Instructional strategies for secondary school physical education,* ed 3, Dubuque, Iowa, 1992, William C Brown.
9. Hunter M: *Teach for transfer,* El Segundo, Calif, 1983, TIP.
10. Zaichkowsky LD, Zaichkowsky LB, Martinek T: *Growth and development: the child and physical activity,* St Louis, 1980, Mosby.

ANNOTATED READINGS

AAHPERD: *Motor learning: Basic Stuff Series I,* Reston, Va, 1987, AAHPERD.
　Features the discussion and application of principles of motor learning to teaching with examples to assist practitioners.
Cardinal BJ: Motivation: strategies for success, *Strategies* 4(6):27-28, 1991.
　Offers helpful strategies that can be readily implemented to enhance student motivation.
Christina RW, Corcos D: *Coaches guide to teaching sport skills,* Champaign, Ill, 1988, Human Kinetics.
　Presents guidelines for designing practices to optimize student learning.
Schmidt RA: *Motor learning and performance: from principles to practice,* Champaign, Ill, 1991, Human Kinetics.
　Offers a clear description of motor learning principles and how they can be applied to teaching.

Teaching Styles and Strategies

CHAPTER OBJECTIVES

- ◆ To discuss the relationship of teaching styles to teaching effectiveness
- ◆ To review the implications for classroom management of the respective teaching styles
- ◆ To describe a number of different teaching styles
- ◆ To discuss the advantages and disadvantages of the styles reviewed
- ◆ To identify the factors which influence the selection of an appropriate teaching style

Some teachers are superb lecturers, while others are excellent discussion leaders. Still others are at their best in one-on-one, individualized sessions. Some teachers reach students with their humor and wittiness, other with their candor, openness, and honesty. Other teachers dazzle students with their scholarship and erudition. Some are stern and firm, while others are relaxed, casual, and informal.

All of the preceding brief descriptions indicate that teaching varies along a broad continuum of behaviors. It should be obvious, then, that successful teaching can come in many forms, styles, and approaches.

There is little argument that the most potent variable in the learning environment, apart from the student, is the teacher. That teaching effectiveness varies greatly and impacts in many ways, directly and indirectly, to influence student learning and performance is not a novel or unique revelation. However, teaching effectiveness, regardless of individual perspective employed, is directly influenced by the strategies and style utilized by teachers of physical education. The issue of teaching style is the focus of this chapter.

EFFECTIVE TEACHING

The AAHPERD has identified the components of a quality physical education program as one which:

1. Helps improve students' mental alertness, academic performance, readiness to learn, and enthusiasm for learning

2. Improves students' self-esteem, interpersonal relationships, responsible behavior, and independence
3. Provides sequential planned objectives:
   - ◆ motor skills (psychomotor)
   - ◆ knowledge and understanding (cognitive)
   - ◆ attitude and appreciation (affective)
4. Is taught by a qualified physical education teacher[1]

Effective, quality programs require effective, well prepared professional educators. There is little question that the teacher is a critical actor in the instructional endeavor, and much of the success of the secondary movement program is dependent upon the competency of the instructor.

In 1986 AAHPERD and NASPE, with the support of the National Association of Secondary School Principals, outlined guidelines for secondary school physical education. In these comprehensive guidelines, rather specific directives were included addressing the required minimum skills, competencies, and knowledge of secondary school physical education teachers. Several of these recommendations centered about the teacher's ability to radiate a repertoire of teaching methods, strategies, and styles in an effort to enhance instruction and to personalize the physical education program.[2]

Effective teachers are interactive beings and masterful decision makers, competent and introspective reflectors, who also must develop a variety of knowledge, skills, and abilities. Teachers must then choose, select, combine, order, and organize the learning activities into sensible and clearly perceivable (to students), logical presentations and productions to accomplish the learning objectives as planned. All of this must be achieved while concurrently considering the previous experiences of the teacher and the student, prior student learning and abilities (long term and short term), curricular, professional, and personal (student and teacher) goals and objectives (for example, student individual and group learning styles and preferred teacher instructional style).

To be effective, then, implies the teacher's execution of carefully organized and planned learning experiences, the teacher's skill in bringing the lesson to successful completion, and the students' learning in one or more of the many dimensions of human development. Included in this process are the following specific steps:

1. The determination of the needs of the students
2. The selection of appropriate learning activities
3. The design of a logical and sequential order of instruction
4. The efficient use of time
5. The relation of activities to the student's world
6. The achievement of the planned objectives
7. The selection of a specific teaching strategy or instructional style to accomplish the lesson objectives

If the instructional program is to be effective, regardless of specific strategy or teaching style employed, the teacher must consider several important factors that influence student learning. These factors can be viewed as common elements that must be addressed in all instructional endeavors and play a secondary role in the determination of teaching style.

It is our belief that all teaching styles include the elements listed in Box 9-1. These elements in and of themselves do not greatly influence the specific teaching style employed, but they must be addressed in an effective manner for lessons to maximize student learning.

Student Motivation

Student motivation is a critical component of the instructional process, one that is influenced greatly by both the teacher's style and specific behavior. However, most styles do not address this factor directly, although teaching style may certainly affect future student motivation. Moreover, teachers who plan lessons that do not include efforts to address student motivation run the risk of destroying the motivation brought to such settings. In effect, these teachers rely upon the students' perception, understanding, comprehension, and ability to filter out or ascertain the motivating aspects of the lesson.

More specifically, if a teacher designs a lesson employing a practice style and plans at least two different activities and divides the class into at least two groups, motivational devices or techniques may or may not be utilized by the teacher. Yet the style remains the same regardless of the specific teaching behavior in the class.

Student motivation is a critical issue in physical education, and one that appears, at times, to be secondary

---

BOX 9-1

COMMON ELEMENTS IN TEACHING STYLES

1. Student motivation
2. Management tasks
3. Anticipatory set*
4. Sequence and progression
5. Activity selection
6. Provisions for feedback
7. Closure/summary

*Anticipatory set is defined as actions by the teacher that will assist students to focus on the subject matter or content of the lesson. In addition, such actions may cause students to relate the topic or focus of the lesson to something in their past experience or prior learning.

---

to the immediacy of the instructional endeavor at hand. Teachers often assume and take for granted that the activities and lesson objectives themselves will be attractive to all students. However, failure to focus on motivation can result in an overdependence on and assumption of the potency of student intrinsic motives, the overreliance inappropriate extrinsic motives (peer pressure) and reinforcers, and the creation of possible negative, long-term effects (that is, the failure to develop strong effective ties to physical activity).

Provisions for Feedback

Motor learning research has validated and supported the critical role that feedback in various forms plays in the learning process. Literally, without feedback of a minimal level, learning will be greatly inhibited if not curtailed entirely. Effects on motivation and information about performance are directly influenced by the regular appearance and provision for feedback (see Chapter 8 for a more extensive review of the literature on the importance of feedback in the learning process).

Presentation of the Lesson

This construct relates to the teacher's ability to relay the essence of the lesson to the learners. This can be accomplished in a variety of ways, but it is a necessary component of quality lessons. Unfortunately, some educators either avoid this important element or execute it in a poor manner, thereby often confusing learners, or at the least causing students to struggle to identify what is important in the lesson and where they should expend their energies. Often, especially with beginners, students commit gross errors, resulting in misdirected and inappropriate efforts and, unfortunately, a high degree of frustration.

Presentation tasks include the introduction and explanation of the skills or content, including obtaining the students' attention and arranging for all students to see and hear the important aspects of the lesson, emphasizing main points, interjecting questions to check for understanding, proceeding in small steps at a fairly quick pace, using sufficient and appropriate examples and employing clear models and demonstrations.

Closure/Summation

Each lesson should be brought to a formal close, preferably with enough time to review the learning and provide time for summarizing, clarification, and checking the students' comprehension and application. In addition, secondary physical education, which has long suffered from the negative image as a glorified "workout," must endeavor to reassert and support its contention that it addresses the many dimensions of the student, that it is instruction that develops the whole person. By providing a time for summation of cognitive, physical, and affective objectives addressed in or resulting from the physical education lesson, not only will the instructional objectives be reinforced, but they will convey to students, teachers, and administrators that the curriculum is viable, important beyond its physical aspects, and contributes much to student learning in a variety of dimensions.

THE IMPORTANCE OF STUDYING TEACHING STYLES

The importance of teaching styles is reaffirmed by Newman's[3] summation of the research on student engagement:

Students naturally find some topics and activities more stimulating and enjoyable to work on than others. However, what a student finds interesting often depends not simply upon the subjects or topics themselves but upon the way the topics are presented and the student's prior experiences with those concepts.

This latter statement provides much impetus for the inclusion of the study of styles in the preservice programs in physical education, as well as the delivery of inservice programs to heighten the awareness of teachers in the field of the importance of the teaching styles agenda.

TEACHING STYLE: A DEFINITION

How is the term *teaching style* defined? Mosston and Ashworth[4] define a style of teaching as "basically a set of decisions made in conjunction with the teaching act." Teaching style can also be used to denote patterns in and related to features of the teaching behavior manifested. Teaching style is not to be confused with instructional or teaching strategy. Teaching style can be used to indicate the general approach taken by the teacher when confronted with a specific teaching-learning situation. The term *instructional strategy,* on the other hand, is the more general, global term and can be described as the plans and actions involved in implementing instruction so that the student goals of a lesson, unit, or total curriculum might be accomplished.[5] Teaching style is the composite of teacher behavior (including responses to a broad set of teaching and learning decisions), strategies, methods, and patterns of interaction with students in efforts directed at being effective.

In an effort to explicate this term fully, let us suppose that a number of high-school physical education teachers approach their classes with an identical set of behavior objectives (instructional plans). If these teachers were to be observed at any length, consistent yet different patterns would undoubtedly be found in the way they operate in the gymnasium. For example, probably differences would be found in the following aspects of each lesson: the grouping of students; warmth-aloofness; orderliness-disorderliness; businesslike-sensitive; variations in type, frequency, and tone in the employment of feedback; and directness-indirectness.

Teacher effectiveness can be defined as the congruence between teacher actions and teacher intent. That is, a measure of teaching effectiveness can be described as that which a teacher does (that is, style) contrasted with the goals and objectives of the lesson as determined by the teacher. However, any measure of teaching effectiveness must also include an indication of student learning, because indeed this must be the ultimate concern for teachers. While some teachers may be reinforced when their planned efforts are accomplished, more effective teachers are encouraged only if student learning occurs in one or more of the various dimensions or domains of learning. It should be noted that the wide spectrum of student responses that often makes teaching simultaneously unpredictable and exciting often results in positive, incidental learning regardless of the teacher's performance.

Why is it important to study teaching styles? Why should the various styles of teaching be of interest to professionals and practitioners in physical education? Specifically, what is to be gained by crystallizing the topic of teaching styles?

There are several important reasons why present and future physical education teachers should be concerned about teaching styles. Knowledge of the various options, as it pertains to styles, facilitates efforts to explore alternative methods, strategies, and approaches to be more effective with a greater range of students. In other words, teachers who have developed the capacity to radiate and employ a variety of teaching styles are more likely to enhance their ability to reach more students and to increase their effectiveness with this increased number of students.

Knowledge and skill in a number of styles maximize

the teacher's efforts to change. Possessing the ability to teach in a number of different ways increases the range of ways of acting/modes of operation from which the teacher can explore and select the most comfortable, most effective, and, more important, the most appropriate style to use with the many and various groups of learners they will face daily. In this way, teaching effectiveness should be improved. With its myriad of contexts and motor skill environments specifically defined by the arrangements of the various sports structures, the use and selection of teaching styles in physical education might be a more critical factor than in other subject areas.

The heightened self-awareness that results from the analysis and study of various instructional styles brings with it other important benefits. The study of teaching styles brings with it the prerequisite attitude, reinforced by many in the profession of education, that there is no one correct way to teach across all groups and all situations.[4,6,7] When a fledgling teacher first comes to understand this critical concept, a major milestone toward professional, pedagogical growth has been mastered. It means, then, that the teacher is not bound to one teaching style, but rather will modulate and select styles based on other critical components of the teaching-learning environment. This enhances the movement of the physical education teacher toward the role of reflective practitioner so greatly needed in physical education.[8] This development is usually accompanied by the start of a serious teacher's self-analysis, with its inherent benefits of increased teacher awareness of self, increased awareness of

teacher and student behavior, and the positive outcomes associated with such analyses.

Selection of a teaching style is neither a random process nor one that should revolve solely about the preferences of the teacher. Rather the process of selecting a specific approach for a lesson should be dependent on a number of factors that will have an impact on the student learning. For example, a lesson involving high-risk activities such as gymnastics often dictates that more commandlike teacher strategies be employed, rather than the more open styles of teaching (for example, problem solving). It is important, at this juncture, to understand that the selection of style is predicated on a rationale, thoughful approach to preparing a lesson and the particular focus therein. A more complete discussion of the factors that teachers should consider in the selection of a teaching approach for a particular lesson is found later in this chapter.

In the next section, selected styles of teaching commonly employed in secondary physical education programs are briefly described and analyzed. For further information as well as additional and specific examples of each style, the reader is referred to the work of Mosston and Ashworth.[4]

TEACHING STYLES
Command Style

The command style is the most teacher-centered style. In this style the teacher provides a demonstration, then

The command style of teaching is used quite frequently in physical education classes.
Courtesy of Cathy Haight, Lansing High School, Lansing, NY.

explains the motor tasks to be performed. On completion of an explanation and demonstration, the teacher leads the entire class as a unit through the various components entailed to the motor activity. Throughout this style, the teacher provides a visual model, and the students are expected to imitate the motor performance exhibited by the teacher.

At the present time, given current practice in secondary school physical education, the command style can be observed in a majority of lessons in the warm-ups, calisthenics, stretching or loosening-up portion of the class, usually provided for within the opening moments of the instructional session. Another common example, albeit a more thorough experience entailing more progression, learning, and follow-through than the class warm-up activities, is the dance aerobics class. Typically the instructor is in front of the class and provides the explanation, demonstration/modeling, walk-through of the steps, and then leads the group through each phase of the music and rhythmical performance.

The student's role in the command style of teaching is the aspect of the style that can be problematic, at least as practiced in physical education. The students are not encouraged to think, to make decisions, or to diverge during the lesson. Rather, students are expected to behave predictably, often passively, and the resulting behavior has been described as mechanistic, rote, or mindless. This style of teaching is often appropriate in certain prescribed circumstances. For example, when the subject matter of the lesson involves dangerous activities such as rock climbing or when the learners are truly beginners and are unable to relate to the activities at any level, teachers must provide much information and direction. These latter examples would, of necessity, force teachers to employ the command style of instruction at least in the early stages of the learning. However, the overuse of the command style can be problematic if the curriculum (as we have suggested throughout this text), the instructional endeavor, and the teacher's goals are based on nurturing the growth and development of the whole person. That is if one believes that physical education contributes to the social, cognitive, affective, and physical development of students, then the style of teaching selected must reflect such beliefs. It should be apparent that the command style, while it may be appropriate in certain select situations such as in high-risk activities, is limited in the contributions it can make to the learning of students. A program of instruction dominated by the use of this style raises questions about the faculty's responsiveness, sensitivity to students, and the curriculum's congruence with its goals.

In the command approach, the teacher is the sole decision maker. It should be clear that the command style, while it implies an autocratic approach, is still dependent on the teacher's exact behavior. That is, different teachers employing the command approach could vary in warmth, responsiveness, and aloofness.

The command style can contribute much if it is employed judiciously. It provides the most direct route to the learning objective, and therefore it can be a timesaver. If time is limited, it may be the most efficient and productive way to convey to students the elements of the performance required. Maximum practice for all can be readily achieved.

Practice Style

This style of teaching requires that teachers relinquish some decisions to the learner. This style is also utilized by many professional physical education teachers in schools. The large classes in many secondary school physical education programs almost dictate the employment of the practice style that encourages the organization of multiple activities and multiple groups conducted concurrently during the lesson. Examples of this style are reflected in the terms often heard in schools (circuit training, station-work, or the center approach to instruction).

The creation of several groups within a lesson is a major move on the part of the teacher away from the command style, as well as from a totally teacher-centered approach. Ceding several decisions to students (location, pace, repetitions, rate, and posture) means a new role is provided to the teacher. The teacher is no longer relied on to provide a continual, visual, or verbal model of performance throughout the learning setting. Therefore while some decisions are transferred to students, other decisions now become available to the teacher that were not apparent within the command style. Specifically, teachers now must choose where to direct their energies once the groups have commenced their activities. The teacher can choose where, when, how, and how long to provide feedback and reinforcement to students. Teachers have the option of providing private, individualized feedback, rather than relying solely on generalized, group, or public feedback. This is a major accomplishment in a number of important dimensions: socially, emotionally, and humanistically.

This style requires more preparation before class begins. Space, equipment, and activities must be clearly determined to efficiently organize at least two groups working simultaneously within the same area. Provisions must be made for providing information to the groups clearly, quickly, and efficiently to avoid students' dependence on the teacher (as in the command style lesson) for direction, visual information, modeling, and explanations.

An example of the use of the practice style follows. The teacher introduces the overhand serve in volleyball. Previous to this lesson, all students had been introduced to and have practiced the underhand serve. The group is

The practice style frequently incorporates use of stations, and students are provided with directions to guide their performance at each station.
Courtesy of Ben Lombardo, Rhode Island College, Providence, RI.

situated so as to see and hear the teacher, who now explains the overhand service, its use, and the points of emphasis. Several demonstrations follow, with the teacher executing the serve a few times and again emphasizing the major points in the execution of the serve. The students are then placed into one of two groups. Group I will practice the new skill (the overhand serve) in area A, while Group II will practice the underhand serve. The teacher is free to move between the two groups, providing feedback and additional instruction as needed. At a predetermined point in the lesson, the groups will switch tasks (from overhand to underhand service and vice versa), and the teacher will move among groups addressing the needs of individual students as needed. At the close of practice, the teacher asks the group to review and discuss the major points of emphasis in the service once again. The teacher would then proceed to the next portion of the lesson.

Reciprocal Style

In the reciprocal style, students are assigned the task of providing feedback for each other. One student performs the task, while the other observes and provides feedback. Then the students exchange roles. In effect, students are provided with some opportunities and decisions normally reserved for the instructor such as evaluation decisions (that is, how well did the student perform). The teacher, filling a role similar to that in the practice style, makes all the prelesson decisions. The

teacher determines the objectives of the lesson, what tasks are to be accomplished, identifies the criteria that will guide the students in their observers' roles, gives the assignments to the students, and assists the observers to improve their ability as observers and their ability to interact in positive, productive ways with their partners.

When using the reciprocal style, one student performs the task while the other observes and provides feedback.
Courtesy of Ben Lombardo, Rhode Island College, Providence, RI.

Performer _____ Class _____
Observer _____ Date _____

The Tennis Forehand Stroke

Performer: Use the forehand stroke to bounce and hit a minimum of 25 balls into the backcourt.

Observer: Observe the performance and, using the check points listed below, provide the performer with knowledge about his or her performance.

At the completing of the task, switch roles. (Use a separate criteria form for each performer.)

Criteria: Indicate accomplishment ("A") or needs work ("N")

_____ 1. Stance (side to the net, weight on rear foot).
_____ 2. Racquet taken back at about hip level.
_____ 3. Eyes maintained on the ball.
_____ 4. Weight transferred onto the front foot.
_____ 5. Racquet brought to the ball in a straight line.
_____ 6. Performer watches the ball until it is hit by the racquet.
_____ 7. The knees are slightly bent throughout the stroke.
_____ 8. The racquet contacts the ball when it is even with the front foot.
_____ 9. Wrist is firm and stroke is made with the whole arm, moved from the shoulder.
_____ 10. The trunk rotates so that the shoulders and hips face the net on follow-through.
_____ 11. Follow-through is completed so that the racquet moves in a forward and upward direction of the stroke.

FIG. 9-1 An example of a criteria sheet for use with the reciprocal style of teaching. Adapted from Mosston M, Ashworth S: *Teaching physical education,* ed 3, Columbus, Ohio, 1986, Merrill Publishing.

The main aspect of this style when contrasted with those previously reviewed, is the teacher's role when working with the observer and only indirectly with the performer. The student is placed in a position to become a skilled observer and thereby must translate the observations made about the performance of another to his or her performance. The teacher provides feedback directly to the observer, not the performer, thereby providing a perceptual check on the observer's understanding of the selected criteria as applied to another's performance. Obviously, the information or materials provided for the students as they complete their observations will certainly facilitate not only the student learning and performance but also the success of this style.

If the teacher has prepared this lesson well and has provided the students with the specific and appropriate criteria as related to the skills and concepts to be studied, the obvious advantage of this style is the increased amount and incidence of feedback provided to the learner. In effect, the teacher will have created many assistant or student teachers within the lesson and in this way maximizes the opportunities for feedback.

The criteria provided for the students, for use as a guide to the feedback provided, becomes an important task for the learner. Fig. 9-1 is an example of a criteria sheet that could be designed not only to inform the observers of the specific aspects of the skills that should be commented on, but also to ease the actual communication of such feedback to the performer.

Potential drawbacks of this style relate to the possibility for social and emotional antagonism among the students. This style might involve more time than anticipated to develop the guidelines for students to act as observers. Steps should be taken by the teacher to prepare students for their role as assistant teachers, or those who provide feedback to the other students.

Guided-Discovery Style

Sometimes referred to as the convergent style of teaching, the guided-discovery style allows students to learn on their own under the direction of the instructor. Discovery is the main focus, and the rationale for use of the style is founded on the notion that the experiences of the learner will remain with the student (that is, learning and retention will be enhanced because of the path traveled to self-discovery).

It is in this style that the teacher takes on yet another role, that is, one of a guide, facilitating the students' self-discovery by means of indirect prodding and a multitude of specifically directed and focused questions. The reader would do well to hold on to the image of a funnel, that is, the students' path to learning is funneled into one direction and to a common endpoint, specifically the teacher-identified set of objectives for the lesson. All learners' thoughts converge to one point of understanding. All students are expected to arrive at the same common knowledge and understanding, albeit the path they take should be individualized and unique.

The teacher plans this type of lesson by starting with a known endpoint and then organizes the lesson about this focus (for example, efficient soccer passing, a powerful forehand tennis stroke, the principles of stability). With this focus in mind, the lesson is developed by preparing a series of specific questions requiring high-order cognitive responses, to enhance the learners' attempts at understanding the lesson content and thereby enhancing the accomplishment of the lesson objectives through self-discovery.

The teacher's task is quite clear and direct. Painstaking as it may be, the teacher constructs a progressive series of logically sequenced questions leading the student to understanding via physical, cognitive, individual, or group learning activities. Yet another important aspect of this style of teaching is the course taken by the teacher when students are puzzled, confused, or arrive at an incorrect answer. The teacher must be ready with additional questions and alternative ways to address or rephrase the question to keep the students focused and moving in the desired direction of uncovering for themselves the concepts, skills, or knowledges that comprise the lesson.

The teacher does not provide answers. Rather, the teacher insists that the students discover for themselves. Therefore another aspect of this style is teacher "wait time" and patience. Teachers must provide sufficient time for learners to come up with appropriate responses. For some teachers, this in and of itself is difficult and must be practiced. Waiting sometimes means permitting the class to be physically inactive, silently composing a response. Many professionals incorrectly believe such behavior to be counter to the notion that the students in physical education must always be physically engaged. Teachers employing this style must learn to allow students to think, to struggle in their efforts to learn for themselves, and to compose a logical response to the situation. In this way, teachers can also develop students' reflective abilities and quite possibly their analytical skills as related to the content of physical education and the study of human movement.

Teacher feedback becomes even more critical than in the previous styles of instruction described. Once they have embarked upon the guided discovery (convergent) style, physical education teachers must create and maintain a climate of relative openness, acceptance, and patience. Once teachers are committed to asking students questions as a style of learning, the following other circumstances must happen:

1. The learning climate "opens up" (in the psycho-socio-emotional sense).
2. Power and authority in the learning setting are shared with the students. This occurs any time the teacher asks a question.
3. Teachers must become "active" listeners.
4. Students actually get to listen to their peers. They too must become "active" listeners.
5. The teacher's response to the students, as feedback and reinforcement, takes on additional significance. Such feedback influences succeeding interactions much more than in other styles because of the public exposure and voice given the students' verbal and cognitive efforts.
6. The resulting physical education becomes more humanistic.

The implications of this style are many. By organizing lessons in this fashion, the teacher not only implies the willingness to commit to all the outcomes affiliated with "crossing the discovery threshold" but also enters a style of inquiry that carries few guarantees.[4] Indeed, any instructional style that is basically indirect, that is, relies heavily on teacher questioning and acceptance, is unable to predict accurately the actions and thoughts of the students. This last factor truly intimidates many professionals, experienced and otherwise.

Trust in the capabilities of the student is implied in any style that relies heavily on the cognitive capacity of students. The teacher must believe in the students' inherent cognitive, physical, and psychosocial capabilities and dispositions. If not, this and other inquiry, conceptual, or discovery styles, which depend on the higher order cognitive abilities of students, are doomed to failure and will be transformed to appear similar to activity-based, teacher-centered lessons.

Merely asking questions does not mean that the teacher is employing this style. Questions must be structured in a logical sequence related to the structure of the subject matter, that is, a defined, identified endpoint or outcome. Random questions are not a part of this style.[4] Readers should keep in mind the funnel metaphor described earlier, when attempting to visualize the processes and procedures inherent in this style. Two short examples of the guided discovery style are shown in Boxes 9-2 and 9-3.

Conceptual Style

An ancient Chinese proverb states that if you give a hungry man a fish, his hunger will be satiated for the

BOX 9-2

EXAMPLE OF GUIDED DISCOVERY IN BASKETBALL

Objective

To discover the ways to respond individually to a pressing defense.

Question 1:	What options are available to you individually when confronted with a pressing defensive player?
Action:	Students work in small groups, physically and cognitively attempting to prepare a response to this question.
Anticipated response:	Stop and go, fake left and go right, and vice versa.
Teacher response:	Correct.
Question 2:	Suppose the defensive player overplays you on the ball side. What can you do?
Action:	Students work in groups to develop possible answers. The teacher suggests possible gamelike drills that might assist students in their efforts.
Anticpated response:	The offensive player should move strongly to the ball and quickly pivot and go "backdoor" to the basket.
Teacher response:	Excellent. That certainly is a fine option for the offensive player.

The teacher and students would continue working in this fashion until the students developed an understanding of the possible options available to the offensive player.

BOX 9-3

EXAMPLE OF GUIDED DISCOVERY IN VOLLEYBALL

Objective

To discover the most efficient method of serving overhand.

Question 1:	In what position should the arm and shoulder be at the point of contact when serving?
Action:	Students work individually, some in pairs or small groups, obviously practicing their overhand serves. Several students perform, while others are apparently observing, describing body parts, and attempting to analyze the skill.
Anticipated response:	The arm should be extended fully above the shoulder.
Teacher response:	Correct. Well done.
Question 2:	How fast should the arm and shoulder be traveling at the point of contact?
Action:	Students practice, drill, and analyze the activity.
Anticipated response:	The server should execute the serve as fast as possible, yet remain in control.
Teacher response:	Well done. Excellent analysis.
Question 3:	Where should the point of contact with the ball be in relation to the body?
Action:	Students practice, observe, and analyze their performance.
Anticipated response:	The ball should be in front of the body, so that the arm and shoulder are extended and forward of the body.
Teacher response:	Well done. That is the correct point of contact when the server desires maximum power.

The teacher and students would proceed in this manner until the lesson objectives are accomplished and the students develop a full understanding of the volleyball techniques and concepts under consideration.

moment, but if you teach him how to fish, he will never feel hunger again. In a nutshell, this proverb defines the essence of the conceptual style.

The conceptual style focuses on subject matter more than all other styles. Its characteristics are most similar to the guided discovery style, and in fact, when the guided discovery style focuses on conceptual matters (force production) rather than activity concepts (baseball batting), this style is in effect a conceptual style. Some believe that the conceptual style is less a style and more a mindset in which the teacher employs the guided discovery style in conjunction with a focus on concepts that can be applied in many situations well beyond the specific application of the activity or sport.

The conceptual teaching style emphasizes the use of the content of motor activity as a vehicle to learning that is broad in nature and has wide applicability. The cognitive basis of this style results in knowledge and understanding that can be applied not only to other sports and

physical activity situations, but also to everyday motor functioning. For example, the concept of force absorption, while critically important to motor performance in the rebound aspects of several activities (such as, gymnastics vaulting and basketball rebounding) also relates to general motor aspects of daily living (such as, transferring and receiving packages from person to person and cushioning falls).

The characteristics of the conceptual style of teaching physical education are most like that of the guided discovery approach. Specifically, the teacher employs a questioning style (that is, an indirect teaching behavior) that requires higher order student thinking well beyond mere rote repetition of the teacher's ideas, memorization, or the knowledge and comprehension level. Student responses are predominantly interpretations, analyses, and applications of specific conceptual knowledge. The resulting student thinking should be at the application level and above.

Once the questions have been posed, the teacher encourages, accepts, and supports the students' efforts to understand the concept being considered. The teacher often probes past the students' initial attempts to respond to the question and forces the students to understand the *why*'s and *how*'s of human movement, and then takes the student to a higher level of understanding of the concept by means of the planned motor/physical activity.

For example, in the conceptual lesson in Box 9-4, the teacher moves the student from the specific comparisons indicated to the broader aspects of the principles and factors of stability and balance. Once these factors are clearly understood, the teacher attempts to have the students apply the knowledge of stability and balance to other motor activities, and then ultimately to motor activities and the physical aspects of everyday living.

Students can practice independently and evaluate their own performance using a checklist.

Courtesy of Ben Lombardo, Rhode Island College, Providence, RI.

BOX 9-4

EXAMPLE OF A CONCEPTUAL LESSON

Objective

The students will apply the concepts of stability to the various positions indicated and respond to the questions that follow.

1. What is the most stable position you can move into? Explain.
2. What is the most unstable position you can move into? Explain.
3. Which position described below is easier to maintain? Why?
   - Lying on one side, one arm stretched along the floor overhead, and the other arm along side
   - Lying on one side, one arm stretched along the floor overhead, with the top hand resting on the floor in front of the body
   - Standing upright on two feet, *or* standing on head and two hands
   - Standing upright on two feet, *or* standing on two hands
   - Standing on two feet and two hands, *or* standing on two hands and two knees

---

Teachers' acceptance (in verbal and nonverbal forms) of student responses is a critical teacher behavior in this style. Teachers cannot expect students to respond willingly if the teachers do not accept and reward good attempts and encourage and reinforce the students in their cognitive efforts.

In much the same way as the guided discovery style, the teacher guides the students' understanding of the concepts under study by means of a series of reflective and specific questions. The teacher must continually maintain the concept under consideration within the attention and purview of the student. For example, when attempting to teach the concept of the mobility/stability relationship to students via a basketball lesson, which focuses on the defensive stance, the teacher needs to maintain the students' focus on the mobility/stability relationship, although most students would prefer to focus on the specific basketball skills within the lesson.

Teachers employing this style can focus on a variety of concepts from a multitude of sources. For example, there are sports concepts (offensive and defensive tactics and the "weave" in basketball), biomechanical concepts (force production and leverage), affective concepts (fear and trust), and physiological concepts (overload). Concepts are readily available within a typical physical education curriculum. Supporters of the conceptual style believe that the physical activity should be the vehicle for broader learning and understanding (conceptual learning). Consultation with the AAHPERD Basic Stuff Series would provide the reader with an excellent and thorough set of materials that would support and facilitate efforts in this direction.[6]

The conceptual approach has the potential to add much to a secondary lesson. By focusing on concepts that have broad application, by encouraging student interpretation and analysis, and by broadening the scope of the physical education curriculum, the conceptual style can heighten the contributions to the development of the whole student and add much to the growth of the student in many dimensions.

Problem-Solving Style

Sometimes referred to as the divergent approach, the problem-solving style, more than any other, encourages students to be independent and creative and to develop solutions to a given problem. While students are encouraged to think at the higher cognitive levels (synthesis and evaluation) throughout the lesson in much the same way as the guided discovery and conceptual style, the problem-solving approach is differentiated from these other styles by subtle yet unique changes in both the learning environment and in the teacher's behavior.

First of all, the teacher creates the lesson by selecting the subject matter and designs one or more problems. In Box 9-5, the teacher has designed a series of problems within a basketball unit. Second, the problems created provide students with opportunities to respond in multiple ways and to generate multiple solutions to one problem, as long as the students' responses satisfy the criteria either specified or implicit in the problem itself. Verification can be completed by the teacher and the student together, or by either alone. As such, evaluation of the various solutions becomes a major part of this teaching style.

The problem-solving style requires a setting in which physical education teachers feel confident and secure, and can invite and accept a wide variety of alternative solutions to a problem.[9] Within this environment, teachers must accept student responses, assess the students' methods and procedures of problem resolution, and avoid evaluating specific responses.[4,9]

Earlier in the chapter, the funnel metaphor was used in reference to the guided discovery style. For the problem-solving style, a more appropriate metaphor would be an inverted funnel, because it is in this style that the learners start with one specific problem and attempt to generate a possible and viable response.

Problem solving has the potential to unleash students' creativity and support their efforts to apply this ability as they experience human movement and study physical education. As such, the use of this style can make unique

BOX 9-5

AN EXAMPLE OF THE PROBLEM-SOLVING TEACHING STYLE

Subject matter: Basketball

Students are asked to develop responses to each of the following problems:
1. What is your most effective shot?
2. At what distance from the basket are you most accurate?
3. Which shot is most difficult for you?
4. Which shot is most difficult for you when using the dominant arm? The nondominant arm?
5. Describe the ideal conditions required for you to be a successful shooter (time of day, type of court, side of court, angle, and position of defense).
6. Respond again to questions 1-5 assuming that you will be shooting from a stationary position.
7. Respond again to questions 1-5 assuming that the shot will be taken off a one-step dribble.
8. Respond to questions 1-5 assuming that the shot will be taken during a fastbreak situation.
9. Respond to questions 1-5 assuming that the shot will be taken off a screen/pick.
10. Respond to questions 1-5 assuming a two-on-one fastbreak situation.
11. How would you get a shot off if two defensive players were guarding you closely?
12. What shot would you prefer to use if closely guarded by two defensive players?
13. Describe your preferred shot selection when playing one-on-one against a defensive player with the following characteristics:
    ◆ Taller and quicker
    ◆ Taller and equal quickness
    ◆ Taller and slower
    ◆ Same height and quicker
    ◆ Same height and equal quickness
    ◆ Same height and slower
    ◆ Shorter and quicker
    ◆ Shorter and equal quickness
    ◆ Shorter and slower

contributions to the student and the secondary school curriculum (Table 9-1).

FACTORS IN SELECTION OF A TEACHING STYLE

Selection of an appropriate teaching style should be a decision greatly influenced by the results of careful and professional reflection. A teaching style should not be determined in a whimsical manner, and certainly not for

TABLE 9-1 Summary Analysis of Teaching Styles

Style	Teacher Decisions	Student Decisions	Special Features	Advantages	Disadvantages
Command	All decisions with one exception are the domain of the teacher	Student chooses to respond and participate, or not	Teacher-centered, teacher-dominated approach; teacher serves as continual model; entire class/group moves as unit	Uniformity; conformity; efficient use of time; maximum potential for physiological changes; minimal preimpact planning	Not sensitive to individual needs and differences; minimal cognitive growth
Practice	Almost exclusively; some impact decisions are ceded to the students	Student has some decisions to make about rate, start/stop times, posture, and location	Students are somewhat independent of teacher; teacher free to move among groups to respond to immediate student needs; several groups involved in different learning activities	Individualization; private feedback; better utilization of space and equipment; opportunities for student socializing	Students can avoid interaction with the teacher; increased need for preimpact planning and preparation
Reciprocal	All prelesson, some impact decisions; teacher still develops content and lesson objectives	Students maintain same decisions as in practice style, but add some evaluation/feedback decisions; students have opportunity to assess student partner	Students act as assistant teachers and provide feedback to other students; teacher responds to the assistant teachers' efforts to help their partners; students work in pairs	One-to-one teacher student ratio; increased and immediate feedback; develops understanding and observation skills; students share responsibility for learning	Potential for physical, social, emotional antagonism among students; takes time to develop guidelines for students as sources of feedback; feedback dependent on student perceptions
Guided discovery (convergent)	Determines objectives of lesson, individual steps, content; many decisions modified, dependent on specific student responses; teacher provides feedback to all responses	Students decide responses (cognitive and motor) as they attempt to answer questions; they participate in postimpact assessment and decisions	Many teacher questions employed to shape or "funnel" student responses to a single learning endpoint; high-level student cognitive involvement	Involves higher levels of cognition; develops understanding of efficient movement; opportunities for improved self-concept	Takes time; requires careful planning; some difficulties with groups with great variability in skills and abilities and large groups
Conceptual	Similar to guided discovery, but the content or subject matter is broad with more integrative concepts that relate and can be applied to many activities and life situations	Students make many decisions as they respond to questions and analyze activities for identification and application of concepts	Conceptual development emphasized; indirect teaching approach; emphasis on student application of concepts learned to broader life activities	Indirect approach; involves high-order cognitive involvement; promotes broader, long-term understanding of concepts foundational to movement study; enhances affection for physical activity	Time-consuming; requires specific and exact preimpact planning; teaching affective and other more complex concepts requires the employment of a large number of relevant examples
Problem solving (divergent)	Teacher makes preimpact decisions; sets limits of problems and challanges; raises open-ended, broad questions to stimulate a variety of possible responses or solutions	Determines how to move and think within boundaries of the problem; makes impact and postimpact decisions about varied and multiple divergent solutions	Multiple and varied responses elicited for the various problems posed by the instructor; reverse "funnel" effect; creative thinking emphasized	Enhanced conceptual development; great cognitive involvement; creativity and individuality enhanced; skill of problem solving developed	Generalized approach; specific skills are secondary; very diverse performance result

TABLE 9-2

Factors Influencing Selection of an Appropriate Teaching Style

Student Factors	Teacher Factors	Subject Matter Factors	Environmental Factors
Skill level	Instructional philosophy	Prerequisite knowledge	Resources (facilities, equipment, space)
Beginner	Personal disposition	Students' view of subject matter	
Advanced	Skill in various styles		Time
Physical maturity	Objectives of lesson	Individual or team	Class size
Cognitive level	Teacher flexibility	Open or closed skills	Noise level
Motivation	Class management abilities	Risk factors	Public or private venue
Activity level	Personal preferences	Complexity of content	Location of teaching station
Difficulty of specific learning tasks			
Learning style			

idiosyncratic reasons. Instead, teachers should consider a variety of factors before employing a particular style. This is the focus of the next section.

Many factors influence the instructor's decision about how to conduct a specific lesson. While some might suggest that this decision rests solely in the hands of the teacher and thereby is dependent wholly on the individual teacher's preferences, others recommend that the decision about teaching style should be included within the broader reflective process employed by thoughtful, mindful physical education practitioners. This latter approach would suggest that the needs, preferences, and abilities of the teachers become merely one aspect (albeit a critical one) of this analysis.

Broadly defined, the factors that can influence decisions about teaching style are categorized as (1) student characteristics, (2) teacher variables, (3) subject matter or content concerns, and (4) context and environmental variables. Each group of factors, when examined closely, reveals an extensive list of constraints, needs, abilities, and influences, all of which may have an impact on the decision process related to specification of teaching style. Table 9-2 summarizes the various factors that have the potential for affecting the determination of teaching style.

The following is a brief analysis of the most salient aspects of each factor. This is presented in an effort to review the unique contributions each factor can make to the efforts of teachers to identify and select the most appropriate and facilitative style for their class.

Student Characteristics

First and foremost, teachers must observe, study, and analyze the characteristics, abilities, needs, and interests of their students, to match accurately their behavior and teaching style to their students. The characteristics of students are the most critical variables in the process of style determination. Thoughtful, reflective teachers strive to understand and know their students. They do this with at least two goals in mind, that is, to understand and become knowledgeable about their students as both individuals and as students functioning within the class to ensure more appropriate and accurate plans. Such necessary planning includes the determination of teaching style. Secondary school physical education teachers must become astute and skillful at selecting styles that closely approximate the characteristics and style of their learners.

Specifically, teachers needs to become aware of students' abilities by answering the following questions:

◆ Can students solve problems independently?
◆ How do they respond to questions?
◆ Can they function well in small group settings?
◆ Have they matured to a level that permits them to provide meaningful and relevant feedback to other students?
◆ How intelligent are they?
◆ How do the students prefer to interact with the instructional process?
◆ What are the predominant learning styles of the students in class? Group learning styles? Individual learning styles?
◆ Do the students respond well to cognitive or conceptually based physical education content?
◆ Are the students active? Verbal? Social? Emotionally stable?
◆ Are the students physically mature? Developed? Strong? Flexible?

The learner's skill level should also play a role in the style selection process. Do beginners learn better operating within the same teaching style provided advanced performers? Many suggest that a more open, exploratory style can be successfully employed for initial lessons in many skilled areas with novice students.[9-11] These are just a few examples of the type of information teachers should seek and comprehend that can facilitate their efforts to select an appropriate teaching style.

Teacher Variables

Variables to consider within this factor relate to the needs, abilities, and characteristics of the individual teacher. Teachers, hopefully via an authentic, reflective process, should analyze their responses to the following questions (some of which truly go way beyond the mere selection of style and strike more at the heart of the instructional endeavor and related decisions) to facilitate the process of selecting an appropriate teaching style:

◆ What role do I need to play during the lesson?
◆ Can I lead the class in a variety of styles?
◆ How much pedagogical flexibility do I possess?
◆ Can I demonstrate or employ?
◆ Do I have the ability to behave in the manner prescribed by various styles?
◆ Which style of teaching do I prefer?
◆ To which style do I object?
◆ Which styles are difficult for me?
◆ Can I perform more than one style well?

Responses to these and similar questions will assist teachers in their efforts to provide lessons for students employing teaching styles that will facilitate student learning and maximize effectiveness.

Subject Matter/Content Concerns

In this area, the teacher should attempt to discover and analyze the students' prerequisite knowledge and familiarity with the subject matter. Is the content new? Familiar? Is the student's prerequisite knowledge adequate? Appropriate? Thorough? Do the students value the content? Do the students consider the subject matter exciting? Dull? Worthwhile?

Often decisions about the exact content to be discussed or presented provide clues as to how the class should be conducted. For example, some styles are more appropriate for individual skills than team activities (reciprocal teaching works well for individual skills, such as the tennis serve). Open skills instruction would lend itself to more open styles of lessons or teaching. For example, the use of the guided discovery style would be more appropriate for teaching basketball skills while the more teacher-centered command style would be a better choice when teaching a cartwheel or other gymnastics skills. Closed skills, those skills performed within an environment with little variation, would appear to be more appropriately conducted within more closed styles of teaching (that is, teacher centered, subject matter focused, and less open ended).

Finally, the risks inherent in the subject matter sometimes dictate the specific style to be employed by the teacher. All others things being equal, the higher the risks of injury within the performance requirements of the activity, the more physical education teachers tend to

Various styles of teaching offer teachers different opportunities for the provision of feedback to their students.
Courtesy of Ben Lombardo, Rhode Island College, Providence, RI.

employ less open, less exploratory teaching styles. In the latter case, teachers often rely on the command style, teacher-directed styles of teaching.

Context and Environmental Variables

These factors relate to the available resources (equipment and facilities), class size, time, and space. Will the lesson be conducted indoors or outdoors? Does location of teaching station have an impact on the instructional style? Is the environment quiet or noisy? Public or private? What styles are more appropriate for large classes? Small groups? Is there equipment for each student? How active can each student be within the assigned space?

The determination of a teaching style for a particular lesson is influenced by the number of students in the class, the location of the class (indoor or outdoor), and the availability of space. The employment of the practice style, which often requires the use of multiple teaching stations, would be precluded if this option were not available to the instructor. On the other hand, the more individualized style of teaching (for example, the guided discovery or problem solving styles) which usually require a piece of equipment for each student, in some cases can be administered well within one teaching station and quite possibly require less space.

While this section does not represent the full spectrum of possible factors that have an impact on teaching style, those reviewed and included in Table 9-2 should be considered during the planning stages of a lesson. Teachers who reflect on these matters are more likely to enhance the learning of their students and personally experience success in their instructional endeavors.

SUMMARY

For too long in education, there has been a search for the one best system of teaching. There has been a major preoccupation with the notion that there is a "best" way to teach and that there is a style that is effective across all subject areas and student groups. Such a notion, however attractive it may appear, has not been supported by the research literature.

It is time to move beyond this position. Alan Tom's[6] work clearly dissects this nonproductive view, and the works of Mosston and Ashworth,[4] Siedentop,[12] and others suggest that teaching style must be adjusted according to the maturation, previous experiences, and needs of the student.[4,6,8]

It is our view that teachers must be encouraged, supported, and, more important, prepared to employ a variety of approaches—what Joyce, Brown, and Peck[7] refer to as being able to radiate a broad repertoire of teaching behaviors and styles. Teacher preparation and in-service programs must support secondary school teachers' efforts to develop these abilities.

In this chapter several styles have been presented and analyzed to prepare the reader to employ a variety of teaching approaches. Each style is appropriate in select situations based on teacher objectives, student characteristics, and environmental and contextual factors (space, time, and class size). The secondary physical education teacher must be able to analyze and size up the effects of such factors and include this information when selecting or matching the style to a particular class. Special note was made of this process, which directly influences the determination of style.

Teachers who proceed through this latter process, thereby reflecting on the many factors that impinge on teaching effectiveness and student learning, will be embarking upon a course destined to improve instruction and learning in secondary school physical education. Such reflective, mindful behavior as regards the determination and selection of a teaching style will bring secondary school physical education to new heights and start it on the path to its rightful place, as a major contributor to the growth and development of secondary students and a positive influence on the health and welfare of students beyond high school and into adulthood.

FOR REVIEW

1. Why is it important for physical education teachers to be able to employ a variety of teaching styles?
2. Select a motor skill or concept that can be taught by more than one style of teaching. Develop a written plan to teach this content for each of the following styles: command, practice, reciprocal, guided discovery, conceptual, and problem solving. Compare the lessons and analyze the roles of the teacher and the student in each plan.
3. Which style(s) discussed in this chapter would you feel most comfortable using in class? least comfortable? Why? Explain fully.
4. Observe several physical education teachers while they conduct a class. Record significant interactions and student and teacher behaviors. Try to classify the teaching styles employed utilizing the styles reviewed in this chapter.
5. What factors should influence the teacher's selection of a teaching style?

REFERENCES

1. AAHPERD: Physical education, *JOPERD* 61(8):2, 1990.
2. AAHPERD: *Guidelines for secondary school physical education: a position paper*, Reston, Va, 1986, AAHPERD.
3. Newman F: Student engagement and high school reform, *Educational Leadership* 40(5):34-36, 1989.
4. Mosston M, Ashworth S: *Teaching physical education*, ed 3, Columbus, Ohio, 1986, Merrill Publishing.
5. Colfer G et al: *Contemporary physical education*, Dubuque, Iowa, 1986, William C Brown.
6. Tom A: *Teaching as a moral craft*, New York, 1984, Longman.
7. Joyce B, Brown C, Peck L, editors: *Flexibility in teaching*, New York, 1981, Longman.
8. Hellison D: *A reflective secondary school physical educator*, paper presented at National Convention of AAHPERD, Kansas City, Mo, 1987, AAHPERD.

9. Harrison J, Blakemore C: *Instructional strategies for secondary school physical education,* ed 3, Dubuque, Iowa, 1992, William C Brown.
10. Dougherty N, Bonanno D: *Contemporary approaches to teaching physical education,* ed 2, Scottsdale, Ariz, 1987, Gorsuch Scarisbrick.
11. Nichols B: *Moving and learning: the elementary school physical education experience,* ed 2, St Louis, 1990, Mosby.
12. Siedentop D: *Developing teaching skills in physical education,* ed 3, Palo Alto, Calif, 1991, Mayfield Publishing.
13. Kneer M, Heitman H: *Basic stuff series II: the basic stuff in action for grades 9-12,* Reston, Va, 1987, AAHPERD.

ANNOTATED READINGS

Mosston M, Ashworth S: *Teaching physical education,* ed 3, Columbus, Ohio, 1986, Merrill Publishing.

This is the classic work on teaching styles. Mosston and Ashworth's spectrum of teaching styles has proven to be the seminal work in the area of style, and students and professionals alike should study this work carefully. Clearly written, it contains many explicit examples of each teaching style and numerous lesson plans. These items amply support the theoretical basis of the authors' work. The material is presented in a manner which facilitates discussion, review, and analysis by students and professionals at all levels of development.

Siedentop D: *Developing teaching skills in physical education,* ed 3, Palo Alto, Calif, 1991, Mayfield Publishing.

Siedentop's excellent work on the preparation of physical education teachers includes a fine section on teaching methods. These methods can be considered teaching styles as we have discussed them. Siedentop presented three categories or methods: direct instruction, task teaching, and inquiry. These styles are reviewed on the basis of Siedentop's main tenet, that is, his belief that the most important characteristics of effective teaching are found in many different styles, yet the "adoption of a style without these characteristics results in form without substance." Readers will find the section devoted to planning and teaching methods to be quite informative and beneficial.

Silvernail D: *Teaching styles as related to student achievement,* ed 2, Washington, DC, 1986, National Education Association.

This comprehensive monograph, now in its second edition, is a summary of the research on teaching style as it relates to student achievement. In its effort to summarize the research findings, the monograph also suggests some underlying principles of effective instruction. In this effort, Silvernail has responded in a comprehensive manner to the following questions: What teaching activities enhance pupil learning? Are certain teaching styles and strategies more effective than others in helping students increase their performance? Readers will find this monograph informative, and it will provide excellent background data pertinent to the teaching style question. While the author does not review the research in physical education, the material will help both novice and experienced teachers in their efforts to respond and adapt to the varied needs of students.

Communication, Motivation, and Discipline

CHAPTER OBJECTIVES

◆ To discuss the importance of communication in the learning setting

◆ To describe communication processes and strategies that enhance learning in the secondary school physical education program

◆ To describe factors that influence motivation in the secondary physical education program

◆ To discuss strategies for increasing and maintaining student motivation for the program of secondary school physical education

◆ To describe the various approaches to discipline

◆ To describe strategies for effective discipline and classroom control

◆ To describe factors that influence discipline in the learning setting

Communication skills, motivational strategies, and class management techniques are foundational elements common to successful education programs. Each factor in this group of teacher abilities, by itself and in conjunction with the others, contributes much to teacher effectiveness, student commitments, educational goals, the establishment and maintenance of a fulfilling school environment, and a productive teaching-learning climate. These three important aspects of teacher efficiency also have a significant impact on the instructional endeavor.

Major problems confronting education today, such as student apathy, rebellious behavior, inappropriately designed learning environments, and teacher incompetence, exert a direct influence on the effectiveness of instructional programs. Analysis reveals that several factors are common to these problems. Significant aspects of these problems relate to the use of appropriate communication techniques in the learning setting, the provision of adequate levels of teacher and student motivation, and the creation and maintenance of an instructional atmosphere impervious to and capable of restricting behavioral disruptions.

This chapter will address the concerns of teacher-student communication, motivation for learning, and the maintenance of discipline. In each case the focus will be on strategies appropriate to the creation of positive, productive learning environments and on the facilitation and enhancement of student learning. It is this latter aspect by which secondary physical education teachers should ultimately elect to have their programs judged.

COMMUNICATION

A major target of educational reformers has been the U.S. high school. Various study groups have criticized secondary education and educators for accomplishing so little with so many students, for failing to reduce the dropout rate, for attempting to implement curricula that are all-inclusive while at the same time superficially addressing subject matter, for causing standards to decline drastically, and for failing to generate an interest in learning.[1,2] Some of the more enlightened reformers have gone beyond mere criticism and negativism and have offered suggestions that can address the concerns indicated and would promote more effective secondary education.[3-5]

Many of the proposals for change focus on teacher-student interaction and communication. Sizer's[3] Coalition of Essential Schools has as one of its main tenets "less is more," that is, reductions in class size and teaching loads and the simplification of class schedules so students can spend more time on fewer subjects. In much the same way, Goodlad[6] recommended a significant reduction in the workload of teachers to stimulate the quality and quantity of student-teacher interactions. The intent of these and similar reports is to maximize that vital part of the instructional endeavor—teaching working and interacting with students, preferably at an individual level.

The point here is that the critical outcomes of the secondary program are dependent on numerous, timely, and facilitative exchanges between students and teachers. Problems of many types (for example, confusion, lack of clarity, behavioral disruptions, and motivational problems) arise when such communications are restricted because of large classes, infrequent contacts or meetings, flexible time, and limited access to teacher assistance. Various approaches to communication and motivation will not only facilitate learning via positive interaction and heightened student motivation, but these approaches also can alleviate the severity and occurrence of disruptions and disciplinary exchanges in the secondary physical education program.

THE IMPORTANCE OF COMMUNICATION

Many physical education teachers are expert planners. Others work wonders by their unique utilization of various teaching techniques. Still others dazzle students with their subject matter expertise. But success, productivity, and effectiveness, all measured in terms of student-learning and development, can be greatly limited unless teachers communicate effectively. The importance of communication to the instructional endeavor can be summarized succinctly: no matter how brilliant teachers may be at developing lessons or how familiar they might be with the special knowledge of physical education content, effectiveness and the facilitation of learning will be affected by the teacher's ability to communicate with students. Check[7] goes so far as to claim, " . . . success in teaching is possible *only* when the teacher is communicating with the students."

There are no quicker ways to decrease learning, diffuse a stimulating environment, reduce student interest, and inhibit development of students in general than to manifest instructional behaviors that create confusion, interject chaos to the gymnasium, muddle through presentations, or to emit mixed signals to students. The destruction of, or failure to establish, communication lines is a definite indicator of nonproductive, negative instructional experiences.[7-9]

How does the secondary physical education teacher create facilitative lessons grounded in positive interactions and sound communication techniques? The next section will respond to this issue and focus on two critical aspects of communication. First, techniques to enhance teacher presentations and demonstrations in physical education will be addressed. Second, communication strategies that promote increased student contributions and participation in physical education classes will be reviewed.

Effective Presentations

Teaching is comprised of a multitude of activities. Teachers today are expected to perform more roles as the expectations, responsibilities, and outcomes for U.S. high schools continue to increase. However, the primary role of the teacher, that is, as the facilitator responsible for learning, is founded upon, and based in competencies related to, effective communication.

Physical education teachers' ability to effect change in student behavior (learning) will depend on their ability to communicate. Moreover, the difference between exciting, stimulating, facilitative physical education teachers and dull, boring, or discouraging teachers is often directly related to communication and interactive skills.

Some teachers are perceived as confusing and sleep-inducing, while others are clearly understood and interesting. More often than not, differences can be traced not so much to subject matter competency but to the teachers' communication of such knowledge. Effective presentations, an essential teaching activity, make the subject interesting and easy to learn, while the teacher with deficient communication skills often makes lessons confusing and concurrently exerts a detrimental effect on learning.

How does a teacher ensure interesting, yet effective, presentations, including demonstrations? What strategies can maximize learning by capitalizing on effective communication processes? The effectiveness of presentations in physical education can be heightened if teachers employ some of the following strategies:

1. Provide the learner with specific information about the task at hand. Many times simply stating the objectives of the lesson clearly will enhance student understanding. For example, if the teacher states to the class, "Today we will learn to score a complete bowling game," students immediately become aware of the teacher's intent and can then apply their energies appropriately. Much research indicates that more effective teachers introduce and explain material more clearly than do less effective teachers.[10,11]

Teachers also need to adjust the amount of information provided for learners based on the students' developmental level. For example, beginners require a minimal amount of information (that is, enough to get started), or else teachers run the risk of overloading them. Beginners in such circumstances will be unable to discriminate or prioritize the more critical aspects from the secondary, less important aspects of the skill under study. When this latter situation occurs, beginners often become paralyzed by the wealth of information and the choices set before them. However, the advanced performers who come to the class with some prior knowledge and experience are better able to deal with and comprehend more material, and thus they are able to filter out less relevant information from the more relevant material presented (see Chapter 8).

2. Present material in a logical order. Employ the principles of progression to sequence material that will ensure comprehension by the students.

3. Provide copious examples. Examples provide learners with concrete images and visuals of often abstract terms or concepts. Examples also bring to life the concepts that may be hard to relate to, difficult to envision, or foreign to the student's experience.

4. Personalize the instruction. Personalizing the material assists the learner in identifying with it. Often seemingly irrelevant information or material can become immediately interesting because of the teacher's efforts to relate it to the students' personal realm of experience.

5. Relate the presentation to the previous learnings and background of the students. By demonstrating that the material being presented intersects with students' previous learnings, teachers can tie the content into the students' experiences.

6. Check on student understanding by asking questions often. Feedback obtained in this manner will prevent teachers from proceeding with the presentation unless the group gives evidence of comprehension. It also serves as a check on the teacher's clarity. Often students remain timid and silent in the face of a confusing or difficult presentation, fearful of asking what they interpret to be stupid or embarrassing questions. Students will often not take the risk of asking questions because they are fearful of losing face with their peers and the teacher. Questions should be posed throughout the presentation, not only at the end of the session. Hunter[12] refers to this practice as *dip sticking* and suggests that such teacher behavior will contribute to the teachers' knowledge of what has been learned and what needs to be retaught.

7. Present material dynamically. Modulation and variation in volume, voice inflection, and timing can do much to enhance communication. Effective use of pauses, wait time after posing questions, and nonverbal gestures can help the teacher avoid desultory and ineffective presentations. General teacher dynamism, teacher enthusiasm, and teacher delivery are almost universally viewed as desirable teacher behaviors, and are supported by a considerable body of research evidence.[13,14]

8. Be sure to keep learning task information separate and distinct from organizational or administrative task information. That is, present information so that students can easily interpret and can clearly understand the differences between the subject matter and learning objectives and the administrative or organizational aspects of the drill, formation, or class structure.

It would be helpful at this point if the reader would review the material on enhancing motor skill acquisition found in Chapter 8. Additional suggestions for preparing and presenting clear, effective explanations are outlined in that section.

Effective Demonstrations

Demonstrations have been commonplace in physical education since its inception. If employed wisely they can increase the effectiveness of the lesson by maximizing the students' conceptualization of the expected performance and by providing a broad overview of the nature of the skill, thereby enhancing student learning.

In addition to showing how a movement is performed, demonstrations can be used to generate interest in a particular skill or activity and certainly can assist in minimizing misconceptions. In addition to the discussion on demonstration techniques provided in Chapter 8, the following suggestions can assist physical education teachers to maximize the effect of demonstrations:

1. Make certain that the demonstrator, whether a teacher or a student, presents an accurate image for the learners. The importance of the presentation of a technically correct model cannot be overemphasized because learners will attempt to model the performance displayed.

2. It is preferable, from the motor learning and pedagogical perspectives, to employ a demonstrator other than the teacher if possible. First, a physical education teacher who can point out the key aspects of the demonstration, call the students' attention to the critical components of the performance, and provide emphasis where needed will be more productive in the dual role of analyzer and presentor, than solely as a demonstrator. Second, the use of a skilled student quite possibly will encourage students via the presentation of a peer model. Such a peer model can convince some students that success in this skill is well within their reach.

3. The demonstration should be conducted in the context of the activity. When demonstrating the forehand volley, for example, the model should be stationed at the net, at the exact point when and where a forehand volley might indeed be executed. This context-driven demonstration assists the learner in comprehending the purpose and the reason why the skill is performed in such a manner.

4. Provide several demonstrations at various angles to maximize the information provided for the students. Have the students move about the model (or reposition the demonstrator for each of the several successive demonstrations) when possible, to view the demonstration from the right, left, front, and rear.

5. Before dispersal and immediately following the demonstration, check the students' understanding. Ask the students questions about the demonstration and the most important elements of the performance just observed.[15] The use of a worksheet to list or diagram the critical components of the performance can be employed to reinforce students' understanding.

6. An expanding body of literature on student learning styles verifies that not all students learn best through the auditory modality, and that when possible, instructors should employ several modalities (auditory, visual, tactile, and kinesthetic) when presenting information. A wide range of learning styles exists in each class. By utilizing several modalities, teachers are more likely to succeed in conveying information to a greater percentage of students. Therefore demonstrations that provide visual information are most effective when accompanied by pertinent auditory information and provisions for tactile and kinesthetic involvement (doing or touching) as soon as possible after the presentation.

The most common problems with ineffective demonstrations appear to be the failure to provide sufficient directions and explanations, the assumption of complete comprehension by students because questions are not raised by students, and the introduction of more difficult material before student mastery of material presented earlier.[16] With a modicum of careful planning and reflection, physical education teachers can avoid these pitfalls. Demonstrators are advised to rehearse the demonstration before class to increase the effectiveness and potency of the scheduled demonstrations.

Physical education teachers need not be public speakers, but with a modicum of attention to their delivery and continued monitoring of their skills, they can ensure stimulating presentations and maximize learning. Reflective teaching behavior and thoughtful preparation go a long way to enhancing teacher presentations and demonstrations. The use of video-recording or audio-recording equipment can support efforts at self-study of these essential instructional endeavors.

Increasing Student Contributions

What are the characteristics of positive appropriate communications of the type that promote learning and self-esteem in students? Effective communication processes in physical education should make students feel good about themselves; enhance self-image; and develop trust in the teacher, the situation, and the group.

Various authorities support the fact that in most learning settings, teachers talk too much. As far back as 1965, Flanders'[17] findings led to his formulation of a "two-thirds rule": "Two thirds of the time in an ordinary classroom someone is talking; two thirds of that time it is the teacher talking; two thirds of that time the teacher is using direct influence."

Goodlad's[6] work nearly 20 years later supported Flanders' findings. In 1984 Goodlad reported, " . . . on the average about 75% of class time was spent on instruction and nearly 70% of this was 'talk'—usually teachers to students. Teachers out-talked the entire class of students by a ratio of about three to one."

In physical education, findings from research reflect similar trends. Templin[18] reported that "the typical pattern in the classroom is that the teacher is the dominant figure in determining the activities and tone of the classs, and is virtually autonomous with respect to classroom decisions." Siedentop, Mand, and Taggart[19] summarized several Academic Learning Time (ALT) studies in physical education and found that students spent 15% to 20% of class time receiving information.

Others have reported similar findings. Lombardo and Cheffers[20] reported a teacher-talk to student-talk ratio somewhat less than that predicted by Flanders' two-thirds rule, but the interaction patterns revealed in their study were indicative of teacher dominance in the gym. Gusthart[21] reported that "informing" (that is, providing information about the task) was the most common substantive verbal behavior observed.

Ritson, Smith, and Twa[22] found that the teacher talking was the most common interaction style in his study of teaching in physical education. Sizer[3] succinctly noted, "a lot of us are teachers because we like to tell the truth, not because we want to help kids find the truth on their own."

In light of this it should be clear that a common communication problem is that of teacher domination of the learning process. A major issue related to communication in secondary school physical education, then, is to develop methods of decreasing or limiting teacher talk while concurrently maximizing student exchanges. A secondary, related problem is that of raising the level or type of student thinking in the learning interactions from rote memorization and comprehension to higher levels of cognitive functioning, such as analysis, application, and evaluation (see Chapter 6).

The crux of the problem is one of creating an environment in which students will feel comfortable and will seek opportunities to share their thoughts. To do this Charles[23] maintains that teachers should concern themselves with developing learning climates imbued with psychological support, that is, teachers need to perform " . . . acts that show students they may speak their minds without fear of punishment, sarcasm, or being put down."

In other words for teachers to facilitate student participation in the learning activities, they must create a setting that is nonthreatening, open, facilitative, and concurrently *not* dominated by teacher talk, teacher concerns, and teacher thoughts.

If developing classrooms and gymnasia typified by psychological support are desirable, then the task becomes one of how to generate and maintain such climates. Several specific approaches are available to teachers that will broaden learning environments, induce student talk, possibly raise the cognitive level of the student thinking, and thereby facilitate learning via more active student contributions and enhanced student-teacher interaction.

The process of creating a learning session that is characterized by facilitative communication and psychological support starts when the teacher (1) generates a high degree of student involvement, (2) regularly responds with acceptance of student behaviors, and (3) employs a high frequency of teacher questions and a minimum of selective use of rejection. Such behaviors will result in a gymnasium full of students ready to share ideas, volunteer information, and think at levels well beyond rote memorization and comprehension.

By involving students in lessons and learning activities, several outcomes can be effected: (1) students will come to view the program as their own if encouraged to participate in its design, pace, and direction; (2) the meaningfulness and relevancy of the program of learning activities will more readily remain current to the needs of the students; and (3) learning will be enhanced because students will be able to apply materials and information immediately. High involvement can ensure immediate application, and quite possibly immediate feedback too of strategies that maximize learning. When students are asked to apply information and material presented, they are more likely to perceive the relevancy of subject matter and thereby would be more receptive to it.

Teacher acceptance of student behaviors when employed in conjunction with a high frequency of questions intended to elicit higher levels of cognitive functioning can activate the learning setting. Once students realize that teachers are willing and prepared to share their authority via the presentation of thought-provoking questions and will also carefully listen to, consider, and, more important, respect their contributions, communication and student-teacher (and if desired, student-student) interaction will be maximized. Indeed, often teachers who employ such techniques find it difficult to curtail or redirect the students' enthusiasm for contributing in class.

THE USE OF QUESTIONS

Of particular importance is the use of questions. Several types of questions are available to teachers. These questions can be broadly categorized as divergent and convergent. The choice of the type of question to be employed depends greatly on the context of the learning setting, including the level and ability of the student, the objectives of the lesson, and the specific material to be addressed. Each type of question possesses limitations that will structure the students' responses.

Teachers who employ a high frequency of thought-provoking (rather than narrow and convergent) questions convey several subtle, yet potent messages to students. Examples of these implicit messages are:

1. Students' thoughts are valuable.
2. Students have much to contribute to the learning encounter.
3. Students should be active, rather than passive, participants in learning.
4. The teacher is willing to share the authority with students.

The following teacher-posed convergent questions, for example, require student responses that require minimal cognitive involvement:

1. Susan, how many players are needed to play lacrosse?
2. Who can define equilibrium for the class?
3. Who remembers the inventor of volleyball?
4. John, what are the three most common serves employed in volleyball?

Contrast the preceding with the following questions, which attempt to elicit higher cognitive responses from students:

1. Who can explain when the instep kick should be employed, rather than the side of the foot pass, in soccer?
2. Jennifer, when is a zone defense appropriate in basketball?
3. What are the differences between an anaerobic and aerobic exercise bout?
4. What type of exercise do you enjoy the most? Why?

The reader should recognize that both sets of questions convey different messages and expectations to students. Both types of questions can facilitate student learning, spur student interest, and encourage other positive outcomes. Each type of question, however, is unique and requires a singular type of response from students. Overdependence on any one type of question quite possibly can lead to unintended or unplanned results. Like all other concerns of teachers, the selection of the type of questions employed should be part of the teacher's preparation and prelesson reflection.

To make the point further, let us examine the earlier interaction. The convergent questions in the first grouping, while inviting students' verbal and cognitive contributions, stop far short of requiring more complex and interpretive cognitions. They also seek factual knowledge from students, which normally elicits responses based on recall and memory. Teacher responses to student replies to convergent questions often tend to be evaluative in nature (right, wrong, yes, no, or correct), putting teachers in a position of being the arbiter of student knowledge as well as the reinforcer. There is a great risk of creating teacher-dependent learners with such practice.

The second set of divergent teacher questions asks students to put forth interpretive, evaluative, analytical responses, requiring a measure of application or synthesis of subject matter. Such questions require students to in-

Promote student-to-student communication in class by encouraging students to work cooperatively together.
Courtesy of Emily Leonardo, Camp Hill High School, Camp Hill, PA.

vest more in their responses and often to go beyond the content as presented. Student responses to divergent questions presented by the teacher normally require teachers to do much more than provide a perfunctory, one- or two-word reply. Rather, teachers are more likely to accept, clarify, and use the students' thoughts, all behaviors that not only convey respect to students and their ideas, but also convey yet another message to students—that the teacher wishes to share the power in the classroom.

Well-composed and timely questions can increase the quality of student talk by encouraging students to go far beyond one-word contributions. Teachers can help students explore, explain, justify, and generalize. In short, teacher questions can lead students to use higher cognitive functions (for example, application or evaluation). Charles[23] offers suggestions for teachers to increase the effectiveness of questions in the classroom:

1. Avoid changing or modifying the question in mid-question.
2. Do not repeat the question except to increase clarity. Often impatient teachers, uncomfortable with silence in the class, continue to repeat the question because of their inability to wait for a response.
3. Teachers should not answer their own questions. Instead, they should lengthen pauses, increase waiting time, or even sip a cup of water to show patience with the students' attempts to respond. Teachers should wait until they are certain students have had a fair opportunity to respond before moving on.

4. Teachers should provide hints, cues, or alternative questions if students have difficulty. Teachers should keep in mind that students need encouragement and support in dealing with the risks involved with responding in public, especially if such response exposes the students' higher level cognitive abilities.
5. Accept responses nonverbally. Teachers should provide nonverbal indications, such as gestures or postures, that convey to students nonverbal acceptance. Such behavior will be further reinforced if used simultaneously with congruent verbal messages.

Another set of teacher behaviors that will increase student contributions relates to the skills of active listening. This strategy is a method of helping students express themselves, without judging their responses. Teachers who are active listeners convey to students that they comprehend the students' meaning.

Active listening occurs when someone engages in a dialogue with another person in response to what the person is saying and feeling.[24] The following active listening guidelines can assist the teacher who wishes to encourage student contributions in physical education.

1. Remain silent while the speaker is making a point or expressing feelings.
2. Always take the feelings of others seriously. The concern is not whether the situation is serious but rather that the feelings expressed by students are real and therefore perceived by the teacher as serious.
3. Listen attentively. Gather information by asking questions if necessary to ensure obtaining the facts before

responding. Before responding, teachers should be sure that they know what was said. Paraphrasing is a dependable technique to employ in this situation.

4. At times, it is more appropriate to deal with feelings rather than facts. Students who are upset are not receptive to giving answers to questions. At that moment, the student's need is less on a response to the question and more directed to communicating feelings. The physical education teacher would do well in this case to respond to the feelings. Accept the student's emotions. Do not deny students their right to their own feelings. Be supportive.

5. Empathetic teacher behavior will consistently support student efforts at responding and contributing in class. Effective teachers remember how it felt to be a student.

These active listening strategies can assist teachers in the creation of an environment in which students will welcome opportunities to talk, to contribute in several ways, and generally to decrease the teacher's domination of the physical education class. Communication is a two-way process. To enhance learning in physical education, teachers must ensure and support students' participation at several levels.

PARENT-TEACHER CONFERENCES

Another area of communication skills secondary teachers must attend to relates to parent-teacher interactions. It is often useful and necessary to meet periodically with parents. At times these meetings are called simply to gather information; other meetings may be required to respond better to special situations that arise during the school year (for example, absenteeism, motivation problems, or inappropriate behavior).

A successful, well-planned conference can assist parents to take actions that will positively affect their children's education. The goal of such parent-teacher meetings is to bring together information about the student from both parties into a knowledge base that can be utilized to design more appropriate resolutions.

Conferences between teacher and parents permit maximum flexibility because most people communicate better in person than in writing. Face-to-face interaction also decreases the possibilities of confusion and misinterpretation because questions can be raised and issues clarified.[25]

Preparation by physical education teachers is required to enhance the success of such meetings. Before the parent-teacher conference, the teacher should be ready to share concerns and problems without assigning blame. A few minutes of thoughtful reflection before the meeting can assist teachers in their efforts to maintain their objectivity and to ensure a fair, unemotional analysis of the important aspects to be considered.

Preparation also will assist the physical education teacher to remain focused on the specific purpose of the meeting. Try to keep thoughts on the immediate reasons for meeting and do not recreate history or open up old wounds.

Finally, a list of questions to ask parents should be included among preparations for the conference. The teachers should list questions that will provide them with information they need to serve the student better, for example, "What does the student do outside of class in leisure time? Does the student work after school? Where? Type of work? How many hours per week? Does the student express feelings about education? School? Physical education?" These kinds of questions can elicit information from parents not easily learned by teachers in school.

To enhance the effectiveness of conferences, Rutherford and Edgar[25] suggest that teachers do the following:

1. Treat parents with respect. Parents have the ultimate responsibility for the well-being of the adolescent and for implementing planned, out-of-school interventions. Success of the conference depends on the parents' willingness to cooperate and follow through on suggestions.

2. Make parents comfortable. In addition to the previous recommendations, avoid using educational jargon. Provide easily understood information. Use prepared, written materials if appropriate. Parents want to know exactly where they and their children stand. Strive to convey to parents that their child's education is truly a cooperative venture between the parents and the school via the physical education teacher's efforts and interactions with their students.

3. Put forth realistic recommendations. A realistic recommendation is one that can be carried out in the home by parents and can be reinforced in school. For example, for a student who has consistently failed to come to class with a change of clothes, a realistic suggestion to parents might be to post the student's physical education schedule at home. Next, parents could assist the student the night before a class by gathering appropriate clothing and footwear and placing them in a spot that the student will not overlook in the morning before leaving for school.

At the time of the conference itself, teachers should encourage the parents to consider questions such as, "What can parents do at home to help? How is our child progressing? How does our child relate to others in class? What are the child's specific strengths and weaknesses?"

Keep in mind that information in this meeting must flow in two directions. Parents must have their concerns addressed. They will be interested in the student's general behavior in school and in the physical education class specifically. An indicator of a productive parent-teacher conference is that both sides depart having gained significant insights into the student that can help both parties to assist the student's growth.

Before the close of the conference, summarize the main points achieved, including any future steps to be implemented. Misunderstandings can be avoided in this way.

If specific interventions are planned, follow-up by the parents and teachers is vital. If Johnny is to be more closely monitored regarding his preparation and dressing for physical education, and a plan has been devised to address this concern, parents and teachers must make plans to remain in communication. Before departure, establish a future date by which communication should take place.

Once the conference has ended, teachers should reflect on and evaluate the discussion that entailed. What did the teacher learn that will facilitate efforts with the student? Was the meeting congenial? Frank? Open? Productive? Did practical, specific suggestions result from the conference that will resolve the problem and assist the student? Teachers should make note of the answers to these and similar questions.

It would be useful to communicate to parents in writing as a follow-up to the conference. In this memo teachers can outline the specific, agreed-on course of action and ask for specific feedback from the parents about the plan. Seek from the parents responses to such inquiries as, Is the plan working? How frequently does the plan work? Should the actions be continued? Modified? Cancelled? Is another conference needed? Certainly, open-ended comments should also be encouraged.

Ultimately, teachers and parents meet to help students. Parent-teacher conferences must remain centered on the abilities and needs of students. Suggestions delineated earlier can enhance the success of such endeavors.

MOTIVATION

Motivation, as defined in Chapter 8, refers to factors and processes that cause individuals to behave and act (or fail to act) in a certain manner or situation. Motives (the underlying reasons for behavior) can be derived and influenced by internal and external factors, and therefore physical education teachers must attend to these factors as potential sources of student motivation.

Before examining motivational strategies and approaches to increase students' desire to participate in and value physical activity, it is important to address the specific types of motives and motivators that should be emphasized when interacting with secondary school students. In general, teachers should strive to develop intrinsic motivation for participation in physical activity. Intrinsic motivators are factors that arise from within the individual that prompt self-initiated and directed behavior, practice, review, and repetition of a particular activity. For example, the adolescent who willingly rises at 6:00

Ongoing communication with parents is emphasized in some schools.

Courtesy of Ben Lombardo, Rhode Island College, Providence, RI.

AM and jogs three miles, for reasons known only to himself and without coercion from others, manifests an internalized motive for such exercise.

The use and development of intrinsic motivation bring about the more desirable type of learning, learning that is not easily disturbed. This type of motivation produces learning that in and of itself is its own greatest reward.

The long-term objective of a secondary physical education program should be the development of independent individuals who value physical activity and incorporate it into their lifestyles and daily regimens. Physical education teachers can encourage and support such behavior by providing accurate, current information about the contributions of physical education and its importance including healthy practices in their daily activities and providing instruction at conceptual levels that nurture students' informed and confident decision making. This latter point is critical because the goal must be to develop students' abilities to make knowledgeable, informed decisions about their activity and to foster self-reliance and independence.

How does the instructor foster intrinsic motivation to promote learning? Many of the strategies reviewed in the next section will address this question. In general, however, educators believe that students who share in the planning of their programs of study are more likely to have a greater interest in their learning. The goals and objectives that students set for themselves are usually those they will sincerely strive to attain. Teachers who establish goals and objectives that take into account the needs and interests of students and who encourage students to share in specific curricular planning can expect more effective learning. Halliwell[26] points out that when people feel their actions are self-determined and gain a sense of personal competence, the higher their level of intrinsic motivation will become. To do otherwise would be to contribute to the development of dependent students, who must rely on others to lead them and make decisions for them. The misuse or overreliance on extrinsic motivators can prevent the development of self-reliant, responsible, and independent movers. Extrinsic motivation is defined as factors external to the individual that influence behavior, and it can result in learners who act only in the presence of another who can provide the external stimulation or inspiration to continue engagement in the activity. For example, the individual who will pay $20 to attend a tennis lesson, but who would not otherwise play tennis, has not yet developed an internalized interest toward participation in tennis. This person is dependent on external conditions and motivators when it comes to tennis.

It is suggested here that physical education teachers make selective use of extrinsic motivational techniques. Overemphasis on extrinsic approaches will encourage a dependent relationship with the subject matter and quite possibly with the instructor. In the future of the youngster, such a dependent relationship could easily be translated to behavior, that is, engagement in physical activity occurs only when led, coached, or instructed formally by others. In other words while the extrinsic motivator might engage the students at the moment or until a grade is assigned, continued use of such motivational strategies often diminishes future self-direction and the internalization of the values of physical education.

However, teachers realize that extrinsic motivational factors are not without value. Grades, trophies, and point systems fall into the category of extrinsic motivators. Certain students will work hard to earn a grade of "A" or a team jacket. Learning often does occur under conditions of extrinsic motivation. Success in using intrinsic or extrinsic motivational techniques is probably dependent on assessment of the readiness or learning state of the student, and then the most appropriate technique is selected. Who would argue with the use of an extrinsic technique to generate interest or catch the students' attention so that at least some minimal, initial effort will be directed toward a unit of study or particular skill? Quite possibly from such an initial exposure, teachers should minimize employment of external motivators and attempt to foster and support development of intrinsic bonds to the activity.

The scope of the next section will be to examine possible causes of student motivational problems and then to discuss strategies and approaches to enhance student motivation for participation in the program and the strengthening of approach tendencies to physical activity. Approach tendencies can be defined as "behaviors of students that indicate that they like and value the subject."[27] These are essential, albeit indirect, influences on student learning in physical education. The direct effects of motivation on learning have been addressed more fully in Chapter 8.

STUDENT APATHY IN THE GYM

Authorities have regularly described secondary physical education programs as plagued with apparently severe student (and sometimes teacher) motivational problems. Indeed, the lack of enthusiasm for secondary physical education programs is seemingly endemic.[28-34] While the magnitude of such behaviors varies dependent on specific locale and the particulars of the educational context, the causes manifest amazing similarity. A survey of this situation derived from selected analyses includes the following reasons:

1. High-school programs that have narrowly focused sports-oriented curricula with a concurrent overemphasis on athletic competition. Student development and growth in the cognitive and affective domains are addressed only in a perfunctory manner.

2. The failure or inability of professionals to provide a clear accounting about "what it is that is distinct about what physical education has to offer"[34] to students, parents, administrators, colleagues, and the community. Similarly, Siedentop[29] suggests that a major weakness of secondary physical education is the "almost total lack of expectations for significant outcome." There are few professionals and students who are aware of and can clearly articulate appropriate outcomes for secondary school physical education. In general, in most programs students are expected to attend class and to be dressed to move, beyond which few precisely stated goals are made public or addressed via curricular activities.

3. Recent analyses of high-school physical education have revealed that the environment is "perceived as sterile (stressing conformity) and unsafe (characterized by embarrassment and humiliation)."[32,33] In such situations is it surprising that students protect their integrity by complying minimally to directives, resisting involvement, attempting to manipulate others (including the teacher), exuding false enthusiasm, becoming rebellious, leaving, or giving up?[33]

4. Secondary programs deny most students the feeling of accomplishment normally accompanying the mastery

of something important[34] and as a result, effect "minuscule achievements by students in the skills being taught."[28]

5. In addition to overcrowded classes regularly observed in physical education, many physical education teachers are teaching one or more activities in which they are not totally competent. Under such circumstances, teachers often are self-conscious about their instructional behaviors, limited in their efforts to generate genuine enthusiasm for the subject matter, and often are stressed by anxiety, which regularly accompanies such situations.

6. Several recent reports indicate that teachers are presenting inappropriate, if not negative, role models in many instances. Studies that indicate that physical education teachers are physically unfit,[35,36] overweight or have high levels of fat tissue,[37,38] and have poor cardiorespiratory fitness,[36] apparently suggest that simply by their appearance, such teachers can greatly inhibit the students' interest and involvement in physical activity.

Faced with seemingly insurmountable problems, what are teachers to do? Certainly professionals who believe in the merits of physical activity and the contributions the secondary program can make to student development will confront such issues in an effort to maintain program integrity and credibility. A number of strategies are available to teachers, some more feasible than others. Such feasibility will depend on several factors such as teacher commitment, resource allocation, professional and collegial support, and other personal and systemwide variables.

STRATEGIES TO ENHANCE STUDENT MOTIVATION

This section will focus on behaviors and curricular techniques physical education teachers can employ to increase student motivation, maintain interest, and maximize student persistence and approach tendencies toward physical activity and the secondary program. A major assumption supporting such suggestions is that teachers must strengthen intrinsic motivation and the student's approach tendencies (behaviors that indicate that students enjoy and value physical education).

1. Curriculum models should be employed that maximize and capitalize on student responsibility for program choices, design, and development. Programs like Hellison's responsibility model, elective or selective programs, will increase the student centeredness of the program and enhance student ownership.[39] Feelings of responsibility, pride, and a sense of making the program succeed (by participating, performing, and learning) usually emerge from such ownership. Chapter 4 includes a more elaborate discussion of Hellison's responsibility model.

2. Professionals must take steps to clarify the distinctiveness of physical education, especially when contrasted with athletics. Students are often unable to distinguish between the instructional and the interscholastic programs. This confusion often is at the foundation of the apathy observed in students who believe that physical competence and sports skills are inseparable. Teachers must work diligently to dispel this common misconception, one that accounts for many "invisible" participants

Teachers need to be good listeners.
Courtesy of Patricia Quinn, Notre Dame High School, Elmira, NY.

in physical education,[39] drop-outs, and counterproductive or maladaptive behavior in physical education.

Many students often underestimate their chances for achieving desirable levels of physical fitness because they are uncoordinated and they consider themselves athletically inept. Relatively simple teacher strategies, like explaining the differences between fitness-related test items and the use of appropriate assessment instruments, would do much to dispel these erroneous beliefs. More complex responses would commit to individualized curricular activities, such as learning contracts or individually prescribed activity units, to promote physical fitness and motor skill enhancement for the purpose of motivating students to value physical activity.

3. Teachers should consider structuring the curriculum to provide longer, but fewer, units of instruction. This strategy will provide reasonable time for students to develop mastery of selected skills and concepts, while simultaneously eliminating superficial, "shotgun" curricular efforts. Such curriculum modifications will enhance student motivation by encouraging in-depth, intense study of concepts and skills or by providing more time for repetitive and supervised practice. It will also increase the professional's motivation by enabling teachers to observe more readily the effects of their lessons, provide more time to work with individual students, and in general, enhance the quality and quantity of student-student and teacher-student interactions. For example, the use of initiative activities, cooperative games, and adventure programs would enhance interaction between all groups.

4. Teachers should strive to reduce the public nature of student learning and performance whenever possible. Motor learning, as presently conducted, is overwhelmingly a public event—highly visible and open to social evaluation and public scrutiny. Even for the highly skilled student, performing for an audience, whether it be teachers, friends, or peers, can be an intimidating and anxiety-inducing experience. For students who possess disabilities, poor coordination, or are overweight, such public displays can be devastating and probably account for Griffin's observation of "invisible" participants and "system-beaters" (dropouts).[39] Students with low self-esteem who are highly self-conscious, timid, or have a poorly developed self-concept will attempt to avoid activities, drills, games, and other activities that force them into the spotlight.

Where and when possible, teachers should try to individualize and privatize the instructional process. A second more feasible choice might be to pair students with peers with whom they feel comfortable. A simple practice would be to ask students with whom they would like to work.

Physical education teachers would do much to address this problem by teaching students how to be supportive when part of an audience. Teachers should plan to discuss and develop sensitivity to their own capabilities and the abilities of others. The inclusion of acceptance of others and self in the curriculum concepts to be mastered by students would also address this issue. Teacher behaviors in the gymnasium that reflect such acceptance of individual capabilities and the abilities of others will provide active models for students to emulate.

5. Evaluation is a critical link connecting behavior, learning, discipline, and motivation. It is known that students who receive poor evaluations often become poor learners, who, in turn, often prefer to drop out—physically or mentally, or both.

The suggestion is to teach and evaluate for success. Teachers must make it genuinely possible for students to receive a grade of "A". This means, in all practicality, that teachers have to provide instruction at several levels to meet needs of students who progress through the program at their own rate based on their individual capacities. Failure to provide instruction for students at their academic level can result in student discouragement, motivation problems, and, quite possibly, rebellion against instructional programs and teachers that refuse to accept them as they are. If at all possible, physical education teachers would do well to incorporate mastery of learning concepts into curricular practices and policies.

Teaching for success also means employing appropriate instructional techniques such as proper sequencing, logical progressions, and carefully structured practice schedules that nurture skill development for everyone. Teachers must be certain to provide adequate instruction in each unit. Opportunities for skill instruction, feedback, and supervision should be maximized, especially for students who do not possess basic skills to enjoy success (and learn) in games. If possible, provisions should be made for extra in- or out-of-class practice (before class, before school, or after school).

Ability groups might be considered for drills, practice, and gameplay. Although it may be time-consuming, matching students by ability and possibly by interest level or styles of participation in certain cases would not only bolster motivation by increasing opportunities for success, but this may be the most appropriate instructional approach. In this way, frustrating beginning students and boring advanced students can be avoided.[34]

Griffin[39] offers a practical suggestion that would maximize opportunities for teaching for success. She suggests that to encourage all students, regardless of interest and ability, teachers should be certain to separate competitive experiences from skill development sessions. She claims, "When all skill drills are competitive the focus is on winning, not learning, and beginners feel responsible for team losses rather than trying to improve skills."

Such a practice will reassert the student as central focus of the curriculum, downplay competition, and clearly demonstrate that learning is more important than winning.

6. Physical education must present positive and attractive role models for students. Role modeling of desired behaviors by physical education teachers has a stronger effect than mere verbal instructions or exhortations. What teachers are and how they act is much more potent than their acclamations. Such modeling can powerfully influence student motivation and interest in physical education.

Several recent reports indicate that often the models presented to students are inappropriate, if not negative. Certainly one could understand students' lack of interest in physical education if teachers' enthusiasm for movement and fitness, as reflected in their appearance, is not readily observed, while simultaneously the results of an inactive or unhealthy lifestyle are regularly presented and quite apparent.

To encourage students, physical education teachers must strive to be models of healthy, conditioned, and active adults. Instructors need to manifest a love for activity and an obvious enthusiasm for motion.

7. Teacher enthusiasm for subject matter is another avenue for the stimulation of students. It is not essential that teachers entertain students, but teachers need to exude positive energy. Teachers seemingly tired or bored with the subject matter usually do little more than go through the motions of presenting information, employ few gestures, and rarely smile. Student boredom and the failure of teachers to exhibit excitement are related. Boredom, like excitement, is contagious.[36] Teachers must demonstrate their interest and excitement for students to observe on a regular basis.

8. Curwin and Mendler[24] provide insight into yet another approach to improve student motivation in physical education:

Students today have been trained by television to be passive learners. They demand variety, a fast pace, a rock soundtrack, a comedian for a teacher, and virtually total control of the image before them. However, stimulating lessons requiring high-level thinking, working cooperatively, and creating products that evoke pride—and that encourage personal discovery—fill a great void created by television. Teachers can use this syndrome to great advantage by building lessons on what students need but are unable to get from television.

The implications of this approach are clear: secondary school physical education teachers must include units of study that enable students to use the higher levels of cognitive functioning (application, synthesis, and evaluation), within the context of the student's study of human movement. Such lessons would require students to be active, vibrant learners, forced to think at levels not encouraged elsewhere. Teachers can gain a fine view of such an approach, including numerous explicit examples of such conceptual methods by perusing *The Basic Stuff Series II*, Levels 9-12.

Making Physical Education Inviting

Building on Purkey's[41] model of invitational education, Chandler[40] provides physical education teachers with additional motivational strategies. Invitations described as messages sent to students are intended to inform students that they are valuable, able, and responsible. Invitational education maintains that each individual possesses relatively untapped potential for intellectual and psychological development, and that this potential may best be realized in a nurturing environment.[41] The invitational approach, as analyzed by Chandler, provides several strategies that can assist secondary physical education teachers in their attempts to motivate students.

1. Arrange a pleasant atmosphere. Bright displays, neat and colorful bulletin boards, and relevant posters can brighten the surroundings.

2. Use music to add spice to class. Let students bring their favorite music to class and employ it to accompany warm-up exercises or to serve as background when appropriate.

3. Take advantage of opportunities to display the physical skills and talents of students at school assemblies, PTA programs, and community club meetings. Show off student skills in activities such as gymnastics, tumbling, dance, and fitness. Teachers should stress group accomplishments and group recognition in these activities.

4. Secure and employ special video or film media to inspire students (for example, NCAA Basketball Finals or World Cup Soccer Tourney).

5. Learn students' names. As the teacher learns names, ask the students what they like to be called.

6. Treat students with the respect and dignity that all individuals deserve, regardless of status.

7. Spread positive rumors. Publicize positive efforts or accomplishments without using names. The purpose of positive rumors is to tell students how good they are and that their efforts and their accomplishments are noticed and appreciated.

8. Display "with-it-ness." Make an effort to better understand the world of the student. Stay abreast of popular heroes, fashions, recent films, actors, and other interests of students. Relate the academic program to the world of the students at every opportunity.

9. Advertise the successes of students. Use the school newspaper, public address system, or bulletin boards to announce special activities, awards, and recognition taking place in physical education.

10. Invite others to become involved in physical education. Principals, supervisors, colleagues, and parents might enjoy being invited to the physical education class for special activities and events. This technique, while not

BOX 10-1

INVENTORY OF PHYSICAL EDUCATION INVITATIONS

Students respond yes, no, or cannot say to each item

1. Are you treated courteously by your physical education teacher?
2. Does the physical education teacher know you by name?
3. Does your physical education teacher help students in class get to know one another?
4. Does your teacher try to recognize special events like birthdays, special achievements, and performances?
5. Does your teacher personally invite you to particpate in activities in class?
6. Are the gym and physical education teacher's office attractive?
7. Do you feel welcome when you come into your class?
8. Is it easy to visit your physical education teacher when you need to?
9. Does your teacher follow through on promises?
10. When you have problems, does your physical education teacher express concern and care?
11. Is your teacher courteous to everyone in class?
12. Is your teacher on time for classes and appointments?
13. Does your teacher seem to really listen to you?
14. Are you invited to give suggestions to your teacher about the physical education program?
15. Do you feel free to communicate your concerns to your physical education teacher?
16. Do your feel free to make an appointment with your teacher?
17. Does your physical education teacher give students a voice in the way things go in class?
18. Is your teacher fair in the enforcement of rules and policies?
19. Is the physical education office usually open?
20. Do the activities provided in physical education class help you in any way in your personal development?
21. Does the weekly newspaper carry information about your physical education program?
22. Does your physical education teacher try to make new students feel at home?
23. Are the bulletin boards and displays in the gym up to date?
24. Does your physical education teacher make positive remarks about students?
25. Does your physical education teacher care about you?

Adapted from Chandler GL: Invitational physical education: strategies in the junior high school, *JOPERD* 59(4):68-72, 1988.

new, works in at least two ways: it provides an interested audience to inspire and stimulate students in physical education, and it enables the physical education faculty to show off the program to the various publics whose support is so dearly needed.

Teachers can determine how inviting their programs and instructional behaviors are by utilizing the Inventory of Physical Education Invitations (Box 10-1). Negative responses from students should be analyzed and addressed. The use of this instrument as a self-evaluation technique can lead to increased self-awareness and quite possibly changes in program policies and student motivation.

Until this point, communication and motivation have been examined and discussed. Implicit in this analysis is the notion that communication, motivation, and discipline are strongly interrelated and interdependent. In the last part of this chapter, then, the discussion proceeds by building on the communication strategies and motivation techniques already reviewed and then focuses directly on discipline and related topics.

DISCIPLINE

Few would argue that maintenance of good discipline is a much needed precondition to the establishment of a physical education climate conducive to learning. Indeed, many teaching professionals believe that effective discipline within the context of effective classroom management is essential to the educational process. Ultimately, the responsibility for discipline within the learning environment rests with the individual physical education teacher, given the realities of the modern high school and the concomitant expectations of minimal assistance from external sources.

Previously, strategies and approaches to communication and motivation have been examined. Effective communication and interaction with students directly influence teacher and student motivation, and certainly motivation for school learning impinges directly on discipline in physical education classes. At this point, methods for maintaining learning environments that maximize opportunities for student learning and limit behavioral disruptions will be addressed.

Discipline in Schools

According to recent surveys of the public's attitudes toward schools, student disruptions and general school discipline are considered one of the pressing problems confronting U.S. educational professionals by parents, students, teachers, and administrators.[42,43] Moreover, the general public has cited the "lack of discipline" first or second in all 20 Gallup polls. Discipline ranked fourth among teachers.[44] Recent analyses of adolescents' views about school stress revealed that students also are concerned about student behavior, disruptions in schools, interrupted learning, and teachers' ability to maintain control of unruly students.[45,46] Certainly such distractions must be counterproductive to student learning and development.

Concern about discipline and maladaptive behavior by students is on the increase. Why? Quite possibly clues can be located in the current effectiveness of social institutions, such as religion or the family, which over the past 25 years have been weakened and have had their authority and ability to affect individuals and groups reduced, thereby also rendering ineffective their capacity to influence the development of adolescents. To compound this situation further, more responsibility has been delegated to the purview of the secondary school, many times by state mandate. Teachers are being asked to fit even more into the curriculum and simultaneously to raise academic standards. Not only have the responsibilities been increased and broadened greatly, but the complexity of these additional responsibilities has been magnified. Heretofore, subjects historically off limits in educational institutions have been transferred to the supervision of educators. Drug education, sex education, family living, the provision of day-care centers, emotional-social-psychological support, and character development are examples of recently added (or reemphasized) areas transferred to schools, apparently ceded to educators in most cases because of the inability of other professional groups and institutions to deal effectively with such concerns.

Most educators are convinced that teaching today is more difficult than ever before. Why? Hellison's[47] profound analysis provides some direction:

Kids face more choices today than ever before—from television, the knowledge "explosion," and exposure to different value systems in an increasingly pluralistic society. They are getting less guidance from home . . . and from neighborhoods that once helped to raise children but are now more mobile and anonymous . . . there is a concern about the quality of life, an effort to reach higher levels of consciousness, a search for self that is at times obsessive, and a leisure lifestyle identity with overtones of narcissism and new consumerism.

Dillon[48] continues in the same vein:

Parents more and more frequently admit that they cannot control their children. Many even abandon them. Many students act as free agents. They do not live at home and are responsible to no one. They have few personal restraints.

More children are coming from homes where there is violence, drug or alcohol abuse, divorce, separation, or a single parent. Increasingly children are being raised by children. Many of them, understandably, are so anxious and insecure that they are unable to concentrate. The

pressure to fit more into the school day, while simultaneously attempting to improve academic standards, creates great stress on students and faculty. If students do poorly, teachers and students feel like failures. The goal of teachers should be to foster self-discipline and autonomy that are essential to a productive, successful learning environment. Teachers and students alike need educational climates that provide uninterrupted, committed study, positive psychosocial interactions, and learning.

WHAT IS DISCIPLINE?

Volumes have been written about discipline, and a multitude of definitions abound in the literature. However, analysis reveals several commonalities, specifically the following elements: (1) students maintaining focus on and engaging in the learning activity, (2) responsible student behavior, and (3) students exhibiting positive relations with others. Behavior that is lacking in one or more of these elements would define a discipline problem or inappropriate behavior. For the purpose of this discussion, discipline is a term used to describe student behavior that is focused on intended learning activities, couched in responsible actions, and manifesting positive interactions with others in the instructional setting. It should be obvious to the reader that teachers intend to develop behavioral patterns in students who will maximize the use of time and effectiveness so that all participants benefit from instruction.

DISCIPLINE PROBLEMS

Physical education teachers face several problems that often contribute to frustrations of students and that evolve from the unique nature of the physical education program itself. In most other subjects, the learning environment is an ordinary classroom. In physical education problems often are magnified because of the excitement aroused by competition and the use of apparatus or large classes. Such conditions require special handling well beyond normal circumstances because of the potential for disruptions. Another source of potential problems relates to students who try to avoid participation in class activities by employing various deceptions. Feigned illnesses or injuries, loss of workout clothing, reluctance to work up a sweat, and unwillingness to dress out for class are among the common strategies employed by students to avoid interacting in the physical education setting. These student behaviors, if not responded to effectively by teachers, can lead to a variety of student responses, ranging from extreme passivity to active involvement or violent outbursts. Teachers must be prepared to react to such situations. Better yet, teachers need to be proactive in preparation to contain and respond to disruptions.

Yet another situation idiosyncratic to physical education relates to the public nature of motor performance.

In physical education, poorly skilled, physically weak, and uncoordinated students often receive minimal validation. On the contrary, Curwin and Mendler[24] identify a potent issue basic to cooperation in physical education:

> There is no greater fear for a growing youngster than to look or feel foolish in front of his peers. Unfortunately, physical education classes show a student's clumsiness and physical vulnerabilities more overtly than English or Math.

Attempts at creating and employing positive classroom management techniques and a proactive disciplinary plan must take into account this complex situation that is unique to physical education.

Other factors that have the potential to fuel the disciplinary situation are large classes characteristic of secondary physical education, the overemphasis on competition, the predominant position of a sports orientation within the curriculum, and instruction too often organized from the athletic coaching model concurrent with a diminished conceptual focus on the study of human movement. Is it any wonder that students, often nonathletic and disinterested in sports, become nuisances, disrupt class, and exhibit maladaptive behaviors? These stu-

Promote student involvement through the sharing of information about students' accomplishments.
Courtesy of Joanne Ruane.

dents become the discipline problems in the physical education class.

Combs'[49] perceptive review of classrooms, schools, and problematic student behavior elucidates the discipline situation in physical education. He identifies characteristics of the modern school that often hinder learning, nurture dull, unexciting classrooms, and dampen enthusiasm. Several of these characteristics speak volumes about the source of problems that often emerge in physical education:

1. Preoccupation with order and categorization
2. Overvaluing authority
3. The elimination of the student's self from the learning experience; what students think is not important
4. Emphasis on force, threat, or coercion

Given the real possibility of disruptive student behavior in physical education, we now turn to a review of suggested solutions. In the next section disciplinary programs regularly found in the professional educational literature will be described.

APPROACHES TO DISCIPLINE

In the section that follows, several of the most popular approaches (models) to discipline are briefly outlined for the reader's use. Included are key concepts, the originator or developer of the model, and selected references (Boxes 10-2 to 10-6).

Some of the models reviewed have been field tested, and literature exists describing their effectiveness and application to other settings. Others have not been examined as thoroughly or implemented to any great extent and, therefore, remain in a more theoretical stage of development. In either case the information provided should assist the practitioner in physical education, especially the novice teacher, by providing an array of disciplinary strategies for consideration. The material presented here should provide teachers with a solid foundation from which to organize initial efforts directed at classroom management and specifically discipline.

A proactive mindset is critical to the formation of a sound disciplinary atmosphere in the learning setting. Careful planning, including preparation for student management concerns, inappropriate behavior, and recalcitrant students will go a long way toward reducing the frequency of such incidents and minimizing the effects of such happenings when they do occur.

Gallahue[50] suggests that teachers who display effective discipline techniques tend to be positive role models, efficient planners, effective communicators, and consistent in their expectations of students. He indicates that to be proactive in regard to classroom management and discipline, teachers would do well to adhere to the following suggestions:

1. Be assertive (rather than aggressive).
2. Be enthusiastic.

BOX 10-2

THE KOUNIN MODEL

Originator: Jacob Kounin

Key Concepts

1. When teachers correct misbehavior in one student, it often influences the behavior of nearby students. This is known as the "ripple effect."
2. Teachers should know what is going on in all parts of the classroom at all times ("with-it-ness").
3. Teachers must correct misbehavior as soon as it occurs. Students will be less likely to misbehave if they perceive that teachers are "with-it" (teachers choose the correct culprit and correct the misbehavior at once).
4. The provision of smooth transitions between activities and the maintenance of consistent momentum within activities is crucial.
5. Teachers must strive to maintain group alertness and to hold every group member accountable for the content of a lesson.
6. Student satiation (boredom) can be avoided by providing a feeling of progress and by adding variety.

Source: Charles CM: *Building classroom discipline: from models to practice,* New York, 1981, Longman; and Kounin JS: *Discipline and group management in classrooms,* New York, 1970, Holt, Rinehart and Winston.

3. Respond in a consistent fashion.
4. Be clear when communicating expectations for students.
5. Set reasonable (rather than unrealistic) goals. Be sure to clearly convey these goals to all students.
6. Have a plan of action ready (rather than planning to react).
7. Prepare thoroughly (overplan) for each lesson.
8. Minimize formation changes and transition time.
9. Create a physical education environment that is safe and pleasant.
10. Be positive and respond to students' attempts to behave in a positive manner.
11. Avoid nagging, teasing, shaming, belittling, and other aggressive forms of communication.
12. Be consistent in meaning and use of verbal and nonverbal forms of communications.

Gallahue's proposals would appear to set an effective proactive agenda for all teachers. Preparation and anticipation are required to avoid, if not prevent, disruptions in the physical education environment.

Other preventive measures teachers can employ to minimize, if not avoid, classroom disruptions include thorough planning that addresses maximizing use of space, equipment, and facilities and minimizing student waiting, administrative tasks, and transition time. Teachers should

BOX 10-3

THE GINOTT MODEL: ADDRESSING THE SITUATION WITH SANE MESSAGES

Originator: Haim Ginott

Key Concepts

1. The most important ingredient in discipline is the teacher's own self-discipline.
2. The best teachers help students build their own self-esteem and trust their own experience.
3. The use of sane messages when correcting misbehaving students is critical. Sane messages address the situation and do not attack the student's character. Sane messages accept and acknowledge how students feel.
4. Teachers at their best use congruent communication, which is harmonious with students' own feelings about situations and themselves. Teachers at their worst attack and label students' character. Labeling students disables them.
5. Teachers should model the human behavior they hope to nurture in their students. Their behaviors should always be genuine. Teachers, when appropriate, should express anger but in appropriate ways.
6. The use of "I" messages ("I am angry," "I am disappointed") are much more appropriate expressions than "you" messages ("you are no good," "you are lazy"). The former expressions tell students how the teacher feels about the situation, while the latter ones attack the student.
7. Sarcasm is always dangerous; praise often is. Use both with great care. Teachers must be careful not to attribute qualities of the student behavior or student performance to the students' personality.
8. Apologies from students should be accepted with the understanding that they intend to improve.
9. Inviting cooperation from students is preferable to demanding it. Teachers need to respect students' ability to behave autonomously. When possible, permit students to decide on their own what their course of action should be. Such teacher behavior invites cooperation, promotes self-choice, and fosters responsibility. Self-image increases with independent choice of productive behaviors.

Source: Ginott H: *Teacher and child,* New York, 1971, Macmillan.

regularly plan lessons that engage all learners at an appropriate level. Knowledge of students' abilities and interests will make the teacher more accurate and minimize discipline problems. It is important to post the rules of conduct in the physical education class and then review these rules with students to ensure comprehension. Teachers must be sure that all students know the consequences of behaviors.

BOX 10-4

THE NEO-SKINNERIAN MODEL: SHAPING DESIRED BEHAVIOR

Originator/chief proponents: BF Skinner and his disciples

Key Concepts

1. Behavior is shaped by its consequences and by what happens to the individual after performing an act. Behavior is strengthened if followed immediately by reinforcers.

2. A strengthened behavior is one that the individual will be more likely to repeat.

3. Behavior is weakened if it is not followed by a reinforcer. A weakened behavior is less likely to be repeated.

4. Behavior is weakened if it is followed by punishment. Punishment is not the same thing as negative reinforcement.

5. The use of reinforcement can shape individuals' behavior. When applied to school learning and discipline, this behavior shaping process is called behavior modification.

6. In the early stages of learning, constant reinforcement produces the best results. Once learning has reached the desired level, it is best maintained through intermittent reinforcement, on an unpredictable schedule.

7. Behavior modification is applied in two ways:
   a. The teacher observes the student perform a desired act; the teacher rewards the student; the student tends to repeat the act.
   b. The teacher observes the student perform an undesired act; the teacher either ignores the act or punishes the student, then praises a student who is behaving correctly; the misbehaving student becomes less likely than before to repeat the act.

8. Various reinforcers are used in behavior modification:
   a. Social reinforcers (verbal comments, gestures)
   b. Graphic reinforcers (marks, stars)
   c. Activity reinforcers (free time)
   d. Tangible reinforcers (food, prizes)

Source: Axelrod S: *Behavioral modification for the classroom teacher,* New York, 1977, McGraw-Hill; and Cooper JO, Heron TE, Heward WL: *Applied behavior analysis,* Columbus, Ohio, 1987, Merrill Publishing.

BOX 10-5

THE GLASSER MODEL: GOOD BEHAVIOR COMES FROM GOOD CHOICES

Originator: William Glasser

Key Concepts

1. Students are rational beings, and they can control their behavior.

2. Good choices produce good behavior. Bad choices produce bad behavior.

3. Teachers must always try to help students make good choices. This is accomplished in two ways: (1) stressing students' responsibility for their own behavior, and (2) teachers demonstrating that they truly care about the student.

4. Teachers who care accept no excuses for bad behavior. A teacher who accepts an excuse says, in effect, that it is acceptable to break a commitment.

5. Reasonable consequences should always follow student behavior, good or bad. These consequences should not be physically punishing or employ caustic language, ridicule, or sarcasm.

6. Class rules are essential and must be enforced. Rules should be established by teachers and students together.

7. Classroom meetings are effective vehicles for attending to matters of class rules, behavior, and discipline.

8. Caring teachers are persistent and constant in helping their students move toward self-discipline.

Source: Glasser W: *Schools without failure,* New York, 1969, Harper & Row.

Teachers will avoid many confrontations if they provide private and individualized feedback, comments, and reprimands (if necessary) to students. Teachers should avoid public confrontations, interactions, and shouting, especially when responding to inappropriate behaviors. Teachers should maintain alertness, "with-it-ness," and interest during the lesson. Finally, teachers should circulate among the students, groups, and various activities, as well as remain visibly involved in the lesson. These and other ideas will help the teacher minimize, if not prevent, many of the commonly observed discipline problems in the physical education setting.

Common elements in these approaches to discipline are quite evident, and the identification of the commonalities can assist teachers as they consider formulating a proactive plan for class management and discipline. These elements are outlined in Box 10-7.

DISCIPLINARY STRATEGIES IN PHYSICAL EDUCATION

Several authorities in physical education have described systems to deal with inappropriate behavior and recalcitrant students as such episodes develop in the gymnasium. Only those plans that are explicit, readily available

BOX 10 - 6

THE CANTER MODEL: ASSERTIVE DISCIPLINE

Originators: Lee and Marlene Canter

Key Concepts

1. Teachers must insist on decent, responsible behavior.
2. Firm control maintained correctly is humane and liberating.
3. Teachers have basic educational rights, including the right to establish optimal learning environments and the right to determine, request, and expect appropriate behavior.
4. Students' basic rights include:
   a. The right to have teachers who help them limit their inappropriate, self-destructive behavior
   b. The right to have teachers who provide positive support for their appropriate behavior
   c. The right to choose how to behave, and a full understanding of the consequences that will follow their choices.
5. Assertive discipline best meets the rights above since the teacher clearly communicates expectations to students and consistently follows up with appropriate actions, but never violates the best interests of the students.
6. The basis of assertive discipline is care—teachers caring about themselves to the point of not allowing students to take advantage, and teachers caring about students to the point of not allowing students to behave in ways that are self-destructive.
7. Assertive discipline consists of the following elements:
   a. Clearly identified expectations and the elimination of negative expectations about student behavior.
   b. Teachers' willingness to express themselves clearly.
   c. Persistence in stating expectations and feelings.
   d. Use of a firm tone of voice.
   e. Maintenance of eye contact.
   f. Use of nonverbal gestures in support of verbal statements.
   g. Use of hints, questions, and "I" messages rather than demands for requesting student behavior.
   h. Follow through with promises (reasonable consequences that are previously established) rather than with threats.
8. Teachers have a right to ask for and receive support from principals and other school personnel.

Source: Canter L, Canter M: *Assertive discipline: a take charge approach for today's educator*, Seal Beach, Calif, 1976, Canter and Associates.

BOX 10 - 7

COMMON ELEMENTS IN DISCIPLINARY APPROACHES

1. Teachers should be clear with instructions, directions, and presentations.
2. Teachers should project "with-it-ness."
3. Misbehavior should be corrected as soon as it occurs.
4. Students should be held accountable to both the lesson and behavioral consequences.
5. Reinforcement can shape student behavior.
6. Teachers must employ sane, humane messages when they communicate with students. The situation should be addressed without attacking the student's character.
7. Teachers should accept and acknowledge how students feel.
8. The modeling of appropriate behavior by teachers is of great significance.
9. Teachers should employ "I" messages instead of "you" messages.
10. Sarcasm and ridicule should be avoided.
11. Class rules are critical to a sound program of discipline. Rules should be established by teachers and students together. Rules should be enforced.

in the professional literature, and field-tested will be reviewed in this section.

The first set of strategies has been developed by Don Hellison and his students, based on extensive field testing with at-risk students. Founded on the tenets of the student-centered curriculum and the humanistic approach, Hellison has devised an effective (and extensive) compendium of explicit techiques that can move students from irresponsible, self-centered behavior, through intermediate stages of self-control, self-responsibility, and high involvement, to the point of caring for others. Critical aspects of these strategies appear to be numerous, high-quality, and intensive student-teacher and student-student interactions; provisions for student options throughout the curriculum; encouragement of student ownership of the program; and unconditional support of and respect for the dignity of the student. Hellison's recommendations, while couched within a broader curriculum framework, are practical and speak volumes to practitioners concerned with student motivation and discipline. Individuals interested in perusing Hellison's ideas further should review his outstanding text.[47]

In 1984 Olson[51] outlined an application of the *LEAST* approach to discipline to physical education. The *LEAST* method, according to Olson, is based on nearly two decades of research and has been field tested, refined, and retested in eight states.[52] The *LEAST* program stresses five concepts or teacher options and, thereby, suggests a specific course of action in response to student misbehavior. The options are listed below:

1. *Leave things alone:* Leaving situations alone means proceeding as planned and making no move to respond to or correct behavior. Teachers should use this strategy when all three of the following conditions exist:
   a. No one will be harmed.
   b. There is little chance of a "ripple" effect.
   c. The behavior will probably disappear if the teacher does not become involved.

2. *End the action indirectly:* Olson suggests ending the action by using any of three progressive steps:
   a. "Eyeball" the offender.
   b. Reduce the distance between the teacher and the offender.
   c. Call the student's name in a quiet, controlled voice.

3. *Attend more fully:* Attending more fully involves two related activities. The first is responding to communicate the teacher's attention and concern to students. The second activity is the use of questioning. Questions (who, what, where, when, why, how) are designed to get a full, factual description of a particular situation. Yes-no questions permit shy or troubled students to respond with a minimum of stress.

4. *Spell out directions:* With as much information as can be acquired, directions must be spelled out for students. As teachers attempt this option, they should specify a positive alternative and then describe the consequences of the continued problem-related behavior.

5. *Track student progress:* Teachers should always track student progress. Such behavior demonstrates to students that the teacher is attending and helping to ascertain the success of a particular approach.

The *LEAST* method is designed to provide simple survival strategies for the teacher. As reviewed by Olson, the *LEAST* method certainly achieves this goal and can support secondary physical educators in their efforts to establish facilitative learning environments and carefully planned disciplinary policies.

Meyer[53] suggests that psychologically safe environments should be established and maintained in an effort to minimize disruptions and maladaptive behavior. Psychologically safe environments protect participants from embarrassment, confusion, and anxiety (all potential stimulators of inappropriate behaviors), while simultaneously providing consistency, support, and predictability. Meyer[53] suggests the following actions:

1. Establish a behavior code which is understood and supported by the class. Discipline can be maintained and embarrassing and confusing situations can be avoided when there is general agreement as to what constitutes appropriate behavior.

2. Refrain from abitrary decision making. Teachers should establish policies and procedures which are followed when making activity- and student-related decisions. A standard decision-making process provides consistency of teacher behavior and predictability for students.

3. Limit the number of things that participants have difficulty understanding or performing. Confusing situations are more likely to increase student errors and create added stress and frustration. Not only does confusion then impede learning, but it can also reduce motivation and enjoyment, both of which are precursors to student disruptive behavior.

4. Acknowledge student actions and efforts. Provide informational feedback which explains what is wrong, why it is wrong, and what needs to be done to improve it. When required, teachers must explain the consequences to the student if improvement is not achieved. Such information should be provided in a nonjudgmental, nonembarrassing manner.

Meyer's[53] suggestions have merit for several reasons, not the least of which are their inherent practicality and simplicity. Several other authorities echo Meyer's recommendations and set forth similar proposals related to

---

BOX 10-8

MANAGEMENT OF THE PHYSICAL ENVIRONMENT

1. Maintain comfortable room or water temperature. Appropriate temperature correlates highly with appropriate behavior.
2. Provide adequate lighting and ventilation. A too-dim or too-bright, stuffy, or smelly environment can sabotage the best of lessons.
3. Use color effectively in the instructional environment. Bright, drab, or distracting colors are factors to consider in planning.
4. Combine music with instruction. Fast tempos may increase movement, while slower rhythms aid in relaxation.
5. Minimize distractions such as extra equipment in close proximity to the students. Restrict equipment to that which is required for the lesson.
6. Maintain a professional appearance with respect to physique, conditioning, and apparel.
7. Lock doors and safeguard equipment to reduce safety hazards.
8. Provide appropriate visual cues and instructions. It is often hard to distinguish boundaries for a volleyball court in the midst of the badminton, tennis, and basketball markings.
9. Use space efficiently. Too little space can cause crowding, and too much space can create distractions.

managing discipline in physical education. Physical education teachers would do well to start with these ideas when establishing a systematic approach to discipline in the gym.[54,55]

Jansma, French, and Horvat[56] provide an additional source of ideas for preventing problem behaviors in physical education that are derived from field-tested behavioral engineering studies of the physical environment. In Box 10-8 practitioners are provided with a list of suggestions that can enhance student behavior.

The suggestions put forth by Jansma, French, and Horvat,[56] while appearing simplistic, are relatively easy to overlook within a typical teacher's fast-paced, stressful, and busy schedule of daily activities. Attention to the various physical factors identified can contribute much to the establishment of sound and stable disciplinary endeavors.

Physical education teachers, novice and experienced, are concerned about class control, disruptive behavior, and recalcitrant students, as well as how to respond to these situations. Teachers are aware that discipline must be maintained if instructional objectives are to be achieved. Therefore the primary goal of teachers is to organize and implement a positive learning environment and an effective disciplinary plan.

This section reviewed various approaches to discipline. These ideas can assist practitioners in their efforts to formulate a sound, preconceived strategy for the establishment of an effective classroom management plan and policies to deal with behavior problems.

SUMMARY

Teachers who conduct effective secondary physical education programs exhibit remarkable similarity in their operating style. While a universal formula or a definitive set of principles that can guarantee effective instructional practice does not yet exist, there are a number of strategies apparently characteristic of successful teachers. Successful teachers tend to be effective communicators who truly listen to students and encourage them to interact in many ways in the gym. They also typically are inspirational motivators, moving students to enjoy learning the content of physical education and to value an active lifestyle. Successful teachers are also skillful managers of behavior and respond proactively, clearly, and quickly to disciplinary enounters. This chapter has examined several critical aspects of instruction (communication, motivation, and discipline), has provided a synopsis of the key elements of each, and has described various strategies to facilitate productive instructional practices.

FOR REVIEW

1. Discuss the relationship between (a) communication and motivation, (b) communication and discipline, and (c) motivation and discipline.

2. Describe a plan that would promote increased participation by disinterested or apathetic students scheduled in a daily, required program of physical education.

3. Describe how a successful parent-teacher conference can influence the performance of a student.

4. Observe several physical education classes at a nearby high school. Describe one or two behavioral disruptions or discipline problems you observed. How did the teachers respond to each episode? What were the outcomes of the teacher's actions?

5. Prepare a code of behaviors to be followed in the locker room before and after class. Be sure to identify a list of consequences for violations or inappropriate student behaviors.

REFERENCES

1. Holmes Group Executive Board: *Tomorrow's teachers: a report of the Holmes Group,* East Lansing, Mich, 1986, Holmes Group.

2. National Commission on Excellence in Education: *A nation at risk,* Washington DC, 1984, US Government Printing Office.

3. Sizer T: Putting ideas into practice: an interview with Ted Sizer, *Harvard Education Letter* IV(4):5-7, 1988.

4. Bishop JH: Why the apathy in American high schools? *Educational Researchers* 18(1):6-10, 1989.

5. Chion-Kenny L: A report from the field: the coalition of essential schools, *American Educator* 11(4):18-27, 47-48, 1987.

6. Goodlad J: *A place called school: prospects for the future,* New York, 1984, McGraw-Hill.

7. Check J: Communication skills in the classroom, *The Physical Educator* 42(2):76-81, 1985.

8. Porter AC, Brophy J: Synthesis of research on good teaching: insights from the work of the Institute for Research on Teaching, *Educational Leadership* 45(8):74-85, 1988.

9. Ratliffe T: Overcoming obstacles beginning teachers encounter, *JOPERD* 58(4):18-23, 1987.

10. Belgard M, Rosenshine B, Gage NL: The teacher's effectiveness in explaining: evidence on its generality and correlation with pupils' ratings and attention scores. In Westbury I, Bellack AA, editors: *Research into classroom processes,* New York, 1971, Teachers College Press, Teachers College, Columbia University.

11. Lawrenz F: The relationship between science teacher characteristics and student achievement and attitude, *Journal of Research in Science Teaching* 12:433-437, 1975.

12. Hunter M: *Mastery teaching,* El Segundo, Calif, 1982, Tip Publications.

13. Roberts CL, Becker SL: Communications and teaching effectiveness in industrial education, *American Educational Research Journal* 13:181-197, 1976.

14. Mastin VE: Teacher enthusiasm, *Journal of Educational Research* 56:385-386, 1963.

15. Rink J: *Teaching physical education for learning,* St Louis, 1985, Mosby.

16. Rosenshine B: Teaching functions in instructional programs, *The Elementary School Journal* 83(4):335-351, 1983.

17. Flanders NA: *Teacher influence, pupil attitudes, and achievement,* Washington, DC, 1965, US Government Printing Office.

18. Templin T: Some considerations for teaching physical education in the future. In Massengale JD, editor: *Trends toward the future in physical education,* Champaign, Ill, 1987, Human Kinetics.

19. Siedentop D, Mand C, Taggart A: *Physical education teaching and curriculum strategies for grades 5-12,* Palo Alto, Calif, 1986, Mayfield.

20. Lombardo B, Cheffers JTF: Variability in teaching behavior and interactions in the gymnasium, *Journal of Teaching in Physical Education* 2(2):33-48, 1983.

21. Gusthart JL: Variations in direct, indirect, and noncontributing teacher behavior, *Journal of Teaching in Physical Education* 4(2):111-122, 1985.

22. Ritson R, Smith R, Twa H: Student and teacher interaction analysis: a comparison of activities, age, groups, and sex of the students in physical education, *Journal of Teaching in Physical Education* 1(2):15-25, 1982.

23. Charles CM: *Educational psychology: the instructional endeavor,* ed 2, St Louis, 1976, Mosby.

24. Curwin RL, Mendler AN: *Discipline with dignity,* Alexandria, Va, 1988, Association for Supervision and Curriculum Development.

25. Rutherford RB, Edgar E: *Teachers and parents: a guide to interaction and cooperation,* Boston, 1979, Allyn & Bacon.

26. Halliwell W: Intrinsic motivation in sport. In Straub W, editor: *Sport psychology: an analysis of athlete behavior,* Syracuse, NY, 1978, Movement.

27. Siedentop D: *Developing teaching skills in physical education, ed 3,* Mountain View, Calif, 1991, Mayfield.

28. Paese PC: Improving secondary school physical education, *The Physical Educator* 40(2):60-63, 1983.

29. Siedentop D: High school physical education: still an endangered species, *JOPERD* 58(2):24-25, 1987.

30. Lambert L: Secondary school physical education problems: what can we do about them? *JOPERD* 58(2):30-32, 1987.

31. Earls N: Distinctive teachers personal qualities, perceptions of teacher education, and the realities of teaching, *Journal of Teaching in Physical Education* 1(1):59-70, 1981.

32. Kollen P: The experience of movement in physical education: a phenomenology, Doctoral dissertation, University of Michigan, 1981, *Dissertation Abstracts International* 42(2):428A-893A, 1981, University Microfilms, No 81-16, 272.

33. Kollen P: Fragmentation and integration in human movement. In Templin T, Olson J, editors: *Teaching in physical education,* Big Ten Body of Knowledge Symposium Series, vol 4, Champaign, Ill, 1983, Human Kinetics.

34. Griffey D: Trouble for sure—a crisis perhaps, *JOPERD* 58(2):20-21, 1987.

35. Brandon LJ, Evans RL: Are physical educators fit?: perceived and measured physical fitness of physical educators, *JOPERD* 59(7):72-75, 1988.

36. Whitley JD, Sage JN, Butcher M: Cardiorespiratory fitness: role modeling by physical education instructors, *JOPERD* 59(7):81-84, 1988.

37. Melville DS, Cardinal BJ: The problem: body fatness within our profession, *JOPERD* 59(7):85-87, 95-96, 1988.

38. Cardinal BJ: Body composition of physical education students at Eastern Washington University. Unpublished masters thesis. Eastern Washington University, Cheney, Washington. In Melville DS. Cardinal BJ: The problem: body fatness within our profession, *JOPERD* 59(7):85-87, 95-96, 1988.

39. Griffin P: Girls and boys participation styles in middle school physical education team support classes: a description and practical applications, *The Physical Educator* 42(1):3-8, 1985.

40. Chandler GL: Invitational physical education: strategies in the junior high school, *JOPERD* 59(4):68-72, 1988.

41. Purkey WW: *Inviting school success,* Belmont, Calif, 1978, Wadsworth.

42. Gallup G: The public schools, *The Gallup Report* 42-57, 227-228, 1984.

43. Gallup A: The 18th Annual Gallup Poll of the public's attitude toward the public schools, *Phi Delta Kappan* 68(1):43-59, 1986.

44. Feistritzer E, editor: *Teacher Education Reports* 10(12), 6-7, 1989, Washington, DC, Feistritzer Publications.

45. Van Oteghen SL, Forrest M: Adolescent stress, *Strategies* 2(2):5-10, 29, 1988.

46. Rothstein A, Lapkin B: Can teachers help? *Strategies* 2(2):6-10, 29, 1988.

47. Hellison D: *Goals and strategies for physical education,* Champaign, Ill, 1985, Human Kinetics.

48. Dillon EA: Did we all let Barry die? *Journal of Teacher Education* 29:30, 1978.

49. Combs A: *The professional education of teachers,* Boston, 1965, Allyn & Bacon.

50. Gallahue D: Toward positive discipline in the gymnasium, *The Physical Educator* 42(2):14-17, 1985.

51. Olson J: Keeping cool: be a teacher who disciplines LEAST, *JOPERD* 55(6):38-39, 1984.

52. Carkhuff R: The LEAST approach to classroom discipline, *A design for discipline,* Infopac, no 72, Washington, DC, 1978, NEA.

53. Meyer L: Creating psychologically safe activity environments, *JOPERD* 59(9):15, 1988.

54. Brandon J: Discipline, choosing teams, square dance, and rope skipping. In Carlson RP, editor: *Ideas II for secondary school physical education,* Reston, Va, 1984, AAHPERD.

55. Rimmer JH: Confrontation in the gym: a systematic solution for behavior problems, *JOPERD* 60(5):63-65, 1989.

56. Jansma P, French R, Horvat M: Behavioral engineering in physical education, *JOPERD* 55(6):80-81, 1984.

ANNOTATED READINGS

Chandler GL: Invitational physical education: strategies in the junior high school, *JOPERD* 59(4):68-72, 1988.

A multitude of practical strategies are provided, all of which can promote student motivation and heighten the attractiveness of any physical education program. Chandler masterfully extends Purkey's work on invitational education to physical education and presents many relevant, inexpensive, and doable suggestions aimed at strengthening students' bonds to physical activity and physical education. Included is *The Inventory of Physical Education Invitations,* an instrument that could be employed to analyze student-teacher relationships and the environment in physical education.

Check JF: Communication skills in the classroom, *The Physical Educator* 42(2):76-81, 1985.

Working from the premise that good teaching is equivalent to professional communication, the author discusses the relationship of specific communication skills and teaching effectiveness. Check, an educational psychologist, carefully reviews the assets and liabilities of verbal and nonverbal communications with the goal of enhancing pedagogical practice. An extensive list of suggestions is provided to assist teachers with the numerous interactions and presentations so characteristic of their daily performance and responsibilities.

Meyer L: Creating psychologically safe activity environments, *JOPERD* 59(9):15, 1988.

Psychologically safe environments protect participants from embarrassment, confusion, and anxiety while providing consistency, support, and predictability. Using this as a starting point, Meyer outlines several steps that create a positive learning environment, foster appropriate behavior, and provide effective strategies to respond to disruptive behavior.

Olson J: Keeping cool: be a teacher who disciplines LEAST, *JOPERD* 55(6):38-39, 1984.

Olson describes a little-known but extremely useful plan called the *LEAST* approach to discipline. The method entails simple survival strategies for the teacher and has great potential for the gymnasium setting.

Rutherford RB, Edgar E: *Teachers and parents: a guide to interaction and cooperation,* Boston, 1979, Allyn & Bacon.

This is a succinctly prepared volume on various topics pertaining to parent-teacher interaction, including an analysis of the potency of such relationships. The authors make many specific and practical recommendations for facilitating positive parent-teacher cooperation.

Meeting Students' Special Needs

CHAPTER OBJECTIVES

◆ To explain legislation that has been enacted to ensure equal educational opportunity for all children

◆ To describe the process by which special needs can be assessed and accommodated

◆ To introduce strategies that can enable all students to achieve success in physical education

All students have the right to a quality physical education program. To help students develop to their fullest potential requires relevant instruction and the utilization of teaching strategies that are sensitive to individual differences.

Considerable differences exist between students within and across grade levels. Students come to a physical education class at varying stages of development, from a diversity of backgrounds, with different levels of ability and needs, and possessing different learning styles. Because of these differences, not all students can accomplish physical education objectives without some special consideration. Some students lack proficiency in prerequisite skills, others exhibit low levels of physical fitness, and still others may be unable to meet the objectives because of a temporary or permanent disabling condition—a broken leg, cerebral palsy, a learning disability, or a visual impairment, for example.

Because the goal of education is to help all children attain their fullest potential, the physical education teacher must plan learning experiences that will address the needs of all their students. Individualization of instruction is the key to accomplishing this goal. This instructional approach emphasizes modifying instruction according to individual differences. Wessel and Kelly[1] note that this does not necessarily mean that instruction is different for each student, but that it is appropriate for each student.

According to Sherrill,[2] the essence of good teaching is the essence of adapted physical education: adjusting the curriculum and instructional process to accommodate a diversity of individual needs while ensuring each student the opportunity to participate fully, successfully, and safely in physical education. Developmentally appropriate physical education that provides for sequential experiences appropriate to the individual's development and recognizes that children learn at their own rate and in their own way is the cornerstone of adapted physical education.

LEGISLATION

Federal legislation within the past two decades has had a profound effect on the education of children with disabilities and the opportunities afforded these children in physical education and athletics (Box 11-1). Passed in 1973, Public Law (PL) 93-112 or Section 504 of the Rehabilitation Act provided that no qualified individual shall be excluded from participation, denied benefits, or be discriminated against by virtue of his or her disability in a program or activity that receives federal funds. Schools are mandated by this law to provide equal opportunities for students with disabilities to participate in all programs offered by the school. This encompasses physical education, intramurals, clubs, and interscholastic sports or athletics. Adaptations and accommodations must be made so that individuals with disabilities can participate in these programs. Architectural, administrative, and instructional barriers to participation must be removed. Provisions must be made to make buildings

BOX 11-1

LEGISLATION IMPACTING ON PHYSICAL EDUCATION AND CHILDREN WITH DISABILITIES

1973	PL 93-112	Rehabilitation Act Amendments, Section 504
1975	PL 94-142	Education for All Handicapped Children Act
1978	PL 95-606	Amateur Sports Act
1986	PL 99-457	Education of the Handicapped Amendment
1990	PL 101-336	Americans with Disabilities Act
1990	PL 101-476	Individuals with Disabilities Education Act

and facilities accessible, to provide appropriate transportation, and to make adaptations in the curriculum and activities to accommodate individuals with disabilities.

One of the most significant federal statutes affecting physical education is PL 94-142, the Education of All Handicapped Children Act of 1975. This landmark law, implemented in 1977, mandates that all students, ages 3 to 21, have the right to a free quality education regardless of their disability. Each child with a disability must have the opportunity to receive an appropriate education with instruction specially designed to meet each child's unique educational needs and in the least restrictive environment (LRE).

PL 94-142 requires that each child with a disability have an individualized educational plan (IEP). Physical education is the only school subject specifically named in the law. Every student with a disability must have access to physical education. The law defines physical education as the development of (1) physical and motor fitness; (2) fundamental motor skills and patterns; and (3) skills in aquatics, dance, individual and group games, and sports (including intramural and lifetime sports). Furthermore, students with disabilities must have access to extracurricular activities, including athletics, that are comparable to those available to their nondisabled peers (Box 11-2).

According to PL 94-142 children with a disability must be educated in the least restrictive environment, which is one in which the child can participate successfully and safely in as near a normal setting as possible. Whenever appropriate, students with disabilities should be mainstreamed and have the opportunity to learn with their nondisabled peers rather than in special education classes.

PL 99-457 (Education of the Handicapped Amendment), the 1986 Amendment to the Education of All Handicapped Children Act, extended the provisions of PL 94-142 to children from birth to age 2 on a discre-

tionary, not mandated, basis. Because these children will begin to receive needed services and interventions at an earlier age, their development will likely be enhanced. Thus by the time these students reach the secondary school level, they will be functioning at a higher developmental level. Schools will need to adjust the services they are now providing to a much higher level to meet more fully the needs of their students.

There have been several other federal statutes that have wide-ranging implications for the education and the conduct of physical education and sports opportunities for children with disabilities. In 1978 the passage of PL 95-606, the Amateur Sports Act, led to recognition of sports organizations of disabled athletes as part of the United States Olympic Committee. The Amateur Sports Act encouraged the development of amateur athletic programs and competitions for individuals with disabilities at all levels. Meaningful participation by athletes with disabilities in programs for able-bodied individuals was also supported.

The Americans with Disabilities Act (ADA), PL 101-336, was passed in 1990 and prohibits discrimination against individuals with disabilities. Individuals with a disability that limits their education are covered under this law. The law forbids discrimination in employment, public accommodations (for example, public recreation facilities), transportation, public services, and communication.

Also passed in 1990, PL 101-476, the Individuals with Disabilities Education Act (IDEA) amended some of the provisions of PL 94-142. It replaced references to "handicapped children" with the words "children with disabil-

BOX 11-2

KEY PROVISIONS OF PL 94-142

- Each handicapped child has the right to a free, appropriate public education, regardless of the type or severity of the disability.
- Placement decisions must be based on nondiscriminatory tests. A comprehensive evaluation must be made; no placement decision can be based on the result of a single test.
- An individualized educational plan (IEP) is required for each child.
- Each child is to be educated in the least restrictive environment (LRE).
- To ensure the rights of children with handicaps and their parents, the school must employ due process safeguards.
- Parents and, when appropriate, the child have the right to be actively involved in educational decisions regarding the child's education.

ities." Transitional services to prepare students to move from the school to the postschool environment were added. The need to develop more programs for minorities with disabilities was recognized. With respect to physical education and athletics, the right of every child to receive an appropriate physical education experience was reaffirmed. Children with disabilities must also be given equal opportunities to participate in athletics. Attention must also be given to helping students make the transition from secondary school physical education to postsecondary participation in community recreation activities.

These federal statutes and related laws at the state level have had a major impact on the education of children with disabilities. They have led to modifications in the curriculum to include a wide array of activities for students with disabilities and changes in instructional practices to reflect a greater sensitivity to the needs of these students. Architectural barriers have been removed and administrative practices changed to provide students with disabilities with greater educational opportunities.

LEAST RESTRICTIVE ENVIRONMENT

PL 94-142 mandates that each student be educated in the *least restrictive environment*. When possible, students with disabilities should be educated with students without disabilities in the regular educational environment. The intent of the law is to prevent unwarranted segregation of students with disabilities from their nondisabled peers. *Mainstreaming* is a popularized term used to describe the integration of students with disabilities with other students in the public schools.

When satisfactory educational progress cannot be made in regular classes with the use of supportive aides and services, then the student with a disability should be placed in a setting where his or her needs can be met. The focus is on meeting the unique needs of the student and placing the student in a setting that is as normal as possible while allowing opportunities for educational success.

The appropriate environment also depends on the subject being taught and the teaching style. With respect to physical education, a student with limited mobility may find a soccer unit to be restrictive and require placement in an adapted setting, whereas the student may be able to achieve success in an archery unit in a regular class setting. A student with mental retardation may find it difficult to succeed when taught using a problem-solving approach but may achieve success with a more structured command-style teaching approach. Thus the least restrictive placement for a student may change during the course of a year.

Schools should provide a variety of placement options for students with disabilities. With respect to physical education services, opportunities range on a continuum from fulltime placement in the regular physical education

---

BOX 11-3

PLACEMENT OPTIONS FOR PHYSICAL EDUCATION FOR STUDENTS WITH DISABILITIES

Full integration into regular physical education
Full integration into regular physical education with special accommodations (limited class size, consultant)
Full integration into regular physical education with adapted physical education on an occasional basis
Partial integration into regular physical education according to the number of days per week prescribed in the IEP (2 days in regular physical education, 3 days in adapted physical education)
Separate adapted physical education
Separate adapted physical education in a school exclusively for children with disabilities

---

class to fulltime placement in an adapted physical education class. A resource room is also an important placement option in the physical education program. These placement options are shown in Box 11-3.

Regular Physical Education

Many times the needs of students with disabilities can be met in the regular physical education program. The more developmentally oriented and individualized the regular physical education program is, the easier it is to mainstream students with unique needs. Mainstreaming is facilitated when the teacher selects and conducts activities to fit the myriad developmental needs of all students. Incorporation of a diversity of activities in the curriculum, utilization of sound progressions to promote achievement while providing for frequent and meaningful success, and employment of a variety of teaching styles contribute to effective mainstreaming.

Additionally, the mainstreaming of students with disabilities may be accomplished by providing students with extra assistance during class. For example, students may work with a paraprofessional or a peer tutor during instruction. One federally validated program that utilizes peer tutors to work with individuals with special needs is the Physical Education Opportunities Program for Exceptional Learners (PEOPEL).[7] This program trains student volunteers to work with students with disabilities. The use of a peer-tutoring model such as PEOPEL offers many advantages. Students with disabilities receive greater attention, personal instruction, and individual feedback, all of which help maximize the benefits accrued from participation in the regular program. The peer tutors learn how to work with individuals with a wide array of disabling conditions and experience personal satisfaction from helping their peers learn.

Adapted Physical Education

Adapted physical education classes are for those students whose needs are such that they cannot be safely or successfully met within the regular physical education program. Students who require special considerations to learn successfully may be assigned to the adapted physical education program on a full-time basis. In this program they have the opportunity to participate in remedial activities and develop competency in physical activities.

Students may also be placed in adapted physical education on a part-time basis. This could be only during certain units of instruction in which their participation in the regular program is not possible. For example, a student who is visually impaired may spend most of the time in the regular physical education program but may participate in the adapted physical education program during tennis and badminton units where it is difficult for the student to successfully participate. Students could also be assigned to adapted physical education for a certain number of days per week, for example, three days of regular physical education and two days of adapted physical education.

Another option is to mainstream the student into the regular physical education class but also provide for additional development through assignment to an adapted physical education class. In this situation the student would receive additional assistance in needed areas, such as in the case of extremely low fitness or poor fundamental skills (for example, throwing or running). Yet the student would have the opportunity to participate with peers in the mainstream setting.

Resource Room

The resource room or learning center is a place where additional help can be provided to students by qualified teachers. Students who need help can be given supplementary instruction and can engage in supervised practice.

In determining which placement option is appropriate, the teacher must review the student's needs on an individual basis. Moreover, all aspects of human development must be considered: psychomotor, cognitive, and affective dimensions. Placement options should be reevaluated periodically, at least once a year, to ensure that the placement continues to be beneficial to the student. While the teacher should remain focused on the student's needs, every effort should be made to maximize the amount of time each student participates in regular physical education class with his or her peers.

I. Student name __John Doe, Jr.__ Date of birth __1-24-76__ Age __16__ School division __Stony Point__
Parent/Guardian __Mrs. John Doe__ Date of eligibility __6-15-92__ Date of IEP implementation __9-6-92__
Address _____1736 Bay Street_____ Categorical identification _____E.M.R._____

II. Present level of performance (summary data)

Academic:	*Piat*		*AAHPERD Physical Fitness Test Items* *(Refer to charts/age group)*	
Key math	Reading recognition	2.3	Pull-up/flexed arm hang	5
3.8	Reading	3.6	Sit-ups (flexed legs)	41
Dolch sight	Spelling	2.0	Shuttle run	10.1
Word inventory	Reading comprehension	4.8	50-yard dash	6.7
263 words mastered	Mathematics	4.2	600-yard run-walk	1:55
	General knowledge	5.9	Standing broad jump	6'9"

Behavior:
John is very shy and lacks physical fitness. There is little eye contact with others. He is well mannered. John gets discouraged easily when working in language areas. He performs well in math. His social skills are limited. John is interested in woodworking. Carpentry may provide a setting for advancement and training after he has obtained the necessary prevocational orientation.

III. Long-term goals
  1. To increase all items of the AAHPERD Physical Best Fitness to the criterion level by the end of the school year.
  2. To increase sight word vocabulary and survival words.
  3. To increase skills in reading through spelling skills and decoding skills.
  4. To increase math processes skills to include banking and savings.
  5. To demonstrate planning of careers, duties of specific jobs, and survival forms of applications.
  6. To provide instruction in local, state, and national governments.
  7. To increase self-confidence and social adaptability.

FIG. 11-1 Sample Individualized Education Plan (IEP).

From Bucher CA, Koenig CR: *Methods and materials for secondary school physical education,* ed 5, St Louis, 1978, Mosby.

IV. Education and related services

services	Date to begin	Anticipated completion date	Environment	Location	Personnel
E.M.R.	9-6-92	through high school	4 periods— self-contained	Virginia High School	Mrs. Green
Physical education	9-6-92	through grade 10	1 period— regular	Virginia High School	Mr. Dean
Vocational orientation	9-6-92	through high school	1 period— regular	Virginia High School	Vocational rehabilitation W.I.N. program

V. Short-term objectives

Objectives	Methods	Special materials and equipment	Dates Begun	Completion	Continuation or modification
Physical education	Establish warm-up stations to be used for following activities:				
1. Student's performance levels should show improvement in efforts to obtain the criterion level	1. To perform sit-ups 3 times/wk 2. To perform pull-ups 3 times/wk 3. To perform stretching exercises 3 times/wk 4. To run two ½-mile run-walk/wk	Tape, stop watch, horizontal bar	9/6 9/6 9/6 9/6 9/6 9/6	5/4 5/4 5/4 5/4 5/4 5/4	Mastered/maintain Cont. (incl. no./wk) Cont. (incl. no./wk) Cont./modif. (no.) Exercise Mastered/cont.
Academic					
1. To master Dolch sight vocabulary and survival words		Flash cards, word finds, crossword puzzles	9/15	6/3	Cont./increase
2. To spell and define 10 words/wk	Cover and write method		9/15 9/15	6/3 6/3	Modif. Cont.

VI. Participants

Date	Signature of persons present	Relationship to student
9-1-92	Mrs. Ann Long	Guidance counselor
9-1-92	Mrs. Louis Green	E.M.R. teacher
9-1-92	Mr. George Dean	Physical education teacher
9-1-92	Mrs. John Doe	Parent
9-1-92	Ms. Matilda Snodgrass	Psychologist
9-1-92	Mr. Oscar Rinklefender	Director of special education

I GIVE PERMISSION FOR MY CHILD _____John Doe, Jr._____ to be enrolled in the special program described in the individualized education program plan. I understand that I have the right to review his/her record and to request a change in his/her individualized education program at any time. I understand that I have the right to refuse this permission and to have my child continue in his/her present placement pending further action.

I did participate in the development of the individualized education program.   YES ___X___ NO_____

I did not participate in the development of the individualized education program, but I do approve of the plan.   YES_____ NO_____

9/1/92	Mrs. John Doe
Date	Signature of parent or guardian

I DO NOT GIVE PERMISSION FOR MY CHILD _____ to be enrolled in the special education program described in the individualized education program. I understand that I have the right to review his/her records and to request another placement. I understand that the action described above will not take place without my permission or until due process procedures have been exhausted. I understand that if my decision is appealed, I will be notified of my due process rights in this procedure.

Date	Signature of parent or guardian

FIG. 11-1, cont'd.   Sample Individualized Education Plan (IEP).

INDIVIDUALIZED EDUCATION PLAN

All students with disabilities who have been identified by the school as needing special education and related supportive services, such as physical therapy, must have an individualized education plan (IEP). An IEP is a written document that includes information about the student's present level of educational performance, assessment of the extent the student can participate in a regular educational program and the type and degree of special services required, specific educational goals and instructional objectives, learning activities, and evaluation procedures and schedules. A sample IEP is shown in Fig. 11-1.

The first step in writing an IEP is to identify students with disabilities who have special educational needs. Once a student is identified as eligible and parental permission has been obtained, a planning conference is held to develop the IEP. By law the IEP must be developed by a committee comprised of the following members: an educator who is qualified to supervise special education, the teachers who will implement the IEP, the student's parents, and, when appropriate, the student. Because physical education is a required subject, the physical education teacher is involved in the design of the IEP. At this meeting, for each subject it is determined whether the student's needs will best be met by assignment to a regular, special, or combined educational placement.

The IEP must contain the following information:

1. *A statement of the student's present levels of educational performance.* A multitude of formal and informal assessment techniques are used to evaluate the student's current status with respect to psychomotor, cognitive, and affective development and to serve as a basis for planning the IEP.

2. *A list of annual goals and instructional objectives.* Goals are broad statements that provide direction for the school year. A series of short- and long-term performance objectives are developed to provide specific direction for the instructional endeavor.

3. *A description of special education and related services to be provided.* A student wtih a disability may require special materials, mechanical equipment, and supportive personnel to attain the educational goals. These must be designated as part of the IEP to ensure that the student will have these needs met. For example, a person skilled in signing may need to accompany a student with a hearing impairment to class, or a student with cerebral palsy may need a voice-augmented computer to communicate effectively. There must also be identification of the extent the student will be able to participate in regular education. Plans for mainstreaming the student into regular class activities, according to the student's special needs, are included. In physical education, the student may safely engage in some activities or units; other instructional units may not be appropriate. In this case alternative activities need to be designated.

4. *Dates and providers of service.* Specific dates for starting and ending special services must be identified. The expected duration of the services needs to be stated. The name and title of the individuals who will be providing the services must also be identified.

5. *Evaluation procedures.* Steps for assessing progress toward the established goals should be outlined. The extent to which the instructional objectives are attained should be determined. These may be through informal or standardized assessments arranged at appropriate intervals throughout the year. The student must be evaluated annually and the IEP updated. A full assessment must be made every 3 years.

Physical education is the only curricular area specifically named in PL 94-142. Because of this legislation, teachers have a unique opportunity to provide a quality educational experience to students with disabilities. Active involvement as a member of the school team in developing IEPs and commitment to helping each student attain the specified goals are responsibilities encumbant on the secondary school physical education teacher.

DETERMINING NEEDS AND SERVICES

By law each state is required to have a plan that describes specifically how PL 94-142 will be implemented within that state. The IEP process, sometimes referred to as the Admission, Review, and Dismissal (ARD) Process, is directed toward identifying students with disabilities, assessing their needs, enrolling students in the school's special education program, implementing the IEP, and providing an annual review to assess progress, and ultimately, if appropriate, fully integrating students from the special education program to the regular education program.[2]

To identify students who have disabilities that may require special consideration, the school system evaluates students using a variety of assessment techniques. Typically, there is a district-wide screening of all students in all school subjects to find children who have special needs and who may be eligible for special services.

After the screening is completed, an assessment is conducted. Those students who appear to have special needs are then referred to the special director. A multidisciplinary team of experts, including the physical education teacher or the adapted physical education teacher, then administer additional tests to gain a more comprehensive understanding of students' abilities and needs. Parental permission must be obtained before this assessment. During these formal assessment procedures, due process for students and their parents must be observed.

Parents and students must be informed about their rights under the law. There are procedural safeguards in

PL 94-142 to protect the rights of children with disabilities and their parents. According to these guidelines, parents must sign consent forms before assessment activities are undertaken to determine special education eligibility. The results of the assessment must be explained to parents. Parents must be told the nature of their child's disability and what services will be provided. If parents are not satisfied with the assessment, they have the right to an external assessment, that is, to an evaluation performed by an agency outside of the school. Parents have the right to appeal the outcome of the assessment if they disagree with it. Parents also have the right to attend the meeting to develop the IEP and indicate their approval by signing the document.

The assessment process is critical because it has a profound effect on the nature of the education received by the children tested. PL 94-142 delineates specific procedures to be used in the selection of the testing instruments, test administration, and evaluation. Tests used must be valid. Multiple measures, including formal and informal assessment procedures, are to be used to ensure an accurate and comprehensive picture of the child's abilities and needs. Care must be taken to ensure that the student's disability does not contribute to a mistaken diagnosis. For example, a student with cerebral palsy that has speech difficulty may be mistakenly classified as mentally retarded because the inability to speak well contributes to a poor test score.

Students with disabilities should be provided with opportunities to learn lifetime sports.

Courtesy of Sarah Rich, Ithaca College, Ithaca, NY.

Implementation Model

One model that may provide teachers with guidance in individualizing instruction to meet the special needs of students is the achievement-based curriculum model, or the ABC model.[1] As shown in Chapter 4, this model conceptualizes teachers as providers of services. The model is comprised of five components: plan, assess, prescribe, teach, and evaluate. This diagnostic-prescriptive model and others like it are helpful to teachers in assessing each student's abilities and designing interventions to meet needs. This model is helpful in designing individualized IEPs.

This model is designed to help teachers answer the following questions:

1. What content should be taught?
2. What is the current level of the student in terms of abilities and needs?
3. What instructional activities are appropriate?
4. What teaching styles and instructional strategies should be used?
5. What procedures should be used to determine whether the student has achieved the desired levels of performance?
6. What changes need to be made to help students achieve the desired levels of performance?

In the first step of the model, the planning step, content appropriate for instruction is identified and sequenced. Goals, broad statements of intent, and objectives (more specific outcomes) are established. Factors such as instructional time, personnel, facilities, equipment, and scheduling variables are considered in determining the nature and number of objectives. These objectives are sequentially arranged by program level, ranging from the preschool through the secondary school years. From this written program plan, instructional units are developed.

The second step involves assessing students' abilities. The written plan is constructed to meet the needs of the majority of students. To meet the needs of all students, the plan must be modified. Preassessment is conducted before the unit begins. Utilizing the stated unit objectives, the assessment process focuses on determining how much students already know and their potential for achievement, instructional activities to be prescribed, and the most effective grouping of students for instruction. This helps the teacher determine what instructional objectives need to be modified and whether any need to be deleted or added. For each instructional objective, class and student expectations are established.

Prescription is the third step in the model. Once the students have been assessed and the objectives modified, planning for instruction occurs. Specific instructional objectives to be learned by the students are identified, students are grouped appropriately for learning, instructional activities are selected, and sequential lesson plans for the unit are developed. Continuous monitoring and reassessment of students during the unit may lead to modification in the lessons.

Teaching the prescribed lesson is the fourth step. This involves engaging students in activities, practices, games, and drills to maximize on-task time relative to the objectives to be learned. Providing feedback and reinforcement, managing behaviors, and assisting students who have problems learning are incorporated into the teaching process. Continuously monitoring students' progress is a critical aspect of teaching.

The last step is evaluation. At the end of the unit of instruction, students are evaluated to determine whether the instruction was effective in achieving the unit's objectives. The teacher seeks to ascertain whether the class and the individual students have achieved the objectives. If the objectives were not achieved, reasons for nonachievement are identified. Thoughtful consideration is also given to other changes that need to be made to promote student achievement.

An integral part of the model is the use of feedback to make changes in the model based on observed results. Changes can be made in any component of the model. This model offers teachers a systematic approach to designing instruction to meet the needs of all students.

Physical Education Placement

Several states have specific guidelines governing the eligibility of children for special services, including adapted physical education. Typically, these guidelines are based on the administration of standardized tests. The norms or percentiles associated with these tests help make the placement process more objective and reduce the subjectivity that may lead to disagreement or inappropriate placement.

One state that has specific criteria for placement in adapted physical education is Alabama. The criteria are as follows:

1. Performs below the 30th percentile on standardized tests of:
   a. Motor development
   b. Motor proficiency
   c. Fundamental motor skills and patterns
   d. Physical fitness
   e. Games/sports skills
   f. Perceptual-motor functioning
   g. Posture screening

2. Exhibits a developmental delay of 2 years or more based on appropriate assessment instruments.
3. Functions within the severe or profound range as determined by special education eligibility standards.
4. Possesses social/emotional or physical capabilities that would render it unlikely for the student to reach his or her physical education goals without significant modification or exclusion from the regular physical education class.

These criteria pertain to the placement of students with disabilities into separate or specially designed physical education. This placement must be formally reviewed within the year.

Some students who may not fit these criteria, and thus are not eligible for special services, may benefit from adapted physical education. Sherrill[2] suggests that students who fall consistently below the 50th percentile on standardized tests should be provided with adapted physical education appropriate to their needs. This may be in the mainstream setting or part-time in the adapted physical education program (2 days a week) in conjunction with regular physical education.

Students who are eligible for special services should have them written into the IEP. Physical education must be written into the IEP to provide a legal basis for the providing of adapted physical education or for modifications in the regular school physical education program.

POPULATIONS SERVED

Many conditions require special consideration with respect to education and physical education. Some students have disabilities to such an extent that they are eligible for special services under PL 94-142. These conditions include mental retardation, auditory impairments, visual impairments, cerebral palsy, orthopedic impairments, epilepsy, learning disabilities, and emotional disorders. Other students may have conditions that also require special consideration. Students who have asthma, diabetes, low fitness levels, deficits in motor abilities, or are obese may require some modification of instructional strategies or programs to meet their needs.

Many adapted physical education textbooks contain a comprehensive description of these conditions, and specific information about how to tailor instruction to meet these students' needs is presented. It is important to use this information as a guide to help you understand the student and his or her needs. However, be careful about labeling students and making stereotypical assumptions about their abilities, for example, saying that all students with hearing impairments have balance problems or all individuals with cerebral palsy have impaired cognitive function. Take the time to know each student in terms of his or her cognitive, affective, and psychomotor abilities. This way you can more readily modify instruction and program content to meet each student's needs. It is important to be familiar with each student's medical restrictions and to use this information as guidelines for instruction. It may also be helpful to use other experts, such as a psychologist, as consultants in designing educational experiences for students with special needs.

Asthma

A chronic lung disease, asthma is typically managed through the use of medication. Many children outgrow asthma during puberty, but it appears that exercise-induced asthma occurs at all ages. Asthma attacks are characterized by breathing distress, wheezing, coughing, and feelings of constriction in the chest. Medication taken orally or through an inhaler is usually effective in treating an attack and should be taken immediately at first warnings of an impending attack. When an attack is severe, the child may suffer from a lack of oxygen, turn cyanotic, and require emergency measures.

When asthma is properly managed, students can participate in vigorous physical activities. Warm-ups are recommended before exercise, and each student's tolerance for exercise duration and intenstiy should be determined. Some students may find activities that are intermittent in nature—vigorous exercise followed by a period of rest (volleyball or sprints followed by a rest period) more suitable to their abilities than activities that are of a longer duration (running distances). It should also be noted that when students with asthma are also overweight and have a low fitness level, they may experience breathing discomfort as a consequence of these conditions, not asthma. Helping these students attain progressively a high level of fitness will alleviate this discomfort. While students should be encouraged to be active, they should also be allowed to be the judge of their condition. Students should be free to step aside during an activity to rest if needed.

Cardiac Conditions

Cardiovascular conditions may be congenital or acquired in nature. Congenital problems, those that exist at birth, may be corrected with surgery. Students with congenital conditions that have been corrected often have no restriction on their physical activities. In other situations where the defect cannot be corrected, the physician may limit physical activity. Acquired heart disease in children and youths often occurs as a result of rheumatic fever, which leaves the heart damaged in some way. The degree of disability varies among individuals, thus the restrictions on physical activity differ greatly.

The physical education teacher should work closely with the student's physician in designing an appropriate physical activity program. The prescribed program should be followed carefully, and no modifications should be made without the physician's approval. Within the limitations imposed, the student should be encouraged to work to his or her fullest capacity.

Cerebral Palsy

Cerebral palsy is a nonprogressive neuromuscular condition resulting from damage to the motor areas of the brain. In nearly 90% of the cases, this damage occurs before or during birth. The degree of involvement may be mild, moderate, or severe. Many children who have cerebral palsy often have other disabilities as well because the conditions that caused the motor dysfunction often affect other areas of the brain. Mental retardation, speech problems, learning disabilities, visual and auditory impairments, seizures, and reflex problems are common. It is important, however, to focus on each individual's condition. Not all cerebral palsy victims have mental retardation—in fact, many are of normal intelligence. Difficulties in speech and language function often hamper the assessment of intelligence. Electronic communication devices are being used increasingly to help individuals with cerebral palsy communicate more easily.

Many individuals with cerebral palsy have difficulty in moving because of the retention of reflexes that are usually lost at an early age by their peers. Some students with cerebral palsy may be ambulatory, while others may require the use of a wheelchair. Helping individuals achieve competency in the control of simple movements is an important goal. Exercises that contribute to the development of strength and increased range of motion are frequently needed. Relaxation and stress control techniques may be particularly useful in helping the student cope with spasticity, a common condition associated with cerebral palsy. There are also a diversity of sports, dance, and aquatic activities that students with cerebral palsy can learn and enjoy. Jones[3] suggests that persons with cerebral palsy may do well in individual sports such as archery, bowling, bicycling, track and field, swimming, table tennis, and weight lifting. The emphasis in teaching should be on the ability of the student, not the disability.

Emotional Disorders

Students with severe emotional disorders may require special considerations to learn. There are a myriad of emotional disorders, such as schizophrenia, depression, anxiety, and conduct disorders such as extreme aggression with which teachers must be prepared to work.

One emotional disorder teachers may encounter is Tourette's syndrome. This syndrome is characterized by involuntary, repetitive, rapid, and purposeless movements of various muscles groups and various vocalizations. These vocalizations may be described as a series of grunts, yelps, barks, sniffs, and words. Many individuals with this syndrome have the uncontrollable urge to utter obscenities. Stress may heighten these symptoms. Teachers should be aware that students with Tourette's syndrome have little control over these muscular movements and vocalizations.

Most students with emotional disorders benefit from a learning environment that is structured, fair, and consistent. Clearly defined rules and expectations for behavior are important. Some students are prone to emotional outbursts, and it may be helpful to give some forethought as to how you will handle these situations.

Students may also benefit from learning how to express their hostility in socially accepted ways. Movement offers many individuals a release for anger; learning how to channel one's anger and aggression into working out rather than toward other people is an important outcome.

Students who are overanxious or withdrawn require extra patience. Students should not be forced to participate in activities they fear or intensely dislike. Students who have difficulty relating to their peers or working in groups perhaps should be introduced to individual sports activities and dual activities first. The complexities of relating to others in team sports may be too difficult for some students until they gain some social skills.

Extra attention should be given to fostering feelings of self-worth and enhancing students' self-esteem. Some students may react excessively to criticism or even helpful suggestions. Consistent standards for behavior and recognition of accomplishments may help these students to benefit from the physical education program.

Auditory Impairment

Students who are deaf or hearing impaired can usually participate successfully in most physical education activities when careful attention is given to their needs. Because much of the instruction is given verbally, a student with an auditory disorder has difficulty hearing what is being said. Many children with severe auditory impairments have speech problems and may experience difficulty when trying to converse with their peers.

When students with severe auditory impairments are mainstreamed into physical education, the teacher can do several things to enhance the quality of the experience for these youths. When the students first enter the class, the teacher should plan activities and instruction to reduce the amount of verbal communication. The teacher should be carefully positioned so that the students can easily see the teacher. This is particularly important for students who lip-read. Using task cards and other teaching strategies that convey information through nonverbal means—demonstrations and videotapes, for example—helps the students learn more easily. It may be helpful to learn simple signs to communicate more directly with students who are hearing impaired.

Some students with auditory impairments have difficulty in relating to their peers. Before involving them in team sports activities, provide opportunities for them to know and be accepted by class members. Individual activities that allow students to be members of the class and gain confidence in their abilities to perform perhaps should be taught first. Then they can progress to team sports activities. Students who wear hearing aids may prefer activities in which they can continue to use this device.

Be sure to develop consistent hand signals for such activities as starting, stopping, moving to an area, or assembling by the teacher for safety reasons. Remember that in team sports games where officiating occurs, hand signals may need to be used.

Some students with auditory impairments have difficulty with balance. Activities that encourage the development of static and dynamic balance should be incorporated in these students' physical education program. Where problems are severe, these students may benefit from more intensive instructions and part-time placement in the adapted physical education program.

Dance can make an important contribution to the development of communication abilities. Dance provides an opportunity for expression of feelings and emotions, an important outlet for those with inadequate speech. Placing the stereo speakers on the floor to provide vibrations and using a metronome or a blinking light can help students gain a sense of the rhythm of the music.

Learning Disabilities

Students who are labeled as learning disabled exhibit a wide range of characteristics. Although this is a heterogeneous group, certain behaviors may be exhibited quite frequently. These behaviors include hyperactivity, distractibility, dissociation, perseveration, social imperception, immature body image, poor spatial orientation, and awkwardness. Students who are hyperactive have difficulty performing academically because they can seldom sit still long enough to complete a task. They may experience dissociation, the inability to perceive things as a meaningful whole, and may have difficulty remembering sequences. They are easily distracted and cannot concentrate their attention on a task or a person. In contrast to distractibility, some students exhibit perseveration, that is, they continue to perform the behavior after it should be stopped (for example, continuing to bounce a ball long after being signaled to stop). Poor social adjustment may be present; some students may have difficulty making friends and interacting with their classmates. Others exhibit a poor body image and spatial orientation; they have difficulty in discriminating directions and estimating distances. Clumsiness may be present.

It is important, as with all disabilities, that the physical education program focuses on the students' abilities and provides opportunities for improvement where possible. Students with learning disabilities may benefit from a program that is highly structured and incorporates the use of routines (for example, set procedures for entering the class, for attendance, and for rotating from station to station). Clear boundaries and behavioral limits are important. If task cards are used, realize that some students may have difficulty in reading and following directions, and assistance should be readily provided. Teaching by the whole-part-whole method may be helpful in instructing students who tend to dissociate. The use of small groups and moving from instruction in individual activities to group activities may be helpful in teaching social skills. Students who are clumsy and exhibit difficulty in eye-hand coordination and balance should be helped to find success in activities suited to their abilities; as success is experienced and one's self-concept is enhanced, other activities can be introduced to help improve areas that need to be strengthened.

Mental Retardation

Mental retardation varies in degree according to the extent of mental impairment and may be mild, moderate, severe, or profound. Individuals who perform two or more standard deviations below the average on intelligence tests, who have an IQ of approximately 70, and who exhibit deficits in adaptive behavior (developmentally delayed) are classified as mentally retarded.[2]

Students who are mildly retarded, with IQs ranging approximately from 50 to 75, are often mainstreamed into the regular classroom and physical education. Those students with IQs below 50 generally cannot function in the regular educational environment and are usually placed in special classes.

Students who are mildly retarded generally are slower to understand and respond to directions, have difficulty with concepts, may require longer to complete tasks, and progress less rapidly. The physical education program should build on each student's level of fitness and motor development.

Fitness programs should start at each student's current level and progress from there. Specific directions and goal setting help students know what is expected of them and provide motivation to persist. Goals that are challenging (yet attainable) and experiences that provide for frequent success help students become physically fit. Be sure to reward effort and reinforce hard work.

Build competency in the fundamental skills and then apply these skills to various sports. Demonstrations and modeling of desired movements rather than verbalization should be used. To avoid boredom and waning of attention, keep practice periods short. Try to decrease frustration by using progressions that provide frequent success. Acknowledging improvements and accomplish-

ments, even if they are small, will encourage students to keep trying.

Orthopedic Disabilities

Physical ailments in a wide range are encompassed within orthopedic disabilities. Some students may have an amputation and wear a prosthesis, others have disabilities that require the use of a wheelchair, and yet other students may have posture disorders that require bracing. It is difficult to offer guidance for the conduct of physical education programs for students with such a wide range of disabilities. As for other disabilities, the best advice is to focus on the students' abilities and needs and make modifications as necessary.

Many orthopedic disabilities interfere with the students' mobility, and activities that require running may need to be modified accordingly. Individualized programs for fitness and teaching styles that allow students to progress at their own rate while learning are beneficial to students with orthopedic impairments. Aquatics and dance activities are important because they are easy to accommodate to individual differences. As with other secondary school students, it is important to help these students acquire competency in lifetime sports, sports that they can participate in with able-bodied individuals as well as with individuals with disabilities.

Special consideration must be given to provide adequate time after class for health care for students who wear braces or prostheses or use a wheelchair. These students may require extra time to wash up and to take proper steps to ensure that related health conditions do not arise, such as pressure sores or rashes from perspiration. It may be helpful to schedule physical education the period before lunch or study hall, or the last period of the day to provide extra time. Some students may be sensitive about changing clothes or performing special aftercare in the locker room and should be given a private place.

Epilepsy or Seizure Disorders

The terms *epilepsy, convulsive disorders,* and *seizure disorders* are used interchangeably to describe a chronic condition of the central nervous system characterized by various types of seizures. A seizure is a sudden change in consciousness accompanied by involuntary motor activity and caused by abnormal electrical activity of cortical neurons. Most individuals are on medication that is highly effective in controlling seizures.

There are several types of seizures. Absence seizures involve a brief impairment of consciousness, usually no more than 30 seconds. During this time the student appears to be dazed or inattentive. The student and often the teacher may not even be aware that this type of seizure has occurred. Myoclonic seizures are brief in nature and manifested by violent contractions of the muscles in some part or in the entire body. Consciousness may be lost. The most easily recognized of all seizures are the tonic-clonic seizures. Complete neurological involvement occurs; continuous contraction of the muscles is followed by intermittent contraction and relaxation of the muscles. Unconsciousness, rigidness and tremors, and loss of control of the bladder and bowels occur.

Teachers should be prepared to recognize the signs of a seizure and take proper precautions so that the chances of the student getting hurt are minimized. Clear the area around the student and make sure that the mouth and nose are clear so that the student can breathe. Seizures must run their course. Teachers and students should remain calm. When the seizure is over, rest should be allowed if the student desires.

The social stigma associated with epilepsy is one of the most difficult challenges. Having a seizure in front of classmates can be embarrassing. Information about epilepsy as well as other disabilities should be a integral part of the health curriculum of the school. Discussing epilepsy as a reaction to a seizure can further contribute to the self-consciousness the student feels. An accepting and caring attitude on the part of the teacher and classmates can help the student feel more comfortable.

Most students with epilepsy are under the supervision of a physician, and medical guidelines regarding participation should be followed closely. Many of these students have virtually no restrictions on their activities. They, like their peers, require good supervision and benefit from a quality physical education program. Students whose seizures are not yet medically controlled may be restricted from certain activities, such as those that might result in a fall, for example, climbing or cycling.

Visual Impairment

Legally blind students may have partial sight, or they may be completely blind. This disability imposes problems in mobility for many individuals. Because of this, participation in certain activities may not be feasible, but this determination should be made on an individual basis. Many students with visual impairments can successfully participate in physical education with their sighted classmates, provided attention is given to their needs.

Students who are visually impaired need opportunities to develop confidence in their abilities to move as freely and safely as possible. Teachers should keep the learning environment stable and be careful not to leave equipment lying around. Classmates should be instructed as to the assistance needed and how it may best be provided. For example, in running activities the student who is visually impaired should hold onto the upper arm of the sighted partner, not vice versa. Sighted students should take the initiative to identify themselves and make their presence and name known when interacting—they should not assume that they can be recognized from the sound of their voice.

Many activities can be successfully performed by students with limited vision, although certain activities that require visual acuity may be difficult, such as badminton. Special equipment may facilitate participation, such as electronic balls with beepers for softball or basketball or guide rails for bowling. Creativity on the part of the teacher can enhance learning as well. A balloon mounted on a target lets the student know when he or she has been successful in archery; other adaptations to activities to provide a sound to help the student's efforts can be made. The ability of the physical education teacher to give precise and vivid verbal instructions is critical. At times the student may benefit from being manually guided through the initial efforts at a skill.

Other Disabilities

In a secondary physical education class, the teacher should be prepared to work with students with a host of disabilities. In addition to those conditions mentioned earlier, the teacher may have students with diabetes, a variety of learning disabilities, eating disorders, arthritis, and multiple sclerosis, for example. Meeting such a diverse range of needs requires commitment to the belief that quality physical education is the right of each student. Special consideration of individual needs and modifying the type, intensity, and duration of activity according to these needs is the cornerstone of a quality physical education program.

At the secondary level, it is important that time be devoted to help students develop competency in lifetime sports so that they can participate in expanding community recreational activities and expanded opportunities for the disabled. Teachers can also help students with disabilities become aware of the competitive sport opportunities available to them and gain the necessary skills to participate in these activities.

MEETING SPECIAL NEEDS

Considerable thought and planning are needed to make mainstreaming effective and physical education a successful experience for all students involved. Teachers can help enhance the acceptance of students with disabilities by helping all students understand the problems related to being disabled and what special assistance may be required. Teachers might incorporate activities especially designed for individuals with disabilities into the curriculum. For example, beep baseball, which is played with a softball that emits a tone, can be used to introduce students to some of the difficulties experienced by individuals with visual impairments. Students should understand that each person is worthwhile and is to be respected.

Several goals are related to the mainstreaming of students with disabilities. First, it is important to help students develop life skills to enable them to be as independent as possible. Motor skills and physical fitness are important to leading a productive and active life. Second, the physical education experience should help contribute to the development of a positive self-concept. This is a difficult task in a society where individuals encounter discrimination because they are different. Physical education can help students accept their abilities and enable them to reach their fullest potential as movers by modifying activities to meet their needs. Third, attention must be given to helping students with disabilities learn appropriate social skills and behavior relating to sports and recreational activities.

Accomplishing Fitness and Motor Goals

Health-related fitness is important for all students, including those students with disabilities. Adequate physical fitness can enhance the ability of students to function independently and accomplish the tasks of daily living, including those associated with school. It also contributes positively to the performance of motor skills.

Fitness programs should emphasize physical fitness objectives appropriate to the student's abilities and needs. The fitness program should offer all students the opportunity to begin at a point suitable to their current fitness status and to progress to higher levels. Fitness principles pertaining to the intensity, duration, and frequency of exercise as well as to overload, warm-up, and cool-down should be followed, with modifications as needed. Students should have the opportunity to choose between several activities according to their preference and needs. For example, a student who is a single-leg amputee may find a swimming program more enjoyable and effective in developing cardiovascular endurance than a running program. Teachers must also know which exercises and activities are not recommended for each student. Task analysis can be used to structure exercises into easy, medium, and difficult progressions and thereby provide students with exercises that are compatible with their present abilities.

The refinement of motor patterns and their application to sports skills should also be emphasized. Where students exhibit poor motor performance, steps must be taken to remediate the problem. The goal is to develop mature movement patterns that are mechanically efficient, or, as Sherrill[2] states, patterns that conform more or less to "good form" for adults. "Good form," however, encompasses a wide range of individual differences and must also be assessed in light of the limitations imposed by the disability. Students who exhibit signs of immaturity in

their movement patterns, such as inconsistency, asymmetry, poor balance, extraneous motions, inability to maintain rhythm or pattern, or inability to control force need help in refining their movements. The emphasis should be on the development of motor skills that are the most functionally relevant.

It is also important at the secondary level to help students learn individual and lifetime sports skills so that they may participate in recreational and leisure activities enjoyed by so many people. Teachers should not hesitate to modify the activity to help students be successful. For example, tennis can be modified by using a wider court (doubles boundaries instead of singles), a different size racquet, a slower-bouncing ball, moving the service line, or by allowing the ball to bounce twice.

Students with disabilities may often have posture problems either as a consequence of their disability or low physical fitness. Exercises are often employed to help strengthen needed muscle groups and improve flexibility. Body awareness and image activities, balancing tasks, and relaxation training are also used to help students develop proper posture.

Some students with disabilities may experience difficulty in physical education because of past inactivity. They may have not been encouraged to be physically active. In some cases parental overconcern and anxiety about safety may have needlessly limited the child's activity. Students may be reluctant to participate because past experiences have resulted in failures and embarrassment in front of their peers.

The students' self-concept may affect their learning of motor skills. Students with disabilities may have a lower self-concept than their able-bodied classmates. Expectations of failure and fear of embarrassment contribute to a reluctance to learn. Teachers must recognize that this may interfere with learning and take steps to deal with these negative feelings. Personalization, individualization, praise, and success can help students gain more positive self-concepts and perceptions of themselves as competent movers.

If the student's level of fitness or motor development is low, placement in an adapted physical education class on a full- or part-time basis may be indicated. Many activities can be successfully modified to accommodate a wide range of abilities within the class. However, there may be students whose needs may best be met through other placement options.

Meeting Cognitive Needs

The level of cognitive functioning must be considered in placing students with disabilities in physical education. The failure to consider this aspect of development in the placement decision can lead to difficulty and failure.

Students whose cognitive development is delayed or

Many students with disabilities enjoy the opportunity to participate in athletic competitions.
Courtesy of Sarah Rich, Ithaca College, Ithaca, NY.

emphasis on repetition and practice, and working in small groups may be helpful. Goal setting and specified outcomes help maintain students' attention and motivation.

Achieving Effective Outcomes

Developing social skills is important for all students in the mainstreamed setting. A supportive learning environment that fosters respect for each individual and discourages discriminatory behavior is essential if mainstreaming is to be successful.

Some students with disabilities may have limited communication skills and may find it difficult to interact with their peers. Students who are deaf or hearing impaired, for example, may have difficulties with their speech, and other students may find it difficult to understand and converse with them.

Adolescence is a critical time for students with disabilities. Peer relationships are important at this stage of development. Structuring the learning environment to provide opportunities for classmates to work together in group activities that require cooperation, sharing, and acceptance of responsibility can be helpful in developing peer relationships. Situations should be structured to allow students with disabilities to experience success in front of their peers. Avoid situations that embarrass students or lead to failure in front of their peers.

Some students require a structured and consistent learning environment to achieve. Students with emotional disorders or cognitive impairments work better in an environment that is highly organized and has clear limits for behaviors. Teachers can help these students by clearly defining the rules, setting consequences, and reinforcing appropriate behavior. Helping students achieve self-control is an important learning outcome.

As a teacher, try not to be overprotective of students with disabilities. Teachers should know the characteristics of each disability and how it may affect learning. Yet the teacher must be aware of the abilities each student brings to the learning situation. Focus on what each student can do, and provide a safe environment in which to learn. Give students confidence in their abilities by promoting independence.

Careful attention needs to be given to the promotion of a positive self-concept and self-esteem in students with disabilities. Help each student with disabilities develop competence in line with their disabilities. Success builds confidence and feelings of self-worth; it leads to persistence and further success. Students who are disabled should have the opportunity to compare their efforts and successes with those of similar abilities and disabilities, not only against the average performer in the mainstream. There are increased opportunities for recreational and competitive participation for students with disabilities with peers who have similar disabilities. This is helpful in promoting self-acceptance.

impaired may experience difficulty in comprehending the material presented and following directions. Problems in processing information, poor vocabulary, short attention span, and difficulty in recalling and retaining material may hinder students' learning. Difficulty may also be encountered in transferring and generalizing the skills learned in one situation to other situations. Some students have trouble asking for help or requesting assistance.

Demonstrations and verbal cueing, short explanations followed by an immediate opportunity to respond, and structured learning experiences are helpful approaches to learning for students with cognitive disabilities. Multisensory approaches to learning should be used. Some students do not respond well to visual or auditory approaches. These students may benefit from being physically guided through the skill. Peer tutors can be helpful in modeling appropriate skills and providing learners with frequent feedback and reinforcement. There should be an

Encourage the establishment of realistic goals and be supportive of efforts to attain them. Be positive and encouraging toward all students because these behaviors communicate feelings of worth. Convey to students that you genuinely care about them as individuals and value them for who they are, not just for their fitness or motor ability.

ENHANCING MAINSTREAMING

Successful mainstreaming and adapted physical education require sound preparation and a high level of commitment to meet the needs of all students. Students' needs are best met when the school is committed not only to complying with the letter of the law but also with the spirit of the law.

Comprehensive in-service training should be provided for all teachers to enhance their ability to work with students with disabilities. Information about various disabilities, special medical needs, contraindications relative to participation, and suggestions about how program content and teaching strategies can be modified to meet students' needs is useful.

Some schools have adapted physical education teachers employed full-time on their staff. These specialists are responsible for conducting the adapted physical education program. Other school districts employ adapted physical education teachers that are itinerant in nature. They travel from school to school within the district. These itinerant teachers may be responsible for conducting the adapted physical education program in each of the district's schools, or they may serve as consultants to the regular physical education teachers in the district, sharing ideas and providing information on how to best meet the needs of students with disabilities.

To ensure public and parental support for physical education for students with disabilities, the teacher must inform people about the contributions a quality physical education program can make to the lives of all students. Information pertaining to the objectives of the program and its content should be shared.

Whether the needs of students with disabilities are successfully met depends on the teacher's ability to individualize the physical education experience to meet the needs of each student. The program of activities must be carefully selected, teaching styles must take into account each student's starting point, and provisions must be made to allow for growth and progress within the capabilities of the individual.

Guidelines for Working with Students with Disabilities

The following general guidelines may be of assistance in working with secondary school students who have disabilities regardless of whether they are mainstreamed in the regular physical education program or placed in an adapted physical education program on a full- or part-time basis.

◆ Check carefully on the student's medical clearance. A written release from the student's physician must be on file before allowing participation. Be sure the physician is thoroughly informed about the nature of the activities offered in the physical education program. If a physician is not informed, the student may be unnecessarily restricted because of inaccurate perceptions about the program. Most students with disabilities can enjoy and benefit from a physical education program that is sensitive to their needs. A physician who is knowledgeable about the program can make a more informed judgment about the student's participation.

◆ Cooperate with the physician and parents in planning the program. They are the individuals who are most knowledgeable about the history of the disability and the student's abilities. Their knowledge and insight are valuable in designing a program to be most beneficial to the student. When appropriate, involve the student in the process. Determine the student's needs and capabilities as well as his or her interests.

◆ Test the motor skills and physical fitness levels of each student. These should be tested in areas where medical permission for participation has been granted.

◆ Consider all aspects of development in determining the appropriate program for the student. Cognitive and affective development needs are as important as psychomotor needs. The development level and needs of the whole person must be considered in planning the program.

◆ Provide challenges for the student. Students with disabilities need and respond to the challenge of a progressive program. They welcome the opportunity to test their abilities. The fun, satisfaction, and success associated with meeting challenges contribute positively to the outcomes of the physical education program. Students' feelings about their physical education experience are important too.

◆ Provide time for extra help. Individual assistance may make the difference between a successful and unsuccessful physical education experience. Extra assistance or one-on-one attention provided by peers, paraprofessionals, or the teacher can do much in helping students with disabilities attain their goals.

◆ Promote acceptance of students with disabilities. Stress acceptance of all individuals and an appreciation of individual differences. Teachers who model acceptance through their words and actions and help students understand and realize the challenges faced by individuals with disabilities do much to engender peer acceptance.

◆ Adapt the activity to the student rather than the student to the activity. Focus on the students' abilities, rather than the disability. Modify the activity to meet the needs of students.

◆ Provide safe facilities and equipment. Although this is essential in any physical education class, extra safeguards must be taken in a physical education class that includes students with disabilities.

◆ Provide suitable extra-class activities. Intramurals, club sports, and athletic opportunities are mandated by law. Moreover, these activities are just as important for students with disabilities as they are for their nondisabled peers. These activities are an integral part of the total physical education curriculum, and opportunities to participate in them are important to all students. Acquaint students with competitive opportunities available for individuals with disabilities such as the Special Olympics or the Paralympics.

◆ Focus efforts on building competency in fundamental motor skills so that students can move effectively. Build physical fitness; it is important for all students' health and well-being. Competency in fundamental skills and physical fitness may contribute to increased independence in students with disabilities.

◆ Incorporate lifetime sport activities into the program. Provide opportunities for students to develop competency in a sport that is enjoyable and appropriate for lifelong participation. Inform students about recreational opportunities in the community so that they can make an effective transition from participation in school programs to those in the community.

◆ Keep the program under constant evaluation. Careful records should be kept showing the student's test scores, activities, and accomplishments. In this way, the physical education teacher will know whether the program is reaching its objectives. Moreover, discussion of the student's progress with the student, parents, school administrator, and student's physician will be easier. A microcomputer may be helpful in recording data and writing reports.

Every student needs a quality physical education program. Whether teaching regular or adapted physical education, teachers must be prepared to make program and instructional adaptations skillfully to meet the needs of their students.

Special Resources

There are several resources available that would be of assistance to secondary school physical education teachers in working with students with disabilities. These specially designed programs offer a diversity of activities and suggestions to help students with special needs safely and successfully participate in physical education.

Project ACTIVE. ACTIVE is an acronym standing for All Children Totally InVolved Exercising.[4] This program offers information on providing direct services to students with psychomotor problems. A diagnostic-based teaching and individualized learning approach is empha-

sized. A test battery and program manuals provide information relative to the following conditions: low motor ability, low physical vitality, postural abnormalities, nutritional deficiencies, respiratory problems, motor disabilities, and communication disorders. In-service training information is also included in this program.

Project UNIQUE. Assessing the fitness status of students with sensory (blind or deaf) or orthopedic disabilities is addressed in UNIQUE.[5] Fitness test items that can easily be administered in a mainstreamed setting and a special setting are included.

Project I CAN. I CAN represents programatic directions: Individualized instruction, Create social leisure competence, Associate all learnings, and Narrow the gap between theory and practice.[6] The three programs included within this model emphasize the development of preprimary skills, primary skills, and sports and recreational skills. Observational assessment techniques, goals, objectives, activities, instructional strategies, and evaluation techniques for each of the three program areas are provided. Five teaching tasks are emphasized within each program: planning, assessing, prescribing, teaching, and evaluation.

PEOPEL. A peer-tutoring approach, Physical Education Opportunity Program for Exceptional Learners (PEOPEL) pairs trained students with students with disabilities.[7] The peer-tutors complete a training program that provides them with the skills to work effectively with individuals with special needs. The use of peer tutors offers students with disabilities more individualized attention and increases their chances for success. The peer tutors learn how to interact with students with disabilities and realize a great deal of satisfaction from their involvment.

Sports for the Disabled

Many students with disabilities have the potential to be excellent athletes. Depending on the nature and severity of the disability, some students can compete equitably with their able-bodied peers. Other students may choose to compete against individuals with comparable disabilities.

Within the past two decades, competitive sport opportunities for individuals with disabilities have grown tremendously. Opportunities may be found at the local, regional, state, national, and international levels. Sport organizations for the disabled include the National Association of Sports for Cerebral Palsy (NASCP), the United States Association for Blind Athletes (USABA), the United States Amputee Athletic Association (USAAA), the National Wheelchair Athletic Association (NWAA), the National Handicapped Sports and Recreation Association (NHRSA), and the Special Olympics (Box 11-4). These competitions may involve specially

BOX 11-4

SELECTED GOVERNING BODIES FOR SPORTS FOR DISABLED ATHLETES

National Wheelchair Athletic Association (NWAA)
1604 E. Pikes Peak Ave.
Colorado Springs, CO 80901

National Association of Sports for Cerebral Palsy (NASCP)
66 East 34th Street
New York, NY 10016

United States Association for Blind Athletes (USABA)
55 West California Avenue
Beach Haven Park, NJ 08008

United States Amputee Athletic Association (USAAA)
Route 2, County Line
Fairview, TN 37062

National Handicapped Sports and Recreation Association (NHSRA)
1145 19th Street NW, Suite 717
Washington, DC 20036

Special Olympics
1350 New York Avenue NW
Suite 500
Washington, DC 20005

American Athletic Association for the Deaf (AAAD)
1134 Davenport Drive
Burton, MI 48529

---

adapted sports such as wheelchair basketball, quadraplegic rugby, or beep baseball, and individual sports such as wheelchair tennis and golf. Sometimes special classification systems are used to help equalize abilities and ensure fair competition.

Another popular trend is the growth of integrated or unified sport teams. In sports such as softball, volleyball, basketball, and bowling, disabled and nondisabled athletes compete on the same team.

All students should have the opportunity to compete in sports. Whether they compete as part of a unified team or in sports specially designed for the disabled, the value of the sports experience makes it important that it be available for those who wish to pursue it. Physical education teachers can help students make contact with associations sponsoring appropriate activities and develop skills, attitudes, and habits.

SUMMARY

Within the past two decades, legislation by Federal and state governments has significantly affected the education of children with disabilities. This legislation has mandated that all children have an equal opportunity for education in our schools. PL 94-142, the Education of All Handicapped Children Act, requires that each child with disabilities have an individualized educational plan and be educated in the least restrictive environment. By law, physical education services are to be included as part of that plan.

Meeting the fitness, motor, cognitive, and affective needs of all children is a challenging task. To accomplish this goal, teachers must individualize instruction, carefully select program content, and provide opportunities for success and achievement within the capabilities of each individual.

FOR REVIEW

1. Identify barriers to effective mainstreaming in secondary school physical education and suggest means by which these barriers can be overcome.
2. Obtain a copy of the state laws pertaining to the education of children with disabilities. What are the implications of these laws for the conduct of physical education programs?
3. Select a specific disability and, using your adapted physical education text, identify characteristics associated with that condition. Next, for a selected lifetime sport, describe how instruction may need to be modified to provide a successful physical education experience for a student with this disability.

REFERENCES

1. Wessel JA, Kelly L: *Achievement-based curriculum development in physical education,* Philadelphia, 1986, Lea & Febiger.
2. Sherrill C: *Adapted physical education and recreation: a multidisciplinary approach,* Dubuque, Iowa, 1986, William C Brown.
3. Jones JA: *Training guide to cerebral palsy sports,* ed 2, New York, National Association of Sports for Cerebral Palsy.
4. Vodola T: *Motor disabilities or limitations,* Oakhurst, NJ, 1976, Project ACTIVE.
5. Winneck JP, Short FX: *Physical fitness testing of the disabled: project UNIQUE,* Champaign, Ill, 1985, Human Kinetics.
6. Wessel J, editor: *Planning individualized educational programs in special education with examples from I CAN,* Northbrook, Ill, 1977, Hubbard.
7. Irmer L: *PEOPEL Project materials,* Phoenix, Ariz.

ANNOTATED READINGS

American Alliance for Health, Physical Education, Recreation and Dance: *Sport instruction for individuals with disabilities: the best of practical pointers,* Reston, Va, 1991, AAHPERD.
  Provides practical suggestions for teaching team, individual, and dual sports and suggestions relating to the organization and administration of programs.
Eichstaedt CB, Lavay BW: *Physical activity for individuals with retardation,* Champaign, Ill, 1992, Human Kinetics.
  Presents characteristics and needs of individuals with mental retardation and methods for the acquisition of fitness and movement skills.

Shepard RJ: *Fitness in special populations,* Champaign, Ill, 1990, Human Kinetics.

A good overview of fitness for children with disabilities, including fitness assessment, training programs, and instructional strategies.

Sherrill C: *Adapted physical education and recreation: a multidisciplinary approach,* Dubuque, Iowa, 1986, William C Brown.

A comprehensive resource for teachers of students with disabilities.

Wessel JA, Kelly L: *Achievement-based curriculum development in physical education,* Philadelphia, 1986, Lea & Febiger.

An excellent resource for designing physical education programs for students with special needs.

Winnick JP, editor: *Adapted physical education and sport,* Champaign, Ill, 1990, Human Kinetics.

Emphasizes a developmental approach to physical education and sports for individuals with special needs, including suggestions to promote effective mainstreaming.

CHAPTER 12

Safety and Administration

CHAPTER OBJECTIVES
◆ To offer guidelines for creating and maintaining a safe learning environment
◆ To describe departmental policies and procedures that facilitate the establishment of an effective instructional situation
◆ To describe how microcomputers can be used effectively in secondary school physical education programs

Students' safety is one of the foremost considerations in planning and conducting the physical education program. Additionally, because of the increasing number of lawsuits involving physical education, teachers should familiarize themselves with the factors that contribute to legal liability. In planning for a safe learning environment, supervisory, instructional, environmental, and emergency health care procedures should be taken into account when teaching.

Class management influences the attainment of instructional outcomes. Establishing, communicating, and implementing departmental policies and procedures should be done in an efficient manner so that the time available for instruction is maximized. Teachers are also using microcomputers to complete a myriad of administrative tasks more efficiently.

CREATING AND MAINTAINING A SAFE LEARNING ENVIRONMENT

A major responsibility of every teacher is to create and maintain a safe environment for learning for their students. By its very nature, physical education involves students participating in physical activities that involve various degrees of inherent risks. In fact, approximately half of all accidents that occur within the school setting occur in physical education.[1] Teachers need to be cognizant of the potential for accidents, be familiar with the inherent safety hazards associated with each activity, and take ap-

propriate measures to reduce the possibility of injuries occurring.

The number of lawsuits in physical education has grown tremendously within the past decade and continues to escalate.[2] For this reason it is important that every physical education teacher has a clear understanding of what constitutes legal liability, the situations and conditions that often lead to legal liability, and the actions that can be taken to minimize these problems.

Legal Liability

Liability is the responsibility and obligation to perform a duty by a particular individual or group that is enforceable by court action. For example, teachers are required by their contracts to fulfill their responsibilities to their students in a reasonable and prudent manner, exhibiting behavior that may be expected of a professional with similar years of training and credentials. Because liability is a legal matter, it must be proved in a court of law.

A tort is a legal wrong that directly or indirectly results in an injury to another individual or property. A tort can occur as a result of an act of omission or commission. An act of omission occurs when an accident results because of the failure to perform a legal duty, such as when a teacher fails to obey fire alarm procedures and an injury occurs. An act of commission occurs when the performance of an unlawful act, such as an assault, results in an accident.

Tort liability, commonly referred to as legal liability, involves a lawsuit for a breach of duty. The individual or group initiating the lawsuit is called the plaintiff(s), and the individual or group, for example, the school board, against whom the action is brought is referred to as the defendant(s). The plaintiff seeks to prove to the court that the defendant is at fault, that this fault or behavior led to an injury or loss to the plaintiff, and that the defendant is legally responsible.

Negligence

Many of the lawsuits involving injuries to participants in physical education activities focus on the issue of negligence. Lawsuits involving negligence assess whether the physical education teacher acted in a reasonable and prudent manner and exhibited the behavior and a standard of care that a trained professional would exhibit in a similar situation.

Teachers are responsible for the well-being of all students in the class. They must provide appropriate instruction, adequate supervision, and conduct the activity in a safe manner. When failure to meet these responsibilities results in an injury, teachers can be found negligent. By law, all of these elements must be present for the teacher to be considered negligent:

1. The individual in charge had the duty or responsibility to ensure the safety of the student.
2. The individual in charge breached or violated this responsibility.
3. Harm or injury did occur.
4. The harm or injury was a direct result or was caused by the violation of the responsibility for the safety of the individual.

Negligence can be attributed to many causes. Negligence can arise when a teacher fails to do what is required or does not carry out a duty that is appropriate under the circumstances, for example, a teacher who fails to instruct a student in the safe use of a piece of equipment or does not administer first aid to an injured student. A teacher who acts incorrectly or who does not perform up to the required standard of conduct, such as giving incorrect information about weight training, spotting incorrectly in gymnastics, or administering a first-aid procedure improperly, can be found guilty of negligence. Performing an illegal or unlawful act, such as administering corporal punishment when prohibited by law, may also be viewed as negligent.

Negligence typically arises from one of five conditions:
1. Failure to supervise students properly.
2. Failure to instruct students properly.
3. Failure to provide safe environmental conditions, specifically facilities and equipment, for participation.
4. Failure to employ proper first-aid measures in an emergency.

5. Failure to provide proper transportation for students.

Teachers who are knowledgeable about the typical causes of negligence can take steps to reduce the possibility of these events occurring.

Foresight is an important issue in the establishment of negligence. Essentially, could the teacher have anticipated or foreseen the potential danger and have taken the appropriate steps to prevent or eliminate the dangerous situation? Would another trained professional have been able to foresee the dangerous situation and taken steps to prevent its occurrence? If so, the teacher is likely to be found negligent.

Teachers should evaluate all activities, actions, facilities, and equipment with a critical eye to determine possible hazards and sources of accidents. The risks involved in each physical education situation should be carefully examined and the reduction of these risks addressed during the planning process. A reasonable standard of care should then be used in conducting the activity to ensure the safety of all participants.

Defenses Against Negligence

There are several factors that may be weighed by the court in determining whether a teacher was negligent. Comparative and contributory negligence, an act of God or nature, and assumption of risk are factors that can be used as defenses in an attempt to demonstrate that the teacher may not be the primary cause of the injury.

Contributory and comparative negligence. When improper or irresponsible actions taken by the student directly contribute to the injury, contributory negligence exists. For example, after being told that eyeguards must be worn when playing racquetball, a student is hit in the eye by the ball after removing his eyeguards while playing. Students are expected to behave responsibly, use sensible care, and follow safety precautions to avoid injury. In determining whether the injured student behaved in a responsible manner, the maturity, ability, and experience of the student is considered by the court.

In some states, if there is contributory negligence on the part of the injured student, the student may not receive compensation for the damages. This applies even if the teacher is found to be negligent. However, some states have comparative negligence laws. Under these laws, the student and the teacher may be held jointly responsible for the injury.

When the injured student and the teacher are both responsible for the accident, comparative negligence occurs. Under comparative or shared negligence laws, the court determines the percentage of responsibility for each person involved. Monetary damages are then accorded proportionately. For example, the teacher could be held responsible for 60% and the student for 40%, and the monetary award would be adjusted accordingly. Typi-

Some activities are inherently more dangerous than others. Proper safety precautions should be established for each activity.
Courtesy of Emily Leonardo, Camp Hill High School, Camp Hill, PA.

cally, under a comparative negligence statute, to recover damages, the student must be found to be less negligent than the teacher.

Act of God or nature. An act of God or nature is considered to occur when an unforeseeable, completely unexpected natural event causes an accident. If, during clear weather, a student is struck by a flash of lightning while playing softball, the accident would be considered an act of God. On the other hand, if the teacher allows students to continue to play softball in the face of an impending electrical storm and a student is struck by lightning, the teacher could be considered negligent.

Assumption of risk. Every physical education activity has inherent risks of injury. Students must fully understand the risks associated with a particular activity. When a student understands and participates in an activity, the student assumes the risks involved. However, the student assumes only the risks associated with the activity, *not* the risk of negligent behavior on the part of the teacher.

Teachers must inform students about the risks inherent in an activity, the reasons for specific safety measures, and the consequences of failing to follow these measures.

Negligence Prevention

Teachers must be aware of their duties pertaining to the safe participation of students entrusted to their care. Teachers must fulfill this obligation in a manner that is consistent with professional standards of conduct and reasonable care. Four major responsibilities need to be addressed:

1. Provision for safe and adequate supervision of the activity
2. Care in selection of suitable activities and their conduct
3. Creation and maintenance of a safe learning environment
4. Proper administration of emergency health care

Teachers have a responsibility to supervise the locker room.
Courtesy of Mary Beth Steffen, Shaker Heights High School, Colonie, NY.

Guidelines relative to each of these responsibilities are offered to help you fulfill your duty to provide for the care and well-being of your students.

Supervision. The nature of physical education activities makes it imperative that adequate and proper supervision be provided at all times. In lawsuits, questions often focus on whether the accident would have occurred if the supervisor had been present or whether the supervisor fulfilled assigned responsibilities and abided by the rules and regulations.

Supervisory process

Supervision is an active process. Teachers must be alert to what is occurring and closely monitor students' behavior. Leaning disinterestedly against the wall or standing on the sideline gossiping with another teacher are just two examples of poor supervisory practices. Good supervision requires vigilance—an awareness of the activities of the students, an orientation toward preventing dangerous occurrences, and a readiness to intervene quickly when appropriate. Actively scanning the class in an organized fashion (left to right) is one effective approach to supervision.

One of the most critical and most often cited principles of supervision is *never leave the class unsupervised,* even for a brief period of time. Regardless of whether the teacher has a phone call, personal emergency, needs to speak to a student privately, or get more equipment, the class should not be left unattended. In an emergency where it is necessary to get help, send a trustworthy student to the physical education, health, or administrative offices for assistance.

Teachers have the responsibility to supervise the class at all times. Should a situation arise that necessitates the teacher leaving the class, another qualified supervisor should be left in charge. If an injury occurs while the teacher is not present, the teacher's absence will be examined to ascertain if it was a contributing factor in the injury that occurred.

Supervisory determinants

In determining the extent of supervision required, several factors must be considered. Generally, students who are younger and less mature need more supervision than older, more mature students. The tendency for students to engage in horseplay should be taken into account, and some classes, because of the nature of the students within them, require more supervision than other classes. Make sure that student behavior does not get too aggressive, malicious, or "out of hand." Become aware of the warning signs of dangerous and inappropriate behavior and quickly intervene to rectify the situation.

Levels of students' skills and previous experience with the activity should be evaluated. Beginners with no previous experience in an activity require more supervision than advanced students with past experience. However, bear in mind that advanced students may be attempting more difficult skills and supervision must be adjusted accordingly. Students typically need more close supervision when an activity is first being introduced to the class than when it is being reviewed. High-risk activities (for example, gymnastics, archery, and diving) require closer supervision than low-risk activities (for example, badminton and dance).

Teacher location

The size and shape of the instructional area are also considered in planning for supervision. Teachers should position themselves carefully to make sure all students are in view. Supervising from the perimeter of the area allows teachers to monitor students' activities readily. When working with a small group of students or individual students, teachers must take care to position themselves in such way so that the rest of the class is visible.

The placement of equipment must also be taken into account. When planning the lesson, a teacher should take care to place the equipment where it can be readily seen and supervised.

Student responsibility

Teachers need to prepare students to assume responsibility for their own behavior. Clearly communicate expectations for behavior to students and reinforce appropriate behavior. As teaching styles shift from teacher-centered and direct to student-centered and indirect, students' responsibility for their own behavior increases. Also remember that some students need more supervision than others. Furthermore, any failure by students to adhere to safety rules or behave in a responsible manner indicates that closer supervision is necessary until the situation improves.

Teacher qualifications

Teachers must be qualified to instruct and supervise the activities they are assigned to teach. If a teacher does not feel competent in a particular area (for example, aquatics), the teacher should not undertake the responsibility. A written note should be sent to the department chairperson outlining specific concerns.

When teachers know their assignments in advance, they can take steps to gain competency. Teachers can attend a clinic or workshop, enroll in a course at a local college, or take advantage of instruction within the community. Colleagues may also be a great assistance in improving skills and knowledge in a particular area.

Off-campus activities

Scheduling off-campus physical education activities has become popular in many schools. Although instruction may take place off campus or be given by nonfaculty members at these sites, considerable responsibility still rests with the school for these activities. The school ad-ministration and teachers must exercise care and prudence in selecting sites to be used for off-campus activities as well as consider the quality of instruction and the supervision provided.

Transportation to these sites must receive careful attention. When transportation is necessary, all travel arrangements should be placed in writing and written approval obtained from school officials. It is strongly recommended that students be transported only via school bus or commercial vehicle. Transportation by teachers, parents, and students driving private cars can dramatically increase the liability risks.

Due care must also be exercised when students must walk from the gymnasium to the playing field or an off-campus site a few blocks away. Although it seems commonsensical, students should be instructed to follow a specific route, obey traffic signals, and use caution in crossing intersections. Teachers have a responsibility to supervise students during this time.

Consent forms and waivers

When arranging for students to participate in off-campus activities, teachers often send parent(s)/guardians consent forms and waivers. Consent forms and waivers are not synonymous. Consent forms provide documentation that the student was granted permission by his or her parent to travel to or participate in an activity. These forms may include information about the inherent risks involved in participating in the activity and method of travel.

A waiver form seeks to relieve the school of responsibility for injury that may occur when a student participates in an activity. Teachers should note carefully that the parent may waive his or her right to sue for damages, but a parent cannot waive the rights of a child who is under 21 years of age. A parent can sue in two ways—from the standpoint of rights as the parent and from the standpoint of the child's right as an individual, irrespective of the parent. Therefore the parent cannot waive the right of the child to sue as an individual. Although consent forms and waivers do not relieve the school or teacher of responsibility, they are a valuable means of informing parents and guardians of their children's activities.

Proper instruction. Providing students with proper and adequate instruction is important in preventing negligence. Lawsuits charging negligence relating to instruction often claim that the instruction provided by the teacher was inadequate or virtually nonexistent.

In the design and implementation of instructional experiences, consideration must be given to the selection of activities, inclusion and communication of safety precautions, planning, curriculum, teaching methods, and grouping of students. These same considerations should be applied when conducting physical education classes at off-campus sites.

Activity selection

When one is selecting activities for inclusion within the curriculum, the potential of these activities to contribute to the objectives of physical education and student development must be weighed carefully. Teachers who include activities in the curriculum because "students like to play it" or because "it's fun" may find their reasons not defensible in a court of law. Activities must be educationally justifiable.

Student characteristics play an important role in determining the appropriateness of activities. The age, developmental level, maturity, skill, background experience, and fitness status must be taken into account. The range of student characteristics within a given class vary widely, and these individual differences must be able to be accommodated within the activities selected to be taught.

Safety precautions

Proper instruction requires safety to be of paramount concern. Safety rules should be formulated. They should be few in number, thoughtfully constructed, stated positively, and applicable to most situations. Examples of safety rules include "use equipment properly," "safety first," and "wear proper attire."

Teach your safety rules to your students. Explain the reasons for the rules, give examples of how the rules are applicable to different situations, and review the rules periodically. Post rules in prominent places throughout the gymnasium, fields, swimming pool, and other areas. Remember, however, safety rules have little impact unless they are consistently enforced.

In addition to the general rules pertaining to safety, more specific rules may need to be developed for each activity unit. To help students learn these rules, teachers can incorporate them into the activity, for example, in softball the batter can be required to place the bat in a marked area on the way to first base or be called out. For each unit, students also need to be informed about the danger inherent within each activity, the risks involved, and how these risks can be minimized.

Students must be gradually educated to assume responsibility for their personal safety. They must be taught to participate carefully, to recognize possible dangers, and to act preventively so as to reduce the possibility of accidents occurring. Some teachers suggest preparing a safety handout and reviewing it with the class. The handout typically emphasizes students' safety responsibilities, such as reporting unsafe equipment or playing conditions that have escaped the teacher's attention, informing the teacher when they feel unwell or fatigued, refraining from trying skills they have not been taught, and requesting help when they have difficulty in performing a skill.

Planning

Careful planning is essential. State, district, and school guidelines should be carefully checked when plans for instruction are developed. A written, approved curriculum provides critical documentation of the scope and sequence of instruction and offers valuable evidence that sound planning for instruction has occurred.

Unit and lesson planning should reflect purposeful orientation toward stated objectives, proper sequencing and progression of skills, incorporation of sound teaching methodologies and accepted teaching practices, provision for individual student needs, recognition of anticipated problems and proposed solutions, and concern for the safety of the participants. Provisions should be made in the lesson plans for explaining and reviewing the risks of the activity and the safety procedures to be followed. Lesson plans should specify where and how the teacher will supervise the activity, how various safety equipment, such as mats for apparatus, will be utilized, and what safety equipment will be required of students, such as eyeguards.

Written unit and lesson plans should be retained and filed for future reference in case of a lawsuit. They offer documentation that you have considered the safety of the students in planning for instruction.

Curricular considerations

Teachers must follow the approved curriculum. The curriculum should be up to date and approved by the school board. The curriculum serves as a guide for teachers, authorizing the teaching of certain activities and often specifying the manner in which they are to be presented. Teachers are responsible for being knowledgeable about its content. Teachers may be found negligent if they are not familiar with the curriculum's content or fail to follow approved procedures.[3]

Any deviations from the approved curriculum should be approved in writing by the administration. Many lawsuits are based on the teacher deviating from approved practices, resulting in the subsequent injury to the student.[4] Changes from approved procedures should be based on well-documented research that offers a sound basis for modifying a previous procedure or incorporating a new one.

Teachers should follow their lesson plans. Often, snap judgments and spur of the moment decisions may prove to be risky and subsequently costly. It is also helpful to plan ahead for various instructional contingencies, such as inclement weather or shortened periods. This way a thoughtful and safe plan for the special instructional situation can be developed, one that is acceptable within the curricular guidelines.

Proper instruction

Students must be informed of the proper techniques before they are allowed to participate in an activity. Students should not attempt a skill without proper instruction, nor should they attempt a skill if they have not acquired the prerequisite skills.

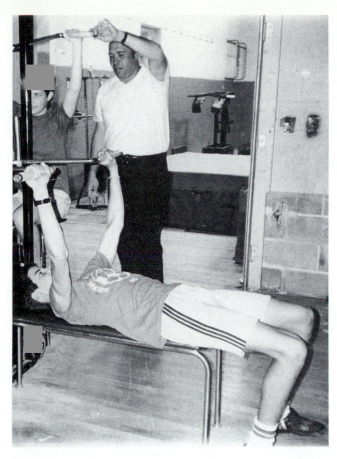

Employment of proper spotting techniques is a critical part of establishing and maintaining a safe learning environment.
Courtesy of Joy Buffan, SUC Oswego, Oswego, NY.

Students should progress in logical fashion from simple to complex tasks. Provision for accommodating individual differences must be made within the progression of the activity, the pace of instruction, and the amount of supervision provided.

Teachers are obligated to inform their students how to use the equipment properly, the inherent dangers of the equipment, the risks involved in the activity, the consequences of not following directions and using proper procedures, and the safety precautions to be taken. Furthermore, in activities that require spotters for safe performance, spotting should be performed by the teacher or trained students. Before students are allowed to spot, they must receive training in the correct technique.

Requirements and risk

When activities are a curricular requirement and students are placed in a position of having to complete the activities in order to pass or if the teacher insists that all students perform a skill, the amount of care required on the part of the instructor increases dramatically.[5,6] When an activity is both high risk and compulsory, teachers must be very diligent and careful in the performance of their duties of supervision and instruction.[5,6]

Moreover, a student should not be forced to participate in an activity against his or her will. Some students may be reluctant to try an activity because they perceive it beyond their abilities, are fearful of being injured, are not feeling well or are injured, or have other valid reservations. If physical or mental coercion is used to force or intimidate these students to participate and an injury occurs, the teacher may be viewed as behaving in a professionally inappropriate manner. Gentle encouragement or a progression that accommodates students' concerns is perhaps the best approach in this situation.

Grouping

Students should be grouped appropriately for activity and competition. Pertinent student characteristics, such as age, height, weight, grade, health status, skill level, maturity, and gender, must be considered in conjunction with the activity being taught when one is assigning students to groups for practice or competition. Students must be thoughtfully matched so that no student is placed at a serious disadvantage. Methods that are mainly convenient may not produce a safe match for practice and competition. Group students carefully to provide a safe as well as a positive learning experience.

Proper learning environment. Teachers have a duty to provide a safe and healthful learning environment for their students. This responsibility encompasses providing safe facilities and proper equipment in good condition as well as ensuring that they are used in a safe and appropriate manner.

Facilities

Responsibility for safe facilities extends to all areas that students use. In addition to the gymnasium, locker room, and shower area, these facilities include, for example, the playing fields, track, swimming pool, and auxiliary rooms such as for weight training.

Inspect facilities regularly and thoroughly for safety hazards. A written checklist is helpful in making sure that all areas are periodically and closely checked. By recording the date of the inspection on the checklist, documentation that these safety checks were completed on a regular basis is provided.

Where hazards exist that require corrective action, the teacher should correct them immediately if able to do so. If this is not possible, the hazards should be reported immediately, in writing, to the proper administrator for prompt remediation. A copy of the signed and dated report should be retained by the teacher for his or her records.

Get in the habit of checking facilities on a daily basis before teaching to make sure that no unforeseen hazards are present, such as broken glass on the playing field or water on the floor in the gymnasium. If a situation cannot be remediated immediately, then steps must be taken to alert students and protect them from harm. Warnings can be verbally given as well as posted to keep students away from danger. Or the area can be locked up or roped off until the situation is remedied.

Rules for the use of each facility must be provided to the students, and these rules must be reinforced consistently. When students use a facility for the first time, such as the pool when starting a swimming unit or the weight room for a fitness unit, review the safety rules for the facility with the students. Posting facility rules is helpful in reminding the students of acceptable standards of conduct.

Particular attention must be given to establishing rules for the safe use of locker rooms and shower areas because of the special hazards they present. Because these facilities are often crowded and congested, used by students usually in a hurry, and may be slippery, numerous opportunities for an injury are present.

For each facility, students must be instructed in emergency procedures. For example, in case of a fire alarm, students in the gymnasium must know which exit to use, what procedures to follow, where to meet outside, and what are acceptable standards of behavior. To reduce confusion, be sure to inform students what to do if such an emergency occurs when they are changing in the locker room or swimming in the pool. Review emergency procedures for each facility before the emergency occurs.

Facility maintenance is critical in providing a safe environment. Where facilities are inadequately maintained, chances of injuries are increased. The surfaces of the gymnasium, playing fields, and other areas, such as the pool or locker room, must be properly maintained. Teachers need to consult with maintenance personnel to ensure that they understand the specific requirements for facility maintenance and that these requirements are carried out in a timely fashion.

Facilities must be used in a safe manner. Because facilities are often used for multiple purposes, teachers must be aware of any conditions that might make the facility dangerous in a specific situation. For example, when playing soccer or basketball, teachers need to make certain that the boundaries are sufficiently far away from the edge of the field or walls of the gymnasium to allow for adequate deceleration or to provide sufficient clearance if the student ventures out of bounds to retrieve a ball during a game. Game boundaries may have to be adjusted to provide for adequate clearance. Where walls and equipment are dangerously close to the playing area, as is often the case with basketball standards, steps must be taken to ensure participants' safety, such as padding the walls or the standards.

Equipment

Equipment should be inspected on a regular basis, and written records should be maintained documenting these inspections. Equipment records should also include the date of purchase, manufacturer, condition of equipment, recommended maintenance or reconditioning schedule, and necessary repairs. Equipment that is dangerous, broken, or outdated should be removed from use and either repaired or replaced. Teachers who try to get by "for just one more day" with inadequate or improperly maintained equipment risk dangerous consequences. Only certified or properly trained individuals should be allowed to adjust, repair, or recondition equipment.

When purchasing equipment, teachers should buy the best equipment they can afford from reputable dealers. Equipment purchased should meet approved industry standards and be suitable for the age and size of the students.

Equipment must be used in accordance with the manufacturer's recommendations regarding proper use, care, and safety. Equipment should not be modified unless adjustments are made extremely carefully and by a trained individual.[7] Additionally, teachers should be alert that students do not alter the equipment in any way.

Equipment must be installed properly. This is critical when one is using equipment that must be anchored, such as apparatus or standards. Only trained individuals should be used to install such equipment, and manufacturer's guidelines for installation must be strictly followed. When setting up equipment for class, teachers should follow manufacturer's recommendations, exercise a high degree of care, and check periodically to make sure that the equipment remains properly installed (for example, volleyball standards).

Before using new or unfamiliar equipment, students need to be instructed in the proper use of the equipment and the possible consequences if the equipment is not used correctly. Teachers must also explain to students the risks associated with using the equipment.

Increasingly, warning labels are being attached to equipment (for example, goalie helmets) to inform users of the proper use and limitations of the equipment. Do not assume that students have read and understood the warning labels. These warnings must be carefully explained to the students so that they are cognizant of the dangers. Information about the proper use of equipment and its dangers should be included in the written lesson plan so as to ensure that all pertinent points are covered. Additionally, no claims should be made for a piece of equipment when the manufacturer does not provide such a warranty. For example, when teaching racquetball, instructors should not claim that eyeguards prevent injuries because they do not; students should be informed that eyeguards reduce the incidence and severity of eye injuries, but that they do not prevent them.[4]

Each student should also be held responsible for inspecting his or her equipment when it is issued to be sure that it is safe for use. Teachers should inform students of the safety guidelines pertinent to the equipment and ask students to report any problems immediately. Under no circumstances should students use unsafe equipment. This is imperative for protective equipment.

Attractive nuisances

Teachers must be aware of "attractive nuisances." This is a dangerous facility or piece of equipment, usually unattended or unsupervised, that is so enticing or attractive that an individual is drawn to its use. Swimming pools, weight training facilities, or gymnastic apparatuses left unattended and unsupervised are examples of attractive nuisances. If a student enters a facility or uses a piece of equipment under these conditions and becomes injured, a law suit could result in the teacher being found guilty of contributing to an attractive nuisance.

Informing students not to use a facility or equipment or posting warning signs is not sufficient. Leaving equipment on the playing field between classes, going to lunch without locking the gymnasium, or not being in the gymnasium when students arrive for class is risky. For safety's sake, keep all facilities and equipment locked up when it is not in use.

Proper health, first-aid, and emergency care. The health status of each student within the program must be considered when one is teaching. Teachers must also be prepared to administer first aid should an accident occur and activate the emergency plan to gain further assistance.

Health status

Most schools require medical examinations of students before the start of the school year. These medical records should be carefully reviewed, and students who have special medical needs or disabling conditions identified within each class. Before the first day of instruction, teachers should familiarize themselves with students' medical needs and any special requirements, such as adapted instruction or restriction from certain activities. Just in case a medical condition may warrant immediate attention, teachers should be knowledgeable regarding the provision of first aid for specific medical conditions (for example, diabetes or epilepsy) possessed by students in the class. It may be helpful to speak privately to each of these students and determine how their needs may best be met in an emergency.

Carefully monitor students' health status as they participate in physical education activities. The yearly physical examination may not identify problems related to participation in physical activity and exercise. In other instances, health problems may arise after the examination during the course of the school year. Be alert to changes in students' behaviors as they engage in physical activities, particularly conditions that may arise during and after exercise. Students who experience excessive breathlessness, pale or clammy skin, unusual fatigue, persistent shakiness, muscle twitching or tetany, fainting, or heart problems should be referred to the school nurse and physician.[8]

Teachers must be knowledgable about first aid procedures and have a carefully formulated emergency plan. Here a teacher attends to a student who was hit in the head during softball class.

Courtesy of Ben Lombardo, Rhode Island College, Providence, RI.

Students returning to participation following a serious injury or long illness should obtain a doctor's release or be cleared through the school nurse before being allowed to enter class. Any special restrictions on activity should be noted. Sometimes students may need to be placed in an adapted program or allowed to participate on a limited basis until they have fully regained their health.

First aid

Specific procedures to be followed in case of a medical emergency should be established and reviewed periodically. Should such a situation occur, teachers are responsible for providing first aid and obtaining professional medical care quickly. Teachers are both required and limited by law to providing students with first aid,[6] which is the immediate and temporary care given in an emergency until proper medical care can arrive. The purpose of first aid is to maintain or restore an individual's life, protect the individual from further harm, and alleviate suffering. Teachers must act immediately when confronted with life-threatening emergencies, such as stoppage of breathing or severe bleeding.

First-aid training should be required of all physical education teachers. In-service sessions in safety conducted by properly trained personnel should be held before the start of each school year so that all teachers are familiar with current first-aid practices and can perform such procedures properly and effectively. Obtaining certification through a recognized program, such as the American Red Cross, is highly recommended, and requiring current, valid certification of all teachers is strongly suggested.

Teachers should be aware from the liability standpoint of some of the common problems that arise in the performance of first aid. Usually negligence results from teachers attempting to do too much, thereby causing further injury, or from doing too little, resulting in permanent damage or harm. Generally, a teacher who moves a student with a suspected back injury, rather than waiting for trained medical help to arrive, is doing too much; this error has resulted in permanent paralysis in some cases. On the other hand, failure to obtain medical help for an injured student can also be harmful. Failure to obtain medical assistance for a student suffering from heat exhaustion or a broken bone can have adverse effects.

Emergency care

If there is an accident, the teacher should administer first aid and activate the emergency care system by calling or sending a responsible student for help. Specific procedures to be followed in case of an emergency should be formulated. A written plan detailing these procedures should be developed by teachers working in concert with the school nurse and physician and approved by school officials.

Emergency care planning also includes identifying conditions under which additional medical assistance, such as paramedics, will be summoned, and who will make this determination. It should also be determined under what conditions the student's parents or guardian will be notified and who will contact them.

Accident reports

An accurate report of each accident should be completed by the teacher promptly while the details of the incident are still clear. The accident report should include a description of the circumstances under which the accident occurred, the nature of the injury, first-aid treatment administered, type of additional medical assistance obtained, names of persons providing services, information regarding parental contact, and names and addresses of witnesses. A sample accident report is shown in Fig. 12-1.

The accident report should be thoroughly and objectively written. It is important to remember that the report may be introduced as evidence in a lawsuit that occurs years later. Copies of the report should be retained by the teacher, department, principal, and administration. It may also be helpful to attach copies of the lesson plan for the class so that all information pertaining to the accident is readily available. The cause of the accident should be investigated so that factors contributing to the accident can be identified and, if possible, corrected or eliminated.

Personal Protection: Minimizing the Effects of a Lawsuit

Teachers must exercise due care and perform their responsibilities in a professional manner. Providing proper supervision and instruction, creating and maintaining a safe learning environment, and utilizing proper first-aid and emergency care procedures are actions that teachers can take to provide a safe physical education experience for students and to minimize the risk of negligence. Guidelines to reduce the possibilities of lawsuits are presented in Box 12-1.

BOX 12-1

GUIDELINES FOR PREVENTION OF LEGAL LIABILITY

- ◆ Be familiar with the health status of each student.
- ◆ Follow the approved curriculum.
- ◆ Provide proper and adequate instruction that is sensitive to individual differences.
- ◆ Group students appropriately for activities.
- ◆ Be sure facilities and equipment are safe and used properly.
- ◆ Provide proper and adequate supervision—remain with the class at all times.
- ◆ Transport students in an approved manner.
- ◆ Act promptly to provide first aid in an emergency and, if necessary, activate the emergency care procedures.
- ◆ Keep accurate and complete records.
- ◆ Anticipate and act to minimize inherent risks.
- ◆ Follow mandated legislation in conducting the program.
- ◆ Keep student safety a foremost concern.
- ◆ Be professional—be reasonable, be careful, and be prudent.

STUDENT ACCIDENT REPORT FORM

This triplicate form should be completed by the supervising teacher and then signed by the supervising teacher, school nurse, and building principal. The original copy of the form will be forwarded to the superintendent's office, the second copy will be filed in the principal's office, and the third copy will be retained by the supervising teacher.

Student Information

Name of injured _____ Age _____ Grade _____

Home address _____

Parent's name _____ Phone _____

Accident Information

Date of accident _____ Time of accident _____

Location of accident _____

Activity at the time of the accident _____

_____

Description of accident (events, conditions, and other contributing factors) _____

_____

_____

_____

Nature of the injury _____

_____

_____

Teacher (supervisor) at the time of the accident _____

Location of teacher at the time of the accident _____

Names and addresses of witnesses

_____

_____

_____

Actions Taken

First-aid treatment administered by whom? _____

Treatment by school nurse? Yes _____ No _____ If yes, was the treatment at the scene or at the office? _____

_____

Ambulance/paramedics summoned? Yes _____ No _____ Time called _____ by whom? _____

Treatment by physician? Yes _____ No _____ Time called _____ by whom? _____

Physician's name _____

Location of treatment _____

Injured sent to hospital? Yes _____ No _____

Method of transportation _____

Parents or guardian contacted? Yes _____ No _____ Time called _____ by whom? _____

Follow-up Information

Remediative measures taken to prevent similar accidents (if taken)

_____

_____

_____

Report prepared by _____ Date _____

Signature of preparer _____ Date _____

Signature of school nurse _____ Date _____

Signature of principal _____ Date _____

FIG. 12-1   Sample student accident report form.

However, despite all due care and preventive measures, accidents do happen. Teachers should familiarize themselves with the liability laws of their states. Physical education teachers should be informed about the insurance coverage provided to them by their school as protection against losses from job-related litigation. Many teachers also purchase personal liability insurance to cover costs of legal services and financial settlements that may occur. Personal liability insurance may be purchased from AAHPERD, the National Education Association, or through commercial insurance companies.

Student safety is of paramount concern in conducting the physical education program. Policies and procedures utilized in the program should reflect this concern. In addition, carefully formulated policies and procedures can help teachers deal efficiently with the various organizational and administrative facets of the physical education program.

DEPARTMENTAL POLICIES AND PROCEDURES

Well-conceived departmental policies and procedures contribute to the effective administration of the physical education program. Written guidelines should be developed to provide consistency in dealing with recurring practices and concerns, such as program objectives, attendance policies, and grading.

Departmental Handbook

A departmental handbook is an effective means to communicate information about departmental policies and procedures. Physical education department handbooks commonly provide information about the following areas:

◆ Program philosophy and objectives
◆ Program scope
◆ Registration and course selection procedures
◆ Medical examinations
◆ Dress requirements
◆ Attendance, participation, excuse, and makeup policies
◆ Grading policies
◆ Locker room policies
◆ Safety considerations

The handbook should be no longer than 10 pages in length and contain clear, concise statements of the guidelines governing the program.

These policies and procedures should be explained clearly to students during the first class meeting of the school year. A copy of the handbook can be sent home so that parents are informed about current practices and requirements, thus reducing misunderstanding about the program. A form for parents and students to sign indicating that the material has been reviewed could be included in the handbook.

Philosophy and objectives. The physical education department's philosophy and objectives should be stated clearly. It is important that parents and students have an understanding of the specific objectives being sought and the approaches that will be taken to accomplish them. This is also helpful in clarifying the perceptions pertaining to the nature of physical education and its importance.

Program offerings. Information about program offerings and a brief description of the content of each unit should be included in the handbook (Fig. 12-2). An annual plan for each grade level can be used to effectively illustrate the activities to be taught throughout the school year.

Registration. In schools where students select their physical education activities, procedures to be followed to register for a course should be listed. This information should include how often registration will be conducted (once a semester), procedures to be followed in selecting and assigning classes (first choice, second choice), and other pertinent information, such as additional fees required for off-campus activities.

Graduation requirements. To avoid misunderstandings, clearly state physical education graduation requirements. These requirements vary from state to state and from school district to school district.

Credit. Activities for which physical education credit is to be awarded must be identified. Credit should only be awarded for activities that fulfill the objectives of the program. Although controversial, some schools award physical education credit for participation in athletics, marching band, ROTC, band, or cheerleading. Although these activities are worthwhile, they do not contribute to the attainment of the objectives of a quality physical education program.

Medical Examinations

Before participating in physical education, each student should be required to have a medical examination by a physician. These results should then be kept on file in the school health office for future reference.

The extent to which each student may participate in the physical education program should be determined by the physician. In situations where health conditions preclude full participation, the physician must carefully define all restrictions and specify the conditions and modifications under which participation can occur.

To assist the physician in making an educated decision about the extent of participation in physical education, he or she should be provided with a list of activities and their description. It may also be helpful for the physical education teacher or the school nurse to communicate directly with the physician regarding individual restrictions. Such communication may reveal that the student's needs may best be served through a restricted program

PHYSICAL EDUCATION

Course	Semester	Credit	Group	Open To
Boys and Girls P.E. 9	Full Year	3	2	9
Boys and Girls P.E. 10	Full Year	3	2	10-11-12
Boys and Girls P.E. Assistant	Full Year	2	1	11-12
Exercise Science	2	3	3	11-12
Leisure Living	1 and 2	2	1	11-12
Lifeguarding	2	2	2	10-11-12
Personal Safety	1 and 2	2	2	9-10-11-12
Water Safety Instructor	1	2	2	11-12

PHYSICAL EDUCATION

NOTE: Physical education will consist of two major components: Physical Fitness and Health Fitness. Both components will help the student do a variety of physical and intellectual tasks. The students will learn concepts pertaining to their own physical fitness and participate in skill activities related to those concepts. Each student will be diagnosed individually as to strengths and weaknesses and then be prescribed with certain activities to help correct the weaknesses and build on strengths.

BOYS AND GIRLS PHYSICAL EDUCATION
9. Full-year course

Total in-class time: 5 mods   Credits: 3   Group: 2
R/P: 5

Each student will complete:
1. Physical fitness tests and activities
2. Preparation and activities pertaining to recreational and lifetime sports
3. Lifetime health fitness principles and activities
4. Written problems and reading assignments concerning fitness principles
5. Nine weeks of swimming based on individual ability
6. Two (2) lab assignments each quarter during unscheduled time
Prerequisite: None
Open to: 9

BOYS AND GIRLS PHYSICAL EDUCATION
10. Full-year course

Total in-class time: 5 mods   Credits: 3   Group: 2
R/P: 5

Each student will complete:
1. Physical fitness tests and activities
2. Preparation and activities pertaining to recreational and lifetime sports
3. Lifetime health fitness principles and activities
4. Written problems and reading assignments concerning fitness principles
5. Nine weeks of swimming based on individual ability
6. Two (2) lab assignments each quarter during unscheduled time
Prerequisite: None
Open to: 10-12

BOYS AND GIRLS PHYSICAL EDUCATION ASSISTANT. Full-year course

Total in-class time: 5 mods   Credits: 2   Group: 1
R/P: 3

Each student will complete:
1. Leadership duties within the class
2. Officiating duties within the class
3. Assignments as they pertain to equipment and locker room duties
Prerequisite: Boys or Girls P.E. (grade of C or better)
Open to: 11-12

EXERCISE SCIENCE. Second semester

Total in-class time: 4 mods   Credits: 3   Group: 3
R/P: 6

Each student will complete:
1. Skills and activities concerning aerobic and anaerobic fitness
2. Experimentation for and preparation of an in-class strength presentation
3. Investigation and analysis of the biomechanical and psychophysiology of specific sports. Participation in discussions and activities related to the physiological, mechanical, and psychological functions of the neuromuscular, cardiovascular, and cardiorespiratory systems
Prerequisite: Boys or Girls P.E. (grade of C or better)
Open to: 11-12

LEISURE LIVING. One semester course, both semesters

Total in-class time: 4 mods   Credits: 2   Group: 1
R/P: 3

Each student will complete:
1. A cluster of three similar activities arranged in 6-week units
2. Physical fitness activities and skills related to each cluster
3. Preparation and activities pertaining to the recreational aspects of sports
4. There will be some additional fees associated with the use of outside building recreational facilities and agencies
Prerequisite: Boys or Girls P.E.
Open to: 11-12

FIG. 12-2   Sample of handbook information on physical education activities from Westside High School, Omaha, Nebraska.

of activities or through placement in the adapted physical education program as opposed to totally prohibiting participation in physical education.

Dress Requirements

Students should be suitably attired for physical education classes so that they can actively participate in a safe and comfortable manner. Some schools require a uniform for physical education, others do not. This is a controversial issue.

Some reasons frequently cited for having all students wear a uniform are that it presents an appearance of discipline and orderliness, reflects school spirit, and ensures that all students are attired in dress that is safe for participation. Using uniforms also makes available clothes for active participation at a reasonable cost and removes the discrimination in dress between wealthier and poorer students.

On the other hand, mandating uniforms can create problems and even lead to teacher-student conflicts. Some students will seek to avoid physical education merely because they do not want to wear the uniform, that is, they think it is ugly or it represses their individuality. Students who are overweight or have certain physical conditions, such as acne or burn scars that they wish to keep covered, find wearing uniforms that expose these conditions to be stressful and embarrassing, especially in a coeducational situation. Requiring uniforms also poses a problem for students who hold religious beliefs that prohibit them from wearing certain types of attire, such as shorts. Additionally, provisions must be made for students who cannot afford to purchase the required uniform.

Where uniforms are required, it may be beneficial to involve students in the selection process. A committee composed of faculty and students can review samples of uniforms from clothing companies and make the selection. Or the committee can present several of their choices to the students in the physical education classes for a vote. It may be desirable to have students select from several options in purchasing the uniform. For example, students could choose from T-shirts in one of the two school colors, select from a long- or a short-sleeve shirt, and have the option to wear either shorts or sweatpants. Allowing students' input in selection and choices about their dress may mitigate some of the concerns about uniform requirements.

While not requiring uniforms, some schools have dress code requirements. The dress code may be strict, specifying in detail what the students must wear for physical education. Or it may be quite simple, requiring only that the students change from street clothes into safe and comfortable attire and wear sneakers. Just as with uniforms, the dress code should offer students some flexibility in attire. For safety reasons, dress codes often specify that students remove all jewelry and secure long hair so it does not interfere with vision.

Teachers should adjust the uniform requirement or dress code depending on the activity. Activity clothes may be required for some physical education units, such as for fitness and basketball. Students can safely participate in street clothes in other activities such as archery.

Proper footwear is critical from the safety standpoint. If students do not have footwear, do not allow participation in stocking feet—it is very hazardous.

Both for attire and footwear, some provision must be made by the department for students who can not afford a uniform, change of clothes, or proper footwear. Often funds are made available through the parent-teacher association for this purpose. Used and unclaimed clothes and outgrown shoes can be cleaned and made available for students who need them. This matter should be handled in a sensitive way so that students are not embarrassed at being unable to afford physical education attire and shoes.

Attendance Policy

Sound guidelines pertaining to class attendance, participation, excuses, and makeup requirements need to be established and communicated to students and parents at the beginning of the school year. These policies should focus on a positive approach to maintaining student involvement and interest in physical education.

Attendance and participation. Structuring the physical education program to be a positive experience for students can help reduce problems with attendance and participation. However, even in a quality, dynamic program, such policies are needed. A positive system of rewarding appropriate behavior creates a more conducive learning environment. Under such a system, dressing for class, attending, and participating could result in students receiving points that can be used toward free time for favorite activities. A negative approach, where students are deprived of privileges or penalized with low grades, contributes to a negative learning environment.

Accurate records of daily attendance are required by the school. Absences, excused absences, tardiness, excused tardiness, limited participation, and nondressing are typically noted. These records can help teachers monitor the involvement of their students. Also, teachers can keep track of those students who may have missed instruction in a particular skill and need to be taught prerequisite skills before proceeding further in class.

Excuses. Requests to be excused from participation because of medical reasons should be handled by the school nurse and information about the excuse communicated to the physical education teacher. A form can be developed to expedite the process and to facilitate the maintenance of accurate records.

School nurses and physicians who are accurately informed about the physical education program can make more knowledgeable decisions about the extent of participation for students. Alternatives to regular participation, such as restricting participation to certain activities or placement in a modified class, may then be prescribed to meet the student's needs. Some schools require that students who are excused for an extended period, such as longer than 1 week, obtain a note from their physician. Clearance by the physician is then required to resume participation.

Some schools require that all medical excuses be cleared through the nurse's office, while in other schools teachers can use their own discretion for certain problems. For example, sometimes students with minor problems, such as a sore throat, headache, stomach or menstrual cramps, or those just having a "bad" day, may directly ask the physical education teacher to be excused from class or a particular class activity. Teachers need to give careful thought as to how best to handle these problems on an individual basis and yet in a fair and consistent manner.

Nondressers. Students who fail to dress appropriately for class present a serious problem. Chronic nondressing may be caused by a strong dislike for physical education, defiance of authority, lack of motivation, or a whole host of other reasons. Some students who feel inept or embarrassed in performing in front of their peers avoid these feelings by the strategy of not dressing for class.

The many different causes for nondressing require a variety of approaches to resolve this problem. Conducting an exciting program that is perceived by students to be relevant to their lives is important in creating positive feelings toward physical education and the desire to be an active participant. Reasons for dressing for activity should be explained to students so they understand its importance. Talking to nondressers is helpful in ascertaining their reasons for this behavior.[9] Such conversations may reveal a possible solution to the problem; for example, students embarrassed about wearing shorts because of obesity or a physical problem may be allowed to wear sweat pants. Rewarding students with time to spend on favorite activities or awarding the class free time when the percentage of students dressing reaches a specific goal is one approach that has been used successfully.[10] Requiring students to make up all classes missed to receive credit for physical education is another solution to the problem.

Students who do not dress for class should not be permitted to participate in activities. As a teacher, you need to decide whether to allow nondressers to sit on the sidelines during class. If nondressers are permitted to remain, they should be involved in some meaningful physical education activities. These activities could include requiring them to read pertinent articles and answer a series of questions or complete a written report. Students who sit on the sidelines without something to do can be negative influences on the rest of the class. Disparaging remarks addressed to participating classmates, social conversation, or horseplay by sidelined students can disrupt learning.

Tardiness. Inform students of the starting time of class, procedures to be followed if they are tardy, and the consequences of being tardy. Tardiness that exceeds a certain time, such as 10 minutes after the start of class, or excessive tardiness, such as when tardiness exceeds three times a marking period, may require that the student make up the class.

Makeup classes. Opportunities to make up classes that were missed because of absences or excessive tardiness should be provided for the students. This could be done by allowing students to attend another physical education class during their unscheduled time or to take a special makeup class.

There are several different ways that makeup classes are scheduled by schools. Before school, during the lunch hour, or after school are all possible times. They may be offered on a weekly basis or held only near the end of the marking period. Coverage of the classes may be assigned to a specific teacher or rotated among teachers on the staff.

Ideally, makeup classes cover the same activities and material that the students missed. Makeup classes are of questionable value when they consist of students just putting in the required time in the gymnasium, lackadaisically doing whatever activity they desire until the time requirement is met. These classes should have a specific focus. They can consist of instruction in an activity or guided opportunities to practice skills covered in classes missed. Students could also be assigned to perform specific activities on an independent basis, such as to complete a 45-minute workout, play a tennis match, or participate in an aerobic class at the community center.

It is important that students have a clear understanding of the policies and procedures governing attendance, tardiness, participation, and makeup work. This information should be covered on the first day of class and reviewed periodically, if necessary. All physical education teachers in the department should consistently follow approved policies and procedures.

Grading

Students and their parents should be provided with information about the criteria that will be used to evaluate student learning in physical education. Before the start of a unit, the teacher should share with the class the procedures that will be utilized to assign a grade. Grading and evaluation of student learning are discussed fully in Chapter 13.

LOCKER ROOM POLICIES AND PROCEDURES

At the beginning of the year, inform students about policies and procedures governing the use of the locker room, including locks, lockers, showers, and towels. Well-defined guidelines are necessary so that time spent on these procedures is minimized, providing more time for class instruction.

Locker Room

Students using the locker room should follow a safe and efficient traffic flow pattern. The doors to be used for entering and leaving the locker room should be specified. Adequate supervision of the locker room must be provided for safety and security. The locker room should be checked regularly for proper use of lockers, unlocked lockers, clothes and books left out, and towels strewn about. A lost and found should be maintained for locks, clothing, and other items. In some schools the locker room is locked during class time to prevent unsupervised use and to minimize thefts. Other schools hire paraprofessionals to supervise locker rooms during classes, while in other schools no supervision is deemed necessary.

Lockers and Locks

Many schools use some combination of large, long lockers for storage of students' street clothes and belongings during the class period and smaller lockers or wire baskets for storage of activity clothing. Teachers must emphasize that activity clothes are not to be stored in long lockers, which are to be reserved for street clothes and belongings during class. When activity clothes are stored in long lockers, the number of long lockers available for use by students during class to store their possessions is reduced. This leads to lost belongings.

Combination locks are used by most schools to secure the lockers. Many schools provide students with locks and often require a lock deposit to ensure their return at the end of the school year. Because school locks usually have a master key, the teacher can easily gain access to the locker in case of an emergency.

When students purchase their own locks, combination rather than key locks should be bought because it is too easy for students to lose the key. Some schools require the purchase of a specific lock brand, so that a master key can be used. If personal locks are used and there is no master key, the lock must be cut off when the student loses the key or forgets the combination.

Locker Assignment

Students in different classes should be assigned adjourning classes to avoid overcrowding. Within a class, assign lockers horizontally by rows in order to spread students throughout the entire locker room. This alleviates overcrowding, reduces safety hazards, and facilitates students dressing more quickly. Typically, older (and usually taller) students are assigned to lockers in the upper rows, while younger students are assigned to those in lower rows. This ensures that most students can reach their lockers.

Record Keeping

Good record keeping facilitates teachers' efforts to identify a student's locker, return a lost lock, or assist a student who has forgotten the lock's combination. There are several different methods that can be used.

A master diagram of each bank of lockers is useful for identifying locker assignments. The student assigned to each locker, the lock number, and the lock combination can be written in the appropriate space on the diagram.

A card file can also be used. The student's name, class period, locker number, lock serial number, and lock combination can be recorded on a locker card, which is then placed in the card file. Teachers can also use a microcomputer to record similar information.

A master lock book, which lists lock serial numbers and combination, often can be gotten from the lock manufacturer. This expedites obtaining information about the lock or the combination.

Showers

Shower policies should be thoughtfully formulated and based on the variety of physical activities offered as well as be sensitive to students' needs. Inflexible and insensitive shower guidelines often lead to student-teacher conflict or students seeking to avoid physical education altogether.

Rather than requiring showers, teachers may find it more effective to spend a few minutes discussing the importance of personal hygiene and why showering is necessary. Help students understand after which activities showering may be necessary. Students should be encouraged to shower after vigorous activities but allowed to make a choice after less strenuous activities. Shower policies that require a shower after every class, even if the students have been relatively inactive, are inflexible and lead to alienation among students. Additionally, such a requirement does little to help students learn how to make appropriate decisions regarding personal hygiene.

When showering is necessary, enough time must be allotted. Usually, 10 minutes is adequate for students to shower, dress, and groom. More time may be needed after swimming classes, because students need to dry their hair. Students at this age are conscious of their appearance, thus having adequate time to fix their hair and clothes before returning to class is important to them.

Some private shower facilities should be provided for students who desire them. Students are often embarrassed or uncomfortable about "gang" showering for a variety of reasons, including menstruation, acne, specific medical conditions, or an under- or overdeveloped body in relation to those of their peers. Be sensitive to these concerns.

Safety in the shower room should be emphasized. Require students to dry off in a specific area so water is not tracked through the locker room causing slippery floors. Horseplay should not be tolerated under any circumstances. Because of the hazard of broken glass, absolutely no glass containers should be allowed in the shower or locker room. Plastic containers should be used for soap and shampoo. Pertinent safety rules should be posted as a reminder at the entrance to the shower area.

Towels

There are several different options regarding the acquisition, laundering, and distribution of towels. Some schools require students to provide their own towels and assume responsibility for laundering them. This often results in students leaving wet towels in their lockers, leading to mildew and odor problems. Furthermore, because students do not have a dry, clean towel, they may not shower. Other students may forget to bring a towel from home.

Other schools provide students with towels and launder them. In this case, arrangements must be made for towel distribution. Each student can be issued a towel at the beginning of the year and allowed to exchange the towel for a clean, dry one as needed. Another method is to issue a student a towel by roll call number and check the number off when the towel is returned.

Well-formulated policies and procedures contribute to the efficient conduct of the physical education program. Many administrative tasks can be expedited with the use of microcomputers. Microcomputers are also used by teachers for instructional purposes.

MICROCOMPUTERS IN PHYSICAL EDUCATION

The use of microcomputers can greatly assist teachers in performing various professional and instructional tasks. Decreased costs, greater ease of use, and increased availability of relevant programs or software have contributed to the increased use of computers by educators to perform a diversity of tasks. Computers can be used for data management, student assessment and prescription, evaluation, instructional preparation, administrative functions, and computer-assisted instruction.

Data Management

Much of the data collected in physical education relates to fitness testing and subsequent analysis of results. Using specially designed computer programs, teachers can enter student fitness test results into the computer; analyze the data; compare results to national norms; establish local

Microcomputers can help teachers more efficiently perform many administrative tasks.
Courtesy of Ann Stevens, Evanston Township High School, Evanston, IL.

norms; compare results from one testing session to another to identify improvements; and generate reports for students, parents, and administrators. Some programs, such as the Fitnessgram[11] or many of the programs available from AAHPERD, like Physical Best,[12] provide for the printing of personalized fitness reports for each student, listing scores, comparisons, and exercise prescriptions to meet individual needs.

There are several ways to enter the large volumes of fitness data typically generated by physical education classes. Optical scanning sheets provide a ready means to enter data. Data may also be entered by teachers, instructional aides, or students themselves. On-line data collection systems exist, allowing for rapid gathering and automatic entering of test results, such as for the sit-and-reach, into the computer where it can be stored and readily analyzed.[13]

Data from students' performance on various skills tests can also be entered and analyzed. The computer makes it easy to keep records of students' performance and to analyze their progress.

Assessment and Prescription

Many programs are currently available for assessment and prescription purposes. Programs designed to assess wellness, nutrition, fitness, or activity interests, for example, ask students to enter pertinent data in response to various questions. The student's responses are analyzed, and a printout is generated listing results and recommendations for maintenance and improvement of one's status. This printout is given to the student and can be shared with the parents.

Also, specially designed programs are available to help write individualized educational plans (IEPs) for students with disabilities. These computer programs facilitate the actual writing of the IEP as well as the progress reports on the student.

Evaluation

Several programs are available commercially for generating student grade reports. Students' test results on a multitude of items can be weighted and grade calculations easily performed. Class performance on a particular test item can be determined and used to compare students' efforts as well as gain insight into the effectiveness of the physical education program.

Test Construction

Test construction programs permit the writing of a diversity of test items. Test banks can be developed for each skill area. When it is necessary to construct a test,

teachers can rapidly select and organize questions from this resource and print a test. Most programs also allow for the printing of tests with questions presented in a different order or multiple forms of a test.

Administrative Functions

Many record-keeping and administrative functions can be expedited with the use of the computer. Attendance, equipment inventory, locker and lock assignments, and facility safety check records are just a few of the many record-keeping tasks that can be more easily and rapidly handled by the computer. The department handbook can be stored on a computer and updated rapidly as needed.

Scheduling can also be facilitated. Facility schedules can be easily monitored and changed as needed. In a selective program, the computer can be used to assign students to classes based on their activity preferences. Tournaments can also be quickly scheduled with the computer.

Instructional Preparation

Instructional materials can be prepared more easily with the use of the computer. Curriculums, units, and lesson plans can be written and stored, recalled for future use, and easily modified. Task cards and a variety of skill checklists can easily be constructed. Preparation of overhead transparencies and handouts is facilitated. Specialized application programs are available for the construction of certificates of achievement, various awards, and signs.

Computer-Assisted Instruction

Computer-assisted instruction allows students to proceed at their own pace and receive immediate feedback about their work. These programs can be used as tutorial tools to help students learn pertinent information relating to such items as terminology, rules, safety, strategies, and concepts. Teachers can also use these programs to test students' knowledge. Simulation and modeling programs can be used to graphically illustrate skill performance or concepts.

Physical education teachers can use computers in a diversity of ways to deal more efficiently with a variety of managerial and instructional tasks in a less time-consuming manner. Computers also offer many exciting possibilities to enhance instruction and student learning.

When one is selecting computer software programs to use, several factors must be considered. These include compatibility with the available computer system, ease of data input, manner in which data are analyzed and results presented, and ease of use. Two sources of software for physical education are CompTech Systems Design, P.O. Box 516, Hastings, MI 55033 and the American Alliance for Health, Physical Education, Recreation and Dance, 1900 Association Drive, Reston, VA 22091. Other sources of software include professional colleagues, professional education and physical education journals, and computer magazines.

SUMMARY

One of the primary responsibilities of physical education teachers is to create and maintain a safe learning environment for their students. Within the past decade, the number of lawsuits involving physical education has increased dramatically. Many of the lawsuits involve allegations of negligence. Therefore it is important that teachers familiarize themselves with the conditions that contribute to negligence as well as actions that can be taken to reduce the likelihood of negligence occurring.

Lawsuits involving negligence focus on determining whether the teacher acted in a reasonable, prudent manner and exhibited a standard of care that a trained professional would exhibit in a similar situation. In determining whether a teacher is negligent, four questions are examined by the court: Was there a duty? Was there a breach of duty? Was there harm? Was the breach of duty a direct or proximate cause of the harm?

Negligence arises frequently from these sources: failure to supervise properly, failure to instruct properly, failure to provide safe environmental conditions, and failure to employ proper emergency health care measures. The potential for injury and a subsequent lawsuit can be reduced when teachers employ proper and adequate safety measures within these areas.

Departmental policies and procedures are essential to the smooth conduct of the physical education program. Guidelines should be formulated to handle effectively the communication of the program's philosophy and objectives and to deal efficiently with course scheduling, medical examinations, and a myriad of administrative tasks. Attendance, participation, excuse, makeup, dress, and grading policies should be clearly communicated to parents and students. Efficient procedures need to be implemented for the use of the locker room, assignment of locks and lockers, towel use and distribution, and record keeping.

Microcomputers are being used increasingly by physical education teachers to perform many tasks. Specialized programs help teachers manage data, assess students' needs, perform administrative tasks, evaluate student performance, prepare instructional materials, and enhance student instruction. They reduce the time required to complete instructional and administrative tasks and have the potential to enhance student learning.

FOR REVIEW

1. Assess the liability of the teacher involved in the following situation: The teacher left the gymnasium to secure additional equipment for volleyball class. The students were warned to sit quietly in their squads until the teacher returned. However, two of the students started practicing serving across the net. The student receiving the serve was struck in the face by the ball and suffered permanent vision damage in one eye. Arrange a mock trial in the class. Have a jury, prosecutor, defendant, plaintiff, witnesses, and judge and resolve this case.

2. Survey the physical education program at your high school or college. Using a checklist that you develop, identify any areas of potential negligence that exist within the program. List specific recommendations to eliminate or reduce any safety hazards.

3. Develop specific departmental policies and procedures dealing with two of the following areas: philosophy and objectives, course selection, medical examinations, attendance, participation, excuses, activity attire, showering, and locker room. Write these policies and procedures in a manner that can be readily understood by secondary school students and their parents.

4. Select an administrative or instructional task performed by physical education teachers. Use a computer program to perform this task. Analyze the advantages and disadvantages of using a computer to perform this function.

REFERENCES

1. Bucher CA: *Management of physical education and athletic programs,* St Louis, 1987, Mosby.
2. Wong GM: *Essentials of amateur sports law,* Dover, Mass, 1988, Auburn House.
3. Baker BB: Unsuitable curriculum and methodology. In Baker BB, editor: *Current issues in sport law,* Reston, Va, 1987, National Association for Physical Education and Sport.
4. Nygaard G, Boone TH: *Coaches guide to sport law,* Champaign, Ill, 1985, Human Kinetics.
5. Drowatzky JN: On the firing line: negligence in physical education, *Journal of Law and Education* 6:481-490, 1977.
6. Harrison JM, Blakemore CL: *Instructional strategies for secondary school physical education,* ed 3, Dubuque, Iowa, 1992, William C Brown.
7. Appenzeller H: Sport litigation and the administrator. In Baker BB, editor: *Current issues in sport law,* Reston, Va, 1987, National Association for Physical Education and Sport.
8. Pangrazi RP, Darst PW: *Dynamic physical education for secondary school students: curriculum and instruction,* New York, 1991, Macmillan Publishing.
9. Placek JH: Involving the nonparticipant: motivation and makeups, *JOPERD* 55(6):27-29, 1984.
10. Paese PC: Effects of interdependent group contingencies in a secondary physical education setting, *Journal of Teaching in Physical Education* 2:29-37, 1982.
11. Institute for Aerobics Research: *Fitnessgram,* 1993, Dallas, Institute for Aerobics Research.
12. AAHPERD: *Physical best,* 1986, Reston, Va, AAHPERD.
13. Dauer VP, Pangrazi RP: *Dynamic physical education for elementary school children,* Minneapolis, 1986, Burgess.

ANNOTATED READINGS

Gray GR: Risk management planning: conducting a sport risk assessment to enhance program safety, *JOPERD* 62:29-32, 78, 1991.

Presents a systematic approach to reduce the occurrence and extent of injuries in physical activity settings.

Horine L: *Administration of physical education and sport programs,* ed 2, Dubuque, Iowa, 1991, William C Brown.

Discusses many managerial and administrative aspects of the physical education program, including leadership, human relations, legal liability, and risk management.

Kolander CA, Grayson JL, Miller LK: Teachers and coaches at risk: how personal insurance policies can help, *JOPERD* 62:76-79, 1991.

Describes the importance of professional and personal insurance policies and offers guidelines to evaluate such policies.

Nygaard G, Boone TH: *Coaches guide to sport law,* Champaign, Ill, 1985, Human Kinetics.

Offers many practical ideas to help teachers provide a safe learning experience for their students. Examples of lawsuits help emphasize the importance of thinking safety first.

CHAPTER 13

The Evaluation of Learning

CHAPTER OBJECTIVES
- To describe the purposes of evaluation in physical education
- To discuss the need for appropriate evaluation procedures
- To describe various methods of evaluating student learning in physical education
- To describe selected grading practices

Parents, community leaders, taxpayers, and administrators have a right to know how well public institutions fulfill their responsibilities. Recently the need for such information has been magnified because of various fiscal and societal imperatives. Moreover, evaluation of student achievement is necessary to support the ongoing process of informed decision making at the classroom, school, and community levels. Information garnered from the evaluative process related to student performance is helpful in determining the effectiveness of the instructional program.

Therefore it is not surprising to learn that evaluation is a critical and common component of the educational process. In fact, many authorities believe that evaluation and education are so closely associated that one cannot and should not occur without the other.

In general, evaluation can be defined as the process of judging worth or determining the value of a product or a process. In educational organizations, evaluation can be defined as the process (usually systematic) of collecting information and data about student performance in order to ascertain the worth of such accomplishments. Dunham[1] defines evaluation as the " . . . process of obtaining information (data) and using it to form judgments which in turn are used in decision making."

Grading, on the other hand, is the selection and display of symbols to communicate the results of an assessment. Usually, grading systems are established to facilitate the evaluative process and simplify it for all concerned parties.

It is this latter aspect that often leads to misuse, if not abuse, of the evaluation/grading process.

There exists a consensus among professionals that evaluation is an important and pervasive aspect of all educational systems. Despite the articulation of various positions on the potential dangers and benefits emerging from the assessment process, the evaluation process remains staunchly entrenched as a cornerstone of education. Therefore, teachers and other school personnel must be prepared to deal with evaluation and related matters.

That evaluation is commonplace in schools and a fact of life for both teacher and student is not startling. The importance of constant monitoring of student progress for maximum learning is widely accepted as fact by students, parents, and teachers. Effective teachers have known for a long time that assessment and the resulting feedback are critical factors in the experience of learning. Indeed, in most instructional programs, a significant portion of the teacher's and the student's time is devoted to activities that involve the assessment of learning. Schafer and Lissitz[2] estimate that 10% of a teacher's professional time is spent on activities related to pupil assessment.

Physical education, as a part of the institution of public education, must respond to these mandates as well and provide reasonable and systematic methods to determine and assign grades for student performance. To do less would be a public admission that what we, as physical education teachers, do and expect of our students is not worth measuring or evaluating.

Physical education teachers have the responsibility for evaluating the degree to which they are accomplishing professional objectives. The process of evaluation should include two general areas: (1) student achievement, which includes the progress report or grade, and (2) curriculum assessment. In Chapter 5 curriculum assessment was reviewed. In this chapter the topic of student evaluation and grading will be addressed. Specifically, this chapter will describe the need and importance of the evaluation process as it relates to secondary school physical education. Second, the various modes of evaluation will be reviewed. In the last section, selected grading methods, procedures, and schema will be presented and analyzed.

THE ROLE OF EVALUATION IN PHYSICAL EDUCATION

Why should physical education teachers evaluate students? What are the purposes of evaluation in secondary school physical education? Before selecting evaluation techniques or grading systems for use with students, teachers need to consider the reasons for employment of such techniques. The primary goal for assessing students in physical education is "to assist in making educational decisions that will be in the students' best interest."[3]

Frequently stated purposes for evaluating student performance are screening, planning, program evaluation, and evaluating student progress. Evaluation for the purposes of screening or selecting students attempts to identify special students who require special services, programs, considerations, etc. For example, screening procedures are often utilized to identify physical education students requiring adapted physical education programs and services.

Planning, a fundamental teacher responsibility, is greatly facilitated by various educational assessment procedures. As discussed in Chapter 6, planning assists teachers and other curriculum planners in their efforts to determine what to teach and how to teach it. Evaluation measures should be an integral part of the planning process and be reflected in the behavioral objectives, and activities of the curriculum.

Another purpose of evaluation is program assessment. Specifically, a program evaluation can determine the effectiveness of the physical education program. However, the concern is more global and not usually directed at the progress or growth of individual students. In Chapter 5 program assessment strategies were addressed, and it was suggested that items such as curricular progressions, administration and organization, facilities and equipment, and time allocation for instructional purposes should be included in this more global approach. However, it should be apparent that the concern in this latter case is of a more general nature than interest in individual student development.

Physical education is a purposeful activity and is directed toward the attainment of certain goals. Regular assessment of student achievements assists educators, at all levels, to recognize the effectiveness of programs and the progress students are making toward predetermined goals.

The reporting of student progress to parents, administrators, and students themselves comprises yet another purpose of the evaluative process. It is educationally sound and useful to determine and to communicate clearly and regularly the level of student achievement in the subject studied. Indeed, this function of the grading system (as part of the evaluative process) is pervasive in schools in the United States and required virtually of all teachers, in all disciplines and in all public educational institutions.

For all teachers, evaluation is critical to the maintenance and improvement of instructional practice. Kindswatter et al[4] suggest that the evaluative process should not only permeate the physical education teacher's every teaching task but also should be central to every teacher's role. Specifically, they point out that evaluation and the assessment process occurs in the initial planning stages, in the selection of strategies and activities, and as lesson objectives are determined. Furthermore, Kindswatter et al make a case for the impact of the evaluative process on the teacher's plan for collecting data on student progress. As a result, much of the way students spend their time learning in a given class is determined by the grading procedures established by the instructor. Finally, they put forth that effective teachers regularly consider evaluation during instruction when they:

. . . observe student behaviors, consider student responses, provide feedback and corrections to students and judge the extent to which instruction has been effective.[4]

Inherent within the physical education teacher's responsibilities is the task of assigning grades or other qualitative measures as a means of assessing student performance. Several issues emerge from this responsibility, not the least of which is the view held by some that physical education skills should not be graded as other subject areas because of the unique conditions readily apparent in the physical education context.[5] Specifically, these professionals feel that the characteristics of the freedom of movement, informality, the psychomotor nature of the learning, and the large classes militate against the employment of traditional grading practices or techniques that parallel those used in the classroom setting.

Another view suggests that if physical education is indeed unique in its disciplinary content and the context of its pedagogical endeavors, then physical education teachers need to devise grading systems that encompass and respond to these distinctive qualities and unique working conditions. Still others carry this line of thinking to another level and claim that teachers need to formulate evaluative schemes that truly evaluate accomplishments in the discipline of physical education and human movement, and set aside concerns about whether the process will be considered equitable to (or acceptable by) teachers in other traditionally classroom-bound academic areas.

Yet another purpose of assigning grades and establishing sound evaluation procedures is the pervasive belief that such practices enhance student motivation. The assignment of good grades is highly valued by students who are highly motivated and achievement oriented. Students who obtain high grades are reinforced for their efforts and obtain other positive outcomes for their achievement of these high grades (for example, enhanced self-esteem, social status). This latter outcome should be contrasted with the view held by some educators, who believe that when students receive poor grades, they are supposed to feel like failures, and such feelings are, in theory, supposed to create a desire to be a success. For most teachers, this theory relates well to their own experiences as high-school students (that is, highly motivated, college-bound students). Failing grades are more likely to motivate students who value high marks. But what about the other students, who possibly represent the majority of secondary school students?

In secondary school physical education, students are required to engage in highly visible, public performances, often judged openly (formally or informally) by the teacher and by audiences (for example, peers). Given the realities of the physical education setting, it is not surprising that the evaluation process and the resulting grades awarded are powerful in effect. Recent studies of dropouts reveal that students' images of themselves as losers are a basic cause of their departure from the educational scene, and this outcome is, in part, attributed to the school for creating this negative impression. Curwin and Mendler[6] suggest that students who receive poor evaluations become poor learners, and poor learners will often prefer to drop out of school.

Regardless of issues such as those described earlier and the position of individual physical education teachers, teachers are required to assess student performances and assign grades. Therefore the matter at hand, is not one of *if*, but *how* to best evaluate student achievement.

THE IMPORTANCE OF EVALUATION

Evaluation affects learners in many varied ways. Crooks[7] indicates that evaluation:

> . . . guides their judgment of what is important to learn, affects their motivation and self-perceptions of competence, . . . structures their approaches to and timing of personal study, . . . consolidates learning, and affects the development of enduring learning strategies and skills.

While the evaluation of learners is apparently a major factor influencing education in general, it takes on added significance in physical education. When one considers that one of the goals of physical education is to develop a lifelong affection toward physical activity, human movement, and wellness, an outcome that teachers will rarely have the opportunity to observe firsthand, it is imperative that the development of such knowledge and attitudes is nurtured by carefully planned assessment practices. Improving students' attitudes toward physical activity has long been considered an important objective of physical education.

Recent evidence indicates that parents, teachers, and physical education teachers rate the development of a good attitude toward physical activity as the primary purpose of physical education, rating it higher than the development of motor proficiency in sport skills.[8] Problems arise, however, when professionals attempt to measure growth[9] in this area.

Physical education teachers must ensure that their efforts to foster appropriate motor skills and attitudes toward a lifestyle that includes and embraces regular physical activity are not undermined by ill-conceived or poorly administered systems of student evaluation. In general, evaluation can be threatening, and in physical education such threats can destroy the students' affection for physical activity. Such threats can be magnified in physical education because of its inherent public nature and, in many cases, the extreme visibility of student performances and abilities. Secondary school physical education teachers must be sensitive to these aspects of the evaluation process and take steps to ensure that learners do not feel pressured, coerced, or threatened by assessment practices. For, unlike other academic areas, physical education gauges its success and effectiveness in terms of life, death, health, wellness, and quality of life. While it may be extravagant exaggeration to suggest that evaluation procedures in physical education potentially may lead to life and death consequences, such assessment practices do have an impact on affective development. An individual's adherence to a physically active lifestyle is directly related to affective bonds to, and feelings for, physical activity.

Crooks,[7] in a masterful review of classroom evaluation practices, outlines the long-term consequences of school evaluation procedures:

Evaluation practices influence

- ◆ Students' ability to retain and apply in varied contexts and ways the material learned.
- ◆ The development of students' learning skills and styles.
- ◆ Students' continuing motivation, both in particular subjects and more generally.
- ◆ Students' self-perceptions, such as their perceptions of their self-efficacy as learners.[6]

Veal[9] recommends that physical education teachers reconceptualize assessment procedures in this light, and that the motivational aspects of evaluation should take precedence within evaluative schema, rather than the testing and grading aspects of the process. Specifically, Veal's[9] work suggests that physical education teachers should (1) shift their thinking from an evaluative only mode to one that employs evaluation techniques to heighten motivation, (2) emphasize formative evaluation rather than continue to utilize traditional testing and evaluation programs, and (3) move to a broader interpretation of assessment and emphasize purposes in addition to testing and grading. In light of the affective imperatives inherent in the physical education curriculum, professionals should consider such a major shift in the objectives of evaluation.

At this point it is important to move on and review the various assessment options and procedures available to physical education teachers. Ultimately, it is from among these possibilities that professionals will select and formulate coherent plans, policies, and practices for student evaluation.

TYPES OF EVALUATION

At this juncture, it is important to review briefly approaches to evaluation. It is from among these general types of evaluation that the secondary physical education teacher must select, organize, and use in any number of possible combinations to formulate a specific grading procedure for students (Table 13-1).

Formal Evaluation

Formal evaluation practices clearly specify in advance the exact nature of the assessment process. Usually, formal procedures encompass the use of written tests, checklists, inventories, observation systems, psychomotor skill batteries, and other teacher- and institution-selected evaluative instruments. During the evaluation encounter, students are fully cognizant that the teacher is collecting data to facilitate the grading process. Evaluation procedures are definitively explained to students, are carried out at predetermined times (for example, each Friday, at the end of each unit of instruction), and result in an "officially" recorded grade for each student.

Formal evaluation practices, all of which attempt to assess student achievement and performance via direct processes, that is, by minimizing the subjective interpretation of the students' progress by a second party such as the evaluator, are more readily verified by other data collection processes, when contrasted with informal or subjective approaches. If physical education teachers can increase the objectivity of their formal attempts at student evaluation, the accuracy of the data will be enhanced even more.

The reduction of subjectivity within the context of formal evaluative approaches will enhance the veracity of the data. The increased objectivity will thereby increase the

TABLE 13-1	
Types of Evaluation	
Formal	Informal
Objective	Subjective
Norm-referenced	Criterion-referenced
Formative	Summative

usefulness of the results of the evaluation process and ensuing assessment of students' achievement.

Often, because of the presence of powerful intervening variables in the instructional environment, teachers are severely hampered in their efforts to institute formal evaluative approaches in the secondary physical education program. Factors such as overcrowded classes and restricted facilities, equipment, lack of time, and faculty and staff often minimize the viability of formal approaches to evaluation in physical education. Such variables listed earlier often challenge the instructor's persistence and creative instincts relative to the establishment of viable and relevant assessment procedures.

There appears to be a mass of data currently being generated by researchers relating to the problem of the assessment of student performance in physical education.[10-12] For example, a recent study of grading practices of teachers indicated that criteria such as attendance, tardiness, showering, and dressing out account for a major portion of a student's grade in physical education.[13] Veal[9] states, " . . . it is critical to make every attempt to address the lack of formal pupil assessment in secondary physical education." Veal[9] also suggests that a new view or rationale for testing and evaluating students be formulated, one that employs assessment "for motivating students rather than for testing and grading."

Formal evaluation is usually closely associated with, or requires the establishment of, specific and explicitly stated objectives and goals for student outcomes. It should be noted, then, that a clear benefit of formal evaluation practices would be the relative ease of addressing program effectiveness questions and specific student progress.

Informal Evaluation

Informal assessment, by far the most commonly employed evaluation procedure in physical education, includes all approaches not associated with the formal evaluation approach. Most common among these methods is teacher observation, often referred to as "eyeballing." During these informal endeavors, teachers simply observe and listen to the students as they respond. Typically, informal approaches are not associated with any preset or explicitly preconceived notion of standards or criteria of performance, other than loosely formed, vaguely or superficially stated goals (for example, to improve motor proficiency). In addition, more often than not, students are not aware when the teacher is evaluating informally. Verification, then, becomes a problem because the use of informal techniques militates against the collection of valid, corroborating data from other sources. The most common form of informal evaluation is, at its very essence, a heavily subjective approach.

However, despite its relative shortcomings, in a very practical sense, informal techniques can contribute much in the effort to ascertain the student's progress. With just a modicum of organization and selectivity, the informal approach can add much to the teacher's knowledge of students' accomplishments. One suggestion to maximize the results of informal assessment would be to employ a multifaceted assessment strategy, that is, several data collection methods should be utilized. In other words, instructors should not rely on one source of information. A second suggestion for using this easiest to employ technique would be to observe students' performance over a long period of time (that is, employ repeated observations).

The practice of informal evaluation clearly makes it difficult, if not impossible, to account for program effectiveness and, more important, student achievement. As a result, it is difficult to support teachers' efforts or to generate data that could justify physical education programs if teachers and administrators rely on data generated solely from informal techniques.

Objective Evaluation

Assessment techniques that can be employed by more than one individual at different times and produce identical results are known as objective evaluation instruments. For example, a volleyball serving test (for example, AAHPERD Volleyball Skills Test) would be identified as highly objective if several physical education teachers, on different occasions, administered the test to the same class and obtained similar test scores.[14]

Objective measures add positively to the evaluation process because they obviously minimize the possibilities of subjective influences on the teacher's judgment of student performance. Students (and teachers) will more readily accept an objective evaluation for no reason other than that the assessment is based on facts, performance, overt behavior, and measurable abilities that are readily apparent to all observers and participants.

Difficulties arise many times because of the need for precise measurement procedures, specialized equipment, staffing needs, large classes, and too little time. Kneer[10] reported that 16% of 128 physical education teachers professed that evaluation procedures take too much time. Such precision and other demands that must, of necessity,

accompany objective procedures often constrain professionals from their use or render them ineffective in the context of high-school physical education.

Objective measures are recommended for use by secondary physical education teachers because they are amenable with program goals and curricular plans and for this reason can assist professionals in their efforts to explain, clarify, publicize, and sometimes defend their programs and policies. If objective measures are employed (either singly or in conjunction with other assessment strategies), objective results thereby obtained can be emphasized to support the various positions of professional physical education teachers. This latter item is a major advantage of the objective approach to the evaluation task and addresses areas subjective data cannot address.

Subjective Evaluation

Subjective evaluation procedures produce data that are often idiosyncratic in nature, difficult to replicate, and exhibit a high degree of variability and inconsistency between successive administrations or between various evaluators. In other words, objectivity of the information collected is in question. What, then, are the values of subjective evaluation practices?

Many feel that the best measure of a student's progress or achievement is the student's work, products, and efforts as observed on a daily, continual, regular basis, not scores from a one-time administration of a text. Professionals who put forth such a view use subjective data collection procedures (for example, teacher observation, student discussions, anecdotal records, student journals, student self-evaluations) to gather data from a large number of sources, usually over a long period of time. Employed in this manner, subjective evaluation endeavors quite possibly can contribute to student assessment in more comprehensive, varied, and complete ways than more singular, focused, summative approaches (for example, an end of the unit written exam, a motor skills test).

A teacher assigned to a small class would seem to be in an optimal position to make good use of subjective techniques over an extended period. In this way, a varied, comprehensive profile of a student can be constructed, with the possibility of commenting on consistency of performance and durability of learning.

Teachers concerned with assessment of many of the most critical learning to occur in physical education (that is, affective outcomes) are more often than not forced to employ subjective techniques because of the lack of appropriate instruments to collect relevant data. It is imperative to keep in mind that despite the lack of precise evaluation systems for assessing growth in the affective domain, outcomes related to lifestyle change and the valuing of physical activity are among the most important

Evaluation in physical education encompasses learning in the psychomotor as well as in the cognitive and affective domains.

Courtesy of Ann Stevens, Evanston Township High School, Evanston, IL.

in the physical education program and must be periodically evaluated.

How does a professional assess such things as cooperation, appreciation of tennis, self-control, love for swimming, and enjoyment of physical fitness activities? These certainly vitally important concerns would make viable, meaningful program objectives. How can professionals measure achievement in these areas and then assign a symbolic grade as required by school administrators? Typically these tasks are accomplished with much difficulty, probably by relying on subjective evaluation techniques. However, it is imperative that physical education teachers make learned attempts not only to assess student achievement in these areas but also to account for their efforts in facilitating student growth in these areas. In a survey of grading practices of Louisiana physical education teachers, it was demonstrated that difficult constructs such as attitude, effort, and sportsmanship were regularly addressed by professionals in the field.[13] While the study did not specify how physical education teachers accomplished such evaluation, the results do indicate the teachers' willingness to struggle with assessment of important, albeit sometimes illusive, concepts.

Valid, reliable, and objective evidence is more readily obtained from psychomotor and cognitive student development and performance, and physical education teachers should certainly employ appropriate measurement policies and instruments to assess such growth. However, in the affective domain there is a dearth of such measurement technology.

Subjective evaluation can contribute to an assessment program by addressing areas that are not amenable to more objective approaches (for example, valuing, appreciation). A subjective approach to assessment can contribute much if it is part of a broader, multidimensional continuum of evaluative processes. Effective teachers across all disciplines attempt to judge students on the basis of multiple assessments, rather than on the basis of one evaluative interaction. The evaluation process should be viewed as a continuum of daily records of progress in the gymnasium, participation in the learning activities, a variety of exams, skill tests, and motor performance analyses. The intent should be to create a composite profile of student abilities, achievements, strengths, and weaknesses.

Norm-Referenced Evaluation

The traditional and (in many disciplines) the most widely employed evaluation system is one in which the instructor evaluates students by differentially ranking or grading them on the basis of their differential performance. It is not unusual for the physical education instructor to give students a psychomotor skill test and a written test on rules and to combine the two scores for each student in some way to arrive at a course average, and on the basis of the distribution of scores on this average, to decide what grades to give to students. Judging performance in this manner, which is on the basis of relative standing within a group, is referred to as norm-referenced evaluation.[15]

Some authorities employ the term *competitive assessment*

for this method of evaluation because students are forced to compete with each other for the best grades. In other words, a student's test score or grade is interpreted in terms of the performance of the group as a whole. For example, John's grade on a volleyball test battery is directly influenced by how his class performs as a whole. Norm-referenced methodology requires that John's scores be compared against the students in the volleyball class before the determination of his grade.

Several disadvantages or weaknesses of norm-referenced grading (also known as "grading on the curve") are identified by several authorities.[16, 17] Such techniques force less capable students to compete with peers and can effectively discourage them and force them to focus on their inadequacies. Competitive assessment practices can pit students against each other, thereby creating an uncooperative learning environment. Other issues relate to policies, which not only generate competition but also ensure student failure. In norm-referenced procedures, for every student success there must be a student failure. Finally, physical education activities, conducted in the context of the gymnasium, often do not lend themselves to the use of norm-referenced policies. Grading on the curve is often not consistent with evaluation based on performance objectives.[18]

Another drawback to the use of norm-referenced assessment relates to affective development, a goal central to the secondary program in physical education. Competitive grading practices, it should be understood, have the potential for seriously undermining the student's attachment to physical activity. This issue was addressed earlier in this chapter. Yet, it is imperative for educators to weigh carefully the use of norm-referenced methodology, when a major part of their professional endeavor relates to nurturing students' interests in physical activity, and supporting students' efforts to include activity in their daily regimen.

Advantages of normative evaluation strategies include the inherent desirability of using a test that can provide information about an individual's performance relative to scores made by other students in the same population (for example, similar developmental level). The use of normative evaluation requires standardized administrative procedures and a level of validity, reliability, and objectivity, which is attractive to theorists and practitioners. In addition, the formalized directions that accompany norm-referenced evaluation procedures provide prepared, ready-to-use test items, often amenable to or congruent with the need for assessment of large numbers of students quickly and as efficiently as possible, given commonly observed constraints of many secondary physical education programs.

Normative approaches are especially useful when assessment is employed for screening purposes (for example, the identification of students in need of special services), and as a measure against which an individual's performance can be contrasted. For example, to better determine an individual student's progress in motor development or physical fitness, the student's scores could be viewed or interpreted in light of data from similar groups of students (for example, age 16 years, female). With the use of such normative assessment data, specific programing recommendations for a particular student or group of students could be identified.

Finally, the use of norm-referenced techniques is often required by school administrators, for reasons that sometimes go beyond the best interests of the individual student. Standardized (that is, norm-referenced) tests are sometimes required by state education units for comparative purposes (for example, to compare schools, or school districts). In other cases, individual school administrators choose to use standardized procedures and impose such tests on physical education faculty. Finally, the many misconceptions about both criterion- and norm-referenced assessment procedures contribute to the often overreliance on norm-referenced, competitive evaluation techniques.

Criterion-Referenced Evaluation

Students assessed via criterion-referenced evaluation strategies are judged against a performance standard rather than against one another.[15] The primary goal of criterion-referenced grading is to provide the learner with assessment data relative to the student's mastery of specific skills, not to identify students who perform at a superior level when compared with other students. In addition, criterion-referenced evaluation requires that expected student outcomes be predetermined and specified clearly as to the level(s) of performance required or acceptable.

Criterion-referenced assessment is so named because each student is evaluated in relation to the course objectives that are employed as the criterion or standard, and students must demonstrate that they have mastered these objectives.[17] Each student is judged solely by preestablished criteria (for example, unit objectives) and independently of the performance of any other student. For example, in a volleyball serving test, the student's score would be based on the number of overhand serves that land in the backcourt areas, according to the following scheme:

Number of serves (out of 20) that land in the backcourt	Grade
16-20	A
13-15	B
10-12	C
0-9	Retest

Notice that if a student's score falls below a certain minimum level, a retest is indicated. This practice capitalizes on the concept of mastery and shifts the focus of instruction to the achievement of specific learning objectives, rather than solely on the determination of the student's grade. The process of criterion-referenced evaluation, however, does not eliminate (as it is often misunderstood to do) the inherently arbitrary nature of the grading process (that is, the teacher subjectively established that A = 16 to 20 successful serves).

Recent analyses of the current grading practices in physical education reveal a movement to greater dependence on criterion-referenced strategies in the evaluation/grading process. King and Aufsesser[19] suggest that changes in societal attitudes and an accompanying concern for social equality has led to an increased interest in the idea of criterion-referenced testing. They suggest that because the focus of the criterion-referenced approach is on the identification of students who do or do not possess skills (not who is better than who), and because group performance is of secondary importance, it can provide the means for individualizing instructional procedures, if not the entire curriculum.[19] The results of criterion-referenced methodology are directly related to instructional goals and strategies, thereby facilitating teacher instructional behaviors and methods quite possibly leading to personalized and individualized programs.

Hensley et al[11] report research results that support the views of King and Aufsesser.[19] In a recently completed survey of the grading practices of physical education teachers in public schools, they reported that 57% of teachers surveyed used criterion-referenced assessment techniques. This is a significant increase from Imwold's[12] 1982 data, which indicated that 33% of Florida teachers surveyed employed criterion-referenced techniques.

It is obvious, then, that many physical education teachers utilize methods other than the normative approach to assessment and grading. Not unlike the normative strategy, however, there are unique problems with the utilization of criterion or mastery assessment. Johnson and Nelson[20] address several of the implementation concerns associated with criterion-referenced strategies:

◆ Schools are not usually structured for mastery learning systems, which criterion-referenced strategies for evaluation support and encourage. In the criterion-referenced approach to learning and instruction, teachers proceed on the premise that all students *can* master the instructional objectives if provided sufficient time. Schools, unfortunately for a variety of reasons, are not organized on this assumption. This latter situation often accounts for the overemphasis on normative evaluation.

◆ Criterion-referenced practices mandate frequent assessment. In fact, adequate time is essential to the success of criterion-referenced evaluation. The burden of continual testing and follow-up of students with respect to mastery and retention of the many specific unit objectives can overwhelm the most enthusiastic teacher or depart-

ment. To a limited extent, computer technology can help, but additional resources in a variety of forms is nearly always required.

◆ There are problems associated with the design of appropriate criterion-referenced tests. Some teachers underestimate or misjudge the problems inherent in preparing both criterion-referenced tests and identifying appropriate standards or levels of achievement that represent mastery. Arbitrarily determined attainment levels can be problematic, and justification for a particular score or skill level may be difficult to ascertain.

◆ Most schools are not structured and prepared, nor do they support or encourage the individualized and humanized approaches that are implicit in criterion-referenced evaluation practices. Failure to provide physical education teachers with such support and resources often undermines the more humanistic, criterion approach to assessment and drives teachers to become dependent and overreliant on normative strategies.

Several options are available to physical education teachers who wish to employ criterion or mastery assessment methodology. Teachers could develop criterion reference tests for use with similar classes in order to conserve time and use it efficiently, to avoid duplicative efforts, and to assess the abilities of groups of learners who present similar educational profiles. Another suggestion that might facilitate the use of criterion methodology would be to utilize computer technology, if available. Teachers could place assessment instruments and tests on computer files and create a system in which students can self-test on various items. This could be established for students at certain intervals or time periods (for example, study hall, free period). A final suggestion relates to the instructor's establishment of comprehensive student learning center within the physical education teaching stations available. Teachers could provide students with time during lessons for students to rotate to a cognitive assessment station, thereby possibly addressing the demands on time often required of criterion/mastery systems.

Formative Evaluation

Formative evaluation refers to the gathering and assessment of data about students' progress throughout a unit of instruction.[20] This mode of assessment contributes in several ways to the learning encounter:

◆ It can provide meaningful feedback to both the student and teacher.
◆ It enhances and supports the learning process.
◆ It enhances student efforts to achieve instructional outcomes.

The importance of formative evaluation as a standardized instructional procedure should not be minimized. Frequent, if not daily, nongraded assessments guide the

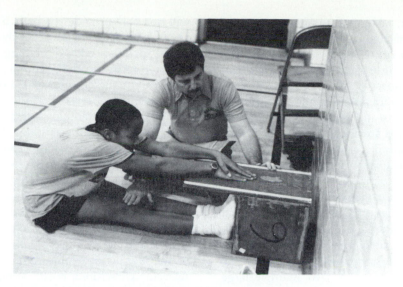

Some physical fitness tests, such as the AAHPERD Physical Best, employ criterion-referenced standards.
Courtesy of Ann Stevens, Evanston Township High School, Evanston, IL.

student toward achievement of goals and assist the instructor by identifying needed modifications in teaching methodology and instructional procedures. The employment of formative assessment can lead to changes in the instructional endeavor and objectives via appropriate and specific feedback, which can be implemented before the students progress too far through the unit of learning. Kindswatter et al[4] believe that teachers should rely heavily on formative assessment (1) to collect information and data on student performance on a regular basis; and (2) to evaluate continually during instructional sessions, as they observe student behavior, consider student responses, provide feedback and correction, and judge the extent to which instruction has been effective.

Krajewski and Shuman[21] suggest that evaluative systems should be continuous (that is, formative). Student evaluations should be given frequently for teachers to assess how they are relating to students and what adaptations, modifications, or corrections, if any, are required to better serve students and address their needs.

Formative evaluation techniques support the view held by many professionals that the best assessment of student performance is derived from observing the students' work and progress on a daily basis. Dunham[1] believes that "continual assessment of student progress should be the norm." Teachers who are well prepared, possess sharp analytical abilities, are observant, and regularly and carefully attend to individual student performance during instruction will find formative assessment to be most accurate and effective in judging student learning.

A commonly observed strategy, employed by many physical education teachers, is the use of an informal assessment procedure during and at the end of each lesson. In such situations, teachers might ask a few questions that focus on the learning objectives of the class. Other teachers employ brief checklists, quizzes, or task sheets to facilitate and enhance these formative assessment efforts. Other professionals attempt to have students analyze their own performance (self-analysis) or assess their peers.

Regardless of specific techniques employed, formative data and strategies can contribute much to the instructional endeavor and enhance student learning. Although it requires a considerable investment of time and is inherently a more complex process, the educational payoffs are significantly greater than the predominant mode of school evaluation, that is, summative evaluation. A discussion of summative procedures follows.

Summative Evaluation

The most common form of school evaluation is summative evaluation, which is defined as evaluation usually conducted at the end of the instructional unit, end of the marking or grading period, or at the end of the school year. Examples would include unit grades, quarter or semester grades, and grades that represent work completed during an entire school year.

When contrasted with formative evaluation, it can be observed that both the purposes and usefulness of summative approaches are quite different. The results of summative evaluation are often directed to groups other than the students (for example, taxpayers, administrators) and thereby are less likely to facilitate or support current student learning. The results of summative evaluation could be employed to enhance future instructional endeavors, however. Summative evaluation also is commonly used as the basis for student grades and to facilitate reports of student progress to parents and the school committee. Grades, by their very nature, are not as useful as formative reports of progress or as specific, criterion-referenced profiles of student performance in physical education. Why, then, are summative approaches so prevalent in educational and physical education circles?[9,10]

First of all, grading is required in some form in all school systems, thereby adding the weight of administrative mandate and institutionalized expectations to the use of summative methods. Summative evaluation, while difficult to accomplish in some settings (for example, large classes), is usually neither as time consuming as nor as dependent on intensive and numerous student-teacher interactions as a program of continual, formative evaluation would be. Also, summative evaluation, usually limited to a one-time administration of a test instrument to the class, is easier to organize and manage.

The various methods, techniques, and strategies reviewed in the previous sections can assist teachers as they attempt to assess student learning and performance in their secondary programs. The intent of the authors, obviously, was not to present an all-inclusive discussion of these methods. Individuals with interests in pursuing any of the various topics or techniques discussed are encouraged to examine some of the fine evaluation and measurement textbooks readily available to students and professionals in the field today.[20,22-25] Rather, the objective was to prepare the reader for the next topic, that is, the process of determining student grades.

DETERMINATION OF STUDENT GRADES

The process of student evaluation begins long before a teacher attempts to calculate a student's grade. It begins, in effect, from the first moment that a professional conceptualizes the results or outcomes of the program and how students will change or grow as a result of program activities. In other words, grading begins from the time that a program is able to identify clearly what their clients should learn, do, and exhibit as a result of the curricular and teacher activities. The process of evaluation is intimately associated with and implicit in the process of formulating program goals and objectives.

In essence, then, grading for our purposes began in an earlier chapter when an attempt was made to define a physically educated person (see Chapter 5). Using this definition as a guideline, a teacher can attempt to determine the various components, which when put together

will not only provide the basis for a grade but also will assess the program's effect on the student's growth.

The specific process of grading involves two steps. The first step relates to the selection of the measurement approach or methods, which will provide information about the student's performance and will comprise the basis of the grade. For example, will the evaluation process include subjective information? Objective data? A combination of both? Or another process? The second step involves the exact process of the calculation of the grade, and the teacher is faced with many choices here. Stated another way, how will the teacher determine the grade based on the accumulated data/information about the student's performance?

As stated earlier, the evaluation process must be related to the instructional objectives to be most effective and relevant. Therefore it is only logical that the instructional objectives form the basis from which to determine the factors on which to grade student performance or progress. Instructional objectives, which can be cognitive, psychomotor, or affective, and the evaluation process, must reflect and be congruent with the objectives of the curriculum. It would be totally illogical, for example, to grade students by means of a written test only in a volleyball unit, if the entire unit was devoted to motor skill development and game play (that is, the students were physically involved 100% of the class time).

A review of the sample grading plan in Table 13-2 reveals four components from which the teacher will determine the students' grade (that is, skill development, knowledge, attendance and participation, and social development). The reader would assume, then, that the instructor employing this system of assessment values much participation in class and cognitive, social, and motor skill development. In effect, if one can assume the employment of relevant and sound measurement techniques, the students will be assessed based directly on their achievement of the objectives of the program and

TABLE 13-2

Sample Grading Plan

Component	Weight (%)
Skill development	30
Knowledge	20
Attendance/participation	20
Social development	30
Attitude (general)	
Cooperation (with teacher; with students)	
Leadership (ability to direct)	
Following directions	
TOTAL	100

TABLE 13-3

Sample Grading Plan #2

Component	Weight (%)	Instruments
Attitude	15	Attendance
Attendance		Teacher observation
Participation		
Preparedness		
Skills	25	Objective skill tests
Form in execution of skills		Teacher observation
Standard of performance		Student self-evaluation
Application in game situations		
Physical Fitness	20	Objective physical fitness tests
Muscular strength		Teacher observation
Muscular endurance		
Cardiorespiratory endurance		
Agility		
Flexibility		
Knowledge and Application	20	Written tests
		Teacher observation
Skills		Self-evaluation
Strategy		
Rules; history		
Conceptual understanding		
Behavior	20	Teacher observation
Social conduct		Self-evaluation
Health and safety practices		
TOTAL	100	

TABLE 13-4

Sample Grading System Based on a Point System

Domain	Points Possible	Total Points Possible
Physical Ability		60
Fitness	30	
Sit-ups test	10	
Pull-ups test	10	
Distance run test	10	
Volleyball skills	30	
Serving test	10	
Set or bump test	5	
Spike test	5	
Game play	10	
Knowledge		20
Written examination (20 questions)	20	
Affective Assessment		20
Instructor's assessment of effort, improvement, attitude, and attendance	20	
TOTAL		100

Grading Scheme

90-100 points = A
80- 89 points = B
70- 79 points = C
60- 69 points = D
0- 59 points = F

in a manner that is in accordance with the usuage of class time or that parallels the program emphases (for example, physical, affective, and cognitive).

Likewise, the reader should be able to discern the important curricular emphases in the schools employing the grading scheme as described in Tables 13-3 and 13-4. Those components to be assessed in each system of evaluation should be the same elements of the program that are regularly and definitively addressed by the instructional programs.

The evaluation of student performance remains a difficult task at best, and the exact process continues to be a matter of seemingly endless debate. Krajewski and Shuman[21] believe that evaluation can be threatening and is often viewed by students in a negative manner. They continue and urge teachers to take precautionary measures to prevent students from feeling pressured or threatened by evaluation techniques.[21]

Although the assignment of grades may be an unpleasant task, professionals are required by administrators and the school system to assign them. Some practical concerns that teachers need to consider in the development of appropriate assessment policies are suggested in the next section.

EVALUATING STUDENT PROGRESS: PRACTICAL CONSIDERATIONS FOR PRACTITIONERS

In light of the fact that physical education is one of the few areas of the school curriculum that addresses student learning in a multidimensional fashion (that is, affective, cognitive, and psychomotor growth), physical education teachers might wish to examine the possibility of reducing the workload associated with the evaluation process. Several investigations have revealed that a common reason put forth by professionals for failing to utilize appropriate measurement and grading practices is related to the enormous blocks of time and professional energy demanded to institute such programs.[7,10,12] In addition, physical education performance tests are generally more complex and time-consuming than other assessment instruments, and they must be administered in classes that are usually shorter than other academic classes.

Teachers should consider the necessity and feasibility of grading all students in physical education each grading period. Can a system be devised whereby a portion of the physical education class is evaluated each marking period? Staggering the evaluation procedure as suggested can alleviate the burden of assessing the large groups of students typically assigned to physical education classes. Physical education teachers might explore the administrative feasibility of this idea.

Major goals of the program should be assessed when appropriate. Teachers need to ask themselves whether it is important that physical fitness be assessed each marking period. Sport skills could be evaluated during each unit because they can be assessed more readily and objectively than attitudes and lifestyle habits. These latter components, equally important in the development of the student, nevertheless tend to develop slowly over extended periods. Quite possibly they should be evaluated in a different pattern than sport skills and fitness.

Yet another idea relates to the use of trained volunteers to assist in the assessment process. In many school districts, organized groups of senior citizens, retired teachers, and physical education leader club members are available to help in the evaluative endeavors normally associated with school physical education.

Adequate planning will enhance the evaluation process. Effective, logical plans are needed to ensure the quality of the evaluation process and teaching. Teachers need to be realistic in the design of such an evaluation strategy. Unwieldy or administratively unfeasible programs help no one.

The development of evaluation plans that emphasize formative assessment concepts tend to be more supportive, nurturing, and less threatening of student efforts. Secondary physical education teachers should consider stressing formative evaluative practices into their evaluation strategies (Box 13-1).

Educators would do much not only for the evaluation-grading process but, more important, also for student learning and performance if they could create, foster, and promote a positive student attitude toward evaluation. How does a teacher accomplish such a seemingly monumental task? The following suggestions should facilitate movement toward the development of more positive student attitudes toward evaluation and grading:

◆ Make expectations and evaluative standards explicit and public.

◆ Eliminate the stigma of failure. A good starting procedure would be to record only successes or positive student performance. When assessing student achievement

BOX 13-1

FACTORS IN GRADING

Psychomotor

Motor ability, motor skills and proficiency, skill in games, and physical fitness components

Cognitive

Mental concepts, knowledge of rules and strategies, skill analyses, mechanical principles, and wellness concepts

Affective

Social behaviors, relations with others, attitudes, appreciation, leadership, cooperation, sportsmanship, and emotional control and development

or progress, award credit for acceptable, passing work and positive accomplishments, but do not "fail" students for unsatisfactory work. Instead, simply do not award credit.

◆ Deinstitutionalize failures. Teachers who can implement the first two suggestions above will find that student attitudes toward grading, the process of evaluation, and failure will be modified.

◆ Teachers should individualize and humanize the evaluative process when possible, and attempt to keep all assessments, grades, and evaluation results private (that is, keep results between the teacher and students). In all practicality, this would mean that teachers would cease calling out test scores across the gym and eliminate the posting of grades with names indicated.

◆ Teachers should emphasize the importance of the evaluation process as a learning experience. Physical education teachers should attempt to stress that information gained from the assessment process should indicate the students' learning capabilities, opportunities for additional learning, and their potential for further learning. The grading process should be viewed as a positive educational experience that can promote growth, development, and desirable behavioral changes.[26]

◆ Finally, teachers should consider carefully the concept of student self-evaluation. It may be worthwhile for teachers to prepare students to evaluate their peers as well as their own performances. Such a practice can facilitate the accomplishment of several evaluation-related tasks as well as other concomitant objectives. This topic will be addressed more elaborately later in this chapter.

Other concerns related to the grading process are directed to efforts of physical education teachers in the development of grading procedures that are fair, reflect studied professional judgments, and are compassionate.

To facilitate the development of appropriate and thoughtful grading systems, the following general guidelines are offered:

1. Grades should be valid. They should accurately represent pupil achievement for which they stand.
2. Grades should be reliable. Grades should be accurate, consistent, and stand for the same results for each student. It is imperative, also, for teachers to be consistent in their expectations for students during the evaluation process.
3. Grades should be as objective as possible. Different teachers, given the same student data, should arrive at the same grade.
4. The process of determining grades must be based on achievement of the educational objectives of the curriculum, rather than on idiosyncratic, irrelevant, or insignificant aspects of the program.
5. Student grades should be based on a sufficient number of observations. Grades should be based on more than one educational objective. Judging students' performances on the basis of multiple observations and assessment techniques increases the accuracy of the evaluation.
6. Grading in physical education should parallel the assessment process in other subjects, yet leave room for the uniqueness of the educational objectives of the physical education curriculum (that is, emphasis on affective growth and development).
7. Student evaluation should be based on, and directly related to, the teacher's knowledge of students' abilities. Grading should not be permitted to be transformed into a system of rewards and punishments, operating independent of student achievement.
8. Grading should enhance teaching efforts (that is, it should be directed to addressing student weaknesses and gaps in knowledge).
9. Grading should address the whole student (that is, cognitive, affective, and psychomotor dimensions).
10. The grading system should be flexible so it can be used with a wide variety of teaching methodologies (that is, the grading system should not be tied to one specific teaching method).
11. Grading procedures should provide for accurate reporting to all concerned parties (for example, parents and students).

A critical aspect in the formulation of a sound grading policy relates to the determination of the weighting for each of the components of the grade. How much should psychomotor development be weighted? 50%? 40%? How much weight should affective growth be assigned? 20%? 35%? How does a teacher determine such weightings? Probably the easiest method of determining such weightings is to analyze program objectives and correlate the percentage of class time devoted to specific areas of the curriculum with a similar weighting in the determination of the grade. Selection of objectives in the initial planning stages of instructional units, and then the determination of the emphasis to be placed on each objective, can make this task easier. Quite possibly a specific example might help clarify this procedure.

If, upon analysis of program objectives and content within a grading period, it is determined that 40% of the program is devoted to psychomotor development (for example, physical fitness, motor skill development, proficiency in various activities), then it would be a fair procedure to assign the psychomotor aspect of the student's grade a weighting of 40%. Likewise, if cognitive growth consumes approximately 20% of the time, energy, and efforts of both students, teachers, and the program as a whole, then it should be assigned a 20% weighting in the calculation of the student's grade.

SYSTEMATIC STUDENT EVALUATION: SOME UNIQUE ALTERNATIVES

Dunham[1] has proposed a systematic yet practical series of steps to facilitate student evaluation. The set of procedures he suggests parallels the conditions normally

A student uses a checklist to evaluate a peer's performance.
Courtesy of Ben Lombardo, Rhode Island College, Providence, RI.

found within the context of high school physical education. This assessment program is based on the teacher's specification of five levels of planning: (1) outcomes; (2) activities; (3) task identification; (4) instructional preparation including determining content, verifying procedures, and recording, summarizing, and interpreting data; and (5) lesson selection. The unique features of Dunham's program include the following:

1. It addresses the affective, cognitive, and psychomotor areas in a comprehensive manner.
2. It emphasizes formative evaluation techniques.
3. It focuses on each student in every class, which allows teachers to make some assessments every instructional period.
4. The selection of lesson content is always based on those competencies students have not mastered.[27]

Dunham's suggestions hold much potential for enhancing evaluation techniques of physical education teachers and strengthening the association of instructional practice and assessment procedures.

Reeve and Morrison[27] reported on efforts to implement Dunham's approach. They prepared and employed a series of skill task sheets and cognitive quizzes. The skill task sheets provide a complete and accurate summary of each skill and are divided into preparation and execution, both presented sequentially. These skill sheets support instructional practice that is complete, consistent, and accurate. During the lesson, students can review the skill sheets. (They are often projected on a wall.) Teachers create skill checklists to indicate the level of skill proficiency demonstrated by students in each class.

Cognitive quizzes of 10 to 15 questions are developed to serve as the basis for cognitive evaluation. Students themselves are expected to select and answer five questions from a much larger list. The cognitive grade is derived from the percentage of total points possible on all the tests.

In the system Reeve and Morrison conceived, grades were determined by weighting cognitive achievement at 50% and motor skill proficiency as determined by the skill check sheets, also weighted at 50%. The motor skill component is the percentage of the total number of skills students complete at a functional level of competency. A skill is considered to be mastered if the student has check marks for the last three teacher observations of that skill. Reeve and Morrison[27] explain that "since we teach to a functional level of competency, all students who work hard in class should get satisfactory grades."

This program has several positive aspects. The comprehensiveness of the approach, its relative simplicity in assessing student growth across several dimensions (affective, cognitive, and psychomotor), and its congruence with the realities of the high-school physical education program are readily apparent. Moreover, it should also be realized that this system, based on Dunham's ideas

and operationalized by Reeve and Morrison, emphasizes (1) the daily use of formal teacher observation of student motor development, (2) the use of prepared checklists to formatively assess motor proficiency and learning, (3) the almost daily use of quizzes to assess cognitive growth, and (4) the maintenance of a notebook recording significant deviations from acceptable standards of behavior.

The system, viewed from a broader perspective, complements instructional practice very well, and by means of the summarization process assists teachers in their efforts to determine what percentage of the class has mastered particular skills. In other words, feedback about group achievement is made readily available to the teacher. Clearly, this approach offers much to the secondary physical education teacher.

A second alternative program is suggested by Ratliffe, who offers a realistic and practical procedure for skill evaluations, based on generic levels of proficiency.[28,29] By employing a general set of descriptors common to all skills, motor performance is classified into four generic levels. These levels parallel the stages individuals progress through as they learn motor skills. This latter fact provides Ratliffe's approach with a sound and logical basis for the formulation of student grades. The four generic levels, as identified by Ratliffe, are precontrol (virtually no control, haphazard), control (more frequent success, trials start to appear similar), utilization (consistent performance, skills can be used in combination with other skills), and proficiency (fluid, smooth appearance to movements, high level of ability, skills can be employed in a variety of situations, movement appears effortless).[26]

Evaluation is based on qualitative aspects (that is, proper mechanical form) and quantitative aspects (that is, how many times the goal is attained). Ratliffe suggests that teachers can employ the generic levels to describe a student's skill proficiency by considering the quality of performance in addition to a quantifiable measure of goal attainment.

The utilization of Ratliffe's practical system hinges upon the establishment of an environment that permits learners to practice independently while the teacher moves into an optimal observation position to facilitate individual assessments. The use of these generic levels of skill proficiency offers teachers some practical suggestions and viable advantages when conducting student evaluations. Once teachers have learned the four generic levels, this program can be easily employed during the course of practice and game situations, because it places few demands on teachers. The use of qualitative and quantitative information ensures more accurate recording of student achievement and motor behavior. Finally, the use of the descriptors within the definition of each generic level will assist teachers and students as they attempt to visualize and describe a student's skill level and in this way can enhance the communication of the results of evaluation to all interested parties (administrators, parents, and students).

These alternative approaches offer much to secondary school physical education teachers and can facilitate objective planning, recording and reporting student grades, and demonstrating program effectiveness. More important they complement and support the evaluation process as it relates to the instructional endeavor and, therefore, enhances student learning. In the next section, the subject of student self-evaluation will be explored as yet another method of facilitating both instructional effectiveness and student learning.

SELF-EVALUATION

In this section the concept of self-evaluation as an assessment strategy will be examined. If educators truly believe that the goals of education include self-determination, appropriate and rational decision making, independent thinking, responsibility for onself, and self-reliance, then at some point students should experience the process of identifying how well they have performed. If physical education teachers believe that a goal of physical education is to develop individuals capable of learning on their own, with appropriate and accurate self-monitoring abilities, they must include such activities in the high-school program. O'Brien[30] believes that responsibility, peer cooperation, and self-motivation are important outcomes of physical education and has designed a self-grading program to achieve these objectives. What follows is a closer look at O'Brien's program.

Within a democratic classroom environment, O'Brien implemented a cooperative, student-teacher planning process to enhance the students' feeling of ownership in the physical education program. The next step involved preparing students to set reasonable and appropriate goals, utilizing assessment data. The program, which included several program components (for example, psychomotor skill development, effort, cooperative ventures, leadership, various knowledges and concepts related to health, wellness, sports) not only facilitated the growth and development of each student, but it also nurtured students' ability to rate, analyze, and evaluate both their own performances and those of their peers. At the close of each 9-week period, students are asked to assign themselves a letter grade. In addition, students must prepare a written appraisal of their skill, knowledge, participation, and fitness level, and they must submit an explanation of why they deserve that particular grade.[30] A basic premise of the program is that students will receive the self-assigned grade unless the grade is wholly indefensible. (Over a period of 1 year, only 5 of 90 grades were different when teacher- and student-assigned grades were contrasted.)

O'Brien concludes that while self-grading has some disadvantages, such as student dishonesty and the need for regular and open communication with administrators, the advantages clearly support its continued use. As a direct result of this program, she noted an increase in personal responsibility, increased awareness of results, and improved quality of work on the part of the students.[30]

Teppler created a grading system for his ninth-grade students, which can be employed with all secondary students. Teppler encouraged and supported students as they not only planned their own unit via a contract learning unit but also assisted in the grading procedure. Specifically, Teppler designed the program so that the unit mark was comprised of 50% teacher evaluation and 50% student evaluation. Students had to indicate the grade they deserved and also had to describe several reasons why they deserved the mark they indicated.[31] Teppler facilitated this process by providing students with detailed behavioral guidelines for each grade classification to assist students in their self-evaluation efforts. For example, the following items (selected from a much longer list of guidelines) would be used by students to determine if their efforts should be assessed in the 85% to 100% ("excellent") category:

1. The student used a variety of resources (people, material, and situations) during the volleyball unit.
2. The students felt the experience was rewarding in that new knowledge and skills related to volleyball were gained.
3. The student can perform volleyball skills and execute related strategies that were not mastered before the unit.
4. Students developed skills, strategies, and knowledge as indicated in the students' contract plans.

Hellison describes strategies to encourage students to develop their own grading systems. While grades provide students with another type of reinforcement, he urges that they be based on improvement. Specifically, Hellison believes that students must be evaluated on an individual basis, starting at a point where they are in their development at the present time. Self-evaluation strategies, given their inherent personal nature, can best foster the achievement of outcomes that can support students in their pursuit of self-understanding and can foster learning via physical education.[31]

Mosston and Ashworth,[32] in their classic work on teaching styles in physical education, put forth many suggestions for the incorporation of self- or peer-evaluation into instructional practice. Among the many styles that would seem to foster student self-assessment would be the practice style, the reciprocal style, the self-check style, and the inclusion style (Figs. 13-1 and 13-2). All of these styles center about students evaluating peers or assessing their performance. Use of such styles by physical education teachers would not only facilitate the task of stu-

Name ————————————————————— Task sheet # —————————

Class ————————————————————— Date —————————

Basketball Shooting

To the Student:

Perform each task as described in the program below and place a check next to the completed task.

		Dates	Teacher Feedback
1. One-hand shot from the foul line			
	25 shots	———	————————————
2. Jump shot from 10 feet			
Center	15 shots	———	————————————
Right	15 shots	———	————————————
Left	15 shots	———	————————————
3. Repeat #2 above from 15 feet			
Center	15 shots	———	————————————
Right	15 shots	———	————————————
Left	15 shots	———	————————————

FIG. 13-1　　Sample task sheet A.

Name ———————————————— Partner ————————————————

Class ———————————————— Task sheet —————————

Date —————————

Badminton—Forehand Overhead Clear

To the students: This task is performed in groups of 3: a doer, a tosser, and an observer.
Tosser: throw a high, clear service to the doer.
Doer: practice the forehand clear 10 times.
Observer: analyze the doer's form by comparing the performance to the criteria listed below. Offer feedback about what is done well and what needs to be corrected. Rotate roles after each 10 attempts.

Task criteria:
1. Backswing taken with racket, as if to throw it.　　————
2. Left side of body turned to the net, as weight shifts to back leg.　　————
3. Shuttle struck overhead but in front of body, with arm fully extended.　　————
4. Racket head contacts bird from below.
5. Body weight put into shot, as weight shifts onto front leg. Strong wrist action.　　————
6. Follow through in direction of intended flight of bird.　　————

FIG. 13-2　　Sample task sheet B.

BOX 13-2

GUIDELINES FOR SUCCESSFUL STUDENT SELF-EVALUATION

1. Clearly explain the criteria for the determination of successful performance.
2. Ensure student comprehension of the assessment procedures.
3. Provide adequate time and psychological support (encouragement) for the assessment system.
4. Teachers must provide abundant feedback.
5. Provide students with clearly stated behavioral guidelines to facilitate the translation of their achievements to a clear assessment and a grade if needed.
6. Grades should not be solely dependent on the self-evaluation process.
7. Teachers should facilitate student follow-up learning plans guided by the evaluation results.

dent assessment but would also foster student self-evaluation abilities.

Clearly, self-evaluation techniques have inherent shortcomings, such as the time required, tracking, organizing, and maintaining written records and related paperwork. However, the advantages, from the authors' perspective, clearly support the use of these and other similar self-assessment methods. These self-evaluation procedures require students to specify their goals and often demand that they create plans to attain their goals and design plans for evaluating their programs.

Guidelines that can facilitate successful student self-analysis and self-evaluations, developed by Dougherty and Bonanno,[33] are outlined in Box 13-2. Teachers interested in this strategy would do well to attempt to incorporate these into their assessment programs.

SUMMARY

The legitimacy and value of the evaluation process, as it relates specifically to the assignment of student grades in any subject, may be a cause for debate, but at the present time it is a function of the school and, as such, must be properly addressed and accomplished.[26] The assessment process is a significant component of the instructional endeavor and should be employed not only to determine grades but also to improve and maintain the positive aspects of the curriculum.

Evaluation procedures and grading systems work best when the student's performance in school not only reflects the institution's instructional goals but also is closely related to the student's future fortunes. In the case of phys-

ical education, this idea translates to convincing students that the program of activities and skills related to human movement, physical development, and the various concepts, which can be studied and mastered via motor activities, are vitally important to the enhancement of students' health and productivity. By stating it this way, physical education teachers can impose standards reflecting the importance of the various curricular concepts included in the school program, and these standards should be reflected in assessment strategies. This latter statement should not be interpreted to mean that the authors favor or support depersonalized or severely restrictive evaluation techniques. The authors are quite opposed to such strategies. Rather, it is suggested here that teachers diligently present arguments that capture the students' interest and convince and persuade them, intellectually, of the importance of an active lifestyle and health and wellness concepts. Effective grading systems can be promoted more readily if they can demonstrate their direct relationship to the future needs, ambitions, and concerns of students. Physical education teachers need to strive toward attainment of this goal. Students who work conscientiously and thoughtfully in school would then be attempting to attain goals relevant to the school curricular goals and toward objectives that will enhance their future personal and professional aspirations. Working industriously within educational institutions, then, would have a direct payoff.

The need for objective evaluation of learning and achievement is obvious, but practical ways to accomplish it in the physical education setting is difficult, if not elusive. Most concerned teachers have wrestled with the problems and issues related to the evaluation process. Instructional procedures and the assessment process (resulting in a grade for each student) should complement each other. As a result of a clearly conceived and articulated evaluation system, teachers will feel more effective and more purposeful, and students will be captured not only by the feelings that normally accompany achievement, but also by the underlying learning process.

FOR REVIEW

1. Discuss the role and influence of the evaluation process in physical education.
2. Develop a personal grading system that is functional, fair, and clear. What factors will be considered in grading? What weighting will be assigned to each factor?
3. Develop an evaluation design for a typical unit taught in secondary school physical education. What sources of evaluative data will you use? Why?

REFERENCES

1. Dunham P: Evaluation for excellence: a systematic approach, *JOPERD* 57(6):34-36, 60, 1986.
2. Schafer WD, Lissitz RW: Measurement training for school personnel: recommendations and reality, *Journal of Teacher Education* 38(3):57-63, 1987.

3. Morris GSD, Stiehl J: *Physical education: from intent to action,* Columbus, Ohio, 1985, Charles E Merrill Publishing.

4. Kindswatter R, Wilen W, Ishler M: *Dynamics of effective teaching,* New York, 1988, Longman.

5. Colfer GR et al: *Contemporary physical education,* Dubuque, Iowa, 1986, William C Brown.

6. Curwin RL, Mendler AN: *Discipline with dignity,* Alexandria, Va, 1988, Association for Supervision and Curriculum Development.

7. Crooks TJ: The impact of classroom evaluation practices on students, *Review of Educational Research* 58(4):438-481, 1988.

8. Loper D et al: Healthful living: the goal, physical education the means? *JOPERD* 60(2):58-61, 1989.

9. Veal M: Pupil assessment issues: a teacher educator's perspective, *Quest* 40(2):151-161, 1988.

10. Kneer M: Description of physical education instructional theory/practice gap in selected secondary schools, *JOTPE* 5(2):91-106, 1986.

11. Hensley LD et al: A survey of grading practices in public school physical education, *Journal of Research and Development in Education* 22(4):37-42, 1989.

12. Imwold CH, Rider RA, Johnson DJ: The use of evaluation in public school physical education programs, *JOTPE* 2(1):13-18, 1982.

13. Nelson J, Moore J, Dorociak J: A survey of grading practices in physical education in Louisiana, *Louisiana Journal for Health, Physical Education, Recreation, and Dance* 28:18-21, 1983.

14. Shay C: *AAHPERD Skills Test Manual: volleyball,* Reston, Va, 1969, AAHPERD.

15. Siedentop D: *Developing teaching skills in physical education,* ed 3, Palo Alto, Calif, 1991, Mayfield Publishing.

16. Henson KT: *Secondary teaching methods,* Lexington, Mass, 1981, DC Heath.

17. Gentile JR: Toward excellence in teaching: grading practices, *The Reporter,* State University of New York at Buffalo, March 25:4, 1971.

18. Harrison JM, Blakemore CL: *Instructional strategies for secondary school physical education,* ed 2, Dubuque, Iowa, 1989, William C Brown.

19. King HA, Aufsesser KS: Criterion-referenced testing—an ongoing process, *JOPERD* 59(1):58-63, 1988.

20. Johnson BL, Nelson JK: *Practical measurements for evaluation in physical education,* ed 4, New York, 1986, Macmillan Publishing.

21. Krajewski RJ, Shuman RB: *The beginning teacher: a practical guide to problem solving,* Washington, DC, 1979, NEA.

22. Baumgartner TA, Jackson AJ: *Measurement for evaluation in physical education and exercise science,* ed 4, Dubuque, Iowa, 1991, William C Brown.

23. Barrow HM, McGee R, Tiatschler KA: *Practical measurement in physical education and sport,* ed 4, Philadelphia, 1989, Lea & Febiger.

24. Safrit MJ, Wood TM, editors: *Measurement concepts in physical education and exercise science,* Champaign, Ill, 1989, Human Kinetics.

25. Clarke HH, Clarke DH: *Application of measurement to physical education,* ed 6, Englewood Cliffs, NJ, 1987, Prentice Hall.

26. Nixon JE, Jewett AE: *An introduction to physical education,* ed 9, Philadelphia, 1980, Saunders.

27. Reeve J, Morrison C: Teaching for learning: the application of systematic evaluation, *JOPERD* 57(6):37-39, 1986.

28. Ratliffe T: Evaluation of students' skill using generic levels of skill proficiency, *The Physical Educator* 41(2):64-68, 1984.

29. Graham G et al: *Children moving: a reflective approach to teaching physical education,* Palo Alto, Calif, 1980, Mayfield Publishing.

30. O'Brien DB: Self-grading to develop responsibility and cooperation. In Carlson RP, editor: *Ideas for secondary school physical education—II,* Reston, Va, 1984, AAHPERD.

31. Hellison D: *Goals and strategies for teaching physical education,* Champaign, Ill, 1985, Human Kinetics.

32. Mosston M, Ashworth S: *Teaching physical education,* ed 3, Columbus, Ohio, 1986, Merrill Publishing.

33. Dougherty NJ, Bonanno D: *Contemporary approaches to the teaching of physical education,* ed 2, Scottsdale, Ariz, 1987, Gorsuch Scarisbrick.

ANNOTATED READINGS

Hensley LD et al: Is evaluation worth the effort? *JOPERD* 58(6):59-62, 1987.

This article explores the evaluation process as it pertains to a typical physical education class. The authors believe that assessment is the least understood and most often abused part of physical education programs today. Data from a 1986 study of almost 1400 physical education teachers are reviewed and ways of improving the evaluation process are discussed.

Hensley LD: Current measurement and evaluation practices in professional PE, *JOPERD* 61(3):32-33, 1990.

This short, excellent article provides an historical review of evaluation practices in physical education. Next, Hensley outlines the procedures currently employed by physical education teachers, referring to an extensive study completed in 1989 by Hensley et al. The author suggests that only minimal changes have occurred since 1967, and the same constraints then are operational as the profession enters a new decade. Suggestions for changes in both pre- and in-service preparation programs are outlined.

King HA: Practitioners and the scholar-theorists of measurement—an uncoordinated alliance, *JOPERD* 61(3):34-35, 1990.

King supports the practitioner's rejection of recommendations emanating from scholars and academicians, and claims that professional preparation programs are out of touch with the realities of the school. Scholars in evaluation and measurement are constrained by the perils of the academic world and produce literature that does not help the practitioner. It is suggested here that the primary function of the evaluation process for practitioners (that is, to assess whether particular outcomes of the instructional process have been attained) have been ignored by university-based professionals. Plans to address such concerns must be developed by both parties in the interests of promoting sound programs.

Marks MC: A ticket out the door, *Strategies* 2(2):17, 27, 1988.

This article focuses on an assessment technique labeled "closure assessment," which, it is suggested, should be employed at the conclusion of a physical education class. It is suggested that closure assessment activities can help students by providing opportunities to demonstrate their mastery of the instructional goals. This approach can help teachers ascertain student success and will provide valuable feedback to be used in planning.

Marsh JJ: Measuring affective objectives in physical education, *The Physical Educator* 41(2):77-81, 1984.

This article provides a guide for the development and evaluation of appropriate affective behavioral objectives for physical education. An extensive list of affective objectives, specific to physical education, is provided to the reader. The author then continues to discuss the process of monitoring and evaluating student achievement of these objectives, suggesting techniques that would facilitate the accomplishment of this task.

CHAPTER 14

Improving Teaching

CHAPTER OBJECTIVES

◆ To identify strategies that will improve instructional practice

◆ To review selected methods of systematically analyzing instruction

◆ To identify methods of collecting information about instructional behaviors

◆ To discuss the translation of the results of systematic analysis to changes in instruction

Schools perform remarkable feats, constantly repeated nationwide on a daily basis, and account in no small way for the quality of life in U.S. society. Each year hundreds of thousands of students from diverse backgrounds, cultures, and family circumstances receive superb instruction and guidance in a wide variety of subject areas. As a result, much growth and learning are achieved.

However, educators in all fields can never become satisfied with the success of schools and the performance of teachers. At all grade levels and in all subject fields, educational leaders must instill a desire, a drive, and a willingness to pursue excellence. It is quite obvious that effective and successful educators relentlessly pursue knowledge, including self-knowledge. In effect, teachers at all levels and in all subjects are constantly in a state of "becoming" and evolving, hopefully in the direction of increasing effectiveness. To do less is to lose sight of an aspect central to the mission of professionally committed educators.

It is with this intent that this chapter is presented. In the spirit of striving for perfection and in an effort to facilitate enhanced, more comprehensive, and broader learning in students, the authors will review techniques of improving instruction. These techniques differ in focus but have the same intent as the material present in other sections of this text, which also can enhance teaching and the instructional process (see Chapter 6).

Increasingly, it becomes quite evident that the contributions that effective physical education teachers can make to society and its populace can be monumental. At the least, an effective high-school program can heighten awareness of the benefits of a healthy lifestyle and the positive effects of a wellness-oriented personal health profile. This goal, by itself, more than justifies the physical education teacher's pursuit of excellence.

However, highly potent contextual factors, not easily overlooked, often constrain the accomplishment of such goals and certainly influence significantly the status and condition of secondary schools today. Budgets are regularly and severely constrained, classes often are oversubscribed, teaching supplies and equipment are scarce, and yet the daily demands for maximizing effectiveness, from various groups (for example, parents, taxpayers, educational reformers, state certifying boards) are seemingly endless. It is not necessary at this point to reiterate the often weak and defensive position secondary school physical education possesses in various parts of the country. Several chapters in this book have dealt with these latter issues, and the reader is referred to those sections for the discussions of accountability in education and the response of secondary programs in physical education (see Chapter 6).

The point here is that practitioners and administrators in physical education must do all that is possible within their means to maximize teaching effectiveness of their faculty (and programs). This latter point, however, should not lead the reader to think that all the problems of the modern high school today will be resolved by increased teaching effectiveness (as some educational reformers and certifying agencies would have the general population believe). This simply is not so! The problems and conditions of secondary education are far too complex and interdependent to be addressed by such a simplistic, unidimensional view. The concerns go well beyond questions of teacher effectiveness.

Problems exist at the level of administrative support and leadership; community support; parental involvement; availability of and access to equipment and supplies; budgetary concerns; and student-teacher ratios, all of which contribute to the current condition of secondary school physical education. Teaching effectiveness is only a part of the problem, and it is potentially part of the answer. The issue to be addressed in this chapter is how instruction and teaching effectiveness can be improved.

Metzler[1] phrases this latter point quite clearly. He states that physical education teachers must strive to make a difference in the lives of those students who are currently in schools and who will soon be in a position to decide the value of physical education programs in their children's schools. Therefore these teachers must demonstrate that they have the abilities required to assist students to attain programatic goals and with a noticeable effect across their lifetimes.[1] Metzler continues and asserts that the best way to achieve this is to maximize teaching effectiveness. Specifically, Metzler[1] states the following:

> The most meaningful differences teachers can make to children is to help them learn motor skills, work toward improved fitness, and develop lasting positive attitudes toward our subject matter. The best way to accomplish this is to ensure they are instructed by competent, effective teachers.

A major premise of this chapter is that to benefit and learn from teaching experiences, and likewise to facilitate continued development and competence in teaching, practitioners must develop skill in the analysis of teaching. While this development may be time-consuming, it is not a difficult process. The outcomes, however, are extremely powerful and certainly more than worth the investment in time.

EFFECTIVE TEACHING

To this point many ideas about how to teach secondary school physical education have been presented (see Chapters 5, 6, and 14). It is hoped that the reader has acquired a sense of what comprises a mature, professional teacher, and how teachers go about their business. The mature teacher manifests respect for teaching as a science applied in an open, constantly changing, and flexible environment; provides appropriate models for students as a scholar and a leader; employs a broad repertoire of teaching methods; and displays tolerance and patience with

the conditions and circumstances that influence instruction but often cannot be directly controlled.

Before commencing the discussion of how to improve teaching, it is necessary to define effective teaching. This is especially important because it should serve to guide teachers in their efforts to improve their instructional behaviors. Teachers need to possess a conceptual, if not practical, model of success to shape and guide their efforts.

Not unexpectedly, there are abundant definitions of effectiveness in the professional literature. An early definition by Flanders[2] guided much early research in teaching effectiveness and centered on the interaction between teachers and students:

> . . . an effective teacher interacts skillfully with pupils so that they learn more and like learning . . . teaching effectiveness is concerned with those aspects of teaching over which the teacher has direct control.

More recently Shulman[3] described an effective teacher as one who is a good classroom manager, has a firm grasp of subject matter, has professional knowledge about how students learn, and possesses pedagogical content knowledge defined as "an ability to select topics and ideas that are central to the content area, and to present them in ways that are comprehensible and interesting to students."

Traditionally, at least in classroom settings, effective teaching has been associated with student gains as measured on standardized achievement tests. Teaching effectiveness research, when viewed broadly, has emphasized the importance of well-managed classrooms, in which teachers spend most of their time actively instructing students and guiding their learning.[4]

Dougherty and Bonanno,[5] professional physical education teachers, believe that

> . . . the teachers of the twenty-first century must learn to anticipate change and make long-range assumptions. They must be informed, future-oriented, adaptable individuals who are capable of envisioning future alternatives and devising suitable courses of action for themselves and their pupils. Teachers must be able to integrate, synthesize, and coordinate diverse concepts representing both psychological and bioanalytic dimensions in such a way that the individual needs of their students are best served.

Mosston and Ashworth[6] believe that effectiveness centers about the relationship between the teacher and the student and can be discerned only when the learner grows as a person and manifests increased motor proficiency. Another prominent physical education teacher, Donald Hellison,[7] has defined a good teacher as "a teacher whose students learn, perceive themselves as learning, and feel good about that learning experience." Other authorities in physical education provide yet another definition, which, simply put, states that effective teaching is defined as the achievement of the intended outcomes of instruction.[1,6] This latter definitional effort would, therefore, imply that a measure of effectiveness would include comparative analysis of the teacher's plans (for example, objectiveness and time management) and the outcomes of the lesson (for example, student learning and student behaviors).

Harrison,[8] in a thorough review of the professional literature on effective teaching, compiled a rather complete profile of the effective teacher. The effective teacher is one who:

1. Has high expectations for students.
2. Manages classes in ways that increase academic learning time and opportunities to learn.
3. Creates a supportive learning environment in which students are treated as individuals and in which they know that help is available.
4. Selects material at an appropriate level of difficulty for students, moves them through it at a rapid pace, and accomplishes this in small steps with high levels of success.
5. Teaches to mastery.
6. Employs active, direct instruction, including teacher-controlled coverage of extensive content through structured learning activities and appropriate pacing, monitoring of pupil performance, immediate academically-oriented feedback, and a task-oriented yet relaxed environment.

A more concise definition is provided by Nichols,[9] who states that "effective teaching results from the combination of carefully planned and organized learning experiences and the teacher's ability to carry the lesson through to successful completion." This includes:

1. Preparing the student for learning (that is, mindset, preparatory set, motivation, attention getting, and focusing).
2. Presenting the lesson material.
3. Guiding the lesson activities to meet the objectives (congruence).
4. The provision of feedback and adjusting the activity (teacher response/sensitivity to student responses; modulating the activities; pace of lesson; and time).
5. Summation, closure, and ending.

Our view (outlined more thoroughly in Chapter 9) of effective teaching is that to be effective implies the teacher's execution of carefully organized and planned learning experiences, the teacher's skill in bringing the lesson to successful completion, and the students' learning in one or more of the many dimensions of human development.

Whether the reader subscribes to the definitions of effective teaching described here or elsewhere is not crit-ical. What is critical, however, is that teachers of physical education can describe clearly their concept of quality and effective teaching, because this view will serve as a basis for future changes, modifications, and, hopefully, improvements.

The term *concept of teaching* refers to those notions teachers have that reflect their beliefs and thoughts about what they think teaching should be. Typically such a concept of teaching should include (1) the most important goals of teaching and (2) the most critical functions teachers should perform to achieve these goals (that is, to be effective).[10]

In this chapter, several systematic techniques directed toward enhancement of instructional endeavors will be described, all of which will possibly result in a wealth of descriptive information about teaching. Anderson[10] suggests that one way to begin deciphering such information is to view the data in light of the aforementioned concept of teaching. In other words, once the data has been gathered, the teacher should interpret such information through the lenses provided by the individual teacher's concept of teaching.

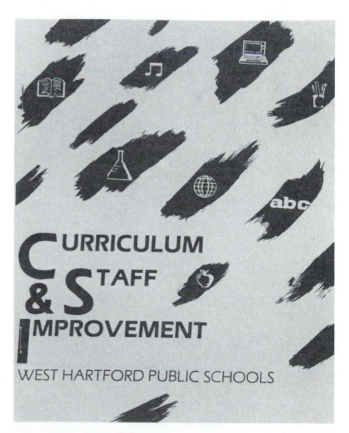

Some school districts have well-designed approaches to the improvement of the curriculum and teachers.

Courtesy of Suzi D'Annalfo, Conard High School, West Hartford, CT.

STRATEGIES FOR IMPROVING TEACHING

In this section, several strategies that can enhance teaching effectiveness will be suggested. The emphasis will be on techniques that will promote continued growth in pedagogical skills. The essential feature of all the strategies employed is the actual experience of teaching, coupled with relevant and specific feedback about the teacher's performance.[11] There is much research that indicates that to produce effective and lasting change in instruction, three elements are required: (1) a descriptive record of the teaching episode; (2) a specific, clearly defined focus; and (3) the presence of an additional person capable of providing an unemotional, objective, and knowledgeable point of view.[12,13]

In essence, then, there is much to suggest that teaching can be improved only if teachers receive well-conceived, specific, and regular feedback about their performance from a competent observer of instructional practice. Because one or more of these critical elements are often unavailable in the secondary setting, strategies are also included that, while somewhat less potent in effect, can facilitate continued growth as a professional teacher in the absence of one or more of the elements previously identified.

Systematic Analysis

The most widely used approach employed by teachers and supervisors alike to enhance teaching effectiveness is based on the views, analyses, perceptions, and interpretations of an observer. Typically, the instructional session is viewed by an observer, whereupon that same individual provides an analysis to the teacher, derived from a personal frame of reference. Although such observations or supervisory episodes can be helpful (especially if the participants are astute, perceptive, and have studied pedagogy), such data can be significantly biased and are often highly inferential. A more beneficial and productive approach, however, is to address the various components of instruction of interest in a systematic manner.

A systematic approach to improved instruction starts with an effort to identify variables of interest or the focus of analysis. It includes an application of a logical, well-conceived, clearly defined data collection and data analysis instrument for the purpose of employing this system in a methodical, reliable, and regular manner. The most widely used systems within the physical education profession have been The Cheffers Adaptation of The Flanders Interaction Analysis System[14] (CAFIAS) and Academic Learning Time in Physical Education[15] (ALT-PE). Many of the systems outlined for use in instructional physical education programs described in Darst et al[16] would serve this function well.

B O X   1 4 - 1

GOALS OF SYSTEMATIC ANALYSIS OF INSTRUCTION

1. Professional development of teachers
2. Improvement of teachers' effectiveness
3. Enhanced student learning
4. Increased teacher reflective abilities
5. Enhanced self-monitoring abilities of teachers

If this process is employed, the teacher and observer must reach consensus about the categories or classifications of behavior (for example, teacher and student) or instructional factors of interest, how such categories are to be defined, coded, counted, and compared. All of these decisions will have to be resolved before the actual observation. In effect, the teacher scheduled for observation will have clear and direct knowledge of the direction, emphasis, focus, and basis of the postlesson discussion and analysis.

Systematic analysis of instruction can be defined as a process of identifying discrete and continuous elements of behaviors, actions, interactions, and pedagogical moves that occur in the instructional setting, for the purpose of analyzing such behaviors and happenings, with the intention of maximizing teaching effectiveness and student learning. A number of researchers and practitioners have suggested several steps in the employment of systematic analysis of teaching which will maximize the results of the process (Box 14-1).* These steps are summarized as follows:

1. *Determine on what aspect of instruction to focus.* Any aspect of the instructional process or events about which data may be obtained may be selected. The focus selected should be based on the perceived needs for improvement in that area as determined by the involved parties (for example, teacher questioning abilities and engaged time).

It is recommended that teachers select a small number of variables, at least initially, rather than attempt to study a large pool of factors. Pangrazi and Darst[11] suggest that, at least at the start, teachers should attempt to evaluate one area at a time. Attempts to record and analyze more than one variable at a time may lead to confusion and frustration. This latter point, of course, would vary dependent on the teacher's experience with systematic analysis and the depth of the teacher's study of teaching. Figs. 14-1 and 14-2 provide the reader with examples of in-

---

*References 10, 11, 14, 15, 17, 18, and 29.

STUDENT VERBAL COGNITIVE RESPONSES

Teacher _____ Observer _____

Date _____ Time _____ Class _____ Lesson topic _____

Time start _____ Time stop _____ Comments _____

Predictable student responses (rote, mechanistic)*	
Somewhat unpredictable student responses (analytical, interpretive replies in response to teacher initiated ideas)*	
Unpredictable student responses (not strongly related to the teacher's initiative)*	

Directions: The recorder/observer tallies each occurrence of student verbal cognitive involvement in the lesson. The recorder/observer needs to discriminate between predictable, somewhat predictable, and unpredictable student cognitive, verbal responses.

*From Cheffers JTF, Mancini VH, Martinek T: *Interaction analysis: an application to nonverbal and verbal activity*, ed 2, St Paul, 1980, Association for Productive Teaching.

FIG. 14-1   Event recording of student cognitive responses.

STUDENT ENGAGEMENT TIME

Teacher _____ Observer _____

Date _____ Time _____ Class _____ Lesson topic _____

Time start _____ Time stop _____ Comments _____

Appropriate (on task) motor behavior/activity	
Inappropriate (off task) motor activity/behavior	
Inactive (no apparent motor activity)	
Transition time*	
Waiting time	
Cognitive involvement	

Directions: The recorder/observer times the duration of each student engagement episode and records this data in the appropriate area.

*Transition time is defined as the time spent moving from one activity to another or the movement from one formation to another.

FIG. 14-2   Duration recording of student engagement time.

struments designed to focus on specific aspects of instruction.

2. *Select or develop an instrument (data-generating tool) that focuses on the targeted skill, method, or other variable of instruction.* (Many useful and appropriate instruments are compiled in Darst et al.)[16] If, for example, time on task is of interest, then ALT-PE, among other instruments, would be an appropriate selection.[15] If student cognitive responses are the focus of the improvement strategies, then CAFIAS could provide the necessary data.[14]

Teachers can also readily develop personally tailored instruments, often in the form of checklists, frequency charts, interval coding procedures, and tallying sheets to obtain quantitative or qualitative data on performance.

Critical to the completion of this task is the individual teacher's concept of teaching that was previously discussed. Most assuredly, the factors teachers choose to study and analyze will be greatly influenced by their vision or concept of those instructional behaviors, skills, and abilities physical education teachers must employ and, therefore, master. This concept of teaching will affect and weigh heavily in the selection and the creation of an appropriate instrument. This is as it should be, because the entire systematic approach is meant to address the specific and personal needs of the teachers involved.

Systematic observation is simple to do. Several excellent sources are available that are designed to assist teachers in their efforts to understand the process and to facilitate the development of systems. Siedentop[18] firmly believes that "the best observation systems are always those created for specific purposes within a local program." Such systems clearly articulate the major emphasis within a program and reflect the immediate constraints on teaching. Therefore these systems are specific to the goal of the teaching episode and should provide appropriate information and feedback.

Siedentop[18] also suggests that the development of systems for a personal purpose (rather than for research purposes) requires some basic understanding and a little practice. Teachers should complete simple summaries of the raw data and avoid compiling sophisticated statistics. Improvement in teaching is not predicated on transforming teachers into number crunchers or on utilization of computer technology. Rather, the emphasis should be on the collection of easily deciphered and relevant data, which can then be translated to practice.

Cheffers, Siedentop, and other authorities* outline a few manageable and doable steps to facilitate the development of personally relevant and professionally productive systematic observation systems:

◆ Performance categories that are reflective of the variables of interest must be clearly and adequately de-

fined. This step not only provides the teacher with the focus of the analysis but is essential if an observer is to observe the lesson and code the variables of interest.

The categories identified above must be well-defined, with minimal overlap (if there are several categories) and should be as objective as possible.

◆ Decide on the specific process. What will be counted? Frequency of occurrence? Duration of events? Sequence of each occurrence?

◆ Design a simple form to collect relevant data. Figs. 14-1 to 14-3 are examples of simple but useful data forms that could be employed to gather information about various aspects of teacher and student behavior.

At this point the teacher needs to prepare to use the system. Self-instruction and practice with live and recorded lessons should assist instructors in their efforts to learn the system to be employed in the overall process.

3. *Teach a lesson and make an audiotape or videotape of it.* The tape recording will provide the means of obtaining data. The most beneficial process is if data can be obtained during the actual teaching event by an observer and later from the recording by the teacher. The ensuring comparative analysis can be especially fruitful. If an observer will be employed, make certain that the categories of behavior are well defined and there is agreement about what constitutes each of the defined behaviors.

4. *Tabulate and examine the data obtained.* The information gathered will provide a realistic, descriptive, and current picture of the present status of the variables of instruction. Convert the data to a form that can be generalized from lesson to lesson (that is, rate per minute, or rate of occurrence per lesson).[11]

5. *From the analysis of the data, determine the status of the targeted variables identified in step 1.* At this point in the process, the individual teacher needs to determine changes to be made. How does a teacher do this? Teachers who employ the systematic process outlined here, utilizing appropriately objective and quantitative instruments, will soon amass an enormous amount of data specifically related to their instructional practices. At this particular point in the analysis, the teacher must interpret the results and in effect, decide what, if any, changes are needed. Those who complete rigorous, more complete analyses can expect the opportunity to make many changes. If the analyses are astutely done, then these changes will constitute improvements.[10]

The key question here, however, is who determines the changes to be made and by what criteria? Certainly the advice and consultation of supervisors and colleagues should be sought and used to facilitate the assessment and interpretation process. However, the ultimate mover in this process is the teacher. For most teachers, this can often be an uncomfortable task, especially those unfa-

*References 1, 7, 10, 11, 14, 15, 18, and 19.

miliar with self-assessment and self-analysis, and especially in light of the way secondary schools are organized. Teachers should consult with others and should refer to the latest research about teaching physical education. But, and this cannot be stressed enough, the final judgments must be those of the teacher.

Why do we suggest this course of action? Several advantages to the self-evaluation strategies are suggested. The authors, along with several others in the field, believe that the willingness to change is greatly enhanced when the source of suggested changes is the teacher and when the role of external supervisors or consultants is minimized. Concurrent with this phenomenon is the fact that teachers are less likely to feel threatened by self-evaluation techniques when compared with evaluations emanating from external sources.[10] Finally, a more practical concern relates to the availability of obtaining the services of observers in schools for the purpose of continued growth as teachers. Teachers often have difficulty finding capable individuals who might provide meaningful feedback about their instructional efforts. This is especially true in the so-called special subject areas, where physical education often is placed.

Administrators are either too busy or unprepared to assist the physical education teacher, especially the way secondary schools are presently organized. Pangrazi and Darst[11] suggest that this "accentuates the importance of learning to self-evaluate one's teaching as the primary avenue for improvement (Box 14-2)."

B O X   14 - 2

STEPS IN THE SYSTEMATIC ANALYSIS OF INSTRUCTION

1. Identify factor(s) of instruction for study.
2. Select or develop and learn how to use an appropriate instrument.
3. Create a video or an audio record of a teaching episode.
4. Tabulate and examine the data.
5. Determine the status of the targeted variable.
6. Set achievable and measurable goals.
7. Repeat the entire process analysis (steps 1-6). Compare and analyze the two data bases.
8. Repeat the entire cycle (steps 1-7) as needed to achieve the goal of improved instruction.

To facilitate the determination of changes to be implemented, the teacher needs to compare the information generated by the systematic process (which should reflect the current status of the items of interest) with the personal goals established in step 1. Discrepancies, however slight, should suggest some directions and possible changes to be made in instructional practice (Fig. 14-3).

One pitfall teachers and supervisors should avoid is

TEACHER QUESTIONING

Teacher _____ Observer _____

Date _____ Time _____ Class _____ Lesson topic _____

Time start _____ Time stop _____ Comments _____

Recall questions	Convergent questions	Divergent questions

Directions: The recorder/observer tallies each occurrence of teacher questioning, discriminating among recall questions (questions requiring recalling material and dependent on memory), convergent questions (focused questions requiring a predictable student response) and those that are more open-ended and requiring a more unpredictable student response (divergent questions).

FIG. 14-3   Event recording of teacher questioning behavior.

one of identification of good instructional practice or bad teaching. This type of thinking or path of analysis tends to be counterproductive to the goal of improved teaching, and it derives from the myth, often articulated in educational circles, of the one perfect method or technique of teaching.[20] Teachers need to realize that the better question to pursue is one that attempts to determine the most appropriate method or technique given specific circumstances, class size, class composition, student needs, and abilities. The more appropriate task is to ask how the teacher can enhance the learning of students given certain, unchangeable factors and circumstances.

The teacher who also can clearly articulate personal goals for improvement will facilitate the collection of pertinent data about such goals and will also have a clearer understanding of the directions for change. The establishment of personal goals, then, is the essential step that must be accomplished to make use of the data generated by the systematic approach in a meaningful, relevant manner.

6. *Repeat the entire process and analysis.* Compare the data from the latter episode with the data base established in the first, and also compare it with the goals established for the second.

7. *Repeat the cycle as many times as seems useful, until the goal(s) in step 5 has been achieved.* With additional practice, the goals may have to be modified or adjusted. Kindswatter et al[17] summarize the benefits of the whole systematic process:

The process of systematic analysis has the potential advantage of describing teaching factors in measurable terms. Determining change in any factor is not dependent on only impression or perception; it is a matter verified by data.

The Reflective Approach

At this juncture we present a strategy for improving teaching and instructional practice that, with some work and careful attention to detail, could facilitate changes without the requirements of an observer. Specifically, the reflective approach provides teachers with a fruitful process for improvement, even when limited to the practitioner's view alone.

Reflective teaching can be defined as a process through which teachers at all levels of development have committed themselves to becoming lifelong students of teaching. Reflective teachers think deeply and analytically about the teaching experience, and such reflection causes teachers to produce insights and wisdom that guide pedagogical practice.[21,22,28] Valverde[23] defines the reflective teacher as one who examines the situation, behavior, practices, effectiveness, and accomplishments to respond precisely and more appropriately to the question, "What am I doing?" and "Why?" Reflective teaching can be thought of as a process of continued self-monitoring, because it pertains to teachers' satisfaction with their effectiveness.

It should be understood that a significant stage of the systematic analysis technique described earlier in this chapter required that the teacher use reflective abilities in the assessment of the changes needed based on the data generated by the systematic process. The significant difference between the two approaches, which by now should be apparent, is that in the reflective approach the practitioner does not rely on others to assist, facilitate, encourage, or nurture the process to the extent normally employed in the systematic approach. This does not mean that those using the reflective approach reject the notion of cooperative ventures if interested observers are available. Rather, the reflective approach should greatly complement the formal analytical approach outlined in the systems approach. More important, however, is the fact that the reflective approach is amenable to all situations and all teachers, once the basics have been mastered. It is a remarkably productive self-growth strategy, freed from the reliance on external sources for completion and also the requirement of quantitative data.

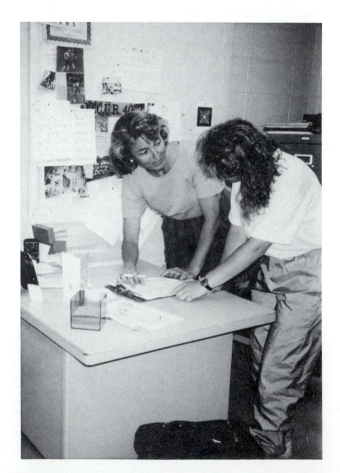

Reflecting on one's teaching with a colleague can help teachers improve their instructional endeavors.

Courtesy of Ben Lombardo, Rhode Island College, Providence, RI.

The systematic and reflective approaches have the potential to stimulate positive growth in all teachers. It would probably be best to view these processes as complementary approaches rather than as competing vehicles for change. Reflective processes for self-growth dovetail nicely with the more systematic approaches, and we encourage the reader to employ both procedures.

A common interpretation of the reflective approach, one that attempts to identify its most basic elements, is offered by Graham et al[24]: "The reflective teacher is one who can design and implement an educational program that is congruent with the idiosyncrasies of a particular school situation." Graham et al[24] convey the notion that effective teaching is situational rather than generic.

Practitioners who practice thoughtful reflection are more attuned to the meaning of each instructional situation for themselves and for their students. This personal engagement in their pedagogical world leads not to final, single, or absolute solutions but rather to continued questioning, reflecting, and tenable solutions continually sought in the face of the complexities of the gymnasium. Such practitioners recognize multiple interpretive frameworks, are able to compare multiple intellectual frames, and believe in the role of subjectivity in constructing knowledge and determining truths.[22,25-28]

There is great need for teachers to develop reflective abilities and to understand the process of reflection. In addition to its ability to facilitate teacher growth with or without the availability of supervisory assistance, reflective strategies can contribute much to the goal of improved instruction. Schools are places of great ambiguities and ill-structured problems that have multiple solutions. The problem space of educational programs is broad, and the parameters are unknown and must respond to the context.[29] Physical education teachers are cast in the role of decision makers and are regularly confronted with situations requiring quick judgments based on their reading and sensitivity to a wide variety of variables. Professional physical education teachers are required to make decisions and judgments about instructional problems that are often steeped in confusion and uncertainties, and these decisions are often subjectively determined.[29]

Teachers must become fully aware that there are many alternative pathways to enhance effectiveness. Tom[20] argues that there is no perfect solution to the question of how to teach. Good teachers collect all possible data and experiences and then go about making learned, informed, reflectively based decisions, based on such information as personal and professional experiences, training, study, and competencies for each group, class, or individual with which they are confronted.

The reflective practitioner acts intelligently, perceptively, and in a methodical, analytical manner. Although the reflective process relies more on intuition when contrasted with the systematic approach (with the required observers) and on the "artful" aspects of teaching, the reflective practitioner attempts to weigh all information (regardless of source) in a logical, dispassionate manner. After the teaching experience, teachers reflect about their actions, assess the experience and outcomes, and this new information, then, is added to the data base to facilitate and enhance future decision making and to enhance the educational experience of their present students.[30]

Reflective Analysis of Teaching

Most teachers, via their professional preparation programs, have studied the various aspects of pedagogy, educational practice, and instruction at some level. It is assumed, therefore, that by the very nature of the admission, selection, retention, and certification-licensing process so commonplace in colleges and universities, physical education teachers have the capacity to develop the necessary abilities required to employ effectively the reflective approach (and thereby reap the benefits of the process). However, the depth and extent of the resulting changes are limited by the commitment, the intensity, and the regularity of the teacher's efforts with reflective strategies.

With the recognition that there should be reflective elements in all procedures designed to improve instruction and teaching effectiveness, there are a few suggestions that will maximize the outcomes of the reflective approach:

1. The reflective process should be methodical and systematic when and where possible. Although this approach is weighted toward the teacher's intuition and subjectivity, regular, logical, and clearly focused attempts will enhance the teacher's efforts. A plan of attack should be created, monitoring of the plan is imperative, and follow-through is required.

2. Record keeping is vital to the process. Records, such as journals, logs, diaries, and notes can help keep the teacher focused; can reduce the occurrence of sporadic or irregular efforts; and can become a viable basis and take-off point for change. Written notations of the sort described here should enhance teachers' self-study and thereby support their personal pursuit of change. Box 14-3 provides the teacher with a list of reflective abilities, many of which describe record keeping techniques. These activities will enhance the teacher's reflective endeavors.

3. A plan of analysis or conceptual framework for the study of teaching is suggested. Mosston and Ashworth's[6] framework for the analysis of teaching, for example, would seem to provide teachers with an excellent, relevant starting point for reflection (that is, preimpact, impact, and postimpact decision-making schema).

4. The initial reflective attempts should probably be more narrowly focused, rather than globally or generally described. As the teacher gains experience with the analysis of teaching in general and the reflective process spe-

cifically, broader and more complex instructional elements can be addressed.

5. It must be recognized that the bottom line of this approach, if not of all improvement strategies, is that the ultimate change agent is the teacher. It is important to keep in mind that the teacher, especially so in this approach, is the final arbiter of the process. Reflection, given its highly personal focus and the fact that the teacher often travels this course in isolation, centers on the individual's perceptions, analytical strengths and weaknesses, and abilities to extrapolate noted happenings into action.

It should be clear that there are reflective elements in all procedures that are designed to improve instruction and teaching effectiveness. However, several steps should be taken to ensure the efficacy of the reflective approach. A good starting point would be to focus on the questions listed below. Specifically, on completion of an instructional episode, the teacher should try to respond to the following:

◆ What happened in general?
◆ Did learning take place?
◆ What did students actually learn?
◆ What might they have learned?
◆ What activities, experiences, and factors promoted learning?
◆ What factors, circumstances, and interactions inhibited or limited learning?
◆ What alternate ways might the material have been taught?

BOX 14-3
EXAMPLES OF REFLECTIVE PROCESSES

1. Question what, why, and how one does things; ask what, why, and how others do things.
2. Emphasize inquiry as a tool of learning.
3. Suspend judgment, wait for sufficient data, or self-validate.
4. Seek alternatives.
5. Keep an open mind.
6. Compare and contrast.
7. Seek the framework, theoretical basis, and underlying rationale of behaviors and methods.
8. View from various perspectives (role playing might help here).
9. Identify and test assumptions; seek conflicting evidence.
10. Put into different/varied contexts.
11. Ask "what if . . . ?"
12. Seek the ideas and viewpoints of others.
13. Adapt and adjust to instability and change.
14. Function within uncertainty, complexity, and variety.
15. Hypothesize.
16. Consider consequences.
17. Validate what is given and believed.
18. Synthesize and test.
19. Seek, identify, and resolve problems.
20. Initiate after thinking through or putting into context.
21. Analyze what makes it work; in what context would it not?
22. Use prescriptive models only when adapted to the situation.

Modified from Roth R: Preparing the reflective practitioner: transforming the apprentice through the dialectic, *Journal of Teacher Education* 40(2): 31-35, 1989.

BOX 14-4
REFLECTIVE STRATEGIES AND ACTIVITIES

1. Free association writing (recording thoughts on a topic as they come to mind, without reorganizing, editing, or structuring them)
2. Self-evaluation—general (daily, weekly, monthly).
3. Self-evaluation—on a specific action (daily, weekly, monthly).
4. Maintain a journal or log. Record experiences, beliefs, feelings, and thoughts within and outside the gymnasium.
5. Use systems for analyzing events in the instructional setting (for example, Flanders, CAFIAS, ALT-PE).
6. Use protocol materials to stimulate inquiry and reflection (for example, audiotapes or videotapes, case studies) on various techniques and issues.
7. Use the reflective teaching exercises as defined by Cruickshank.[21] This requires the use of one or more observers and a rather structured approach, which may be too cumbersome in the real world of secondary school physical education.
8. Employ situational analysis. Analyze the setting, context, the instructional environment, community, administrative leadership, students.
9. Analyze issues (control, decision-making processes, diversity of student population, learning, teacher's role, and school and society).
10. Consider why students should learn the subject matter of physical education. Why should students be interested?
11. Conduct an analysis of planning procedures. How to plan? Methods employed to plan. What should be planned? Unplanned? The planning process for specific subject matter?

The second step would be to utilize several of the strategies itemized in Boxes 14-3 and 14-4. Roth[31] enumerates a number of possible alternatives to facilitate the reflective process once the teacher has addressed the first set of questions. The use of these strategies will result in the generation of many ideas, thoughts, and alternatives about the teaching episode, which should facilitate the change needed to improve instructional practice and teaching behavior.

A key point to keep in mind is that the reflective process is not a one-time happening. The reflective process is continual process that indicates the teacher's commitment to the pursuit of excellence and perpetual change.

Once the results of the reflective process are summarized, the teacher has many choices to make regarding the translation of these indicators into everyday practice. For example, if the results of the teacher's reflective efforts centered on maximizing the students' engagement with the physical education curriculum manifested a need to create greater or more positive social support systems within the gymnasium and provided students with a clear sense of ownership in the program, the teacher could make several moves to accomplish these goals. Students could be invited to propose or react to specific curricular initiatives, or student input could be solicited regarding specific activities to be utilized to achieve selected program concepts. In addition, the use of anonymous journal writings or the provision of opportunities for students to submit written suggestions for change could be a vehicle for curricular changes initiated by students. The teacher could redesign the social environment to increase the individual students's psychological comfort and take steps to reduce antagonistic behavior, extreme competitiveness, and other inhibiting factors that can diminish the positive effects of the social setting in the gymnasium. In such ways, teachers can translate the results of the reflective analysis inherent in this approach into relevant, significant changes in instructional practice.

Benefits of the Reflective Approach

The reflective approach holds much promise as a technique to improve teaching. A relatively recent arrival as a tested instructional strategy, daily it becomes more accepted in preservice and in-service programs. The benefits of the approach are:

1. The use of reflective strategies ensures that teaching becomes less random. The regular self-examination and intensive self-study will increase the purposefulness and meaning of the teacher's instructional practices and behaviors.[32] In this way, reflection can provide an alternative to behaving purely on impulse, tradition, and authority. Too often, secondary physical education programs appear to be typified by randomness and suffer concurrently from a lack of cohesiveness or direction. These programatic characteristics have been attributed to secondary physical education programs by many detractors in recent years that many observers of physical education feel that such weaknesses are endemic to the profession.

2. Reflection creates a sustained commitment to teaching as a profession, as well as an enhanced pedagogical practice. Teachers who employ reflective strategies are committed to improvement and constant pursuit of alternatives. Only truly motivated and enthusiastic professionals embark on this path. Hellison[32] believes that excellent teaching is accomplished by those who truly love what they do and are reflective in doing it.

3. The reflective approach empowers teachers in the sense that the instructional process becomes "their stuff," after considerable review and introspective analysis. In other words, the intensive self-study that characterizes the reflective approach results in a deeper personalization and self-awareness of the teacher's practices. Teachers truly come to know not only what they are doing, but also why they are doing it. They confront their beliefs.[32] The process also reduces the randomness of pedagogical practice and heightens the purposefulness of the teacher's actions. These latter two weaknesses are often characteristic of teaching in physical education and thereby deserve the attention of all secondary teachers.

4. The use of reflection creates and demands the implementation of a developmental approach or attitude that never ceases once begun. It puts the teacher on the path to the continual pursuit of self-knowledge, the examination of reasons justifying instructional decision making and teaching behavior, and the process of curriculum building.

5. Cruicksank[21] claims that users of the reflective approach come to appreciate and understand the complexities of teaching and learning. The introspective analysis characteristic of reflective strategies creates a deeper awareness of the profession and its professional and moral responsibilities and nurtures mindful, inquiring teachers.

6. The fiscal demands of this approach are minimal. This is an important concern because historically teacher education and efforts to improve instruction have been poorly supported relative to other professions. Innovative approaches to improvement have been and must continue to be inexpensive. Clearly the reflective approach is not costly. It requires neither special facilities nor equipment.[25]

Reflective elements in all procedures are designed to improve instruction and teaching effectiveness. However, the specific reflective strategies as described in this section have the potential to contribute much to enhanced teacher effectiveness and thereby maximize student learning. These outcomes are derived primarily from the introspective, self-analytical processes inherent in reflective strategies. The reflective process, as a vehicle for change, can provide teachers with a sense of ownership of the modifications, a more acute sense of control of their pedagogical actions, and more confidence in their self-directional abilities. These latter aspects provide teachers with a more personal basis for changing and growth, which usually translates to implementation in areas of need and significant changes in instructional behavior.

As a strategy to improve instruction, reflective teaching has been demonstrated to have powerful effects.[21] Physical education teachers should study this approach and utilize it to improve instructional practice.

SUMMARY

The strategies reviewed in this chapter are designed to enhance teacher effectiveness and improve student learning. Systematic analysis and the reflective approach can assist teachers to study and improve their behaviors. Regardless of which strategy is employed, teachers and administrators need to pursue excellence in teaching.

The question remains, then, why physical education teachers have been reluctant to utilize these strategies. Given the potency of the systematic approach and the reflective process, why are efforts to improve teaching so idiosyncratic, random, and seemingly without direction? This situation is quite perplexing when one comes to understand that student performance is directly related to teaching effectiveness and instructional competence. Newman[33] makes the point that what students find interesting in schools often depends more on the teacher's skills and instructional manuevers, and not, as many believe, solely on the topics or the students' interest in such subject matters. In an era of reform and attention to maximizing the effectiveness of schools and teachers, the failure to systematically address enhanced teacher performance would seem to be a major shortcoming of the profession and a movement destined to diminish further the legitimacy of physical education within the educational hierarchy.

Moreover, Siedentop,[34] in a thorough summary of much of the literature on teacher education, found that:
1. Teacher behavior can be modified.
2. Modifications do, indeed, have the potency to positively affect student learning and performance.
3. Learned behaviors do transfer to the real world.
4. Strategies for improvement are well within the capabilities of most teachers.

In essence, then, we know that teaching behavior can be changed and that teachers possess the ability to do so. The major issue, then, is the teachers' desire and commitment to study teaching and attempt to improve their instructional endeavors. Once such a decision has been made to do so, the teacher can be confident that positive growth will result.

The two major approaches to improved teaching in physical education have been presented and analyzed.

Various strategies have been discussed, all of which require only the time, effort, and most important, the commitment of the teacher to effect positive changes in instructional practice and teaching behavior.

FOR REVIEW

1. Define reflective teaching. How does the process of reflection relate to the teacher's efforts to improve teaching effectiveness?
2. Improved teaching based on a thorough analysis of instructional procedures and teaching behavior resides in the hands of the individual teacher. Do you agree or disagree with this statement? Explain your position fully.
3. With a colleague, informally observe an entire physical education class. Both observers should individually keep notes on what happens. Be sure to record the most important aspects of the class. After completing the observation, compare and discuss the notes each observer recorded.
4. Make arrangements to have the class you are teaching to be videotaped or audiotaped. Use systematic, analytical techniques to record and analyze a sample of your own teaching. Upon completion of your teaching assignment and before viewing the videotape or listening to the audiotape, write a self-analysis, making certain to describe and emphasize the most important aspects of the class. Then have a colleague, teacher, or suprvisor view the same sample of teaching and compare and discuss the results of the analyses.
5. In a class you are assigned to teach, ask the students to write an evaluation of the experience. Identify the common characteristics of these evaluations. How do they compare with your perceptions of the class? Select one or two changes suggested by the students. Try to implement those changes during future classes.
6. Select a descriptive analytical system (refer to the source by Darst PW, Zakrajsek DB, Mancini VH). Study the category definitions, coding procedures, ground rules, and examples of coding. Practice coding several times until you can do so accurately and efficiently.
7. Select a class and code the teacher's behavior (or code a sample of your teaching from a videotaped recording). Compute the total frequency and percentage of time spent performing each function. Discuss the record with the teacher. What does the description indicate about the lesson? The teacher's behavior? The class in general? Compare the views of the teacher who was observed with your view.
8. Have an observer code your teaching behavior using a system selected from Darst PW, Zakrajsek DB, Mancini VH (use a videotape of your teaching performance if available). Code your own performance as well. Compare your analysis with that of the observer. What did you learn? Describe your feelings about the entire process.

REFERENCES

1. Metzler MW: *Instructional supervision for physical education,* Champaign, Ill, 1990, Human Kinetics.
2. Flanders NA: *Analyzing teaching behavior,* Reading, Mass, 1970, Addison-Wesley Publishing.
3. Shulman L: Knowledge and teaching: foundations of the new reform, *Harvard Educational Review* 57(1):1-22, 1987.
4. *Harvard Educational Letter:* Volume V (3), May/June, 1, 1989.

5. Dougherty NJ, Bonanno D: *Contemporary approaches to the teaching of physical education,* ed 2, Scottsdale, Ariz, 1987, Gorsuch Scarisbrick.

6. Mosston M, Ashworth S: *Teaching physical education,* ed 3, Columbus, Ohio, 1986, Merrill Publishing.

7. Hellison D: *Goals and strategies for teaching physical education,* Champaign, Ill, 1985, Human Kinetics.

8. Harrison JM: A review of the research on teacher effectiveness and its implications for current practice, *Quest* 39:36-55, 1987.

9. Nichols B: *Moving and learning: the elementary school physical education experience,* ed 3, St Louis, 1994, Mosby.

10. Anderson W: *Analysis of teaching physical education,* St Louis, 1980, Mosby.

11. Pangrazi RP, Darst, PW: *Dynamic physical education curriculum for secondary school students,* Minneapolis, 1985, Burgess.

12. Fuller F, Manning B: Self-confrontation reviewed: a conceptualization for video playback in teacher education, *Review of Educational Research* 43:469-482, 1973.

13. Peck R, Tucker J: Research on teacher education. In Travers R, editor: *Second handbook of research on teaching,* Chicago, 1973, Rand McNally.

14. Cheffers JTF, Mancini VH, Martinek T: *Interaction analysis: an application to nonverbal and verbal activity,* ed 2, St Paul, 1980, Association for Productive Teaching.

15. Siedentop D, Tousignant M, Parker M: *Academic learning time—physical education: 1982 revised coding manual.* Unpublished manual, School of Health, Physical Education and Recreation, Columbus, Ohio, 1982, The Ohio State University.

16. Darst PW, Zakrajsek DB, Mancini VH: *Analyzing physical education and sport instruction,* ed 2, Champaign, Ill, 1989, Human Kinetics.

17. Kindswatter R, Willem W, Ishler M: *Dynamics of effective teaching,* New York, 1988, Longman.

18. Siedentop D: *Developing teaching skills in physical education,* ed 3, Palo Alto, Calif, 1991, Mayfield Publishing.

19. van der Mars H: Basic recording tactics. In Darst PW et al, editors: *Analyzing physical education and sport instruction,* ed 2, Champaign, Ill, Human Kinetics.

20. Tom A: *Teaching as a moral craft,* New York, 1984, Longman.

21. Cruickshank D: *Reflective teaching: the preparation of students of teaching,* Reston, Va, 1987, Association of Teacher Educators.

22. Richards JC, Gipe JP: *Reflective thinking and the teaching abilities of prospective teachers,* Paper presented at Annual Meeting of AERA, New Orleans, 1988.

23. Valverde L: The self-evolving supervisor. In Sergiovanni T, editor: *Supervision of teaching,* Alexandria, Va, 1982, Association for Supervision and Curriculum Development.

24. Graham G et al: *Children moving: a reflective approach to teaching physical education,* Palo Alto, Calif, 1980, Mayfield Publishing.

25. Lee DM: *Relativistic operations: a framework for conceptualizing teachers' everyday problem solving,* Paper presented at AERA Convention in Boston, 1990.

26. Stoiber KC: The effect of technical and reflective preservice instruction on pedagogical reasoning and problem solving, *Journal of Teacher Education* 42(2):131-139, 1991.

27. Freidus H: *Critical issues in the curriculum of teacher education programs,* Paper presented at AERA Annual Meeting, Chicago, 1991.

28. Posner GJ: *Field experience: a guide to reflective teaching,* New York, 1985, Longman.

29. Lee DM: Everyday problem solving: implications for education. In Sinnott IA, editor: *Everyday problem solving: theory and applications,* New York, 1989, Praeger.

30. Howey KR, Zimpher NL: Preservice teacher educators' role in programs for beginning teachers, *The Elementary School Journal* 89(4):451-470, 1989.

31. Roth R: Preparing the reflective practitioner: transforming the apprentice through the dialectic, *Journal of Teacher Education* 40(2):31-35, 1989.

32. Hellison D: *Reflective teaching: secondary level,* Paper presented at AAHPERD National Convention, Kansas City, Mo, 1988.

33. Newman F: Student engagement and high school reform, *Educational Leadership* 40(5):34-36, 1989.

34. Siedentop D: The modification of teacher behavior. In Pieron M, Graham G, editors: *Sport Pedagogy: The 1984 Olympic Scientific Congress Proceedings,* Volume 6, Champaigne, Ill, 1984, Human Kinetics.

ANNOTATED READINGS

Cruickshank D: *Reflective teaching: the preparation of students of teaching,* Reston, Va, 1987, Association of Teacher Educators.

In this monograph, Cruickshank successfully outlines the theory, research, and practice of reflective teaching. A thorough review of the various interpretations of this approach is provided. The author also provides a step-by-step program for utilizing the reflective approach in the preparation of new teachers or assisting in-service teachers.

Darst PW, Zakrajsek D, Mancini VH, editors: *Analyzing physical education and sport instruction,* ed 2, Champaign, Ill, 1989, Human Kinetics.

A compendium of observer systems that can be used to analyze interactive and environmental events that occur in physical education and athletic settings, this volume possesses a wealth of instruments for the student of pedagogy. Readers will find Part I, which provides an excellent introduction to the systematic process, especially helpful.

Harrison JM: A review of the research on teacher effectiveness and its implications for current practice, *Quest* 39:36-55, 1987.

A thorough review of the research literature on teaching physical education is presented by Harrison. The author deftly analyzes and presents the implications in a clear manner and one that will enhance the reader's efforts to translate theory into practice.

Metzler MW: Using systematic analysis to promote teaching skills in physical education, *Journal of Teacher Education* 37(4):29-33, 1986.

Metzler presents a general model for integrating teaching effectiveness research with systematic observation to evaluate physical education teaching. He effectively argues against holding physical education teachers accountable for student achievement until some pervasive instructional constraints are eased.

Public Relations

CHAPTER OBJECTIVES
◆ To define public relations
◆ To describe the scope of public relations and its importance to physical education
◆ To identify principles of public relations
◆ To offer suggestions for secondary school physical education public relations programs

Gaining and maintaining support for the physical education program is an important responsibility of each physical education teacher. A well-planned, effective public relations program can help accomplish this objective. Physical education is constantly changing, and the public needs to be informed about these changes. Furthermore, public relations efforts in physical education must be directed at ensuring that physical education is perceived as an educational basic, not a frill. In these times of increasing budgetary constraints and calls for educational accountability, it is important that physical education be recognized by the public as an integral part of the secondary school curriculum.

Effective communication is the key to the physical education public relations program. Many channels of communication can be effectively employed to inform students, parents, school personnel, community members, and decision makers about the physical education program and its contribution to the education and well-being of the students it serves.

PUBLIC RELATIONS: AN OVERVIEW
Public Relations Defined

Simply defined, public relations is the establishment and maintenance of effective two-way communication between an organization and its public that is designed to promote public understanding, confidence, and support.[1] Within the educational realm, public relations involves ongoing communication between the school and its public, specifically students, parents, school personnel, community members, and decision makers.

Scope of Public Relations

Public relations is broad in scope, encompassing many different functions, activities, and individuals. It involves everything that contributes to the school's public image.

Public relations is typically viewed as a management function, that is, it is viewed as the responsibility of the leader. Although the responsibility for public relations for physical education may be delegated to the department chairperson, every teacher has an important and critical role in the public relations endeavor. Physical education teachers must remember that they greatly influence the image that the public holds of physical education through their dress, personal conduct, and the manner in which they perform their teaching responsibilities on a daily basis. Often, what we do or do not do speaks louder than words.

The public relations program should be planned and should be one of action. It should neither be left to chance nor given attention only during a crisis. There should be an ongoing effort to promote physical education to the public.

Public relations can encompass a wide range of activities. It can involve working with the media on an ongoing basis to communicate information about the physical education program, such as the activities offered or the gains made by students in health-related fitness. It can involve promoting special events, such as a community fitness clinic, to gain support for the program. Public relations can involve working with various community decision makers and legislative groups. Efforts within this sphere could be directed at increasing the time requirement for physical education from 3 to 5 days a week or using proactive strategies to prevent reduction in the time allotment for physical education. Regardless of the type of activity, public relations is concerned with favorably influencing the image of the school and its programs in the mind of the public, thereby generating support and understanding.

Although there are many dimensions to the public relations program, an effective program does not need to be complex. Simple programs that focus on establishing and maintaining an ongoing exchange of useful, meaningful information between the school and its various publics can be highly successful.

GOALS OF PUBLIC RELATIONS PROGRAMS

To be effective, public relations should be planned and directed toward attainment of specific goals. Several goals are appropriate for physical education public relations programs. They include the following:[1-4]

1. To communicate to the public information about the physical education program and its accomplishments.
2. To foster public confidence in the physical education program.
3. To generate sufficient support and funding for the physical education program.
4. To promote awareness of the importance of physical education for all individuals and the contribution of physical education to the education and lives of students.
5. To strengthen the partnership between the school and students, parents, and community members.
6. To clarify information and rectify misunderstandings that may occur between the school and its many publics.

Physical education public relations efforts must be specifically directed toward achieving public understanding and support for its programs. It is important that information is disseminated to the public about current physical education practices. Because physical education has changed since students' parents and other adult members of the community were in school, the public must be informed about how contemporary physical education differs from physical education programs 30 to 40 years ago. Physical education teachers must also make the effort to familiarize the public about the contributions of physical education to the child's education and well-being. Additionally, public relations can enhance the staff's morale. Recognition of physical education teachers' perfor-

mance and contributions helps build pride while encouraging teachers to achieve at even higher levels because they know their efforts will be appreciated. Last, public relations is important in gaining financial and curricular support for the physical education program.

Today a planned program to build public support for the school is essential. Public dissatisfaction with the schools is increasing. Calls for accountability, educational reform, and improved student performance abound. In many communities throughout the United States, public dissatisfaction with the schools has led to a failure to approve much needed tax levies or school bond issues. Schools find it difficult to improve and maintain high-quality programs without adequate financial support. Additionally, some people feel that physical education and other subject areas such as music and art are not a necessity but rather a frill. Thus these people may be reluctant to vote to spend public funds on these areas. Planned programs to build public support for physical education are a necessity today.

PUBLIC RELATIONS: PRINCIPLES AND GUIDELINES

Many factors must be considered in the development and implementation of a strong public relations program. Some principles that will be helpful in planning and conducting a physical education public relations program are described in this section and shown in Box 15-1.[1,4,5]

A quality program is the foundation of a successful public relations program. A sound program that leads to the development of stated objectives and attainment of desired benefits adds credibility to the public relations effort. There must be congruence between what physical education teachers say they accomplish and the results that are attained.

Programs that are poorly conducted or misrepresented to the public do little to enhance the image of physical education. Although many physical education teachers labor in less than ideal situations, they should strive for quality within the context and constraints of the situation. Having demonstrated what they can accomplish adds credibility to requests for more equipment or time to accomplish additional objectives or to improve learning outcomes.

Quality professionals are essential to the public relations program. Committed, dedicated professionals are the key to achieving a quality physical education program. Physical education teachers who carefully plan their programs, have stated objectives for their students to reach, and conduct their classes so that their students can attain these objectives help promote a positive image of physical education in the minds of the public.

Physical education teachers must also realize that, as educators, they may be highly visible within the community. Their actions in the gymnasium, school, and

BOX 15-1

CHECKLIST FOR THE PUBLIC RELATIONS PROGRAM

_____ A person is designated to be in charge of the physical education public relations (PR) program.

_____ The PR committee/advisory council meets on a regular basis.

_____ Money is set aside in the budget for PR.

_____ The PR program is based on a quality physical education program.

_____ The PR program is based on truth.

_____ PR planning is done on an annual basis.

_____ Specific objectives for the PR program are identified.

_____ Specific responsibilities for the PR program are assigned to individuals.

_____ Each physical education teacher understands and carries out his or her PR responsibilities and role.

_____ Information about the various publics' characteristics and their knowledge of the physical education program is obtained on a regular basis.

_____ Messages focus on conveying information about the various aspects, outcomes, and values of the physical education program.

_____ Multiple channels of communication are used to reach the various publics.

_____ Emphasis is based on ongoing communication between the physical education department and the various publics.

_____ PR efforts are evaluated on a regular basis.

community may often be closely scrutinized by the public, and judgments about the physical education program are often formulated on the basis of these impressions. These teachers must be cognizant of the powerful effect their image and their conduct have on the public's perceptions of the physical education program.

Physical education teachers who fail to "practice what they preach," for example, those who are overweight, smoke, fail to exercise, or whose appearance and actions conform to the stereotypical "jock" image, may have little credibility as spokespersons for physical education. On the other hand, teachers who do "practice what they preach" enhance the stature of physical education and their credibility with the public. Physical education teachers who exemplify a healthy, active lifestyle—who are physically fit and engage in healthy, personal habits—reinforce the public relations message they are trying to send to the public: physical education is valuable and beneficial to one's quality of life. These instructors are believable spokespersons for physical education.

The truth should be the basis for the public relations program. Information communicated to the public should be based on the truth. Programs should be accurately and honestly presented. Misrepresentation of the facts is dishonest. Moreover, when the true facts become known, the negative reaction will probably be greater than if the facts had been presented correctly in the first place.

Problems should be addressed truthfully. For example, if the fitness scores of the students decline, this information should be reported. Reasons for the decline in the scores should accompany the report as well as information on how this problem will be remediated. The adage "honesty is the best policy" should be followed in public relations work. Honesty enhances the credibility of the spokespersons and builds public confidence.

The public relations program should be planned. An effective public relations program requires planning. Goals of the public relations program should be thoughtfully delineated, target public groups identified, and strategies to achieve these goals developed. Planning does not imply that the public relations program needs to be elaborate. Planning does ensure a thorough approach to public relations, one that may be more effective than a hit-or-miss effort. Specific responsibilities for carrying out various facets of the program should be assigned to the appropriate individuals.

The public relations program should be continuous. Ongoing effort and commitment are important to accomplishing the goals of a public relations program. Public relations should be a year-round effort. Public relations activities should be designated for a particular purpose and placed within a specific time frame. Communication with the various publics should be ongoing if good will is to be developed and maintained. Moreover, messages need to be repeated to ensure that they have a lasting effect.

A program that is proactive in nature, rather than reactive, is generally more effective. A proactive program that generates a high level of support for physical education may even prevent the raising of some issues, such as reducing the time requirement or cutbacks in funding.

Times will occur when a special public relations effort may need to be mounted, such as when there is an unforeseen budgetary crisis. However, public relations campaigns that are only put into action when a crisis occurs are ineffective in the long run.

Public relations is an educational endeavor. Physical education teachers must actively seek to educate the public about physical education. Students should understand the goals of the physical education program and the benefits to be derived from participation. Encourage students to share what they have learned with their parents. Knowledgeable, enthusiastic students are some of the best public relations agents.

Teachers also need to promote the benefits of physical

education to parents, school personnel, and the community at large. The value and contributions of a quality physical education program to the education of the children and its potential impact, both in short- and long-term effects, on one's health and well-being should be emphasized.

The public relations program should be based on accurate information. A multitude of techniques should be used to assess the various publics' knowledge of physical education. This information is useful in determining the objectives of the public relations program. Surveys, conversations, public forums, and conferences can be used to ascertain the public's perceptions of physical education and to solicit input and feedback about the physical education program.

The public relations program should be focused. Specific target publics should be identified and the public relations program should be structured to reach them. At times the public relations program may be narrowly focused, designed to reach one particular group, such as parents. At other times, a broader focus may be necessary to accomplish the objectives of the public relations program. The message and the channels of communication need to be appropriate to the public that the public relations program is seeking to reach for maximum effectiveness.

The public relations program should begin internally and then move to an external focus. Support of individuals within the school should be attained before endeavoring to gain support among the external publics. The public groups that are most directly affected by the physical education program should be the initial focus of the public relations efforts. This generally means students, school personnel, and parents. The focus should then be widened to include those less directly affected by the physical education program, such as the community at large.

Two-way communication is important in an effective public relations program. Steps must be taken to ensure that two-way communication is an integral part of the school's public relations program. Often, the emphasis is placed on disseminating information to the various publics with no provision for public input and feedback. Planned mechanisms for public input and feedback should exist. For example, students may be surveyed about their satisfaction with the physical education program, parents may be invited to observe classes and give input regarding various issues, and community members' suggestions may be solicited.

It is important to determine what is known and not known about the physical education program. This is essential if misperceptions regarding the program are to

The public relations program should have an internal and external focus.
Courtesy of Suzi D'Annalfo, Conard High School, West Hartford, CT.

be corrected. Input, suggestions, and criticisms from the public should be evaluated carefully. Some suggestions and criticisms may offer sound ideas for program improvement, while other input may show the need for clarification of various program aspects and offer direction for public relations efforts.

Multiple channels and avenues of communication should be used. A diversity of approaches should be used in the public relations program. Newspapers, radio, television, public meetings, open houses, community programs, videotapes and slide shows, letters to parents and the public, and face-to-face conversations can all be used effectively as part of the public relations program. Selection of the communication medium requires consideration of the public that is to be reached, the content of the message, the time available to prepare and disseminate the message, and the costs involved. Use of various forms of communication helps ensure that the most effective ways of communicating to the target public are selected.

Evaluate the public relations program periodically. Periodic evaluation is necessary to assess the effectiveness of the public relations program. Are the right publics being reached? Is the message being communicated effectively? Are the public relations program objectives being attained? Should different approaches be utilized or the timing of various public relations efforts be changed? Systematic evaluation of the impact of the program is essential. Formal methods, such as surveys and various data collection approaches, and informal methods, such as listening to different publics, may be used to ascertain the effectiveness of the public relations program. This information may also help analyze the direction of the program and strengthen it when needed.

PLANNING THE PUBLIC RELATIONS PROGRAM

In some schools, the entire physical education department, under the leadership of its chairperson, is responsible for planning and conducting the public relations program. In schools with a large physical education staff, the responsibility for public relations may be delegated to a committee. Yet in other schools an advisory council is responsible for the public relations program.

The advisory council is typically composed of individuals representing the various publics within the community, such as school board members, students, teachers, parents, administrators, and media representatives. The composition of the council should be balanced, composed of individuals from a diversity of backgrounds so that the interests and concerns of various publics are represented. Additionally, when council members are selected, consideration should be given to the various abilities each potential member could bring to the public relations effort. For example, one individual may bring

expertise in writing, while another possesses skill in fundraising. Care should be taken to keep the number of individuals on the council to a manageable number, such as seven to nine members.

Regardless of who is responsible for the public relations program, these individuals need to analyze the physical education program, identify which facets of the program are to be promoted, and determine how best to accomplish this task. This group should then develop a sound public relations plan. This can be accomplished by taking the following steps[1,3,6]:

◆ Develop a sound public relations policy that adheres to the principles of public relations. This policy should provide for the dissemination of information and provide a means for public input and feedback.

◆ Obtain information about what the various publics do or do not know and believe about physical education. This will help determine what areas need to be addressed by the public relations effort.

◆ Determine what facts need to be presented to the public and identify a priority listing for these facts. Present the facts that will enable the public to realize fully the benefits that can accrue from a good physical education program and to elicit their support for improvements that will further increase these benefits.

◆ Identify specific strategies to achieve stated public relations objectives.

◆ Agree on which individuals will perform specific tasks. A timetable for the performance of these tasks should be established.

◆ Evaluate the effectiveness of the public relations program on a periodic basis. This information can then be used to adjust the program and improve it.

A planned rather than a haphazard approach to public relations increases the potential to promote physical education successfully to various publics. An example of an annual plan for a physical education public relations program is shown in Table 15-1.

METHODS AND TECHNIQUES FOR PUBLIC RELATIONS PROGRAMS

Many different methods and techniques can be used successfully in the physical education public relations program. Newspapers, radio and television, films, newsletters, brochures, bulletin boards, posters, and exhibits can all be used to communicate information about various aspects of the physical education program. Sponsoring special events, demonstrations, and awards ceremonies are additional approaches that can be used to highlight the physical education program. Physical education teachers can also promote their program through speaking engagements and by providing opportunities for pub-

Model of a Public Relations Calendar in Physical Education

Month	Goal	Method	Responsibility
September	Plan PR program for the year	Staff meeting	Department head and staff
	Inform parents of program goals for the year	Department handbook	Instructors A and B
	Inform students of program goals for the year and acquaint them with curriculum offerings	Department handbook, bulletin board, posters, and school newspaper	Instructor C and students
October	Familiarize community leaders with the physical education program philosophy and content	Presentations to various community organizations	Department head and staff
	Form a physical education advisory council of community members, faculty, parents, and students	Letters explaining the purpose of the council and inviting people to join	Department head
November	Inform parents of student's progress	Letter and invitation to parent-teacher conference or to observe classes	Each instructor
	Promote interest in fitness within school and community	Community, faculty, parent, and student "Turkey Trot 5 K Prediction Walk/Run"	Instructors A and C
December	Inform school board members about the program	Presentation and showing of *Fit To Achieve* video, *Making the Case for Daily Physical Education*	Department head
	Promote interest in leading a physically active lifestyle within the school and community	Night or weekend miniinstructional clinic in winter sport activities	Each instructor in area of expertise
January	Educate the general public about the changes in physical education	Public service announcements on TV or radio	Department head
	Promote physical education and curriculum offerings to students	School newspaper, bulletin board, posters	Instructor B and students
February	Inform community about the contributions of physical activity and fitness to cardiovascular health	"Jump Rope for Heart" project	Instructor A and students
	Inform parents about the changes in physical education	Address Parent-Teachers Association meeting and show *Fit to Achieve* video *Making the Case for Daily Physical Education*	Department head and instructor C
March	Promote physical education within the school to faculty and administrators	Presentation at inservice workshop and health-related fitness assessment	Instructor B and students
	Share with parents what students are learning in physical education	Evening activity program for students and parents twice a week for 3 weeks	Each instructor is responsible for 1 week
April	Promote interest in leading a physically active lifestyle within the school and community	Mini-instructional clinics at night or weekend for spring/summer sport activities	Each instructor in area of expertise
	Promote student interest in physical education and sport	Work with students to plan activities to promote National Physical Education and Sport Week	Instructors A and B
May	Inform community of National Physical Education and Sport Week	Proclamation by mayor, radio and TV announcements, and newspaper articles	Department head and instructor C
	Involve students and school in celebration of National Physical Education and Sport Week	Various activities planned by students	All staff and students
June	Recognize all students' accomplishments in physical education	Letters to parents informing them of students' achievements	Each instructor

Modified from Nelson JE: Communication: the key to public relations, *JOPERD* 57(4):64-67, 1986.

lic involvement within the program. Also, many professional public relations programs exist that physical education teachers may find helpful in publicizing their programs. Regardless of the approach utilized, the purpose remains the same: to promote a favorable image of physical education and gain support for the program.

Newspapers

Because the local newspaper reaches a large audience, it can be an effective means to promote physical education to the public. Local newspapers are often looking for feature stories that appeal to community interests. Stories may focus on an overview of the physical education program, benefits of physical education to students now and in their future years, students' accomplishments, new or interesting units of instruction, special events, or cooperative school-community ventures.

Contributions should be timely, newsworthy, and factually correct. In preparing the article, the physical education teacher should follow the format and writing guidelines of the local paper.

Newspaper writers generally advise telling the story using short paragraphs, usually one to three sentences in length. The first paragraph is a critical one because it serves to interest the reader in reading the article further. It should relate to the reader the who, what, why, when, where, and how of the story. The remainder of the points to be presented in the article should be written in paragraphs arranged in descending order of importance. Newspapers often have space constraints and may not be able to print the entire article as submitted. By arranging the paragraphs appropriately, it is easier for the editor to cut the article without significantly affecting the presentation.

Photographs that illustrate the key points being presented should accompany the article when possible. Black and white photographs that depict people and action are preferred. Suggested captions and the name of the photographer and the subject(s) should be typed and affixed to the back of the photograph.

Physical education teachers should work collaboratively with local reporters to develop an ongoing flow of material. They should also take the initiative to invite the local press to cover special departmental events, such as a tennis clinic for community members. Positive press relations, interesting features, and adherence to specific newspaper guidelines for article submission will increase the chances of the newspaper being a positive source for the public relations program.

The school newspaper can also be used as an effective public relations medium. Information about upcoming units, guest speakers, intramural activities, and special events can be conveyed effectively to students and school personnel through the school newspaper.

Radio and Television

Radio and television provide the best means for reaching a large number of people at one time. Local stations are always looking for newsworthy items and events. Physical education teachers who cultivate professional contacts with reporters can more easily bring such items and events to reporters' attention.

Physical education teachers should also endeavor to take advantage of public service announcements, educational programing, and community access television and radio opportunities. Free air time is available to broadcast items and events in the public's interest. This time may range from a 30-second public service announcement to a 1-hour educational program. Radio and television opportunities such as these are valuable in promoting the educational value of physical education to the public.

Films

Photographs, slides, and videotapes can be used to vividly portray the physical education program in action. This communications medium can informatively present and dramatically highlight stories about the physical education program. They can capture the public's attention, create interest, and formulate lasting impressions in the public's mind while educating them about the physical education program. Slides and videotapes can also be used effectively as part of presentations to community groups.

Newsletters and Brochures

Periodically some school districts send home newsletters to parents containing information about various school programs. Physical education teachers should take advantage of this avenue of communication and make sure that their program receives coverage similar in scope and content to that provided to other programs within the school.

Newsletter features can inform parents about the goals, benefits, activities, and accomplishments of students in physical education. They are also effective means to reach students' parents to explain certain policies and procedures, such as the grading system or the physical education graduation requirement.

Some teachers have developed brochures to explain their programs. Similar to newsletters, these brochures highlight the value of physical education and provide information about the various aspects of the program.

Other schools use brochures to stimulate student interest in the elective physical education program or intramural and club activities. Students are provided with a listing and short description of the various courses and opportunities available and encouraged to participate in the program.

Bulletin Boards, Posters, and Exhibits

Bulletin boards, posters, and exhibits can be used effectively within the school and community to promote the physical education program. Bulletin boards should be attractive and well designed to capture the attention of the public. The message should be readily apparent to viewers and arouse interest in the subject. In constructing the bulletin board, care should be taken to use large letters that are visible from about 20 feet. Photographs and artwork draw the viewer's attention to the presentation. Information should be presented clearly, and, if appropriate, the name of the person to contact for additional information should be provided.

Posters are also an attractive means of conveying information about the physical education program. Posters are available from various organizations, such as AAHPERD, that promote physical education. Additionally, students who are artistically talented may be willing to volunteer their services to make posters. Some schools have allowed students to paint locker rooms, gymnasiums, and hallway walls with pictures of people participating in various physical education activities.

Exhibits set up in a display case in the main hall or at a location in the community can also be used to promote physical education. Exhibits during an open house at the school or during National Physical Education and Sport Week can help familiarize many people with the physical education program.

Special Events

Special events can do a great deal to stimulate interest and generate a positive image of physical education. Schoolwide playdays and competitions, parents' nights, special school and community activities, and award ceremonies are just a few examples of special events that can be used for public relations purposes.

Schoolwide playdays and competitions include a variety of activities, such as fitness and sport competitions or novel events. The emphasis is on participation. Students may be formed into teams, and often faculty and school staff are invited to join. These events may take place during the school day or held as a special evening activity.

Parents' nights provide an opportunity for students and parents to participate together in physical education activities. These events may include instruction in specific skills or simply the opportunity to enjoy these activities together. Students and parents may also participate together on a regular basis as part of an ongoing fitness program. This program offers opportunities for fitness assessment and time to participate in fitness activities on a regular basis.

To generate support for physical education among

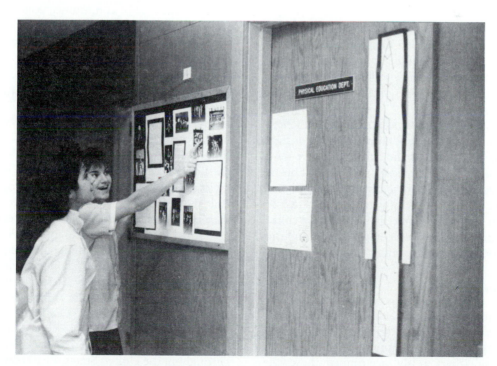

Bulletin boards are an effective means of creating interest in the program.
Courtesy of Joanne Ruane.

school personnel, some physical education teachers have successfully designed and conducted faculty fitness programs similar to those found in the corporate setting. School personnel receive instruction in various aspects of fitness and opportunities to work out under the guidance of the physical education teacher. Joint faculty, parent, and student recreation programs are other means to promote physical education. Opportunities to participate in a variety of activities, such as badminton or volleyball, after school or in the evening are popular.

It may be helpful to direct some special events at community members. Instructional and fitness workshops and clinics are typically well received by members of the community. Increasingly, more schools are opening up their facilities to the community when they are not in use during the evenings, weekends, or summer. Additionally, schools are providing instruction by professionals to adults in a variety of subjects, including physical education.

Some physical education departments hold special assembly programs or award ceremonies during which students' physical education achievements are recognized. Awards may recognize the attainment of a certain level of fitness, achievement of proficiency in an activity, or personal improvement. Certificates of achievement are often presented to the students. Parents may be invited to these ceremonies and a guest speaker invited to address the audience on the value of physical education.

Public Speaking

Public speaking can be an effective means to interpret physical education to the public. Community and civic organizations are always looking for speakers for their meetings. A thoroughly prepared, well-delivered presentation can enhance the image of physical education within these groups.

To be effective as a speaker, physical education teachers should prepare thoroughly, speak clearly, convey enthusiasm and a sincere interest in the subject, adhere to a reasonable time limit for the speech, and, when appropriate, provide opportunities for members of the audience to ask questions. It may be helpful to supplement the presentation with additional materials, such as a brochure about the program or slides or videotapes illustrating the physical education program in action.

Public Involvement

Involving members of the public in the physical education program is another way to build support for physical education. Parents and community members can be used effectively as teachers' aids. Once trained, these volunteers can assist in classes in various capacities, such as helping students learn new skills or administering a component of a fitness test. This involvement will allow the public to see firsthand what students learn.

Parents and community members with special expertise can be invited to serve as guest instructors in the physical education classes. A parent who is skilled in yoga may be invited to present a lesson to the students, the local bicycle shop owner may be asked to speak on bicycle repair during a bicycle unit, an aerobic dance instructor may request to lead a demonstration lesson, and the local golf professional may be called to teach a lesson on putting.

Many schools are increasing their use of off-campus facilities for physical education. Students may participate in a swimming unit at the local YMCA, use local park facilities for a cross-country skiing or an orienteering unit, or work out at a local fitness club as part of their fitness unit. Physical education teachers who incorporate the use of off-campus facilities in their program promote positive public relations when they work cooperatively with facility managers and personnel in planning the students' use of the facility. Good public relations occur when teachers take the time to write these professionals a note of appreciation for their work with the physical education program.

Parents and community members may also be invited to serve as spokespersons for physical education. These spokepersons may have more impact on public opinion because of their positions in their communities. A prominent physician speaking to community groups about the benefits of exercise and the importance of physical education in the lives of community youth or a community leader writing in the newspapers on behalf of more funding or a new facility may be instrumental in favorably influencing public opinion.

Professional Public Relations Approaches

Several public relations programs are sponsored or cosponsored by the American Alliance for Health, Physical Education, Recreation, and Dance (AAHPERD) that may be effectively employed within the secondary school physical education public relations program. These include the Physical Education Public Information project, National Physical Education and Sport Week, Jump Rope for Heart, and Fit to Achieve. Physical education teachers concerned with influencing legislative decision makers may fine the AAHPERD publication, *Shaping the Body Politic,* to be extremely useful in their endeavors.[7]

Physical Education Public Information. Physical Education Public Information (PEPI) is a national program designed by the National Association for Sport and Physical Education (NASPE), an association of AAHPERD. Throughout the United States, PEPI coordinators in each state actively work to promote the value of physical education through the various media. Among the values

FIG. 15-1 Poster promoting National Physical Education and Sport Week.
Reprinted by permission of the National Association for Sport and Physical Education.

emphasized are the contribution of physical activity to health, academic achievement, one's self-concept, and the learning of sports skills for lifetime participation.

PEPI has focused its efforts on getting these and other messages across to the public, particularly taxpayers, students, parents, teachers, administrators, school boards, and funding agencies. The 600 coordinators organize and interpret physical education to the various publics in their own geographical areas. Currently PEPI is stressing how physical education has changed to become more relevant to the times.

National Physical Education and Sport Week. Sponsored by NASPE, National Physical Education and Sport Week (May 1-7) provides an opportunity for physical education teachers to showcase their programs and proclaim the benefits of quality physical education programs. During this week, physical education teachers throughout the country make special efforts to promote their programs. This week may be commemorated through the use of activities such as public service announcements, special events such as a community or legislative fitness day, or promotional displays. Students can also be involved in many ways in promoting the program.

Each year a different theme is selected for this week that highlights the importance of physical education. For example, the theme for 1990 was *Fit to Achieve through Quality Daily Physical Education*. Previous themes also reflect the importance and contribution of physical education to individual's lives: *Physical Education: Essential for Excellence, Physical Education is for Every Body,* and *Physical Education: A Requirement for Life*. Each year posters proclaiming the theme are made available to AAHPERD members for use in promoting National Physical Education and Sport Week (Fig. 15-1).

Jump Rope for Heart. Sponsored by AAHPERD and the American Heart Association (AHA), the Jump Rope for Heart (JRFH) program is a successful public relations event. The program promotes the health value of aerobic exercise, specifically rope jumping, through demonstrations and rope jumping events. Students participate in JRFH events while raising money through pledges for the AHA. This program has served to inform millions of youths and children of the importance of maintaining physically active and healthy lifestyles.

The JRFH program benefits the AHA's research and educational programs aimed at fighting cardiovascular diseases. Through the JRFH program, schools are provided with educational materials to facilitate the instruction of students in the areas of health, fitness, and nutrition.

The JRFH program offers a highly visible means for physical education teachers to promote the value of physical activity and the contribution that physical education can make to enhance the quality of life of people of all ages. It also affords teachers the opportunity to present a positive, professional image to the community and dem-onstrate their willingness to be an active, involved member of the community.

Fit to Achieve. In an effort to educate the public about the potential benefits of daily quality physical education, AAHPERD designed the *Fit to Achieve through Daily Quality Physical Education* program. A public relations initiative, the Fit to Achieve program focuses on educating parents, educational policymakers, and the community about the value of physical education and motivating them to improve the status of physical education in their schools and states.

Through AAHPERD, physical education teachers may obtain Fit to Achieve promotional materials to help educate the public about physical education and the need for daily, quality programs. These promotional materials include a videotape, preplanned slide presentation with a script, various brochures, and a Grass Roots Action kit. This action kit contains materials that can be used for professionals to promote physical education. These materials include sample news releases (Fig. 15-2), feature stories, editorials, public service announcements, and special event ideas. Strategies that can be effectively used to create change are also presented as part of this program.

Shaping the Body Politic. Throughout the country, physical education teachers and professional organizations are becoming increasingly involved in efforts to influence decision makers' votes on issues pertaining to physical education. These issues include decisions pertaining to funding, staffing, curricula and time allotment, and facilities. Many teachers realize the importance of becoming more active in influencing decisions that affect the future direction of physical education programs for our country's youth.

To help teachers more effectively influence decisions, AAHPERD has published a resource manual entitled *Shaping the Body Politic*.[7] Information about how public policy is made and the role of the state legislatures in the formulation of educational policy is presented. It also gives information about how to mount a successful legislative campaign, planning strategies, and how to involve people effectively in these efforts. Techniques that can be used to influence public opinion and suggestions about using the media are also presented. Case studies and examples are used frequently to illustrate various approaches. Finally, the manual contains a research section that provides documented answers to frequently asked questions about the value of physical education. This resource manual would be helpful to physical education teachers in influencing decisions at all levels of government and policy-making, including the local level.

PUBLIC RELATIONS IN PRACTICE

The physical education department's public relations program should be directed primarily toward four publics: students, school personnel, parents, and community

Wanted: Quality Physical Education Programs
By (Your Name, Title, and School)

Educating the mind and not the body is one of the most serious mistakes being made in schools across the nation. Many school physical education programs are in trouble. These programs are being reduced or eliminated from more school curricula every day. More frequently classroom teachers are also being called upon to teach physical education.

Americans must be convinced that quality physical education for every child is a necessity—not a luxury—for the health of our children now and as adults in the 21st century. The benefits of vigorous physical activity through quality physical education have been well documented. Children who are fit, skillful, and healthy are better students and more positive about learning than those individuals who are not. Other benefits that illuminate from a physically active child is improved self-confidence, muscular strength, and endurance level.

Physical education also helps children establish lifelong healthy habits such as not smoking, exercising regularly, eating well and achieving goals in all aspects of life. That is why NASPE, the National Association for Sport and Physical Education, believes that every student, from kindergarten through grade 12 in our nation's schools, should participate in quality physical education programs.

Too often parents believe children are naturally active enough to stay healthy. However, recent research indicates most children spend more time watching television in one day than they spend engaged in moderate to vigorous activity in a week. Children are driven most places, play computer games, watch movies, and do little in the way of physical chores. More than 40% of children between the ages of 6 and 17 are at risk for coronary heart disease because of high blood pressure, high cholesterol, obesity, or inactivity. According to the National Health Examination Survey, obesity increased 54% among children ages 6 to 11 and 39% in adolescents ages 12 to 17 between 1963 and 1980.

These health statistics give us a warning. We must act now to reverse this frightening trend. Increased health care costs, reduced productivity in the workplace, and a reduced quality of life are the consequences of an inactive

and unfit population. While most adults support and understand the importance of academic education, many do not understand the impact of quality physical education for their children. But unless children are taught how and the importance of why to be physically active and to feel physically competent, they will not enjoy the benefits of being active and healthy as children and as adults.

A quality physical education program provides for the development of motor skills, the introduction of fitness concepts, and assessment of children's progress in ways that complement and support the academic program to make a complete educational package. The physical education program should be taught by a specially trained teacher who understands the scientific basis of physical activity and the learning of motor skills. Such a teacher should also have the support of an appropriate faculty, equipment, class size, and schedule.

NASPE believes a physically educated person is one who:
- Has learned skills necessary to perform a variety of physical activities
- Is physically fit
- Does participate regularly in physical activity
- Knows the implications of and the benefits from involvement in physical activities
- Values physical activity and its contributions to a healthful lifestyle.

To achieve those goals, NASPE believes a quality physical education program should:
- Be taught every day
- Be taught by a certified physical education teacher
- Provide a logical progression in skill development, from kindergarten through 12th grade
- Provide children with a basic understanding of their own bodies
- Focus on individual success and participation
- Encourage children to enjoy nonschool physical activities.

A new century of challenges, opportunities, and experiences awaits our children. But to enjoy their lives fully they must be physically active and competent. As concerned parents and adults, please help us educate both our children's mind and body.

FIG. 15-2   Example of a press release from the Fit To Achieve public relations program. Reprinted by permission of the National Association for Sport and Physical Education.

members. Additionally, increased attention is being given to influence the votes of decision makers at all levels. The public relations program can effectively reach these publics in many different ways. Regardless of the approach chosen, efforts should be directed toward helping the public better understand physical education's purposes and gain support for the program.

Student Relations

The most important public is the students. Students who hold a positive impression of physical education will communicate this liking through their enthusiasm to their

parents. Teachers who share with students the reasons why certain activities are being taught, communicate the benefits of participation, exhibit genuine concern about students' well-being, provide opportunities for achievement, and recognize students' accomplishments create a favorable image of physical education in students' and parents' minds.

On the other hand, students who dislike physical education communicate this dislike to their parents. Parents with negative perceptions of physical education will be reluctant to support the program. Furthermore, when these students reach adulthood and can exercise their influence as voters, they will be unlikely to support the physical education program if they disliked it as students. Offering a quality program that is relevant to students' needs now and in the future is the foundation of the public relations program.

Creating a positive image of physical education may be particularly important at the secondary level. In schools where physical education is an elective course, the impressions students hold of physical education will affect the enrollment in these courses. In schools where physical education is perceived positively and as relevant to students' lives, student enrollment in the elective program is likely to be high.

Involving students in the promotion of the physical education program is an effective public relations approach. Students can help conduct special events; they can assist others and utilize their talents in designing posters, exhibits, and displays to promote physical education; and they can speak to various groups, such as the Parents-Teachers Association, about the physical education program and its value to them as individuals.

Parents

Most parents willingly support programs that contribute significantly to their children's well-being. To ensure this support, physical education teachers must conduct a quality program so that these desired outcomes will be achieved. Moreover, teachers must make an effort to communicate to parents information about the educational nature and positive contributions of physical education to children's lives.

The best public relations spokespersons for physical education are excited, enthusiastic students sharing with their parents what they have learned in physical education. However, for parents to gain an accurate impression of physical education, the teachers must ensure that students understand the purposes and sought-after outcomes for the activities presented in class. Students who lack this understanding may convey an inaccurate image of physical education.

Student grade reports are another excellent way to communicate with parents. Traditional grade reports typically do not offer parents much information about what was covered in physical education class or about their children's performance during the marking period. Some teachers are supplementing grade reports with additional reports, such as fitness or wellness profiles. Information about what skills and knowledge were covered in specific units during the marking period and students' attainment of unit objectives may also be sent to parents. Microcomputers can be used to expedite the development of such reports.

Handouts, brochures, and newsletters can be used to explain successfully the physical education program to the parents. Certificates of achievement and effort are other techniques that can be used to help parents become aware of their children's accomplishments.

Parent participation nights, on which a variety of activities are presented by teachers to parents and their children, are a great way to familiarize parents with the physical education program. Participation nights also allow teachers to meet the parents of their students and to speak personally with them.

School Relations

The importance of maintaining a positive image of physical education among other teachers, administrators, and school staff should not be overlooked. All too often, physical education is perceived by many school personnel as a frill, not as an integral part of the educational curriculum, and physical education teachers are relegated to a lesser status than teachers of more academic subjects.

These negative perceptions can have an adverse effect on the program in several ways. Physical education may be shortchanged when it comes to program funding. It may not be allocated sufficient time within the curriculum to accomplish its objectives. Physical education may not be given the same considerations as other instructional areas. Subsequently, little attention is given to controlling class size or grouping students homogeneously. These consequences can have a direct, harmful effect on program quality.

Physical education teachers must make an effort to educate school personnel about physical education. This can be accomplished in many ways. Collaborative teaching efforts, such as working closely with other faculty in the areas of math, science, and health on special units of instruction, can help build a sense of common educational purpose.

Sponsoring special events for school personnel can also contribute to a positive image of physical education. Some teachers conduct special fitness programs for school personnel, modeled after corporate fitness programs. These programs may include such activities as fitness assessment, exercise classes, stress management, and nutritional counseling. Faculty may work out before or after school or during their free time. Establishment of recreational sport leagues, such as volleyball, and other participation opportunities such as student-faculty intramurals, can help create a more favorable impression of physical education among school personnel.

Community Relations

Community members should also receive attention when implementing the public relations program. They support public education with their tax dollars. Even though some community members may have no children in the school, it is important to keep them informed about the physical education program and how their tax dollars are being used. Additionally, many community members may not be aware of the differences between the physical education program and the athletics program. It is important to clarify these differences.

Community members can be informed about the physical education program through the use of the local media: newspapers, radio, and television stations. Physical education teachers may also reach community members through speeches to local community and civic organizations, community clinics, demonstrations, and exhibits.

Special school events for community members can pay big dividends in terms of support. Special clinics, evening classes, and other activities can help community members more fully understand the instructional nature of the physical education program. Increasing numbers of schools around the nation are opening up their gymnasiums and facilities at night, on weekends, and during the summers to serve as community centers. These instructional programs and recreational opportunities are welcomed by many community members.

Some physical education teachers invite community members with specific areas of expertise to serve as guest lecturers within the physical education program. Other teachers have extended the physical education program into the community, using community facilities such as swimming pools, golf courses, hiking trails, and health clubs as sites for physical education classes and involving community members working at these sites as instructors within the physical education program.

Decision Makers

Decision makers at all levels have increasingly become the focus of physical education teachers' public relations efforts. Because of the profound influence that legislative and policy decisions can have on the physical education program, efforts must be made to interpret accurately the content and the worth of physical education programs to these decision makers. One of the most important groups of decision makers that need to be targeted for a public relations effort are the members of the local school board. The degree of support offered by the local school board for the physical education program can have a major impact on the conduct of the program within the community's schools.

Physical education teachers acting independently or in conjunction with their professional organizations can use proactive strategies to gain decision makers' support for physical education. These strategies include providing decision makers with current research about the contributions of physical education to well-being, letter-writing campaigns to urge decision makers to adopt a particular position on votes pertaining to issues of interest, and using the media to address specific issues of concern.

Some teachers sponsor legislative fitness days where legislators receive a personalized fitness assessment and prescription to enhance their fitness status. Other teachers have invited legislators to speak at conventions and other events to promote physical education. Proactive stances help create a favorable climate for physical education and can often head off crises, such as budget cuts, that may require reactive approaches to remediate.

These are just a few examples of public relations approaches that may be effectively used to promote physical education. Further information about these approaches is available from AAHPERD, 1900 Association Drive, Reston, VA, 22091.

SUMMARY

Gaining and maintaining support for the physical education program are important responsibilities of each secondary school physical education teacher. This objective may be accomplished effectively where there is a well-planned public relations program.

Public relations is the establishment and maintenance of effective two-way communication between an organization and its publics. This communication is designed to engender public understanding and support. Physical education public relations programs should focus on communicating the value of physical education to students, parents, school personnel, community members, and decision makers.

In designing and implementing a physical education public relations program, principles of effective public relations should be followed. The foundation of the public relations program is a quality physical education program and its teachers. The public relations program should be planned, truthful, based on research findings, and evaluated periodically. Communication emanating from the public relations program should be continuous and should utilize multiple avenues of communication to reach the intended public.

Many different techniques can be used effectively in the public relations program to gain support for physical education. Newspapers, radio, television, films, newspapers, brochures, bulletin boards, exhibits, and posters can be used effectively to communicate information to the various publics about the physical education program. Special events, demonstrations, public speaking, parent communication, and professional public relations efforts can be incorporated as part of the physical education public relations program.

FOR REVIEW

1. List the principles that should be observed in a public relations program. Using these principles, describe how you would communicate the importance of including physical education as an integral part of the educational curriculum.

2. The public often has difficulty understanding the differences between the physical education program and the athletic program. How would you effectively communicate the differences between these two programs to the public?

3. One of the primary goals of the public relations program is to promote the value of physical education to the various publics. What values would you highlight in a speech to parents?

4. In many secondary schools, physical education is an elective in grades 11 and 12. What public relations strategies would you use to ensure that enrollment by juniors and seniors in the physical education program is at a high level?

5. Design a multidimensional physical education public relations program to promote National Physical Education and Sport Week.

REFERENCES

1. Cutlip SM, Center AH: *Effective public relations,* Englewood Cliffs, NJ, 1982, Prentice Hall.
2. Horine L: *Administration of physical education and sport programs,* ed 2, Dubuque, Iowa, 1991, William C Brown.
3. Bucher CA: *Management of physical education and athletic programs,* St Louis, 1987, Mosby.
4. Bivins T: *Handbook for public relations writing,* Lincolnwood, Ill, 1989, NTC Business Books.
5. Rolloff BD: Public relations: objectives for physical education, *JOPERD* 56(3):69-71, 1985.
6. Nelson JE: Communication: the key to public relations, *JOPERD* 57(4):64-67, 1986.
7. Seiter MM, Goggin M: *Shaping the body politic: legislative training for the physical educator,* Reston Va, 1984, AAHPERD.

ANNOTATED READINGS

Bivins T: *Handbook for public relations writing,* Lincolnwood, Ill, 1989, NTC Business Books.

Practical suggestions for writing press releases; radio and television announcements, advertising, newsletters, and speeches are included.

Nelson JE: Communication: the key to public relations, *JOPERD* 57(4):64-67, 1986.

Keys to effective communication and an example of a yearly public relations program are presented.

Schneider RD: Don't just promote your profession—market it! *JOPERD* 63(5):70-71, 1992.

Suggestions of how to improve the public image of physical education are presented.

Seiter MM, Goggin M: *Shaping the body politic: legislative training for the physical educator,* Reston, Va, 1984, AAHPERD.

Information about how to use legislative power effectively, guidelines for presenting cases effectively, and approaches for molding public opinion are included in this resource.

PART IV

Wellness and Fitness

Wellness is an optimal state of health and well-being. Helping students understand the dimensions of wellness and how to achieve this state is an important contribution that secondary school physical education can make to the lives of students.

The health benefits of incorporating regular and appropriate physical activity into one's lifestyle are increasingly recognized. Students should understand the effects of exercise on the human body and know how to assess and improve each component of health-related fitness. Teachers should provide experiences that will help students incorporate enjoyable physical activities into their lifestyle.

OUTLINE

CHAPTER 16

Wellness for Secondary School Students

CHAPTER OBJECTIVES
- To define wellness and describe its components
- To discuss the contribution of physical education to wellness

During the past decade, the nation has experienced an increasing interest in wellness and a growing awareness of the benefits of leading a healthy lifestyle. Today public health programs emphasize disease prevention and health promotion, not only the treatment of illness. If education is to prepare individuals for life and if education is to enhance the quality of individuals' lives, then wellness education should be an integral component of every school's curriculum.

The U.S. Public Health Service is committed to improving the health of all Americans through a comprehensive health promotion and disease prevention program. The principle goals of this effort are to increase the span of healthy life, reduce disparities in health status among different population groups, and increase access to preventive services.[1] Improving the health and fitness of the nation's children and youth is the cornerstone of this effort to improve the health profile of all Americans. The report *Healthy People 2000* outlined 300 specific health objectives to be achieved by the year 2000, 192 of which related to improving the health of children and youth.[1] Effective school physical education and health programing is critical to achieving these objectives.[2]

WELLNESS: AN OVERVIEW AND DEFINITION

Wellness is an optimal state of health and well-being. It is the capacity to live life to its fullest potential, to be fully alive. In the past, traditional approaches to health have emphasized alleviating or treating disease. From this traditional perspective, good health was viewed as freedom from disease; therefore an individual who was not sick was considered to be healthy.[3] Wellness goes beyond this perspective. Not only does wellness involve freedom from disease, it also involves an optimal state of well-being.[3]

Wellness depends on the individual making responsible and appropriate lifestyle decisions. Experts recognize that many decisions we make pertaining to our lifestyle can significantly influence our health status. These decisions can influence not only our current quality of life but also our length of life. For example, the decision to smoke cigarettes or not to smoke them is a personal choice that will ultimately have an impact on the state of one's health. Furthermore, experts also believe that many diseases experienced later on in life have their roots in childhood. For example, obesity and physical inactivity, two risk factors for coronary artery disease, hypertension, and non−insulin-dependent diabetes, appear to begin in childhood.[4] Therefore it is important that professionals help people develop healthy lifestyles early in life.

Attainment and maintenance of a high level of wellness require the individual to properly manage his or her own lifestyle. Wellness emphasizes making informed choices and taking thoughtful actions that will result in the prevention of disease and the promotion of health. It is estimated that over 50% of illnesses can be prevented or their severity lessened by individuals taking responsibility for their health and making sound choices based on current medical knowledge.[3] The choices individuals make can lengthen or shorten their lives and enhance or adversely affect their quality of life, depending on whether their health habits are good or destructive in nature. Personal responsibility is the key to developing a wellness lifestyle.

DIMENSIONS OF WELLNESS

Wellness emphasizes the development of the whole person and, thus, is multidimensional in nature (Fig. 16-1).[3,5] Its components include physical health, emotional health, social health, intellectual or mental health, and spiritual health. These components are highly interrelated. A poor level of health in one component may adversely affect other components, altering the balance so necessary for well-being. Attainment and maintenance of a high level of wellness require that each of these components be balanced according to individual needs and goals.

Physical Health

To be healthy, individuals must commit themselves to enhancing the physical condition of their bodies. Attainment and maintenance of a high level of physical health require careful attention to physical fitness, especially those health-related components of cardiovascular endurance, muscular strength and endurance, flexibility, and body composition. Proper nutrition, avoidance of tobacco and excessive alcohol consumption, and refraining from drug abuse are important to maintain good physical condition. Individuals must also take steps to ensure that they get adequate sleep and maintain a balance between work and leisure. Safety, medical self-care, and appropriate use of the medical system also contribute to attaining a high level of physical health.

Emotional Health

Emotional health is another important dimension of wellness. Emotions play a major role in healthful living, influencing feelings about oneself and feelings toward and interactions with others. The ability to deal with stress and to adjust and adapt to changes in the environment is influenced by one's emotional outlook.

Understanding the close relationship between the mind and the body is important. For example, anxiety, a mental state, is associated with increased levels of muscle tension in the body. Prolonged stress can adversely affect the immune system, increasing the risk for developing disease.[6] Illnesses, such as cancer, a physical state, may be associated with feelings of sadness or depression. The connection between the mind and the body cannot be overlooked in a quest to achieve optimal health.

FIG. 16-1 Dimensions of wellness.
From Prentice WE: *Fitness for college and life,* ed 4, St Louis, 1994, Mosby.

Social Health

Social wellness encompasses healthy interactions with others. The development of social skills, communication skills, and interpersonal relationships is critical to healthy living. Social health includes our ability to carry out our responsibilities associated with the various roles in life, for example, as a son or daughter or as a friend. It also embraces fulfillment of such critical needs as intimacy, love, and companionship.

Intellectual Health

Intellectual development is also an important facet of wellness. Learning through formal and informal educational activities leads to an acquisition of knowledge. Increased knowledge and skills expand one's horizons, not only in the area of work but also in relation to others. Creative, stimulating mental activities are important to good health. Additionally, intellectual activity is necessary if the individual is to be able to integrate successfully the many facets of wellness—emotions, social skills, physical activities, and spiritual values.

Intellectual skills such as critical thinking and decision making are essential to attaining wellness. Achieving and maintaining wellness involve making responsible choices that will lead to a high level of well-being. Intellectual skills are essential to this endeavor.

Spiritual Health

Spiritual wellness means different things to different people. The meaning of spirituality held by an individual

Participation in physical activities can contribute to social development.
Courtesy of Emily Leonardo, Camp Hill High School, Camp Hill, PA.

is influenced by several factors, including religion, familial beliefs, culture, and nationality. To some individuals spiritual wellness involves a belief in an omnipotent entity, while to others it may encompass the establishment of values, morals, and ethics. Spiritual wellness also includes seeking purpose and meaning in human existence and appreciating the depth and expanse of life and the natural forces that exist within the universe.

CONTRIBUTION OF PHYSICAL EDUCATION TO ACHIEVEMENT OF WELLNESS

Wellness—how can this optimal state of health be achieved (Fig. 16-2)? Attainment of this high level of well-being requires achieving and maintaining physical fitness, following sound dietary practices, and managing one's stress. Sound safety practices should be incorporated into all aspects of one's life. Deterrents to wellness should be eliminated. Wise decision making in relation to lifestyle choices is necessary. Positive feelings of self-worth help individuals make these important lifestyle decisions. And, most important, wellness requires individuals to assume the responsibility for their own health.

Within the secondary school physical education program, there exists a tremendous potential for physical education teachers to help students develop the attitudes, skills, and knowledge essential to achievement of lifetime wellness. The potential of physical education to have a favorable impact on an individual's quality of life grows when attention is given to wellness education in the curriculum.

Development of Decision-Making Skills

Throughout the secondary school physical education experience, students should be given opportunities to develop their decision-making skills. One's level of wellness is directly influenced by the choices one makes pertaining to one's lifestyle. Should I work out today? Should I eat pizza or a salad for lunch? Should I use tobacco because all my friends are using it? Should I use drugs or alcohol to cope with stress? Should I use my seatbelt when driving a car? Decisions such as these on a daily and long-term basis will have an impact on one's health and well-being, ultimately affecting one's quality of life.

Help students develop a systematic approach to decision making. The first step is defining the problem and the choices available. Gathering reliable information about the problem, examining the potential solutions to the problem in terms of their consequences, selecting a

W . . .	Wise decision making and self-responsibility in lifestyle choices
E . . .	Exercising appropriately and regularly
L . . .	Level of stress effectively managed
L . . .	Liking and high regard for oneself—a positive self-concept
N . . .	Nutritionally sound dietary practices
E . . .	Elimination of health deterrents and reduction of risk factors
S . . .	Sound safety practices
S . . .	Satisfying balance between rest, work, and leisure

FIG. 16-2   Steps to wellness.

course of action from among the alternatives, implementing one's choice, and evaluating the effectiveness of the decision are steps involved in the process.[7] Students also need opportunities to examine the impact of their attitudes, values, and feelings on their decision making. Moreover, students should learn that the ultimate responsibility of the decision rests within each person.

Opportunities are plentiful within the secondary school physical education program to teach decision-making skills. Providing students with opportunities to choose among different fitness activities, to select different individuals with whom to work, to choose to accept or not accept responsibility for one's own actions during a unit of instruction are just a few of the many ways that decision making can be incorporated into the curriculum. Teachers can further help students learn about decision making by explaining some of the decisions they have made regarding the content and conduct of the physical education class. Explaining why certain activities are selected in place of others or why certain rules are necessary helps students understand the reasoning and process involved in the decision.

Students who have developed good decision-making skills can make meaningful decisions throughout their lives, even when teachers or parents are no longer present to guide them. For example, increasing numbers of adults are joining health and fitness clubs. Some of these clubs are highly reputable, employ trained professionals, and follow sound fitness and health practices in helping clients attain their fitness goals. Other clubs leave a lot to be desired, utilizing untrained leaders and questionable practices in working with their membership. Students should be able to evaluate a health and fitness club and make a well-informed decision about joining.

Physical education can offer students the skills and knowledge necessary to make well-informed personal decisions about their health and fitness activities. Such decision-making skills allow students to become independent, autonomous, lifelong learners. Moreover, shifting increased responsibility for decisions to students via choices of activities, styles of teaching, and exercising on an independent basis also helps students learn self-responsibility.

Risk Factor Reduction

The attainment of wellness requires the reduction of health risk factors, which increase one's probability of disease. In the case of coronary heart disease, risk factors include cigarette smoking, elevated serum cholesterol, physical inactivity, hypertension, obesity, diabetes, heredity, age, race, and a high-stress lifestyle.[3] Many of these risk factors are a function of individual lifestyles and behavior patterns. With the exception of heredity, age, sex, and race, these risk factors can be altered through lifestyle modification. That is, individuals can reduce their chances of coronary heart disease by making thoughtful, sound decisions about their lifestyles.

Although coronary heart disease and associated risk factors may be addressed in health or science classes, coronary heart disease and risk factor reduction should be mentioned in conjunction with the cardiovascular fitness program. Providing students with information about how fitness activities can alleviate certain risk factors and lead to a more positive health profile helps them more fully understand the purpose and value of what they are doing.

Deterrents to Wellness

To achieve wellness, deterrents to health must be eliminated from the individual's lifestyle. Substance abuse is a serious problem among adolescents. Drug abuse, that is, taking a drug for other than its intended purpose, the use of so-called recreational drugs, such as marijuana or cocaine, alcohol consumption, and use of tobacco have become increasingly prevalent among junior and senior high school students. For example, it is estimated that 88% of high-school seniors have used alcohol.[8] Students usually abuse these substances for any of the following reasons: curiosity, peer pressure, desire to be more mature and adultlike, rebellion against adult authority, and imitation of adult role models.[9,10]

Because substance abuse is detrimental to wellness and can adversely affect fitness, physical education teachers may wish to discuss this problem with their students or follow up on material covered in health and science classes. If students are expected to make wise and meaningful decisions in this area, they need to be knowledgeable regarding the impact of various substances on their physical and psychological well-being. Teachers should present facts pertaining to substance abuse, the short- and long-term effects, in a nonjudgmental manner. The use and misuse of these substances should be discussed objectively with students, because much of the information they receive is from biased sources, such as parents, peers, and media formats.

Students need to understand the effects of substance abuse on their health. Along with this knowledge, they should examine why people choose or choose not to engage in these abusive behaviors. Enhancing students' level of awareness helps them learn about the alternatives and consequences of their behavior. Before students can make a decision about their behavior, they need to understand thoroughly the ramifications of substance abuse.

The increased attention given to the media regarding substance abuse by athletes provides a fruitful area for discussion. The media have reported on athletes' use of pep pills, steroids, and pain killers; presented students with images of athletes smoking and drinking; and examined the use of drug testing in athletics. Moreover, the reported increased use of steroids by high-school students to improve their athletic performance and to enhance their appearance merits discussion.

Physical education teachers must also be prepared when students who are experiencing substance abuse problems seek them out for counsel and assistance. As a teacher, be cognizant of the limits of your ability to deal with these serious problems. When necessary be prepared to assist students in locating capable trained professionals. Be familiar with the various resources in the community where students can locate and find help for their problems.

Stress Management

Effective stress management is necessary to attain a high level of wellness. Stress is the physiological response of the body to demands placed on it. These demands or stress-producing agents are called *stressors*.

There are many different types of stressors. Some stressors are physical in nature. Physical stressors are changes in the body's internal or immediate external environment that place a demand on the body to adapt. Examples of physical stressors include diet, noise, drugs, exercise, illness, and temperature.[6,11]

Other stressors are cognitive in nature, that is, whether a demand is stress producing or not depends on the individual's interpretation of it. In other words, stress occurs as a consequence of the individual's perception. How an individual perceives a demand and chooses to react to it influences the stress experienced. Cognitive stressors elicit emotional feelings and arousal, which are subsequently manifested in physiological arousal. Cognitive stressors include interpersonal relationships, worrying about an exam, peer pressure, value conflicts, and family problems.[6,11]

Individuals' perceptions can influence the intensity and duration of the stress. The same situation or demand can be interpreted differently by each individual. Some individuals will perceive the situation as a nonstressor, others as an insignificant stressor, and still others as a major stressor. Moreover, individuals' perceptions influence their handling of the stressor. Some individuals may interpret a demand as a challenge to be overcome and handled, while other individuals may interpret the same demand as a threat to their well-being. Life's stressors, when perceived as challenges, foster personal growth and development; the same stressors, when interpreted as a threat, can contribute to disease.

Stressors produce a vast array of physiological changes in the body, thus altering the homeostatic balance. These changes result in an elevated level of arousal, preparing the body to deal with the stressor. Examples of changes include increased levels of cardiorespiratory function and skeletal muscle tension. This heightened state is often referred to as the fight or flight response.

When individuals experience a significant amount of stress over a prolonged period of time, illness can occur. Stress has been found to play a role in coronary heart disease, cancer, hypertension, respiratory disease, gastrointestinal disease, eating disorders, and depression.[6,10,12] This link between stress and disease is a threat to wellness.

Learning how to manage stress is an important life skill. Stress management requires that the individual recognize the stressor, become aware of one's reactions to the stressor (that is, bodily tension, increased heart rate, sweaty palms, anxiety), and take steps to alleviate the stress either through the elimination of the stressor or the reduction of its effects.

Several methods and techniques can be used effectively to manage stress. These include relaxation training, participation in physical activity, cognitive strategies to change an individual's perceptions of stressors, time management, and biofeedback. Unfortunately, some individuals may choose to deal with stress through the use of inappropriate coping techniques, such as alcohol and drug use. The selection of a method to manage stress depends on several considerations, including the stressor, one's reaction to the stressor, and the individual's personality.

Secondary school physical education programs can assist individuals to learn how to manage their stress in several different ways. Students need to be aware of the sources of stress in their lives. Adolescence may be a particularly turbulent time for some students. Expectations imposed by parents, identification of a career choice, pressure to excel in school, the often impersonal educational environment, achievement of sexual identity, and balancing work or extracurricular activities with school responsibilities are some of the stressors confronting high-school students. Physical education teachers should also be sensitive to the stressors associated with this age group. As teachers, we must also take care that our teaching does not contribute to students' stress (for example, create fear of failure or embarrassment).

Sports activities provide a ready means to illustrate to students the effects of stress on an individual's performance. Achievement of a high level of performance depends to an extent on the individual having an appropriate level of stress or arousal for the task. An individual who falls short of this optimal state or is too aroused experiences decrements in performance. The amount of stress needed to achieve an optimal performance depends on the nature of the task and the individual.

Sports activities also offer opportunities for students to examine how their perceptions influence their appraisal of stress. Well-posed questions at the conclusion of the activity can help students become more aware of the role their perceptions play in the amount of stress they experience. Students can explore competition as a threat or a challenge and examine their reactions to this situation. The meaning of success can be discussed from different perspectives, such as defining success as beating an opponent versus doing one's best. Students can examine the impact of interpreting their signs of physiological arousal just before competition as an indicator of nervousness or as a sign that they are ready to perform at their optimum level.

The secondary school physical education program can help students acquire competency in many stress management approaches. Helping students to understand the role of physical activity in relieving stress is one of the most important contributions physical education can make to the area of stress management. Physical activity has long been acknowledged as a means of releasing tension and pent-up emotions. Additionally, physical activity helps the body deal with the elevated levels of physiological arousal associated with stress response, returning the body to a normal state more quickly. Physical activity can have a beneficial effect on the psychological state of the individual as well.[10] And when an individual is actively engaged in activities that are enjoyable, the concentration involved in participation helps divert the individual's attention from the stressors.

Students should be cognizant that high levels of fitness help individuals be more resistant to various stressors they encounter in their lives. Conversely, low levels of fitness increase individuals' vulnerability to stress. Moreover, improperly managed stress is a deterrent to fitness.

For some individuals, their appearance and body image is a stressor. This may be particularly true during the adolescent years when individuals are conscious of their appearance. Individuals who are overweight, extremely underweight, or have poor muscular development or poor posture may experience difficulty in coping with these conditions. Proper exercise can assist individuals in regulating their weight and improve muscular development and posture. In turn, the individual's self-image is enhanced, and stress is reduced.

Relaxation techniques can be incorporated into many physical education programs. Through planned movement experiences, students can be taught to become aware of their stress as manifested by bodily tension. Progressive relaxation is a popular approach to relieve the muscle tension associated with stress. Each muscle group within the body is tensed, then slowly relaxed, one at a time. Individuals may begin at their toes and systematically work on relaxing the various muscle groups, working their way up the body. As students become more skilled at performing relaxation, their awareness of tension in their body will increase, and they will be able to relax and release tension on command.

Yoga is another popular relaxation technique that can be incorporated into the physical education curriculum. Yoga is an integrated approach to achievement of relaxation, involving the mind, body, and spirit. Yoga uses a combination of mental and physical approaches to reduce stress. Various postures are practiced, leading to increased mobility and suppleness or flexibility of the body. Slow, deep diaphragmatic breathing is utilized in conjunction with the postures as the individual tries to achieve a tranquil state. Achievement of breath control itself can be helpful in reducing arousal and for calming oneself in stressful situations. Another benefit associated with yoga is increased somatic awareness. This greater awareness of bodily sensations and tensions can help individuals recognize early when they are experiencing stress. The philosophy, postures, and breathing techniques of yoga can be taught within a unit of instruction at the secondary level.

Finally, physical education teachers can help students learn activities that they can use during their leisure time. A healthy balance between work and leisure is important in managing stress. Students should be exposed to a variety of activities so that they can identify those activities that are enjoyable to them. Opportunities to develop competency in these activities need to be provided so that students can participate in them during their leisure time.

Self-Enhancement

One of the most significant influences on an individual's behavior is his or her self-concept. The beliefs individuals hold about their abilities (that is, physical, mental, or social abilities) and competencies with respect to specific situations (that is, school, physical education class, or social settings) exert a profound influence on their behavior. Whether an individual sees himself or herself as being strong or weak, competent or incompetent as a mover, or highly intelligent or less intelligent will influence self-appraisal and ultimately behavior in various situations.

An individual's behavior is also influenced by his or her perceptions of self-worth or self-esteem, which reflect an individual's feelings of worth and dignity. These feelings are an important part of health and well-being.

An individual's self-concept and self-esteem can influence physical and mental health.[6,10,13-16] Individuals who possess a negative self-concept and a low sense of self-esteem appear to be more susceptible to many diseases than individuals who possess a positive self-concept and high levels of self-esteem.

Moreover, an individual's self-concept and self-esteem can influence the amount and intensity of stress experienced and the eventual development of psychosomatic disease. Individuals with a negative self-concept and low self-esteem often have more difficulty in coping with stress. They typically have high levels of fear, tend to perceive more situations as threatening, and generally have inadequate coping skills.[13] They are likely to believe that they are victims of fate and are unable to prevent bad things from happening; consequently, they are less interested in preventive measures.[13]

On the other hand, individuals with a positive self-concept and high self-esteem are less likely to interpret situations as threatening or stressful.[13] Additionally, they usually cope with stressful situations better.[13] Moreover, their self-concept and self-esteem are further enhanced by their successful coping actions. These individuals often believe that they are in control or in charge of their lives and can take steps to prevent bad things from happening.[13] These individuals would be more likely to employ preventive measures.

In addition to playing a role in the onset of disease and susceptibility to stress, low levels of self-esteem have been implicated in substance abuse.[3,10] Individuals with low self-esteem are more likely to abuse drugs and alcohol. Their low levels of self-esteem make them vulnerable to peer pressure. In contrast, individuals with high self-esteem are better able to make decisions in the face of peer pressure. Many schools, recognizing this link between self-esteem and substance abuse, have instituted special programs to enhance the self-esteem of their students.

Because of its significant role in the governing of behavior, its relationship to disease and stress, and its influence on substance abuse, enhancement of an individual's self-concept and self-esteem is an important part of any wellness program. Physical education can contribute to the development of a positive self-concept and high self-esteem in many ways.

An increasing amount of evidence supports the fact that participation in physical exercise on a regular basis can increase self-esteem.[14,15] Individuals who are fit feel good about themselves, mentally and physically. Moreover, individuals who participate successfully in physical activities enhance their self-concept. They further learn to recognize and accept their limitations, while striving to attain their fullest potential.

If teachers are to be successful in helping their students become lifelong participants in physical activities, they must foster within their students a positive perception of their physical abilities. In other words, they must help students view themselves as movers.[16] Students who see themselves as active and physically capable will be more likely to continue to participate in physical activities once

they leave school. Successful experiences in movement activities help students view their physical abilities in a positive light and encourage them to continue to participate. On the other hand, students who perceive themselves as inept or incapable of performing physical skills will likely join the ranks of sedentary adults.

It is important to recognize that physical education teachers at the secondary level may be faced with the task of helping students change their perceptions and image of themselves as movers. By the time students reach high school, they have already formed certain ideas and conceptions about their movement abilities. Those students who have a positive image of themselves as movers need to be encouraged to develop themselves to their fullest potential.

A more difficult task faces teachers in working with students who have negative images of their abilities as movers. These students must be helped to develop more positive views of their movement abilities. Teachers can help these students by providing them with opportunities to develop movement competencies and being supportive and encouraging of their efforts. More so than other students, these students need repeated opportunities for success. Students who have negative images of their movement abilities may attribute success to luck, rather than their ability. Repeated successes help students realize that their ability, rather than luck, was responsible for their achievements. This approach helps students gain confidence in their movement abilities.

While it is important to help students develop their physical abilities and provide them with frequent opportunities for success, it is important that students learn how to deal with failures and disappointments. This is part of the maturing process. Students must also be able to accept their strengths and weaknesses, and like themselves as they really are.

Physical education teachers can do much to facilitate feelings of self-worth and enhance self-esteem. Encouragement and positive feedback are important in helping students view themselves as worthwhile. Teachers and students should focus on the positive aspects of students' performance. While it is important to detect errors in performance to correct them, it is equally important to give praise and positive feedback for what was performed correctly.

The climate for learning established by the teacher can also exert an influence on students' self-esteem. A warm, supportive learning environment in which the worth and dignity of each individual are recognized and respected contributes to enhanced self-esteem. Learning environments in which students' feelings and rights are not respected, such as when a student is publicly embarrassed in front of the class or experiences repeated failure, do little to foster high self-regard. Teachers must remember that their behavior, how they treat students, is mirrored in students' behaviors and interactions with each other.

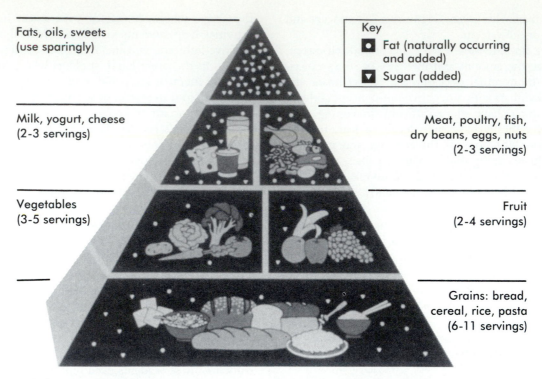

Key
■ Fat (naturally occurring and added)
▼ Sugar (added)

Fats, oils, sweets (use sparingly)

Milk, yogurt, cheese (2-3 servings)

Meat, poultry, fish, dry beans, eggs, nuts (2-3 servings)

Vegetables (3-5 servings)

Fruit (2-4 servings)

Grains: bread, cereal, rice, pasta (6-11 servings)

FIG. 16-3 USDA's Food Guide Pyramid—A Guide to Daily Food Choices. This guide lists the food groups and number of servings to consume of each. Note for children, teenagers, and adults under age 25, three servings should be chosen from the milk, yogurt, and cheese groups.

Adapted from the US Department of Agriculture: US Department of Health and Human Services, August, 1992.

Sound Nutritional Practices

"You are what you eat" is a frequently quoted remark that accents the importance of proper nutritional habits for one's fitness and wellness. Eating the right foods in the right amounts contributes to wellness; eating the wrong kinds of foods in the wrong amounts can be a deterrent to wellness. Diet has been found to play a significant role in 5 of the top 10 causes of death in the United States: heart disease, cancer, stroke, diabetes mellitus, and atherosclerosis.[3,17] Obesity can also adversely affect an individual's health.

It is important that secondary school students understand the importance of adhering to proper nutritional practices. Careful consideration of what one eats and the selection of foods for their nutritional value should be emphasized. The U.S. Department of Agriculture's food guide pyramid can be used to explain daily food choices and their relationship to proper diet (Fig. 16-3). The pyramid presents the grain group at the base, and the vegetable group and the fruit group above it. The dairy group and the group comprised of meat, poultry, fish, dry beans, eggs, and nuts is placed next. At the apex of the pyramid are fats, oils, and sweets, with the note to use these products sparingly. Typically, it is recommended that the ideal diet be composed of 58% carbo-

hydrates, 12% protein, and 30% fat.[3,17] In selecting foods, care must also be taken to ensure that the recommended daily requirements of vitamins and minerals are met. Students should be knowledgeable regarding the sources of specific nutrients and the contributions of various foods to one's diet.

In an effort to improve health and reduce the frequency of illness, the U.S. Senate Select Committee on Nutrition and Human Needs recommended dietary guidelines for Americans (Box 16-1).[17] These guidelines offer students valuable suggestions for constructing a healthy diet.

Through physical education instruction, students should also become knowledgeable regarding the various approaches to weight maintenance and management. The importance of balancing caloric intake with caloric expenditures should be understood. Thus not only should students be familiar with caloric tables for various foods but caloric expenditure tables as well. Students should understand that the energy cost of physical activities varies, and they should have the opportunity to see how many calories are burned by participating in their favorite physical activity (Table 16-1).

Obesity is a serious health problem. There is a 13% increase in the death rate for individuals who are 10% overweight, a 25% increase in the death rate for individuals who are 20% overweight, and a 40% increase in the

TABLE 16-1

Energy Expenditure During Physical Activity

To determine the number of calories expended during an activity, multiply the number of calories per minute per pound by your body weight in pounds. Then multiply this figure by the number of minutes you were involved in the activity.

Activity	Cal/min/lb	Activity	Cal/min/lb
Archery	.030	Jumping rope	
Badminton	.044	70 per min	.074
Baseball	.031	80 per min	.075
Basketball	.063	125 per min	.080
Billiards	.018	145 per min	.089
Boxing (sparring)	.062	Lacrosse	.095
Canoeing		Lying at ease	.010
Leisure	.020	Painting (outside)	.035
Racing	.047	Racquetball	.081
Circuit training		Running	
Hydra-fitness	.060	11.5 min per mile	.061
Universal	.053	9.0 min per mile	.088
Nautilus	.042	8.0 min per mile	.095
Free weights	.039	7.0 min per mile	.104
Climbing hills	.055	6.0 min per mile	.115
Croquet	.027	5.5 min per mile	.131
Cycling		Cross-country	.074
5.5 mph	.029	Sailing	.002
9.4 mph	.045	Sitting quietly	.009
Racing	.079	Skiing	
Dancing		Cross-country	.074
Aerobic, medium	.047	Downhill	.064
Aerobic, intense	.061	Water	.052
Ballroom	.023	Skindiving	
Eating (sitting)	.010	Considerable motion	.125
Field hockey	.061	Moderate motion	.094
Fishing	.028	Soccer	.059
Football	.060	Squash	.096
Gardening		Swimming	
Digging	.057	Backstroke	.077
Mowing	.051	Breast stroke	.074
Raking	.025	Butterfly	.078
Golf	.039	Crawl, slow	.070
Gymnastics	.030	Crawl, fast	.071
Handball	.063	Side stroke	.055
Hiking	.042	Treading, fast	.077
Horseback riding		Treading, normal	.028
Galloping	.062	Table tennis	.031
Trotting	.050	Tennis	.050
Walking	.019	Volleyball	.023
Ice hockey	.095	Walking (normal pace)	.036
Jogging	.069	Weight training	.032
Judo	.089	Wrestling	.085
		Writing (sitting)	.013

From Prentice W: *Fitness for college and life,* ed 4, St Louis, 1994, Mosby.

BOX 16-1

DIETARY GUIDELINES

In an effort to improve health and reduce the frequency of illness, the U.S. Senate Committee on Nutrition and Human Needs recommended the following dietary guidelines be followed:

1. Consume only the number of calories expended.
2. Increase intake of complex carbohydrates and naturally occurring sugars, such as those found in fruits, vegetables, and whole grains.
3. Reduce the ingestion of refined and processed sugar, such as those found in candy, soft drinks, and desserts.
4. Reduce overall fat consumption, such as that found in red meat.
5. Reduce the consumption of saturated fats found mainly in animal products, which result in high levels of blood cholesterol.
6. Limit intake of cholesterol. Diets rich in eggs, sausage, cheese, hamburgers, steak, and butter are also high in cholesterol. Try to limit cholesterol to about 300 mg/day.
7. Limit the intake of sodium by controlling the consumption of salt and processed foods high in salt.

death rate for individuals who are 30% overweight.[18] Because obesity is a major health problem and a deterrent to fitness, the different approaches to weight loss should be discussed. These include decreased caloric consumption, increased physical activity, or a combination of caloric restriction and increased physical activity. It is suggested that a moderate decrease in caloric intake coupled with a moderate increase in physical activity is the best approach to weight loss. Students should learn to monitor the amount of calories consumed as well as the amount of calories used by various types of physical activity.

Various dietary practices should be discussed. Different fad diets should be examined in relation to sound nutritional practices. Students may also benefit from examining different dietary strategies, such as carbohydrate loading in relation to physical performance.

Because fast foods and "junk" food (foods that supply energy but do not have any other nutritional value, that is, sugar) typically comprise a large part of the adolescent diet, students may benefit from examining the nutrients contained in these foods as well as the calories they supply. More healthful alternatives can then be suggested.

Information on nutrition can be presented in class as a minilecture. Students can be given homework assignments, such as keeping a record of caloric consumption and physical activity for a day, that help reinforce nutritional concepts and their relationship to fitness and health. Additionally, there are a wide variety of microcomputer software programs available that present nutritional concepts and allow students to self-assess their nutritional status.

Regular and Appropriate Exercise

Engaging in appropriate exercise on a regular basis is important for attaining and maintaining a high level of wellness. Fitness is important to one's health. The physical activity found to produce the greatest health benefits is aerobic activity. To realize these benefits, the individual must engage in vigorous activity on a regular basis, specifically a minimum of 3 times a week for at least 20 minutes with sufficient intensity to elevate the heart rate to at least 60% of its age-adjusted maximum.

It is also recognized that engaging in low to moderate amounts of physical activity (activity below the threshold required for cardiovascular fitness) can also have beneficial health results.[15,19,20] Making an effort to incorporate regular physical activity, such as sustained walking, into one's lifestyle should also be emphasized.

Numerous health benefits have been ascribed to exercise.[21] Regular physical activity can lower the risk of disability and death from heart disease, one of the nation's greatest killers. Physical activity helps strengthen the cardiovascular system, maintain normal blood pressure, decrease blood cholesterol, increase toleration of stress, and maintain weight within acceptable limits. In addition to its contribution to the reduction of cardiovascular disease, regular exercise increases the energy level of the individual for work and play; leads to improved sleep; strengthens the body, better enabling it to cope with illness or acci-

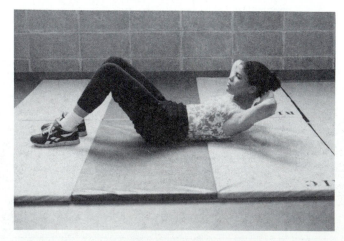

Students should learn how to design and conduct a personal exercise program to maintain satisfactory levels of health-related fitness.

Courtesy of Ben Lombardo, Rhode Island College, Providence, RI.

dents; increases the ability to withstand fatigue; improves concentration and alertness; improves posture; and enhances body appearance.

In addition to its effects on the physical health of the individual, regular exercise can positively improve the individual's mental health. Exercise can reduce anxiety, help alleviate depression, and aid in handling stress.[10] Exercise provides individuals with a heightened sense of well-being; gives people a feeling of accomplishment, which in itself makes them feel better; and can lead to an improved body appearance that helps individuals feel good about themselves.[10]

It is through helping students attain competency in a variety of physical activities, acquiring knowledge, fostering positive attitudes toward physical activity, and engendering an appreciation for the important role physical activity plays in achieving and maintaining a favorable health status that physical education can make its most direct and important contribution to wellness. It is also important that wellness activities, such as development of decision-making skills, discussion of sound nutritional practices, and stress management, be carefully incorporated into a balanced, physical education program.

Safety and Accident Prevention

Adhering to sound safety practices is another consideration in achieving and maintaining a high level of wellness. Safety involves following proper procedures and having concern for one's health and well-being. Accidents are one of the leading causes of death and injury within this age group. Many accidents can be prevented by following accepted safety precautions and using a little common sense. Accidents can be attributed to several causes: inadequate knowledge of potential hazards, risks, and safety rules; lack of knowledge and understanding of the risks; insufficient skill and competence to perform the tasks safely; errors in judgment; emotional states such as anger, frustration, fear, and immaturity that lead individuals to take risks or to suspend judgment; fatigue or illness that may impair mental or physical performance; and the use of drugs and alcohol.[3]

Within the secondary school physical education program, physical education teachers should establish general safety guidelines for all students to follow, that is, no horseplay, warm up and cool down properly, or wait for the teacher to enter the gymnasium before starting activity. Additionally, during each unit that is taught within the physical education curriculum, specific safety guidelines pertaining to the activity should be posted and reviewed with the class before the commencement of activity, that is, in gymnastics always use a spotter or in softball stand behind the backstop while waiting for a turn to bat. These safety guidelines should be presented to the students and discussed so that students understand the reasons for these guidelines. Additionally, these guidelines should be periodically reviewed. Following safety guidelines at all times should be emphasized, because physical education and sports account for more accidents in school than any other area of the secondary school curriculum.

Instruction in proper body mechanics can also help to prevent injuries and accidents. Back injuries disable many people each year. Often these injuries are chronic in nature, persisting for a long period of time. Within the

Students should know how to use each piece of exercise equipment properly and be familiar with recommended safety precautions.
Courtesy of Ben Lombardo, Rhode Island College, Providence, RI.

physical education program, students should learn the correct manner for lifting and moving objects. Attention should also be given to proper posture.

Some secondary school physical education programs include a short unit on safety and first aid within their curriculum. Students learn how to administer basic first aid and perform cardiopulmonary resuscitation (CPR), and they may often attain American Red Cross or American Heart Association certification in these areas. A few schools offer a course in sports medicine for interested students. This course generally deals with the prevention and treatment of sports injuries.

Numerous accidents, often serious, occur to individuals who are out on the road bicycling. In schools where bicycling is offered as a fitness activity, information about bicycle safety—the "rules of the road"—should be included. Additionally, many schools present information about bicycle maintenance and basic bicycle repairs as part of their bicycle fitness unit.

Drownings also account for a great number of accidental deaths among adolescents. Many drownings occur when individuals unexpectedly find themselves in the water. Another contributing factor is the use of alcohol. Ingesting alcohol and then swimming may prove to be fatal. Other contributing causes are "showing off," exhaustion, being swept into deep water, losing one's grip on a floating object such as a raft, becoming trapped or entangled, striking an underwater object, or cramps. Most drownings occur in places where no lifeguard is present. All students should be knowledgeable about aquatic safety, know what their capabilities are in case of an aquatic emergency, and when possible know how to swim. Aquatic offerings at schools vary, ranging from drown-proofing and basic swimming to advanced lifesaving and swim instructor courses. In schools that lack aquatic facilities, students are often bused to off-campus facilities for swimming instruction.

Traffic accidents account for many fatalities and injuries each year within this age group. Some of these accidents are caused by inexperience, because many students are just learning to drive. Many deaths could be prevented or the severity of injuries lessened by drivers using seatbelts. Alcohol and drug abuse increase the risk of having a driving accident. Driver education and promoting student awareness of the possibility of serious injury from automobiles should be a part of the wellness program.

Broadly interpreted, safety can also mean taking reasonable precautions to safeguard one's health. Regular physical examinations by physicians and taking advantage of screening programs (that is, for hypertension and cancer) on a periodic basis that is appropriate for one's age and sex is an important part of wellness. Students should also be cognizant of the need to attain medical clearance before embarking on a fitness program. This is especially important in adulthood, when an individual may desire to start a fitness program after a prolonged period of inactivity.

Promoting Self-Responsibility

Self-responsibility is the key to wellness. Attaining and maintaining a high level of wellness requires that individuals make responsible choices concerning their lifestyles. Making the right choices can help individuals prevent disease and attain a high level of personal health. Making the wrong choices can increase susceptibility to illness and have an adverse impact on an individual's quality of life.

As discussed, an individual's personal habits and lifestyle can increase susceptibility to disease and injury. Taken together, smoking, misuse of alcohol and drugs, poor dietary habits, lack of regular exercise, and stress place enormous burdens on the health and well-being of the individual. However, the individual has control over habits and can change them, if he or she chooses to do so. Self-responsibility is the key.

Physical education can help promote responsibility in several ways. Teachers need to gradually shift the responsibility for decisions pertaining to fitness and wellness to the students. This must occur if students are to become independent, autonomous, lifelong participants in physical activity. Students should have the opportunity to explore the many approaches to fitness and wellness and to select the approach that is most beneficial and satisfying to them.

Students need to learn how to exercise independently, without being directly under the supervision of the teacher. Thus they must have the physical skills and the cognitive skills to make knowledgeable decisions about fitness and wellness. Opportunities to develop fitness outside of the class time should be available. These opportunities may include open gym in the morning, afternoons, and nights as well as when the school is not in session; drop-in fitness and recreation programs when facilities are not scheduled during the day; intramural fitness activities; and homework assignments.

Finally, a health-promoting lifestyle is largely a matter of personal choice—personal discipline and will. Fitness and wellness require personal investment and commitment. Helping secondary school students develop health-promoting lifestyles so that life can be lived to the fullest is an important legacy of secondary school physical education.

Physical education professionals through their teachings can have a tremendous impact on the current and future health of their students and their quality of life. In many school settings where teachers also provide instruction in health education, the potential to have an impact on the lives of students is even greater. If we, as a nation, are to achieve our public health goals and significantly and positively alter the health profile of our citizens, then the critical role of physical education in this endeavor must be recognized.

SUMMARY

Wellness is an optimal state of health and well-being, the capacity to live life to its fullest. A multidimensional phenomenon, wellness encompasses physical, emotional, intellectual or mental, social, and spiritual health. Wellness requires attention to each of these dimensions and achieving a balance between them according to individual goals and needs.

Wellness involves individuals making informed and responsible decisions about their health and accepting responsibility for their own well-being. It encompasses physical fitness, sound nutritional practices, effective stress management, balancing work and leisure, safety and preventive measures, and elimination of destructive health habits.

Physical education teachers can help their students improve their health and quality of life through attention to wellness in the curriculum. A carefully constructed and balanced physical education curriculum can help students learn the skills, knowledge, and attitudes conducive to lifetime participation in physical activity, an important component of wellness. Other aspects of wellness can also be skillfully incorporated into the curriculum. Skills in decision making, promotion of self-responsibility, enhancement of self-concept and self-esteem, safety education, competency in leisure time activities, stress management approaches, and nutritional information can be taught within the physical education program.

FOR REVIEW

1. Discuss the contribution of physical education to each dimension of wellness: physical health, emotional health, social health, intellectual or mental health, and spiritual health.
2. Construct an eight-lesson unit on wellness for secondary school students. What components of wellness would you emphasize within your unit?
3. One way to incorporate wellness into the curriculum is by introducing a single wellness concept, via a 2- to 3-minute minilecture, in each lesson. Make a list of concepts that you would introduce in the course of a marking period (3 lessons a week for 9 weeks).

REFERENCES

1. U.S. Public Health Service: *Healthy people 2000: national health promotion and disease prevention objectives,* Washington, DC, 1990, US Government Printing Office.
2. McGinnis JM, Kanner L, DeGraw C: Physical education's role in achieving national health objectives, *Research Quarterly for Exercise and Sport* 62:138-142, 1991.
3. Levy MR, Dignan M, Shirreffs JH: *Life and health: targeting wellness,* New York, 1992, McGraw-Hill Book.
4. Baranowski T et al: Assessment, prevalence, and cardiovascular benefits of physical activity and fitness in youth, *Med Sci Sports Exerc* 24(suppl 6):237-247, 1992.
5. Prentice WE, Bucher CA: *Fitness for college and life,* ed 2, St Louis, 1988, Mosby.
6. Everly GS, Jr: *A clinical guide to the treatment of the human stress response,* New York, 1989, Plenum.
7. Dunne G, Schilling D, Cowan D: *Impact! A self-esteem based skill development program for secondary school students,* Spring Valley, Calif, 1990, Innerchoice.
8. The American Council for Drug Education: Some facts about drugs and alcohol in the United States, *The Drug Educator,* Spring: 3, 1992.
9. Pangrazi RP, Darst PW: *Dynamic physical education curriculum and instruction for secondary school students,* New York, 1991, Macmillan.
10. Brannon L, Feist J: *Health psychology: an introduction to behavior and health,* Belmont, Calif, 1992, Wadsworth.
11. Allen RJ: *Human stress: its nature and control,* Minneapolis, 1983, Burgess.
12. Rice PL: *Stress and health: principles and practices for coping,* Belmont, Calif, 1992, Brooks/Cole.
13. Johnson H: *How do I love me?* ed 2, Salem, Wis, 1986, Sheffield.
14. Dishman RK: Mental health. In Seefeldt V, Vogel P, editors: *Physical activity and well-being,* Reston, Va, 1986, AAHPERD.
15. Nieman DC: *Fitness and sports medicine: an introduction,* Palo Alto, Calif, 1990, Bull.
16. Nichols B: *Moving and learning: the elementary school physical education experience,* ed 4, St Louis, 1994, Mosby.
17. Select Committee on Nutrition and Human Needs, United States Senate: *Dietary goals for the United States, 1980,* Washington, DC, 1980, US Government Printing Office.
18. Edlin G, Golanty E: *Health and wellness,* Boston, 1982, Science Books International.
19. Haskell WL et al: Cardiovascular benefits and assessment of physical activity and physical fitness in adults, *Med Sci Sports Exerc* 24(suppl 6):201-220, 1992.
20. McGinnis JM: The public health burden of a sedentary lifestyle, *Medicine and Science in Sports and Exercise* 24(suppl 6):196-200, 1992.
21. Seefeldt V, Vogel P, editors: *Physical activity and well-being,* Reston, Va, 1986, AAHPERD.

ANNOTATED READINGS

Brannon L, Feist J: *Health psychology: an introduction to behavior and health,* Belmont, Calif, 1992, Wadsworth.

Explores the links between behavior and health, including such topics as stress and illness, pain, behavioral factors in diseases, adherence, alcohol and drug use, and weight management.

Dunne G, Schilling D, Cowan D: *Impact! A self-esteem based skill development program for secondary school students,* Spring Valley, Calif, 1990, Innerchoice.

Contains exercises to promote decision making and self-responsibility, self-esteem, management of stress, self-awareness, goal setting, peer relations, and communication.

Levy MR, Dignan M, Shirreffs JH: *Life and health: targeting wellness,* New York, 1992, McGraw-Hill Book.

A comprehensive approach to wellness and lifestyle management.

Rice PL: *Stress and health: principles and practices for coping,* Belmont, Calif, 1992, Brooks/Cole.

Discusses the nature of stress and its impact on health and practical strategies for management.

CHAPTER 17

Fitness for Secondary School Students

CHAPTER OBJECTIVES

◆ To provide an overview of physical fitness and its components

◆ To introduce exercise variables of frequency, intensity, time, and mode and their application in designing an exercise program

◆ To describe principles of training and their application to the development of fitness

◆ To present various techniques for assessment of fitness

◆ To offer program and instructional guidelines for the development and maintenance of fitness

The physical fitness of people of all ages in this country needs to be improved. Although interest in physical fitness is high, research indicates that only a little more than 10% of the adult population engages in exercise of sufficient intensity, duration, and frequency that is generally recommended to gain cardiovascular benefits.[1] Moreover, available data on the fitness level of children and youth have raised concern about their fitness status.[1] It appears that the fitness profile of many children and youth needs to be improved. Improving the fitness status of children and youth is essential if the country's public health goals, as outlined in *Healthy People 2000,* are to be achieved.[1]

Physical fitness has long been held as one of the primary objectives of physical education. Given the increased awareness of the important role of physical fitness in promoting health and reducing risk of chronic diseases (such as coronary heart disease), providing students with the skills, knowledge, and values conducive to incorporating appropriate physical activity into their lifestyle, both during their school years and after they graduate, takes on added importance.

PHYSICAL FITNESS: AN OVERVIEW AND DEFINITION

One of the most important contributions secondary school physical education can make to students' lives is in the area of physical fitness. As a part of their physical education program, students should learn the knowledge and skills necessary to select and participate in physical activity throughout their lifetimes. Equally important, students should be motivated to incorporate physical activity into their lifestyles to maintain an optimal level of physical fitness. Individuals who are physically fit accrue many benefits, including a more favorable health status. Specifically, individuals who are physically fit experience a reduction in risk factors associated with cardiovascular disease, a heightened sense of well-being, an improved appearance and posture, and a more positive self-image.[1-4] An increased energy level contributes to greater productivity for physical and mental tasks.[1-4] Additionally, fitness serves as the foundation for participation in a wide range of physical activities. Because of these and numerous other positive contributions to an individual's life, physical fitness should receive strong emphasis in the secondary school physical education curriculum.

The term *physical fitness* means that the organic systems of the body (circulatory, respiratory, and musculatory) are healthy and functioning efficiently so that fit individuals can fully and vigorously engage in activities associated with daily living.[2] Physical fitness includes health- and skill-related components.

Health-Related Fitness Components

Health-related fitness is comprised of those fitness components closely associated with functional health. Satisfactory levels of fitness of these components have been identified as contributing measurably to a healthy lifestyle and to prevention of health problems.[4,5] The health-related fitness components are as follows:

- *Cardiorespiratory endurance.* Cardiorespiratory endurance, often referred to as cardiovascular endurance, is the entire body's ability to exercise vigorously for extended periods of time without undue fatigue.
- *Muscular strength and endurance.* Muscular strength is the ability of a muscle or muscle group to exert force in a single effort against resistance. Muscular endurance refers to the ability of the muscle or muscle group to repeatedly exert force against resistance for an extended period of time.
- *Flexibility.* Flexibility is the ability of the various joints of the body to move through their full range of motion.
- *Body composition.* Body composition refers to the percentage of total body weight that is fat as opposed to lean tissue.

Skill-Related Fitness Components

Skill-related fitness is concerned with those physical qualities that enable the individual to perform movement and sports skills effectively. The five skill-related fitness components are as follows:

- *Agility* is the ability to rapidly change direction or body movement while moving.
- *Balance* is the ability to maintain the body's equilibrium while in various positions while moving and in stationary positions.
- *Coordination* is the ability to integrate sensory and motor systems (that is, eye-hand coordination or eye-foot coordination) to produce efficient movement.
- *Power,* often referred to as explosive strength, is the ability to effectively integrate strength and speed to produce maximum muscular force at maximum speed.
- *Speed* is the rate of movement and often refers to the ability to move rapidly.

The development of health- and skill-related fitness components should be addressed in the secondary school physical education curriculum. However, because of the importance of health-related fitness to the individual's health, priority should be given to assisting each student to learn the skills and knowledge and to instill the commitment necessary to develop and maintain satisfactory levels of health-related fitness. The school years are an optimum time to develop favorable health habits.

Contribution of Health-Related Fitness to Health

Research indicates that maintaining satisfactory levels of health-related fitness can have a positive impact on an individual's health in terms of disease prevention and health promotion.[1,2,6] In the United States, the greatest single cause of death is coronary heart disease (CHD).[1,2,4] The probability of an individual developing CHD is related to the risk factors one possesses or to which one is exposed. The risk factors for CHD are shown in Table 17-1. The greater the number of risk factors, the greater the likelihood of developing CHD. Some of these risk factors, such as heredity, age, sex, and race, cannot be changed. However, many of the primary and secondary risk factors associated with CHD, such as smoking, sedentary lifestyle, obesity, and elevated serum cholesterol are a function of an individual's lifestyle and behavior patterns.[2,7] Thus the likelihood of developing CHD can be reduced through the modification of lifestyle and behaviors to eliminate these risk factors.[2]

Individuals who choose to abandon a sedentary lifestyle and poor nutritional practices can decrease the probability that they will acquire CHD. More specifically, individuals

TABLE 17-1

Coronary Heart Disease Risk Factors

Primary Risk Factors	Secondary Risk Factors
Cigarette smoking	Obesity
Hypertension	Diabetes
Elevated serum cholesterol	Age
	Sex
	Race
	Sedentary lifestyle
	Pulmonary function abnormalities
	High-stress lifestyle
	Family history (heredity)
	High uric acid levels
	Electrocardiographic abnormalities during exercise
	Personality and behavior patterns

From Prentice W: *Fitness for college and life,* ed 4, St Louis, 1994, Mosby.

who make a commitment to develop and maintain appropriate levels of health-related fitness—that is, those who exercise regularly to maintain satisfactory levels of cardiorespiratory endurance and follow sound nutritional practices—will reduce many of the risk factors associated with CHD. Because there is evidence that the genesis of CHD can begin in youth, it is critical that physical education teachers at the elementary and secondary levels help students develop the skills, knowledge, and attitudes necessary to leading a healthy lifestyle and to reduce the threat of CHD.

Another health problem experienced by many Americans is obesity. It is estimated that as many as 50% of all children are overweight, and many obese children grow to be obese adults.[8-10] Being obese can lead to a number of health problems. In addition to being a risk factor for CHD, obesity has also been shown to play a role in stroke and the onset of diabetes. Additionally, during the adolescent years, when there is a great deal of emphasis placed on appearance, individuals who are obese may experience loss of self-esteem.

Developing and maintaining optimal body composition is an integral part of health-related fitness. In addition to overeating, lack of physical activity contributes to obesity. Therefore observation of good nutritional practices in conjunction with proper exercise can help individuals to attain and maintain the proper ratio of fat to lean body tissue.

Some health problems are related to lack of muscular strength, muscular endurance, and flexibility. One prevalent health problem experienced by many Americans is back disorders. Weak, tense muscles that are strained further when performing daily activities, inflexibility caused by inactivity, and poor posture caused by weak abdominal muscles contribute to back problems. A program of exercises that focuses on strengthening the muscles, improving muscular endurance, and increasing flexibility can help alleviate and prevent back disorders. Additionally, proper levels of muscular strength, muscular endurance, and flexibility help individuals perform their daily activities more easily and result in less fatigue.

Because of its contribution to the health and life of individuals, considerable attention should be given to health-related fitness in the secondary school curriculum. To develop effectively the four components of health-related fitness, the program must be conducted properly.

PRINCIPLES FOR DEVELOPING PHYSICAL FITNESS

In designing personal exercise programs, students should be familiar with the exercise variables of frequency, intensity, and time (duration) and be able to apply these factors to different modes of exercise. Additionally, several principles must be followed if desired changes in fitness are to occur. These include the principles of over-

load, progression, and specificity. Exercise programs should also provide for individual differences in the initial level of fitness and opportunities to warm up and cool down. Students should also be aware of the consequences of failing to exercise on a regular basis.

Exercise Variables

When one is designing an exercise program or writing an exercise prescription, attention must be given to the frequency, intensity, and time (duration) of exercise. The acronym FIT may be used to help remember these variables. These variables are used to express the specific training requirements that must be met for the individual to realize the benefits of exercise.

Frequency (F) refers to how often the individual should exercise and is often expressed in days per week. For example, to develop cardiorespiratory endurance, an individual must participate in vigorous exercise for a minimum of 3 days per week. It is important that exercise occur with regularity for benefits to be realized.

Intensity (I) refers to the degree of effort expended during exercise. How intensity is measured varies according to the component of fitness being developed. When one is developing muscular strength and endurance, intensity is measured in terms of the amount of weight lifted; in flexibility, it is the distance beyond normal stretching; in cardiorespiratory exercise it is often measured by heart rate.

Time (T) refers to the duration or amount of the exercise performed. For example, to develop cardiorespiratory endurance, the individual must exercise for at least 20-30 minutes.

The FIT variables influence the total energy cost of the exercise program or the amount of work expended. This may be represented by the following formula:

$$\text{Energy cost} = \text{frequency} \times \text{intensity} \times \text{time.}^{[7]}$$

These factors are interrelated and can be manipulated to produce an exercise program appropriate to the needs of the individual and the desired objectives. For example, to increase the amount of exercise performed, any one of the FIT factors could be increased while the others were held constant. Or all three factors could be increased a moderate amount. Or one factor, such as intensity, could be increased, while another factor, such as duration, could be decreased. Additionally, not only does manipulation of the FIT variables improve physical fitness, but it also introduces variety and enjoyment into the exercise program.

Mode is another exercise variable that must be considered when one is designing an exercise program. The mode refers to the type of exercise activity, such as running, cycling, lifting weights, or stretching.

When manipulating the frequency, intensity, time, and mode of exercise to improve fitness, physical education teachers must be guided by the principles of exercise physiology if they wish to ensure optimum fitness development in their students. Moreover, students should learn about the FIT variables and exercise physiology principles as part of the cognitive aspect of physical education. To plan and implement personal fitness programs and to be able to modify these programs for lifetime participation, students should understand and be able to apply these principles.

Training Principles

If students are to improve successfully and to maintain desired levels of fitness, their exercise program must follow certain principles. These principles also hold implications for the structure of the curriculum and the design of instruction.

Principle of overload. If fitness gains are to be realized, it is essential that the principle of overload be followed. According to this principle, an individual must exercise more than he or she is generally accustomed to doing to improve the fitness level.[8] Essentially, to attain desired physiological changes, the individual must work harder than usual. Physiological changes occur as the human organism, the body, adapts in response to a stimulus, the exercise program. Systematic manipulation of the FIT variables is used to create overload. For example, if improvement in cardiorespiratory endurance is desired, the

Cardiorespiratory endurance is typically assessed in schools with the use of a run/walk test.

Courtesy of Patricia Quinn, Notre Dame High School, Elmira, NY.

individual must exercise more than is customary; a change in the normal routine is needed. Thus a jogger may choose to increase the distance covered, increase the pace, or increase the number of times a week exercised to create an overload situation. It should also be noted that once the desired level of fitness is attained, less work is needed to maintain this level than was needed to improve or achieve it.

It is important to note, however, that some provision must be made for rest and recuperation within the program. Exercise places stress on the body, and the body needs time to adapt to this stress and become stronger. Failure to provide for recuperation can result in injuries from overuse.

Principle of progression. According to this principle, when overload is introduced into the exercise program to improve a fitness component, it should be done slowly. The exercise work load should be gradually increased in a systematic fashion by manipulating the FIT variables. Thus as the individual becomes adjusted to the exercise program, the amount of exercise being performed should be gradually increased. Progression should be slow but steady so that the individual is challenged by the exercise session but not overwhelmed. Steady progression also helps prevent some of the problems associated with exercise programs, such as high levels of fatigue, muscle soreness, muscle and joint injuries, and a negative attitude toward exercise.

Principle of specificity. This principle states that the physiological adaptations to exercise are specific in nature.[2,8] The type of exercise program undertaken determines the benefits accrued by the individual. Thus training programs should be designed to achieve specific objectives. To illustrate, to achieve maximum gains in cardiorespiratory endurance, the structure of the exercise program and the activities used should be selected to realize this specific outcome. Because of the specific nature of exercise, it is essential that fitness objectives be carefully defined and then the program planned to achieved these desired outcomes.

Initial level of fitness. Within a given class, the physical education teacher will notice that students possess a wide range of fitness levels. These fitness levels range from relatively low levels of fitness to high levels of fitness. These individual differences in fitness levels must be accommodated. Each student's current level of fitness should be taken into account when one is planning an exercise program.

Once students have been medically cleared to participate, each student's level of fitness should be assessed. Following this assessment, an exercise program should be designed to accommodate the current fitness level of each health-related component while leading gradually to the achievement of fitness goals. For all students to benefit, individuals who have a relatively low level of fitness should follow a different exercise program than individuals with high fitness levels. This requires that teachers utilize instructional strategies and teaching styles that focus on individualized instruction. Instructional strategies and teaching styles that require all students to do the same activities with the same frequency, intensity, and time fail to provide for individual differences in fitness levels.

Provision for warm-up and cool-down activities. Opportunity for adequate warm-up and cool-down must be provided for students. Warm-up prepares the body for vigorous exercise that follows. A proper warm-up increases the body's temperature, stretches ligaments and muscles, and increases flexibility. Each exercise session or workout should be preceded by a 5- to 15-minute period devoted to warm-up exercises. Warm-up activities should include stretching and gross motor activities, such as light jogging. Proper warm-up helps prevent muscle and joint soreness, prevents injuries, and prepares the circulatory and respiratory systems for exercise. Warm-up activities should gradually progress into vigorous exercise.

A cool-down period of 5 to 10 minutes should follow each exercise session. The intensity of the exercise should lessen gradually before the exercise is stopped. Similar to the warm-up period, the cool-down period should include stretching and gross motor activities, such as light jogging or walking. The cool-down period helps return the blood to the heart for reoxygenation and prevents the pooling of blood in the muscles of the arms and legs. Failure to incorporate a cool-down period into the exercise program can lead to dizziness, faintness, and nausea because not enough blood may circulate back to the brain, heart, and intestines. The cool-down period assists the body in recovering from the workout and returning to its normal state.

Principle of disuse. To realize fitness gains, an individual must exercise on a regular basis. Gains in fitness can be lost rapidly when an individual ceases to exercise. Students may ask, "How long will it take to lose what I have gained?" Cardiorespiratory gains disappear most rapidly.[8] Gains realized as a result of a 4-week training program can be lost within 2 weeks following the cessation of exercise.[9] Gains in muscular strength and endurance appear to be more stable than cardiorespiratory gains, with some training gains still evident 6 months to 1 year after cessation of training.[8] Fitness cannot be stored or saved. Achievement and maintenance of fitness require that appropriate physical activity be integrated into an individual's lifestyle.

DEVELOPING HEALTH-RELATED FITNESS

Programs for the improvement of health-related fitness components—cardiorespiratory endurance, muscular strength and endurance, flexibility, and body composition—should incorporate the principles of training. Gen-

---

BOX 17-1

GUIDELINES FOR THE DEVELOPMENT OF HEALTH-RELATED FITNESS

Cardiovascular Endurance

Frequency: 3 to 5 days/week
Intensity: 60% to 85% of maximum heart rate
Time: 20 to 30 minutes
Mode: Aerobic activity

Muscular Strength and Endurance

Frequency: 3 days per week
Intensity: Strength requires high resistance; endurance requires low resistance
Time: Strength requires 3 sets of 6 to 8 repetitions each; endurance requires 3 sets of 10 to 12 repetitions each
Mode: Isotonic exercises commonly used; alternatives include isometric and isokinetic exercises

Flexibility

Frequency: 3 to 7 days/week
Intensity: Stretch past normal length until resistance is felt
Time: Hold the stretch from 5 to 10 seconds initially, building to 30 to 45 seconds
Mode: Static stretching exercises preferred

Body Composition

Maintain present level of physical activity and reduce caloric intake
Maintain present level of caloric intake and increase level of physical activity
Reduce caloric intake and increase level of physical activity

---

eral guidelines for the development of these fitness components, including development of exercise prescriptions using the FIT variables, are presented in this section and are summarized in Box 17-1. More specific information can be found in the many excellent exercise physiology and fitness references, textbooks, and videotapes available on the market today.

Cardiorespiratory Endurance

When programs are designed to improve cardiorespiratory endurance, the frequency, intensity, and time of exercise must be taken into account. In terms of frequency, three exercise sessions per week are the minimum frequency necessary to achieve a minimum level of desired outcomes. Individuals who work out four to five times a week will accrue greater gains.

The intensity and time or duration of exercise are critical factors in determining whether the individual will experience gains in cardiorespiratory endurance. Because heart rate has been shown to be related to oxygen consumption and intensity of exercise, it provides a convenient means by which to identify the intensity of exercise necessary to experience benefits from training.

To experience benefits, the individual must exercise at an intensity of 60% to 85% of the maximal heart rate. This range of 60% to 85% is frequently referred to as the target zone, that is, the heart rate must be elevated to at least 60% and no more than 85% of the maximum for the duration of the workout.[2,4,9]

Maximum heart rate is age-related. To calculate the maximum heart rate for a specific age, the age of the individual is subtracted from the maximum value of 220 beats per minute (bpm). One simple way to calculate the limits of the target zone is to multiple the age-adjusted maximum heart rate by the desired intensity of exercise. The following formula may be used:

Training heart rate =
    age-adjusted maximum heart rate × desired % intensity,

or

$$(220 - age) \times \% \text{ intensity}$$

For a high school sophomore, age 15, the age-adjusted maximum heart rate would be 220 − 15 or 205 bpm. To calculate the limits of the target zone, 205 bpm is multiplied by 60% and 85%. Thus the target zone for a 15-year-old high-school sophomore is between 123 and 174 bpm. Therefore the sophomore student must exercise aerobically at a sufficient pace to elevate his or her heart to at least 123 bpm and no more than 174 bpm and maintain it within this zone for an acceptable duration to benefit from training. Training heart rates for secondary school students are given in Table 17-2.

The heart rate can be measured easily at several anatomical points. It can be measured by palpating the radial artery located on the thumb side of the wrist joint. A strong pulse can be located by placing the index and middle fingers on the thumb side of the flexor tendon. Each pulse represents one heart beat. Heart rate can also be measured by palpating the carotid artery in the neck. The index and middle fingers should be placed on the Adam's apple and then slid into the groove on either side. Only slight pressure should be applied to allow the blood to continue to flow while taking the pulse.

To accurately compute the heart rate, the individual must stop exercising and begin to count the pulse within 5 seconds because heart rate changes rapidly when exercise slows down or stops. Count the pulse for only a short period of time. Typically, the pulse is counted for 10 seconds, and the result is then multiplied by 6 to give the heart rate per minute. Or, count for 6 seconds and multiply by 10 seconds (simply add a zero to this count to obtain the heart rate). Charts may be posted throughout the gymnasium to help individuals readily calculate their heart rate.

Monitor the heart rate several times during the exercise period until the individual can subjectively determine that he or she is exercising at an appropriate level of intensity to be within the target zone. When an individual is exercising, the heart rate should be elevated and maintained within the target zone. The heart rate can be increased or decreased by making adjustments in one's pace, either by speeding up or slowing down. Because heart rate increases proportionately with the intensity of activity and will plateau after 2 or 3 minutes, heart rate should be checked after this time to make sure the exercise is of sufficient intensity (Fig. 17-1).

T A B L E 17 - 2							
Training Heart Rates (HR) for Secondary School Students							
			Student Age				
	12	13	14	15	16	17	18
			Maximum HR				
	208	207	206	205	204	203	202
Intensity (%)							
60	125	124	124	123	122	122	121
65	135	135	134	133	133	132	131
70	146	145	144	144	143	142	141
75	156	155	155	154	153	152	152
80	166	166	165	164	163	162	162
85	177	176	175	174	173	173	172

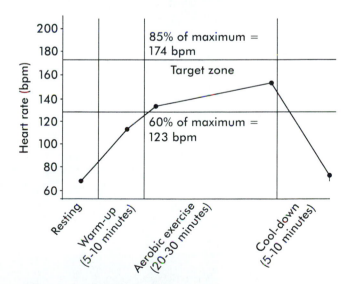

FIG. 17-1   Guidelines for the design of a training program.
Modified from Hockey R: *Physical fitness: the pathway to healthful living,* ed 7, St Louis, 1993, Mosby.

Duration or time of exercise is also a critical factor. To experience significant training effects, the individual must work with sufficient intensity to stay in the target zone for at least 20 minutes. Additionally, vigorous exercise should always be preceded by a warm-up period of 5 to 15 minutes and followed by a cool-down period of 5 to 10 minutes.

Because the exercise variables of intensity and time are interrelated, they can be readily manipulated when one is designing an exercise program. Exercise workload can be varied in many ways, depending on the objective and the condition of the individual. The individual can exercise at low intensity for a long period of time, high intensity for a short period of time, or at moderate intensity for a moderate period of time. Regardless of how these factors are manipulated, the prerequisites for minimal improvement in cardiorespiratory endurance must be met. In summary, to see *minimal* improvement in cardiorespiratory endurance, an individual must exercise for a period of 20 minutes 3 times a week with the heart rate elevated to an intensity of no less than 60% of its maximal rate.

In training to improve cardiorespiratory endurance, the mode or the type of activity used is important. The activity must be aerobic in nature. Aerobic activities are those activities that require a continuous supply of oxygen to be delivered to the muscles and the amount of oxygen supplied is sufficient to meet the demands of the working tissues. Aerobic activities elevate the heart rate and maintain it at an elevated level for an extended period of time.

These activities are typically continuous and rhythmical in nature, involving repetitive, whole-body, large-muscle movements performed over an extended period of time. Running, jogging, walking, cycling, swimming, aerobic dancing, rope skipping, and cross-country skiing are examples of aerobic activities. The intensity of these activities can easily be regulated by altering the pace, either speeding it up or slowing it down. Because an individual works at a relatively steady level during these activities, it is easy to monitor the heart rate to ensure that a sufficient workload is imposed for the specified period of time.

Aerobic activities offer an advantage over activities that are more intermittent in nature, such as tennis or basketball. In intermittent activities, the intensity of effort can vary greatly, and this causes the heart rate to fluctuate.[2] Thus it is difficult to monitor the intensity of the effort and to be sure that the appropriate level of effort is sustained for an adequate duration to yield beneficial effects. Although these activities will lead to some improvements in cardiorespiratory endurance, it is more difficult to determine the intensity of the workload and to ensure that it is sufficient in nature to lead to a training effect.

In contrast to aerobic activities, anaerobic activities are highly intense in nature and can only be sustained for relatively short periods of time. These activities are so intense that the system cannot keep up with the oxygen demands. Consequently, an oxygen debt is incurred that must be paid back during the recovery period. Activities

A variety of activities can be used to develop cardiorespiratory endurance.
Courtesy of Ben Lombardo, Rhode Island College, Providence, RI.

that require an all-out effort, such as sprinting, are anaerobic in nature.

One last consideration in planning for the development of cardiorespiratory fitness is the current fitness status of the students. Some students possess such poor levels of fitness that they are unable to meet the minimal intensity and duration requisites. These individuals require an individualized program that will gradually allow them to attain the levels of fitness necessary to begin to exercise at the appropriate levels.

Muscular Strength and Endurance

The development of muscular strength and endurance is an important aspect of health-related fitness. Muscular strength is concerned with the maximal amount of force that can be exerted in a single contraction. Muscular endurance is the ability to perform a movement repeatedly and is generally measured by time or the number of repetitions.

To improve muscular strength and endurance, the overload principle must be applied, increasing the workload for the individual. This increase in workload can occur by increasing the number of repetitions to be performed, the amount of resistance, or both. For strength training, overload is achieved by progressively adding more resistance, thus increasing the amount of weight lifted. For endurance training, overload involves gradually adding more repetitions. Generally, when one is utilizing weight training to improve strength, heavy weights (resistance) with a low number of repetitions are used. When one is improving endurance, relatively light

Push-ups can be used to develop upper body strength and endurance.

Courtesy of Ben Lombardo, Rhode Island College, Providence, RI.

weights are used and a great number of repetitions performed (Fig. 17-2).

Although several methods can be employed to develop muscular strength and endurance, the most popular method in the secondary schools is the use of isotonic exercises. Isotonic exercises require the individual to exert dynamic force against a resistance through a range of motion. As the individual performs, the muscle changes in length. The muscle can shorten; this is referred to as a concentric contraction. Or the muscle can lengthen;

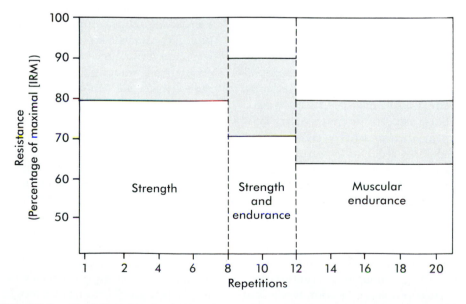

FIG. 17-2   Guidelines for the design of a training program for muscular strength and endurance.

From Wuest DA, Bucher CA: *Foundations of physical education and sport,* ed 11, St Louis, 1991, Mosby.

this is called an eccentric contraction. For example, when performing a biceps curl, as the individual lifts the weight from the starting position, the biceps muscle contracts and shortens in length (concentric contraction). When the weight is being lowered, the individual controls its descent by continuing to contract the biceps muscle while lengthening it (eccentric contraction). Concentric and eccentric contractions should be utilized when training.

Various types of equipment can be employed to perform isotonic exercises. These include free weights; barbells; and Universal, Eagle, and Nautilus machines. Most calisthenics and other sport activities, such as bicycling, involve the use of isotonic contractions.

In improving muscle strength and endurance, systematic progressive overload is necessary. The amount of resistance, the number of repetitions, and the number of sets (groups of repetitions) performed can be manipulated to produce overload conditions.

For strength development, it is suggested that a weight should be selected that will allow the individual to successfully perform 6 to 8 repetitions in each of 3 sets.[2] If at least 3 sets of 6 repetitions cannot be accomplished, the weight is too heavy and should be reduced.[2] On the other hand, if more than 3 sets of 8 repetitions can be completed by the individual, the weight is too light and should be increased.[2]

For endurance development, the amount of weight selected should allow the individual to perform 3 sets of 10 to 12 repetitions.[2] The amount of resistance used should be changed if the individual finds it too difficult or too easy to accomplish the task. Muscular endurance tends to improve with muscular strength, and adjustments in the exercise program should be made accordingly.

To achieve improvements, exercise should be done at least 3 times a week for 8 to 10 consecutive weeks.[2] Attention should be given to the development of the various muscle groups of the body. Some individuals will engage in weight training every day, exercising different muscle groups on nonsuccessive days (upper body muscles one day, lower body muscles the next). Safety considerations are important when students engage in weight training. Students should be required to warm up sufficiently before lifting. Instruction in proper lifting and breathing techniques should be given before allowing students to work out. Spotters should be used when appropriate. Students should be taught to work within their own limitations.

In addition to weight training, various other activities, such as calisthenics and partner exercises, can be used to develop muscular strength and endurance. Many excellent texts are available to assist physical education teachers in designing and conducting quality and innovative exercise programs.

Flexibility

Flexibility is the range of motion possible about a given joint or series of joints. In terms of fitness, an individual who possesses good flexibility can move through the full range of motion. Flexibility is joint specific; an individual may be quite flexible in one joint and quite inflexible in another joint. For example, an individual may possess excellent shoulder joint flexibility, yet exhibit poor hip joint flexibility.

To increase flexibility and thus improve the range of motion around a joint, the extensibility of the musculotendinous units that produce movement at that joint must be increased. This can be accomplished through the use of various stretching exercises. Two types of stretching exercises have commonly been employed: ballistic stretching and static stretching. Ballistic stretching involves the use of repetitive bouncing movements to increase the range of movement. Because these rapid, jerky movements may cause injuries to the muscle and increase muscle soreness, this approach to stretching has decreased in popularity.[2,8]

Static stretching encompasses the use of slow, steady, gentle stretching movements. The individual gently and smoothly stretches the muscle to the point of where tightness or resistance to the movement is felt, eases off slightly, and holds the stretch for an extended period of time. Because static stretching does not involve bouncing movements, there is less soreness and danger of injury associated with this type of stretching.

When performing static stretching exercises, the individual should perform stretching exercises a minimum of 3 times a week. The length of time to hold the stretch can vary from 5 to 10 seconds during the initial training and can gradually increase to 30 to 45 seconds. Each exercise should be completed at least 3 to 4 times. When flexibility exercises are done in conjunction with cardiorespiratory endurance training or muscle strength and endurance training, they should be performed as part of the warm-up and cool-down periods, that is, before and after the other training exercises.[2]

Body Composition Fitness

The body composition of an individual is an important aspect of the individual's total fitness. The frequently used age-height-weight tables to determine ideal body weight may provide misleading information. They often give broad ranges for acceptable weight and may fail to take into account different body types. Moreover, because they are based solely on gross body weight, they may not accurately reflect an individual's health status. For example, it is possible to be overweight, yet not be overfat. Overweight implies having excessive weight relative to physical size and stature, where overfat or obese refers to

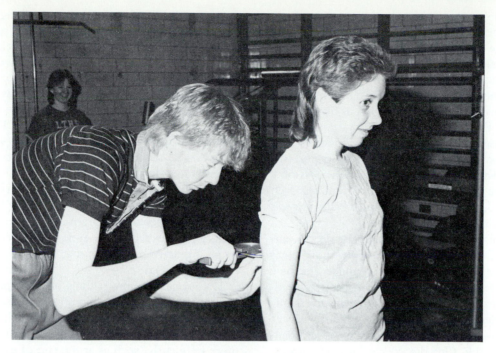

Skinfold measurement as part of a health-related fitness assessment at Lyons Township High School, LaGrange, IL.

Courtesy of Bucher C: *Management of physical education and athletic programs,* ed 9, 1987, Mosby.

excessive fat. An athlete, for example, who is muscular may be overweight for his or her age and height, yet be lean in terms of body composition. On the other hand, an individual may be average for his or her age and height, yet possess an undesirable excess of body fat. Thus assessment of body composition may provide the best indication of the individual's health status and fitness level.

Body composition fitness refers to the attainment and maintenance of the appropriate proportion of lean body tissue to fat body tissue. The degree of fitness is often expressed as the percentage of body fat. In terms of body composition, individuals who are fit possess an appropriate percentage of body fat for the age, sex, and height. The young male adult who is considered fit has 10% to 15% body fat, while the young fit female adult has 20% to 25%.[2] Highly trained athletes may exhibit even lower body fat percentages. It is also possible to be too lean, thereby possessing too low a percentage of body fat. It is recommended that the body fat percentage not go below 3% for men and 10% to 12% for women because of potential health problems.[2,8]

Although a certain amount of body fat is essential for good health, an excessively high or low level is unhealthy. Individuals who possess too high or too low levels of body fat need to undertake a program to improve their body composition.

The balance between caloric intake (energy input) and caloric expenditure (energy output) is a critical factor in weight control and structure of body composition. Caloric intake is a function of the food ingested. Calories are used through processes involved with basal metabolism, work (activities that require more energy than sleeping), and excretion.

The caloric balance influences the individual's weight. When caloric intake and expenditure are balanced, one's weight is maintained. Weight gain occurs when there is a positive caloric balance, that is, more calories are taken in than are used. This can occur as a consequence of eating more, exercising less, or both circumstances. Weight loss occurs when there is a negative caloric balance, that is, more calories are expended than consumed.

For individuals who are overweight and possess poor body composition values, three approaches can be taken for improvement:

◆ Caloric intake can be decreased and the present level of physical activity maintained.
◆ The level of physical activity can be increased and the present caloric intake maintained.
◆ The level of caloric intake can be decreased, and the level of physical activity can be increased.

It appears that combining caloric restriction with increased caloric expenditures is the best approach to achieving appropriate body composition values.[2,8]

To decrease the percentage of body fat, it is suggested that moderate caloric restriction be combined with a moderate increase in caloric expenditure to create a negative caloric balance. Using this approach, the individual could make relatively small changes in his or her lifestyle, yet be successful. For example, if caloric intake is reduced by just 250 calories a day and activity level increased to expend just 250 calories a day, over a 7-day period this will result in a deficit of 3500 calories or the loss of 1 pound. When one is losing weight, a long-term approach should be adopted, emphasizing slow but steady progress toward one's goals.

Achievement of weight loss and appropriate body composition values often requires changes in the individual's lifestyle. Old habits may need to be changed and new ones adopted. These changes should be introduced gradually for the individual to incorporate them successfully into his or her lifestyle.

Having excessively low levels of body fat is also dangerous to one's health. One disorder associated with extremely low levels of body fat is anorexia nervosa, which is characterized by obsessive dieting and extreme weight loss. Bulimia, another type of eating disorder, involves recurrent episodes of binge eating followed by purging the body of the food through self-induced vomiting and the use of laxatives. Because these disorders are widespread and commonly seen in adolescent women, secondary school physical education teachers should be alert to these problems. However, treatment of these disorders requires trained professionals. Teachers can encourage students suffering from these disorders to seek professional help. Moreover, they should communicate to their students the importance of maintaining an appropriate level of body fat, neither too high nor too low.

When working with individuals who possess extremely poor body composition values, a team approach is suggested. The physical education teacher should involve the school nurse, the student's parents, the student, and, when appropriate, other trained professionals when designing a weight management program. In terms of exercise, the physical education teacher should be prepared to make modifications in the exercise prescription for the student, altering the FIT variables to meet individual needs.

ASSESSMENT OF HEALTH-RELATED FITNESS

Periodic assessment of health-related fitness is an important aspect of the secondary school physical education program. As an integral part of the program, test results can help students personalize information about fitness and wellness concepts by giving them the opportunity to apply this information to the improvement of their own fitness levels. Tests also aid in identifying the strengths and weaknesses of each individual. Test results can help students form individualized fitness goals and help teachers determine whether the students have achieved the fitness program objectives and to monitor student progress. When properly conducted, testing is motivating to students; students can readily discern the results of their efforts to improve their levels of fitness. Through fitness testing, students can be shown how to self-assess their fitness levels so that they know how to evaluate their fitness status throughout life.

Fitness test results are also important in evaluating program effectiveness. Students' scores can be used to determine whether the program is effective in helping students attain desired goals. Areas of the program that need to be improved and areas that are particularly effective can be identified.

Traditionally, many schools have administered fitness tests in the fall, at the beginning of the school year, and in the spring, at the conclusion of the school year. Many schools are now incorporating assessment procedures more frequently, such as at the end of each marking period.

Physical Fitness Programs

Numerous physical fitness programs have been developed to educate students about fitness and to evaluate students' status relative to the different fitness components. Four of these programs are the AAHPERD Physical Best, the Prudential Fitnessgram, the President's Challenge Fitness Program, and the Chrysler Fund-AAU Physical Fitness Program.

It should be noted that some fitness assessment programs use norm-referenced standards, while other programs use criterion-referenced standards. Norm-referenced tests compare an individual's performance against the performance of other persons of the same age and sex. A percentile rank is used to indicate an individual's standing, that is, the 85th percentile for sit-up performance compared to the norm group. Criterion-referenced tests, such as Physical Best and the Fitnessgram, link performance on the test to health outcomes. Student performance on the test is assessed with respect to a health standard (criteria) associated with low health risk.[4] Thus a 13-year-old girl who completes the 1-mile walk/run in a time of 10 minutes, below the criterion health standard of 10 minutes and 30 seconds, is considered to have an acceptable level of aerobic fitness with respect to health and is a lower health risk for health problems associated with this fitness parameter than individuals who do not meet this criterion standard (from Physical Best).[10]

Physical Best. In 1988 AAHPERD inaugurated the Physical Best fitness program.[10] The Physical Best program uses five tests to measure the components of health-related fitness.

Aerobic endurance is assessed by the 1-mile walk/run, in which the student is instructed to run the 1-mile course in the fastest time possible. Students are encouraged to use the fastest pace that can be sustained for the distance. The shorter the time to complete the distance, the greater is the level of cardiovascular endurance.

Body composition is assessed through the use of skinfold measurements. Skinfolds are taken at two sites—the triceps and the calf—and summed to provide information about the percentage of body fat. The smaller the value for the sum of the two skinfolds, the more fit the individual is in terms of body composition.

Flexibility of the lower back and hamstring muscles is measured through the use of the sit-and-reach test. The student sits in the proper position at the test apparatus, leans forward, and extends the arms as far forward as possible along the ruler on top of the box. The greater the distance reached, the more flexibility the individual possesses.

Abdominal strength and endurance is assessed by the use of modified sit-ups. The number of correctly executed sit-ups completed in 60 seconds is recorded. The more sit-ups the student can complete, the greater is the student's level of abdominal strength and endurance.

Upper body strength and endurance is measured by the use of pull-ups. The number of correctly executed pull-ups that are completed is counted. The more pull-ups the student can complete, the greater is the student's level of upper body strength and endurance.

Information on the administration of the test items and evaluation of results is contained in the Physical Best manual. The Physical Best program uses criterion-referenced standards to determine the student's status on each of the fitness components. Computer programs are available to facilitate analysis.

The Physical Best award system recognizes students who participate in physical activities outside of the regular school physical education program (Fitness Activity Award), students who attain individual fitness goals established by contract with the teacher (Fitness Goals Award), and students who attain mastery of health fitness standards (Health Fitness Award). In addition to health assessment, the Physical Best program offers educational materials to physical education teachers to help them teach and motivate their students. These educational materials include lesson plans, wall charts, and report cards. Complete information on this program can be obtained from AAHPERD, 1900 Association Drive, Reston, VA, 22091.

Fitnessgram. Developed by the Cooper Institute for Aerobics Research, the Prudential Fitnessgram assesses the principal aspects of health-related fitness.[11] Aerobic capacity, muscle strength and endurance, flexibility, and body composition are measured.

Aerobic capacity is measured by the 1-mile walk/run. Students are asked to complete a distance of 1 mile as

quickly as possible. They may intersperse walking with running, if needed. Time to complete the distance is recorded, and this time is compared with the criteria.

Body composition is calculated through the use of skinfold measurements. Measurements are taken at the triceps and the calf, and these data are used to determine the percentage of body fat.

Both abdominal and upper body muscular strength and endurance are measured. Abdominal strength and endurance are measured by the use of curl-ups. The number of correctly performed curl-ups completed at the appropriate pace (1 every 3 seconds to a maximum of 75) yields the score. The higher the score, the higher is the level of abdominal strength and endurance. To measure upper body strength and endurance, push-ups are used. The goal is to complete as many push-ups as possible at the appropriate cadence (1 push-up every 3 seconds).

Trunk extensor strength and flexibility are assessed using the trunk lift. Lying in a prone position, the student slowly lifts the upper body off the floor. The distance of the student's chin to the floor in inches is the score, and the maximum score is 12 inches. The higher the score, the greater is the flexibility.

Criterion-referenced standards are used by the Fitnessgram. These standards identify a level of fitness that offers some degree of protection against diseases associated with a sedentary lifestyle. The student's performance is classified either as "needs improvement" or "healthy fitness zone." Students should endeavor to achieve a level of fitness that allows their score to place them within the healthy fitness zone.

After the students are tested, teachers can use the school's computer to generate a personalized, printed report for each student. The report contains information about student's performance relative to health-fitness criteria. The report also contains recommended activities for improving fitness based on each student's individual performance.

The Fitnessgram program offers a recognition system that acknowledges those students who are physically active and achieve a level of fitness that places them in the health fitness zone. The program emphasizes lifetime fitness for all people through promotion of regular physical activity habits. Complete information about the Fitnessgram can be obtained from the Cooper Institute for Aerobics Research, 12330 Preston Road, Dallas, TX, 75230.

President's Challenge. The President's Council on Physical Fitness and Sports sponsors the President's Challenge fitness program.[12] Unlike the Physical Best and Fitnessgram programs, the President's Challenge uses norm-referenced standards for evaluation of students' fitness level. The five items that comprise the program measure aerobic endurance, muscle strength, muscle endurance, flexibility, and body coordination.

The 1-mile run/walk is used to assess aerobic endurance. The student is instructed to cover the 1-mile distance as quickly as possible. Walking can be interspersed with running, but completion of the distance in the shortest amount of time is encouraged. The shorter the time to complete the distance, the greater is the level of aerobic endurance.

Abdominal strength and endurance are assessed by the use of curl-ups. The maximum number of curl-ups that are performed correctly in 1 minute are counted. The greater the total of curl-ups completed, the higher is the level of muscular strength and endurance.

Upper body strength and endurance are determined by the maximum number of pull-ups completed. The greater the number of pull-ups correctly completed, the higher is the level of muscular strength and endurance. Students who cannot complete one pull-up may perform the flexed-arm hang. The longer the time the student can hang with arms flexed and the chin clearing the bar, the higher is the level of strength and endurance.

The flexibility of the lower back and hamstrings muscles is assessed by use of the V-sit reach. The student sits on the floor, with the soles of the feet placed immediately behind the baseline, heels about 8 to 12 inches apart. Hands together, the student reaches forward as far as possible. The greater the distance reached beyond the baseline, the higher is the level of flexibility. An alternative option to the V-sit reach test is the sit-and-reach test.

Body coordination is measured by using the shuttle run. Two parallel lines are drawn 30 feet apart, and two blocks are placed behind one of the lines. Starting from the opposite line, the student runs to the blocks, picks one up, returns to the starting line, places the block down, runs and picks up the second block, and runs back across the starting line. The faster the student can complete the task, the higher is the level of body coordination.

The President's Challenge has an award system based on student's performance compared to the established norms. Three different levels of physical fitness are recognized. The Presidential Fitness Award recognizes outstanding achievement and is awarded to students who score at or above the 85th percentile on all five test items. Students who score at or above the 50th percentile on all five test items are eligible for the National Physical Fitness Award. The Participant Physical Fitness Award acknowledges the efforts of students who attempted all five test items but scored below the 50th percentile on one or more of the five test items. Further information about the President's Challenge program can be obtained by writing to the President's Challenge, Populars Research Center, 400 E. 7th Street, Bloomington, IN, 47405.

Chrysler Fund-AAU Physical Fitness Program.[13] This program assesses cardiovascular endurance, abdominal strength and endurance, flexibility, and upper body strength and endurance through the use of four required tests. Then one of seven optional tests is used to assess additional fitness components. Like the President's Challenge fitness program, norm-referenced standards are used to evaluate students' fitness level.

Cardiovascular endurance is measured through the use of a 1-mile run. Students are encouraged to complete the distance as rapidly as possible. The more quickly the distance is covered, the higher is the level of fitness.

Bent-knee sit-ups are used for assessment of abdominal strength and endurance. The number of correctly completed sit-ups in 1 minute is recorded for the score. Upper body strength and endurance are assessed through performance on the pull-ups. The greater the number of correctly performed pull-ups, the higher is the level of fitness.

Flexibility is evaluated through the use of the sit-and-reach test. Sitting on the floor, legs straight and feet 12 inches apart, the student places the hands together and reaches forward as far as possible. The greater the distance reached, the greater is the flexibility.

Each student must also complete one of the optional tests. These include the Hoosier Endurance Shuttle Run, the standing long jump, the isometric push-up, modified push-ups, phantom chair or isometric leg squat, shuttle run, and sprints (50 or 100 yards depending on age).

There is an award system that recognizes different levels of fitness achievement. The awards are Certificate of Outstanding Achievement, Certificate of Attainment, and Certificate of Participation.

Educational materials focusing on fitness development and nutrition are available. Further information about the program can be obtained by writing to the Chrysler Fund-AAU Physical Fitness Program, Populars Building, Bloomington, IN, 47401.

State and school fitness tests. Many states have their own physical fitness tests, standards, and educational programs. Physical education teachers can obtain information about these programs from the state education department.

Some school districts have developed their own fitness assessment procedures. These tests typically reflect the fitness objectives deemed important by physical education teachers within the school system. Teachers should ensure, however, that these tests are valid and reliable measures of fitness components.

Assessment Measures

In addition to various fitness assessment programs, teachers may choose other tests to assess health-fitness components. There are a variety of other approaches to measure cardiovascular endurance, body composition, muscular strength and endurance, and flexibility from which teachers can choose depending on program objectives, situational variables, and students' needs.

Cardiovascular endurance. Cardiovascular endurance is typically measured through running. Measures include the time to run a certain distance, usually 1 mile or 1.5

miles, and the distance covered in a specific amount of time, such as the distance covered in 9 minutes or 12 minutes. Another test that may be used is the Harvard Step Test. Maximal and submaximal tests of oxygen consumption using a treadmill and various exercise protocols may also be employed. Performing these oxygen consumption tests requires trained personnel and extensive laboratory equipment.

It is important to note that the principle of specificity should be taken into account in the measurement of cardiovascular endurance. The mode of exercise that a student has used to train may influence test results. Students who train aerobically using swimming or cycling may not test well on the distance run, because they are not being tested in the mode in which they trained. With these students, teachers may wish to employ some of the bicycle ergometer measures available or a specific swimming test.

Body composition. Although body composition is usually measured using the skinfold technique, there are several other means available to assess this fitness component. The body mass index (BMI) may be calculated. The BMI is the ratio of body weight, measured in kilograms, and the square of body height, as measured in meters. (See Physical Best test manual for further information.[10]) Another technique is the use of underwater weighing. While this technique provides accurate information about an individual's body composition, the equipment is expensive and not generally available to physical education teachers, and the procedure is time consuming. A new method that has gained in popularity for measuring body composition is the use of the body composition analyzers. By measuring the resistance to the flow of electrical current through the body between selected points, the percent of body fat is determined.

Muscular strength and endurance. Often, improvement in muscular strength and endurance is assessed from

inspection of the records kept while the individual was training. Carefully designed record keeping allows the teacher and the student to identify areas in which progress was made and areas in which further work is needed. Another means to assess strength is through the use of grip dynamometers.

Flexibility. Flexibility can be measured through a variety of simple tests, such as those of trunk flexion, trunk extension, and shoulder flexibility, all of which evaluate how far the individual can reach or move in relation to a specific reference point. Joint flexibility can also be measured using a variety of devices. One of the simplest and most widely used is the goniometer. The goniometer is a large protractor, with measurements in degrees. The range of motion can be attained by aligning the two arms parallel to the longitudinal axis of the two segments involved in motion around a specific joint.

Fitness laboratories. Although some of the tests that measure fitness require fairly expensive equipment and specialized training and are time consuming, some teachers are beginning to incorporate these measures into their physical education programs. Exercise physiology laboratories, motor fitness laboratories, and physical education learning centers in some secondary schools may contain a variety of equipment to conduct sophisticated fitness tests, such as motorized treadmill and equipment to conduct submaximal oxygen tests. Budgetary funds previously allocated to purchase more sports equipment are being used to purchase exercise physiology equipment, such as bike ergometers and electronic body composition analyzers, to use in fitness programs.

It should be noted that some teachers are able to receive financial support for specialized training in exercise testing from their school boards. In other situations, teachers work out collaborative arrangements for training with faculty at neighboring colleges and universities. Yet, in other situations, teachers take it upon themselves to obtain necessary training to implement these programs.

Fitness Assessment for Students with Special Needs

Physical education teachers should also be cognizant that some students in their classes, because of a disability, may not be able to perform successfully on standardized fitness tests. One fitness assessment program designed for students with special needs is Project Unique.[14] Project Unique is appropriate for use with individuals who have orthopedic impairments, cerebral palsy, visual impairments, and auditory impairments. Fitness norms are provided for these special populations as well as for nonhandicapped individuals.

Many fitness program packages offer information on assessing the fitness status of youths with special needs. The Physical Best, the Fitnessgram, the President's Challenge, and the Chrysler Fund-AAU physical fitness pro-

Grip dynamometer used to measure muscular strength.
Courtesy of Ben Lombardo, Rhode Island College, Providence, RI.

grams all contain information about fitness for youths with disabilities.

Test Administration

Fitness testing should be efficiently planned so that it does not take up an inordinate amount of class time. Teachers should be familiar with the test items and how to score the tests. Students should also be informed as to the purpose of each test item, procedures for performing the test item and scoring, and how the tests will be administered. As students become familiar with the administration of the test items, the entire process can be expedited.

The use of volunteers can help streamline the testing process. Parents, community members (such as, senior citizens), leaders club members, and other responsible students can, after a training period, be entrusted to administer the tests. The teacher should give each assistant specific responsibilities to fulfill. The use of volunteers allows a large class to be divided into smaller, more manageable groups for test administration.

Students should also learn how to self-assess their fitness levels. This way, students, particularly those students who are working hard to improve their fitness levels, can see their progress more readily. Students, once trained, can self-assess their fitness levels or work cooperatively with a peer to complete the assessment process.

Record Keeping

Record keeping is an important part of fitness assessment. Accurate records make it easier to monitor student progress throughout the year and to keep track of students' fitness status during all of the secondary school years. Such documentation may be helpful to teachers in wagering successful campaigns to increase the time allocated to physical education and to increase funding. Record keeping is also important in evaluating program effectiveness. Good record keeping assists teachers in determining the extent to which program goals have been obtained as well as establishing future directions for the program.

An increasing number of teachers are using microcomputers to facilitate the record-keeping process. The Physical Best, the Fitnessgram, the President's Challenge, and the Chrysler Fund-AAU physical fitness programs have computer software available to assist teachers in reporting results and record keeping.

PROGRAM AND INSTRUCTIONAL GUIDELINES FOR FITNESS

In designing programs to promote student fitness, teachers need to structure these programs to take into account the training principles of overload, progression, specificity, initial level of fitness, and provision for warm-up and cool-down. Program structure must also take into account the minimum exercise criteria for fitness development in terms of frequency, intensity, and time as well as introduce students to a variety of fitness activities to develop cardiovascular endurance, muscular strength and endurance, flexibility, and body composition.

Additionally, physical education teachers must consider safety, goal setting, incorporation of periodic assessment, and communication of results. The importance of fitness as a personal responsibility must be emphasized. Fitness activities should be designed to provide for individual differences in fitness levels and other abilities. Equally important, teachers should give students encouragement and positive reinforcement and strive to make fitness development fun and enjoyable. Teachers should serve as positive models of fitness for their students, and they should incorporate a variety of curricular and instructional approaches within their programs.

Safety

Safety should be a primary consideration in designing exercise programs. The exercise principles discussed previously are not only important in terms of maximizing fitness gains but also in terms of ensuring the safety of participants. When the principles of overload and progression are inappropriately incorporated into the exercise program, students may experience injuries. Injuries can also occur when the student's initial level of fitness is not taken into account when planning the exercise program or students do not have the opportunity to adequately warm up or cool down.

Equally important in terms of safety is consideration of the environmental conditions, specifically the climate. In areas of the country where the climate is hot, humid, or both, special care should be taken when one is exercising. Exercise programs should start out at reduced levels of intensity and duration and be gradually increased as the students become acclimated. Students should have free access to water and be encouraged to drink when needed. Additionally, if the relative heat and humidity rise above critical levels, the levels of intensity of activities that last 30 minutes or more should be reduced.[2,8] Finally, teachers should be especially aware of the dangers that heat and humidity pose to students who are obese. Students who are obese should reduce the intensity and duration of their exercise programs. Teachers should carefully monitor all students when they are exercising in hot or humid climates. They should be aware of the signs and symptoms of heat-related problems, such as heat cramps, heat stroke, and heat exhaustion, and know the basic first-aid procedures to deal with these problems. Teachers may find the purchase of a heat stress indicator, which gives readings of temperature and humidity, helpful in providing for student safety in hot and humid climates.

When students exercise in cold weather, teachers must be careful of hypothermia. Hypothermia occurs when the body's ability to produce heat is impaired and the body's temperature drops below 95° F.[2,8] Hypothermia typically occurs when the temperature is between 50° and 60° F and when the weather is damp and windy.[2,8] Teachers should be aware of environmental conditions that may indicate a predisposition to hypothermia and be prepared to deal with this serious problem should it arise.

It is also the responsibility of each physical education teacher to keep up with current research and developments in the area of fitness. Failure to keep abreast of current findings may lead to the employment of contraindicated exercise practices with harmful results.

Goal Setting

Goal setting is an important part of fitness programs. Well-defined goals allow students to identify desired outcomes. Intermediate and long-term goals, such as for the year's end, should be developed. These goals should encompass fitness activities, knowledge, and values.

When students have specific goals to strive for, their activity becomes more purposeful. Students can more readily see the value of what they are doing and the payoff for their hard work, commitment, and investment in fitness. Short-term, specific objectives allow students to track their progress as they work toward their long-term goals. This helps students remain adequately motivated to achieve the desired outcomes, rather than giving up because they could not discern their progress.

While goals should be realistic, it is important that they challenge the students to work hard. Students should also be encouraged to participate in specific activities based on their personal interests outside of class to help them meet their fitness goals.

Periodic Assessment

As previously discussed, periodic assessment of fitness levels of students should be an integral part of the secondary school program. Assessment should be scheduled at regular intervals throughout the school year.

In addition to formal testing, students can work independently or with a peer to perform a variety of self-testing activities. Besides providing students with information about their fitness status, self-testing activities can allow students to apply various concepts to the development of fitness. As part of the evaluation program, teachers should readily make available to students information about health standards. For example, teachers can post standards for the Physical Best tests on the gym-

nasium bulletin board so that students can easily evaluate their performance by comparing it to information on the chart. If available, students can input their data into the microcomputer and receive an immediate printout of their results.

Communication of Results

Results of fitness tests should be reported to the student and the parents. This report should include a little background information on each fitness component, a description of test items and test scores, and an explanation of how to interpret them. Prescriptive activities to improve fitness deficiencies should also be included. In cases where a student scores extremely poorly on the fitness items, his or her parents should be encouraged to contact the teacher to discuss the results and possible cooperative approaches to remedy these deficiencies.

Informing students of test outcomes allows them to see the results of their efforts. Informing parents not only helps them become more aware of their child's fitness and health status, but also helps parents become more knowledgeable about what is being taught in physical education and its value.

It may also be beneficial to provide administrators with a summary report of a student's fitness status. Accountability is important. Physical education teachers who are able to document students' fitness development may be able to gain additional support for their program, either in terms of funding or time allocation.

Some teachers report the results of fitness assessments to the public. This frequently takes the form of a short article written for the local newspaper highlighting the progress students have made in fitness development throughout the year and the accomplishments of the physical education program. This approach is also useful in generating public support for physical education programs.

Use of a computer can expedite analysis of students' performance and reporting of information. Many fitness software programs quickly analyze the student's data, provide an interpretation of the results, graphically illustrate the student's fitness profile, and present prescriptive exercises.[10-13]

Personal Responsibility

Teachers must emphasize that fitness and wellness are the individual's personal responsibility. This responsibility cannot be delegated to others, such as one's parents or one's teacher. Fitness requires the assumption of responsibility for incorporating exercise as part of one's lifestyle. Moreover, fitness requires personal investment. Fitness demands hard work, self-discipline, and a strong commitment to include fitness activities as part of one's life. Individuals who fail to exercise regularly will not realize the benefits. Students who exercise for 6 weeks as part of a fitness unit and then fail to continue to exercise upon its conclusion will quickly lose the benefits they have gained. Therefore it is imperative that students develop the skills, knowledge, and attitudes that lead to lifelong fitness.

Furthermore, in many schools, the time constraints involving the physical education program require that students assume responsibility for the development of fitness outside of class. In schools where physical education classes meet only twice a week, for example, the frequency criteria for training for cardiovascular endurance cannot be met unless students exercise outside of class.

Individuality

The individual's characteristics, needs, and objectives must be taken into account when one is planning an exercise program. The rate of fitness improvement varies for each individual and is influenced by such factors as age, body weight, current fitness and health status, nutritional status, and level of motivation. Nutritional habits must be taken into account when one is helping the individual obtain an appropriate value for body composition. Individual objectives and needs differ as well. Furthermore, fitness programs should take into account individual likes and dislikes. Some individuals prefer to exercise by jogging, while others may prefer swimming, bicycling, or cross-country skiing.

Students should be introduced to a variety of activities and have opportunities to develop movement competencies necessary for participation. Students should also be knowledgeable about the potential of each activity to develop physical fitness. Students who have opportunities to experience success and to learn skills necessary to participate in activities that are personally meaningful and satisfying will be more likely motivated to participate on a regular basis.

Fitness is for Everyone

Being fit is important for everyone. Yet, often those students who may need fitness the most are not reached by traditional fitness programs. Teachers must make a special effort to reach out and involve these students. The fitness needs of students who are unfit, obese, and disabled should be accommodated within the secondary school curriculum.

Helping these youths obtain better fitness levels requires teachers to move away from the traditional approach where all students perform the same exercises at the same pace for the same number of repetitions. Individualized programs that allow students to start at their own level of fitness and progress at a pace appropriate to their abilities is important if the needs of these students are to be met.

For students whose needs are such that they cannot be met in the regular program, alternative approaches should be explored. Many of these special needs students may require additional time or guidance to develop minimal levels of fitness. To meet these needs, some schools have developed special programs.

Reinforcement

Reinforcement of students' efforts and achievements can help students develop and maintain desirable levels of physical fitness. Support and recognition by the physical education teacher, students' peers, and students' parents can help motivate students. Because it may require a period of at least 8 to 10 weeks of regular participation in fitness activities before significant improvements can be seen, reinforcement and encouragement can be critical in helping students adhere to the exercise program through these long weeks, rather than giving up.

Developing and maintaining fitness is hard work, requiring self-discipline and commitment. When teachers, parents, and peers care about the feelings and needs of students and support students' efforts, not only do they encourage them to persist in their endeavors but enhance their self-esteem as well.

Fun

Enjoyment may be one of the most critical factors in a successful fitness program. Students should be exposed to a variety of fitness activities so that each student may find an activity that he or she enjoys. Enjoyment increases the probability that an individual will incorporate the activity as part of his or her lifestyle.

Even though some activities may be popular with the public, such as running, and effective in developing fitness, some individuals would prefer to engage in other activities. They may not like to run and may prefer to develop fitness through cycling or swimming. Students should have opportunities to select an activity that is enjoyable for them, while contributing to the attainment of fitness goals. When an activity is enjoyable to students, their interest and motivation are maintained, and they will be more likely to continue participation so that they can realize fitness improvement. Students must be allowed to find the approach to fitness development that works best for them. Students should learn how to manipulate creatively the fitness variables of frequency, intensity, and time and apply them to different modes of exercise. If students are expected to incorporate exercise into their lifestyles, they must learn activities that are enjoyable to them.

Modeling

Modeling by teachers can exert a significant influence on the development and maintenance of fitness in secondary school students. Physical education teachers who believe that fitness is important and provide opportunities for its development and maintenance within the curriculum reinforce their message to students.

Physical education teachers' behaviors and appearance can have a powerful influence on the fitness development and maintenance of their students. Instructors who "practice what they preach," that is, who are fit and incorporate fitness activities into their lifestyles, serve as positive role models for students.[15] Teachers who exemplify healthy, active, fit lifestyles and whose appearance and activities mirror their commitment to fitness may bring additional credibility to their teaching.[15]

On the other hand, teachers who are not fit may not be as effective in accomplishing curriculum fitness objectives.[16] Students may find it difficult to believe in the importance of fitness to health and daily living when teachers' appearances belie this message.[15] Moreover, students may perceive these teachers as less knowledgeable and may be less influenced to exercise.[16]

Physical education teachers need to think carefully about their beliefs concerning the importance of serving as a role model to their students. Being fit and exercising regularly, perhaps sometimes with students in their classes, can be a powerful testimony to the importance of physical fitness to well-being.

SUMMARY

Health-related physical fitness has been increasingly linked with health outcomes. Cardiovascular endurance, muscular strength and endurance, flexibility, and body composition are the components of health-related fitness. One of the most important contributions teachers can make to the lives of their students is to help them acquire the skills, knowledge, and attitudes to lead healthy, active lifestyles.

When one is planning a fitness program, the exercise variables of frequency, intensity, time, and mode are used to design the program. Additionally, if fitness gains are to accrue, training principles must also be incorporated into the exercise program. These include the principles of overload, progression, specificity, and disuse. Individual differences in fitness levels must be taken into account and provision made to include a warm up and cool down within the program. Periodic evaluation of fitness should also be an integral part of the program.

When one is designing instructional experiences for students, safety, goal setting, positive reinforcement, and frequent communication of results should be given attention. Teachers should strive to be a positive role model for their students. And, most important, fitness is for everyone and should be fun!

FOR REVIEW

1. Make a list of 10 team sports and 10 individual and lifetime sports. Construct a chart showing the potential contribution of each sport to the development of each component of health-related fitness: cardiovascular endurance, flexibility, body composition, and muscular strength and endurance.

2. For each sport listed previously, describe what changes you would make in each sport to maximize the contribution of the sport to cardiovascular endurance.

3. Secondary school physical education classes contain individuals whose fitness levels vary considerably. Select two health-related fitness components. For each component, plan a lesson that would provide for individual levels of fitness while promoting the development of the component. The actual class time available for fitness development is 30 minutes.

4. One important responsibility facing physical education teachers is helping students make the transition from high school to the world of work or college. What strategies can teachers incorporate into their program to help students learn how to exercise independently and incorporate physical activity into their lifestyles once they graduate?

REFERENCES

1. Public Health Service: *Healthy people 2000: national health promotion and disease prevention objectives,* Washington, DC, 1990, US Government Printing Office.

2. Prentice WE, Bucher CA: *Fitness for college and life,* ed 2, St Louis, 1988, Mosby.

3. Neiman DC: *Fitness and sports medicine: an introduction,* Palo Alto, Calif, 1990, Bull.

4. Schoenborn CA: Health promotion and disease prevention. In *Vital and Health Statistics: Series 10, No 163,* Department of Health and Human Services Pub No (PHS) 88-1591, Public Health Service, Washington, DC, 1988, US Government Printing Office.

5. Going SB, Williams DP, Lohman TG: Setting standards for health-related youth fitness tests—determining critical body fat levels, *JOPERD* 63:19-24, 1992.

6. McGinnis JM: The public health burden of a sedentary lifestyle, *Med Sci Sports Exerc* 24 (suppl 6):196-200, 1992.

7. AAHPERD: *Lifetime health-related fitness test manual,* Reston, Va, 1980, AAHPERD.

8. Nobel BJ: *Physiology of exercise and sport,* St Louis, 1986, Mosby.

9. Allsen PE, Harrison JM, Vance B: *Fitness for life: an individualized approach,* Dubuque, Iowa, 1989, William C Brown.

10. AAHPERD: *Physical Best test manual,* Reston, Va, 1988, AAHPERD.

11. The Cooper Institute for Aerobic Research: *The Prudential Fitnessgram,* Dallas, Tex, 1993, The Cooper Institute for Aerobic Research.

12. The President's Council on physical fitness and sport: *The President's Challenge physical fitness program,* Bloomington, Ind, 1993, The President's Council.

13. Amateur Athletic Union: *Chrysler fund-AAU physical fitness program,* Bloomington, Ind, 1992-1993, AAU.

14. Winnick J, Short FX: *Project Unique Fitness Test,* Champaign, Ill, 1984, Human Kinetics.

15. Johnson MW: Physical education-fitness or fraud? *JOPERD* 56(1):33-35, 1985.
16. Melville DS, Maddalozzo JGF: The effects of a physical educator's appearance of body fatness on communicating exercise concepts to high school students, *JOTPE, 7*:343-352, 1988.
17. Wilmore JH: *Objectives for the nation—physical fitness and exercise,* *JOPERD* 53(3):41-43, 1982.

ANNOTATED READINGS

Corbin C, Lindsay R: *Concepts of physical fitness with laboratories,* Dubuque, Iowa, 1991, William C Brown.
An excellent resource for teaching fitness through a "hands-on" approach.
Going SB, Williams DP, Lohman TG: Setting standards for health-related youth fitness tests—determining critical body fat levels. *JOPERD* 63(8):19-24, 1992.
Discusses the linking of health outcomes to fitness testing and presents an excellent discussion of the criteria for body composition fitness.
Melville DS, Maddalozzo JGF: The effects of a physical educator's appearance of body fatness on communicating exercise concepts to high school students, *JOTPE* 7:343-352, 1988.
Investigates the effects of a physical education teacher's appearance on the credibility and success in teaching fitness concepts to students.
Neiman DC: *Fitness and sports medicine: an introduction,* Palo Alto, Calif, 1990, Bull.
A comprehensive approach to fitness testing, condition, benefits of fitness, and precautions for physical activity.
Shepard RJ: *Fitness in special populations,* Champaign, Ill, 1990, Human Kinetics.
Offers helpful suggestions on meeting the fitness needs of those students with disabilities.

Wellness and Fitness Programs in Action

CHAPTER OBJECTIVES

◆ To offer general guidelines for wellness and fitness programs
◆ To provide examples of wellness and fitness programs in action

Throughout the nation, teachers are using a variety of curricular and instructional approaches to educate their students about fitness and wellness. Increasingly, teachers are using computer technology in a diversity of ways within their programs. This chapter provides examples of program models in practice to offer physical education teachers ideas to implement within their own programs.

WELLNESS AND FITNESS CURRICULUM AND APPROACHES

A variety of curriculum and instructional approaches can be successfully used for wellness and fitness instruction in the secondary school. In designing programs and in planning for instruction, teachers must take into account the exercise science criteria that specify the requirements for training (for example, to develop cardiovascular endurance the individual must exercise at least 3 times a week, for 20 minutes, with an intensity of at least 60%) and the principles governing the design of exercise programs (for example, principle of progression). In addition, teachers must consider situational factors (for example, frequency and length of class meetings) and students' needs. Furthermore, some thought must be given to the proportion of time that will be devoted to fitness development as compared with skill development. If time is not sufficient for students to achieve competency in selected motor skills, acquire necessary knowledge, and

develop favorable attitudes toward physical activity, then the likelihood that students will incorporate physical activity into their lifestyle diminishes.

Creative planning and nontraditional approaches may be called for if students are to attain the fitness objectives set forth in the curriculum. When the exercise science criteria and situational factors are congruent, planning for the attainment of fitness objectives by students may be fairly easy. However, when the exercise science criteria and situational factors are not congruent, innovative approaches need to be employed. For example, to develop cardiovascular fitness, the student must have the opportunity to exercise a minimum of 3 times a week, 20 minutes a session, with an intensity of at least 60%. In a school setting where physical education classes meet only twice a week, alternative strategies must be used to achieve the stated exercise science criteria of exercising 3 times a week. This may involve expecting students to exercise outside of school and keep weekly exercise logs or providing opportunities within the school setting, other than the time when physical education class meets, to allow students opportunities to meet the exercise science criteria. During the school day, this could include drop-in fitness sessions scheduled in the gymnasium or other physical education areas or intramurals scheduled before or after school. In some schools the gymnasiums are open at night and during the weekend for community use. Students could then use this time to work on their fitness development. In short, teachers must seek creative

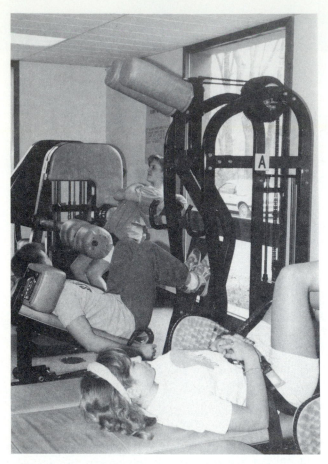

Some schools use off-campus health clubs to conduct their fitness unit. Students at Camp Hill High School work out at the local health club as part of their physical education program.
Courtesy of Emily Leonardo, Camp Hill High School, Camp Hill, PA.

approaches to fitness development that provide a match between the exercise science criteria and situational constraints.

Equally important, the fitness development and wellness should be incorporated into a balanced physical education program. If students do not have the opportunity to develop adequate physical skills and knowledge, they will lack the abilities and understanding necessary to participate in activities that lead to fitness development. Moreover, without adequate skills, knowledge, and opportunity to develop a positive attitude toward physical activity, students may be less likely to participate in physical activities during their leisure time and incorporate these activities into their lifestyles. Physical education teachers should endeavor to use the time allocated for physical education to the fullest, employing creative approaches to maximize fitness and skill development. Once students have learned fitness activity skills and are able to write a personal exercise program, students should be expected to exercise independently. Once students reach this point, teachers can reduce the time directly allocated to fitness development within the class period and curriculum, while providing alternative opportunities to students to improve and maintain their fitness levels.

Curricular Approaches

Unit approach. Many physical education programs provide a unit of instruction once or twice each year focusing on fitness development. These units may last from 2 to 4 weeks at the junior high-school level and to 6 to 9 weeks at the high-school level. Typically, students are introduced to a variety of fitness activities and training techniques, such as circuit training, interval training, aerobics, weight training, calisthenics, flexibility exercises, and jogging. Fitness concepts and guidelines for physical development are also covered in these courses. Some teachers choose to start and conclude the unit with the administration of selected fitness tests.

At the upper secondary school level, students often have the opportunity to elect units focusing on instruction in different activities that can be used for fitness development. Units commonly offered include weight training, aerobic dance, aerobic exercise, and jogging. Some schools offer units on swimming, bicycling, and cross-country skiing.

A few schools have made arrangements with off-campus local health clubs to conduct the fitness unit on its site. In addition to being exposed to various fitness activities and having the opportunity to work out, students learn to be wise health fitness consumers. Students receive information on how to select a health club for use in their adult fitness program.

A few schools offer an elective unit on exercise physiology. Basic concepts of exercise physiology are presented, and students frequently have the opportunity to engage in a variety of laboratory experiences designed to help them apply various concepts. Students may learn how to conduct various fitness assessment measures as part of this course.

Other schools have established a motor learning or motor fitness learning center. Students receive instruction in motor learning and exercise physiology and have the opportunity to conduct a variety of experiments focusing on the application of principles discussed in class.

Some schools elect to teach a unit on wellness as part of the physical education program. Information on developing and maintaining a high level of wellness is presented. This may include information about nutrition, safety and accident prevention, decision making, and various stress management techniques.

Comprehensive approach. Some schools choose to have a comprehensive fitness curriculum. Although other skill activities may be taught, many of the units within the curriculum focus on fitness activities. Furthermore, fitness development activities are incorporated into every lesson, regardless of unit content.

Within the comprehensive program, fitness development is emphasized, and other sport activities may be modified to increase their potential contribution to fitness. For example, reducing the number of participants per team, using mini-games to involve more individuals, and instituting role changes to make game play relatively nonstop are some strategies teachers can use to increase the amount of time students are actively moving during skill activities. When students are standing on the sidelines waiting for their chance to participate during game play, such as waiting to go up to bat in softball, they can work on fitness development rather than just watching the action. Waiting students can engage in flexibility exercises, jog, lift weights, perform calisthenics, engage in partner resistive exercises, or perhaps take a test on fitness concepts.

In schools where physical education is scheduled on a daily basis, 3 days a week may be devoted to fitness development and the remaining 2 days to motor skill development, or vice versa.

Some schools have chosen to integrate wellness concepts throughout the entire curriculum. Each time the class meets, students may receive a minilecture on a particular wellness concept or participate in a short activity designed to develop or promote an awareness of wellness.

Conceptual approach. Increasing numbers of physical education teachers are choosing to employ the conceptual approach within their curriculum. Key concepts underlying fitness development and wellness are identified. Often, these concepts are presented to students in a brief lecture. Students then have the opportunity to apply these concepts while performing specific activities. Some teachers utilize problem-solving approaches that allow students to discover concepts underlying performance or to take previously learned concepts and apply them to different situations. An example of the conceptual approach is the *Basic Stuff* series published by AAHPERD.

Remediation approach. For individuals who are in need of a great deal of help in the area of fitness and wellness, many schools have established remedial programs. Criteria for inclusion in the program are established by the school. For example, a student who scores in the 10th percentile or below on three of the five items comprising the Physical Best fitness test would be earmarked for inclusion in this program.

These programs may take on a variety of structures. Students who meet the requirements for inclusion in the remedial program may be assigned to the class in lieu of their regular physical education class. Or students may be assigned to take remedial classes in addition to their physical education classes. Classes may meet before school or during the school day, perhaps in lieu of the students' study hall. Students receive individual attention in these classes, instruction in fitness and wellness, and oppor-

tunities to develop their fitness levels. Students may test out of these classes on a periodic basis, typically at the end of a marking period. At that time, students who meet the established criteria, such as scoring in the 50th percentile on all fitness test items, may discontinue participation in these classes.

Special classes in weight management are offered by some schools to meet the needs of students who are overweight or underweight. These classes involve fitness development as well as considerable instruction in nutrition and dietary management. These classes may be conducted collaboratively with other school health professionals, such as the school nurse or physician.

Individualized approach. Another way individual special needs may be met is through the design of an individualized fitness program to be conducted outside of the school setting. The teacher, the student, and sometimes the student's parents meet to evaluate the student's needs and to design an exercise program specifically to meet these needs. The teacher then reviews the program with the student and parents and explains each person's responsibilities. The parents may exercise with the student and help the student monitor his or her progress. Often parental support and positive modeling can help the student adhere to the fitness program. Periodic meetings are held to assess the student's progress and to update the fitness program as needed. This approach may prove particularly valuable in reaching students who exhibit poor levels of fitness.

Teaching Approaches

Within each fitness and wellness unit or program, a variety of teaching approaches may be employed. Traditional approaches, such as direct command instruction, may be used to initially teach various exercises and techniques or to present information. Individualized approaches may then be employed during the workout portion of the class. Individualized approaches better provide for individual differences in students' abilities and needs than the more traditional approach, which emphasizes all students performing the same exercise at the same pace for the same number of repetitions.

Individualized teaching styles, such as using several different teaching stations and task cards, working reciprocally with a partner, and working by oneself following an individually prescribed program, accommodate individual differences in the initial level of fitness, allow students to work at their own pace, and take into account differences in students' abilities and interests.

The use of multiple teaching stations and task cards allows students to work on different aspects of fitness and wellness. Students can rotate from station to station, performing the activity specified on the task card. Task cards can be written to allow students to choose from different levels of difficulty of the same activity. Some stations may require that students perform certain exercises, while at other stations students may take a test on fitness concepts, take part in small group discussions pertaining to wellness, or engage in problem-solving activities.

Guided discovery and problem-solving approaches may be used as part of different learning experiences to help students understand various fitness and wellness concepts and allow them to apply them to different situations. Such experiences help students make a connection between theory and practice and make the learning experiences more meaningful for students.

COMPUTER TECHNOLOGY, FITNESS, AND WELLNESS

Increasingly, computers may be found in the gymnasium. More teachers throughout the nation are incorporating computer technology into their fitness and wellness programs. Computer technology can be utilized to provide students with information about their physiological responses. Many pieces of exercise equipment incorporate computerized displays to give users feedback about their efforts. Instructional software in the area of fitness and wellness is becoming more widely available. Computerized assessment instruments facilitate the measurement of fitness components, and computers can greatly expedite data analysis and record keeping.

Computers and Physiological Monitoring

In recent years, more equipment has become available to help individuals readily monitor their physiological responses. Computerized heart rate monitors are being used by some teachers in their physical education pro-

grams. The monitor is worn on the wrist, similar to a watch, and the electrodes are contained in an easy to use chest strap. The monitor can be set for an individual student's training zone, and an auditory signal lets the student know when that training zone is reached. Some heart rate monitors store information about the individual's heart rate during an exercise period and then, via a computer interface, this information is transferred to the computer. The computer printout shows the heart rate of the student during the exercise or class period. This information allows the teacher and the students to examine more closely the effects of class activities on physiological functioning.

These heart rate monitors can be used in many ways within the physical education program. They can be used as instructional aids, helping reinforce such fitness concepts as target heart rate and working within the training zone. They can be used to help assess the effects of various activities on fitness development. A student can wear the heart rate monitor while participating in a volleyball game. This heart rate information can later be analyzed by the teacher and students to examine the potential contribution of this activity to fitness development. Teachers can also use the heart rate monitor to examine the effects of activity modification on fitness development. For example, teachers can see whether changing the rules of a game enhanced the potential of the game to contribute to cardiovascular endurance.

These heart rate monitors are relatively inexpensive, ranging from $200 to $300, and the prices continue to decrease. Prices for the computer interface vary depending on the computer used. Some teachers have purchased four or five of these monitors and set up a rotation system for student use within the class. Students enjoy using

Students take advantage of different exercise stations in completing their fitness program at Evanston Township High School, Evanston, IL.
Courtesy of Ann Stevens, Evanston Township High School, Evanston, IL.

these monitors and receiving immediate feedback about their efforts. Additionally, these heart rate monitors can make fitness concepts more meaningful to the students.

Electromyographic (EMG) machines can be used to provide students with information about their levels of muscle activity. Typically, three electrodes are positioned over a muscle group, and information about the activity of those muscles is transmitted to the machine where it is displayed. Some of these machines interface directly with a computer, providing not only a display of the muscle activity but a printout as well.

These machines can be used to monitor the effects of different types of exercise on muscle activity. These machines can also be used to help students see firsthand the effects of different types of relaxation programs on levels of muscle tension. Additionally, these machines can be used as part of a biofeedback program where students can learn how to reliably control their muscle activity and move toward a lower level of physiological arousal.

These machines have also become less expensive. Some teachers have included such machines as part of their exercise physiology or motor learning laboratories. These machines can also be used on a rotational basis by students within the physical education class.

Computerized Exercise Equipment

Many rowing machines and bicycle ergometers now use computerized displays. Typically, these displays provide the individual with information about the work load, work rate, and time exercised. Some computerized displays may give information about caloric expenditure and heart rate. In addition to providing students with immediate feedback about their efforts, this readily available information helps students make connections between their subjective feelings of effort and their bodily sensations. These displays are also motivating to the students.

Computerized displays are also being incorporated into some types of weight-training equipment. These displays provide information about the number of repetitions performed and weight lifted. Some displays even store information about the individual's previous workout efforts.

Exercise equipment with computerized displays varies in cost. Bicycle ergometers with computerized displays range in price from $300 to $1500. Weight-lifting equipment with computerized displays is expensive. However, some health and fitness clubs have such equipment, and teachers may be able to make arrangements for off-campus visits for their classes to these clubs.

Computer Software for Instruction

Computers can also be used as part of the instructional process in fitness and wellness programs. There are an increasing number of interactive software programs available in the areas of physical education and health. These instructional programs can be used to teach fitness and wellness concepts. Computer programs are also available so that students can design their own exercise programs.

Self-assessment programs allow students to analyze their behaviors and lifestyles. Assessment programs are available to analyze leisure and activity preferences, diet, health risk factors, level of stress, values, and coping strategies.

Teachers can provide time for students to perform these instructional tasks and self-assessment inventories by setting up the computer as one of many activity stations. Another alternative would be to have students perform these activities independently in the computer room at school and bring the results to class.

Computerized Assessment Instruments

Body composition analyzers rely on computer software. The computer provides a complete body composition profile. It gives information on the percent of water, lean tissue, and fat; provides recommendations on weight and caloric intake; and lists suggestions for an exercise program. In terms of skinfold measurement, skinfold calipers that interface directly with the computer are available, facilitating the recording of students' scores and record keeping. Digital skinfold calipers are available as are grip dynamometers.

Computers and Record Keeping

Computers have greatly facilitated the record-keeping process for many teachers. With the increased types of computer software available, the record-keeping process has become much more efficient. Longitudinal fitness information can be maintained on each student for the entire school career. Data analysis programs facilitate calculation of norms and other data, which is useful in evaluating the effectiveness of the program in meeting fitness goals.

Students can input their own fitness data, or the teacher can perform this function. Some computer programs not only provide an analysis of the student's fitness scores but also supply information on percentile ranking and suggest exercises that can be done to improve low-status fitness items. When students can input their own fitness data and get a printout of their scores and evaluation of their performance, it is motivating to them. These printouts can also be sent home to parents to inform them of the progress of their child and to develop an awareness of what is being learned in physical education. Other computer software programs can generate an individualized physical fitness program for the student. Students can then follow this personalized exercise prescription to develop and maintain a high level of fitness.

WELLNESS AND FITNESS PROGRAMS IN ACTION

Throughout the country, many dedicated physical education teachers are involved in conducting exemplary fitness and wellness programs. Examples of these programs are presented in this section. Included are examples of comprehensive fitness and wellness programs, programs designed to promote self-responsibility and enhancement of the student's self-concept, the use of a physical education learning center, conceptual approaches to secondary school physical education, and wellness and fitness units.

These programs are presented to illustrate different approaches to the development of fitness and wellness and to provide a starting point for physical education teachers charged with developing or modifying fitness and wellness programs within their schools. Each teacher must assess these programs in terms of situational constraints within the school, the physical education program, program objectives, personal preferences and philosophy, and the needs of the students.

◆ Physical Education: Being and Becoming
(New Trier Township High School, Winnetka, IL)

Attainment of optimal wellness requires that individuals develop decision-making skills and assume responsibility for their own health. As students move toward adulthood, they need to accept more responsibility for their own wellness and fitness. Students should move from dependence on teachers and parents to independence and self-responsibility. This shift should be progressive in nature, with students undertaking more responsibility as they gain in knowledge and maturity.

These important qualities of student growth, decision making, and self-responsibility are emphasized in the

---

TABLE 18-1

New Trier High School Physical Education Curriculum: Being and Becoming

Quarter			
1	2	3	4

Freshman

A = Exercise foundations	A = Gymnastics/I can cope	A = Basketball/swimming	A = Soccer/badminton
B = Exercise foundations	B = Gymnastics/swimming	B = Basketball/I can cope	B = Soccer/badminton
C = Exercise foundations	C = I can cope/gymnastics	C = Swimming/basketball	C = Badminton/soccer
D = Exercise foundations	D = Swimming/gymnastics	D = I can cope/basketball	D = Badminton/soccer
	A = Wrestling/I can cope	A = Gymnastics/swimming	A = Lacrosse/badminton
	B = Wrestling/Swimming	B = Gymnastics/I can cope	B = Lacrosse/badminton
	C = I can cope/wrestling	C = Swimming/gymnastics	C = Badminton/lacrosse
	D = Swimming/wrestling	D = I can cope/gymnastics	D = Badminton/lacrosse

←———————————————— Physical education special opportunity class ————————————————→

Sophomore

A = Healthful living	A = Weight training/aerobic fitness	A = Volleyball/team handball	A = Swimming/soccer
B = Healthful living	B = Weight training/aerobic fitness	B = Team handball/volleyball	B = Soccer/swimming
C = Healthful living	C = Volleyball/team handball	C = Weight training/aerobic fitness	C = Healthful living
D = Healthful living	D = Team handball volleyball	D = Weight training/aerobic fitness	D = Healthful living

←———————————————— Physical education special opportunity class ————————————————→

Junior/Senior

Tennis/badminton	Volleyball/conditioning	Volleyball/conditioning	Team sport/tennis
Badminton/tennis	Lifeline	Lifeline	Tennis/badminton
Lifeline	Aerobic dance	Aerobic dance	Lifeline
Speedaway/football	Court sports	Court sports	Speedaway/softball
Football/speedaway	Advanced weight training/aerobics	Advanced weight training/aerobics	Softball/speedaway
	Basketball	Basketball	

←———————————————— Physical education special opportunity class ————————————————→

Courtesy of New Trier Township High School, Winnetka, IL.

New Trier Township High School physical education curriculum (Table 18-1).[2] This curriculum combines a traditional approach to the development of skills, knowledge, and appreciation of and for many popular sports activities engaged in during leisure time, with health education. It incorporates the teaching of decision-making skills and promotes the assumption of responsibility for one's lifestyle.

The theme of the physical education curriculum is *Physical Education: Being and Becoming.* Curricular subthemes assigned to each of the 4 years reflect the progressive development of knowledge and skills and the shift from exploration to independence and self-control. The theme for the freshman year is entitled *The Inner and Outer Me,* and the theme for the sophomore year is *Decisions on the Way.* The shift toward assumption of one's own responsibility for wellness and fitness is reflected in the junior and senior years' theme, *The Responsibility is Mine.*

Physical education and health education are combined in the New Trier program. Freshman students begin their wellness and fitness education through enrollment in a 10-week unit entitled *Exercise Foundations.* Objectives for the unit include understanding of basic movement fundamentals and principles and their application to appropriate activities, ability to distinguish between aerobic and anaerobic activities, attainment of a degree of proficiency in aerobics and weight training, and identification of sound nutritional practices and their effects on human growth and activity.

The introductory course is followed by a unit entitled *I Can Cope With . . .".* This unit emphasizes recognition of factors that can influence mental health and the application of their factors to the student's life. Students receive information about drugs and chemical use that lead to dependency, acquire decision-making skills and problem-solving techniques, and learn how to evaluate their individual lifestyle choices.

Healthful Living, a unit taken in the sophomore year, focuses on the development of positive interpersonal relationships and understanding the anatomy and physiology of the human reproductive system as it relates to health and disease. By building on information presented during the freshman year, decision-making, problem-solving, and lifestyle choices are further discussed and explored. Additionally, students enroll in a unit on weight training and aerobic fitness.

During the junior and senior years, students build on their earlier foundations in wellness and fitness. As part of the *LifeLine* unit, students are required to demonstrate proficiency in various aerobic activities, reflect commitment to aerobic exercises as illustrated by daily participation, and engage in a variety of laboratory experiences related to fitness. Additionally, students learn about the role of physical activity in the management of stress, weight, and a variety of cardiovascular conditions. Furthermore, students learn and participate in a variety of relaxation techniques. The synergistic effect of wellness

components is emphasized, and personal decision making in regard to individual lifestyle choices is stressed as a function of responsible citizenship.

Students also enroll in units on advanced weight training techniques, aerobic conditioning, and aerobic dance during these years. These units emphasize not only fitness and skill development, but also the acquisition of knowledge. Students gain experience in designing personal exercise programs and applying fitness concepts to various physical activities.

In addition to the emphasis on fitness and wellness throughout the high-school years, students receive instruction in traditional team sports activities as well as individual and lifetime sports activities. These units of instruction emphasize skill development and acquisition of knowledge. For each activity, the instructors seek to help students relate their knowledge of fundamental movements to other activities they learn. Furthermore, for each activity its potential contribution to the overall fitness and wellness of the individual is analyzed and discussed.

Students who require additional instruction in physical education to meet their special needs are accommodated in a special course entitled *Physical Education Special Opportunity Class* (PESO). This course is offered every quarter.

The New Trier physical education program reflects an integrated physical education and health education program. Multidimensional and progressive in nature, this program emphasizes the acquisition of skills, knowledge, and attitudes necessary to attain an optimal level of wellness and fitness. Moreover, it emphasizes student growth and assumption of self-responsibility.

◆ The New Design in Secondary Physical Education (Prospect High School, Mt. Prospect, IL)

The New Design in Secondary Physical Education program emphasizes the physical, mental, social, and emotional development of students.[3] This well-balanced, comprehensive program strives to prepare students for a lifetime of participation in physical activities that sustain personal fitness (Table 18-2). This program focuses on the development of a high level of personal fitness and knowledge pertaining to fitness concepts. Knowledge and understanding of basic movement concepts and acquisition of skills in a variety of lifetime activities are equally important outcomes. Development of socialization skills and a healthy competitive spirit are also emphasized.

Frequent evaluation of fitness components is included in the program. Students are tested five times a year, using a battery of eight tests: 1-mile/12-minute run, sit-ups, grip dynamometer, sit-and-reach, standing long jump, shuttle run, ball toss, and soccer dribble. Students are tested on all eight items at the beginning and the end of each year. They are tested on four fitness items (1-mile/

TABLE 18-2

Mt. Prospect High School Physical Education Curriculum: The New Design in Secondary Physical Education

	Freshman 851	High 891	Medium High 892	Medium 893	Low 894
Unit 1 8/26-9/26 23 days	Fitness concepts Fitness testing Cross country	Fitness concepts Fitness testing Flickerball (8) Rugby (2)	Fitness concepts Fitness testing Touch football	Fitness concepts Fitness testing Touch football	Fitness concepts Fitness testing Cycling Jogging
Unit 2 9/29-10/31 23 days	Cross country Soccer Speedball	Touch football (8) Rugby Flickerball (2)	Tennis	Badminton Weight training	Cycling Jogging Speedball
Unit 3 11/3-12/5 21 days	Basketball (8) Weight training Conditioning (2)	Power volleyball	Team handball Indoor soccer	Floor hockey	Weight training Aerobics
Unit 4 12/8-1/23 22 days	Basketball (2) Conditioning Weight training (8) Circuits	Basketball (1) Team handball (9) Indoor soccer	Power volleyball	Cross country Skiing Circuits Basketball	Floor hockey
Unit 5 1/27-2/25 21 days	Power volleyball	Basketball (8) Team handball (2)	Floor hockey Weight training	Power volleyball	Cross country Skiing Team handball Circuits
Unit 6 2/26-3/27 20 days	Square dance	Floor hockey Weight training	Basketball	Team handball Indoor soccer	Volleyball Lifelines
3/23-4/10	Fitness testing	Fitness testing	Fitness testing	Fitness testing	Fitness testing
Unit 7 3/30-5/8 24 days	Track & field	Floor hockey Weight training	Golf Softball	Tennis Aerobics	Pickleball Rope jumping
Unit 8 5/11-6/12 22 days	Badminton Softball	Tennis Paddle tennis Softball	Softball Weight training	Golf Softball	Softball Roller skating

Courtesy of Mt. Prospect High School, Mt. Prospect, IL.

12-minute run, sit-ups, grip dynamometer, and sit-and-reach) at the end of each quarter. The improvement the student makes on these four fitness items is incorporated into the student's grade for the marking period. The use of microcomputers facilitates the testing process, allowing rapid calculation of each student's cumulative score, determination of the student's status relative to national norms and the rest of the class, and production of a fitness report for each student. Parents are sent a letter explaining the program at the beginning of the school year and a report of their child's score twice a year, once at the beginning and again at the end of the school year.

Students in grades 10 to 12 are grouped for physical education class on the basis of their cumulative score on the test battery. The counseling department schedules students according to this score, just as they would schedule students into other academic classes. Students may advance to another group only at the beginning of the semester.

The homogeneous grouping of students provides a teaching environment in which the curriculum and instructional techniques can be tailored better to the specific needs of individual students. Four ability groups are used: high performance, medium high performance, medium performance, and low performance. Learner outcomes are identified specifically for each of the ability groups.

Freshman students receive an orientation to the physical education program and learn about the various types and the value of fitness. They also work to develop movement skills in a variety of sports activities.

In grades 10 to 12, the curriculum, program objectives, and specific course content vary according to the level of fitness. Students with a low level of achievement concentrate on the improvement of physical fitness and basic motor skills. Improvement of students' attitude toward fitness and physical activity and an appreciation of the value of fitness physical activity are emphasized. Students learn how to develop a personal prescription for a fitness

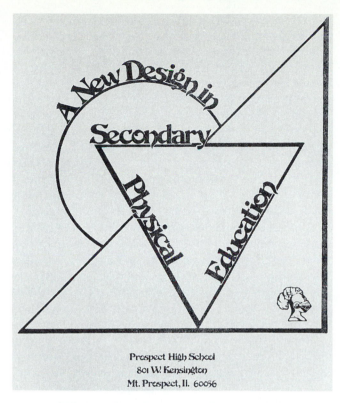

Courtesy of Sandy Pifer, Prospect High School, Mt. Prospect, IL.

lifestyle and strive for self-improvement. Students with a medium level of achievement work on the improvement of their fitness and motor abilities and the design of an individual exercise prescription. Additionally, these students learn intermediate movement skills and develop a healthy, competitive spirit. Students who score high in fitness concentrate maintaining these high levels and designing personal programs to accomplish this objective. Intermediate movement skills are refined and integrated into more advanced movement skills.

All students, regardless of fitness level, gain skills, knowledge, and appreciation for a wide variety of team and individual sports, many of which are lifetime in nature. Students are also exposed to many different types of fitness activities, providing them with the opportunity to select those that best fit their needs and interests.

Prospect High School's *The New Design in Secondary Physical Education* program has been successful in improving the fitness level and skill abilities, knowledge, and attitudes of their students. Fitness development and testing are an integral part of the total physical education program. Homogeneous grouping and cooperation by the administration in scheduling students into appropriate classes and program and instructional techniques designed to meet students' needs have led to a physical education program that makes a difference in the lives of the students.

◆ Ultra Physical Education (Tilford Middle School, Vinton, IA)

The development of each student's self-concept is the focus of the *Ultra Physical Education* program at Tilford Middle School.[47] The student's self-concept is developed through four avenues: mental development, skill awareness and improvement, emotional and social development, and health development. Classes are structured to provide a climate for achievement of success by all students. Program goals include acquisition of knowledge pertaining to principles of fitness and achievement of an average or above average level of health-related fitness; full participation and improvement by each student in the 18 physical activities presented; knowledge and application of wellness concepts to each student's lifestyle; and development of positive attitudes, as reflected in students' acceptance of differences in others and encouragement of others' efforts (Fig. 18-1).

CURRICULUM

Activities/Units	Positive Living Skill
Soccer	Releases for stress
Flag football	Cooperation
*Individual fitness assessment	Lifestyle awareness
Power volleyball	Responsibility
Badminton	Focus/concentration
Table tennis	Strategy alternatives
Shuffleboard	Interaction
Team handball	Acceptance
Cross-country skiing	Confidence
Basketball	Motion
Wrestling (boys only)	Independence
Gravionics	Relaxation
Tennis	Planning ahead
Golf	Balance/patience
Archery	Precision
Softball	Contributions/you
Aerobic dance	Expression
Outdoor recreation	Positive/peace

(Units last from 2 to 4 weeks)

1. Cardiorespiratory (ergometer/heart monitor)
2. Pre-exercise heart rate (quantum heart monitor)
3. Recovery heart rate (quantum heart monitor)
4. Blood pressure (digital sphygmomanometer)
5. Lung volume (spirometer)
6. Body fat percent (skin calipers)
7. Posture efficiency (Martin posture assessment)
8. Stress awareness (biofeedback—electromyograph)

*Individual fitness assessment—Fall and Spring.

FIG. 18-1 Tilford Middle School physical education curriculum: ultra physical education.

Courtesy of Tilford Middle School, Vinton, IA.

These goals are accomplished by dividing the 48-minute class period into two segments: a wellness segment and an activity segment. The wellness segment focuses on health development. At the beginning of the class, students participate in gravionics, while the teacher takes attendance. Gravionics are a series of exercises that focus on flexibility and balancing agonist and antagonist muscles; these exercises take the students through six postures, including postures that work to offset the effects of gravity. During this portion of the class, there is a 2-minute mini-lecture during which the concept of the day is presented. Over 100 different concepts are covered during the school year, ranging from principles of fitness to positive thinking to stress reduction. Students are also introduced to the muscle of the week. By the time these students complete 3 years of middle school, they will have learned over 100 muscle groups. A 9-minute aerobic exercise period is next, followed by a 1-minute cool-down and a pulse check.

The activity segment of the class lasts 21 minutes and emphasizes effort and participation throughout each of the 18 different activity units. Typically, skills are developed in the first half of each unit, and the remaining time is devoted to game play. Students also become familiar with the rules governing the activity, because each student is required to serve as an official during game play. Serving as a referee allows students to apply rules and develop an appreciation for sportsmanship. Positive living skills are also incorporated into this segment of the class. Through physical activities, students learn such living skills as listening, concentration, and investing in oneself.

The ultra shuffle is used during this segment of the class. The ultra shuffle is a system by which students rotate to different stations as they complete specified activities at each station. Students move from skill development stations to a cognitive station, where they complete a worksheet on scoring and rules, skill techniques, safety, and fitness and wellness concepts. Students also substitute in and out of the several mini-games that are being played, without time being called. Consequently, team composition changes randomly, and students learn to play with and accept each other. No scores are kept for the games; participation and skill development are the focus. As part of the rotation scheme, students also serve as referees. Because the students move at their own pace and take responsibility for their behavior, the teacher is free to provide individual help as needed. All of these activities enhance social and emotional growth while accomplishing the objective of skill development.

Computer technology is employed as an instructional aid for assessment and for record keeping. Each day six students in the class use microcomputer heart rate monitors. These visually display the heart rate and emit an auditory signal that allows the student to readily monitor whether the heart rate is within the training zone. The memory recall function interfaced with a microcomputer allows heart rate data to be recalled and a computer printout of heart rate activity to be generated during class. The teacher and student can use this data to monitor the contribution of each class activity to cardiovascular fitness. Heart rate monitors also help reinforce fitness concepts presented, such as maintaining the heart rate within the target zone to achieve a training effect. These monitors serve an important safety function as well, allowing the student and teacher to ensure that the students exercise within the appropriate range for their own physical condition. The use of these monitors is rotated throughout the class. Computerized running shoes also allow students to monitor their workload during exercise.

A microcomputer electromyograph (EMG) biofeedback machine allows students to become aware of their own level of muscle tension and to learn how to reduce this tension to more acceptable levels. The heart rate monitors can also be used to help students become aware of their levels of stress and practice various strategies to reduce their levels of physiological arousal.

Record keeping is facilitated with the use of the microcomputer. Results of fitness tests can be readily analyzed. It is also used to print student reports.

Each student's fitness level is assessed in the fall and spring of the school year. Cardiovascular endurance is assessed through the use of the Astrand Condition One Step Test using an ergometer and heart rate monitor. Preexercise heart rates and recovery heart rates are also recorded. A digital sphygmomanometer expedites the assessment of blood pressure, and digital skinfold calipers are used as part of the assessment process to determine the percentage of body fat. Lung volume is measured using a spirometer. Posture efficiency is determined by employing the Martin posture assessment instrument. Students' awareness of and their ability to control their muscle tension is assessed through the utilization of the EMG biofeedback instrument.

Ultra Physical Education offers a comprehensive approach to wellness and activity development. By providing a climate for success, teachers help students to achieve their fullest potential and develop the skills, knowledge, and positive attitudes necessary for lifelong fitness and health.

◆ Physical/Motor Fitness Learning Center
(Rock Springs High School, Rock Springs, WY)

Students at Rock Springs High School are involved in a fitness-based curriculum that utilizes a variety of laboratory experiences to teach fitness and wellness concepts.[5] The *Physical/Motor Fitness Learning Center* at the school houses a vast array of sophisticated exercise equipment.

Equipment within the learning center includes a motorized treadmill with a metabolic measurement cart and a computerized body composition analyzer. Students work out using bicycle ergometers, a cross-country ski

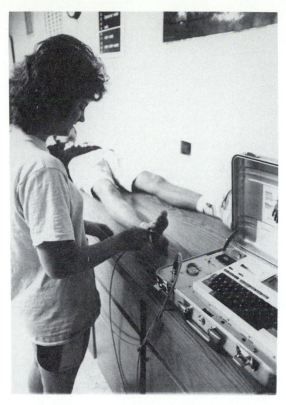

Student uses computerized bioelectrical body composition analyzer at Rock Springs High School, Rock Springs, WY.
Courtesy of Paul Grube, Rock Springs High School, Rock Springs, WY.

machine, and a rowing machine. Computerized heart rate monitors allow students to readily monitor their heart rates. A digital grip dynamometer and skinfold calipers, including an electronic caliper, facilitate the assessment of various fitness measures. An Apple IIe computer is utilized as part of the fitness assessment process and to expedite record keeping and reporting of fitness results.

It is important that physical education teachers be aware of how all this equipment was obtained. Initially, after the submission of budgetary requests and rationales by teachers for all this equipment, only enough money was approved to purchase the computerized bioelectrical body composition analyzer. This machine was used as part of an extensive public relations effort to secure parental, administrative, and community support for funds to purchase the rest of the desired equipment. As part of this effort, the computerized body composition analyzer was used to analyze the body composition of all students within the physical education classes, and this information was sent home to students' parents along with a letter explaining the body composition profile (Fig. 18-2). Each profile detailed information about the student's body composition—percent body water, lean body weight, and fat and weight, calorie, and exercise recommendations.

To engender support from the administration and the community, physical education teachers took it upon themselves to speak to the school administration and numerous community groups about fitness and wellness. These talks included information about the contribution of fitness to a healthy lifestyle, fitness principles, and the importance of fitness and wellness education in the schools. As part of these talks, the computerized body composition analyzer was used to provide audience members with assessments of their body compositions. Not only were these talks helpful in informing the school administration and community members about the value of physical education, but the individual body composition profiles also created a great deal of enthusiasm about fitness. This administrative and community support resulted in money being found within the school budget for the *Physical/Motor Fitness Learning Center*. Space was initially a problem, but physical education teachers volunteered to work during the summer to build the center from a storage room. Hard work, strong public relations efforts, and dedication by the teachers reaped dividends for the physical education program and its students.

Within the learning center, students participate in a variety of mini-laboratory experiences designed to enhance their understanding of various fitness principles. Students also engage in a variety of fitness development activities, such as using the rowing machine, ergometers, and cross-country ski machine. Heart rate monitors are used by students to monitor the intensity of their training. Students can also work on improving muscular strength and endurance using different training approaches. Workout videotapes, tailor-made for these high-school students and produced by fitness instructors at a local health club, are used also in the program.

Frequent assessment and screening are integral components of this program. Health-related fitness components are evaluated periodically. Students take an active role in the administration of fitness tests, computing the data, and interpreting the results. In addition to the traditional ways of measuring these components, more sophisticated tests are used. As previously mentioned, the computerized body composition analyzer is used to compute the percentage of body fat. Additionally, students have the option of taking a submaximal oxygen consumption test.

The submaximal oxygen test is one of the most accurate methods that can be used to measure cardiovascular endurance. Physical education teachers received training for the administration of the test from faculty at the University of Wyoming. Members of the Rock Springs physical education faculty also spent time during the summer at the university's exercise physiology labs, which further familiarized them with the administration of the submaximal test. Parents are sent a letter explaining the test, and the parents and the student must sign an informed

BODY COMPOSITION PROFILE

Rock Springs Physical Education

April 22, 1988
9:17 AM

Kevin

Sex: male
Height: 63.0 in
Resistance: 430 ohms
Reactance: 69 ohms

Age: 15
Weight: 145.0 lbs
Activity level: moderate

Body composition calculations:

Percent body water: 63%
Total body water: 41 L

The average range of water for a male is 55% to 65%. The amount of water in your body is determined by the dominant tissue type. Lean tissue is generally 71% to 75% water, while fat tissue is generally 14% to 22% water.

Percent lean: 84%
Lean body weight: 122 lb

The normal range of percent lean for a 15-year-old male in good physical condition is 84% to 88%. The normal range of lean weight for a male of 15 years and 145 lb is from 122 to 128 lb. Your lean to fat ratio of 5.3 can be used as a convenient index of your body composition. A value of 6.1 or higher is desirable for you.

Percent fat: 16%
Fat weight: 23 lb

The normal range of percent fat for a 15-year-old male in good physical condition is 12% to 16%. The normal range of fat weight for a male of 15 years and 145 lb is from 17 to 23 lb. Your body fat is within the average for a male of your age.

Weight recommendations

Your optimal weight is 141 to 149 lb. Your weight is above the average for a male of your height. Should you wish to further increase your lean body mass, a regular exercise and nutrition program should be maintained.

Caloric recommendations

Based on your age, sex, and lean body mass, your estimated basal metabolism is 1721 kcal. This is the minimum number of calories needed to maintain your lean body mass. Calories expended by daily activity (about 344 to 516) and exercise (see chart below) must be added to this amount to maintain lean mass.

Your body composition is within the normal limits for your age and sex.

Exercise recommendations

Aerobic exercises should be done at least 3 days per week, a minimum of 20 minutes per session, and at a minimum intensity level of 60% to 80% of your maximum heart rate. In your case, your training heart rate zone is 123 to 164 beats per minute. Regular exercise will promote optimal body composition (proportionate fat and lean mass).

| | | | | Time in minutes | | | | | |
Exercise	10	20	30	40	50	60	80	90	120
				(Calories expended based on your weight)					
Sitting	14	28	41	55	69	83	110	124	166
Walking (15-17 min/mile)	53	105	158	210	263	316	421	473	631
Jogging (10-12 min/mile)	108	216	324	431	539	647	863	971	1294
Running (9 min/mile)	127	254	381	508	635	761	1015	1142	1523
Swimming (breast stroke)	107	213	320	426	533	639	852	959	1278
Cycling (9.4 mph)	66	132	197	263	329	395	526	592	789
Basketball	91	181	272	363	454	544	726	817	1089
Racquetball	115	230	345	460	575	690	921	1036	1381
Weight training circuit	73	146	219	292	365	438	584	657	876
Gardening	61	121	182	243	303	364	486	546	728
Aerobics (continuous)	112	224	335	447	559	671	894	1006	1341
Tennis (continuous)	72	143	215	287	358	430	573	645	860
Golf (carrying bag)	56	112	168	224	279	335	447	503	671
Skiing (moderate speed)	78	157	235	313	391	470	626	704	939
Football	87	174	260	347	434	521	694	781	1042
Soccer	88	176	264	352	441	529	705	793	1057

This or any other exercise/nutrition program should not be undertaken without the advice of your health care professional.

FIG. 18-2 Body composition profile for high-school student.
Courtesy of Rock Springs High School, Rock Springs, WY.

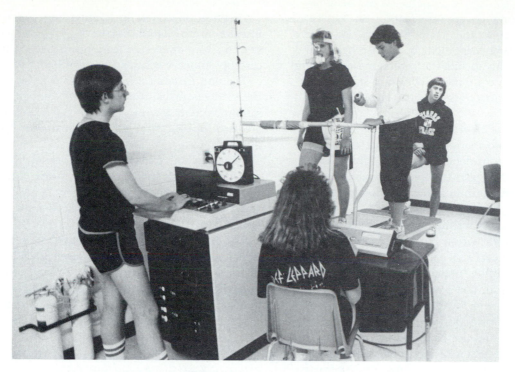

Students perform an exercise test to assess cardiovascular endurance.
Courtesy of Paul Grube, Rock Springs High School, Rock Springs, WY.

consent form. Students take an active role in the administration of the test, such as monitoring the various physiological functions, under the supervision of the instructor.

The use of physical education learning centers offers exciting directions for fitness and wellness education in the public schools. The incorporation of the learning center into the school physical education program provides students with opportunities to understand more fully the principles of fitness as well as to be able to apply them to their personal exercise programs.

◆ Fitness for Life: A Conceptual Approach (Westside High School, Omaha, NE)

Fitness for Life: A Conceptual Approach is the focus of the secondary school physical education at Westside High School.[6] This program reflects the integration of health fitness concepts within the physical education curriculum. The program for students in grades 9 and 10 consists of broad-based health concepts and a physical activity approach. Students in grades 11 and 12 can elect classes in advanced health concepts and leisure time activity courses.

Students meet for two 80-minute activity periods and one 40-minute health concepts class each week. The 80-minute classes are divided into three phases. During the first 5 to 10 minutes of class, students engage in various stretching exercises. The aerobic activity phase, 15 to 20 minutes, follows this stretching period. A variety of aerobic activities such as group calisthenics, aerobic dance, run-walk-jog, rope jumping, and cycling are included in this phase. The last phase of class is devoted to instruction and participation opportunities in a variety of physical activities. These activities include volleyball, strength training, badminton, wrestling, basketball, pickleball, floor hockey, team handball, and swimming.

Students receive instruction in health fitness during the 40-minute class period. Various teaching approaches, such as lecture, small group discussion, multimedia, and guest lectures, are used to present this information to the students. Four units are offered: *Cardiovascular Fitness, Positive Healthy Lifestyles I, Positive Healthy Lifestyles II,* and *Neuromuscular Fitness.*

Cardiovascular Fitness is a 4- to 6-week unit. Discussions within this unit emphasize basic anatomical and physiological information, disease and risk factor analysis, and target zone exercise theory. Laboratory experiences, such as an analysis of blood pressure during rest and following exercise, allow students to relate concepts discussed to actual practice.

Positive Healthy Lifestyles I is an 8- to 10-week unit. The importance of chemical dependency awareness, appropriate knowledge of nutritional concepts, and learning alternatives to life's pressures are the topics emphasized.

The next unit, *Positive Healthy Lifestyles II,* is a 6- to 8-

week unit. This unit covers information on skin care, communicable diseases, and AIDS. Students also receive information that will help them be a wise health and fitness consumer. This includes information on selecting appropriate exercise equipment, choosing suitable exercise attire, and factors to consider when choosing a health or fitness center.

The *Neuromuscular Fitness* unit lasts for 4 to 6 weeks. Within this unit, information on muscular and skeletal structure, postural considerations, and flexibility is presented. The use of a physiograph helps students further understand muscle function through simple EMG analysis.

Health-related fitness testing is incorporated into the overall program. Information is gathered on percentage of body fat, resting heart rate, grip strength, sit-ups, push-ups, hamstring flexibility, upper back and trunk flexibility, 1-mile run, height, and weight.

Microcomputers serve several functions in this program. They store information on each student's performance on the various test items and can provide students with a printout of their test results, which also expedites the calculation of district fitness norms. This normative information is then used as a basis for the development of individual exercise programs that will accentuate aerobic fitness, strength and endurance exercises, and stress reducers as part of the comprehensive wellness package. Construction of these individualized exercise programs is facilitated by the use of the microcomputer.

Elective classes for the upper secondary grades are designed to further students' involvement in physical education. Students can enroll in courses in many different activity areas, including exercise science, certification in safety, and leisure living.

The exercise science course provides opportunities for the advanced study of anatomical, physiological, and psychological principles of exercise. Students can take this course on an independent study basis.

Certification classes in lifeguarding and water safety instruction are offered. As part of a personal safety course, students can attain certification in standard first aid and cardiopulmonary resuscitation (CPR).

The unit *Leisure Living* has proved to be popular with the students. This class meets off campus for two 80-minute periods a week. Commercial recreation facilities are used for courses in golf, volleyball, bowling, and racquetball.

Departmental activities also promote fitness for life. The department sponsors such fitness events as *Jump Rope for Heart*, student poster projects on various topics such as nutrition and cardiovascular disease, and a school health fair.

The conceptual approach to health fitness in conjunction with opportunities to develop fitness and skills in physical activities contributes to the total educational development of Westside High School students. These students develop the skills, knowledge, and attitudes essential to lifelong participation in physical activity.

◆ Physical Education, Sport, and Wellness: A Comprehensive Approach (West Hartford Public Schools, West Hartford, CT)

The West Hartford Public Schools secondary school physical education curriculum is comprehensive in its approach (Fig. 18-3).[7] Students develop skills and knowledge in a wide range of activities, with the instructional emphasis on promoting positive social interaction, fun, and success through movement. Students acquire competencies in several lifetime sports skills, allowing them to choose the activities that meet their needs and their ability levels.

Physical education teachers strive to promote within each student a positive attitude toward physical fitness. Students' fitness levels are assessed periodically, and this information is used to establish personal fitness goals.

Team	Individual/Dual	Fitness/Wellness	Wednesday Series (Grades 9 and 10)
Basketball	Archery	Fitness assessment	Cardiovascular fitness
Field hockey	Badminton	Physical fitness	Stress reduction
Floor hockey	Cycling	Weight training	First aid
Football—flag/touch	Dance fundamentals	Aerobics	Sports series/sportsmanship
Hockey	Fencing	Yoga	
Lacrosse	Golf	CPR/First aid	
Speedball/speedaway	Gymnastics	Sports medicine	
Soccer	Jogging		
Team handball	Project adventure		
Ultimate frisbee	Tennis		
Volleyball	Skiing		
	Outdoor education		

FIG. 18-3 West Hartford secondary school physical education and sport curriculum: course offerings.

SECONDARY SCHOOL PHYSICAL EDUCATION AND SPORT CURRICULUM

Grades 7-12

West Hartford Public Schools/West Hartford, Connecticut

Courtesy of Suzi D'Annalfo, Conard High School, West Hartford, CT.

Students learn appropriate, safe techniques for developing and maintaining fitness throughout their lifetime.

Fitness and wellness education is an important aspect of the total school physical education curriculum. Students receive instruction in fitness and wellness as part of an integrated elementary school program, starting at the first grade. At the secondary level, teachers strive to further students' skills, knowledge, and values in this important area.

Within the secondary school physical education program, students have the opportunity to develop and maintain high levels of personal fitness. Units on personal fitness are offered as part of the core program for 9th and 10th grade students and as part of the elective program for 11th and 12th grade students. These units emphasize awareness of the individual components of personal fitness, learning to establish personal goals for lifetime fitness, and understanding of the importance of the training factors of frequency, intensity, and duration for the success of any personal fitness program. Students are exposed to a variety of activities designed to develop the various fitness components and learn how to design appropriate exercise programs. The potential contribution of various sport activities to fitness development is discussed, and students learn how activities can be modified to further enhance their fitness potential. Mini-laboratory experiences allow students to investigate the application of fitness concepts to a variety of physical activities. Students learn how to measure and assess their fitness status and how to monitor their progress. This includes information on how to measure and interpret their resting, working, and recovery heart rate. Knowledge tests help teachers assess students' mastery of the fitness concepts. Students are also required to keep a fitness log in which they record their fitness activities within and outside of school.

In addition to a unit on personal fitness, students have the opportunity to enroll in units on weight training and aerobics. Fitness testing is conducted periodically throughout the school year to monitor student progress and help students set appropriate fitness goals.

Wellness is also an integral part of the curriculum. Students in grades 9 and 10 take in a special series of wellness courses entitled *The Wednesday Series*, named after the day on which they are offered. These courses focus on cardiovascular fitness, stress reduction, first aid, and sportsmanship.

Students in all grades have the opportunity to receive additional instruction in the wellness area. For example, students can elect to enroll in a unit on yoga. Within this unit, students explore the tenets and philosophy underlying the practice of yoga and learn basic yoga techniques—movements, postures, and controlled breathing are practiced. As part of this unit, students also receive instruction in progressive relaxation. A series of progressive relaxation exercises increases students' awareness of their own levels of muscle tension. In a systematic fashion, muscles are isolated and contracted, with the tension then being slowly released. These experiences help students become more aware of the difference between muscle tension and relaxation. This awareness helps students more readily discern when they are experiencing stress and associated high levels of muscle tension. Students can then use various relaxation techniques to reduce their levels of arousal.

As part of wellness education, students also receive training in first aid and learn cardiopulmonary resuscitation (CPR). These skills in conjunction with safety techniques presented as part of every sports unit prepare students to deal with injuries and emergencies that they may encounter. Sports medicine as a career choice is also discussed with students.

This comprehensive secondary school curriculum prepares students for a lifetime of physical activity by teaching them various sports skills, while developing positive attitudes toward participation and promoting understanding of various sports activities. Additionally, students learn how to develop and maintain a satisfactory level of personal fitness, construct a personal exercise program, and value the contribution of fitness to their well-being.

Students use Par Cours at Mahar Regional High School, MA.
Courtesy of Kathy Pinkham.

◆ **Par Cours** (Mahar Regional High School, Orange, MA)

Students at the Mahar Regional High School improve their fitness levels by using the *Par Cours* program. This par cours is built on the school grounds.[8] A par cours is a series of stations set around a jogging course. At each station students perform a specified number of exercises and then jog to the next station. An instruction board at each station provides guidelines and directions for the performance of the exercises. Often, different levels of ability are provided for at each station. Heart rate checks are interspersed throughout the course. The circuit may be completed once or several times, depending on the individual's needs and the time available. Following a warm-up period, students are divided into small groups, and each group is assigned to start at different stations. This reduces congestion at the start of the par cours and allows all students the opportunity to complete the course. Once students begin, they can move at their own pace from station to station.

If a school does not have a par cours facility, one can be built rather inexpensively if volunteers are used to build the course. As part of a physical education project, students can design the par cours keeping in mind the specific training requirements for fitness development. Design specifications should include the total distance of the course, number of stations, distance of each station from the previous station and layout of the stations, degree of emphasis given to each fitness component, specific exercises and number of repetitions to be completed at each station, provision for multiple levels of ability, and so on. Cooperation from other curricular areas within the school can be helpful in completing the project. Industrial design class students can be involved in the construction of the exercise equipment placed at each station (such as pull-up bars). Students in art classes can use their talents to illustrate the exercise charts at each station, for example, drawing a picture of how an exercise is properly performed, printing directions for each exercise on the board, and producing maps of the course.

A par cours offers a different approach to the development of various fitness components. Cardiovascular endurance as well as other components of fitness are developed as students proceed through the circuit. A par cours can accommodate large numbers of students while allowing them to work out at their individual paces. Additionally, students enjoy this different approach to fitness development and like to work outdoors. Another benefit of the par cours is that students can use the par cours during their free period. School staff, faculty, and community members may also enjoy using the par cours for fitness development.

SUMMARY

Throughout the country, many different approaches to the incorporation of fitness and wellness education within the physical education curriculum can be found. These programs reflect the commitment of physical education teachers to providing their students with quality instruction leading to the development of skills, knowledge, and attitudes for lifelong participation in physical activity and attainment of high levels of fitness and wellness.

FOR REVIEW

1. Obtain a physical education curriculum from your high school. Examine the curriculum and determine its primary focus. How could the curriculum be modified to include greater emphasis on fitness? What are the consequences of these changes? Is the curriculum promoting lifetime participation in physical activities?
2. Obtain a science and a health curriculum for secondary schools. After reviewing the curriculum, identify how specific concepts presented in science and in health can be reinforced within the physical education program.
3. Select a specific sport. If you were teaching a 12-day unit, how could the unit be structured and activities be modified to increase the amount of physical activity experienced by the students during the unit?

REFERENCES

1. Koslow RE: Can physical fitness be a primary objective in a balanced physical education program? *JOPERD* 59(4):75-77, 1988.
2. Beach B: New Trier Township High School, Winnetka, Ill, 60093.
3. Pifer S: Prospect High School, Mt Prospect, Ill, 60056.
4. Kirkpatrick B: Tilford Middle School, Vinton, Iowa, 52349.
5. Grube P: Rock Springs High School, Rock Springs, Wyo, 82902.
6. Krecklow D: Westside High School, Omaha, Neb, 68124.
7. D'Annalfo S: West Hartford Public Schools, West Hartford, Conn, 06107.
8. Mahar Regional High School, Orange, Mass, 01355.

ANNOTATED READINGS

Koslow RE: Can physical fitness be a primary objective in a balanced physical education? *JOPERD* 59(4):75-77, 1988.
   The specific exercise science requirements for achieving fitness and whether fitness development is a realistic goal within a balanced program are discussed.
Smith TK, Cestaro N: Saving future generations—the role of physical education, *JOPERD* 63(8):75-79, 1992.
   Contains suggestions to integrate fitness development and concepts into a secondary school curriculum.

PART V

Teaching Activities

Sport, dance, and outdoor activities are an integral part of the physical education curriculum. Teachers should provide students with the opportunity to develop skills and competency in such activities. Physical education experiences that are thoughtfully designed and implemented in meaningful ways can promote desirable student development in the cognitive, affective, and psychomotor domains.

The chapters devoted to teaching individual, dual, team, and outdoor program components include a wide variety of activities. Included are knowledge, skills, teaching strategies, and safety concerns. Each section also addresses the pedagogical strategies and teaching points related to learning tasks for the development of skills, the provision of appropriate teaching cues, references for rules of the games, alternative lesson ideas and strategies (for those days when teaching stations may not be available), and information pertinent to the facilitation of timely and appropriate feedback, knowledge of result, and skill analysis to students.

OUTLINE

Team Sports

CHAPTER OBJECTIVES
- ◆ To review basic teaching points for teaching team sports
- ◆ To introduce the basic fundamental techniques used in various team sports
- ◆ To show how team sports can be adapted to meet the needs of students with varying skill levels
- ◆ To provide some ideas for modified games and activities to be used in team sports units

Team sports have traditionally been a part of secondary school physical education curricula. In some schools team sports have been the primary focus of the entire physical education curriculum. There is no doubt that team sports are an important part of our physical education curriculum in the secondary schools. There is some question, however, as to how much emphasis should be placed on team sports in the secondary school physical education program.

CONTRIBUTIONS

Team sports are familiar activities to most children. Through television and live games, they see highly skilled athletes perform skills with little effort and watch them engage in exciting competition. Many young children identify professional athletes as heroes or as supernatural beings and want to emulate their performances. What was once reserved only for boys is slowly becoming available to girls. Many young girls have and still do identify with male athletes. Although not nearly as common as viewing male athletes, young girls are beginning to see female athletes engaged in national competition on television. It is becoming more possible for young girls to identify with professional athletes of their own gender.

Parents are great advocates for team sports. Many parents purchase sporting equipment for their young children as gifts. In addition, parents enroll their children in recreation sports leagues or send them to summer sports camps to develop their skills. Many communities have

recreational athletic leagues for children, such as soccer leagues, little league baseball, and football leagues. Children who participate in these leagues come to physical education classes with more skills and experience in certain sports than others. Some may be fairly accomplished at certain sports, while others are exposed to team sports only in their physical education classes.

By the time students reach high school, they bring with them a wide range of skills, abilities, and experiences in various team sports. As a result of differences among high-school students, secondary physical education teachers should not assume that all high-school students are ready to participate in traditional team sports. On the contrary, much work is still left to do on the basic fundamentals (Box 19-1).

Basketball

General information. It should not be assumed that because students have reached high school, that they are proficient in all the skills required to play traditional competitive basketball. Basketball, played in its competitive form, is a highly complex activity that requires a wide range of skill proficiency on the part of individual players. In addition, it is a complex team sport that requires tremendous amounts of teamwork to execute appropriate offensive and defensive strategies.

High-school students will vary in their basketball skills in part because of the amount of exposure they have had to the sport. A typical physical education class will range

PLANNING CONSIDERATIONS FOR TEAM SPORTS

Before beginning a unit on any team sport, the teacher should consider the following six points:
1. Check students for abilities in the basic fundamental skills of the sport before putting them in to any type of competitive situation.
2. Teach basic fundamentals if they have not yet been learned.
3. Develop and implement strategies for sports units that will benefit students at all ability levels.
4. Instead of the traditional full games that limit the numbers of participants and require high levels of skill mastery, use mini-games, stations, and task cards designed to challenge all students at their own levels.
5. Vary your use of teaching styles to account for differences in learning styles.
6. Provide students with experiences that offer them opportunities to realize satisfaction and experience some level of success.

---

in skill level from students who play on the school's interscholastic basketball team to students who have managed to avoid the sport completely. Basketball can be a frustrating game for those who are expected to play in game situations with others whose ability levels are significantly different from theirs.

Fortunately, basketball is a game that can be appreciated and enjoyed by people with varying ability levels because it lends itself easily to modified games, such as one-on-one and two-on-two, and activities, such as shooting games like around the world, that can be used to challenge all individuals. Therefore it is important to develop classroom experiences in which all students, regardless of their ability levels or their familiarity with the sport, are encouraged to practice skills that will help them enjoy and improve their ability to play basketball. This may mean, with the exception of highly skilled classes, steering away from the traditional five-on-five full court game and moving toward modified half-court games and challenging drills with similarly skilled students.

Equipment and facilities. Basketball can be played on either an indoor or outdoor playing court with a smooth playing surface. A regulation court is 94 feet by 50 feet and is divided by a center line. At each end there is a marked area that designates the free-throw lanes. A semicircle around each free-throw lane marks the 3-point shooting line.

The backboards are usually made of plastic, glass,

wood, or some synthetic material and are usually rectangular (although some are fan shaped). The backboard is attached above the playing court (4 feet inbounds) at a height of 9 feet from the playing surface. The basket is attached to the backboard at a height of 10 feet from the playing surface. The basket is an 18-inch ring with a nylon or cotton net suspended from it to slow the ball as it comes down through the rim.

There are two official basketball sizes. Boys and men play with a ball with a circumference between 29½ and 30¼ inches. Girls and women play with a ball with a circumference between 28½ and 29 inches. Before 1984 men and women played with the same size ball. A smaller ball was introduced into womens' play because of the generally smaller size of their hands to enable them to have better control of the ball.

Game play. The game of basketball is played by two opposing teams. Points are scored by throwing the ball through the hoop at the opponents' end of the court while defenders attempt to prevent their opponents from scoring. The ball must be advanced by passing or dribbling while opponents attempt to intercept it.

Violations result in loss of possession of the ball. Examples of violations include taking steps while holding the ball, double dribble (dribbling the ball, carrying the ball, dribbling the ball again), stepping on or over a boundary line while in possession of the ball, and holding the ball for more than 5 seconds before passing while closely guarded.

Fouls result when personal contact is made between two opposing players. Examples include pushing, holding, blocking, and tripping. Fouls are penalized by allowing the opposing team free throws after certain conditions are met.

For every field goal made from inside the 3-point radius, 2 points are awarded. For every free throw made from the foul line, 1 point is awarded. For every field goal made from outside the 3-point radius, 3 points are awarded.

Adapting to meet students' needs. Because basketball requires the student to be proficient at a variety of different skills such as ball handling, passing, catching, shooting, rebounding, and defending, classes can be designed to focus specifically on individual skills. Modified games, drills, and activities can be created to challenge individual students' abilities to perform these skills.

Modified games can be played on smaller courts, on half courts, or under baskets that line the side of a gymnasium or that are available on playgrounds. Basketball skills can be practiced anywhere there is a smooth surface, such as a gymnasium, a multipurpose room, a recreation hall, a tennis court, or an outdoor parking lot. Passing skills, with the exception of the bounce pass, can even be practiced on grassy fields.

Baskets are not needed for practicing many of the skills in basketball. Shooting, however, is probably the most

One-handed set shot.
Courtesy of Ben Lombardo, Rhode Island College, Providence, RI.

exciting and the most popular skill for high-school students to practice. Baskets can be purchased that are adjustable in height. In addition, makeshift targets can be created for shooting practice (after all, the first known baskets were merely peach baskets adapted for the task).

Different balls can be used when one is practicing basketball skills. Changing the type of ball used by a student can add variation to the skill that can help challenge individuals at different skill levels. It is important to encourage your school to purchase enough equipment so that all students in a given class can practice their skills simultaneously if possible.

Design warm-up activities that are related to basketball using the court, hoops, and ball in some way, such as jog around the court or jog around the court dribbling; use the lines on the court to designate different skills in warm-up, such as defensive slides on end lines or crossover dribble on sidelines; shoot at the hoops practicing different shots; rebound the ball; and vary skills and patterns of movement.

Stations can be an effective way to work on individual skills. Design stations so that students can work independently or in small groups. Task cards or checklists may be useful ways to assign specific tasks. *Keep-away*

games may be used with or without the dribble. Assign two teams of equal numbers to match up in a person-to-person defense. The game starts with one team (offense) having the ball. Defensive players must try to prevent the offense from receiving a pass. Offensive players must free themselves to become open to receive a pass. Offensive and defensive teams change as the ball is intercepted.

Shooting games such as *Around the World, Out,* and *Twenty-one* are popular activities and can be challenging if groups are small and students are equally matched according to skill level.

Around the World

When playing *Around the World,* five specific shooting spots are designated around the key. The goal is to successfully complete 10 shots (beginning at spot 1 through 5 then coming back 5 through 1). Students begin at the first spot and attempt a shot. If the shot is made, they move to the next spot, and so on. If the shot is missed, they may either wait for their next turn or request a second attempt. If the second attempt is successful, they move on as before. If they miss the second attempt, they must go all the way back to the beginning.

Out

When playing *Out,* students line up and shoot in a specific order. The first student shoots. If the shot is successful, the next student in line must shoot from the same spot. If the second student's shot is successful, the third student in line must also shoot from the same spot. If the second student's shot is unsuccessful, he or she gets the first letter in the word *out* and the third student in line is free to shoot from anywhere on the court. Students are eliminated from the game when they have accumulated all three letters in the word *out.* The game continues until there is one student remaining in the game.

Twenty-one

Students line up and shoot in a specific order. The goal is to be the first to accumulate 21 points by shooting from two designated spots. The first shot is taken from behind the free-throw line (worth 2 points). Once one successful free throw has been made, a second shot, a lay-up can be taken (worth 1 point). Students continue to shoot until they miss. The first student to reach 21 points wins.

Sport-specific skills. See Box 19-2 for teaching tips for basketball.

Receiving

Move to the ball. Reach toward the ball with both hands. Elbows are flexed, fingers spread and relaxed. Fingers point down for balls anticipated to be received below the waist, and fingers point up for balls anticipated to be received above the waist. Watch the ball come into the hands. The ball is caught in the fingers. Cushion the impact by "giving with the ball." Gradually bring the ball into the body.

Passing

The *chest pass* is used for short, unobstructed distances. Assume the athletic stance. The ball is held in two hands slightly out in front of the chest. The elbows are close to the body, and the fingers are spread with the thumbs pointed inward. See the target (chest level of the receiver). The pass is initiated by stepping toward the receiver and pushing the ball away from the body. As the ball is released, snap the wrists, fingers, and hands. Exaggerate the follow-through. Hands should finish pointing at the target spot with palms facing out and thumbs pointing down.

The *two-handed bounce pass* is used for short passes when the high-level passing lane is being defended or when it is appropriate for a teammate to receive the ball at waist level. Assume the athletic stance. The ball is held in two hands slightly out in front of the abdomen. See the target (a designated spot on the floor about two thirds of the distance between the passer and the receiver). The pass

---

BOX 19-2
TEACHING TIPS FOR BASKETBALL

Receiving
Move to the ball
Ready hands (relaxed)
See the ball into the hands
Give with the ball

Passing
See target
Execute a precise "crisp" pass
Follow through to target

Dribbling
Assume the athletic stance
Fingers spread
Push the ball with the pads of the fingers
Relax with head up and eyes alert

Shooting
Balance
Eyes on target
Elbow under the ball
Follow through

Rebounding
Get into position slightly in front of the basket
Form a wide base of support for stability
Ready position for jumping—flexed ankles, knees, and hips
Elbows at shoulder level and arms and hands extended toward the basket
Jump up and pull the ball down in front of the head with elbows out to protect the ball

---

is initiated by stepping forward and pushing the ball to the floor (target spot). As the ball is released, snap the wrists, fingers, and hands. Exaggerate the follow-through as with the chest pass. Hands should finish pointing at the target spot with palms facing out and thumbs pointing down.

The *one-handed bounce pass* is used while one is on the move or to pass around a defender who is closely guarding the ball handler. Fingers of the passing hand are placed behind the ball. The nonpassing hand supports the front of the ball until it is in its ready position at the hip on the throwing-hand side. See the target. Once the ball is in the ready position, the nonshooting hand comes off the ball, and the throwing hand extends, pushing the ball toward the target. The throwing hand follows through to the target.

The *two-hand overhead pass* is used for short passes over the heads of the opponents. Assume the athletic stance.

The ball is held in the fingers of both hands. The fingers are spread with the thumbs behind and to the side of the ball. See the target (a spot slightly above the head of the receiver). The ball is brought back slightly behind the head. The elbows are flexed. The pass is initiated by stepping forward and extending both arms forcefully. Hands follow through to the target as the wrists and hands snap.

The *baseball pass* is used for long distances. The mechanics of the baseball pass resemble the overhand throw. The ball is held in the fingers and thumb of the throwing hand. The ball is brought back to about ear level, which initiates movement. As the ball is brought back, the body turns slightly so the hip of the nonthrowing side faces the receiver, and the weight is on the foot under the throwing arm. Step toward the receiver with the opposite foot. The elbow leads the throw. The wrist remains flexed until the final release. The throwing arm follows through in the direction of the throw and continues down across the body.

Dribbling

Dribbling is used to move the ball down the court. The fingers are spread, and the wrist, elbow, and shoulder are relaxed. The head is up with the eyes looking ahead. Push the ball to the floor with the pads of the fingers with a force that will make the ball bounce back at waist level.

Shooting

The *lay-up* shot is executed while moving and dribbling. The last step should be taken by the foot opposite the shooting hand. Stop the dribble while the shooting foot is on the floor. See the target (top inside corner of the square on the backboard just above the rim). Raise the shooting-side knee up toward the basket and jump off the nonshooting foot. Shift the ball to the shooting hand. Extend the shooting hand as high as possible and in front of the head. The ball is released from the finger tips with a slight snap of the wrist laying the ball softly against the target.

The *one-handed set shot* is a common technique used to shoot from the floor. Assume the athletic stance. The lead foot (same side as shooting hand) is slightly forward. The ball is held in the fingers of both hands with the shooting hand behind and slightly under the ball and the non-shooting hand to the side and slightly toward the bottom supporting the ball. The wrist of the shooting hand is cocked back. Ankles, knees, and hips are slightly flexed. The shot is initiated by extending from this flexed position while the ball is taken solely into the shooting hand. The shooting arm is extended forward and upward. Shooting hand follows through forward and upward with a snap or the wrist at the end of the full extension giving the ball a slight backspin.

The *foul shot* is the shot taken from the foul line. The one-handed set shot is executed from the foul line.

The *jump shot* is used to shoot above the reach of an opponent's block. The ball is held the same as in the previous two shots. The shooter stands square to the basket. The shot is initiated by jumping vertically into the air. As the shooter begins the jump, the ball is brought up and in front of the head. At the height of the jump, the ball is shot using the same technique as in the one-handed set shot.

Rebounding

For *offensive rebounds*, anticipate the shot and the direction of the rebound. Use a fake to lose your defender and gain an opportunity to get into a good rebounding position (avoid getting forced too far under the basket). Once in position, assume a wide stance and a ready jumping position. Elbows should be flexed and at shoulder level with arms and hands reaching upward. Anticipate the timing of the ball coming off the rim. The offensive rebounder has three choices: (1) jump up and tip the ball back into the basket; (2) jump straight up, grasp the ball in the hands, and pull it down and go right back up with a shot; or (3) pass to another teammate who is in a better position to make a shot or resume the offensive strategy.

The *defensive rebounds* are the same as the offensive rebounds except once the ball has been obtained, the objective is to pass it out to a teammate who is away from the basket toward the sideline. For more information, contact USA Basketball, 1750 E. Boulder Street, Colorado Springs, CO, 80909, or call (719) 632-7687.

GOAL GAMES

Field hockey, lacrosse, soccer, and team handball are four goal games that have been grouped together because they are similar in strategy. The object of each game is to protect a goal at your own end while trying to score in a goal guarded by your opponent. Each goal is defended by a goalkeeper. For safety reasons, in high-school play it may be advisable to play these games without a goalkeeper. Students can be challenged by varying the size of the goal, setting up targets within the goal, or by adding an extra defender in place of the goalkeeper. If a goalkeeper is used, protective equipment should be worn.

Adapting to meet students' needs. Because these goal games are similar in strategy, they can, in many cases, be adapted in similar ways. Drills can be designed and with little variation be used for any one of these games. One common adaptation is eliminating the goalkeeper and changing the size of the goals to make shooting easier or more difficult. Targets can be placed inside goals to make scoring more challenging.

Using smaller areas, reducing the number of players per team, and matching students according to skill level are all good ideas. Six-by-six grids can be marked off with cones, and modified games and drills can be practiced within these grids. Small, modified games allow students

Floor hockey is a popular sport offered in many schools.
Courtesy of Suzi D'Annalfo, Conard High School, West Hartford, CT.

the opportunity to handle the ball more often, which gives more students opportunities to practice skills in game situations.

Field Hockey

General information. In the United States, field hockey is thought of as predominately a women's sport, whereas in other parts of the world, it is a popular men's activity. Until the late 1800s hockey was predominately a men's sport and is still played by men throughout the world.

Like other field games, the goal of field hockey is to pass the ball down the field and score by putting the ball into the other team's goal. Field hockey is a wonderful game for secondary school physical education classes for two primary reasons. The first reason is that field hockey can easily be divided into smaller, modified games. This allows more students to have opportunities to handle the ball and, therefore, practice their skills. In addition to small modified games (1 vs. 1, 2 vs. 2, 3 vs. 3, and 6 vs. 6), drills can be creatively designed to challenge students' individual skill levels and to provide adequate practice time for skills to be learned.

The second reason why field hockey is a good game for high-school students is because most boys and girls have little exposure to field hockey before entering high school and, therefore, will be fairly equal in terms of skill level. This allows for more opportunities in coeducational classes. High-school students who do have exposure to field hockey before reaching high school usually are female students who have played either on a junior high-school team or in recreation leagues. These girls will be exceptionally skilled compared with the majority of the class. They could be used as peer teachers in your class to help other students master their skills.

Some high-school students will have had exposure to ice hockey, which will provide them with knowledge of some general hockey concepts. These students will be tempted to use both sides of the stick, which is not allowed in field hockey. Most students will probably have had some experience playing similar games such as floor hockey, pillow polo, or broom ball. All of the previous situations will provide opportunities for the teacher to encourage students to call on their experiences with similar activities when learning the skills associated with the game of field hockey.

Equipment and facilities. The beauty of field hockey is that it can be played on almost any flat surface. Although a grass field is the most typical surface, it is not necessarily the easiest for beginners or even novice players. A smooth surface, such as the gymnasium floor, reduces obstacles and allows for more success when one is handling a ball with a hockey stick. Indoor hockey leagues are becoming more popular and are played with 6 players on a side instead of the 11 players required for regulation field hockey.

A regulation field hockey field is comprised of either natural grass cut relatively short or artificial turf. The field dimensions are 100 yards by 60 yards with goal cages centered at opposing ends of the field. Regulation goal cages are 4 yards long, 7 feet high, 3 to 4 feet deep, and covered with a net to keep the ball contained when a goal is scored. The field is divided in half by a center line and again in quarters by an additional two 25-yard lines. Inside each of the 25-yard lines and in front of each goal there is a semicircular area called the shooting circle or the striking circle.

Field hockey sticks are traditionally made of wood and have one flat side (left side) and one rounded side (right side). Unlike in most other hockey derivatives, such as ice hockey, street hockey, and floor hockey, only the flat side of the stick, which is called the face of the stick, can be used to contact the ball. Sticks vary in length from 30 to 36 inches and also vary in weight from 12 to 23 ounces for women and 28 ounces for men.

The regulation field hockey ball weighs 5 to 6 ounces with a circumference between $8\frac{13}{16}$ and $9\frac{1}{4}$ inches. Traditionally field hockey balls have been white in color and covered with either leather or plastic. However, field hockey balls are now available in a rainbow of bright colors.

Shin guards should be made available to high-school athletes to prevent injury from being hit in the shins with a stick or ball. Shin guards vary in style and can be used in field hockey and soccer classes. The goalie needs extra protection in relation to pads. Goalie equipment consists of goalie pads to protect the shins and thighs, special shoes or pads that cover the regular shoes, a mask similar to a catcher's mask used in baseball or softball or a goalie's mask in ice hockey, a chest protector, and gloves.

Game play. A regulation hockey team has 11 players. Specific positions consist of offensive players or forwards, defensive players or backs, and a goalkeeper. Only the flat side of the stick is allowed to be used to advance the ball. Players may not advance the ball by using their hands, feet, or bodies. The ball must first be advanced inside the striking circle before shots on goal are allowed. One point is scored each time the ball is hit into the opponents' goal.

Sport-specific skills

See Box 19-3 for teaching tips for field hockey.

There is no difference between a left-handed and a right-handed stick in field hockey. All students, regardless of which hand is dominant, must learn to hold the stick in the same manner.

Dribble

The stick is held with the left hand at the top and the right hand further down the shaft. Beginners many want to move their bottom hand further down the stick, while more advanced players may want to position their bottom

Students practicing field hockey passing skills.
Courtesy of Kathy Pinkham.

BOX 19-3

TEACHING TIPS FOR FIELD HOCKEY

Dribble

Hands are relaxed
Bend at the ankles, knees, and hip
Head is up with eyes focused on play
Keep the ball under control

Shooting and Passing

Position hands
Adjust face of stick
Contact through the ball and follow through in a continuous motion

Receiving

Move to the ball
Reach forward with the blade of the stick down
Assume the athletic stance
Give with the ball as it makes contact with the stick

Tackling

Line up with the opponent
Watch the ball
Contact the ball when it is off the opponent's stick
Control the ball, then dribble or pass

The *tight dribble* is used when a player is tightly guarded. The ball is kept as close to the stick as possible.

Shooting, passing, and receiving

The following can be executed either as passes or as shots on goal. The ball is hit directly through the middle of the field.

The *push pass* has no backswing. The pass begins with the blade of the stick in contact with the ball and the top of the stick facing forward in the direction of the target. The left hand is at the top of the stick, and the right hand is midway down. The left foot is forward. The ball is pushed by a quick wrist snap of the right hand.

The *flick* is executed much like the push pass, only the ball is lofted slightly. The same mechanics are followed as in the push pass, but the stick starts behind and slightly under the ball.

The *drive* is used for passing and shooting. The back of the left hand faces the target. The right hand slides up and is placed directly under the left hand. The Vs formed by the thumb and index finger of both hands are in line with the toe of the stick. The wrists and arms are out in front of the body, while the heel of the stick rests directly behind the ball. The stick is brought back with the arms and wrists until the wrists reach about waist level; the wrists are then cocked so that the head of the stick is higher than the wrists. Hit and follow through in a continuous motion.

In the *scoop,* the feet are in a forward-stride stance with the right foot forward. The ball is to the right and out in front of the right foot. The left hand is at the top of the stick, and the right hand is a little over halfway down. The stick is held at an angle to the ground with the face of the stick facing up. The body is flexed at the hips with weight forward. The toe of the stick is placed under the ball, and the ball is scooped by with a forward motion. Follow through by pointing the toe of the stick toward the target.

In *receiving the ball,* students should be taught to stop the ball with their stick or to *catch* the ball. When the ball comes from the front, this is done much in the same way as catching a ground ball. The student runs to meet the oncoming ball and reaches forward with the blade of the stick on the ground. The left hand is at the top of the stick, and the right hand is a little more than halfway down. The hips are flexed with the body weight over the front foot. The stick is at an angle with the blade of the stick back and the top of the stick forward. The student reaches out for the ball and gives with it as the ball comes in contact with the stick. If the ball is coming from the left side, the student must let the ball pass in front, where it can be fielded on the stick side and quickly brought under control in a dribble. If the ball is coming from the right side, the student must turn the body to the right to get the face of the stick to face the oncoming ball.

---

hand closer to the top hand. The palm of the right hand faces the direction of the dribble. The left wrist controls the stick. The wrist is flexed with the elbow out in front of the body. Encourage students to keep their heads up and eyes focused on what is going on around them.

An *Indian dribble* or a *zig-zag dribble* is used to move the ball from left to right in a zig-zag pattern, making the dribbler's moves more deceptive to the opponent. The top hand (left) turns the stick, while the bottom hand (right) remains loose, allowing the stick to turn freely. The ball is pulled left with the flat side of the stick and then pushed right with the flat side of the stick.

The *push dribble* is used on a smooth surface. The stick and the ball remain in close contact as the ball is pushed along by the stick and kept slightly ahead of the right foot.

The *tap dribble* is used on uneven surfaces. The ball is continuously tapped out ahead of the dribbler (approximately 1 to 2 feet). Keep the ball slightly to the right so it will not be stepped on.

Dribbling styles

The *loose dribble* is used when the player is open and running down the field. The ball is hit further out in front.

Tackling

Box 19-3 presents teaching tips for tackling.

Dodging

Dodging is a skill used by the dribbler to avoid an opponent. Each dodge is executed as part of the dribble. The stickside dodge or pull dodge is done by turning the face of the stick to the left by turning the left wrist. The ball is quickly dragged to the left, and then the dribble is continued or the ball is passed to a teammate. The nonstickside dodge or Y dodge is done as the dribbler approaches the tackler and the ball is tapped to the left or to the nonstick side of the opponent. The dribbler then runs around the tackler (passing right shoulder to right shoulder) to recover the ball. The scoop dodge is done by scooping the ball over the tackler's stick and then running to recover the ball. The scoop is executed the same as described earlier. For more information on field hockey, contact the United States Field Hockey Association, 1 Olympic Plaza, Colorado Springs, CO, 80909, or call (719) 578-4567.

Lacrosse

General information. The game of lacrosse is a continuous running and passing game that requires players to catch and throw a ball by use of a stick referred to as a crosse. Scoring in lacrosse is done by shooting the ball into a 6- by 6-foot goal. Rules are significantly different for men's and women's lacrosse. In the men's game, body contact is allowed, and, as a result, helmets and pads are needed for protection. In the women's game, players are not allowed to hit the other players with their sticks or their bodies. It is for this reason that women's rules are suggested for use in physical education classes.

Equipment and facilities. For play during physical education classes, a basketball court can be used for indoor play (small teams of 6 vs. 6), or an existing field hockey, football, or soccer field can be used for outdoor play.

Game play. Lacrosse is played on an outdoor field. There are no boundaries except those designated by the person in charge. By using women's rules, body contact is not allowed. Each shot is worth 1 point. The emphasis should not be placed on force of the shot but on placing the shot well. Encourage students to shoot from different angles around the goal. For safety, the following are violations that are not permitted:

◆ Warding off. The offensive player, while in possession of the ball, cannot protect the crosse with the arm from the opponent's stick check. Shielding is permitted in men's rules.
◆ Protecting a ground ball with the body or the crosse. Once an opponent has begun to move toward a ground ball, the opponent cannot step into and protect the ball with the body.

◆ Dangerous play. When the defender establishes a legal position, an offensive player cannot force the crosse into the defender's crosse in such a way that the crosse slides back and hits the offense player's body or the defender's body.
◆ Shooting or throwing a ball dangerously or following through. Once a defender has established a legal position, it is the offensive player's responsibility to pass around the defender. As the offensive player finishes the shot or pass, the follow-through cannot be such that the stick hits the defender.

BOX 19-4

TEACHING TIPS FOR LACROSSE

Cradling

Hold the stick perpendicular to the ground and vertical to the body
The top hand and bottom hand move together as one unit
The left elbow acts as a hinge at the waist
"V on V"—the thumb and forefinger form a V at the V of the stick
Complete action across the face from ear to ear

Receiving a Pass

Show (target) the open basket toward the passer
Give with the ball
Wrap it across the face into a complete cradle

Passing

Crosse up with the basket open to the target
The top hand makes an up-and-over motion toward the receiver's target
The bottom hand is used as a lever—it is pulled into the armpit
Follow through in the direction of the pass (toward the target)

Picking up Ground Balls

The feet are behind the pickup, knees are bent, and the head is over the ball
Prepare the stick head flat and low (the bottom hand is very low)
Push through with bottom hand
Begin the cradle action as soon as possible while pulling the crosse into the body

Shooting

The stick should be vertical—the bottom hand directs that shot, and the top hand places the shot
Lift the crosse just before the shot—follow with a snap
Continue to run through the shot (do not fall away)
Attempt to shoot out of the cradle action

◆ Dangerous shot. Placement of any shot should not be aimed directly at the goalie, executed with extreme force, or shot forcefully from a close distance. The goalie must have a fair amount of time to react to any shot. If the shot is well placed (not at the goalie), it can be forceful.

Sport-specific skills. See Box 19-4 for teaching tips for lacrosse.

Cradling

The *grip* used for catching is the same as that used for cradling. Place the stick on the ground with the head of the crosse facing up. Straddle the stick. Bend down and pick up the stick with the natural throwing hand at the top of the stick where the crosse begins to form a V. The V formed with the thumb and the pointer finger should line up with the V formed by the crosse. The fingers wrap around the stick firmly. The nonthrowing hand is wrapped around the bottom of the stick.

Cradling is used to keep the ball in the crosse while moving the ball down the field. Place the throwing hand on the top of the stick and the nonthrowing hand on the bottom of the stick. Cradling is motion that creates a force that keeps the ball in the pocket of the crosse. This is done by swinging the arms and the stick (as one unit) from side to side. The crosse should be held perpendicular to the ground with the elbows relaxed. Be sure to keep the crosse straight. The bottom arm creates the motion by acting as a hinge moving from the hip. The elbow remains relatively stationary at the hip, while the forearm opens and closes. Both wrists move with the motion, but the hands maintain the proper grip.

Receiving

When *receiving* a pass to the forehand side, the player should ask for the ball by extending the head of the crosse toward the passer to provide a target. Watch the ball into the crosse. As the ball enters the crosse, give with the force by bringing the stick into the body and up into the cradling position. Wrap the ball into the cradling motion. When receiving a pass to the backhand side, the stick is brought across the body to the nondominant side, and the basket is rotated around to face the oncoming ball. Give as the ball enters the crosse. Immediately bring the ball into the cradling motion.

Passing

Passing is done overhand and underhand. The overhand throw in lacrosse is similar to the overhand throw in softball. Place the throwing hand at the top of the crosse. See the target. With the ball in the crosse, bring the crosse back beside the throwing-side ear, turning the shoulders slightly. Step forward with the opposite foot. The elbow and the butt end of the crosse lead the motion with the throwing hand remaining at ear level or slightly

above. The follow-through with the crosse is an up-and-over motion with the bottom of the stick being pulled into and ending in the armpit of the throwing arm and the head of the crosse pointing toward the target. The underhand throw in lacrosse is like a shoveling motion. The throwing side of the body faces the target. Bring the stick back over the opposite hip with the bottom hand coming slightly above the throwing hand. From this position the throwing hand pulls the crosse down and across the body while the bottom hand pushes. The top hand follows through to the target.

When picking up ground balls, the player should step beside the ball with the dominant foot, bend the knees, and keep your head over the ball. Scoop the ball into the crosse. Push through with the bottom hand while stepping through in the same direction. Begin cradling as soon as possible by bringing the crosse with the ball up to the full cradling position. Picking up a ground ball rolling away from you is similar, but be sure to bend down low getting the stick level with the moving ball.

Picking up a ground ball rolling toward you starts with positioning yourself directly in front of the oncoming ball. Place the head of the crosse down in the path of the ball while keeping the end of the stick up at an angle allowing the ball to roll into the crosse pocket. Give with the ball, push down with bottom hand, and bring the crosse up to the cradling position and begin cradling.

Shooting

The *overhand shot* is similar to a pass and is executed like the overarm pass, except the wrist snap is exaggerated, and the top hand may slide down the shaft of the stick to gain more power.

The *side arm shot* is executed like the side arm pass, except it requires a good cradle and a quick wrist snap.

For the *reverse stick shot,* pull the stick to the weak or nondominant side. The player turns the head of the stick and whips the ball out with the wrist.

The *bounce shot* is like the overhand shot except the follow-through is down. For more information about lacrosse, contact the United States Women's Lacrosse Foundation, 45 Maple Avenue, Hamilton, NY, 13346, or call (315) 824-2480.

Soccer

General information. Soccer is presently the most popular sport throughout the world in terms of spectators and participants. In the United States, soccer is one of the only team sports in which boys and girls have equal opportunities for exposure to skills at an early age. Many city recreation departments offer boys', girls', and coeducational soccer leagues for young children. For this reason, soccer is usually a very successful coeducational activity for secondary school physical education programs.

In addition to youth programs, many recreation departments are also offering soccer leagues for adult participation, thus providing more lifetime opportunities for adults in soccer. Soccer requires little equipment and can be added to any program at little cost. Like other field games, soccer can be modified to accommodate smaller numbers of players to give more students an opportunity to contact the ball and thereby practice executing skills in gamelike situations.

Equipment and facilities. Soccer is played outdoors on a grassy playing field. The only equipment needed is a soccer ball and goal posts for two goals. Shin guards are suggested to prevent students from getting hurt. A regulation soccer field is 100 to 120 yards × 60 to 75 yards, but smaller fields (60 × 70) are suggested to accommodate modified game play (6 vs. 6). The field should have a marked center line and penalty boxes in front of each goal. Goals are centered on the end lines and are 8 yards × 8 yards covered by a net to capture the ball. Soccer balls are made of leather, rubber, or synthetic materials and are between 27 and 28 inches in circumference. Softer playground balls or foam balls can be used when practicing skills that require contact with the body.

Game play. The game is started by a kickoff. One team (usually determined by a flip of a coin) is awarded a free unobstructed place kick from center field. A kickoff is done after each goal is scored by the opposite team. Teams score one point for each goal. When the ball goes out of bounds (over the sideline), the ball is put back in play by a member of the opposite team using a throw-in. When the ball goes out of bounds (over the end line) by a member of the offensive team, the defense is awarded a free unobstructed kick, called a goal kick, from the goal area. When the ball goes over the end line when kicked by a member of the defensive team, the offense is awarded a free kick or a corner kick from a designated spot near the corner of the field where the ball went out. Once a player has taken a kickoff, a throw-in, a goal kick, or a corner kick, the player cannot touch the ball again until it has been touched by another player (from either team).

Sport-specific skills

Box 19-5 lists teaching tips for soccer.

Shooting or passing

Some skills can be executed either as passes or as shots on goal. When shooting the ball on goal, the shooter wants to propel the ball so it will be difficult to stop by a defender. When a player is passing to a teammate, however, the ball needs to be passed so that it can be easily controlled. The degree of power used will determine the speed of the ball. The point of contact on the ball will determine the loft of the ball. When the ball is hit directly through the middle, it will stay closer to the ground. Generally, a good pass stays close to the ground, so it can be easily received. The one exception given here is the instep drive, which is intended to be lofted.

The *inside of the foot pass* or *push pass* is done with the inside of the foot. (The nonkicking foot is placed beside the ball with the knee slightly bent.) The kicking leg is brought back, and the leg is turned to the side. Contact the ball through the center by the inside of the foot. The leg follows through to the target.

The *outside of the foot pass* or *flick pass* is used for diagonal passes either ahead or behind. This pass is done off the run. The nonkicking foot is placed beside the ball. The kick is initiated from the knee by a short backswing. The ball is contacted at the center with the outside of the foot. The foot and leg follow through to the target.

The *instep drive* is used to loft the ball for greater distance. The nonkicking foot is planted next to the ball. The target is determined. The head and the kicking leg knee are over the ball, and the eyes are focused on the ball. The hip is extended, and the knee is flexed so that the kicking foot comes back to the buttocks. The kick is initiated by flexing the hip and extending the knee. As the foot comes through, the ball is contacted on the lower half of the ball with the instep of the foot (shoelaces). The ankle is snapped at contact to add extra force. The foot and the leg follow through to the target.

Receiving or collecting

Trapping is used to bring the ball under control. The ball can be trapped with any part of the body except the arms and the hands. The ball can be trapped by putting the sole of the foot on the moving ball and pushing it to

---

B O X   19 - 5

TEACHING TIPS FOR SOCCER

Passing

Firmly plant the nonkicking foot
The head is over the ball
Eyes are focused on the ball
Kick through the ball
Leg follows through in the direction of the pass

Receiving a Pass

Move to meet the ball
Give with the ball
Gain control of the ball with feet

Dribbling

The head is up
Maintain rhythm of run
Contact the ball with the foot
Keep the ball within the playing distance

Trapping the soccer ball.
Courtesy of Ben Lombardo, Rhode Island College, Providence, RI.

the ground. The inside of the foot or the inside of the leg can also be used to trap the ball. This is done by using the instep or thigh as one would a hand. Reach for the ball and give with the force as the ball comes in contact with the body part. A ball can also be trapped anywhere between the chest and the thighs by allowing the ball to hit the body, giving with the force and deflecting the ball downward so the feet can gain control.

Dribbling is a controlled tapping or pushing of the ball with either foot while one is advancing down the field. The ball is contacted with the inside, the outside, or the top of the foot (shoelaces). A dribbler can vary the style of dribble used or vary the speed of the dribble. For more information about soccer, contact the American Youth Soccer Organization, 5403 W. 138th Street, Hawthorne, CA, 90250, or call (310) 643-6455.

Team Handball

General information. Team handball is an ideal sport for secondary school physical education classes. It can be played inside on a basketball court or outside on a soccer field. It is very much like other field games in that the object of the game is to move the ball downfield or downcourt and score while avoiding the defensive team. The basic skills of the game are very much like basketball with goals at each endline as in other goal games (field hockey, lacrosse, soccer). The ball is thrown into the goals. For

play in physical education classes, small playground balls or small foam balls can be used.

Equipment and facilities. A field or a court, a ball (slightly larger than a softball and slightly smaller than a volleyball), and two goals are needed.

Game play. The game is started by a throw-off from the center of the field in any direction. At the time of the throw-off, both teams are positioned on their respective sides of the field. When the ball goes out of bounds (over the sideline), the ball is put back in play by a member of the opposite team using a throw-in, which may be executed with one or two hands. When the ball goes out of bounds (over the end line) from an action of a member of the offensive team or from being touched by the goalkeeper on a shot on goal (when the goalkeeper was the only defender touching the ball), the defense is awarded a throw-off from anywhere within the goal area, while the offensive players stay behind a 9-meter marker. When the ball goes over the end line by a member of the defensive team (other than the goalie), the offense is awarded a corner throw, which is executed at the corner where the sideline intersects with the goal line. Players must keep one foot in contact with the ground when taking a throw-off, a throw-in, a corner throw, or a penalty throw. A goal is worth one point and is scored when the ball is thrown into the goal area.

The best way to think of team handball is as a combination of other team games. Players are penalized for fouls by being suspended from play as in ice hockey. The ball can be dribbled the same as in basketball. The ball is passed and shot. Players can hold the ball for up to 3 seconds. Players cannot double dribble or kick the ball. A free throw is awarded for double dribbling, taking more than three steps, holding the ball for more than 3 seconds, charging, holding, illegal picking, pushing, and unnecessary roughness.

Free throws are awarded at the point of infraction unless the foul occurs between the 6- and 9-meter markers. Then the ball is put into play from the 9-meter marker closest to the point where the infraction occurred. A goal can be scored from the free throw.

A penalty shot is a free unobstructed shot taken from the penalty mark with only the goalkeeper defending the goal.

For *passing*, practice those passes used in basketball: the chest pass, baseball pass, bounce pass, overhead pass, and underhand pass.

Shooting the handball at the goal is similar to throwing a softball. Shooters should aim at the four corners of the goal.

Dribbling in team handball is the same as in basketball. For more information on team handball, contact the United States Team Handball Federation, 1750 E. Boulder Street, Colorado Springs, CO, 80909, or call (719) 578-4582.

Flag Football

General information. Touch and flag football are very popular team games played in high-school physical education classes. These modifications of U.S. (tackle) football require far less protective equipment and are much safer games to play. As a result, these games can be played by people with varying skill levels and are popular as recreational pick-up games. Although boys usually have more opportunities to learn the basic fundamental skills required in football (throwing, catching, and kicking a football), girls are genuinely interested in the game as well. When huge variations in skills level appear between the boys and the girls, both become easily frustrated. It is important, therefore, to be sure that skill development for football is encouraged in all students regardless of gender.

Adapting to meet students' needs. The game of football can be adapted slightly to accommodate variations in skills level and availability of equipment. Touch football needs only a ball and an end line, and it requires the tackler to touch the ball carrier with two hands or with one hand (depending on predetermined rules). Requiring the tackler to use two hands makes the game more difficult.

Flag football requires the ball carrier to wear two flags on a belt worn around the waist. The flags are usually attached by Velcro and can be bought or made. The tackler must rip one of the flags off the belt of the ball carrier to be credited with a tackle. The tearing of the flags provide a more accurate account of the tackle: It is much easier to determine whether or not a flag has been acquired than it is to determine if a person has made a successful tag with either one or two hands. In game play, encourage students to switch positions so everyone will have the opportunity to handle the ball.

When one is practicing skills, especially throwing and catching, small or softer (foam) balls can be used to accommodate smaller hand size or fear of getting hit with the ball. The kicks can be practiced first with round balls, and once the technique is mastered, students can transfer their learning to the football.

Running plays and general football drills can be exciting for students as long as consideration is given to ensure that all students get plenty of attempts to practice their skills.

Equipment and facilities. Regulation leather footballs, rubber-covered footballs, or rubber-covered foam balls are all options to be considered for physical education classes. Flags are needed for flag football games (described earlier). Flag or touch football is played on a grass field. Dimensions of the field may vary. A regulation football field (100 yards by 50 yards) may be used but smaller spaces with fewer players per team is best (seven to nine players on a team).

Game play. When the ball is either passed or carried into the opponent's end zone, 6 points are scored. The ball is advanced toward the goal by either running with it or passing it. The ball carrier is stopped by being either touched (one hand or two) or by having a flag removed. The offensive team has four attempts, called downs, to move the ball every 10 yards. (This distance may vary depending on specific field dimensions.) Once they have reached the 10-yard mark, they have four more attempts. On small fields the offensive team may be required to score within those four downs. If not, the ball is turned over to the defensive team. A safety occurs when the ball

---

BOX 19-6

TEACHING TIPS FOR FLAG FOOTBALL

Forward Pass

Hold ball slightly behind the middle with fingers on laces
Turn your side in the direction of the throw
Bring the ball back and transfer your weight to the rear foot
Pass the ball forward in an overhand motion, and transfer your weight to the forward foot
Follow through in the direction of flight

Catching

Look toward the passer and the ball
Extend the arms and hands forward toward the ball
Watch the ball *into* the hands and *give*
Pull the ball in toward the body

Hand Off

Keep ball close to body
As receiver approaches, shift the ball to the hand closest to the receiver
Hand the ball to the receiver

Center Snap

Straddle position
On signal, center extends the arms back between the legs and tosses the ball to the player

Punting

Hold the ball in front of and away from the body
The end of the ball faces downward
Step on the kicking foot
Drop the ball parallel to the ground, step on the nonkicking foot
Contact the ball on instep, point the toe out with the body leaning away
Kicking leg follows through

carrier is "tackled" behind his or her own goal line. Field goals (3 points) and conversions (1 point) are not always used in flag or touch football because cones are often used as goals instead of regulation goal posts.

The game begins and is resumed after every field goal and after the halftime with a kick-off, which is a place kick made by one team to the other. The team receiving the ball becomes the offensive team. Fumbled (dropped) balls are considered dead and are automatically given to the team that fumbled. Any player on the offensive team is eligible to receive a pass. The ball must be passed by the quarterback before crossing the line where the ball was first put into play (called the line of scrimmage, which is an imaginary line running through the center of the ball from sideline to sideline).

Roughing a player (tackling, tripping, or pushing) is not allowed and results in loss of yardage. The hands cannot be used in blocking. Players must remain on their own side of the line of scrimmage until the ball is put into play by the center snap.

Sport-specific skills. See Box 19-6 for teaching tips for flag football.

The *offensive line stance* is used by the players on the offensive line. Offensive players must be within 1 foot on their side of an imaginary line of scrimmage until the ball is snapped. This imaginary line runs through the ball from sideline to sideline. Players assume the athletic stance with weight on the balls of their feet so they are ready to move in any direction.

Offensive players in the backfield assume the athletic stance. Hands rest gently on the knees with the head and eyes up and focused on the play.

The *defensive line stance* is used by the players on the defensive line. Defensive players must remain on their side of an imaginary line of scrimmage until the ball is snapped. The defensive stance is similar to the offensive stance, only the center of gravity is lower, and the weight is forward more so the players are ready to charge forward. Defensive players in the backfield assume the athletic stance with the head and eyes up and focused on the play.

Passing and receiving

Catching a football requires many of the same fundamental techniques as catching in other sports. Practice with a football should be encouraged to become familiar with its shape and size.

The *forward pass* is used to advance the ball downfield. The ball is gripped toward its middle by the throwing hand by placing the fingers laterally over the lace of the ball and the thumbs under the ball. The ball is then thrown with an overhand throw with emphasis on the release. At the time of release, the hand comes under the ball to impart spiral spin on the ball. The hand and fingers follow through to the target. Only one forward pass is allowed for each play.

Passing the football.
Courtesy of Ben Lombardo, Rhode Island College, Providence, RI.

The *lateral pass* is used to pass the ball to the side or behind the passer. This is done with either a one-handed or a two-handed underhand throw.

The *handoff* is used to hand the ball to a teammate. The ball is held in two hands close to the body. The passer steps toward the receiver and extends the ball at waist level. The ball is held until the passer is sure that the receiver has possession of the ball.

The *center snap* is used to initiate play by snapping the ball from the line of scrimmage by a line player to a player in the backfield. The ball is snapped from its position on the ground to the receiver, who stands between 1 and 6 feet behind the center snapper. The center assumes a straddle position facing the opposing end line with the ball approximately 2 feet out in front and equally between both feet. The center of gravity is low, and the ball is held in both hands. The ball is snapped between the legs of the center to about waist level of the receiver.

Blocking is used to prevent an offensive player from moving to a particular area on the field or to move an offensive player away from a particular area. The blocker must cross the arms in front of the body and assume the athletic stance, keeping the center of gravity low with back straight and head up. The block is executed by pushing the offensive player with the upper body, using short, steady steps, in a direction determined by the blocker.

Ball carrying is when the ball is advanced by carrying it while the player is running. The ball should be carried close to the body. When a player is running with the ball, one end of the ball is tucked between the body and the inside of both the upper arm and elbow. The other end is protected by the palm and fingers of the same hand. When the player is closely defended, the other hand should come in for added protection.

Kicking

For the *place kick,* the soccer place kick is used.

Punting is used by the offensive team to move the ball further downfield when they have failed to make the first down. Punting is a complicated skill and should be practiced if used in classes. Place kicks can be substituted in situations where students are not successful or students can be given a choice of which kick to use. The punt is done by dropping the ball and kicking it before it hits the ground. The ball is held (laces up) in both hands out in front of the body. The kicker steps forward with the nonkicking foot. At the same time, the kicking leg is bent backward, and the knee is bent. The punt is initiated by flexing the hip and extending the knee while at the same time dropping the ball. The ball is contacted by the instep of the foot just before it reaches the ground. The entire leg follows through with an exaggerated forward and upward motion. For more information on football, contact the US Flag & Touch Football League, 7709 Ohio Street, Mentor, OH, 44060, or call (216) 974-8735.

Softball

General information. Softball is becoming more popular with adults. Because softball can be played coeducationally and can be easily adapted to meet a wide range of ability levels, organizations throughout the country are creating softball leagues for people of various ages. There are leagues for the young and the old and for the highly skilled and true beginners. College intramural leagues, corporate leagues, church leagues, recreational leagues, and professional leagues, are all developed to provide different levels of play.

While softball is a team sport that can be active, exciting, and provide social opportunities for its participants, it must be carefully planned so as not to create negative experiences. In many situations, students playing softball spend large amounts of time standing around waiting for their turn to hit or waiting for a ball to come to them in the field. For these students, softball can become frustrating and boring.

For this reason, it is important to emphasize skill development throughout a secondary program and to incorporate alternatives to full game play, such as drill stations, situational drills, and modified game play. With large classes, it is important to get as many students as active as possible. Try to play two or more games simultaneously when possible. Large teams increase students' opportunities for standing around and becoming bored with the game.

Adapting to meet students' needs. Softball can be modified to suit a variety of different skill levels and educational objectives. A number of different situations should be considered by the physical education teacher to vary the difficulty of the game. For example, softball can officially be played by three distinct sets of rules: fast-pitch, modified fast-pitch, or slow-pitch rules.

Fast pitch relies heavily on skilled pitching and solid defensive skills. It is generally a low-scoring game and is played primarily in competitive leagues such as interscholastic and intercollegiate leagues. Fast pitch allows for stealing and bunting, which are not allowed in slow pitch.

Modified fast pitch and slow pitch were essentially developed as recreational games to generate more opportunities for offense (hitting). Therefore they are usually higher scoring games and more fun to play in physical education classes. In slow pitch, the distance of the pitcher from home plate is further, and the ball must be delivered with an *arc.* The defensive field consists of 10 players instead of the 9 used in fast pitch. The tenth player may be used anywhere but is usually used as an additional outfielder.

To make the game exciting to all students, teachers need to be creative by establishing their own rules and varying the equipment used to accommodate large class sizes and diverse ability levels. An example might be to vary the size of the ball or the type of ball used. A soft leather-covered fleece ball or a plastic whiffle ball can be used to play indoors, in situations where students do not have gloves, or with lower-skilled students and beginners who are afraid of being hit with the ball.

Other ideas for adapting the game are to vary the distance of the base paths or to change innings only after every person has had an opportunity to bat. Batting averages could be increased by allowing the batters to hit from a batting tee, fungo hit their own ball, throw the ball into play—or choose from any combination of the above.

Equipment and facilities. The equipment needed to play softball consists of balls, bases, bats, catcher's equipment, helmets, and gloves. Ideally, there should be enough balls so that each student can have one. This will allow more opportunities for individual practice. Many students will have their own gloves, but it should not be assumed that all students will be able to afford one. Therefore the school should provide enough gloves so everyone on a team can have one. For class use, fielders' gloves are sufficient for all positions. Be sure, however, to purchase right-handed and left-handed gloves. Gloves should be properly broken in and carefully oiled each season to increase their comfort and longevity.

In addition, several bats should be provided in a variety of sizes and weights to allow for differences in individual size and strength. Properly fitting catchers' equipment and batters' helmets should be used for safety. Finally, bases are needed. Rubber bases can be used for indoor and outdoor use.

BOX 19-7

TEACHING TIPS FOR SOFTBALL

Throwing

The ball is held in the fingers and thumb
Bring the ball back to the rear—rotate the body so the glove side faces the target
Step forward with the opposite foot
Elbow leads the throw—follow through

Catching

Move in line with the ball
Watch the ball into the glove
Give with the ball
Protect the ball with the nonthrowing hand

Fielding a Ground Ball

Ready position—head up and glove open
Get in front of the ball
Keep the glove down
Watch the ball into the glove

Fielding a Fly Ball

Begin in the ready position
Get under the ball
Reach with both hands above the head
Bring the ball and glove into the body with both hands

Batting

Side to pitcher
Bat held up and off the shoulder
Focus on the pitcher and the ball
Shift weight, contact, and follow through

Game play. The game of softball can be played indoors in a large, open gymnasium with a fleece ball or whiffle ball, and outdoors on a diamond-shaped field.

For *positions,* all players hit on offense and play the following defensive positions: pitcher, catcher, first baseperson, second baseperson, third baseperson, shortstop, left fielder, center fielder, right fielder, and short fielder (in slow pitch only).

Sport-specific skills. Box 19-7 lists teaching tips for softball.

In competitive softball games, good *pitching and catching* are crucial. Fast-pitch games, in particular, require a well-trained and highly disciplined pitcher and catcher (called the *battery*). A good battery will prevent batters from hitting and discourage base runners from stealing bases. The pitcher's primary goal is to make the ball more difficult to hit and, ultimately, attempt to strike batters out.

Although stealing and bunting are not allowed in slow-pitch softball, good pitching and catching are still important for the quality of the game. The pitch in slow pitch must be delivered at a moderate speed with an *arc* of at least 6 feet from the ground and no more than 12 feet from the ground. A legal pitch in modified rules is any ball that is delivered to the batter with an underhand motion.

Recreational softball can be played with any pitching style. In situations where time is limited, the teacher can pitch, or each offensive team can provide their own pitcher.

For the *infielders' ready position,* infielders begin in a defensive position with knees and hips bent, feet shoulder width apart with weight distributed evenly on the balls of both feet. The hands are close to the ground with fingers pointing down (start with the glove down), palms facing forward (glove open), and head up.

For the *outfielders' ready position,* outfielders begin in a defensive position with knees and hips slightly bent, feet shoulder width apart with weight distributed evenly on the balls of both feet. The hands are open, palms out, and the head is up.

Throwing and catching

Throwing and catching are fundamental movement skills that are usually taught in elementary school. It is not uncommon, however, for students to reach junior high and high school and still throw and catch with an immature pattern. It is important, therefore, to begin with the basic fundamentals of throwing and catching. Once these two skills are developed, students can concentrate on throwing and catching skills specific to the game of softball, such as overhand throw, overhand snap, underhand toss, fielding a ground ball, and fielding a fly ball.

For the *overhand throw,* the ball is held with the fingers and thumb of the throwing hand. The ball is brought back to about ear level, which initiates the movement. As the ball is brought back, the body rotates so the glove side faces the target, and the weight is on the foot under the throwing arm. The player steps forward with the glove side foot, and the elbow leads the throw while remaining at ear level with the hand slightly above. The wrist remains flexed until the final release. The throwing arm follows through in the direction of the throw and continues down across the body. The throwing-side foot comes through to a balanced position. For shorter distances, a overhead snap or an underhand toss can be used.

Fielding a ground ball

In *fielding a ground ball,* begin in the ready position. Move into a position directly in line with the oncoming ball (get in front of the ball). The glove remains close to the ground, fingers are pointed down, and the eyes remain on the moving ball (watch the ball into the glove).

Fielding a ground ball.
Courtesy of Ben Lombardo, Rhode Island College, Providence, RI.

Both arms reach out toward the oncoming ball, and it is caught in front of the feet (keep the ball in front).

As contact is made in the glove, the glove is squeezed shut, and the throwing hand covers the glove to protect the ball from falling out (use two hands). Both hands are brought in toward the body to absorb the force (give with the ball). Simultaneously, the body comes up to an erect position and moves into a ready position to begin the throwing motion.

Fielding a fly ball

In *fielding a fly ball,* begin in the ready position. As the ball is hit, move into a position under and behind the ball. Stand with legs spread and the glove side of the body facing the target (ready position for the throw). Reach with both hands above the head. The glove should be open with the fingers pointing up and slightly back. Catch the ball slightly in front of the throwing arm shoulder to accelerate the transition to the throwing position. As the ball enters the pocket of the glove, protect it with the throwing hand while simultaneously bringing the ball into the body and stepping forward to begin the throwing process.

Hitting

Hitting fundamentals include using a firm but relaxed grip. Hold the bat in the base of the fingers with the fingers and thumbs wrapped around the bat. The dominant hand is placed above the nondominant hand. The second joints of the fingers of your dominant hand form a straight line down the bat shaft with the knuckles of your nondominant hand.

The feet are shoulder width apart, and weight is dis-tributed evenly on both feet. The knees are bent at a comfortable distance. The hands with the bat are held back by the rear shoulder. The bat is held out away from the body, and the head of the bat is held still and in a horizontal position pointed back at the backstop. The head is turned toward the pitcher with eyes ready to focus on the ball. The head remains fixed throughout the swing.

Batting stance.
Courtesy of Ben Lombardo, Rhode Island College, Providence, RI.

Slow pitch softball, in which the ball is pitched with an arc, is a popular recreational activity in many communities.

Courtesy of Ben Lombardo, Rhode Island College, Providence, RI.

As the ball is pitched, the weight is shifted slightly onto the back foot. The swing is initiated by a short step forward in the direction of the oncoming ball. With this step, the hips rotate and open up toward the pitcher while the trunk and shoulders follow. The arms extend as the batter pulls the bat forward with the bottom hand. Contact is made out in front of home plate. The top hand rolls over as the batter snaps the wrists at contact. Watch as the bat makes contact with the ball. After contact, continue to swing the bat around.

Using a *batting tee* to hit from eliminates the uncertainty of a pitched ball and allows a student to concentrate on the mechanics of the swing. A batting tee can be used in a game situation as an alternative to a pitched ball or can be used as a drill station to practice hitting.

Fungo hitting can be used as an alternative to hitting a pitched ball in modified game play or in practice drills where students help other students practice their fielding by hitting them practice balls. To fungo hit, first stand square to home plate. Hold the bat in the dominant hand. Toss the ball up in front as you would for a tennis serve. Step toward the target with forward foot. As the ball

comes down, swing through the ball. Keep eyes on the ball throughout the toss and contact with the ball.

Baserunning

Baserunning in softball requires an explosive sprint. After the ball is hit, the runner must run to first base. If the ball is hit to the infield, and it is anticipated that the runner will only get a single, the runner sprints as quickly as possible down the base path toward first base. Run full speed in a straight line and run through first base. Do not break stride. Once the base has been crossed, turn to the right into foul territory and decelerate.

If the ball is hit to the outfield, and it is anticipated that the runner can make it to second base or beyond, then a different technique is required. The runner runs out of the base path into foul territory about two thirds of the way down the base line. Without slowing down, the runner makes a wide turn and steps on the inside corner of first base with the left foot and continues on the way to second. This technique is repeated at both second base and third base if the runner plans to move on to the next base. For more information on softball, contact the Amateur Softball Association, 2801 NE 50th Street, Oklahoma City, OK, 73111, or call (405) 424-5266.

Volleyball

General information. Volleyball is a sport that is being played by all age groups at a variety of different ability levels. It is common for adults to have opportunities to continue their interest in volleyball long after high school. Serious players can play power volleyball, which is highly competitive and requires advanced skills and conditioning. Beach volleyball leagues are becoming very popular and offer highly competitive leagues and tournaments; some city recreational leagues provide fairly competitive volleyball leagues for adults. Most students, however, will not go on to play competitively. Volleyball is a sport that can also be played for pure enjoyment. Volleyball games are becoming popular activities at family gatherings and summer barbecues; recreation leagues also offer less formal volleyball leagues for men, women, and coeducational teams.

Adapting to meet students' needs. Volleyball is probably one of the most adaptable of all team sports. It can be played with one or two people on a side (like tennis), or it can be played with large teams of 12 on a side. As suggested earlier, it can be highly competitive or purely recreational. The game can be easily adapted to accommodate varying skill levels by changing the size and weight of the ball—such as regulation ball, foam ball, beach ball, balloons, cage ball—or the height of the net. Volleyball can be played almost anywhere. It can be played inside on a regulation court, outside on a grass or sand court, in the deep snow for outdoor winter fun, or in the pool. The game of volleyball has even been adapted to be played in a racquetball or handball court and is called *walleyball*.

Equipment and facilities. Volleyball is played on a rectangular court (60 feet × 30 feet) divided in half (two 30-foot squares) by a net (7 feet 11⅝ inches from the floor for men, 7 feet 4⅛ inches from the floor for women). A center line is directly under the net, and each half of the court is divided by an attack line, which is 10 feet back and runs parallel to the center line. Equipment needed for volleyball is a regulation volleyball, the net, and net supports.

Game play. In regulation play, a volleyball team consists of six players on a side. The object of the game is to hit the ball back and forth over the net (volley), preventing the ball from hitting the floor on your side while at the same time trying to make the other team miss or hit the ball out of bounds. A volley is started by one team serving to the other. The server must serve the ball from the right side just outside of the court (behind the end line). The ball must clear the net on the initial serve. During the volley, however, each team is allowed three hits before the ball has to go over the net (the ball must go over on the third hit). No one player, however, can hit the ball twice in a row. The ball cannot be caught or thrown.

Only the serving team can score and does so only if they win the volley. The same server continues to serve as long as the serving teams continues to win the volley. If the nonserving team wins the volley, they get to serve next (called side out), thus winning the opportunity to score. Each time the receiving team wins the serve, players rotate positions (usually a clockwise rotation) so that a new server moves into position. Players must maintain stationary positions until the ball has been served but can move strategically on the court once the ball has been served.

A game consists of 15 points, but if the score is close, play must continue until a team wins by 2 points. A match consists of winning 2 out of 3 games or 3 out of 5 games.

Sport-specific skills. Box 19-8 lists teaching tips for volleyball.

Passing

The *forearm bounce pass (bump)* is used when one anticipates that the ball will be below waist level. Step toward the ball with either foot (forward-backward stride). Clasp the hands together by interlocking them. The forearms extend forward forming a flat hitting surface (approximately 2 inches above the wrists). Get under the ball by bending the knees and slightly forward at the hips. The ball should be contacted as close to the midline of the body as possible. The pass is initiated by swinging the arms upward and forward from the shoulders and continuing this motion by following through after the ball.

The *one-hand bounce pass (dig)* is used against a spike or against balls of varying speeds when there is little time

---

BOX 19-8

TEACHING TIPS FOR VOLLEYBALL

Forearm Bounce Pass (Bump)

Forward-backward stride with hips, knees, and ankles bent

Create a flat surface

Extend the ankles, knees, and hips while striking the ball

Follow through in the intended direction

Overhead Volley

Assume the athletic stance under the ball

Hands move to a ready position (form a triangle)

At contact, flex

Extend with an upward force

Forearm pass.
Courtesy of Ben Lombardo, Rhode Island College, Providence, RI.

Volleyball set.
Courtesy of Ben Lombardo, Rhode Island College, Providence, RI.

to get into position. Reach for the ball with one arm. Create a flat hitting surface. Strike the ball and follow through in the intended direction of the ball.

The *overhead volley, overhead pass, or set* is used to pass a high ball or to set the ball to a teammate. The receiver moves into position directly behind and under the flight of the ball. Assume the athletic stance. Hands move to a ready position above and in front of the forehead with elbows flexed and pointing out to the sides. Form a triangle with thumbs and the index finger of each hand. Watch the ball make contact with the fingers of the hands. As the ball makes contact, flex slightly at the joints. The pass is initiated by extension of the arms and legs simultaneously while an upward force on the ball is applied. Snap the wrists and follow through in the direction of the ball.

The *back set* is used to pass the ball back to a teammate. Use the same technique as earlier, only the back is arched slightly as the pass is initiated, and the hands extend over the head with the palms up and pointing back in the direction of the intended pass.

The *serve* is used to put the ball in play. All players get a turn to serve.

The *underhand serve* is the easiest serve for the server to perform and for the receiver to handle. Assume the athletic stance with the foot opposite the serving hand forward. The ball is held still in the nondominant hand slightly below the waist, or the ball can also be tossed. Create a flat surface with the striking hand (fist with hand facing upward or sideways or an open hand). The striking

Underhand serve.
Courtesy of Ben Lombardo, Rhode Island College, Providence, RI.

arm is brought straight back and then forward (in a pendulum motion) striking below and behind the ball. The hand and arm continue through the motion.

The *overhand serve* is more difficult to execute and more difficult to return. Stand with the foot opposite the serving hand forward. The serving arm is back with the striking hand raised. Weight is on the back foot. As the ball is tossed straight up, the weight is shifted forward, and the ball is contacted with an extended arm and open hand. (Timing must be practiced.) The arm follows through in an upward and forward motion. For more information on volleyball, contact the United States Volleyball Association, 3595 East Fountain Blvd, Colorado Springs, CO, 80910, or call (719) 637-8300.

SUMMARY

Team sports have long been a part of the secondary school curriculum, although the percentage of time devoted to them at each level and in each school varies. It is interesting to note that across the nation, opportunities are being provided for participation in team sports for adults of all ages in recreational leagues. These opportunities offer adults who enjoy team sports the chance to continue to participate throughout their life.

When one is teaching team sports, it is important to make sure that students have acquired the fundamental skills before moving on to the more advanced sports skills. Teachers should employ a variety of strategies to adapt the sports to students' abilities and to maximize participation while promoting skill development. Modified games should be employed to enhance participation by students of all abilities and to enable all students to experience satisfaction and success.

SUGGESTED READINGS
Basketball

Krause J: *Basketball skills and drills,* Champaign, Ill, 1991, Human Kinetics.

Moore B, White J: *Basketball theory and practice,* Dubuque, Iowa, 1990, William C Brown.

Whiddon S, Reynolds H: *Teaching basketball,* Minneapolis, 1983, Burgess.

Field hockey

Kentwell R: *Field hockey techniques and tactics,* Brooklyn, Mich, 1976, Sauk Valley.

Kostrinsky D: *Field hockey coaching drills,* Ithaca, NY, 1987, Mouvement Publications.

Wein H: *The science of hockey,* London, 1985, Pelham.

Lacrosse

Brackenridge C: *Women's lacrosse,* Woodbury, NY, 1978, Barrons.

Soccer

Luxbacher J: *Soccer: steps to success,* Champaign, Ill, 1991, Human Kinetics.

Luxbacher J: *Teaching soccer: steps to success,* Champaign, Ill, 1991, Human Kinetics.

Team handball

Cuesta JG: *Team handball techniques,* Colorado Springs, Colo, United States Team Handball Federation.

Mood D, Musker FF, Rink JE: *Sports and recreational activities,* St Louis, 1991, Mosby.

Neil G: *Modern team handball: from beginner to expert,* Montreal, 1976, McGill.

Football

Fuoss D: *Complete book of winning football drills,* Boston, 1984, Allyn & Bacon.

Mood D, Musker FF, Rink JE: *Sports and recreational activities,* St Louis, 1991, Mosby.

Stanbury D, DeSantis F: *Touch football,* New York, 1991, Sterling.

Softball

Potter DL, Brockmeyer GA: *Softball: steps to success,* Champaign, Ill, 1991, Human Kinetics.

Potter DL, Brockmeyer GA: *Teaching softball: steps to success,* Champaign, Ill, 1991, Human Kinetics.

Volleyball

Schaafsma F, Heck AJ, Sarver CT: *Volleyball for coaches and teachers,* Dubuque, Iowa, 1985, Williams C Brown.

Viera BL, Ferguson BJ: *Volleyball: steps to success,* Champaign, Ill, 1989, Human Kinetics.

Viera BL, Ferguson BJ: *Teaching volleyball: steps to success,* Champaign, Ill, 1989, Human Kinetics.

Individual Activities and Sports

CHAPTER OBJECTIVES
- To review basic teaching points for individual activities and sports
- To discuss the value of including individual activities and sports in secondary school physical education programs
- To discuss the role of the teacher when teaching individual activities and sports
- To provide examples of individual activities and sports that could be used in a secondary school physical education program

Individual activities and sports provide students with opportunities for lifelong involvement in physical pursuits. The knowledge of, and participation in, these activities will enhance the health and wellness of individuals at any age.

The provision of opportunities to study and experience individual sports and activities within a physical education curriculum contributes much to the achievement of the profession's goals of encouraging and facilitating lifelong learning and participation. From the teacher's point of view, these curriculum units are also attractive because in many cases equipment demands are relatively minimal.

AQUATICS

As a matter of one's personal safety and welfare, it is important that an individual be able to perform basic swimming and survival skills and feel safe whether the aquatics environment involves an indoor or outdoor pool, an open body of water, or a boating situation.

A physical education teacher must earn the American Red Cross's (ARC) Water Safety Instructor's (WSI) certification to be qualified to serve as a swimming instructor. Additionally, when a teacher is certified to teach swimming by the ARC, a certified ARC lifeguard must also be present in the teaching environment. Contact your local or area ARC chapter office for more information regarding certification requirements and upcoming courses for the foregoing certifications.

The ARC's WSI course provides its students with information regarding (1) physiological training and conditioning principles; (2) the physical laws of swimming, such as buoyancy and propulsion; and (3) psychosocial concepts, such as fear reduction via students' readjustment of their perceptions and attitudes of being in an aquatics environment in addition to learning assurance of their safety by their progress and their encouraging instructor's support. Furthermore, the ARC WSI course also provides for the proper sequencing of swimming skills and knowledge.

Aquarobics

One alternative program or additional instructional program to the traditional swimming and diving unit is aquarobics. Aquarobics follows the concepts and principles pertinent to cardiovascular endurance training, or aerobic exercising, which were presented in Chapter 17. Aquarobics is a type of activity in which all skill and age levels can successfully participate.

An aquarobics program involves individual exercises performed in a body of water without a support (free aquarobics) as well as by holding onto an object such as the pool's gutter or a flotation structure in an open body of water.

Examples of free aquarobics exercises are (1) jogging in water and using the arms as in running; (2) marching in water with high knee positions; (3) walking in the

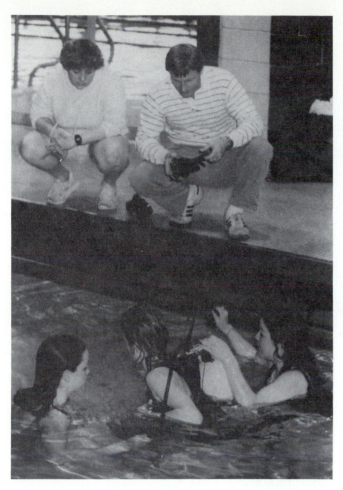

Some high schools offer scuba diving as part of their aquatic program.

Courtesy of Emily Leonardo, Camp Hill High School, Camp Hill, PA.

water opposing the resistance of the water; (4) performing jumping jacks; (5) performing arm swings forward and backward against the resistance of the water; and (6) combining jogging and marching with arms extended while the body is moving forward.

Examples of exercises while holding onto a pool gutter or a flotation structure are as follows: (1) utilizing the flutter kick while on one's stomach; (2) utilizing the flutter and bicycle kicks while on one's back; (3) utilizing the flutter and bicycle kicks while on one's side(s); and (4) with one's back to the pool wall or a flotation device, either hanging on and extending the feet to the center of the body of the water followed by bending the knees toward the chest and then extending them or standing and raising one leg straight up followed by swinging it across the body and back and then reversing the performance of the legs.[1]

Aquarobics also involves partner work. Examples are (1) partners standing back to back, extending the arms

out to their sides at shoulder level, facing palms backward and grasping the partner's arms, with one partner leaning to the left and the other leaning to the right and finally, both partners straightening up and then the partners reversing the pattern; and (2) both partners facing each other and holding hands while one partner bends the knees and squats down as the other partner raises up on the toes and finally, the partners reverse positions.[1]

Last, aquarobics involves performing simple routines to music. Music appropriate for aerobic dance in a studio or gymnasium is also appropriate for aquarobics routines.

Coed Inner-Tube Water Polo

An alternative to water polo in an aquatics unit is coed inner-tube water polo. Unlike regulation water polo, inner-tube water polo provides its participants with an equalizer because it requires that all participants are seated in an inner tube. A student's swimming skills and endurance are not factors in inner-tube polo.

Some of the inner-tube polo rules that vary from regulation water polo rules are (1) each team of six must have an equal number of women and men or more women than men, (2) the goalie for both teams must be a male, (3) players may not utilize a side of the pool to pull or push in an attempt to propel him- or herself in the tube except at the start of each period, and (4) no player shall deliberately hold the ball under the surface of the water.

ARCHERY

Archery is a closed activity. A closed sport is defined as one that is performed in a relatively stable environment. This means that the conditions are similar for performing the activity from one day to the next with an exception being the effect of wind direction and wind resistance on outdoor performances. For the most part, the success of an archer's accuracy and consistency of performance is based on the effective repetition of the sequential and temporal components of target shooting.

Equipment Terminology and Selection

The two types of bows most commonly used by the novice are the recurved bow and the compound bow. Because of the cost of the compound bow, the recurved bow remains popular. A bow should be selected that can be drawn back and held steady while one is aiming.

The proper length of the bow is related to the length of the draw. For example, if the draw length is 24 inches or less, then the recommended bow length is 60 to 64 inches. The bow string consists of varied numbers of threads coated with beeswax with loops at both ends. This type of bowstring is economical and requires the least maintenance. Key points to consider in selecting a

Courtesy of Emily Leonardo, Camp Hill High School, Camp Hill, PA.

bow include the following: (1) the upper and lower arms bend similarly; (2) the drawn bow bends evenly from the handle to the tips; (3) when the bow is strung, the string divides it in half, (4) it feels comfortable in the hands; and (5) it returns to its original shape after it is unstrung.

In the selection of arrows, the novice should check to be certain that the arrow is straight and that its length is appropriate for the length of his or her arm. One method for determining arrow length is to place one end of an arrow against the sternum and, while keeping the shoulders back, reach forward with both arms and use an arrow of such length that it extends 2 to 3 inches past the fingertips. It is important to emphasize that if the shaft of the arrow is too short for the individual, then it is possible to overdraw the arrow beyond the arrow rest of the bow, which can result in injury to the novice or a peer.

Finger protection is necessary for all students. Without it the archer's shots will be inaccurate and unpleasant. Additionally, an armguard protects the dominant forearm from string contact.[2]

Safety Precautions

All students must abide by the following procedures when shooting from a group line: (1) no jewelry is to be worn during class; (2) before shooting, each bow must be checked for cracks and a frayed string; (3) arrows are not to be retrieved until a signal is given by the instructor; (4) arrows may be drawn only when they are directed at the target; (5) bows and arrows are not to be left unat-

tended where careless people might mishandle them; (6) arrows are never to be shot straight up into the air; and (7) nobody is permitted to shoot with a faulty bow or faulty arrows.[2]

Stringing and Unstringing the Bow

The step-through method is one of several ways to brace a bow. The student begins in a side stride position with the bow's upper limb being held by the dominant hand and the bow being placed diagonally in front of the body with the face of bow up. The lower limb's curve is placed over the ankle of the outside foot. With the non-dominant hand, the student separates the string from the bow. With the inside leg, the student steps between the bow and the bowstring and raises the bow until the handle is behind the upper thigh. The dominant hand is moved to a position just below the loop in the string. The stepping leg straightens and pushes back against the bow, while the dominant hand's heel pushes the upper limb forward to create a bend in the bow. With the free hand, the student slips the string into the bow. As a matter of safety, it is important to keep the head away from the bow at all times during the stringing process. To unstring the bow, the foregoing procedures are reversed.[3]

Potential Errors in Performance

Errors in the stance may include (1) both feet on the same side of the line, (2) feet too far apart or too close, and (3) weight placed too much on one foot. Errors in the draw may include (1) nondominant arm being too straight or hyperextended at the elbow or the elbow being bent too much or the nondominant shoulder being hunched; or (2) the dominant arm's anchor point being too high, too low, or too far forward, some part of the hand other than the distal segment of the index finger touching the anchor point, or the elbow being too low or too high. Possible errors in aiming and releasing are (1) both arms and shoulders being relaxed at the moment of release, (2) point of aim not being achieved before the release of the string, (3) aiming with the nondominant eye, (4) sighting with both eyes, and (5) if shooting outdoors, not taking into consideration wind resistance and wind direction.[2]

Suggestions for Instruction

Some suggestions for instruction are: (1) practice the stance, draw and aim without an arrow with instructions not to release the string, and then practice nocking the arrow, draw, anchor aim, and release; (2) teach students how to properly retrieve arrows from the target face[2]; (3) place novices 10 to 20 feet from the target so that they experience success; (4) allow for reciprocal peer teaching regarding error analysis[3]; and (5) provide for novelty shooting activities such as team relay involving each team having one target and each team member having one arrow with the first person shooting followed by the second and so on with the team having the highest score being the winner; and tic-tac-toe involving balloons placed in three rows of three on the targets with the object being to hit three balloons in a row either horizontally, vertically, or diagonally.

BICYCLING

Bicycling has become a popular aerobic activity in the United States. Whether individuals are interested in becoming involved with recreational touring or competitive racing, the best place to start is by learning the proper selection and care of equipment, basic cycling maneuvers, rules of the road, and other safety considerations. It is recommended that bicycle enthusiasts eventually join a local club after participating in a physical education unit on cycling. Information regarding the nearest club can be obtained by contacting the U.S. Cycling Federation, E. Boulder St., Colorado Springs, CO, 80909, or calling (719) 578-4581.

It is strongly recommended that physical education teachers who wish to conduct a class bicycle tour off school property receive approval from an administrator. Additionally, a student's parent or guardian will need to complete and submit a permission form. Furthermore, and as a matter of legal liability, each parent or guardian should be informed of all aspects of the tour including physical demands.

Basic Bicycling Techniques

Mounting the bicycle. The proper method for mounting the bike is to raise one leg over the back of the bike and swing the foot onto the pedal, while standing motionless. Place that foot into the toe clip at the top of the pedal stroke. Next, push down with that leg and insert the other foot into its toe clip as the bike rolls forward.[4]

Riding position. There are three basic positions for one's hands on the handlebars: on the tops, behind the brake levers, and on the bottoms.

One of the key elements in cycling is maintaining a relaxed body position. When utilizing any of the three basic positions, the cyclist should keep the elbows bent. The amount of bend in the elbows acts as a performance multiplier. The cyclist can increase the amount of flexibility in the elbows as a means of adjusting the angle of the back below 45 degrees so that the powerful gluteus maximus muscles are being utilized during the pedal stroke.[4] When riding a bike, the cyclist's comfort is an important concern. To avoid arch and knee problems, the seat must be adjusted to fit the rider so that a cyclist's legs are never straight while pedaling.[5]

To avoid saddle soreness, it is recommended that a leather saddle that is wide enough for sufficient support be selected. A leather seat absorbs moisture; a plastic seat does not.[2]

Chafing of the legs can be avoided by wearing cycling shorts as opposed to running or tennis shorts. Cycling shorts are designed for the motion of pedaling.[5]

Neck stiffness can be avoided in riding by stretching the neck muscles whenever the cyclist stops. Also, to avoid injuries, a protective safety helmet is mandatory for each student.[5]

Pedaling. The most efficient pedaling stroke is one that utilizes the natural walking motion of the feet. In pedaling, it is important that the lower leg functions properly. The instructor or a student partner can best watch the cyclist's calf muscles appropriately expanding and contracting during the pedal stroke by standing behind the rider. The rider's calf muscles should only be tight on the down component of the pedal stroke. Tight calf muscles on the upward portion of the stroke indicate that the cyclist is pushing with the toes instead of pulling the foot in an upward direction. If the calf muscles are under tension, they will become prematurely fatigued.

As individuals become more familiar with their bikes, they will observe that minor adjustments in body positions will affect cycling. One illustration is that sitting toward the front of the saddle will allow the cyclist to move the legs faster. In terms of pedaling up steep hills, one may prefer either selecting a lower gear and pedaling while sitting back on the saddle or selecting a higher gear and sitting forward on the saddle.[4]

Controlling the bicycle. Pedaling a bike around a corner is not a problem if the cyclist is moving at a slow speed. It is not as easy, however, to control a lightweight,

Courtesy of Kathy Pinkham.

multiple-speed bike at high speeds on a corner. Safe cornering involves understanding the best *line* around the corner. Cornering speed is maximized whenever a cyclist turns a corner with the least amount of actual turning. When cornering, the cyclist needs to consider the crucial factor of centrifugal force, which involves pushing the bike outward on the curve. When cornering, a cyclist needs to enter a corner from the far side of the road, proceed to the inside of the corner (the apex), and then move to the outside of the road for the exit.[4]

Shifting gears. The concept of variable bicycle gear ratios on multiple speed bikes is that the cyclist is most efficient when pedaling at a constant rate in revolutions per minute. One revolution is defined as two complementary leg strokes with one from the left leg and one from the right leg. Because the cyclist faces various wind and terrain conditions, it would be impossible to keep a constant speed with only one gear.

To shift a gear, the student should keep pedaling but with little force, then shift the gear lever until the derailleur clatters. Derailleurs are front and rear mechanisms for shifting gears by moving the bike chain from one cog or chain ring to another. It is important that a cyclist practices shifting smoothly on a flat terrain so that it can be achieved quickly and safely on all terrains.[2]

Braking. The front brake provides approximately 75% of the braking action. If the front brake is applied too hard, then the rider might sail over the handlebars. The back brake provides stability to the process of braking the bike. To use the brakes properly, apply the back brake slightly before the front brake. Then increase the pressure on the front brake to control the amount of deceleration.

When you are cornering, brake as the corner is approached, ride past the apex, and accelerate smoothly out of the corner. This technique provides for maximum traction and stability.[4]

Riding with one hand. When cycling, a rider will occasionally need to remove one hand from the handlebars to signal for a turn, to shift gears, or to reach for a water bottle. To avoid personal injury, it is important that the cyclist places one hand near the center of the handlebars with the weight of the rider being equally distributed on the handlebars.[4]

Safety Checking the Bicycle

Before beginning a ride, the student must safety check the bicycle. This process involves gripping the brake levers to be certain that they work as well as looking for worn brake blocks, loose cables, handlebars, saddle seat, and wheels and inspecting the tires for proper inflation. A safety check will prevent not only personal injury but also a long walk home.

Rules of the Road

Cyclists must follow the same rules of the road as drivers of motor vehicles. Cyclists have a right to a safe traveling area along a road or street. It is important that a cyclist does not ride in a vehicle motorist's blind spot, especially when approaching driveways or intersections when a motorist may execute a right-hand turn.[4]

BOWLING

Bowling is another lifelong sport that appeals to individuals of all ages and skill levels. It is a recreational sport that can be enjoyed with friends and family, and it can be a competitive pursuit. Bowling is definitely a social sport. It is an activity that can be learned in a gymnasium with plastic pins and bowling balls. Many teachers make arrangements for their classes to bowl at commercial alleys within the community.

Skills Progression and Techniques

Selecting a bowling ball. In selection of a bowling ball, the ball should neither be too light nor too heavy. The finger holes for the dominant thumb and two middle fingers must neither be too wide nor too narrow for the finger spread from the thumb to the two fingers. To determine the appropriate finger span, insert the thumb into the ball up to the second joint, and then place the hand flat on the surface of the ball with the fingers spread over the holes. The knuckle joints of the two middle fingers should reach approximately ¼ inch beyond the inside near edge of the finger holes. Allowing a slack of ¼ inch between the palm and the ball will permit a comfortable grip.

Picking up the bowling ball from the rack. To avoid strain on the dominant hand while picking up the ball, you should place both hands on opposite sides of the ball and lift the ball to a position in front of the body. Last, place the thumb and fingers in their respective holes according to the method indicated next.

Gripping the bowling ball. While supporting the ball with the nondominant hand, you should place the two middle fingers of the dominant hand in the holes and then insert the thumb into the thumbhole. To maintain contact with the ball, slightly press the palm side of the thumb and fingers toward the palm area of the ball as opposed to squeezing the ball with the fingertips. The index finger and little finger are flat on the surface of the ball, and they are relaxed.

Stance. Before delivering the bowling ball, the bowler assumes a stationary position with the body facing the pins, and the bowler is either standing erect or in a slightly crouched body position. The nondominant foot is slightly in front of the dominant foot with the weight on the nondominant foot and both knees slightly bent. The head is up, and the shoulders, hips, and feet are square to the foul line. The ball is held at waist level and slightly to the dominant side of the body, with the dominant arm being straight from the shoulder to the wrist.

Aiming. Two methods of aiming are called *pin bowling* and *spot bowling*. Because spot bowling is recommended, beginners should be initially taught spot bowling. Teaching beginners pin bowling and then expecting them to learn spot bowling can result in many students finding it

To offer students the opportunity to learn bowling, many teachers arrange to use community facilities.
Courtesy of Emily Leonardo, Camp Hill High School, Camp Hill, PA.

difficult to eliminate the habit of pin bowling during the transitional phase of learning.

Pin bowling

The bowler looks at the pins and pictures an imaginary line between the point of releasing the bowling ball and the point on the pin deck at which the ball will be aimed. The line becomes the path of the ball. For right-handed bowlers delivering the first ball of each frame, the point of aim is the 1–3 pin pocket. For left-handed bowlers, the point of aim is the 1–2 pocket.

Spot bowling

The bowler pictures in the mind an imaginary line from the point of releasing the ball to a triangular spot or mark on the alley bed.

Approach and delivery
One-step approach and delivery

The one-step delivery should be presented to novices before the recommended four-step delivery. Also, the stance, approach, and delivery should be practiced initially without a bowling ball.

The stance for the one-step delivery is different from the previously described stance. The one-step stance involves the nondominant foot and leg being slightly behind the dominant foot. The dominant arm is extended with the dominant hand being dropped slowly to the side and the body simultaneously leaning forward with the knees bent. Throughout the pendulum swing, the dominant arm remains relaxed with its wrist straight. The pendulum swing of the dominant arm involves moving the arm forward, back to waist level, and then forward again to eye level. As the ball is pushed away, then brought backward, and, as the dominant arm swings forward, the nondominant foot and leg are simultaneously slid forward. Throughout the approach and delivery, the shoulders are square to the foul line.

Four-step approach and delivery

After assuming the starting stance with the nondominant foot forward of the dominant foot, the bowler moves forward beginning with the dominant leg and with a total of three brisk walking steps followed by a fourth step being a slide. At the completion of the slide, the weight of the body is on the nondominant sliding foot, which is pointed toward the pins. As with the one-step delivery, the four-step approach and delivery should first be practiced without a bowling ball.

The coordinated approach and delivery involve the bowler assuming the stance, pushing the ball away, then swinging it down, backward, and forward so that the dominant arm movements are synchronized with the three brisk steps and the fourth sliding step. As the nondominant foot slides on the fourth step, the ball comes forward and is released. At the point of release, the thumb comes out first, and the fingers and wrist are laying the ball on the alley bed in a smooth manner. The bowling ball should never be lofted onto the alley bed. The dominant leg swings forward to balance the body, and the dominant arm, which was straight, bends at the elbow for the follow-through. On the follow-through, the dominant arm should continue moving in the direction of the pins.

Two styles of delivering the ball are the straight ball and hook ball. The beginner should learn the straight ball first and then learn the hook ball delivery. The hook ball delivery is the most efficient style of bowling.

Straight ball

For straight ball delivery, the wrist and forearm remain straight throughout the entire delivery. For the right-handed bowler, the thumb is on top of the ball at a 12 o'clock position, and the index finger of the dominant hand is at the 2 o'clock position. For left-handed bowlers, the thumb is at the 12 o'clock position, and the index finger is at the 10 o'clock position.

Hook ball

For a *hook ball* delivery, the ball is held throughout the approach, delivery, and release with the thumb at the 10 o'clock position and the index finger at the 12 o'clock position for right-handed bowlers. For left-handed bowlers, the thumb is at the 2 o'clock position, and the index finger is at the 12 o'clock position. For all bowlers, if the ball hooks too much, move the thumb toward the 12 o'clock position.

Spare Bowling

For a bowler to have satisfactory scores, effective spare bowling is important. The concepts of converting spares are as follows:

1. Determine the key pin (usually the one closest to the bowler) and where it must be contacted to convert the spare.
2. Deliver the same style of ball for converting a spare as used for the first ball delivery in each frame.
3. Concentrate more fully on the second ball delivery than on the first, because there is less opportunity for pin action and, therefore, less margin for error.[2]

Scoring System and Symbols for Scoring

Provide the students with the knowledge of scoring and an opportunity to apply it by preparing a scoresheet with pin counts per frame and a request to determine the frame-by-frame score and the final game score. Box 20-1 provides a quiz to test the students' knowledge of this information.

subtracts one point. The winner is the first student on a lane to reach zero points.

Scotch bowling. This event can also be played in the gym or in a bowling center. Students select a partner and decide who will deliver the first ball. Partners then alternate throughout the game. A strike in any frame will change the order of the partner to deliver the first ball in the next frame.

Red pin. Another activity that can be conducted in a gym or in a bowling center is *red pin*. The bowler rolls only one ball in each frame. The bowler scores for each frame only if the red pin is knocked down. A variation of red pin is to stipulate that if the red pin appears as the head pin and the student delivers a strike, then a prize will be awarded.[2] For more information on bowling, contact the American Bowling Congress' Youth Bowling Program, 5301 S. 76th Street, Greendale, WI, 53129, or call (414) 421-9000.

GOLF

Golf is a lifetime sport that involves many closed skills performed in a relatively stable environment. It is a sport that requires accuracy and consistency in the performance of the skills associated with it. Golf can be enjoyed as a leisure pursuit and as a competitive sport in a league or tournament setting.

Skills Progression

Novice golfers should first be introduced to the terminology pertinent to the clubs such as the toe, heel, neck, and clubface followed by an overview of the nature of a golf hole.

Safety

Before the presentation of skills and the swinging of the clubs, it is necessary to outline the safety rules for class. Some safety rules are: (1) students are to inform the instructor if a club is in need of repair, especially if a club grip is worn or a clubhead appears to be loose; (2) there must be adequate space between students so that a student's swinging of a club will not injure another; (3) students are not to swing toward one another, even if a ball is not on the floor or ground; (4) golf balls shall not be retrieved until the instructor signals to do so; and (5) golf clubs are to be left behind the hitting line when balls are retrieved.

Putting

For novices to experience initial success, it is recommended that the first skill introduced be putting. Beginning a golf unit with the full swing of an iron or wood

---

Rules of Etiquette

Before students practice at a commercial bowling center, they must be aware of the following rules:
1. Food and beverages are not permitted in the area of the lanes.
2. The bowler to the right has the right-of-way.
3. Stay on your own approach.
4. Use only your own bowling ball.
5. Respect all equipment and the bowling center, and do not loft the ball onto the alley bed.
6. Return a bowling center's bowling ball to its proper place.

Novelty Activities

Three pins. In a gymnasium or a bowling center, the student attempts to knock down the 1-2-3 combination by contacting the 1-3 pocket if right-handed, or the 1-2 pocket if left-handed. One delivery is permitted for each turn. Each student begins with a score of 15 points. Three pins knocked down subtracts three points, two knocked down subtracts two points, and one pin knocked down

Teachers may wish to culminate their golf unit by arranging for students to play golf at a community course.
Courtesy of Emily Leonardo, Camp Hill High School, Camp Hill, PA.

usually results in students not experiencing much success because of the complexity of the full swing. A second reason for introducing the putting stroke first in the unit is that theoretically 50% of the strokes required to make par (a numerical standard of scoring excellence per hole on the course) are utilized on the putting green.

Putting, like the approach shots of pitching and chipping, are referred to as stroke savers. Putting and approach shots are categorized as directional swings. The second category of basic swinging skills, known as distance swings, are important from the tee area (the beginning of each hole) to within 50 yards of the green.

The *four key concepts* pertinent to putting are *square, solid, steady,* and *smooth.* Grip the putter by utilizing either the overlapping, interlocking, or baseball grip. Choose one grip and always utilize the same grip for the putting stroke. For each grip, the golfer will be able to look down at the hands on the club and observe two knuckles on the nondominant hand and the letter V formed with the thumbs and forefingers pointing toward the inside of the dominant shoulder. When one grips the putter, the hands, arms, and shoulders will form a triangle tilted toward the nondominant side of the body. The putting stance will involve placing the putter head *square* to the target with the blade of the putter being at right angles to the intended line of the putt. The word *solid* refers to keeping the putter low to the ground on the backswing, forward swing, and follow-through. *Steady* means keeping the body quiet throughout the stroke with the wrists remaining firm. It also involves counting to three before looking at the direction of the putted ball as a means of keeping the head down and steady. *Smooth* refers to moving the head of the putter in a back and through pendulum motion and completing the stroke by moving the putter through the ball toward the cup.[6]

Some learning tasks for practicing putting in the gym, on a rug at home, or on a practice putting green at a golf course are as follows:

1. *Cluster putting.* Starting with four golf balls, the first putt becomes the target for the remaining putts. Try to group or *cluster* all four balls. The second, third, and fourth putts should touch the target ball.

2. *Stop, look, and listen.* Utilizing five balls, start the practice 1 to 2 feet from the hole. Then increase the distance from the hole only after five consecutive putts drop into the hole.

   a. *Stop.* Before each putt, lighten the grip on the putter. The hands should be positioned down on the grip for control, and the head should be over the ball.

b. *Look.* Look at the target and the ball. Check the alignment. Then, close the eyes and take the head of the putter back and through the ball toward the hole.

c. *Listen.* Listen for the ball to drop into the cup before the eyes are opened.

3. *Circle putting.* Practice putting six balls that are arranged the same distance from the cup in a circular formation. Start with a distance of 1 foot from the cup, and, when all putts have been made, then move to greater distances.

4. *Lag putts.* Practice "touch" or "feel" for long lag putts from 10 to 15 feet from the cup.[6]

Chip Shot

In the chip shot, the ball is lofted for the first few feet of its flight, and then it rolls. Chipping involves the ball being in the air for one third of its flight with a two-thirds roll. This shot is utilized from or near the fringe of the green. Selecting a lower-numbered iron such as a 5 or 7 iron will result in less loft and more roll, and, conversely, a higher-numbered iron such as a 9 or wedge will provide for more loft and less roll.

Teaching cues for the chip are as follows: (1) utilize either the overlapping or the interlocking grip with the hands in the down position on the club's grip, (2) assume an open stance (the nondominant foot is closer to the ball than the dominant foot) with the feet close together and the weight on the nondominant foot, (3) the hands on the club grip are ahead of the ball, (4) the arms and shoulders form a triangle that acts like a pendulum, (5) the triangle swings along the track (direction or line of flight of the ball) toward the target, (6) the wrists remain firm with the back of the hand leading to the target, and (7) the head remains steady over the ball for consistent stroking of the ball.

One illustration of a chipping drill is to chip 10 balls within the radius of the length of club that is being utilized.

Pitch Shots

Pitch shots are utilized from 50 yards away from the hole to within 10 yards of the edge of the green. Pitch shots are executed with the higher lofted clubs, such as the 9 iron or pitching wedge, and travel two thirds of the way to the green in the air with a one-third roll.

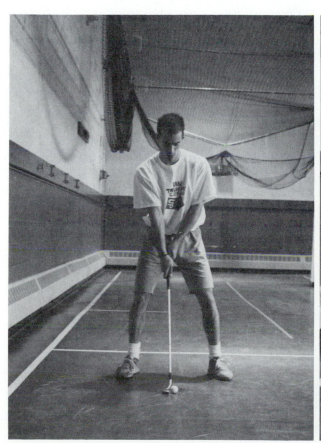

Courtesy of Ben Lombardo, Rhode Island College, Providence, RI.

Teaching cues for pitching are: (1) the stance is narrow (the feet are less than shoulder-width apart) and slightly open with the weight on the nondominant foot and leg; (2) the hands are slightly ahead of the ball as in chipping; (3) the swing is longer than for a chipping shot, and it involves a natural cocking and uncocking of the wrists; (4) the nondominant arm swings through the ball while the head maintains a stationary position; and (5) the knees remain close together during the stroke.

One practice drill for developing the pitching shot is to place a tee in the end of the club's grip. Then, swing the club to waist level on the backswing and on the follow-through. Have a partner check to see if the tee is aimed at the ball on the backswing and follow-through.[6]

Full Golf Swing

The full swing should first be practiced without a club, and then begin with the 9 iron followed by the 5 iron, the 3 wood, and then the driver. For students to experience success with the full swing, it is important to follow the graduated-length method by practicing with a short club followed by increasing the length of the club. Students should be informed of the average yardages for all irons and woods that can be achieved by an experienced golfer. Such information will provide them with goals for distances. Refer to Fig. 20-1 for this information.

The cues for teaching the full swing are as follows: (1) place a golf ball or a tee on the ground or floor as a reference point for assuming the stance; (2) turn the body so that the nondominant shoulder is sideways or toward the target; (3) place the feet together with the nondominant foot in line with the ball or tee; (4) move the nondominant foot about 2 inches toward the target, and then move the dominant foot until the inner borders of the shoes are shoulder width apart; (5) the weight is on the inner borders of the shoes with the knees flexed and knock-kneed and the buttocks are "out"; (6) an overlapping, interlocking, or baseball grip is utilized on the club;

(7) the arms and shoulders form a tilted triangle toward the nondominant side of the body; (8) the head is behind the ball during this address position with the eyes focusing on the back of the ball and the dominant eye in line with the dominant knee; and (9) the club is taken back and then brought through the ball into the full follow-through with a slow rhythm in the backswing and an acceleration into the downswing and follow-through as the body weight shifts to the dominant side in the backswing and to the nondominant side in the downswing, point of contact, and follow-through.

Some drills for developing the full swing are:

1. Towel drill—using the address position, twist a towel and grasp it with the hands shoulder width apart with the nondominant hand facing down and the dominant hand facing up. Then take the towel back, keeping the nondominant arm firm, release the dominant hand from the towel, and shift the weight toward the nondominant side of the body followed by a full follow-through with the towel being grasped by the nondominant hand.

2. Three-tee drill—place three tees in the ground. The tees should be 3 inches apart. The tee in the middle represents the ball. Then address the middle tee with a club. Execute the full swing, and if the club is moving slow and low to the ground in its track, then all three tees will be popped out of ground.[6]

Common errors of the full swing include directional errors and distance (or power) errors. For a list of these errors with their causes and corrections, refer to Tables 20-1 and 20-2.

Because golf is performed in a relatively stable environment, at times the golfer's full swing must be modified to contend with uphill, downhill, and sidehill lies of the ball, playing from the rough and playing from a sand bunker. For example, an uphill lie of the golf ball on a course involves the golfer needing to utilize a straight-faced (or lower-numbered) club, keeping the body weight on the nondominant foot and leg, shortening the swing, and aiming the shot to the right of the target.

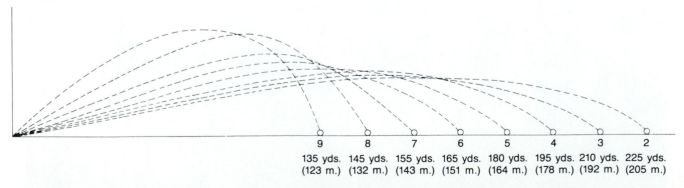

	9	8	7	6	5	4	3	2
	135 yds.	145 yds.	155 yds.	165 yds.	180 yds.	195 yds.	210 yds.	225 yds.
	(123 m.)	(132 m.)	(143 m.)	(151 m.)	(164 m.)	(178 m.)	(192 m.)	(205 m.)

FIG. 20-1 Distances and flight of ball using the same swing with each iron (male golfer).

From Mood K, Musker F, Rink J: *Sports and recreational activities for men and women,* St Louis, 1991, Mosby.

T A B L E   20 - 1

Directional Errors of the Full Golf Swing

Name of Error	Ball Flight Result	Either Clubhead Path Through Impact Area and . . .	Clubface Position in Relation to Clubhead Path at Impact is	Clubhead Path through Area is, but . . .	Clubface Position in Relation to Clubhead Path at Impact is
Slice	Ball curves right of the target	Outside to inside	Open	Straight (correct)	Open
Hook	Ball curves left of the target	Inside to outside	Closed	Straight (correct)	Closed
Push	Ball is straight but right of the target	Inside to outside	Square	N/A	N/A
Pull	Ball is straight but left of the target	Outside to inside	Square	N/A	N/A

Courtesy of the National Golf Foundation.
NOTE: The information in this table is from the perspective of a right-handed golfer.

T A B L E   20 - 2

Analyzing the Golf Swing for Power (Distance) Errors

Name of Error	Defining the Error (or Cause)	Correcting the Error
Turtle position	To observe the ball better at the address position, the golfer drops the head until the chin almost rests on the chest. This restricts the nondominant shoulder turn on the backswing and destroys the body's coiling action.	"Peep" at the ball through the bottom of the eyes, keeping the chin high at address and throughout the swing. This allows the nondominant shoulder room to run under the chin for a full coiling action.
The shrug	The nondominant shoulder turns correctly on the backswing; however, the dominant shoulder, instead of turning, shrugs upward. Because only one half of a turn is executed, a golfer achieves only one half of maximum power.	Use the neck as a reference point. Be sure the dominant shoulder turns behind the neck as the nondominant moves in front of the neck.
The toe dance	Rising up on the nondominant toes prematurely in the backswing gives the golfer a turn, but not a coiling action because the twisting motion is lost. On the downswing, also rising up on the toes of the dominant foot prematurely releases the resistance created on the backswing.	During the swing, concentrate on keeping the heels on the ground until they are pulled away from the ground by the hips turning. If one does not follow the procedure, then a major source of power, which is the resistance of the ground, will be lost. The nondominant heel is on the ground until it is pulled up by the dominant hip on the backswing, and the dominant heel resists until released by the pull of the nondominant hip on the downswing.

From Tomasi TJ: How to maximize your personal distance, *Golf Illustrated* 4:44-45, 1992.

Rules of Etiquette and Safety

Several rules of etiquette and safety exist when playing golf. These rules are as follows: (1) only one golfer hits at a time; (2) the person farthest away from the hole hits first; (3) the person with the longest putt on the green putts first; (4) golfers are to play without delay (for example, they should walk to the ball without delay, be discriminate in the number of practice swings, leave the green immediately after concluding play, and record the scores en route to or at the next tee area rather than on the green); (5) allow faster players to play through; and (6) in a loud voice, say "fore" if your shot is going to land in the vicinity of other golfers on the course.

Suggestions for Instruction

1. For indoor practice in a gym with either plastic whiffle balls or short-flyte balls (which travel no more than 90 feet), have students pitch over an obstacle such as a badminton net or volleyball net.
2. Consider purchasing short-flyte balls instead of plastic whiffle balls, because the short-flyte indoor or outdoor balls provide the learner with an indication of whether there is a tendency to hook, slice, push, or pull the ball.
3. When new skills are introduced, present the appropriate rules of golf for each new skill. For example, when you are teaching the drive from the tee area, explain the tee area rules regarding the stance in relation to the imaginary line between the two tee markers.
4. Offer the students opportunities to participate in several different types of novelty golf events. Some illustrations are presented next.
   a. Approach and putting contest: Each student approaches and holes out three balls from 25, 50, and 100 yards off the green. The winner is the one holing out the three balls in the fewest number of strokes.
   b. Driving contest: Each student is allowed five drives with only the best three counting. For immediate determination of distances, erect markers 25 yards apart from 125 yards to 300 yards from the tee area. Only drives that land in the fairway or other specified area on school property count.
   c. Target contest: Using athletic field marking paint or lime, you should mark four circles around the cup with the radii being 35, 25, 15, and 5 feet. Establish three tee areas at distances of 50, 75, and 100 yards from the cup. Students play one shot from each tee using the club of their choice. If the ball lands within the 35-foot circle, then one point is scored. Two points, three points, and five points are scored, respectively, if the ball lands in the 25-foot, 15-foot, or 5-foot circle. A hole-in-one counts

as 25 points.[7] For more information regarding golf, contact the following organizations: National Golf Foundation, 200 Castlewood Drive, North Palm Beach, FL 33408, or call (305) 844-2500; US Golf Association Golf House, PO Box 2000, Far Hills, NJ 07931, or call (201) 234-2300; or AAHPERD/NASPE School Golf Development Program, 1900 Association Drive, Reston, VA 22091, or call (703) 476-3400.

GYMNASTICS

Gymnastics is a sport that involves the performance of skills comprising routines on a floor exercise mat and on apparatus. The competitive events for girls and women are the balance beam, side horse vaulting, uneven parallel bars, and floor exercise. Boys' and men's competitive events include the long horse vault, pommel horse, horizontal bar, parallel bars, still rings, and floor exercise.

In a class teaching and learning environment, all stu-

Spotting should be emphasized in a gymnastics unit.
Courtesy of Ben Lombardo, Rhode Island College, Providence, RI.

dents should receive instruction and have practice opportunities on each type of apparatus, regardless of the equipment's appropriateness for girls or women and boys or men at the competitive level.

Many skills and movements performed on the apparatus are unique to each piece of equipment. However, some skills performed on the floor exercise mat can also be performed on an appropriate piece of equipment. For example, a cartwheel can be performed on the balance beam, and a front handspring can be performed in the vaulting event.

A physical education teacher who wishes to offer a gymnastics unit must have the appropriate professional preparation to be qualified fully to offer students safety rules, sequencing of skills, and spotting techniques, including the proper utilization of overhead spotting belts, and error analysis skills.

General Safety Rules

Students in a gymnastics unit must follow several rules to ensure the safety of all participants. These rules are:

1. Jewelry cannot be worn during the unit, and the clothing worn must allow for freedom of movement.
2. Each student must warm up at the start of each class.
3. Equipment must be checked for its safety, including the condition of mats and their location in respect to the equipment.
4. All skills must be learned and practiced in a progressive manner with the assistance of properly trained spotters.
5. The instructor must authorize all skills to be practiced.
6. The spotter must be informed of the skills to be performed by a student in advance of their performance. Additionally, students must be familiar with the three types of safety mats (the basic panel, the landing cushion, and the skill cushion). Students must also be informed that gymnastic mats, no matter how thick they are, are not the complete answer to reducing or eliminating personal injury.[8]

Selected Floor and Apparatus Skills

I. Front handspring
   A. Floor exercise mat, parallettes, panel mats, and a springboard are equipment required for this exercise.
   B. Teaching progressions and cues
      1. On the floor exercise mat lunge to a switcharoo followed by a handstand with a round-off.
      2. On parallettes, use the same skill progression as previously stated, using the parallettes to locate the balance point of the body by arching the back and locking the elbows.
      3. The panel mats should be folded with spotters on each side using the previous progressions of lunge to a handstand to a round-off. Next, have the student go all the way over with total spotting assistance. Then have the student gradually increase the kick into the handstand while the spotters decrease the amount of assistance that they have been providing. As the student improves, reduce the height of the folded panel mats until the student is performing the skill on the floor.
      4. With an approach and utilization of a springboard, place the length of the mat perpendicular to the student's approach and have the student first approach the mat with a walk followed by gradually increasing the speed of the approach. At the same time, the two spotters must again begin with a total spot and then reduce their assistance as the student improves. Last, add a springboard at the end of the approach to help the student reach the handstand position.
   C. Spotting techniques
      1. Using folded panel mats on the floor and parallettes, a spotter will stand on the opposite side of the person's round-off for the spotter's safety. The spotter will grasp the student's hips and twist them in the direction of the round-off.
      2. On the mats with an approach and the use of a springboard with two students spotting, each spotter stands on opposite sides of the performer. One hand of each spotter is on the lower back, while their other hands reach for the performer's upper shoulders.[9]
II. Front handspring vault on a horse
   A. Prerequisites
      1. A controlled handstand on the floor
      2. A front handspring on the floor
   B. Teaching cues
      1. A fast run and a hard takeoff
      2. The arms must be straight with the elbows locked.
      3. The head should remain slightly back of the body during the entire vault.
   C. Teaching progressions
      1. Using a springboard and several stacked mats the student takes a three-step approach to the board and places the hands on the mats followed by jumping upwards to gain the feel of the board.
      2. With two spotters, one on each side of the stacked mats, and with the springboard close to the mats, the performer will take a three-

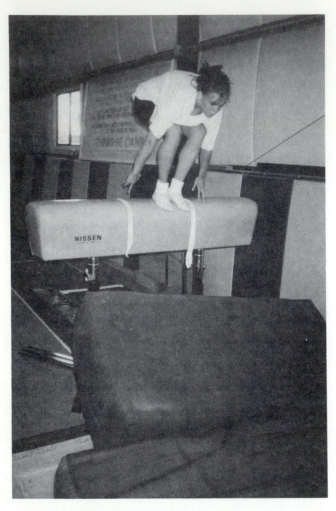

Courtesy of Ben Lombardo, Rhode Island College, Providence, RI.

step approach followed by springing off of the board into a handstand on the mats. This will be immediately followed by a front somersault.

3. With two spotters, one on each side of the mats, the performer will execute a front handstand onto the mats with the spotters providing 75% to 100% of the forward rotation into the landing.

4. The springboard is to be moved farther away from the mats so that the performer can utilize a running approach. The spotters will provide 50% of the performer's forward rotation.

5. The performer will execute a full front handspring onto the mats without spotters.

D. Spotting techniques

1. The vault requires two spotters.

2. Each spotter places one hand under the performer's hips and thighs and the other hand under the upper back.[10]

III. Forward roll on the balance beam

A. The prerequisite for this skill is an effective forward roll on the floor.

B. Teaching progressions and cues

1. A forward roll on a line on the floor must first be demonstrated by the learner.

2. On a floor beam (or minibeam) with mats stacked on both sides of the beam, the student will perform the forward roll with the assistance of a spotter.

3. On a slightly higher beam, the student will practice the forward roll as previously described.

4. The mats are gradually removed until they are no longer needed; however, the spotter remains in position.

5. The spotter performs less assistance until 100% of the skill is being executed by the performer.

C. Spotting techniques: The spotter will stand at the side of the beam facing the performer, and as the performer's arms are bending and the head is tucked, the spotter will grasp the hip and waist areas and assist in lowering the performer's back and hips to the beam.[9]

IV. Double leg circle on the pommel horse

A. Teaching progressions and cues

1. To learn to keep the body straight, the student should utilize the mushroom. On the mushroom, which is low to the floor, the student learns to swing around the mushroom in a conelike manner. The body will become straighter as one's strength improves. To begin on the mushroom, place the hands shoulder width apart. The arms must remain straight as the student jumps around to the left for a rear support. As this becomes easier, the student will complete a circle by shifting to the left, turning in, and bringing the body back to a front support. The student should continue this action until he can perform circles continuously.

2. The same procedure described previously applies to the floor buck; however, it does not force the same conelike path. While on the buck, the student should perform circles sideways as well as crossways.

3. The low floor pommel horse will reduce the chances of the performer hitting a leg on the horse because it will force the performer to swing high over the horse.

4. The student should gradually progress to the regulation pommel horse height for performing this skill.

B. Spotting techniques: Spotter stands behind the student and lifts at the waist to provide support and to assist in lifting the performer onto the horse. Be careful not to get hit by the performer's moving legs.[9]

V. Back scissors turn

    A. Definition: The student supports him- or herself first on the right hand, then on the left, as he or she moves from one side of the horse to the other side.

    B. Teaching progressions and cues

        1. On the floor, begin in a straddle push-up position. Push up with the hands and feet and rotate the body 180 degrees so that the body faces up. One hand remains on the floor at all times for support.

        2. On the pommel horse, straddle the horse at one end, and place both hands on one handle while facing in. Begin rocking forward and backward to gain momentum for the back scissors turn. Perform a half of a turn the same way as on the floor by switching support from one hand to the other.

        3. On the parallel bars, support the body on the bars and start the body moving forward and backward. When the swing is high enough so that the legs rise above the bars on the backswing, then straddle the legs, placing support on one hand, and turn the body 180 degrees. Again, change hand support from one hand to the other and then back to both hands. The legs should fall on the bars in a straddle position.

    C. Spotting techniques

        1. On the pommel horse, the spotter should be on the opposite side of the direction in which the performer is turning to avoid being hit by the swinging legs. The spotter must grasp the sides of the performer's waist to assist in the execution of the skill.

        2. On the parallel bars, the spotter should place the hands under the bars in the event that the performer falls. The panel mats should also be provided so that the spotter's height is increased.[11]

Culminating Activity for a Gymnastics Unit

One culminating activity is to conduct a gymnastics meet at the conclusion of the unit either within each class or between classes (intramural meet). Colleagues and varsity gymnasts can participate as judges.

JOGGING AND BRISK WALKING

Jogging and brisk walking are two aerobic activities that can lead to efficient and effective cardiovascular endurance if the student's training program follows the principles presented in Chapter 17.

It is important to distinguish between the activities of brisk walking, jogging, and running. *Running* involves moving faster than 9 minutes per mile, and moving slower than this rate of speed refers to *jogging*. Jogging or slow running is different from *brisk walking* in that both feet leave the ground during the airborne or flight phase. When walking, one foot is always in contact with the surface. *Brisk walking* can provide aerobic conditioning benefits if the student beginning a walking program moves at a speed of 3.5 to 4.5 miles per hour.[12]

Jogging Form

Some jogging suggestions are as follows: (1) jog *tall*, which means in an upright position with the head level because leaning forward or backward can contribute to back and leg pain; (2) hold the arms slightly away from the body with the elbows bent so that the forearms are parallel to the surface with the arms balancing the jogger and the relaxed hands being positioned near the waist; (3) land lightly on the foot's heel, and then rock forward to drive off of the ball of the foot; (4) keep the steps short by letting the foot touch the surface beneath the knee instead of reaching the foot out in front of the body; and (5) breathe from the abdomen and through the mouth. If you cannot talk while jogging, then you are overdoing it.[12]

Suggestions for Joggers

Several suggestions are: (1) always warm up and cool down as described in Chapter 17; (2) purchase a pair of jogging shoes that have effective arch support, resilient soles, and heel cushioning; (3) wear comfortable and loose fitting clothing, and remember to begin jogging wearing layers of clothing in cool weather; and (4) to avoid injuries, do not exceed jogging for more than 25 miles per week.

Suggestions for Brisk Walkers

The intensity of walking can be increased by (1) alternating periods of walking with jogging or running, (2) walking up and down hills (however, exercise caution when walking down hills by not allowing one's speed to result in haphazard foot placement), and (3) use hand weights appropriately by carrying them with the arms bent and swinging freely. Using a weighted belt or carrying hand weights passively at one's sides is not effective. It is important to note that ankle weights do increase the intensity of the walk; however, they may result in injury caused by fatigue in the lower extremities and changes in foot placement and walking style.[12]

Suggestions for Instruction

Six suggestions for instruction are: (1) provide students with a mileage card or chart that will indicate their total miles jogged or walked during each session over a period of time; (2) another motivator is to have students indicate their progress, on a map of a geographic area, toward a specified goal such as jogging or walking to accumulate miles from one's hometown to a designated community in one's state; (3) encourage students to participate with friends and family members in the YMCA Folksmarch program that involves a 5- or 10-kilometer walk or jog through area communities once per month; (4) conduct a cross-country meet for individual and coed teams such as a turkey trot during the month of November; (5) design and create a vita par cours, or fitness trail, on school property that consists of a variety of stations for stretching and strengthening muscle groups with students jogging from one station to the next; and (6) encourage students interested in basketball or soccer to dribble a ball while jogging.

RESISTANCE TRAINING

Resistance training, or the development of muscular strength and endurance, is an important component of physical fitness. The training principles associated with this type of training were presented in Chapter 17.

A resistance training program may be conducted without weights (with substitutions such as push-ups and pull-ups), with free weights (dumbbells and barbells) or resistance machines (Universal and Nautilus). If expensive equipment is unavailable, then items such as a towel or inner-tube band ("powerband") with or without the assistance of a partner can be used. Additionally, partner resistance training without any equipment can also be introduced to students.

Resistance Exercises without Weights

Three exercises requiring a towel are rowing, towel pulldowns, and towel curls. *Rowing* is a movement to strengthen one's arms and back. Start by sitting on the floor with the legs spread and facing the partner. Fold a large bath towel lengthwise and place it in the hands by holding the towel in the middle. Then, have the partner pull the ends of the towel with his or her elbows to the sides while your arms are fully extended.

Next, pull your elbows back to the sides slowly, with the partner providing resistance until his or her arms are fully extended. Repeat this rowing motion until the set is complete.

Towel pulldowns will firm the back and side muscles as well as add to flexibility. Start by grasping a towel at each end and place the center of the towel on a doorknob or

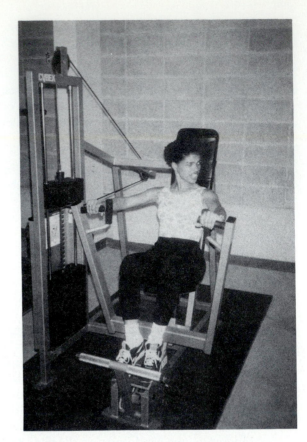

Weight training is a popular high school offering.
Courtesy of Ben Lombardo, Rhode Island College, Providence, RI.

corner of a chair. Then, kneel down and lean forward to an extended position. Pull yourself upward and forward while bending the elbows. Then, slowly return to the starting position using the same motion, and repeat this process. To increase flexibility, stretch at the starting position with each repetition. One can also have a partner provide resistance by pressing on the upper back during the exercise.

Towel curls will shape and tone the front of the arms. Start by facing a partner with a towel held at each end, and the other partner holding the center of the towel, while you keep the arms bent and hands close to the neck. Let the partner pull your arms slowly down until they are fully extended. Then pull your arms back up to the starting position, as the partner applies resistance. Do not allow your upper body to sway during this exercise.[13]

Four examples of *inner-tube strip* or *powerband exercises* follow.

1. *Hips:* Place the band around both legs and above the knees while lying on the stomach with the forehead on the floor, and press the hips against the floor and slowly raise one leg as high as possible. Repeat this exercise with the opposite leg.

2. *Hamstrings:* Place the band around both legs at the ankles while lying face down on the floor with both legs straight and the forehead and hips on the floor. Slowly bend the left leg upward as far as possible while the right leg is straight. Repeat the procedure with the opposite leg.

3. *Quadriceps:* Place the band around both legs at the ankles while sitting in a chair or on a table high enough for the feet to clear the floor, and keep the left leg bent at 90 degrees while slowly straightening the right leg until the leg is straight. Reverse leg positions.

4. *Ankles:* Place the band around both feet while sitting on the floor with the legs straight and the feet turned in. Follow by slowly turning the feet out without rolling at the hips or knees.[13]

Some examples of other partner exercises without equipment are push-ups, leg extensions, and leg curls.

Push-ups strengthen the chest area and arms. Begin by lying face down on the floor, placing the hands slightly wider than shoulder width apart, and keeping the legs together. Extend the arms while having a partner place a hand on the back for resistance. Slowly lower the body downward as the partner applies resistance, until you touch the chest to the floor. Then, push yourself back up to the starting position and repeat. Keep the palms facing inward and have the partner apply resistance throughout the exercise.

Leg extensions strengthen the thighs and increase knee flexibility. Begin by sitting on a bench and bracing yourself at the sides of the bench. Bend one knee so that the leg is at a 90-degree angle. Slowly raise the leg to a fully extended position as the partner applies resistance by pushing against the ankle during the movement. Move slowly and in a controlled manner throughout the exercise for the best results. Repeat using the opposite leg.

Leg curls strengthen the hamstring muscles. Begin by lying face down with the legs together and bent back as far as possible. Next, have the partner slowly pull the legs by their heels until they are fully extended. Increase the resistance slowly. Do 8 to 10 repetitions per session.[13]

Suggestions for Instruction

1. Physical education teachers who wish to conduct a resistance training unit must possess professional preparation in the use of free weights, Universal equipment, and Nautilus equipment, as well as proper training principles, lifting techniques, spotting techniques, and safety rules.

2. Students should be encouraged to establish goals, and they should be provided with a worksheet that indicates the weight being lifted, the number of repetitions per set, and the number of sets during each workout.

3. When conducting the unit, it is strongly recommended that an instructor inform students that the Amer-

ican Medical Association (AMA) has declared that the use of anabolic steroids as a shortcut to enhancing muscular performance is dangerous to the safety and welfare of an individual. *Because of the harmful side effects of illegal steroid abuse, there is no substitution for a 100% commitment to an appropriately designed resistance training program.*

4. Female students should be informed that it is a myth that participating in a resistance training program with free weights, Universal equipment, or Nautilus equipment will cause them to look muscular and less feminine. Inform girls and women that although the quality of muscle in females and males is the same, endocrinological differences such as hormonal secretions of androgen, testosterone, estrogen, and progesterone between females and males will not permit females to achieve the same increase in muscle size, or hypertrophy, as males.[12]

ROPE JUMPING AND SKIPPING

Rope jumping or skipping is another lifelong and enjoyable recreational and aerobic activity. Other benefits of jumping or skipping rope are as follows: (1) it improves fine and gross motor coordination, (2) it provides rhythmic training, (3) it improves timing and speed, (4) it helps to relieve tension, (5) it enhances a positive self-esteem, and (6) it provides basic movement skills for effective body management.[14]

In terms of comparing jumping or skipping rope with other aerobic activities, it is important to state that 15 minutes of rope jumping is equivalent to performing the following activities: (1) 100 yards of swimming in 17 to 23 minutes, (2) walking 2 miles in 20 minutes, (3) running 1 mile in 8 minutes, and (4) bicycling 3 miles in under 9 minutes.[14]

Appropriate Length of a Jump Rope

The length of a jump rope is determined by the height of the student. The person should stand on the rope with the feet together, and the handles should reach the armpits. As gudelines, K-3 students utilize ropes that are 7 to 8 feet long with intermediate students utilizing ropes that are 8 to 9 feet long. Middle school students need to select ropes that are 8 to 10 feet long, and the length of ropes for high-school students is 9 to 10 feet long. Double dutch ropes are 12 to 14 feet in length. Double dutch refers to two rope turners using two long ropes as one or more jumpers enter, jump, and exit without touching the ropes.[14]

General Jumping Hints

Hold the rope loosely by utilizing the thumbs and index fingers for control. The elbows remain at waist level with the arms extended sideways at approximately 90-

degree angles. The body should remain erect while a circular wrist motion is employed to turn the rope. Last, jump or skip on the balls of the feet with a soft landing. Flat-footed landings can cause ankle, lower-leg, or knee problems.[14]

Basic Skills

The *basic skip* involves alternating the feet and swinging the free leg back. Skip over the rope with the right foot as the left foot swings back. Then hop on the right foot as the left foot swings forward. Next, skip over the rope with the left foot as the right foot swings back. Last, hop on the left foot as the right foot swings forward.

Jumping rope involves keeping the knees relaxed and landing on the balls of the feet. This skill involves the feet executing a two-foot takeoff from the floor with a two-foot landing.

Rocking skip is executed by placing the right foot forward and, without utilizing the rope, rocking forward on the right, then back on the left foot. After a brief period of rocking practice, begin to rock over the rope on every forward rock. Change, putting the left foot forward, by performing a few jumps in between right and left rocks.[14]

Assisting the Student Who Has Difficulty with a Single Rope

The following teaching cues are designed to assist students who may be snapping or whipping the rope for utilizing only one arm.

1. Turn the rope over the head and then catch it under the toes.
2. Hold the rope stationary and jump forward and backward over it.
3. Swing the rope slightly while jumping forward and backward over it.
4. Increase the swing of the rope gradually until a full turn of the rope has been completed.
5. Jump to the sound of the rope touching the floor.

Double Dutch Techniques

Suggestions for the *two rope turners* are as follows:
1. Each turner should hold one end of each of the ropes waist high, in front of the body and shoulder width apart.
2. Keep the elbows close to the body and turn the ropes by rotating the right forearm counterclockwise and the left forearm clockwise.
3. Keep the thumbs up during the circular motion of the hands as the ropes are turned.
4. Avoid crossing the midline of the body with the hands while turning the ropes.
5. Establish a cadence of 1-2 for the ropes as a means

of controlling the tempo of the ropes alternately touching the floor.

Cues for *double dutch jumpers* are as follows:
1. Stand close by the side of a rope turner and say "go" each time the rope farthest from the jumper touches the floor to establish a rhythm.
2. Run into the ropes as the rope farthest from the jumper touches the floor and then begin jumping.
3. Jump in the center of the ropes facing one of the two turners.
4. Exit the ropes by jumping toward a turner, and then run close to the turner after a predetermined last jump.[14]

Suggestions for Instruction

Some suggestions for instruction are as follows:
1. Teach two to four skills per class session.
2. Conclude each class with record-breaking attempts such as a 15-second speed test or the number of turns of the rope without missing.
3. Consider involving the students in the *Jump Rope for Heart* educational program sponsored by the American Heart Association (AHA) and our national and state professional organization, American Alliance for Health, Physical Education, Recreation, and Dance (AAHPERD). The mottos of this program are *Jump for the Health of It* and *Give Yourself a Lift*. Contact your local AHA chapter office or AAHPERD for additional information. The AHA/AAHPERD program provides educators with information related to the myriad of skipping and jumping skills with teaching cues.[14]

SELF-DEFENSE

It is important that individuals prepare themselves to avoid dangerous situations that have the potential of threatening their safety and welfare. *Practical* self-defense is defined as (1) being prepared to minimize the possibility of assault by following preventive measures to avoid becoming a victim; (2) being prepared to minimize the possibility of engaging in a physical confrontation by utilizing psychological defenses when facing a potential attacker; and (3) being prepared to utilize a group of simple, but highly effective, physical actions if no other alternatives are available.

Practical self-defense for all is the process of learning how to avoid being a submissive and nonaggressive victim. Self-defense training and practice allows one to be self-confident and assertive. The assertive person refuses to be taken advantage of.[15]

Preventive Measures

Many specific situations allow an individual to become vulnerable to an attack if appropriate precautions are not practiced to avoid becoming a victim. Some preventive measures for protecting one's home are (1) installing and utilizing quality deadbolt or cylinder locks on doors including sliding glass doors, (2) stopping all deliveries including newspapers and mail and placing some lights on automatic timers when away from home, (3) utilizing an identification engraving system for expensive personal property that is on record at the local police station, (4) not opening a door until a stranger has been identified, and (5) using commonsense precautions regarding the telephone such as not revealing the phone number indiscriminately and not allowing people to know that you are home alone.

Other specific situations requiring precautions to protect an individual are traveling by car or public transportation, walking on a street when no one is available to walk with you, staying overnight in a motel or hotel, and visiting public arenas. For these foregoing situations, assign the class to prepare a list of preventive measures to avoid becoming a victim of a personal assault.

Psychological Defense

Psychological defense involves remaining calm, listening carefully to exactly what the potential attacker is saying, communicating with the attacker in a rational manner, and attempting to identify the attacker for later verification and reporting of the incident to the police.

To illustrate this technique, a young woman living alone in a two-story apartment building took a waste-paper basket to the trash bin behind her building at 1:30 P.M. When she returned, a strange man was sitting on her sofa. One psychological defensive strategy for the woman might be to calmly and quickly comment, "I did not know that Carol had company." By pretending not to be the resident of the apartment and then calmly leaving the stranger alone in her apartment, this potential victim was able to avoid a confrontation with the stranger. It is suggested that the instructor present other specific situations to the students for them to prepare plausible psychological defenses in those situations.

Physical Self-Defense Techniques

The *four principles of physical self-defense* are (1) focus, (2) advantage, (3) leverage, and (4) balance. *Focus* refers to attacking the weakest or vulnerable parts of the assailant's body such as the mastoid process, bridge of the nose, temples, throat, solar plexus (located below the sternum), kidneys, and groin. The principle of *advantage* means utilizing your strength to redirect the attacker's movements rather than to directly oppose the attacker. *Leverage* is the concept of gaining a biomechanical advantage by utilizing the powerful leg and back extensor muscles. *Balance*, the most important concept, refers to placing the attacker in a position whereby body stability can no longer be maintained. It is necessary that the victim widen the base of support by placing the feet and legs in a forward and backward stance with the knees bent.[15]

Self-defense class.
Courtesy of Emily Leonardo, Camp Hill High School, Camp Hill, PA.

These principles are to be applied to attacks from the front and back of the body. A number of front and rear attacks should be introduced and practiced by students such as the front wrist holds (1-on-1 and 2-on-2), front shoulder grab, front choke (with one hand and two hands), front hair pull, front bear hug, 2-on-2 rear-wrist hold, rear choke (with one hand on the mouth, with two hands around the throat, and with a forearm), rear hair pull, and rear bear hug. The physical education teacher must receive special training in all of the foregoing physical self-defense techniques before presenting them to students.

One example of a physical self-defense technique is releasing a front-wrist 2-on-2 hold. This type of hold involves the assailant facing the victim and grasping both wrists. Even though this is a confining position for the victim, it can place the assailant in a neutral position. Because the assailant is using both hands to hold the victim, he has to let go of one or both wrists to further attack the potential victim. The victim must immediately maintain balance and then distract the assailant to loosen the hold. To distract the attacker, the victim should yell, stomp on his instep with the heel of one foot, or employ a front or side kick directed toward the assailant's knee or shin. If these actions do not result in the assailant releasing his hold, then the victim should swing the hands and arms outward followed by quickly pulling them inward, up and away from the attacker. The victim must pull against the attacker's thumbs and forefingers because this is the weakest part of one's grip. When the release has occurred, the victim should quickly retaliate with a side kick to the knee and then run from the scene. Practicing the foregoing release with a peer requires carefully and slowly moving through the procedures with the "assailant" applying different degrees of force to the hold as well as using over, under, and side grips on the "victim." The "victim" should also practice the movements with the eyes closed.[15]

Self-Defense Applied to Specific Populations

A self-defense unit should also include information regarding child sexual abuse, battered women, and abused senior citizens.

Regarding child sexual abuse, educators should provide students with a guest speaker representing a local task force. Educators also have a legal and moral obligation to report a suspected case of child abuse to the appropriate school personnel designated by the school district. When a woman is battered or abused by a partner, it is advised that she contact the local police, seek medical attention if need be, have photos taken of the injuries, reside at a temporary shelter for battered women and their children, and seek legal advice. Regardless of a battered woman's financial situation, she can obtain all of these services as well as a legal order of protection to

require the abuser to remain away from her and her children.

Different types of abuse are directed toward senior citizens. All forms of abuse involve the personal needs of the elderly, especially the needs that must be fulfilled by others who are close to the victim such as family members, friends, or other individuals serving as caretakers. The needs may be emotional, psychological, financial, or physical.

It is recommended that adults, before having a need for a caretaker, make all decisions about what will happen to them in the future. Aging adults should predetermine who will care for them and manage all of their affairs if they become mentally or physically incapacitated.[16]

Other Suggestions for Instruction

Throughout the self-defense unit, reinforce the concept that adhering to precautions in specific situations will reduce the possibility of ever being confronted by an assailant.

When presenting psychological defenses, it is suggested that the students also learn how to describe an assailant in detail. The instructor should stage a scene in class in which an "assailant" attacks the instructor. Refer to Fig. 20-2 for a sample of a form that the students can complete

---

I. Specific description of the clothing worn by the assailant
   Type of garment   Color of garment
   A.
   B.
   C.
   D.
   E.
II. Was the assailant wearing any rings?
   Yes _____ No _____
   If yes, the number of rings was _____ , and they were located on the _____ hand(s).
III. Did the assailant have any scars?
   Yes _____ No _____
   If yes, where were the scars located? _____
IV. Did the assailant have any tattoos?
   Yes _____ No _____
   If yes, where were the tattoos located? _____
V. Describe the voice quality of the assailant.

VI. Describe any other noticeable physical characteristics of the assailant.

VII. Other observations:

FIG. 20-2   Describing an assailant in specific detail.

after the "assailant" has left the classroom. Then request the "assailant" to return to the classroom so that the students can determine the accurateness of their descriptions.

CROSS-COUNTRY SKIING

Because cross-country skiing is a seasonal sport and a physically demanding aerobic activity, an instructor is advised to encourage students to develop the components of physical fitness by engaging in other aerobic activities 8 to 12 weeks before the beginning of the ski unit.

Selection of Equipment and Clothing

With the introduction of the skill of marathon skating, which involves side-to-side movements of the hips and legs similar to ice skating and roller skating, skis are now manufactured stiffer than they were before the advent of skating. Because the skating technique involves pushing off with one leg and ski, not only do the skis need to be stiffer, but also they need to be shorter. The skis should be of a length that allows the skier to rest the tails of the skis on the floor or ground, and, with the skis in a vertical position, their tips should be in line with the top of the head.

The poles are important for the effective execution of the skating technique. The poles need to be of sufficient length to allow for the upright skating position. To determine the appropriate length, use the following formula:

$$\text{Skier's height (inches)} \times 2.3 = \text{Ski length}$$

A general rule of thumb is that the poles should be long enough to plant them in the snow with the gripping end of the poles being in line with the skier's facial area between the upper lip and the bottom of the nose. No wax skis have a special pattern on the bottom that permits backslip; however, they are not constructed for gliding purposes. Students interested in skiing as fast as possible should consider skis requiring the application of a wax.

The placement of bindings on the skis is critical so that the gliding quality of the skis is not destroyed. Bindings on skating skis should be moved forward so that the tips of the skis do not rise up. A reputable ski shop will ensure the appropriate positioning of the bindings.

When one purchases boots, they should be stiff with sufficient lateral stability so that the skier does not roll off of the side of the boot along with medial stability, which will prevent the arches from collapsing.

Loose-fitting clothing should be worn to allow for a wider range of motion. The skier should wear several

Cross-country skiing.
Courtesy of Suzi D'Annalfo, Conard High School, West Hartford, CT.

light and warm layers, which provide for more ventilation. To avoid heat loss, a hat is essential. Gaiters worn on the lower legs will keep the boots and socks dry in deep-snow conditions. Last, when touring, it is important that a skier pack an extra pair of dry socks.[2]

Skills Progression

Students should first practice walking on skis and learn how to fall and to rise from a fall. Other skiing skills are presented in the following paragraphs.

The *diagonal stride* is used on level and slightly uphill terrains. This skill is learned by (1) grasping each pole at its midpoint and then placing the pole in each hand parallel to the snow, followed by swinging the arms naturally to the rhythm or beat of each leg stride; (2) the leg action involves kicking with one leg and gliding on the other; (3) proper grasping of the poles involves inserting the hands into the poles' strap loops, grasping the upper portion of the poles, and gripping them with the entire relaxed hands; (4) the body does not move from side to side because the weight of the body is transferred from one ski to the other; (5) the skier should be able to look down and observe that the knee on the gliding ski has covered the toes of the boot; and (6) the skier shortens the arm and leg movements on an upward terrain with the weight of the body being forward on the balls of the feet.

Double poling involves (1) the position of both arms and the weight of the upper body shifting forward as the downhill slope and speed of the skier increases; (2) when planting both poles simultaneously, the skier bends at the waist and feels that he or she is falling forward; (3) when poling, the skier has a firm grip on the pole plant and a relaxed grip on the backswing of the poling action with the palms facing upward in the follow-through of the poling action; and (4) to further streamline the body for more speed by reducing wind resistance, the skier will assume a compact, tuck position so that the back muscles can be rested.

Climbing uphill involves either the herringbone or sidestepping techniques. The herringbone climb is used for steep uphill terrain, and it involves the tips of the skis being apart, the inner edges of the skis gripping the snow, and the body weight being forward. Each pole plant supports the side of the body when a ski is lifted. As the incline of the hill decreases, the width between the skis also lessens.

Sidestepping is employed when the uphill terrain is too steep for an effective herringbone technique. The skier proceeds uphill by moving the skis parallel to each other and perpendicular to the length of the trail. The uphill ski is moved up by lifting the tail of the ski up and then placing the uphill edge into the slope with the body's weight on the uphill ski. Then the downhill ski is moved up parallel to the uphill ski and with its inside edge "biting" the snow.

Downhill techniques include the snowplow and sidestepping. When on steep and narrow downhill trails, the skier can use the snowplow as the means of braking the descent. This technique involves placing one ski tip slightly ahead of the other, pushing the heels outward, and pressing the knees inward. Pressing the knees inward will place the skis on their inner edges. The hands and arms are forward of the body. Decreasing or increasing the degree of flexed knees or the amount of weight placed on the inside edges of the skis will control the skier's speed of descent. Refer to the previously mentioned sidestepping techniques.

Turning the skis to the left or right involves knowledge of the snowplow turn, step turn, and parallel turn. (Refer to the discussion on the basic snowplow position.) Additionally, the snowplow turn involves the body's weight being placed on the inside edge of one ski, which results in a turn in the opposite direction. When the right ski is weighted, the skier will turn to the left, and conversely when the left ski is weighted, the skier will move to the right.

In the *step turn,* initially the skis are parallel and apart for stability. Then the skier lifts up the ski in the direction of the turn while placing the body weight on the other ski. That ski is placed in the direction of the turn, and the body weight shifts to it. The trailing ski is then placed alongside the ski that led the turn.

In the *parallel turn,* the heels are down on both skis, and then both heels thrust sideways to turn the skis. To accomplish this type of turn, the pole is planted on the side of the body toward which the turn is to be made, and the body rises to unweight that ski. The knees then turn the skis in the desired direction followed by the body's weight moving to the outside or downhill ski. The uphill ski slips parallel to the downhill ski.

The *marathon skating skill* involves two phases: the glide and the kick. During the gliding phase, the body weight is on the flat ski in the track of the trail. The flat ski is then edged into the snow, and the body weight is transferred onto the opposite leg in the kicking phase. The kicking foot is lifted off of the snow, angled out at about 40 degrees, and pushed back as in an ice skating motion. At the conclusion of the kick, the leg is extended. The kicking leg is then brought back completely over the ski track and is followed by a glide phase. The head leads the body for the skating technique with the head over the foot on each glide phase. The head then moves laterally over the other foot on the kicking phase. The arm phase includes a double-pole plant, which initiates the skate, with the upper body collapsing to a 90-degree angle and a parallel back position to the ground. The pole action is finished before the kicking begins. Both arms then snap backward and follow through. The leg action should be mastered before the arm action is introduced. It is important to emphasize that the opposite arm and leg work together.[2]

TRACK AND FIELD

Track and field activities have a long history as part of the high-school physical education program. Students have been interested in the various events because of the variety of skills addressed; the challenges presented by the throwing, jumping, running aspects of the sport; and the appeal of the inherent personal self-testing aspects track and field presents.

Track and field is a complex sport involving many different types of events and consists of four different types of events: (1) weight throwing, (2) vaulting, (3) running, and (4) jumping. Students of all types, sizes, shapes, and physical makeup can find avenues to success in one or more track and field activities. Unlike other popular activities that have highly specific and demanding physical requirements (such as height for basketball and physical weight and size for football), track and field remains a sport open to most high-school students. In addition, track and field is a relatively inexpensive activity. For these and other reasons, track and field should continue to be an important part of the secondary school physical education program.

Because track and field includes a large number of specific skills and activities encompassing a wide variety of techniques within several running, jumping, and throwing events, it would be impossible to attempt to provide sufficient analysis in the space provided here. However, many well prepared books and pamphlets are available to physical education teachers. Teachers should refer to the reading list provided to facilitate planning and development of units of instruction in track and field. Additional information can be obtained from Hershey's National Track and Field Youth Program, 14 E. Chocolate Avenue, Hershey, PA, 17033, or call (717) 534-7636; or The Athletic Congress, 200 S. Capitol Avenue, Suite 140, Indianapolis, IN, 46225, or call (317) 638-9155.

SUMMARY

A wide variety of individual activities and sports appropriate to a secondary school physical education program have been reviewed. Included were various elements of knowledge, skills, teaching strategies, and safety concerns. It is important to keep in mind that (1) all of these activities are lifetime activities; (2) efficient and effective student learning and performance are the result of proper sequencing of skills, the presentation of appropriate learning tasks, and the ability of the instructor and students to engage in successful error detection and correction of skills; (3) the instructor should emphasize the physical and mental aspects of the skills, and mental practice should be a regular component of the instructional program; and (4) the instructor should provide opportunities for the students to be videotaped while performing skills, with the instructor and peers providing feedback after students have been given time to evaluate their performances.

REFERENCES

1. Mowatt G: *Aquarobics,* Unpublished class handout, 1991.
2. Mood D, Musker F, Rink JE: *Sports and recreational activities for men and women,* ed 10, St Louis, 1991, Mosby.
3. Seidel BL et al: *Sport skills: a conceptual approach to meaningful movement,* Dubuque, Iowa, 1975, William C Brown.
4. de la Rosa DM, Kolin J: *Understanding, maintaining, and riding the ten-speed bicycle,* Emmaus, Pa, 1979, Rodale Press.
5. Shermer M: *Sport cycling: a guide to training, racing, and endurance,* Chicago, 1985, Contemporary Books.
6. Clark B: *Successful progressions for golf skills,* Unpublished presentation at NYSAHPERD Conference in Rochester, New York, 1985.
7. National Golf Foundation: *Golf novelty events,* National Golf Foundation.
8. George G: *USGF gymnastics safety manual,* Indianapolis, 1985, USGF Publication Department.
9. Turoff F: *Artistic gymnastics,* Dubuque, Iowa, 1991, William C Brown.
10. Bare F: *The complete gymnastics book,* USA, 1980, Vollet Publishing.
11. Tatlow P: *The world of gymnastics,* New York, 1978, Atheneum.
12. Thygerson AL: *Fitness and health: life-style strategies,* Boston, 1989, Jones & Bartlett.
13. Leon E: *Complete women's weight training guide,* Mountain View, Calif, 1984, Anderson World.
14. American Heart Association and AAHPERD: *Jump for the health of it! intermediate style and double Dutch skills,* information packet, Dallas, 1992.
15. Peterson SG: *Self-defense for women: the West Point way,* New York, 1989, Simon & Schuster.
16. *Domestic mistreatment of elderly: towards prevention,* ed 4, Washington, DC, 1989, AARP Publications.

SUGGESTED READINGS
Aquatics

YMCA of the USA: *Aquatics for special populations,* Champaign, Ill, 1987, Human Kinetics.

Ballatore R, Miller W, O'Connor B: *Swimming and aquatics today,* St Paul, 1990, West Publishing.

Forbes MS: *Coaching synchronized swimming effectively,* ed 2, Champaign, Ill, 1989, Human Kinetics.

Krasevec J, Grimes D: *Hydrorobics,* Champaign, Ill, 1985, Human Kinetics.

Schubert M: *Sports illustrated competitive swimming: techniques of champions,* New York, 1990, Sports Illustrated.

Thomas D: *Teaching swimming: steps to success,* Champaign, Ill, 1989, Human Kinetics.

Thomas DG: *Advanced swimming: steps to success,* Champaign, Ill, 1990, Leisure Press.

Vickers BJ: *Swimming,* ed 5, Dubuque, Iowa, 1989, William C Brown.

Archery

Haywood K: *Archery: steps to success,* Champaign, Ill, 1989, Leisure Press.

McKinney WC, McKinney MW: *Archery,* Dubuque, Iowa, 1990, William C Brown.

Bicycling

Burke ER: *Science of cycling,* Champaign, Ill, 1980, Human Kinetics.

Burke ER, Margaret M: *Medical and scientific aspects of cycling,* Champaign, Ill, 1988, Human Kinetics.

Snowling S, Evans K: *Bicycle mechanics: in workshop and competition,* Champaign, Ill, 1986, Human Kinetics.

Weaver S: *A woman's guide to cycling,* Berkeley, Calif, 1991, Ten Speed Press.

Bowling

Martin JL, Tandy RE, Asne-Traub C: *Bowling,* Dubuque, Iowa, 1990, William C Brown.

Strickland RH: *Bowling: steps to success,* Champaign, Ill, 1989, Human Kinetics.

Strickland RH: *Teaching bowling: steps to success,* Champaign, Ill, 1989, Human Kinetics.

Golf

Ballesteros S, Andrisani J: *Natural golf,* New York, 1991, Collier Books/ Macmillan Publishing.

Enhaser K: *Quantum golf,* New York, 1991, Warner Books.

Nance VL, Davis EC: *Golf,* Dubuque, Iowa, 1990, William C Brown.

Ostroske W, Devaney J: *Correct the 10 most common golf problems in 10 days,* New York, 1991, Putnam Publishing.

Owens D: *Teaching golf to special populations,* Champaign, Ill, 1984, Human Kinetics.

Owens D, Bunker LK: *Golf: steps to success,* Champaign, Ill, 1989, Leisure Press.

Gymnastics

Carpenter LJ: *Gymnastics for girls and women,* West Nyack, NY, 1985, Parker Publishing.

Fodero JM, Furblur E: *Creating gymnastic pyramids and balances,* Champaign, Ill, 1989, Human Kinetics.

Pica R: *Dance training for gymnastics,* Champaign, Ill, 1988, Human Kinetics.

Jogging and brisk walking

Cantlay J, Hoffman R: *Running together: the family book of jogging,* Champaign, Ill, 1981, Human Kinetics.

Glover B, Shepherd J: *The runner's handbook: a complete fitness guide for men and women on the run,* New York, 1978, Penguin Books.

Resistance training

Gain W, Hartmann J: *Strong together: developing strength with a partner,* Toronto, 1990, Sports Books.

Fahey TD: *Basic weight training,* Mountain View, Calif, 1989, Mayfield Publishing.

O'Connor B, Simmons J, O'Shea P: *Weight training today,* St Paul, 1989, West Publishing.

Stone WJ, Kroll WA: *Sports conditioning and weight training: programs for athletic competition,* Dubuque, Iowa, 1991, William C Brown.

Rope jumping and skipping

Nichols B: *Moving and learning: the elementary school physical education experience,* ed 3, St Louis, 1994, Mosby.

Elliot ME, Anderson MH, LaBerge J: *Play with a purpose,* ed 3, New York, 1978, Harper & Row.

Mitchell C: *The perfect exercise—the hop, skip and jump way to health,* New York, 1976, Simon & Schuster.

Smith P: *Aerobic rope skipping,* Freeport, NY, 1981, Educational Activities.

Self-defense

Seidler AH, Seidler TL: *Defend yourself: scientific personal defense,* Dubuque, Iowa, 1990, Kendall/Hunt Publishing.

Cross-country skiing

Borowski L: *Ski faster, easier,* Champaign, Ill, 1986, Human Kinetics.

Chamberlain L, Chamberlain T: *Cross-country skiing in New England,* Chester, Conn, 1990, Globe Pequot Press.

Endestad A, Teaford JL Jr: *Skating for cross country skiers,* Champaign, Ill, 1987, Human Kinetics.

Sharkey BJ: *Training for cross-country ski racing,* Champaign, Ill, 1984, Human Kinetics.

Track and field

Brown M: *Track and field rules in pictures,* New York, 1990, Perisee Books.

Carr GA: *Fundamentals of track and field,* Champaign, Ill, 1991, Leisure Press.

CHAPTER 21

Dual Sports and Activities

CHAPTER OBJECTIVES
- ◆ To review basic teaching points for dual sports and activities
- ◆ To discuss the value of including dual sports and activities in secondary school physical education programs
- ◆ To discuss the role of the teacher when teaching dual sports and activities
- ◆ To provide examples of dual sports and activities that could be used in a secondary school physical education program

A wide variety of activities are included in the area of dual sports. Their values are numerous in terms of challenges to the individual student to develop and improve physical skills and therefore should be included in the physical education curriculum. Many of these dual activities provide opportunities for lifelong participation and contribute in many ways to the individual's health and wellness.

BADMINTON

Badminton is an exciting lifelong sport that may be played indoors or outdoors. The badminton court has a 5-foot net and is marked for singles and doubles play. The game is played with a racket and a shuttlecock.

Skills Progression

The appropriate sequencing of skills involves first teaching the forehand grip and ready position, followed by the high and low serves, forehand overhead shots (clear, drop, and smash), backhand grip and backhand shots (clear and drop) and underhand shots (forehand and backhand net clears and net drops). The instructor should indicate the similarities and differences in the flight patterns and sequential/temporal patterns of the clears, drops, and smashes.

Learning Tasks for Facilitating Performance

Alley rally for down-the-line placement. Have students work with partners, with the object being to rally with the shuttlecock in the alley. Students will position themselves opposite each other, near the alley so that the racket head is swinging through the alley, and midway between the net and baseline. One student will be hitting forehands and the other will be hitting backhands. Students then practice from forecourt to forecourt and then backcourt to backcourt. Then, the partners switch to the opposite alleys, so each experiences the forehand and backhand shots.

Crosscourt rally. Partners stand near the alley and behind the service line diagonally opposite each other. The object is to rally crosscourt with partners hitting forehand to forehand or backhand to backhand, if both partners are right-handed. The student's body position is slightly open with the nondominant shoulder for the forehand and the dominant shoulder for the backhand pointing toward the target area. Players should reverse the corners of their courts so that they can experience forehand and backhand practice.

Combination crosscourt and down-the-line rally. Partners begin near the alley as in the alley rally. The student beginning the rally hits down the line. The partner then hits crosscourt as in the crosscourt rally. The first person

375

runs across and returns down the line as the other student slides across the court and hits crosscourt, and so on. Thus one person is always hitting down the line, while the other is always hitting crosscourt. The partners will switch roles so they both have experience with these two types of placement shots. This drill should be practiced from the net area, midcourt, and backcourt.

Center out-of-bounds (modified game). Four players are on a court. Each doubles team plays up and back with the court being divided in half from the net to the baseline. All rules are the same as in regulation doubles; however, a shuttlecock landing in the center area is considered out-of-bounds.

Short serve to the wall. A line is marked on the wall at net height, and a short service line is marked on the floor. The student stands behind the short service line and serves to the wall. For skillful players, this drill may be modified by marking several narrow lines at 2-inch intervals above and below the line representing the height of the net. The student may score the serves according to their proximity to the net line.

Four-corner task for clearing the shuttlecock. Partners begin in the center positions on the court, where this drill starts with a singles serve and continues with clears only. The first student will always remain in the center position, hitting clears to the four corners designated on the partner's side of the net. The second student will start in the center position and run to the corners to which the shuttlecock is directed. After the shuttle is returned with a clear directly to the first student, the second student will quickly return to the center position for the next hit. Both students should reverse their roles.

Overhead dropshot and underhand clear task. Both students start in the center position with the drill beginning with a singles serve by one student to a back corner. The receiver returns it with an overhead drop shot to a front corner. An underhand clear to the same or other back corner follows as the drill continues with a drop, clear, drop, and clear until one partner fails to successfully return the shuttle. Instead of using a dropshot, the overhead clear or overhead smash can be performed, and the concept of deception in terms of disguising overhead shots can be incorporated into this task.[1]

Novelty Events for Badminton

1. Sponge or balloon badminton: Instead of playing with a shuttlecock, a sponge or balloon is substituted.

2. Tin plate badminton: Players use tin plates (aluminum pie plates) as rackets and fleece, Nerf, or ping-pong balls as shuttles during regulation play.

3. One racket–four player badminton: This event is played as regulation badminton; however, the two players on each side of the net must alternate shots.

4. Shuttle badminton: Players are in a single file in a shuttle turn-back formation on a volleyball court. The first person in each file hits the shuttlecock and then gives the racket to the next person in line before going to the end of the line. Failure to execute a legal return results in the student being eliminated.

5. Call shot badminton: As contact is made with the shuttle, the student will indicate to the opponent the shot that must be utilized for returning the shuttle. If the opponent is successful, then 1 point is earned. If the opponent is unsuccessful, then 1 point is lost. The game continues until one player has scored 21 points.

Singles Strategies

Some strategies in singles play are as follows: (1) hit down on every shuttle that can be contacted with an attacking stroke so that the opponent must hit upward, (2) do not move until the opponent contacts the shuttle so that you will not be "faked out" of position, (3) aim every return to a definite place on the opponent's court, (4) use a long and high service for most points, (5) the player who uses the round-the-head stroke rather than the backhand is vulnerable to a combination of drops to the forehand and clears to the backhand because one or two extra steps backward must be taken to execute the round-the-head shot, and (6) maintain a position on the court in the center of the angle of possible return (or the direction a returned shuttle takes in relation to the width and length of the court), and be alert to a shot that falls outside of the angle of possible return.[2]

Doubles Strategies

The three basic systems for badminton doubles are (1) side-by-side, (2) up-and-back, and (3) rotation system. In the side-by-side system, each person is responsible for half of the court, from the front to the back. The up-and-back system requires one person to play the front court and the partner to play the back court. In the rotation system, the partners rotate in a counterclockwise direction. The advantages of the *side-by-side* system are that each partner's area is clearly defined and it is a good defensive formation because it is difficult for the opposing team to "smash through" it. The disadvantages of this system are that an opposing team will play only the weaker opponent by running the player up and back in his or her area; it is difficult to attack effectively from this formation, and the backcourt area might be left unprotected when one of the players is forced to the net.

The advantages of the *up-and-back* formation are that it clearly defines each player's area of responsibility, an effective attack can be initiated from this formation, and a weak partner can be hidden at the net position. The disadvantages of this system are that it places a burden on the back player, and players limit their experiences to the shots required for only the net area or backcourt area.

The advantages of the *rotation system* are that it provides

Name of Student _____   Date of Rating _____

	Excellent	Very good	Good	Needs improvement
I. Ready position A. Racket head high				
B. Weight on balls of the feet				
C. Assumed this position after each stroke				
II. Footwork A. Return to home base				
B. Weight transfers to nondominant foot during forehand strokes				
C. Weight transfers to dominant foot during backhand strokes				
III. Use of strokes A. Chooses appropriate strokes for the game situation				
B. Hits to unprotected court area				
C. Serves accurately and consistently				
IV. General play A. Attempts to score whenever possible				
B. Tries to return all legal shots				
C. Calls shots near lines				
D. Varies strokes effectively				
E. Applies the appropriate playing rules				

V. Other comments

FIG. 21-1   Badminton rating sheet.

for equal distribution of play among teammates, and it provides both partners with more variety for making the shot. The disadvantages of this system are that it assumes equal playing abilities for both teammates in all aspects of the game, and the system can break down if a teammate is forced to move forward or backward in a clockwise movement instead of the preferred movement of partners in a counterclockwise direction.[3]

Rules of Etiquette

Some rules of etiquette are as follows: (1) never walk on or close to a neighboring court while play is in progress; (2) during warm-up, rally with the opponents; (3) call your own (and your partner's) faults; (4) do not serve until the receiver is ready; and (5) following the playing of a point, return the shuttle quickly and accurately to the server. See Fig. 21-1 for a badminton rating form.

DANCE AND RHYTHMS

The curricular area of dance consists of two general forms: recreational and concert (or performing). Recre-

ational forms include aerobic, international folk, ballroom (or social), and square dances. Individuals interested in leisure activities involving social interaction may achieve their goals by utilizing their dance skills. Examples of concert forms are modern dance, ballet, and jazz. The nature of the concert dance forms requires the use of the body as a means of communicating with an audience.

Movement Fundamentals

Before dance can be utilized as a means of expression, an understanding of movement fundamentals is important. Eight basic locomotor movements are the foundation for all dance forms. The eight locomotor skills are (1) walk, (2) run, (3) leap, (4) jump, (5) hop, (6) skip, (7) slide, and (8) gallop. These skills are performed in any meter, tempo, or direction in space when applied to dance forms.[4]

Rhythm and Dance

Rhythm is a series of pulsations that can be weak or strong as well as uneven or even. A dancer is concerned

Teacher leading warm-up exercises in dance class.
Courtesy of Ann Stevens, Evanston Township High School, Evanston, IL.

Social dance.
Courtesy of Emily Leonardo, Camp Hill High School, Camp Hill, PA.

with the rhythmic elements of accent, phrase, tempo, and underlying beat.[2]

Policy Statement on Dance as Education by the National Dance Association

The National Dance Association (NDA) has identified the goals of dance as education as follows:

1. Dance provides a unique aesthetic experience for students because the dancer's body, mind, and emotions are all directly involved in unified expressive opportunities.

2. Dance offers the opportunities for teaching and learning that are designed to encourage and enhance the personal creativity of students.

3. Dance provides an important medium for exploring the history, attitudes, and customs of people of other lands, and it leads to intercultural and integrative experiences.

4. Dance is a form of exercise that leads to improved physical fitness.

5. Dance, because of its aesthetic, social, intellectual, and social values, is a lifelong activity enjoyed at any age level.

6. Dance provides an opportunity for meaningful and constructive social group involvement.

7. Dance offers the potential for a future career as an educator, a choreographer, a dance therapist, or a dance critic, historian, or writer.[4]

Other Considerations Related to a Dance Curriculum

One technique of involving secondary level boys in dance activities has been to encourage members of athletic teams to join dance classes. Dance training can be extremely helpful to student athletes (and nonvarsity students) in developing coordination, gracefulness of moving, and related qualities of movement.

Instructors can also foster interest in their programs by linking dance to other school activities. For example, an instructor may volunteer to work with the school's choir, band, theater group, cheerleaders, and gymnastics teams by using dance instruction to develop timing, precision, rhythm, and performance routines. Whenever possible, physical education (including dance) should be linked to other school educational disciplines.[4]

FOIL FENCING

The lifetime sport of fencing is an exciting and unique activity. It requires students to think quickly and to react to the opponent's movements and blade actions. The three weapons of fencing are the foil, the epee, and the sabre. Each weapon has its own style and slightly different rules, but the goal of the fencer is identical, and that is to score touches on the opponent's valid target area.

Skills Progression

It is recommended that the skills of fencing be presented in the following order:

1. Safety rules, which include students carrying their foils point up or point down, but never under the arm or over a shoulder, never pointing a foil at someone who is not wearing a mask and sweat pants or loose fitting slacks as opposed to shorts, and alerting students to constantly check their blades to be certain that the plastic tips are in place on the ends of the blades

2. Stance or on-guard position

3. Advancing and retreating footwork

4. Lunging

5. Simple thrust

6. Salute leading to on guard with an opponent

7. Explanation of valid target area

8. Explanation of engagement of blades and lines of engagement

9. Direct thrust on both sides of an opponent's blade

10. Demonstration and practice of parry 4 with a direct riposte

11. Use of disengage to avoid opponent's parry

12. Demonstration and practice of parry 6 and riposte

13. Explanation of the right-of-way fencing rule

14. Beat attacks to 4 and 6

15. Explanation of beat-disengage attacks

16. Explanation of rules for competitive fencing along with the duties of judges and the director

Learning Tasks for Developing Selected Skills

Footwork drill. As the teacher advances, the students retreat and vice versa. The teacher attempts to "fake out" the students by providing unexpected changes of direction.

Sneak attack. *Sneak attack* is played in pairs with paper foils (made from several sheets of newspaper rolled into a circular tube and secured with tape). Students will understand that the extension of the dominant arm means that they are on the attack. Withdrawal of the arm by bending it means that the fencer is giving up the attack or preparing to parry, which is a defensive move. The defender must be aware of the fact that to parry the attack, the attacking foil needs to be pushed or tapped aside by a lateral movement of his or her foil. The defending student must learn to judge when a real attack is in progress as opposed to a feinting movement. For making a successful parry, 2 points are scored. When the defender makes an unsuccessful parry, 1 point is scored. The game consists of 10 points. Partners then switch their roles. Sneak attack is an effective game because it teaches fenc-

> ## T A B L E   2 1 - 1

Error Analysis of Selected Fencing Skills

Skill and Errors	Cause of Errors	Correcting Errors
Footwork		
Inability to move forwards (advance) and backwards (retreat) quickly	Taking steps that are too long while advancing and retreating	Practice taking smaller steps in front of mirror without foil in dominant hand
Bobbing up and down while advancing and retreating	Taking steps that are too long	Think of advancing and retreating in a room with a ceiling 1 inch above head
Slow recovery to on-guard position following lunge	Overextension on lunge	Keep weight off of dominant foot Weight should be two shoe lengths behind dominant foot
	Rolling nondominant foot on medial side during lunge	Keep nondominant foot flat on floor during lunge
Falling off-balance in lunge	Dominant foot pointing inward or outward as it lands	Point dominant foot straight ahead towards opponent
	Knees rotated inward	Keep knees over insteps; work on lateral stretching exercises
Simple attacks		
Straight thrust attack		
Blade bends downward or its point glances off target as it contacts opponent	Pommel dangling below wrist or attempting to go around opponent's blade by approaching it from side	Press pommel against wrist and inside of forearm; move dominant arm forward from dominant shoulder
Hitting target after completing lunge	Failing to extend dominant arm before lunging	Do not retract arm after it has been extended
Disengage attack		
Failure to hit on disengage	Disengaging too soon	Disengage just as arm reaches full extension
Hitting underside of opponent's arm on disengage instead of hitting valid target area	Lunging before dominant arm is extended, thus disengaging too late	Complete disengage before foil tip reaches opponent's bell guard
Lateral parries (4 and 6)		
Driving opponent's blade into your legs while parrying	Parrying downward when using a parry 4 or 6	Movement of parry 4 or 6 should be in a lateral, horizontal plane as opposed to a downward movement
Sliding or swishing sound of blades throughout an attack and parry	Anticipation of attack by defender	Wait to parry until you know an attack is really an attack and not just a feint
Opponent's blade overpowers parry 4 or 6 and hits in spite of an attempted parry	Failure to move bell guard laterally and completely to edge of target	Be sure elbow is "in" and line from elbow to foil tip is straight
	Pommel leaves dominant wrist allowing "break" in foil arm's defense	Press pommel firmly against dominant forearm throughout parry

ing basics without the distraction of utilizing a regulation foil.[5]

Error Analysis

Table 21-1 presents causes and corrections for common errors associated with selected fencing skills.

General Fencing Strategy

Some general fencing strategies are as follows:

1. Observe an opponent's stance, speed, aggressiveness, and weaknesses early in a bout to effectively plan attacks and counterattacks.

2. Attempt to control the fencing rhythm or cadence throughout the bout.

3. Vary the types of attacks and parries.

4. Be aware of the opponent's baiting or invitation tactics and react with caution.

5. Remember that the sport of fencing demands total concentration and alertness of the body, of the mind, and of timing.

Fencing Etiquette

Etiquette involves the following key behaviors:

1. Respect all decisions of the officials without questions.

2. Acknowledge all touches and refuse all doubtful touches.

3. Respect an opponent's signal to cease play (with a foot stomp) by immediately stopping an attack or planned attack.

4. In the event that the opponent drops the foil, withhold attacking while the foil is recovered and the opponent resumes the on guard position.

5. Always salute the opponent and officials before and after the conclusion of the bout.[2]

FRISBEE

Frisbee is a unique lifetime sport that participants can play indoors or outdoors. A frisbee unit is a cost-effective addition to the physical education curriculum because a frisbee costs less than $10.00. The sport can offer individual challenges as well as serve as a team sport activity. Additionally, frisbee can be enjoyed as a coeducational activity.

Skills Progression

Throwing the frisbee involves three basic techniques: the backhand, overhand, and sidearm throws. The *backhand throw* involves gripping the frisbee with the thumb on top and the index finger just under the rim. The middle finger should be extended toward the center with the fourth and little fingers curled back against the rim. Next, the dominant arm is extended toward the target, and the frisbee is rolled toward the body as the dominant arm is swung backward. The wrist and forearm should be coiled like a spring, and the edge of the frisbee facing the target is slightly raised. The arm is then swung forward, and the frisbee is released.

The *overhand throw* involves gripping the frisbee with the thumb underneath the disk and the fingers on top with the wrist cocked backward. The throw is made by keeping the arm straight and close to shoulder level. The wrist is snapped forward at the point of release.

The *sidearm throw* requires holding the frisbee with two fingers on the underside of the disk with the thumb on top and the wrist cocked backward. The arm is swung downward at about a 30-degree angle to the body. The leading edge of the frisbee must remain tilted down. The wrist is snapped forward at the point of release.

A variation of the backhand throw is the *curve,* which requires tilting the frisbee in the direction of the desired curve. For the right-handed thrower, tilting the edge of the disk being gripped by the fingers in a downward position will result in a curved flight pattern to the right.

Tilting the edge of the frisbee away from the grip on it in a downward position will result in a curve to the left. The *skip* is produced by starting with the same position and motion as for a curve to the left. This skill results in the frisbee contacting the ground on its forward edge about halfway to the target and then rebounding into the catcher's hand.

Consistent *catching* of a frisbee requires reading the flight of the disk and positioning the body to effectively catch the frisbee. Some of the basic catches are (1) between the legs, (2) behind the back, (3) behind the head, (4) finger catch, and (5) tipping. Tipping means keeping the frisbee aloft and in control by lightly touching the discus in the center of its bottom surface with one finger. Regarding the skill of catching a frisbee, it is important to remember that catches made above waist level should involve the thumb being in a down position. When one catches a throw below waist level, the thumb should be in the up position.[6]

Learning Tasks for Developing Selected Skills

Throwing for accuracy. One partner stands in the center of a 6-foot diameter circle and serves as the catcher. The throwing partner has five turns from 20, 30, 35, and 40 feet from the center of the circle. For the thrower's attempt to be scored, the frisbee must land within the circle. The scoring system is 2 points per valid attempt from 20 feet, 3 points from 30 feet, 4 points from 35 feet, and 5 points from 40 feet.

Throwing for distance. Mark an area on a field or on a gym floor at intervals of 25, 35, 45, 55, and 65 yards parallel to the throwing line. Also, mark sideline boundaries. For an attempt to count, the frisbee must land within the sideline boundaries. For middle-school students, the point system is as follows: 6 points for a throw over 35 yards, 5 points for over 30 yards, 4 points for over 25 yards, 3 points for over 20 yards, 2 points for over 10 yards, and 1 point for under 10 yards. For high-school students, a throw over 45 yards yields 6 points, 5 points for over 35 yards, 4 points for over 30 yards, 3 points for over 35 yards, 2 points for over 20 yards, and 1 point for under 20 yards.[6]

Frisbee Novelty Events

Twenty-one. Players stand 10 yards apart and throw the frisbee back and forth to each other. The throws must be accurate so that they can be caught by the partner. For a two-handed catch, 1 point is awarded, and for a one-handed catch, 2 points are awarded. The player to first accumulate 21 points by a margin of 2 points wins.

One step. Opponents stand 10 to 30 yards from each other. The goal is to throw the frisbee accurately to the opponent so that he or she can catch it without taking a step or by taking only one step. If the receiver has to take more than one step, then the thrower receives 1 point. If the throw is accurate and the receiver drops it, then the receiver earns 1 point. The first player who accumulates 10 points loses the contest.

Adaptation of frisbee to sports. *Frisbee or disk golf* involves the use of traffic cones as tee markers, and holes can be represented by hula hoops, tires, or boxes. Regulation golf rules apply. A class can be subdivided and started at all 9 or 18 holes in a *shotgun* formation with instructions to follow the course in the sequential order of the holes. Frisbee golf involves one stroke being scored each time the frisbee is thrown toward each hole. A one-stroke penalty is in effect if anytime the frisbee lands 6 or more feet above the ground and is unplayable (such as lodged in a bush or tree) and if the frisbee lands out-of-bounds.

Frisbee soccer. Soccer rules can be modified to permit two goalies, particularly for outdoor soccer, and limitations on the number of permitted steps with the frisbee in one or both hands can also be stipulated.

Frisbee softball. The pitcher throws the frisbee to the batter at home plate, who must catch it and throw it into play past the pitcher's plate. If the batter does not throw the frisbee beyond the pitcher, the batter is out. If the batter drops the pitched frisbee, it is a strike. Bunting and stealing are not permitted in this modified game.

Frisbee tennis. Each serve must travel to the receiver's backcourt area beyond the service line. When the frisbee is in play, each singles player or member of a doubles team must catch the frisbee and throw it over the net from the spot where it was caught.[6]

Ultimate frisbee. The object of ultimate frisbee is to gain points by scoring goals. The frisbee may only be passed, and a goal is scored when a player successfully passes the frisbee to a teammate in the end zone. It is recommended that middle school students play the game on a field that is 30 yards wide and 50 yards long with 10 yard end zones. High-school students should play the game on a field 40 yards wide and 60 yards long with 15-yard end zones. For secondary level students, each frisbee team should consist of seven players.[6]

Suggestions for Instruction

In terms of equipment used during the stage of learning throwing and catching skills, an instructor may wish to substitute the following items for the official frisbee disk: (1) a flying foam disk that reduces a student's fear of catching the harder, regulation frisbee; and (2) flying *inflate-o-disks*, which are made of soft, durable vinyl. Additionally, aerobic disks, which are in the form of a ring, are available for use in a frisbee unit. The aerobie disk allows greater throwing distances to be achieved.

As a means of providing students with creative experiences, it is suggested that students be encouraged to

---

BOX 21-1

ULTIMATE FRISBEE RULES QUIZ WITH ANSWERS

1. Teams flip a coin for choice to (receive) or choice of (goals).
2. A goal is worth (one) point(s).
3. If your team is in possession of the disk, or frisbee, then you are on (offense).
4. When running to catch a pass, you are allowed (two) steps in which to stop before being called for traveling.
5. The player in possession of the disk may (pivot) on one foot as in the sport of basketball.
6. A player in possession of the frisbee may not score by (running) into the end zone.
7. To score a goal, (two) feet must be in the end zone.
8. The disk must be (passed) from player to player. It may not be (handed) from player to player.
9. The number of people who may legally guard the person with the frisbee is/are (one).
10. If you hold the disk while guarded for 15 seconds, a (stalling) violation is called.
11. Three types of fouls in the game are (pushing), (holding), and grabbing.
12. The disk cannot be (taken) or (knocked) from an offensive player's hands.
13. A regulation game consists of (seven) players on each team.
14. After every (throw-off), the clock starts when the receiving team touches the disk.
15. Bobbing to gain control is permitted; however, no (tipping) to one's self is permitted.

---

adapt frisbee to other sports not presented in the foregoing subsection.

Administer the quiz on ultimate frisbee rules that is provided in Box 21-1.

PADDLEBALL, HANDBALL, AND RACQUETBALL

Racquetball, involving a strung racket, is a variation of paddleball and handball. Paddleball involves the use of a wooden paddle, and handball involves a player wearing a pair of gloves and striking the game ball with a gloved hand. These sports may be played on one-wall, three-wall, or four-wall courts. If the sports are being offered indoors or outdoors on school property, then the units are usually conducted on one-wall courts.

To avoid eye injuries in these sports, it is strongly recommended that students wear protective glasses.

The remainder of this section will focus on instructional information pertinent to racquetball. For more information on handball, contact the US Handball Association, 930 N. Benton Ave., Tucson, AZ, 85711, or call (602) 795-0434.

Skills Progression

Before students contact a ball with the racket, it is necessary for them to learn and practice the possible angles and heights that a ball can travel and rebound from the walls. Introducing the concepts of the angle of incidence and the angle of reflection, followed by allowing students to practice them by tossing a ball against the wall, will facilitate learning.

Court positioning. Effective court positioning is the basis of efficient performance. Court positioning begins with the serve return. To receive serves, the student should be positioned an arm and a racket's length away from the back wall and halfway between the side walls or side boundary markings. Once the serve has been received, work your way into the center of the court. Center court position is an area 5 feet in diameter equidistant between the side walls, or sidelines, and divided in half by the receiving line. Hitting shots that do not pass through this area will allow a player to maintain this position. Holding this position forces an opponent to hit shots outside of the center area, and it allows you to cover the entire court.

Footwork and balance. A proper ready position involves the feet being shoulder width apart so that the player is balanced for any shot. The body weight should be moving forward toward the ball as it approaches and toward the front wall as it is contacted. As the opponent contacts the ball, determine where it is directed and then locate the position on the court so you can hit the ball squarely.

The kill shot. In the kill shot, the ball is hit low on the front wall and rebounds so close to the floor that it is virtually unreturnable by the opponent. The kill shot is the most commonly used offensive shot. The four types of kill shots are:

1. *The straight kill:* the ball is hit straight into the front wall as low as possible with the ball rebounding parallel to the side wall.

2. *The front wall kill:* the ball is hit low, with the racquet face opened slightly, then it rebounds off the front wall, and the shot dies.

3. *The front-wall–side-wall kill:* the ball is hit into the low corner of the front wall, then it rebounds into the closest side wall and low onto the floor.

4. *The off-the-back-wall kill:* this shot is performed by waiting for the ball to drop low, placing the racket face under it, and with a forceful point of contact directing the ball into the front wall and away from the opponent.

Passing shots. The passing shot is an offensive shot and one of the easiest to use. Types of passing shots are down the line, crosscourt, and angle. *Down-the-line* pass-

Courtesy of Emily Leonardo, Camp Hill High School, Camp Hill, PA.

ing shots require the ball hitting the front wall about waist high and rebounding into deep court without hitting a side wall. Hit a passing shot down the right wall when the opponent is standing to the left of the center of the court and vice versa. *Crosscourt* passing shots are used when both players are on the same side of the court. The ball should hit the front wall at about waist level and near the midpoint of the court. The ball will then rebound crosscourt opposite the opponent and into the back corner of the court. *Angle* passing shots are used only when the opponent is in the center court area. Contact the ball so that it hits either the left or right wall at waist level.

Drive, lob, and Z serves. *Drive serves* are hard-hit, offensive serves that strike the front wall and rebound in a straight line to deep court. *Lob serves* are contacted using a lifting motion that results in a soft service. *Z serves* should rebound close to the receiving line and then into a deep corner. The lob and drive Z serves place pressure on an opponent's reaction time and mobility. The high, or lob, Z serves reduce offensive return opportunities and tempt an impatient opponent into low-percentage kill attempts. To keep an opponent guessing, vary the type of serve that is being delivered.[7]

Learning Tasks for Facilitating Performance

Accuracy drill. Mark the court with targets on the floor and walls by using traffic cones, boxes, or gym floor tape. Challenge the students to execute three forehands, backhands, drive serves, lob serves, and Z serves to the target area. Kill shots can be directed to marked areas on the front wall.

Ready position.
Courtesy of Ben Lombardo, Rhode Island College, Providence, RI.

Six-ball rally. After the serve, each player must contact the ball three times before a point can be scored. This drill encourages a longer rally.

Forehand or backhand exchange. After the serve, each student must hit a designated number of forehand or backhand shots before a point is scored or a side out is awarded.

Head of the class. This activity involves all students in the class playing 10-minute singles or doubles games. At the conclusion of 10 minutes, the students move to the court to their left if they won, or they remain on the same court with new opponents if they lost the game. The object of the game is to move to the left to the last court.

Cutthroat. Cutthroat is played with three people and the server playing the other two players. For more information on racquetball, contact the American Amateur Racquetball Association, 815 North Weber, Colorado Springs, CO, 80903, or call (719) 635-5396.

TENNIS, PICKLEBALL, AND PLATFORM PADDLE TENNIS

Tennis singles and doubles played indoors or outdoors are popular lifelong sports. Pickleball and platform paddle tennis are variations of the sport of tennis. Pickleball is an exciting and enjoyable game that can be played indoors or outdoors and is an effective lead-up game to tennis. Lightweight pickleball wooden paddles and a plastic, perforated baseball are used for singles and doubles pickleball. Indoor pickleball is played on a doubles badminton court (20 feet wide by 44 feet long) with the top of the net being at a height of 3 feet from the gym floor, and the net is attached by badminton and volleyball standards. Pickleball playing equipment, including nets, outdoor standards, instructional written materials, and an instructional videotape can be obtained by writing to the following address: Pickleball, 801 N.W. 48th Street, Seattle, WA, 98107.

Platform paddle tennis is a game of paddleball played on a platform 30 feet wide by 60 feet long that is covered on its sides, ends, and overhead by wire mesh. Platform tennis paddles are constructed of wood, and the game ball is made of light sponge rubber. In platform paddle tennis, the ball may be played off the ceiling, end, and sidewalls of the court as in four-court handball and racquetball. Platform paddle tennis is popular in some of the country's snowbelt areas as an enjoyable outdoor winter activity.[2]

The remainder of this section will be devoted to tennis.

Tennis Skills Progression

It is recommended that a tennis unit begin with the forehand and backhand high and low volleys. The compact stroke of the volley will allow students to achieve initial success. After the volleys have been presented and practiced, they should be followed by the forehand and backhand flat drives, forehand and backhand drives with forward spin and backspin, forehand and backhand passing shots, forehand and backhand defensive lobs and offensive lobs, flat smash, smash with slice spin, followed by singles and doubles strategies.

When one is introducing the forward spin and the backspin for the forehand and backhand drives, it is important to provide students with the means and results of applying each type of spin on the flight characteristics of the tennis ball as well as the advantages of each type of spin.

The term *forward spin* is more appropriate than *topspin* because the latter connotes the wrong image of applying this type of spin. Topspin suggests closing the racket face over the top of the tennis ball, which is incorrect. Forward spin is properly applied by placing a flat or slightly open racket face on the back of the ball and moving the racket face from a low to high plane on the forward swing and follow-through.

Applying forward spin results in the top of the ball being forced downward sooner than a flat groundstroke. This means that forward spin allows a player to hit with greater power and at the same time keep the ball within the opponent's half of the court.

A backspin is applied by moving the racket face forward from a high-to-low-high forward swing and follow-through so that the underside of the ball is contacted with a slightly open racket face. Backspin causes the ball to have a low rebound, which forces the opponent to hit up on the return. Many players do not like attempting to return low rebounding balls.

Learning Tasks for Facilitating Performance

Rapid fire volleys. Two students stand at the baseline and on each side of the center mark and with a bucket of balls. A third student takes the volleyer's position on the opposite side of the net. The two students on the baseline alternate feeding drives to the volleyer, which forces the volleyer to respond as quickly as possible.

Down-the-line and crosscourt forehand and backhand drives with and without spin. Refer to the drills indicated for the sport of badminton in the first section of this chapter.

Approach shot. The feeder stands on the baseline with two tennis balls in the nondominant hand, while the receiver stands on the baseline crosscourt from the feeder. The feeder feeds the receiver a short hit that lands near the *T- position* (the area inside the intersection of the sideline and service line) on the other side of the net. The receiver moves forward and hits a down-the-line approach shot. Regardless of the result, the receiver moves toward the net position. The feeder then feeds the second ball to the receiver for a volley setup. The receiver then volleys the ball crosscourt for a put-away. The partners

should also practice this drill from the opposite side of the court.

Smash task. The feeder feeds high lobs to the receiver so that the receiver can practice the overhead smash from the forecourt, midcourt, and backcourt. As the receiver moves backward deeper into the court, he or she must concentrate on pressing the ball out and over the net before breaking the wrist to bring the ball down into the opponent's court.

Service accuracy task. The receiver of the service designates to the server to which third of the deep service court box the serve will be delivered. The receiver can designate the inside, outside, or center deep areas of the service court.

Speed and accuracy serving contest. Consult with a local law enforcement agency regarding the feasibility of borrowing a radar gun to clock the speed of students' serves. A fast-serve contest involves the serve having to be legal for the attempt to count. Inform students that the flat serve as opposed to a spin serve will result in the fastest serves because applying spin to a serve causes it to move slower than a flat service.[2]

How Good Are You?

All strokes consist of four components and in order of priority, they are consistency, depth, placement, and power. *Consistency* involves getting the ball over the net. *Depth* refers to hitting the ball deep into the opponent's court so that it is difficult for the opponent to attack. *Placement* involves accurately hitting a target area on the opponent's court. *Power* is added to the shots after the foregoing goals of each shot have been achieved.[8]

Refer to Boxes 21-2 and 21-3 regarding the scoring for the four components on selected shots and tips for improving all four components.

Error Analysis

Table 21-2 presents the causes and corrections for common errors associated with selected skills.

Anticipation

Tennis, like the other racket sports, is a sport involving a number of open skills with the exception being the serve. Open sport skills are performed in a constantly changing environment. Predicting when and where the tennis ball will land on one's side of the net requires anticipation so that the player can prepare the body and racket as soon as possible for an effective return. Two factors that lead to anticipatory timing behavior are contextual cues and game expectations, or strategies.

Contextual cues involve watching an opponent prepare and make contact with the tennis ball to determine the placement and velocity of the shot just before the point

B O X 2 1 - 2

ACCEPTABLE STANDARDS FOR THE COMPONENTS OF SELECTED TENNIS SKILLS

Use hula hoops as targets for developing consistency, depth, placement, and power. The location of the hoops on the court for each selected skill is stated below with acceptable performance standards. Note that a shot must land within a hula hoop for it to be acceptable.

1. Forehand and backhand volleys from the forecourt: Place one hula hoop within the court at the intersection of the service line and sideline on both sides of the court, and hit angled volleys. Acceptable performance is 8 out of 10 shots.
2. Forehand and backhand drives down-the-line and crosscourt from the backcourt: Place one hula hoop deep in

each corner of the court within 3 feet of the baseline and 3 feet from the sideline. Acceptable performance is 8 out of 10 shots.
3. Forehand and backhand approach shots from the midcourt with the approach shots being hit down-the-line: Same positioning of hula hoops as for Skill #2. Acceptable performance is 8 out of 10 shots.
4. Serve: Place one hula hoop deep within each service court's inside and outside corners with a third hula hoop between both corner hoops. Acceptable performance is 7 out of 10 serves for the first serve and 8 out of 10 serves for the second serve.

B O X 2 1 - 3

TIPS FOR IMPROVING THE COMPONENTS OF TENNIS

I. Improving consistency and placement
   A. Practice grooving strokes by using a hitting wall and an automatic ball machine, or rallying in patterns with a practice partner. Aim for targets.
   B. Concentrate on the tennis ball by looking for its logo. Although the eyes are not keen enough to detect the logo on a fast-moving tennis ball, this technique will facilitate your focus of attention.
   C. Practice anticipating when and where the tennis ball will arrive on your court as per the information provided in this subsection.
   D. Practice movement learning tasks such as the figure 8 in which one player hits every shot crosscourt while the other player hits every shot down-the-line.
   E. Practice half-court learning tasks in which you use half of the doubles court with one player standing at the net and the other player in the backcourt area.
   F. Practice two-on-one learning tasks in which two players are in the forecourt and the third player is behind the baseline, or two players are on the baseline and the third player is at the net.
   G. Use match-play learning tasks requiring players to hit the designated spots on the court while playing sets.
   H. Avoid *killing* the tennis ball.

II. Keeping the tennis ball deep on a baseline rally and on approach shots
   A. Remember that the speed of the tennis ball is not necessary as long as shots consistently land within the court.
   B. To hit deep in a baseline rally, aim your shots at least 3 feet over the top of the net. If off-balance or on the run, then allow for 6 to 10 feet of net clearance.
   C. Use a forward spin, which allows you to hit the tennis ball high, hard, and deep without hitting it out-of-bounds.

III. Improving power without sacrificing accuracy
   A. Avoid a vice grip on the racket because it not only restricts one's swing but also it leads to premature fatigue.
   B. When racket speed is desirable, depending on the purpose of the skill, swing the dominant arm from the shoulder, transfer body weight from the foot farthest away from the net to the one closest to the net, and turn the hips and shoulders away from the net on the backswing followed by turning them towards the net to initiate the forward swing.
   C. When returning the serve, a student can move the racket faster when the elbows are close to the sides of the body. This technique shortens the radius of the swing, reduces the inertia of the racket, and requires less effort to move the racket with more muscular force being available for speed.
   D. Maintain effective body balance.

T A B L E   21 - 2

Error Analysis of Selected Tennis Skills

Stroke and Common Errors	Cause of Errors	Correcting Errors
Forehand and Backhand Volleys		
Volley too deep into opponent's court	Ball stroked instead of contacted with a punching action	Place student with the back to a wall or fence to eliminate backswing Use rapid setups so that the student does not have time to take an unnecessary backswing
Volley does not clear net	Failing to open racket face on low volleys or using the appropriate degree of a closed racket face for high volleys Grip too loose at point of contact	Toss balls so that the student can learn the degree to which the racket face must be either opened or closed Tell the student to squeeze the grip just before and during the point of contact
Popping the ball up on backhand volleys	Dominant elbow higher than dominant hand at point of contact	Have a student place an empty can of tennis balls under the dominant arm so that if the elbow is raised, the can will drop to the court
Groundstrokes with forward spin		
Drive lacks depth	Improper application of spin caused by racket face closing on top of ball or not having a long and high follow-through	Place the student close to the net with a ball in the nondominant hand resting against the band on top of the net; the upper one third of the ball is above net level, and then the student contacts it
Drive has too much height	Student is failing to stroke forward and upward through the ball	Tell the student to apply spin to the actual tennis ball and to stroke through four imaginary tennis balls
Flat Service		
Inaccurate service toss (The student should toss to the swing of the racket and not swing at the toss.)	Inconsistent or inaccurate tosses because the student is unclear on how high the toss should be and how far away from the body it should be tossed	Mark the maximum height for the toss on a wall or fence post; then ask the student to place the racket on the floor or court with the grip away from the feet and the sweet spot shoulder width away from the nondominant toes; last, have the student toss the ball upward; if the toss is accurate, it should land in the vicinity of the racket face A second student can stand behind the tosser and check for the height of the tossed ball
	Using the wrist to give the toss the desired height	Reemphasize that the fingers "pop open" to give the toss its maximum height after the nondominant hand and arm have reached as high up as possible

Source: Murphy C, Murphy B: *Tennis for the player, teacher, and coach,* Philadelphia, 1975, WB Saunders.

Courtesy of Ben Lombardo, Rhode Island College, Providence, RI.

of contact. Contextual cues are a valuable factor after a learner has acquired the knowledge of the sequential/temporal patterning of each skill. For example, if an opponent is executing a forehand drive and the player contacts the ball with the weight on the dominant foot instead of the nondominant foot, then the force production for the shot will be diminished. Furthermore, observing the direction in which the player's racket is facing at the point of contact will indicate in advance the direction of the return.

Game expectations refer to the patterns of play and strategies that an opponent uses. If, during a match, a player realizes that an opponent hits each approach shot down the line, then the player can anticipate the opponent following the same pattern of play and move accordingly to effectively return the shot.

Rules of Etiquette

Some of the rules of etiquette in tennis play are as follows:

1. Wait until a point is over before walking behind a court where a match is in progress.

2. To retrieve a ball from another court or to return a ball to another court, wait until the players have completed the point.

3. It is your obligation to call all balls on your side.

4. If you have any doubt as to whether the ball is out or good, you must give your opponent the benefit of the doubt and call it good.

5. Any "out" or "let" call must be made instantly.

6. If you call the ball "out" and then realize it was good, you should immediately correct your call.

7. To avoid controversy over the score, the server should always announce the game score before serving each point and the set score before starting each game.

The United States Tennis Association and Benefits

The United States Tennis Association (USTA) promotes the lifelong benefits of the sport of tennis for youth, and it provides instructional services for educators. Examples of USTA services are as follows: (1) providing clinicians for school assemblies conducted in a gymnasium, (2) providing in-service training for teachers by its provision of clinicians whose emphasis is on conducting classes for large groups in or on limited facilities, (3) providing instructional materials relevant to conducting a tennis unit when tennis courts are not available, and (4) providing schools with used playing equipment and a catalog citing sources of low-cost equipment.

It is important to note that the USTA also has a publications department and film library. For more information, contact the staff at the USTA Education and Recreation Center, 707 Alexander Road, Princeton, NJ, 08540, or call (609) 452-2580.

SUMMARY

A wide variety of dual activities and sports appropriate to a secondary school physical education program were reviewed in this chapter. Included were elements of knowledge, skills, teaching strategies, and safety concerns. Dual activities have long been a part of the U.S. way of life. The inclusion of these activities in secondary school physical education has been recognized as vital to the preparation of healthy students and the development of worthwhile lifetime recreational pursuits. Development of knowledge, attitudes, and proper skills will provide lasting enjoyment to each student.

It is important to recognize that success—learning—will accrue from appropriate progression in skill development, the presentation of relevant learning tasks, and the ability of the student and the teacher to engage in successful analysis of performance. Also, teachers should emphasize the physical and mental aspects of the skills and that mental practice should be a regular component of the instructional program. Finally, instructors should use video technology to provide additional feedback to students. This should be completed after the students have been given opportunities to assess their own performances.

REFERENCES

1. *Teaching badminton,* unpublished document prepared by physical education major students at SUNY College at Cortland, Cortland, NY, 1984.
2. Mood D, Musker F, Rink JE: *Sports and recreational activities for men and women,* ed 9, St Louis, 1987, Mosby.

3. Seidel BL et al: *Sport skills: a conceptual approach to meaningful movement,* Dubuque, Iowa, 1975, William C Brown.

4. Kraus R, Hilsendager SC, Dixon B: *History of the dance in art and education,* Englewood Cliffs, NJ, 1991, Prentice Hall.

5. Busch RE: *Fencing classes can be fun: A hand-out for the physical educator.*

6. *Introduction to Frisbee* (information packet), Virginia Beach, Va, Wham-O.

7. Total racquetball, *Ektelon Promotional Magazine,* 1992, San Diego, Calif.

8. Gullikson T, Zeitchick N: How good are you? *Tennis,* June, 40-47, 1992.

SUGGESTED READINGS

Badminton

Bloss MV, Hales R: *Badminton,* Dubuque, Iowa, 1990, William C Brown.

Davis P: *Badminton,* London, 1988, Ward Lock.

Wadood T, Tan K: *Badminton today,* St Paul, 1990, West Publishing.

Dance and rhythms

Block S: *Aerobix plus: how to sweat with class,* Champaign, Ill, 1982, Human Kinetics.

Clarkson P, Skrinar M: *Science of dance training,* Champaign, Ill, 1988, Human Kinetics.

Duffy NW: *Modern dance: an adult beginner's guide,* Englewood Cliffs, NJ, 1982, Prentice Hall.

Gray JA: *Dance instruction: science applied to the art of movement,* Champaign, Ill, 1989, Human Kinetics.

Long RA: *The black tradition in American dance,* New York, 1989, Rizzoli.

Shell CG: *The dancer as athlete,* Champaign, Ill, 1986, Human Kinetics.

Sherber E: *On the count of one: modern dance methods,* ed 2, Palo Alto, Calif, 1975, Mayfield Publishing.

Watkins A, Clarkson PM: *Dancing longer dancing stronger: a dancer's guide to improving technique and preventing injury,* Pennington, NJ, 1990, Princeton Book.

Wilmoth SK: *Leading aerobic dance-exercise,* Champaign, Ill, 1986, Human Kinetics.

Paddleball, handball, and racquetball

Adams L, Goldbloom E: *Racquetball today,* St Paul, 1991, West Publishing.

Reznik JW: *Championship handball,* Champaign, Ill, 1976, Human Kinetics.

Turner E, Hogan M: *Skills and strategies for winning racquetball,* Champaign, Ill, 1988, Human Kinetics.

Tyson P, Turman J: *The handball book,* Champaign, Ill, 1983, Human Kinetics.

Tennis

Borsos JD: *Tennis any style, scientifically,* Matawan, NJ, 1991, Third Level Books.

Douglas P: *Learn tennis in a weekend,* New York, 1991, Alfred A Knopf.

Groppel J et al: *Science of coaching tennis,* Champaign, Ill, 1989, Leisure Press.

Murphy C, Murphy B: *Tennis for the player, teacher and coach,* Philadelphia, 1975, WB Saunders.

Squires RC: *How to play platform tennis,* 1973, Norman Levines Editions.

German Tennis Federation: *Step by step tennis skills,* New York, 1990, Barron's.

Yandell J: *Visual tennis: mental imagery and the quest for the winning edge,* 1990.

Outdoor Adventure Activities

CHAPTER OBJECTIVES

◆ To review basic teaching points for outdoor adventure activities

◆ To discuss the value of including outdoor adventure activities in secondary school physical education programs

◆ To discuss the role of the teacher when teaching outdoor adventure activities

◆ To provide examples of outdoor adventure activities that could be used in a secondary school physical education program

Outdoor adventure activities are becoming popular additions to secondary school physical education programs. They can include a wide variety of outdoor pursuits that provide students with challenging yet meaningful experiences. They include a wide range of outdoor activities, such as backpacking, camping, canoeing, cooperative games, hiking, kayaking, orienteering, ropes courses, rock climbing, and walking. Particular activities will vary depending on school resources and the individual teacher's personal interests and qualifications. Box 22-1 contains specific items a teacher should consider for cooperative games or outdoor activities.

Outdoor adventure activities can be fun; they require little to no equipment (except those that take place on the low ropes course), they can accommodate any number of students, and they are designed to challenge students either individually or collectively. Specific examples of outdoor adventure activities that have become widespread are the cooperative games and ropes course activities. Cooperative games emphasize group cooperation as opposed to competition. Also included within this category are games and activities that encourage communication and trust among people working together to meet specific challenges.

Ropes courses are designed and built on school grounds to provide a variety of specially planned obstacles that challenge individuals and groups. Ropes courses have been traditionally built outdoors in wooded areas but can also be built inside. They are constructed from trees, cables, ropes, nets, walls, beams, and tires and are built on two levels. These two levels are referred to as high elements and low elements.

Low elements emphasize group cooperation, trust, and group and individual accomplishment. They also serve as a leadup to prepare students for the high elements. Most of these low-element activities take place a few feet above the ground and require students to call on different skills than those used in most traditional activities. This creates an atmosphere in which students are challenged by new tasks and are encouraged to work individually and cooperatively with others setting personal goals and meeting group challenges. Because of the unique nature of these activities, students should be taught to spot one another on all activities that take place above the ground, such as on beams, cables, walls, or tires suspended from trees.

High-element activities focus more on individual challenges. They are geared toward enhancing students' self-confidence by challenging them to take controlled risks and go beyond their personal limits. Activities are designed so that students can progress through a series of activities that gradually require more challenge and more risk (walking on a stationary beam 4 feet off the ground and then walking across a moving beam high in the air). Safety precautions are paramount, and because most activities take place in high trees and on cables stretched

---

The activities in this chapter are adaptations reproduced courtesy of Project Adventure, Inc., Hamilton, Mass.

CONSIDERATION FOR COOPERATIVE GAMES OR OUTDOOR ACTIVITIES

Before beginning a unit on cooperative games or outdoor activities, the teacher should consider the following points:

1. Think of creative ways to divide students into groups. Try to prevent individuals from feeling left out of a group. For example, have students get into groups according to their date of birth or color of eyes, hair, shirt, shoes, or socks.

2. Emphasis is on *trying*. Encourage all students to try their best and praise them for their attempts. Encourage students to do the same.

3. Trust is important. Students must learn to be trustworthy. Spend extra time on this if necessary.

4. In cooperative games there is no *right* or *wrong* way to meet challenges. Encourage students to be creative and to elicit input from all members of their groups.

5. Help students to reflect on their experiences. Encourage students to talk about their feelings. This is often difficult among high-school students but is important to the group process.

6. The teacher's role is that of a facilitator. Encourage students to make their own decisions even when you know that there are more expedient methods. The enjoyment is in the process!

high above the ground, physical education teachers should be specially trained before attempting to teach high elements. Project Adventure, Inc., conducts workshops for teachers in various sections of the country. For information on training, contact Project Adventure, Inc., P.O. Box 100, Hamilton, MA, 01936, or call (508) 468-7506.

Examples of outdoor adventure activities that will be included in this chapter are tag games, cooperative games, trust games, initiative activities, and group challenges on the low-element ropes course.

CONTRIBUTIONS

Teachers are finding that cooperative games and outdoor activities provide students with experiences that are much different from those offered by individual, dual, and team sports. Cooperative games and outdoor activities challenge students to work individually and cooperatively while building self-esteem and developing cooperation, communication, and problem-solving skills.

Activities are specifically designed to encourage students to cooperate, support, and trust one another while at the same time challenging individuals to go beyond their personal limits. A philosophical underpinning of these activities is that no one is forced to do anything until they are ready and that trying is more important than actually succeeding. The teacher and classmates learn to encourage gently and to praise others for trying new challenges.

Students practice on low elements on the ropes course at Mahar Regional High School, MA.
Courtesy of Kathy Pinkham.

Many activities emphasize cooperation to achieve stated goals.
Courtesy of Deborah A. Wuest, Ithaca College, Ithaca, NY.

Lessons for cooperative games and outdoor activities require a great deal of forethought. Emphasis should be placed on careful planning and organizing to ensure that all students benefit from the experience. Because of their unique purpose, these activities work best with teaching styles that are less teacher directed and more student directed. Students, not the teacher, become the primary decision makers in these classes. The teacher provides students with a particular challenge, and they determine a correct response for meeting the challenge. There are no predetermined right and wrong responses to these challenges. Specific teaching styles that are especially good are guided discovery, problem solving, and exploration. Things to consider may include safety, student grouping, allowing adequate time to complete the activities, and planning for time at the end to process the experience.

Once the class has begun, the teacher's primary responsibilities are to describe the activities, provide adequate time for students to participate in the activities, and facilitate a discussion at the end of each activity or class (debriefing, or processing). Debriefing provides an opportunity for students to reflect on the experience and their roles in the process. See Box 22-2 for sample questions for debriefing.

Tag Games

Tag games are fun and nonthreatening. They require a high degree of activity with a low level of risk on the part of the students. They are great warm-up activities for an outdoor adventure unit.

Chain tag. Designate a space with distinct boundaries (size depends on number of students participating). One student is "it." All other students spread out within the boundaries. On a signal to begin, the person who is "it" tries to tag someone. When a person is tagged they hold hands with the person who was originally "it," creating a *chain*. Each time a person is tagged they join the chain by holding hands. Only the people on the ends can tag others. Once the chain consists of six people, it splits into

BOX 22-2

SAMPLE QUESTIONS FOR DEBRIEFING

What did you enjoy most about this activity?
What was your first impulse?
How did you feel when . . . ?
What was the biggest challenge?
What were some of the questions that came up?
Did you consider more than one solution?
How did you go about including everyone?
What do you think about some of the other ideas that were tried?
If you were to try this again what might you do differently?
What did you learn about your group? About yourself?

two chains working together. This continues until everyone is tagged.

Musical tag. One student is "it." Once the person who is "it" tags another student, that person becomes "it." To protect oneself from being tagged, students can join hands with another student and sing one phrase of a song. Once they are done with their *one* phrase, they must break up and move on.

Tag-team tag. Students form a straight line and squat down side by side with every other student facing in an opposite direction. The student at one end of the line becomes the runner, and the student at the other end of the line becomes the chaser. The object of the game is for the chaser to tag the runner. The runner must run around the line of squatting people. The runner may run in either direction (clockwise or counterclockwise) but cannot change direction once a choice has been made. The squatters are also participants. The chaser, at any time, can tag a squatter on the back. The squatter then becomes the chaser, and the previous chaser takes the place of the squatter. Once a new chaser has been tagged, the runner may change direction.

Keep-away tag. This game is a combination of tag and keep-away with the object being for one team to maintain possession of an object for a predetermined period of time (for example, 30 seconds or 60 seconds). The class is divided into two teams, and specific boundaries are designated. A ball (or some other piece of equipment) is used to play keep-away. A timer keeps track of the amount of time each team has possession of the ball. If the student who has possession of the ball is tagged with two hands above the waist, the student must stop and get rid of the ball immediately. If a member of the same team picks up the ball, time continues for that team. If a member of the opposite team intercepts the ball, time begins for that team. A point is scored for every time a team maintains possession for the predetermined amount of time. Continuous time can also be kept, and the team that maintains possession for the longest amount of time wins.

Everyone is "it". Create a space with designated boundaries. Everyone is "it." The class spreads out within the boundaries, and on a signal to go they begin chasing and fleeing. The object is to tag someone else before getting tagged. If a tag is received, the student is eliminated and must sit down (either where he or she was tagged or on the side line). Play continues until only one player remains.

Cooperative Games

Cooperative games should be taught before trust games. Cooperative games put students into situations that require group communication, and they begin to build trust. Cooperation games will help to build the group cohesion and trustworthiness that will be needed in later activities.

Back-to-back sit/stand. Students begin in pairs. Sit on the ground (floor) with backs leaning against each other. Lock elbows and pull knees up to chest. While pushing against each other, stand up. Try this with groups of four, six, eight, or more sitting in two lines back-to-back. A variation to this is a front-to-front position with feet together and holding hands.

Mimicking. Done one-on-one. Students stand facing each other. One student makes various random movements while the other copies them as if he or she were looking in a mirror. Switch roles.

Sitting circle. Students form a tight circle standing shoulder to shoulder. Once the circle is as tight as it can possibly be, have everyone turn in the same direction. Everyone should now be facing the back of the person in front of them. Tighten the circle even more by having students move in toward the center so they are standing heel-to-toe with their hands on the shoulders of the person in front of them. At the count of three, have everyone in the group gently sit on the lap of the person behind them. Once everyone has a seat, challenge them even further by asking them to walk in a circle.

Quiet line-up. Have the group line up in order of their birthdays, heights, ages, or names (alphabetically), without talking. Any form of communication is allowed except sound.

Hoop or ring pass. Have students stand in a circle holding hands. Break the circle long enough to put a hula hoop over the arm of one student. Close the circle. Challenge students to pass the hula hoop around the circle without letting go of hands. Add a second hula hoop. Send it in the opposite direction.

Group juggling. Begin by having students stand in a circle. The object is to get as many balls in motion as possible. Establish a pattern by using one ball first. Throw the ball across the circle to one student. Have that student pass to another and continue that process until the ball has been passed to everyone in the circle. Repeat the pattern with one ball, and gradually add as many more as the group can handle.

Trust Games

Trust games require a great deal of trust and trustworthiness among group members. Discussions about trust and the importance of being trustworthy may be helpful in both the preparation of class and in the reflection of the activities.

Palm energy. Students work in pairs. Partners stand facing each other approximately arms length apart. Touch hands (palm-to-palm) and close the eyes. Keeping the eyes closed, drop the hands and turn around in place three times. Without peeking, try to touch hands again.

Trust churn. Use smaller groups of approximately 8 to 10 students. Ask students to stand in a tight circle. Have one student stand in the center with arms crossed

Group approaches to solving challenges are emphasized. Here the group tries to get a tire to go over the top of the tree.
Courtesy of Deborah A. Wuest, Ithaca College, Ithaca, NY.

in front of his or her chest. Everyone in the circle puts their hands up in front of them at about shoulder height with palms facing out. Once everyone is alert and ready, the person in the center closes his or her eyes and, maintaining a stiff body position with feet planted firmly in the center of the circle, gently falls in any direction. The group gently passes the person back and forth around the circle. The activity may be stopped when the teacher deems it appropriate.

Passing ships. Divide the class into two groups. (You may use three or four groups if numbers are high.) Create a space full of obstacles. Each team must have all of its members "navigate" their way through the obstacle-filled space. Members of the group (ships) cross one at a time and must be blindfolded. Teammates help them through by giving verbal cues.

Eye contact. The group stands in a circle. Each person attempts to make eye contact with another person in the circle. Once mutual eye contact has been made, the two people change positions while maintaining the eye contact and avoiding other pairs who are attempting to do the same thing.

Trust walk. The entire group is blindfolded with the exception of one person. This one person is the leader and must lead the group on a trust walk describing to them where they are going and what obstacles (real or imaginary) of which to be careful. The group holds hands and forms a single line. The leader must be positioned so that all participants can hear.

INITIATIVE ACTIVITIES

Many of the initiative games are designed to be used with the ropes course. Because of this, teachers should not attempt to construct any of the obstacles needed without the assistance of a competent ropes course builder.

Individual Challenges

Individual initiatives require individuals to create their own response to a particular challenge presented by the teacher. Creativity should be encouraged, and trying is more important than succeeding.

Triangle balance. A triangle is created using cables stretched around three trees. The cable forms a triangle that is about 3 feet off the ground. Students attempt to walk around the triangle while balancing on the cables. They may use only a rope tied to a tree to help them balance. They attempt to make it all the way around the triangle without falling off.

Cable walk. A single cable is stretched between two trees approximately 20 feet long and 3 feet up off the ground. Students attempt to walk across the cable using only a rope tied to a tree to help them balance.

Beam walk. A balance beam is made from logs built 4 feet from the ground. Students must attempt to walk the full length. Spotters must be used on each side of the log.

Suspended log balance. A log is suspended with two ropes from a tree. The student must walk across the swinging log. Spotters must be used on each side of the log.

Group Challenges

Group initiatives require a group of people to work together to originate ideas or methods for solving a particular challenge presented by the teacher.

Human knots. Students stand in a group, and everyone puts their right hands into the middle of the group and grasps the right hand of another person. Next ask students to put their left hand into the middle and grasp the left hand of a different person. (Students should try *not* to grasp the hands of the people on either side of them.) Without letting go of hands, the group tries to untangle themselves from the knot that was created by grasping hands. In some cases the group will be able to untangle themselves, and in some cases they will not.

The wall. A wall approximately 12 feet high exists between two trees. The group's challenge is to get everyone over the wall. Once a person is over the wall, they may not come back to help. They may, however, help from the other side. The challenge can be adapted by requiring the group to complete their task as quickly as possible.

Platform huddle. The challenge is to get the entire group up onto a platform with no one touching the ground for 10 seconds. The challenge can be adapted by making the platform smaller or increasing the number of people in the group. If it is still too easy, continue to add challenges, such as everyone face in or out or stand on one foot.

Two-way street. Use a balance beam or a long, large log. Have the entire group stand on it. (They may have to have smaller groups or take turns.) Split the group in two with half of the group turning to face the other half. Students are then challenged to get their entire group to the opposite end of the beam.

Nitro crossing. A climbing rope is suspended from the ceiling of a gymnasium or from a tree limb on a certified ropes course. Students stand in a large group at a starting point. (This can be done in two or three smaller groups if necessary.) A finishing point is located 15 feet away. In between is a mat or an *out-of-bounds* area. Students must get their entire group and a can of *nitro* (water) from the starting point to the finishing point without touching the ground or spilling a drop of nitro. (Use a large coffee can. Punch two holes in it and put a string through to form a handle.)

Tire pass. The challenge is to get the entire group safely through a tire that is suspended between two trees. The ropes supporting the tire and the outside of the tire cannot be touched.

The river ride. This activity uses a swinging log suspended from the trees. The challenge is to get the entire group on the log. (Smaller groups can be used if necessary.) The group must maintain balance for 10 seconds.

Spider web. A spider web is created by criss-crossing rope back and forth between two trees. Make sure holes are large enough for students' bodies to pass through. The challenge is to get the entire group through the web. If anyone touches the web while a student is attempting to get through, the student must return to start again.

Teachers should be properly trained before teaching adventure activities. Safety should be emphasized at all times. (Note that students are wearing safety helmets.)
Courtesy of Kathy Pinkham.

Add a rule that once a particular hole has been used one time (two times or three times depending on the size of the class), it cannot be used again.

SUMMARY

Outdoor adventure activities are becoming an increasingly popular component of the secondary school curriculum. They include a wide variety of outdoor pursuits that offer students the opportunity to challenge themselves in the outdoor environment.

Two popular activities that were presented in this chapter are cooperative games and ropes course activities. Cooperative games challenge students to solve problems, promote trust among students working together, and facilitate communication among students as they collaborate to solve various challenges.

Low rope activities also challenge students to work to solve challenges and to promote confidence in their abilities. These activities take place on ropes courses. These courses include a series of specially designed obstacles. The activities designed around these obstacles challenge students to achieve individually and as a member of a group as they seek to complete a series of tasks. For safety reasons, it is important that teachers receive proper training for these activities before implementing them in the curriculum.

SUGGESTED READINGS

Games for this chapter were adapted from the following list of recommended readings for teachers.

Darst PW, Armstrong GP: *Outdoor adventure activities for school and recreation programs,* Minneapolis, 1980, Burgess Publishing.

Fluegelman A, editor: *The new games book,* Garden City, NY, 1976, Doubleday.

Fluegelman A: *More new games,* Garden City, NY, 1981, Doubleday.

New Games Foundation: *The new games book,* Garden City, NY, 1976, Doubleday.

Orlick T: *The second cooperative sports & games book: over two hundred brand-new noncompetitive games for kids and adults both,* New York, 1982, Pantheon Books.

Rhonke K: *Cowtails and cobras,* ed 2, Hamilton, Mass, 1989, Project Adventure.

Rhonke K: *Silver bullets: a guide to initiative problems, adventure games, and trust activities,* Hamilton, Mass, 1984, Project Adventure.

Rice W, Yaconelli M: *Play it! great games for groups,* Grand Rapids, Mich, Zondervan Publishing.

Weinstein M, Goodman J: *Playfair,* San Luis Obispo, Calif, Impact.

Index